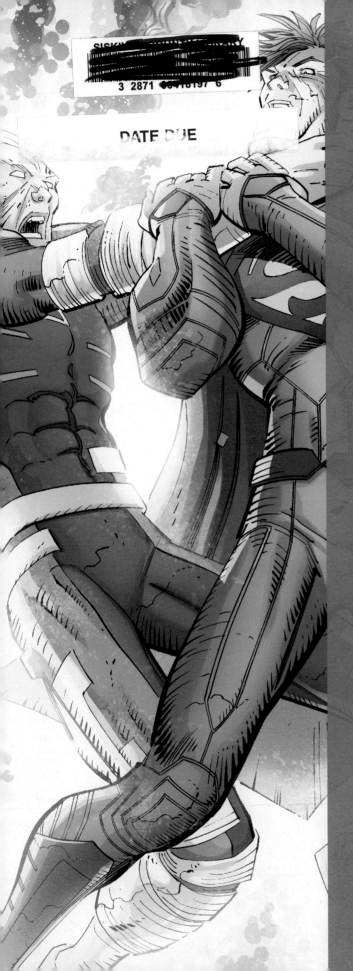

TOMORROW

SUPERMAN

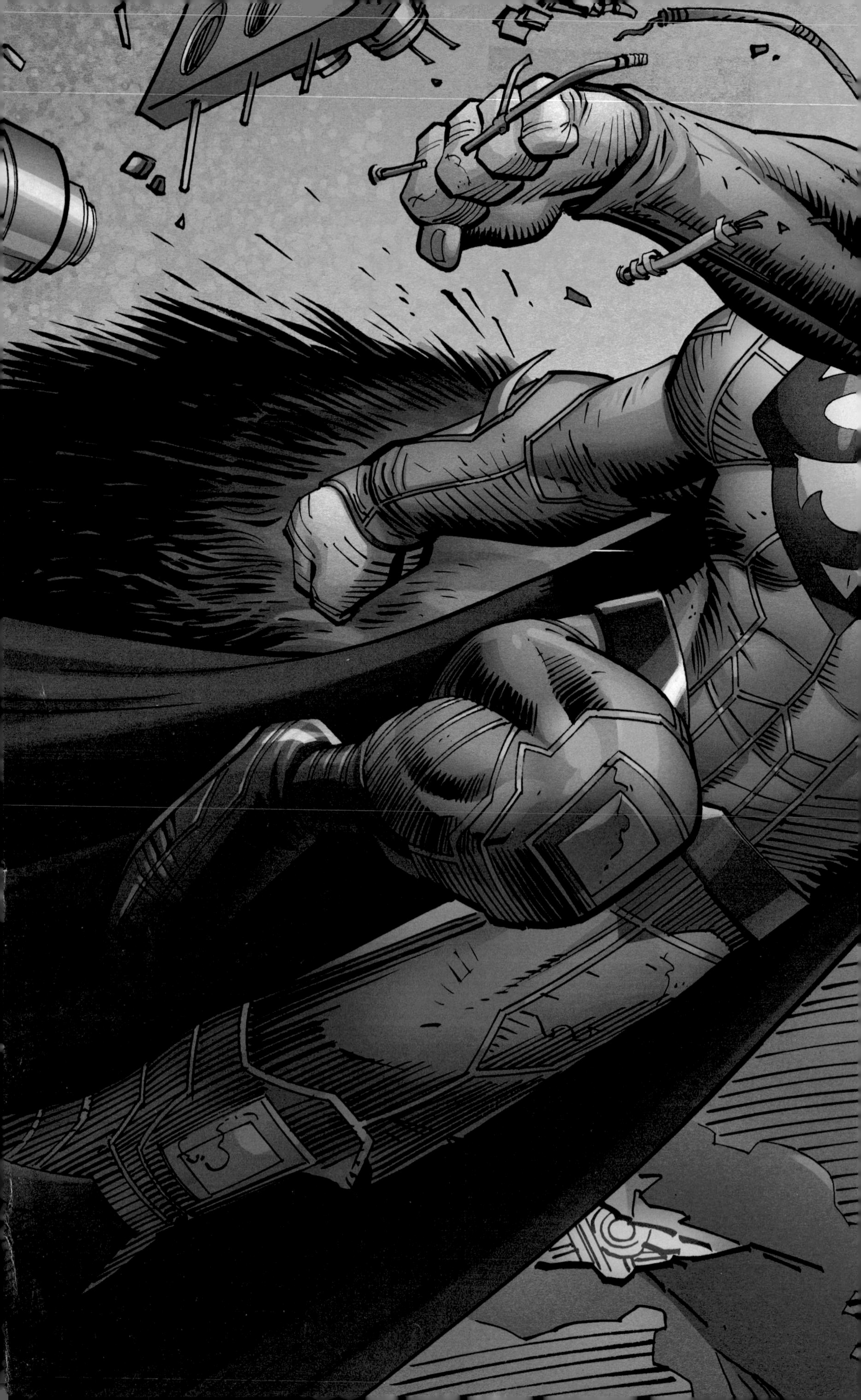

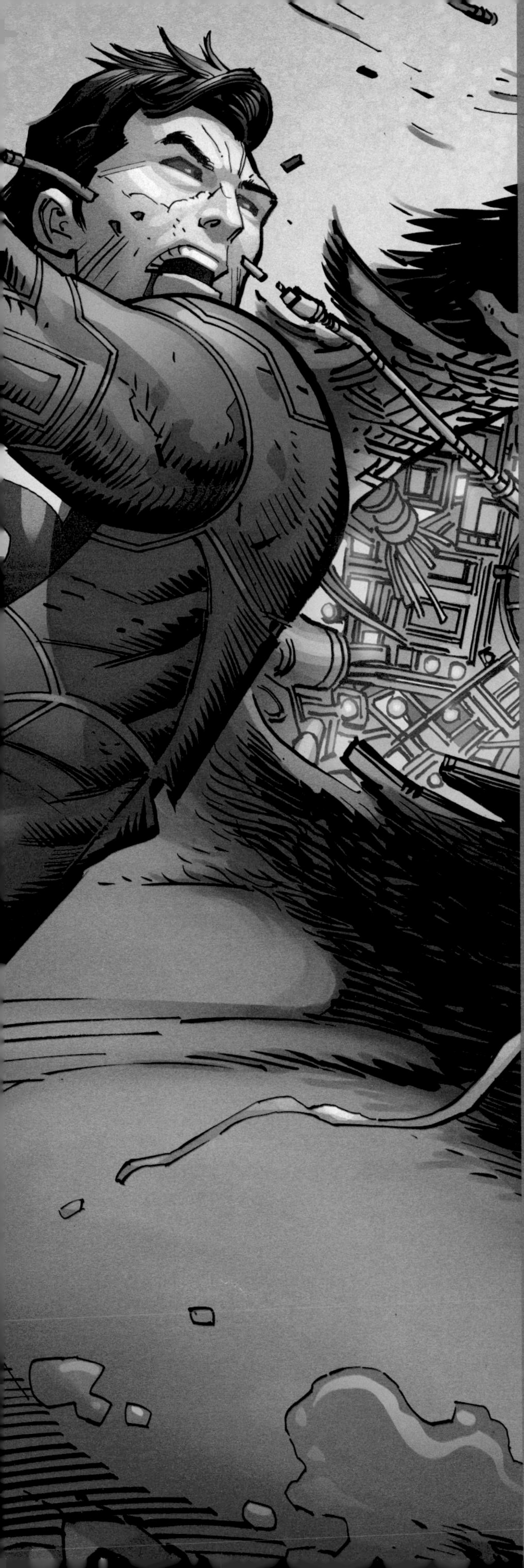

SUPERMAN

THE MEN OF TOMORROW

WRITTEN BY
GEOFF JOHNS

PENCILS BY
JOHN ROMITA JR.

INKS BY
KLAUS JANSON

COLOR BY
LAURA MARTIN
HI-FI
ULISES ARREOLA
DAN BROWN
WIL QUINTANA

LETTERS BY
SAL CIPRIANO
TRAVIS LANHAM

ORIGINAL SERIES &
COLLECTION COVER ART BY
JOHN ROMITA JR.,
KLAUS JANSON &
LAURA MARTIN

SUPERMAN CREATED BY
JERRY SIEGEL &
JOE SHUSTER
BY SPECIAL ARRANGEMENT
WITH THE JERRY SIEGEL FAMILY

EDDIE BERGANZA Editor – Original Series
RICKEY PURDIN Associate Editor – Original Series
ANTHONY MARQUES Assistant Editor – Original Series
JEB WOODARD Group Editor – Collected Editions
ROBIN WILDMAN Editor – Collected Edition
STEVE COOK Design Director – Books
DAMIAN RYLAND Publication Design

BOB HARRAS Senior VP – Editor-in-Chief, DC Comics

DIANE NELSON President
DAN DIDIO and JIM LEE Co-Publishers
GEOFF JOHNS Chief Creative Officer
AMIT DESAI Senior VP – Marketing & Global Franchise Management
NAIRI GARDINER Senior VP – Finance
SAM ADES VP – Digital Marketing
BOBBIE CHASE VP – Talent Development
MARK CHIARELLO Senior VP – Art, Design & Collected Editions
JOHN CUNNINGHAM VP – Content Strategy
ANNE DEPIES VP – Strategy Planning & Reporting
DON FALLETTI VP – Manufacturing Operations
LAWRENCE GANEM VP – Editorial Administration & Talent Relations
ALISON GILL Senior VP – Manufacturing & Operations
HANK KANALZ Senior VP – Editorial Strategy & Administration
JAY KOGAN VP – Legal Affairs
DEREK MADDALENA Senior VP – Sales & Business Development
JACK MAHAN VP – Business Affairs
DAN MIRON VP – Sales Planning & Trade Development
NICK NAPOLITANO VP – Manufacturing Administration
CAROL ROEDER VP – Marketing
EDDIE SCANNELL VP – Mass Account & Digital Sales
COURTNEY SIMMONS Senior VP – Publicity & Communications
JIM (SKI) SOKOLOWSKI VP – Comic Book Specialty & Newsstand Sales
SANDY YI Senior VP – Global Franchise Management

SUPERMAN: THE MEN OF TOMORROW

DC Comics, 2900 West Alameda Ave., Burbank, CA 91505
Printed by RR Donnelley, Salem, VA, USA. 3/11/16. First Printing.
ISBN: 978-1-4012-5868-9

Library of Congress Cataloging-in-Publication Data

Johns, Geoff, 1973- author.
Superman. Volume 6 / Geoff Johns, writer ; John Romita Jr, Klaus Janson, artists.
pages cm. — (The New 52!)
ISBN 978-1-4012-5868-9
1. Graphic novels. I. Romita, John, illustrator. II. Janson, Klaus,
illustrator. III. Title.
PN6728.S9J57 2015
741.5'973—dc23
2015008050

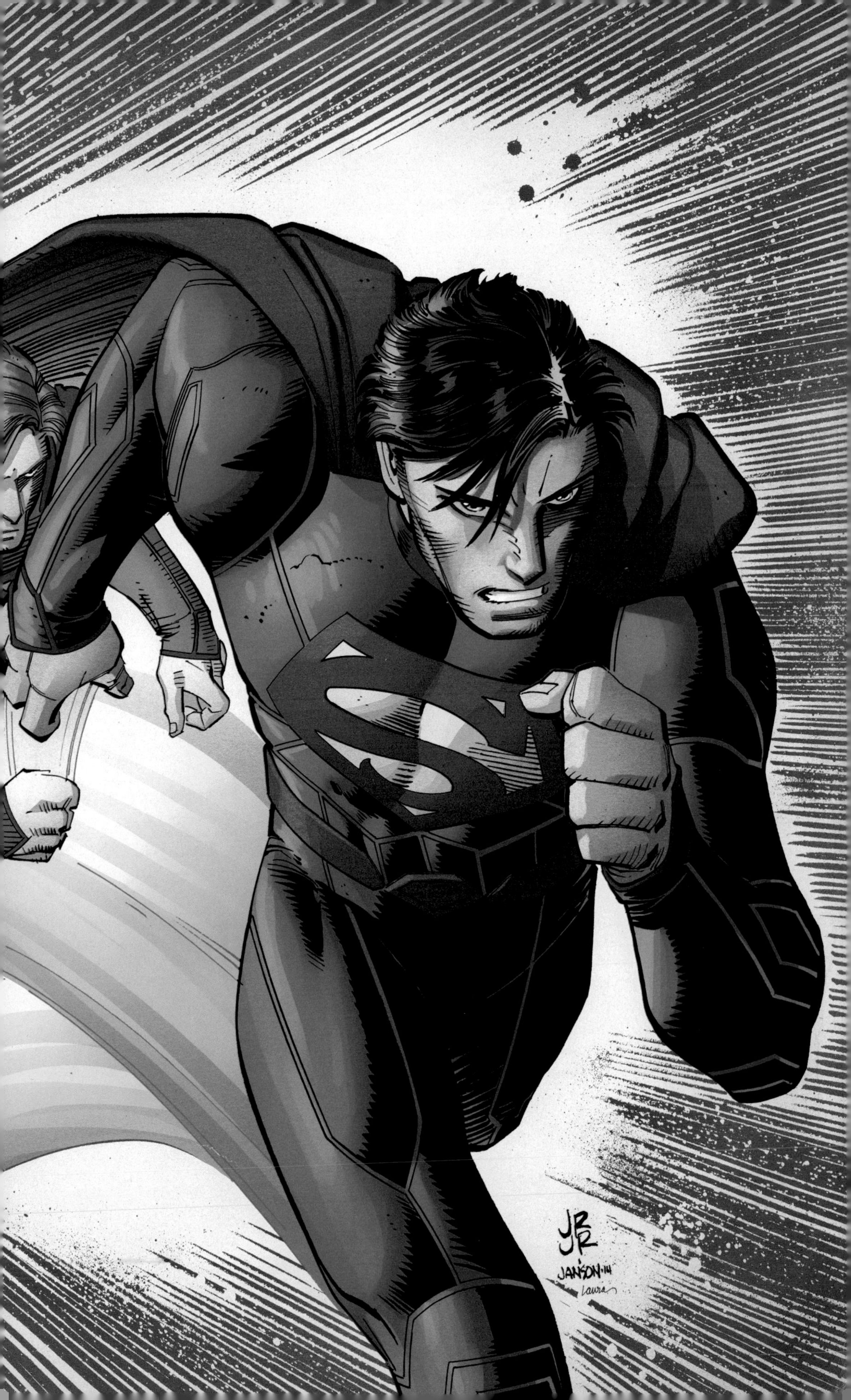
JR JR
JANSON·14
Laura

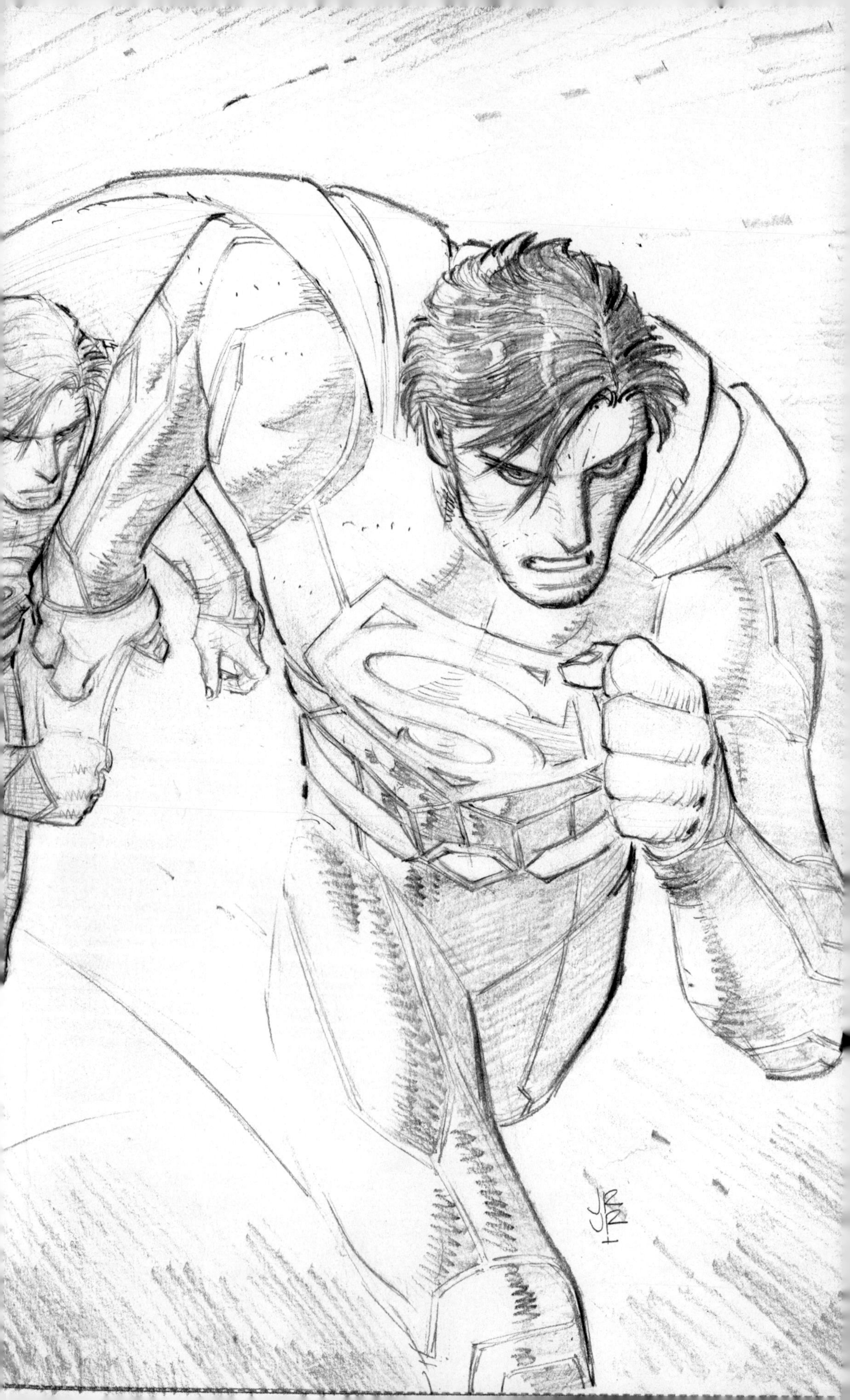

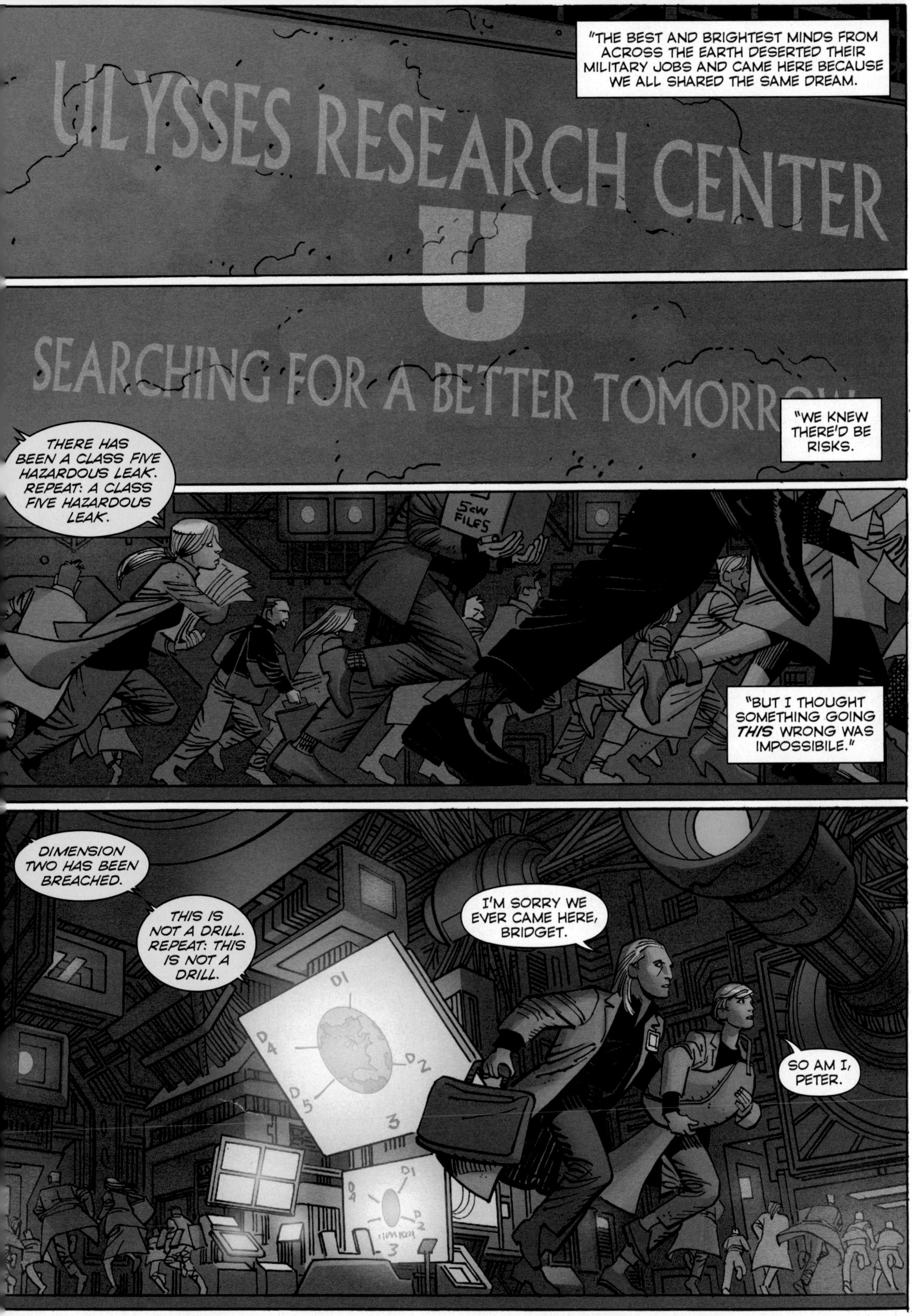

"THE BEST AND BRIGHTEST MINDS FROM ACROSS THE EARTH DESERTED THEIR MILITARY JOBS AND CAME HERE BECAUSE WE ALL SHARED THE SAME DREAM.
ULYSSES RESEARCH CENTER
U
SEARCHING FOR A BETTER TOMORR
"WE KNEW THERE'D BE RISKS.
THERE HAS BEEN A CLASS FIVE HAZARDOUS LEAK. REPEAT: A CLASS FIVE HAZARDOUS LEAK.
"BUT I THOUGHT SOMETHING GOING *THIS* WRONG WAS IMPOSSIBILE."
DIMENSION TWO HAS BEEN BREACHED.
THIS IS NOT A DRILL. REPEAT: THIS IS NOT A DRILL.
I'M SORRY WE EVER CAME HERE, BRIDGET.
SO AM I, PETER.

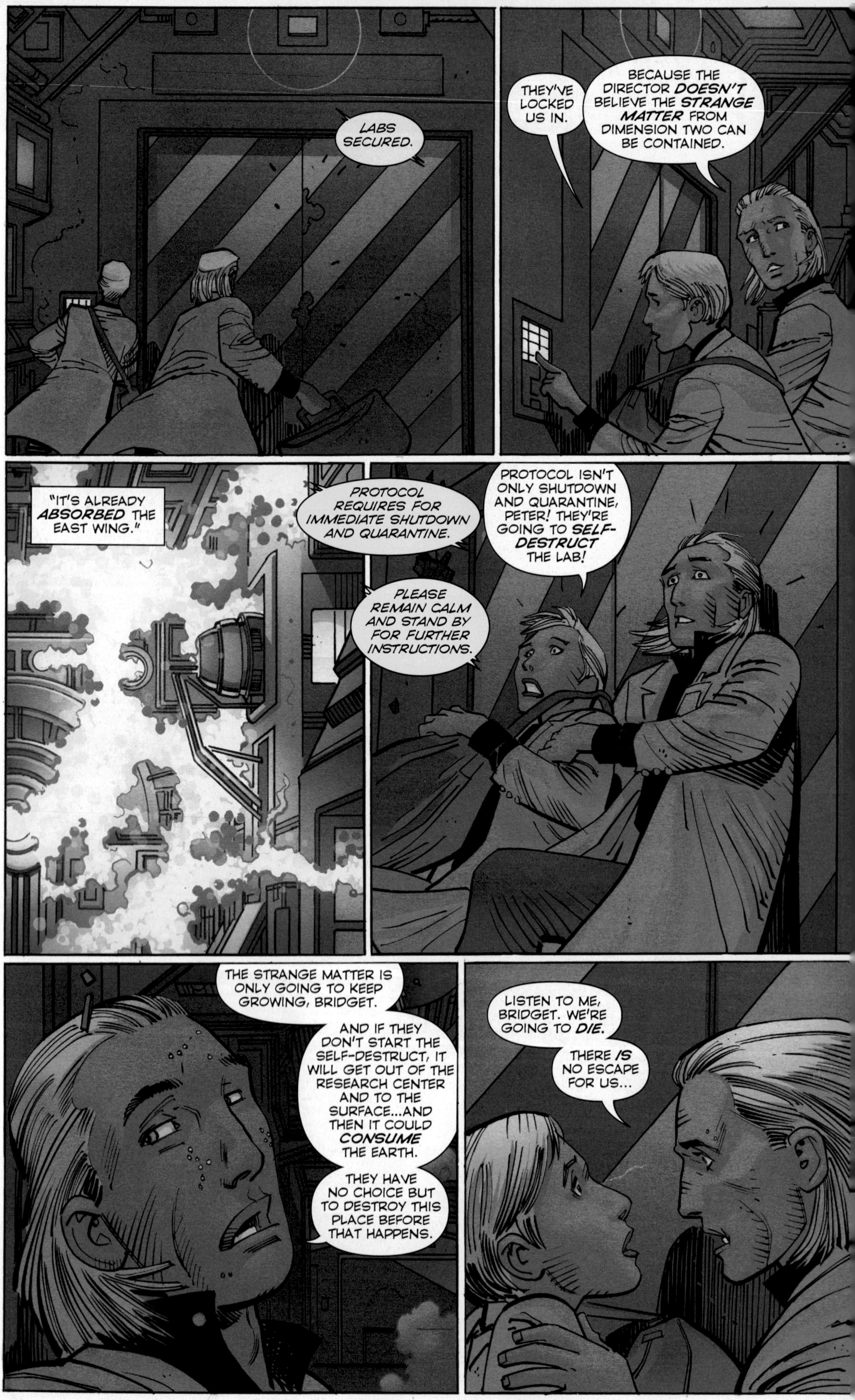

LABS SECURED.
THEY'VE LOCKED US IN.
BECAUSE THE DIRECTOR DOESN'T BELIEVE THE STRANGE MATTER FROM DIMENSION TWO CAN BE CONTAINED.
"IT'S ALREADY ABSORBED THE EAST WING."
PROTOCOL REQUIRES FOR IMMEDIATE SHUTDOWN AND QUARANTINE.
PLEASE REMAIN CALM AND STAND BY FOR FURTHER INSTRUCTIONS.
PROTOCOL ISN'T ONLY SHUTDOWN AND QUARANTINE, PETER! THEY'RE GOING TO SELF-DESTRUCT THE LAB!
THE STRANGE MATTER IS ONLY GOING TO KEEP GROWING, BRIDGET.
AND IF THEY DON'T START THE SELF-DESTRUCT, IT WILL GET OUT OF THE RESEARCH CENTER AND TO THE SURFACE...AND THEN IT COULD CONSUME THE EARTH.
THEY HAVE NO CHOICE BUT TO DESTROY THIS PLACE BEFORE THAT HAPPENS.
LISTEN TO ME, BRIDGET. WE'RE GOING TO DIE.
THERE IS NO ESCAPE FOR US...

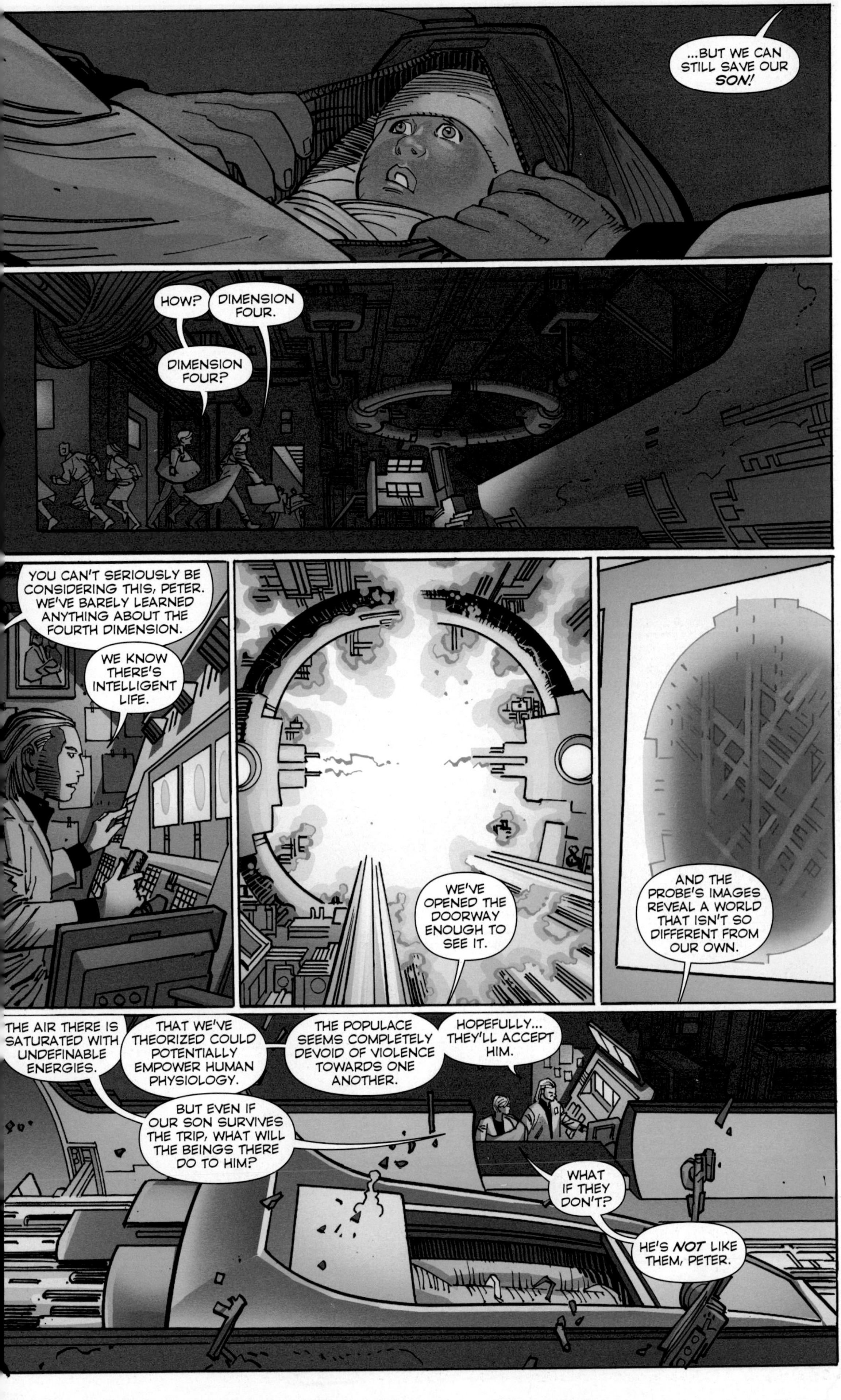
...BUT WE CAN STILL SAVE OUR SON!
HOW?
DIMENSION FOUR.
DIMENSION FOUR?
YOU CAN'T SERIOUSLY BE CONSIDERING THIS, PETER. WE'VE BARELY LEARNED ANYTHING ABOUT THE FOURTH DIMENSION.
WE KNOW THERE'S INTELLIGENT LIFE.
WE'VE OPENED THE DOORWAY ENOUGH TO SEE IT.
AND THE PROBE'S IMAGES REVEAL A WORLD THAT ISN'T SO DIFFERENT FROM OUR OWN.
THE AIR THERE IS SATURATED WITH UNDEFINABLE ENERGIES.
THAT WE'VE THEORIZED COULD POTENTIALLY EMPOWER HUMAN PHYSIOLOGY.
THE POPULACE SEEMS COMPLETELY DEVOID OF VIOLENCE TOWARDS ONE ANOTHER.
HOPEFULLY... THEY'LL ACCEPT HIM.
BUT EVEN IF OUR SON SURVIVES THE TRIP, WHAT WILL THE BEINGS THERE DO TO HIM?
WHAT IF THEY DON'T?
HE'S NOT LIKE THEM, PETER.

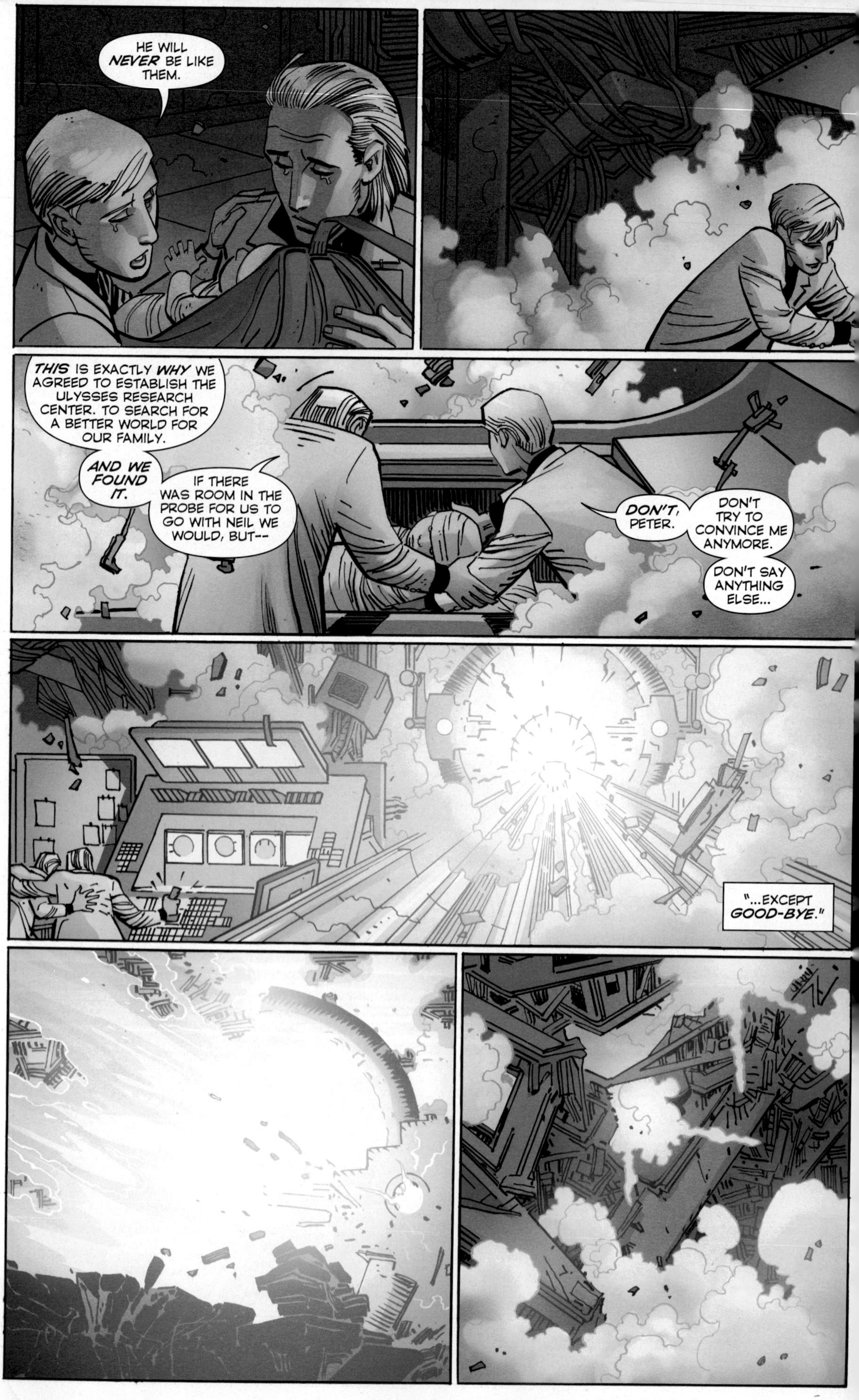
HE WILL NEVER BE LIKE THEM.
THIS IS EXACTLY WHY WE AGREED TO ESTABLISH THE ULYSSES RESEARCH CENTER. TO SEARCH FOR A BETTER WORLD FOR OUR FAMILY.
AND WE FOUND IT.
IF THERE WAS ROOM IN THE PROBE FOR US TO GO WITH NEIL WE WOULD, BUT--
DON'T, PETER.
DON'T TRY TO CONVINCE ME ANYMORE.
DON'T SAY ANYTHING ELSE...
"...EXCEPT GOOD-BYE."

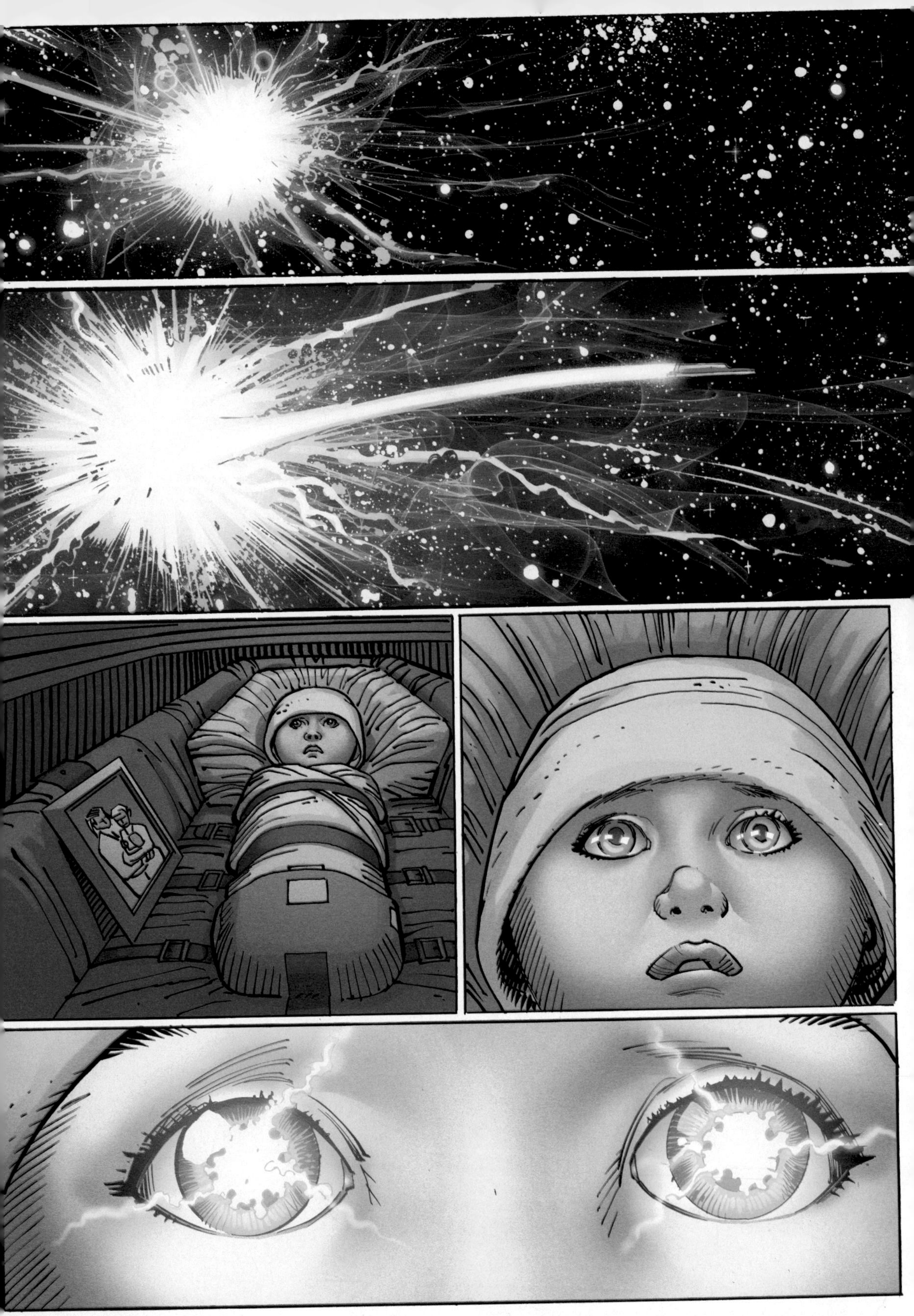

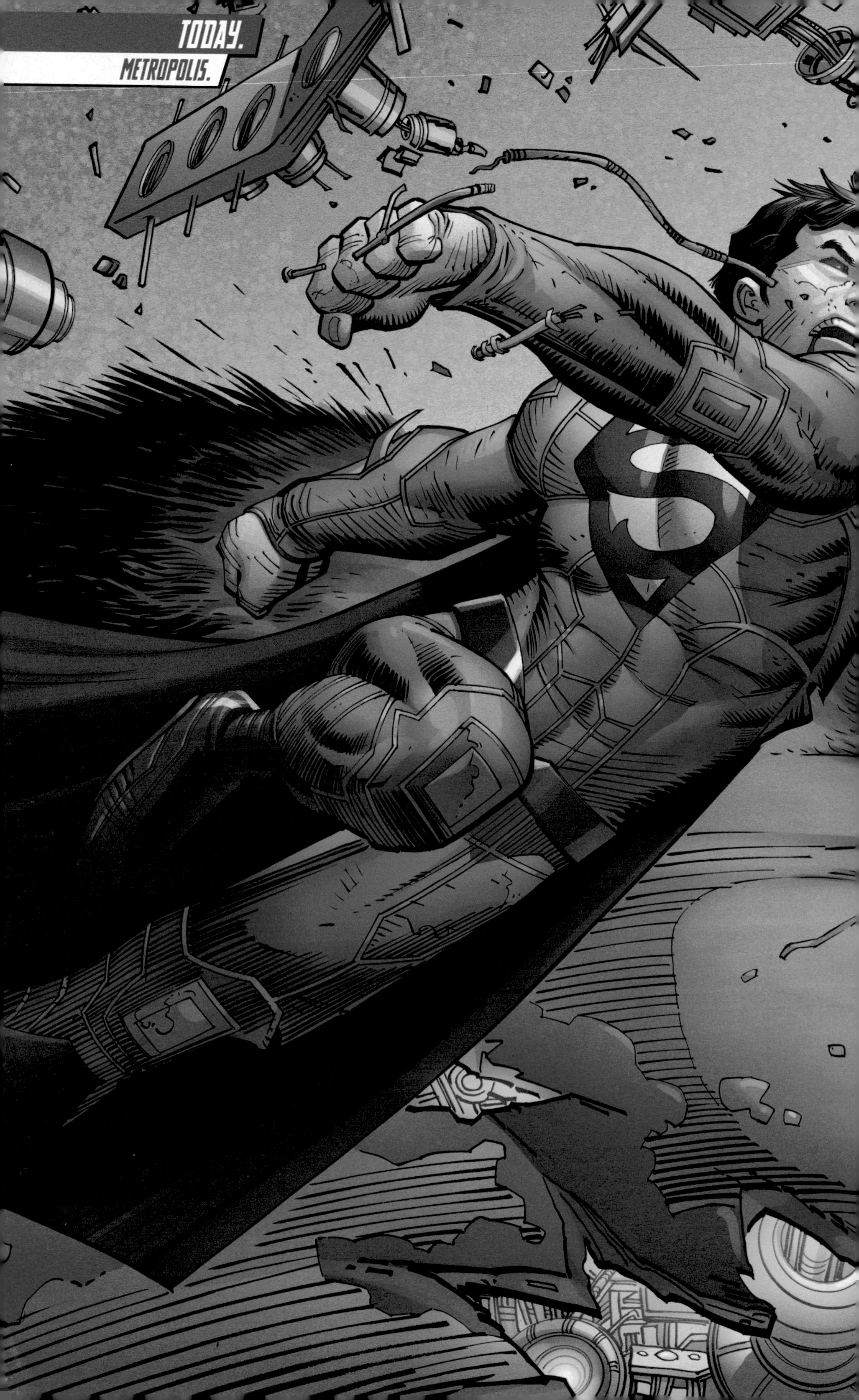
TODAY.
METROPOLIS.

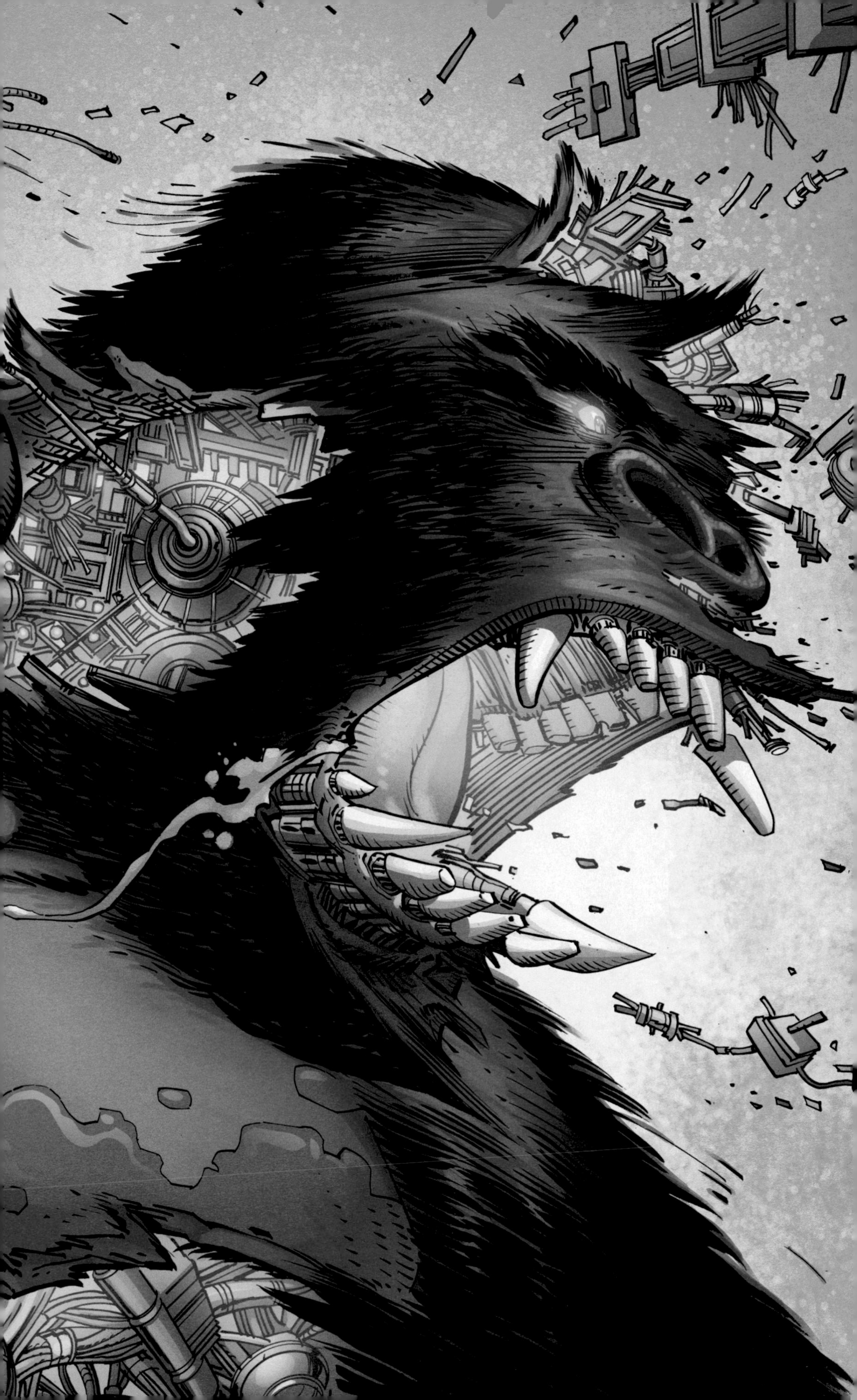

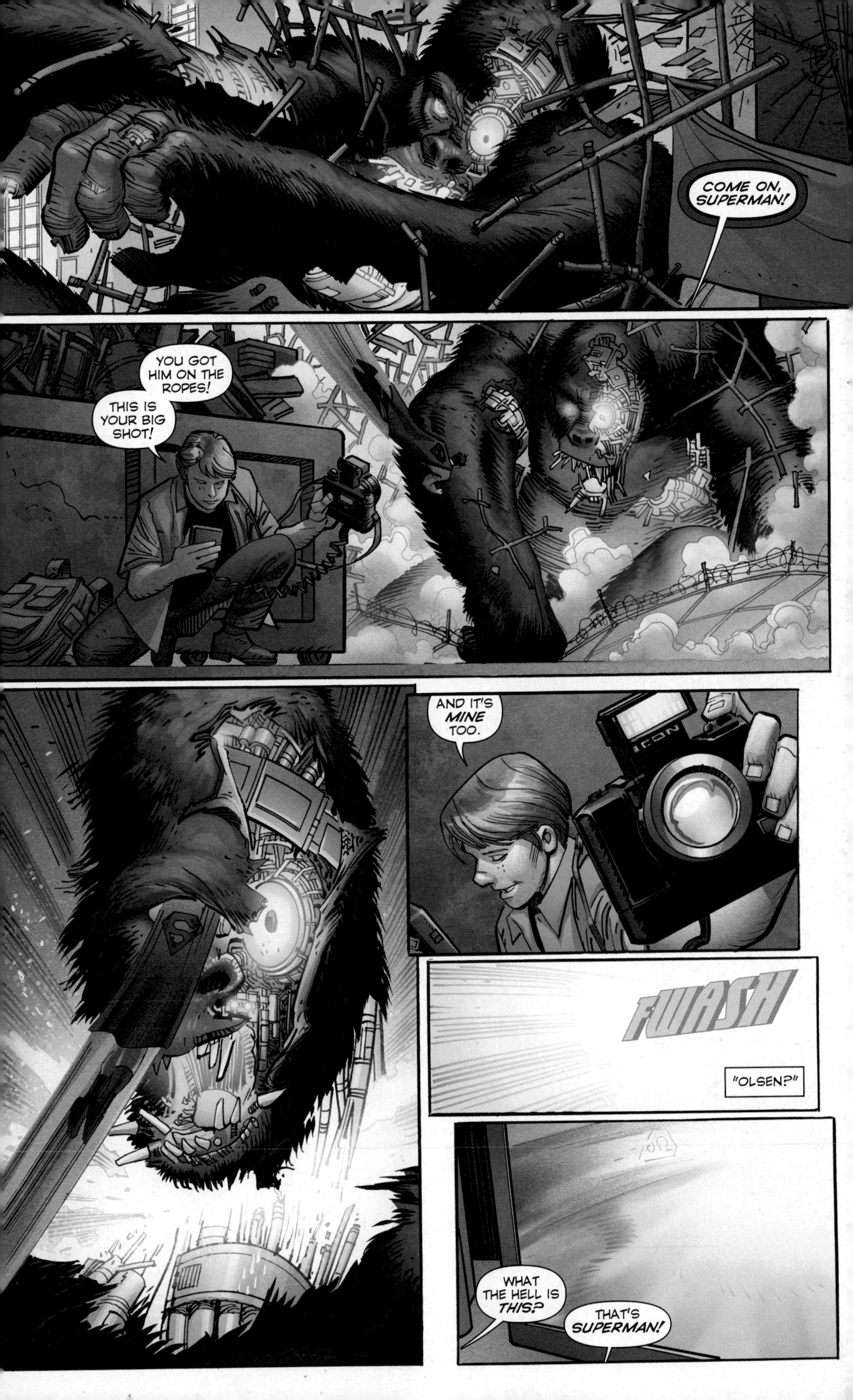
COME ON, SUPERMAN!
YOU GOT HIM ON THE ROPES!
THIS IS YOUR BIG SHOT!
AND IT'S MINE TOO.
FWASH
"OLSEN?"
WHAT THE HELL IS THIS?
THAT'S SUPERMAN!

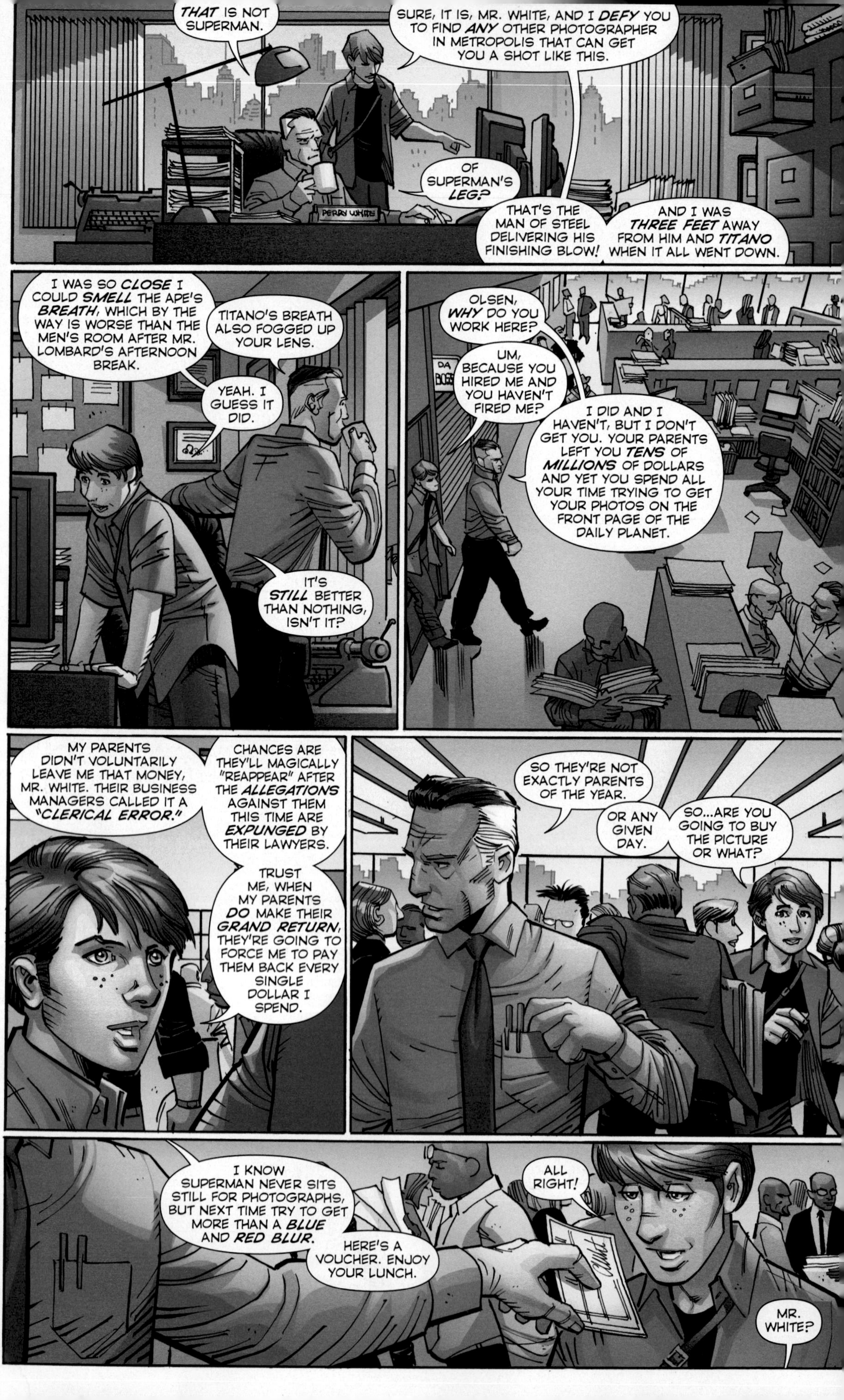
THAT IS NOT SUPERMAN.
SURE, IT IS, MR. WHITE, AND I DEFY YOU TO FIND ANY OTHER PHOTOGRAPHER IN METROPOLIS THAT CAN GET YOU A SHOT LIKE THIS.
PERRY WHITE
OF SUPERMAN'S LEG?
THAT'S THE MAN OF STEEL DELIVERING HIS FINISHING BLOW!
AND I WAS THREE FEET AWAY FROM HIM AND TITANO WHEN IT ALL WENT DOWN.
I WAS SO CLOSE I COULD SMELL THE APE'S BREATH, WHICH BY THE WAY IS WORSE THAN THE MEN'S ROOM AFTER MR. LOMBARD'S AFTERNOON BREAK.
TITANO'S BREATH ALSO FOGGED UP YOUR LENS.
YEAH. I GUESS IT DID.
IT'S STILL BETTER THAN NOTHING, ISN'T IT?
OLSEN, WHY DO YOU WORK HERE?
UM, BECAUSE YOU HIRED ME AND YOU HAVEN'T FIRED ME?
I DID AND I HAVEN'T, BUT I DON'T GET YOU. YOUR PARENTS LEFT YOU TENS OF MILLIONS OF DOLLARS AND YET YOU SPEND ALL YOUR TIME TRYING TO GET YOUR PHOTOS ON THE FRONT PAGE OF THE DAILY PLANET.
MY PARENTS DIDN'T VOLUNTARILY LEAVE ME THAT MONEY, MR. WHITE. THEIR BUSINESS MANAGERS CALLED IT A "CLERICAL ERROR."
CHANCES ARE THEY'LL MAGICALLY "REAPPEAR" AFTER THE ALLEGATIONS AGAINST THEM THIS TIME ARE EXPUNGED BY THEIR LAWYERS.
TRUST ME, WHEN MY PARENTS DO MAKE THEIR GRAND RETURN, THEY'RE GOING TO FORCE ME TO PAY THEM BACK EVERY SINGLE DOLLAR I SPEND.
SO THEY'RE NOT EXACTLY PARENTS OF THE YEAR.
OR ANY GIVEN DAY.
SO...ARE YOU GOING TO BUY THE PICTURE OR WHAT?
I KNOW SUPERMAN NEVER SITS STILL FOR PHOTOGRAPHS, BUT NEXT TIME TRY TO GET MORE THAN A BLUE AND RED BLUR.
HERE'S A VOUCHER. ENJOY YOUR LUNCH.
ALL RIGHT!
MR. WHITE?

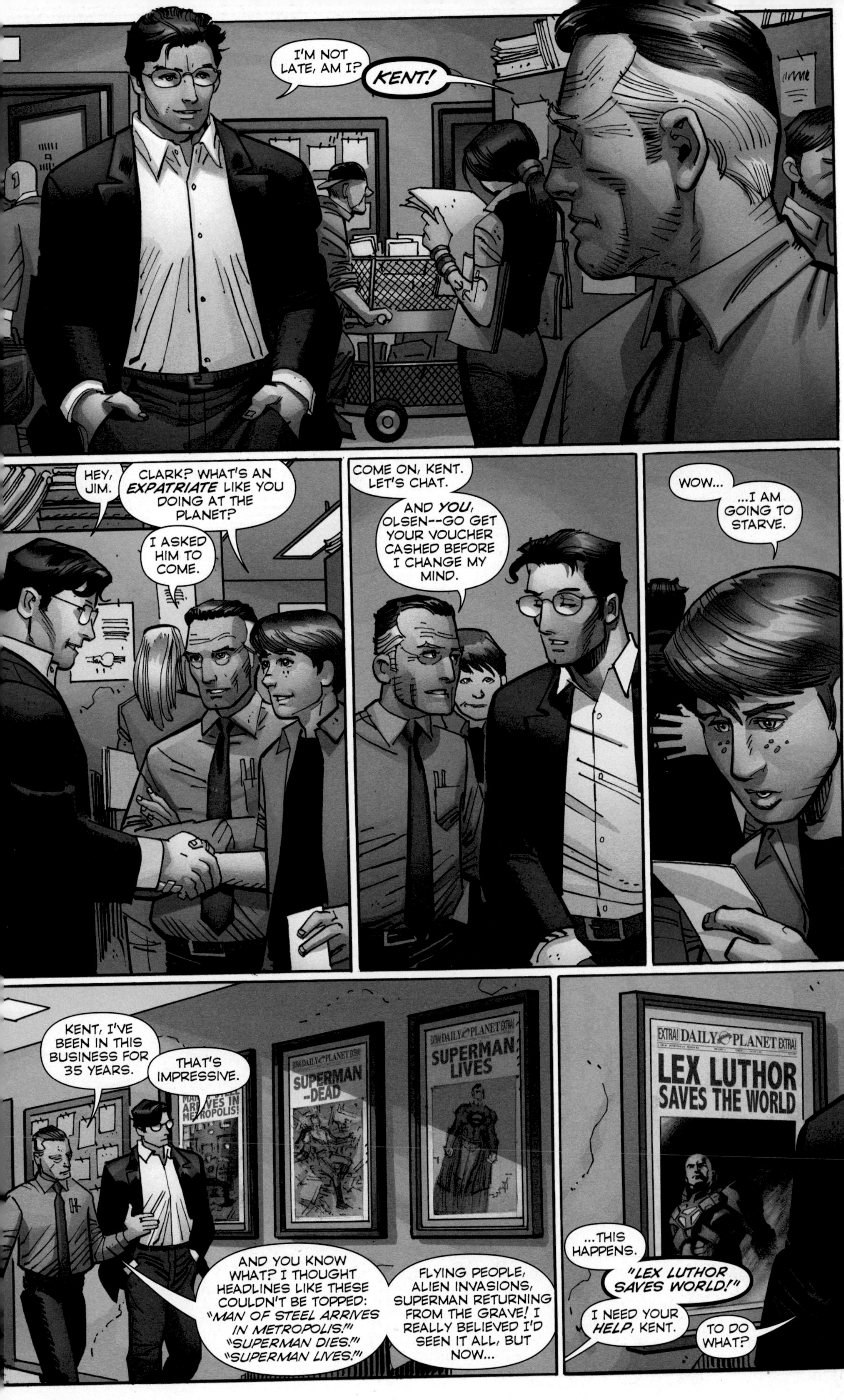
I'M NOT LATE, AM I?
KENT!
HEY, JIM.
CLARK? WHAT'S AN *EXPATRIATE* LIKE YOU DOING AT THE PLANET?
I ASKED HIM TO COME.
COME ON, KENT. LET'S CHAT.
AND *YOU*, OLSEN--GO GET YOUR VOUCHER CASHED BEFORE I CHANGE MY MIND.
WOW...
...I AM GOING TO STARVE.
KENT, I'VE BEEN IN THIS BUSINESS FOR 35 YEARS.
THAT'S IMPRESSIVE.
SUPERMAN -DEAD
SUPERMAN LIVES
AND YOU KNOW WHAT? I THOUGHT HEADLINES LIKE THESE COULDN'T BE TOPPED: *"MAN OF STEEL ARRIVES IN METROPOLIS!" "SUPERMAN DIES!" "SUPERMAN LIVES!"*
FLYING PEOPLE, ALIEN INVASIONS, SUPERMAN RETURNING FROM THE GRAVE! I REALLY BELIEVED I'D SEEN IT ALL, BUT NOW...
EXTRA! DAILY PLANET EXTRA!
LEX LUTHOR SAVES THE WORLD
...THIS HAPPENS.
"LEX LUTHOR SAVES WORLD!"
I NEED YOUR *HELP*, KENT.
TO DO WHAT?

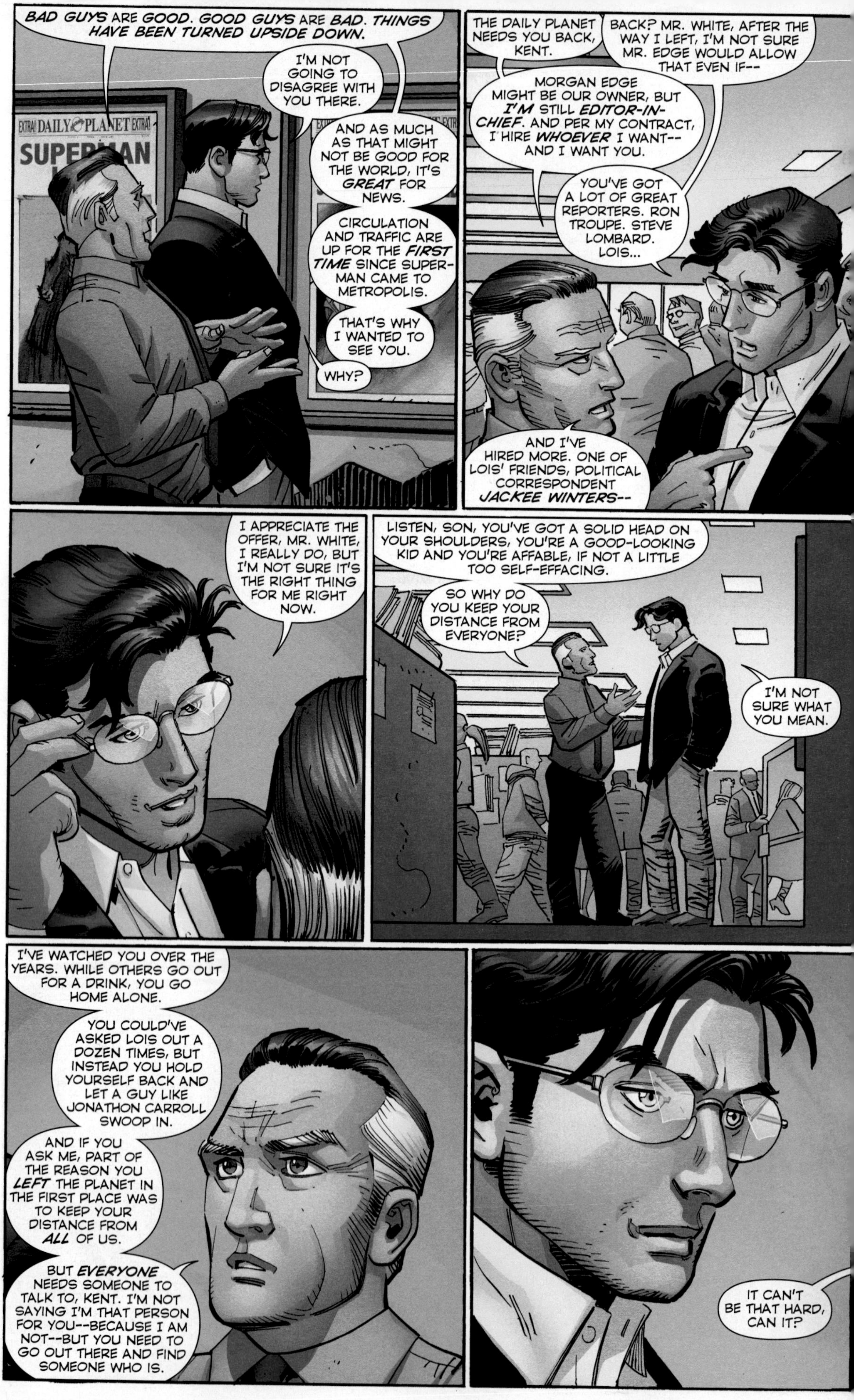
BAD GUYS ARE GOOD. GOOD GUYS ARE BAD. THINGS HAVE BEEN TURNED UPSIDE DOWN.
I'M NOT GOING TO DISAGREE WITH YOU THERE.
AND AS MUCH AS THAT MIGHT NOT BE GOOD FOR THE WORLD, IT'S GREAT FOR NEWS.
CIRCULATION AND TRAFFIC ARE UP FOR THE FIRST TIME SINCE SUPERMAN CAME TO METROPOLIS.
THAT'S WHY I WANTED TO SEE YOU.
WHY?
EXTRA! DAILY PLANET EXTRA!
SUPERMAN
THE DAILY PLANET NEEDS YOU BACK, KENT.
BACK? MR. WHITE, AFTER THE WAY I LEFT, I'M NOT SURE MR. EDGE WOULD ALLOW THAT EVEN IF--
MORGAN EDGE MIGHT BE OUR OWNER, BUT I'M STILL EDITOR-IN-CHIEF. AND PER MY CONTRACT, I HIRE WHOEVER I WANT-- AND I WANT YOU.
YOU'VE GOT A LOT OF GREAT REPORTERS. RON TROUPE. STEVE LOMBARD. LOIS...
AND I'VE HIRED MORE. ONE OF LOIS' FRIENDS, POLITICAL CORRESPONDENT JACKEE WINTERS--
I APPRECIATE THE OFFER, MR. WHITE, I REALLY DO, BUT I'M NOT SURE IT'S THE RIGHT THING FOR ME RIGHT NOW.
LISTEN, SON, YOU'VE GOT A SOLID HEAD ON YOUR SHOULDERS, YOU'RE A GOOD-LOOKING KID AND YOU'RE AFFABLE, IF NOT A LITTLE TOO SELF-EFFACING.
SO WHY DO YOU KEEP YOUR DISTANCE FROM EVERYONE?
I'M NOT SURE WHAT YOU MEAN.
I'VE WATCHED YOU OVER THE YEARS. WHILE OTHERS GO OUT FOR A DRINK, YOU GO HOME ALONE.
YOU COULD'VE ASKED LOIS OUT A DOZEN TIMES, BUT INSTEAD YOU HOLD YOURSELF BACK AND LET A GUY LIKE JONATHON CARROLL SWOOP IN.
AND IF YOU ASK ME, PART OF THE REASON YOU LEFT THE PLANET IN THE FIRST PLACE WAS TO KEEP YOUR DISTANCE FROM ALL OF US.
BUT EVERYONE NEEDS SOMEONE TO TALK TO, KENT. I'M NOT SAYING I'M THAT PERSON FOR YOU--BECAUSE I AM NOT--BUT YOU NEED TO GO OUT THERE AND FIND SOMEONE WHO IS.
IT CAN'T BE THAT HARD, CAN IT?

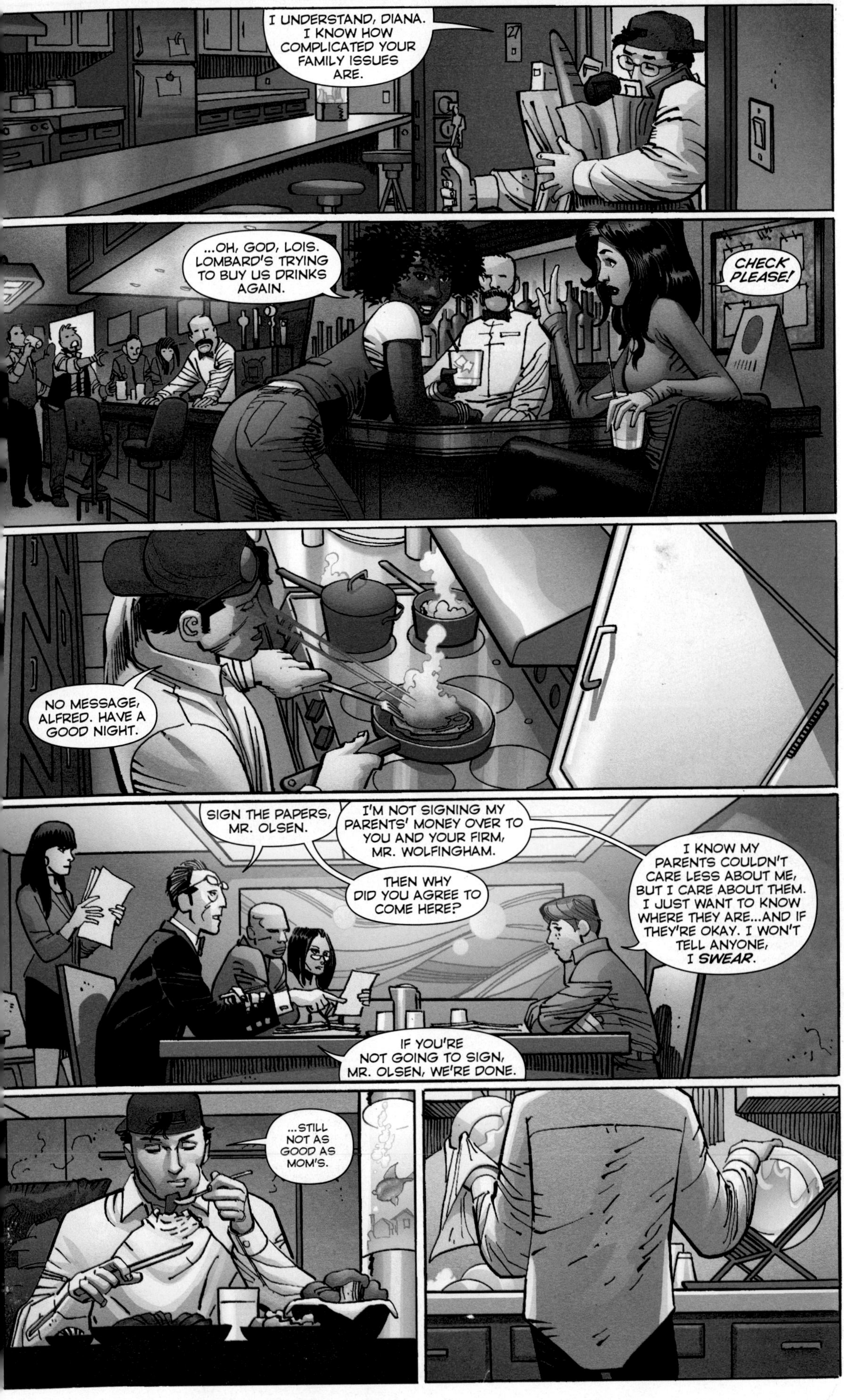
I UNDERSTAND, DIANA. I KNOW HOW COMPLICATED YOUR FAMILY ISSUES ARE.
27
...OH, GOD, LOIS. LOMBARD'S TRYING TO BUY US DRINKS AGAIN.
CHECK PLEASE!
NO MESSAGE, ALFRED. HAVE A GOOD NIGHT.
SIGN THE PAPERS, MR. OLSEN.
I'M NOT SIGNING MY PARENTS' MONEY OVER TO YOU AND YOUR FIRM, MR. WOLFINGHAM.
THEN WHY DID YOU AGREE TO COME HERE?
I KNOW MY PARENTS COULDN'T CARE LESS ABOUT ME, BUT I CARE ABOUT THEM. I JUST WANT TO KNOW WHERE THEY ARE...AND IF THEY'RE OKAY. I WON'T TELL ANYONE, I *SWEAR*.
IF YOU'RE NOT GOING TO SIGN, MR. OLSEN, WE'RE DONE.
...STILL NOT AS GOOD AS MOM'S.

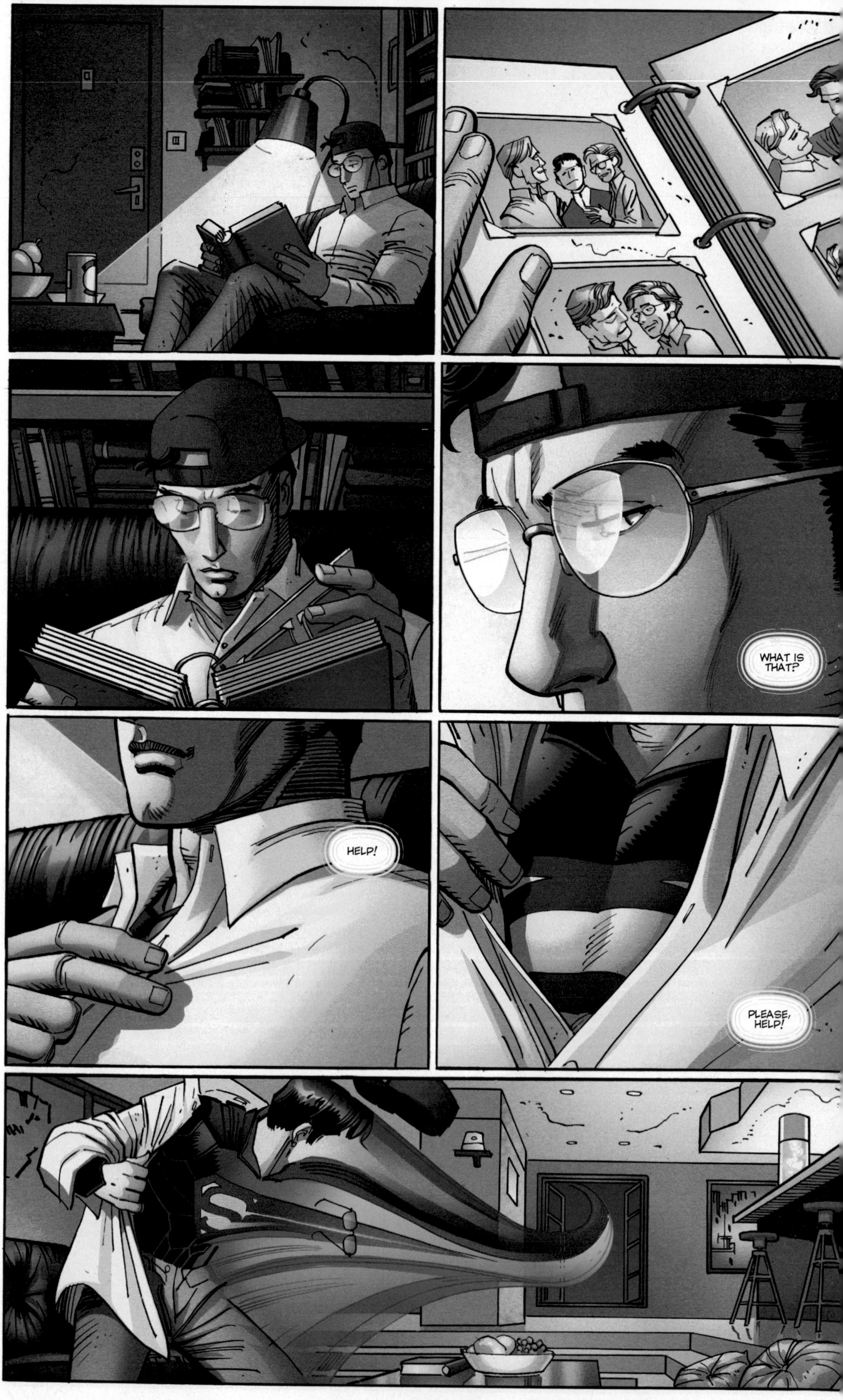
WHAT IS THAT?
HELP!
PLEASE, HELP!

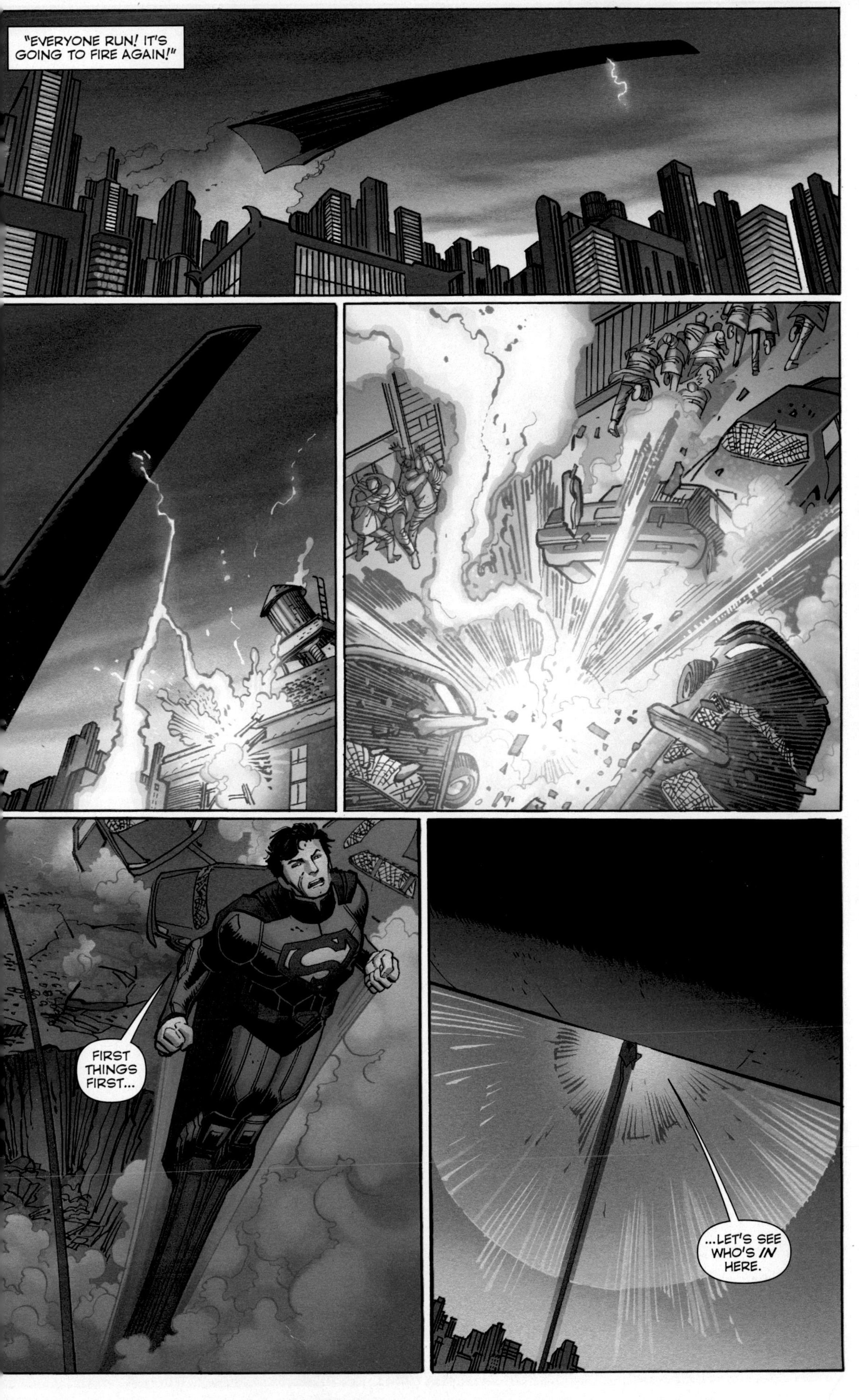
"EVERYONE RUN! IT'S GOING TO FIRE AGAIN!"
FIRST THINGS FIRST...
...LET'S SEE WHO'S *IN* HERE.

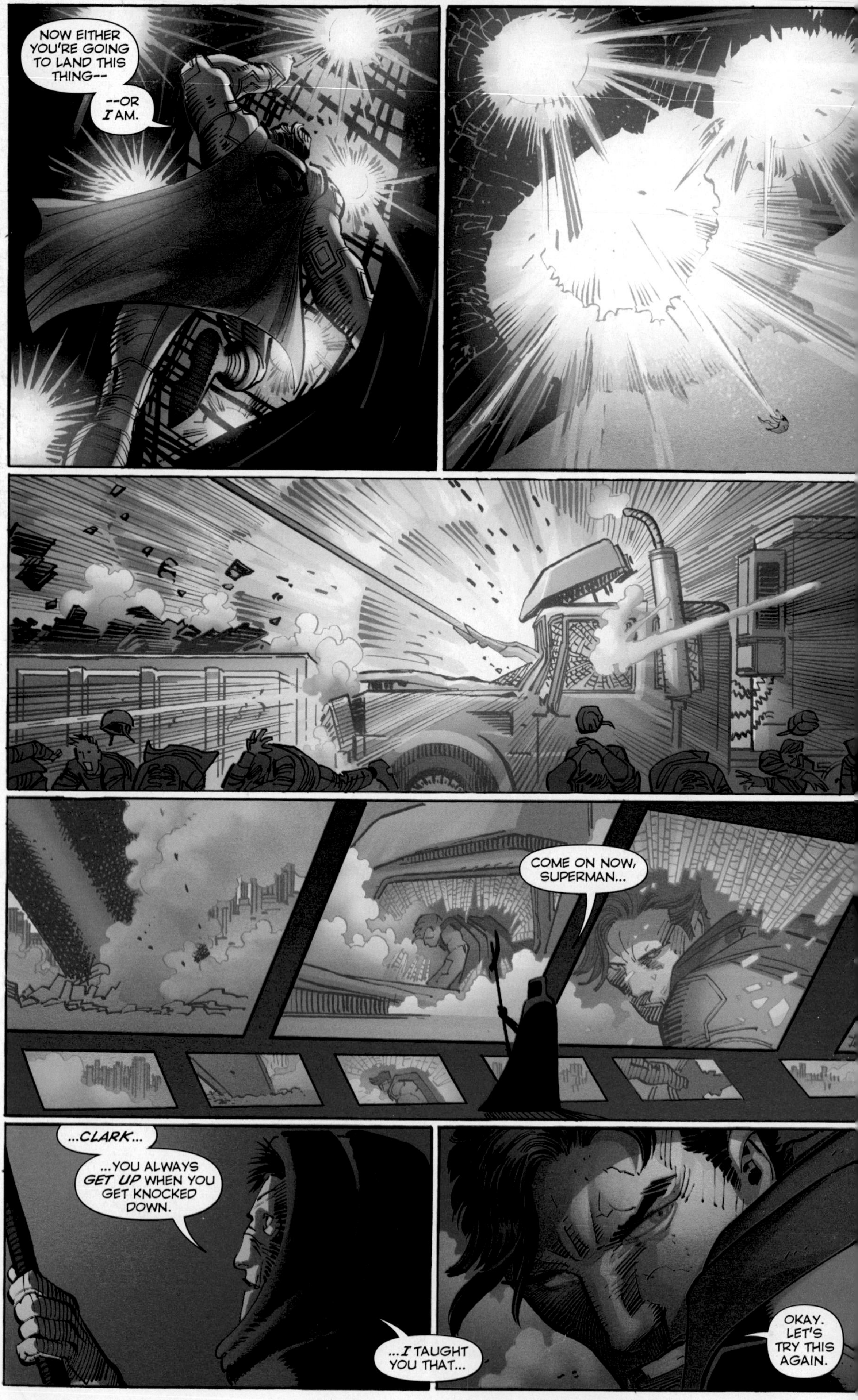
NOW EITHER YOU'RE GOING TO LAND THIS THING--
--OR *I* AM.
COME ON NOW, SUPERMAN...
...*CLARK*...
...YOU ALWAYS *GET UP* WHEN YOU GET KNOCKED DOWN.
...*I* TAUGHT YOU THAT...
OKAY. LET'S TRY THIS AGAIN.

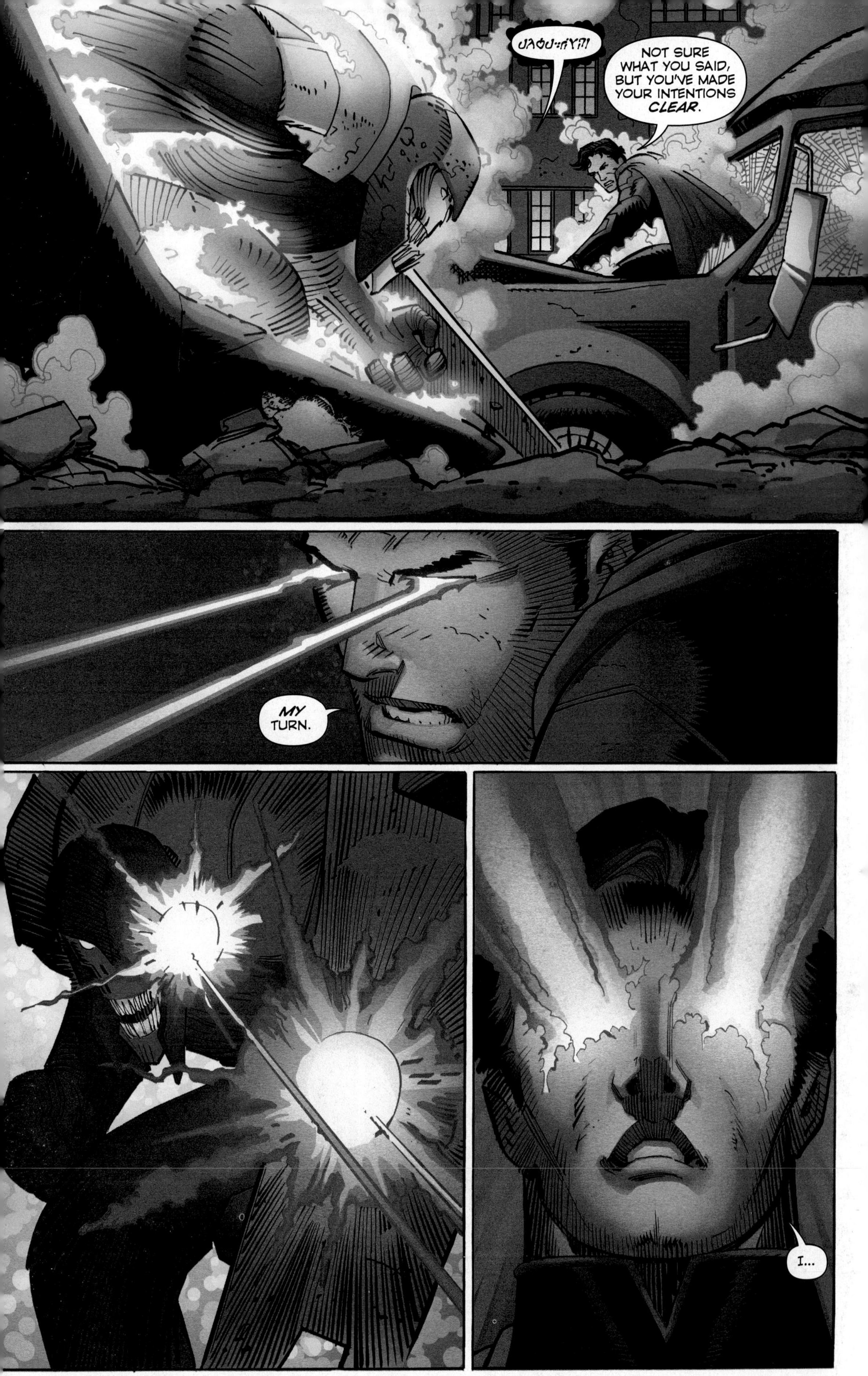
NOT SURE WHAT YOU SAID, BUT YOU'VE MADE YOUR INTENTIONS CLEAR.
MY TURN.
I...

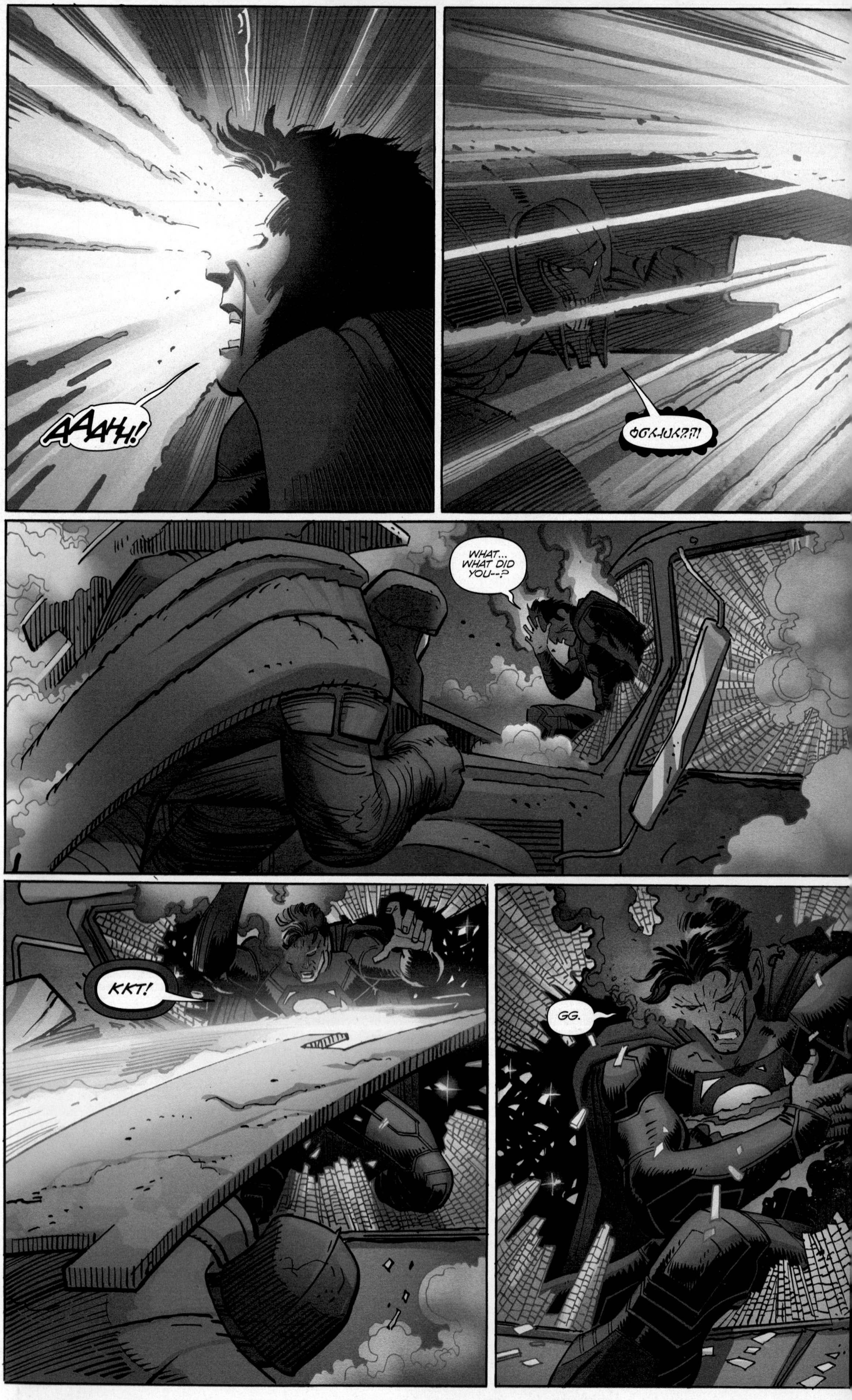
AAAHH!
WHAT... WHAT DID YOU--?
KKT!
GG.

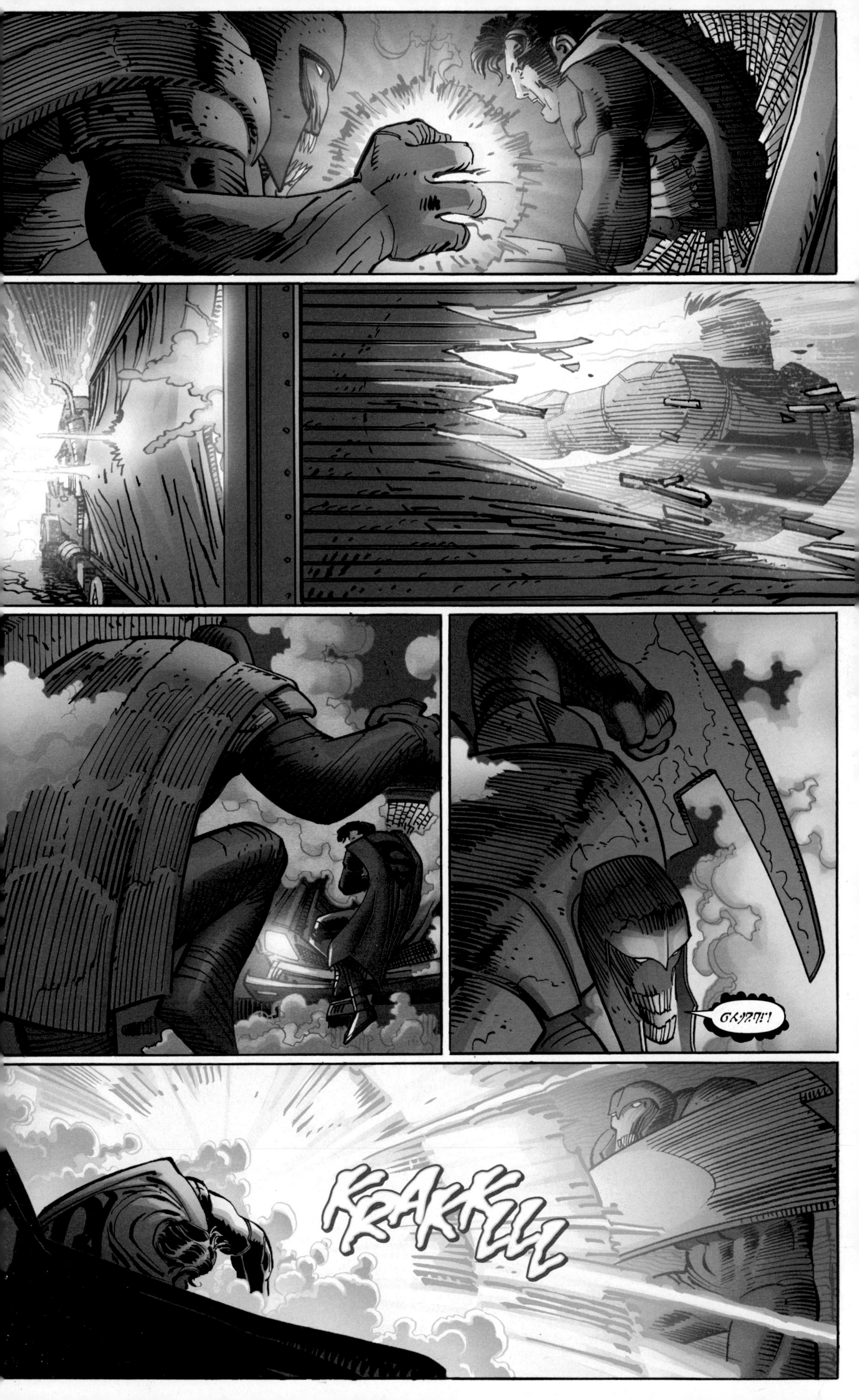
KRAKKLL

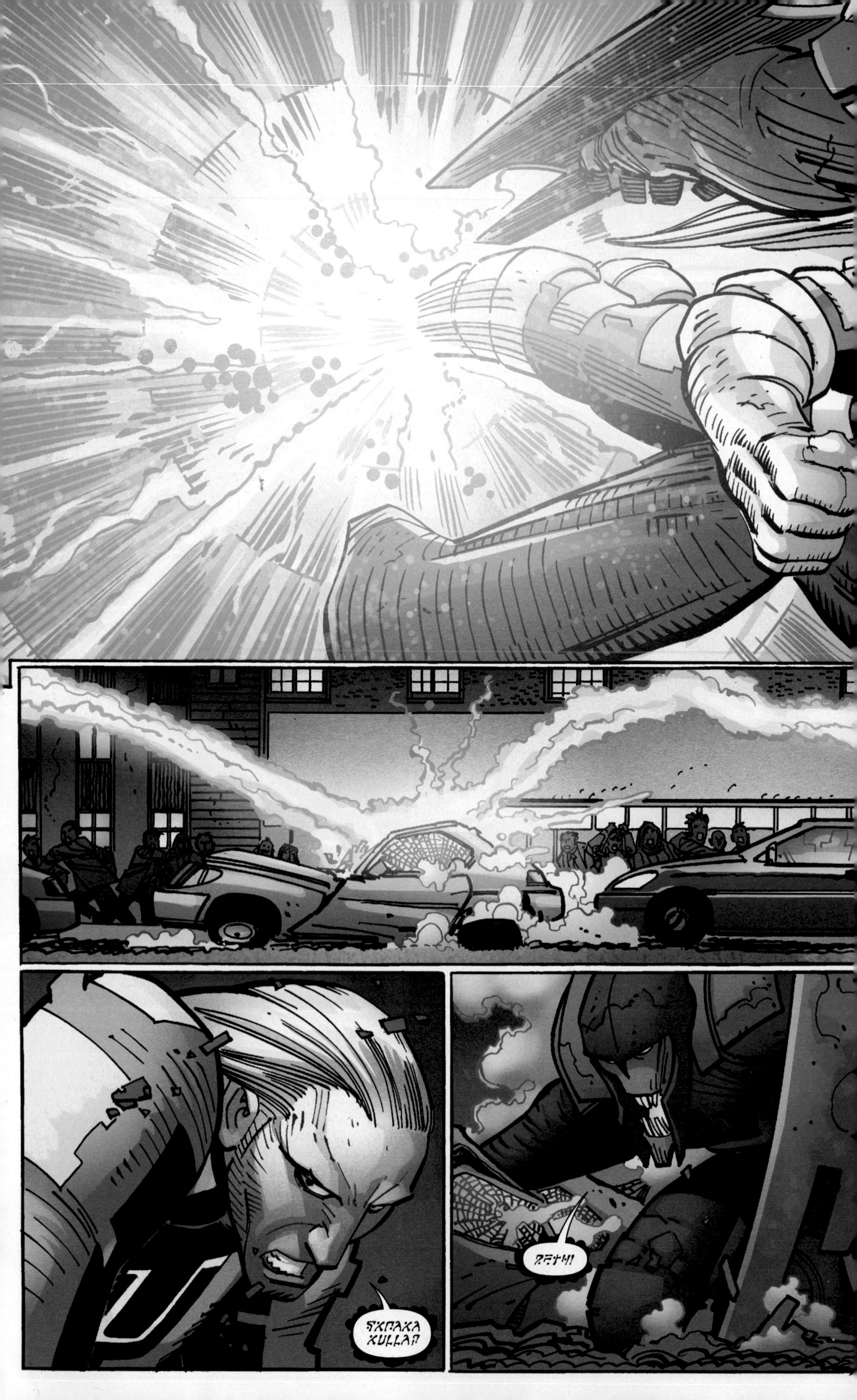

GAAAAH!

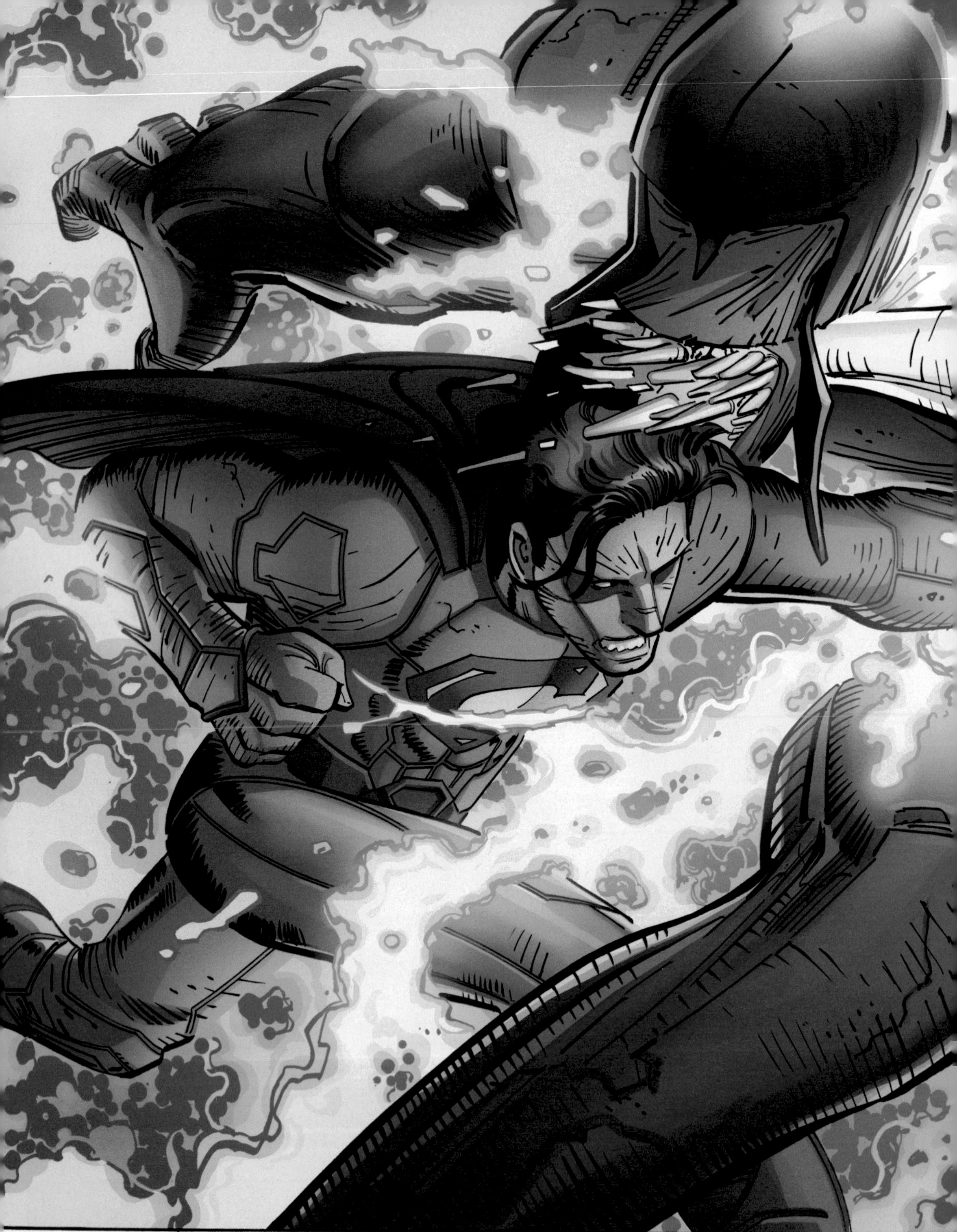
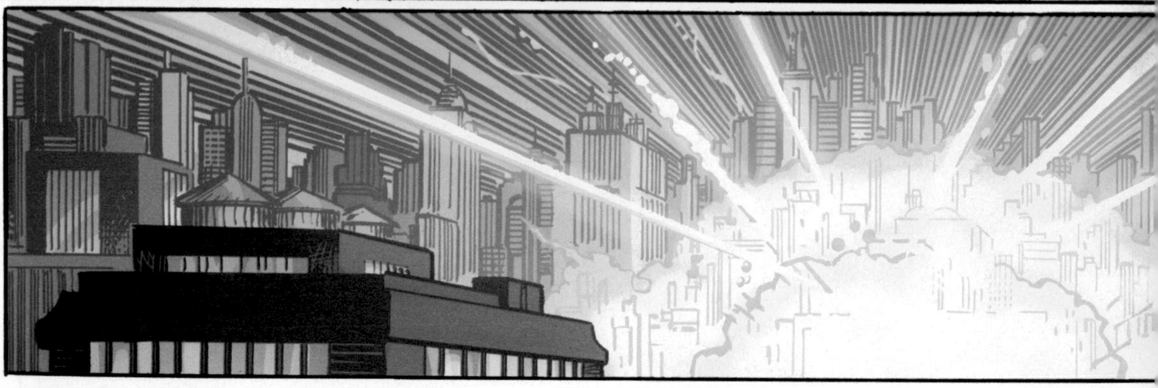

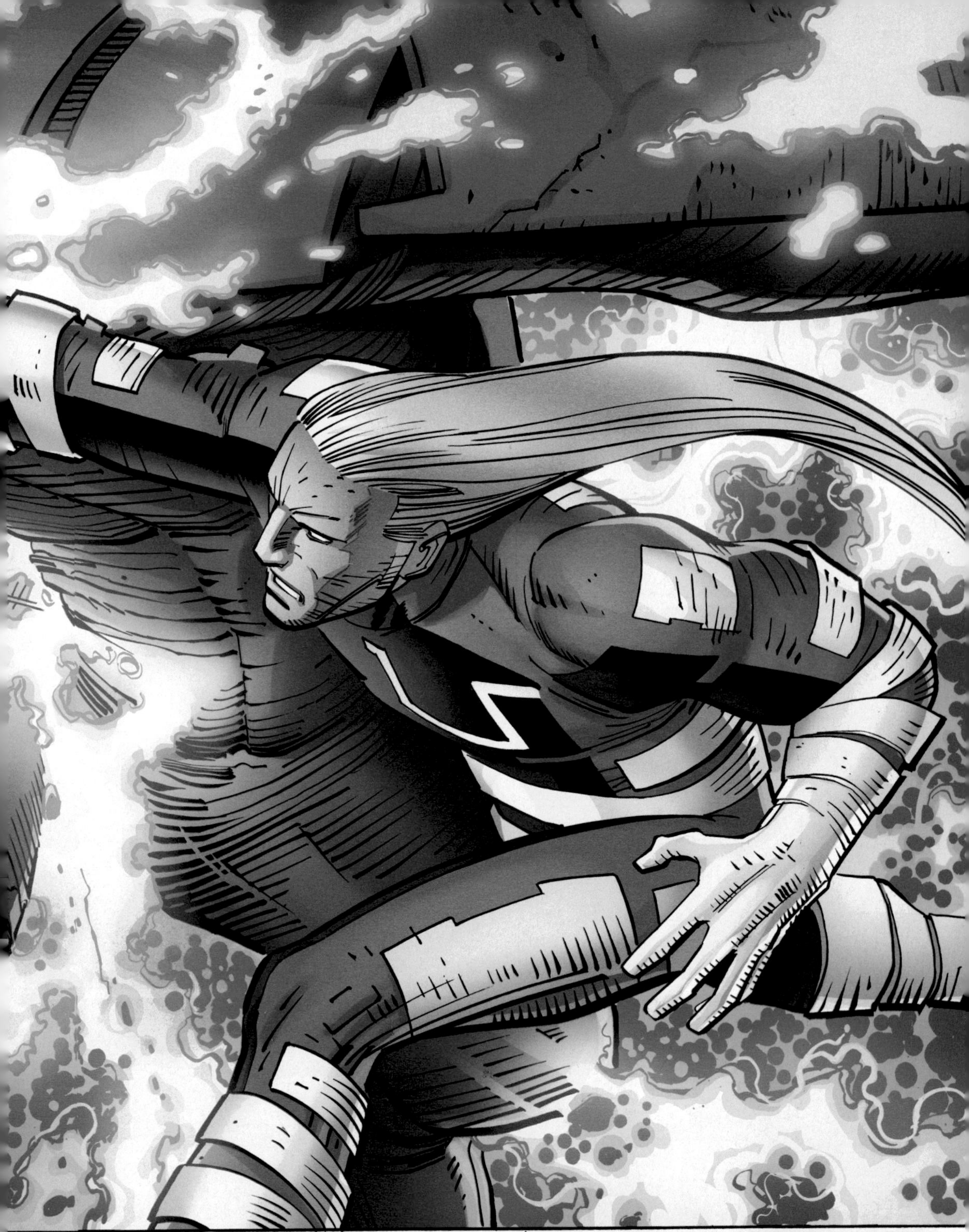
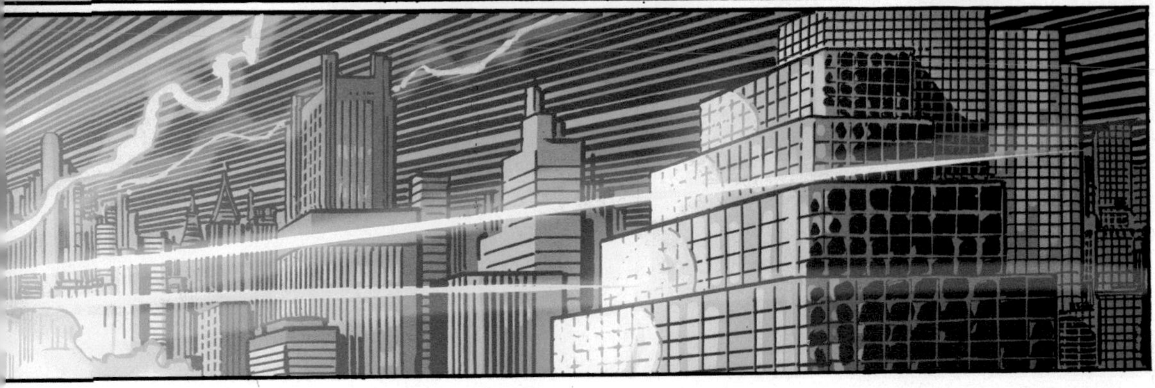

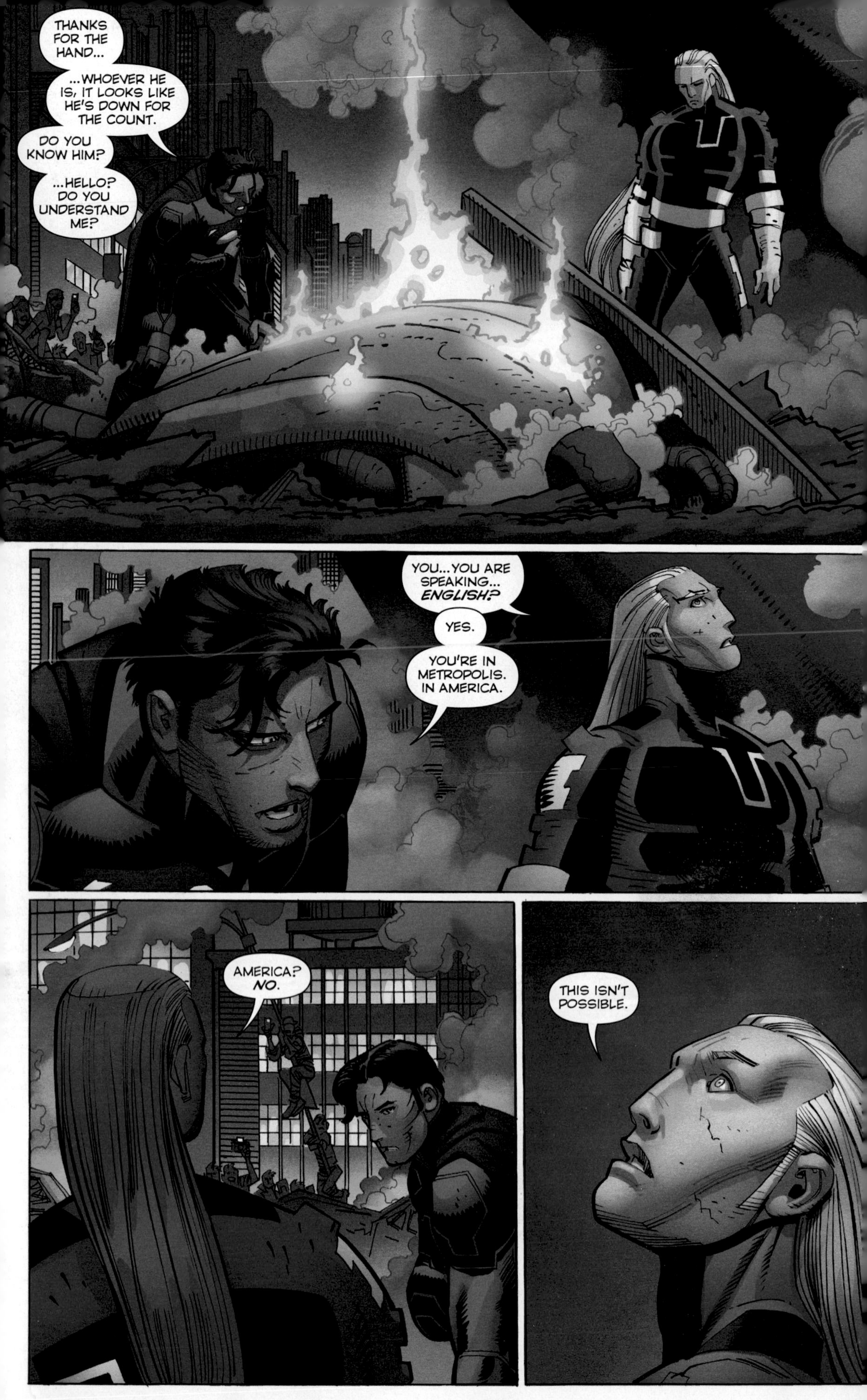
THANKS FOR THE HAND...
...WHOEVER HE IS, IT LOOKS LIKE HE'S DOWN FOR THE COUNT.
DO YOU KNOW HIM?
...HELLO? DO YOU UNDERSTAND ME?
YOU...YOU ARE SPEAKING... ENGLISH?
YES.
YOU'RE IN METROPOLIS. IN AMERICA.
AMERICA? NO.
THIS ISN'T POSSIBLE.

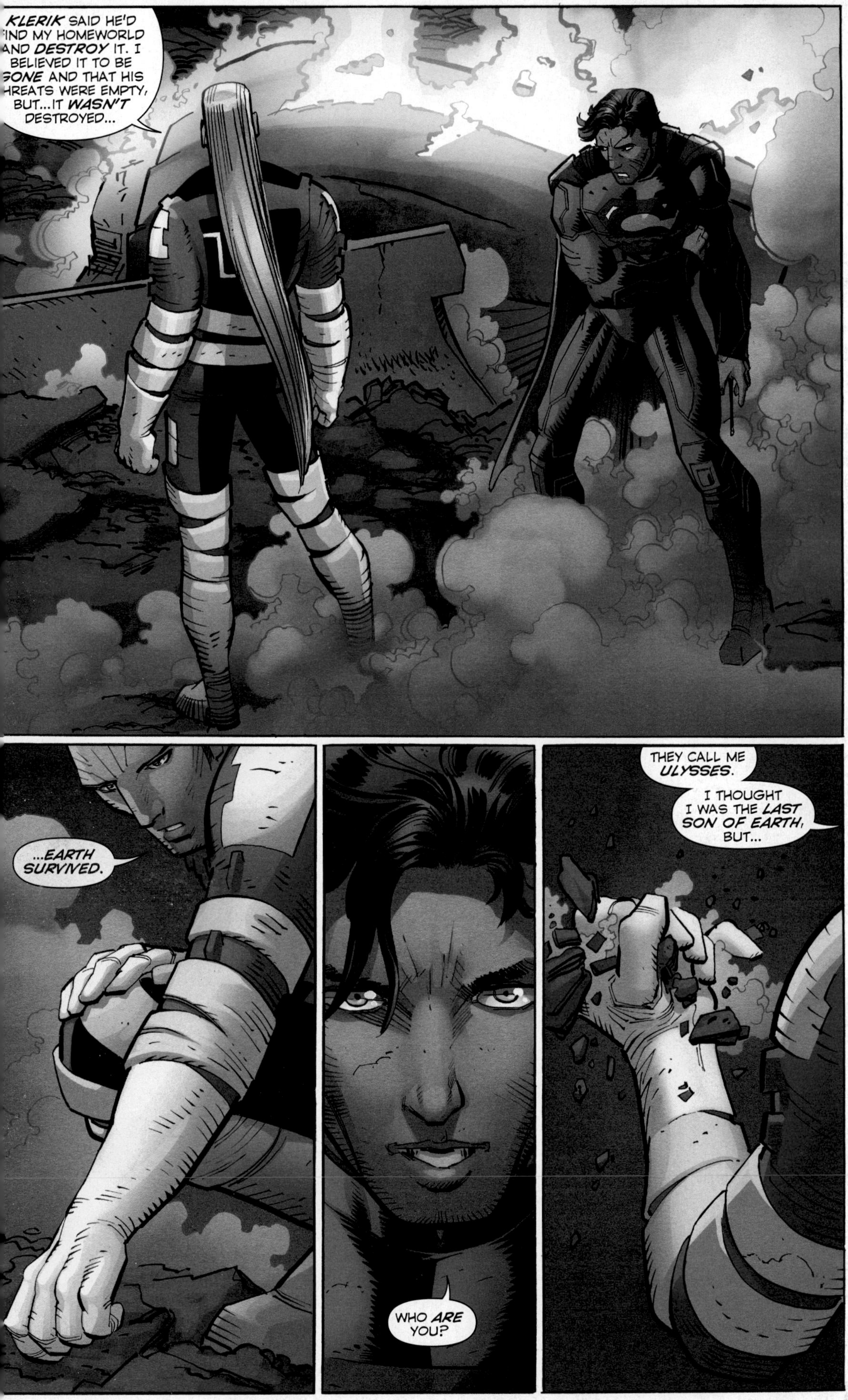
KLERIK SAID HE'D FIND MY HOMEWORLD AND DESTROY IT. I BELIEVED IT TO BE GONE AND THAT HIS THREATS WERE EMPTY, BUT...IT WASN'T DESTROYED...
...EARTH SURVIVED.
WHO ARE YOU?
THEY CALL ME ULYSSES.
I THOUGHT I WAS THE LAST SON OF EARTH, BUT...

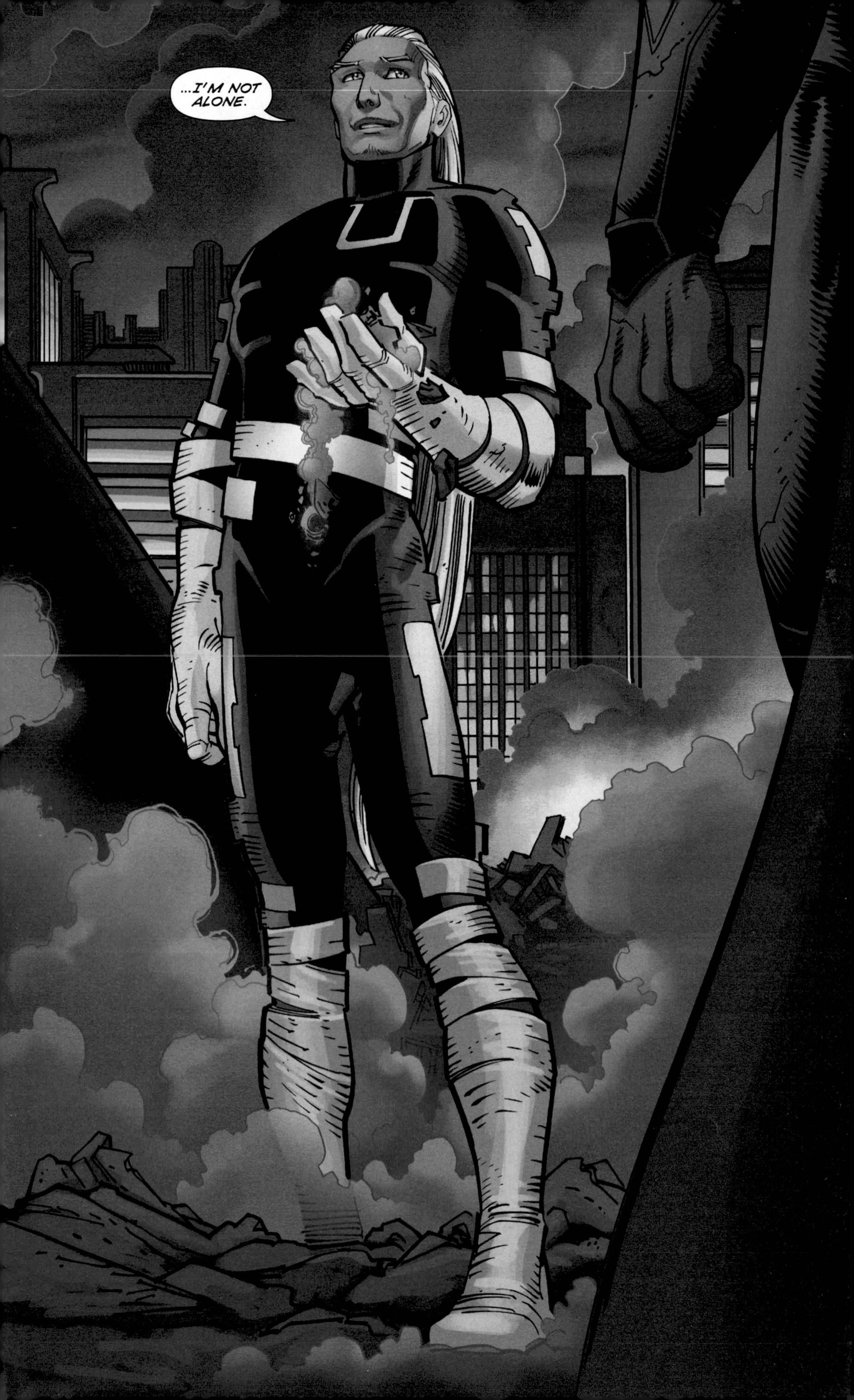
...I'M NOT ALONE.

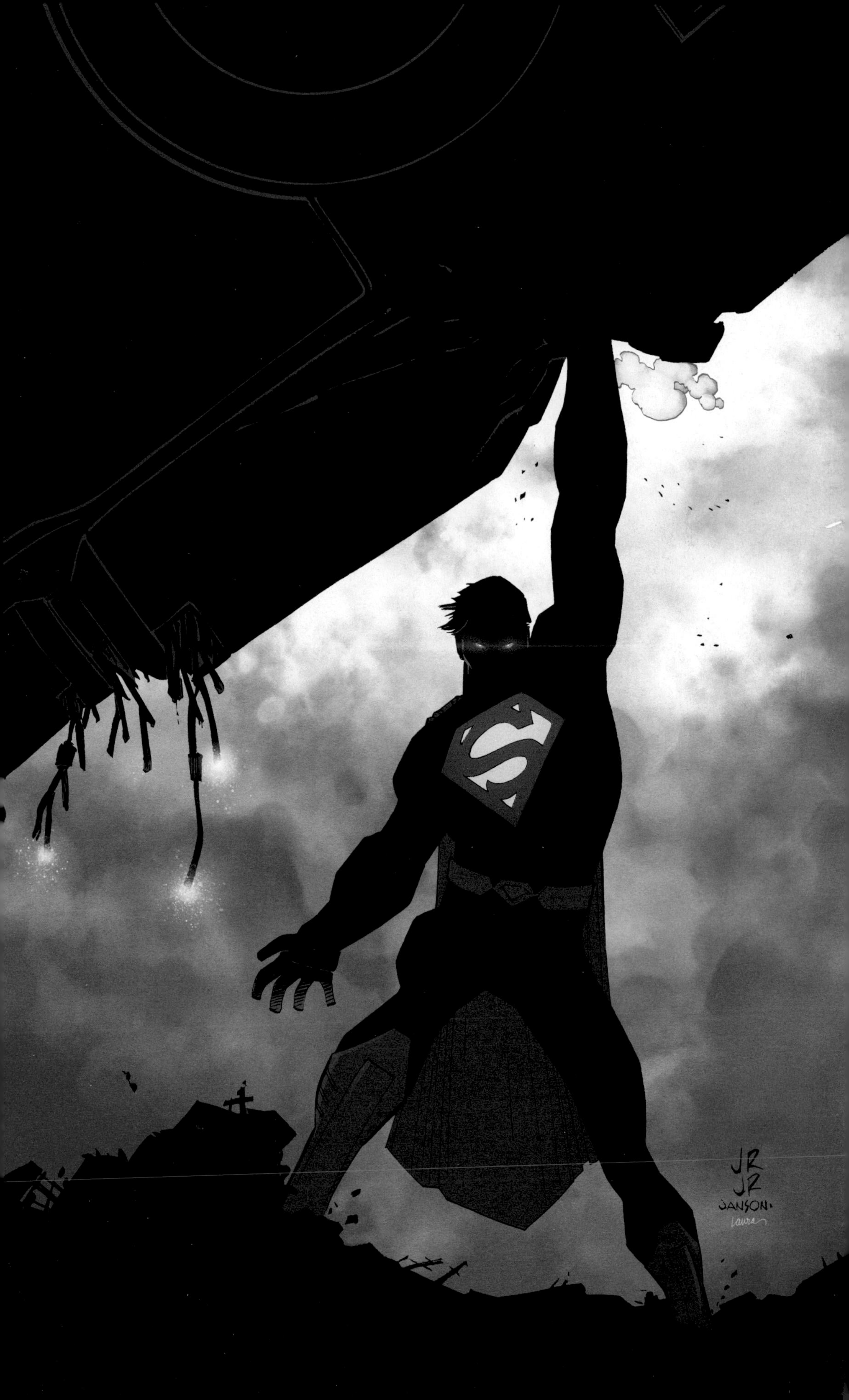
JR
JR
JANSON.

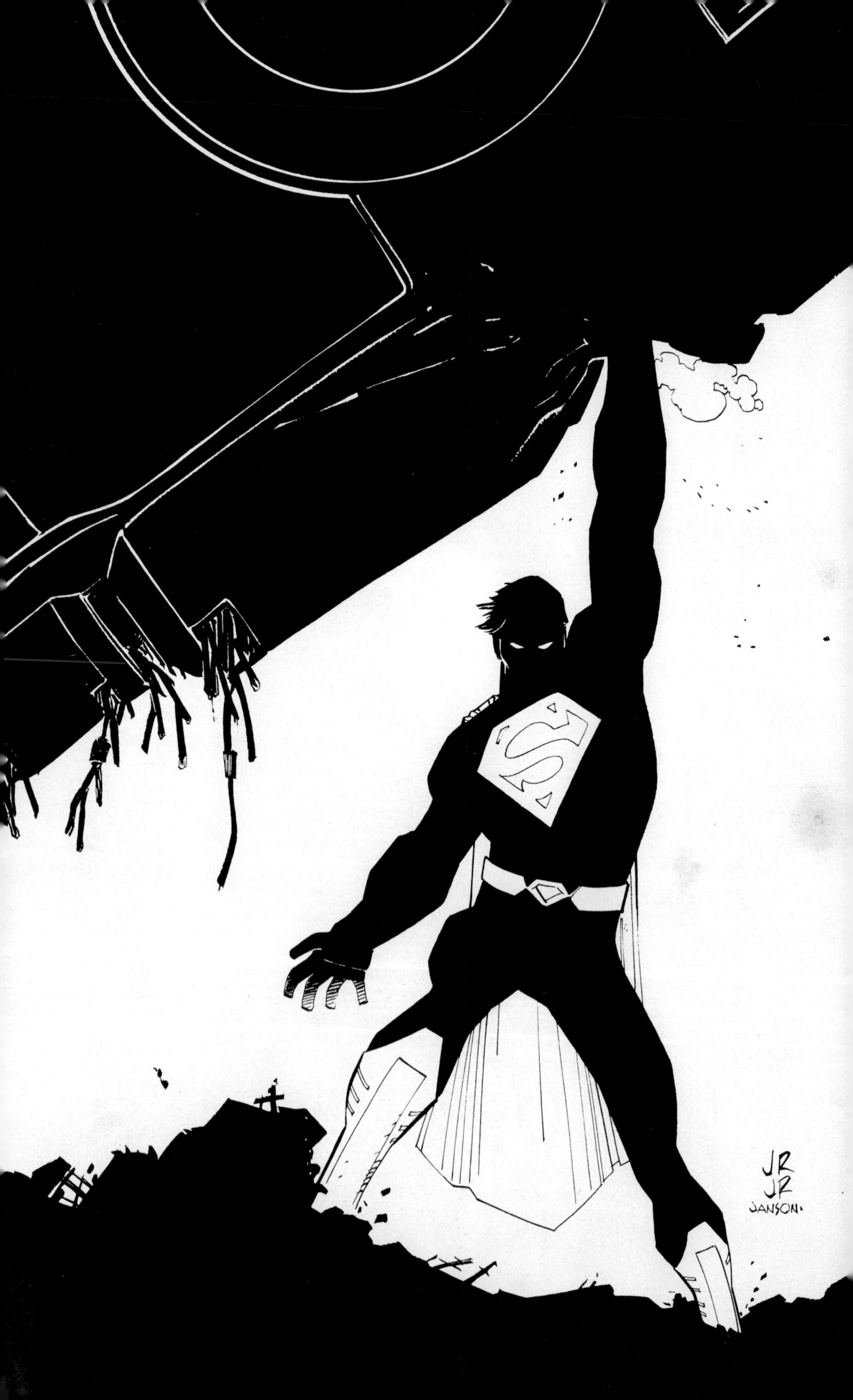
JR
JR
JANSON.

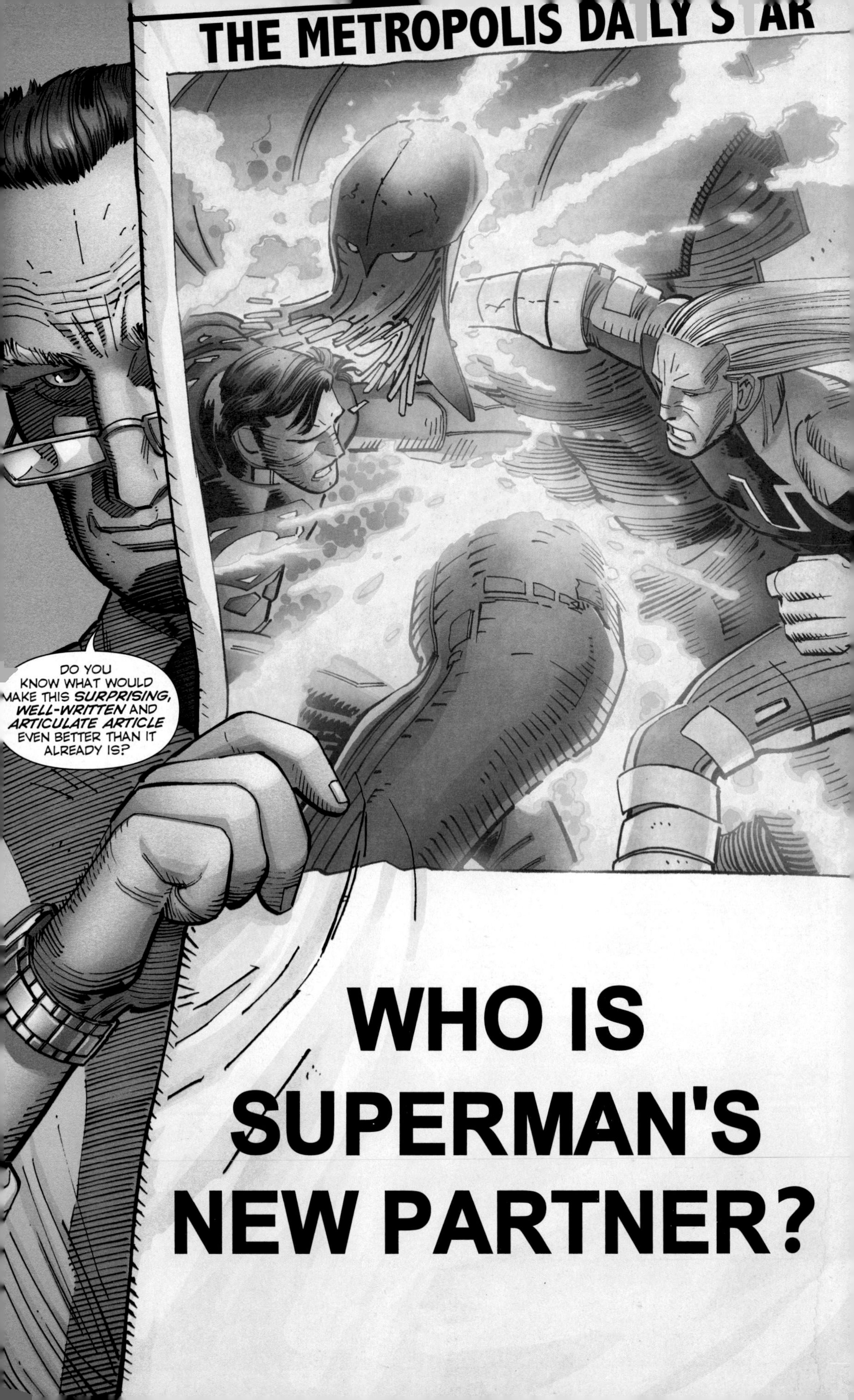
THE METROPOLIS DAILY STAR
DO YOU KNOW WHAT WOULD MAKE THIS *SURPRISING, WELL-WRITTEN* AND *ARTICULATE ARTICLE* EVEN BETTER THAN IT ALREADY IS?
WHO IS SUPERMAN'S NEW PARTNER?

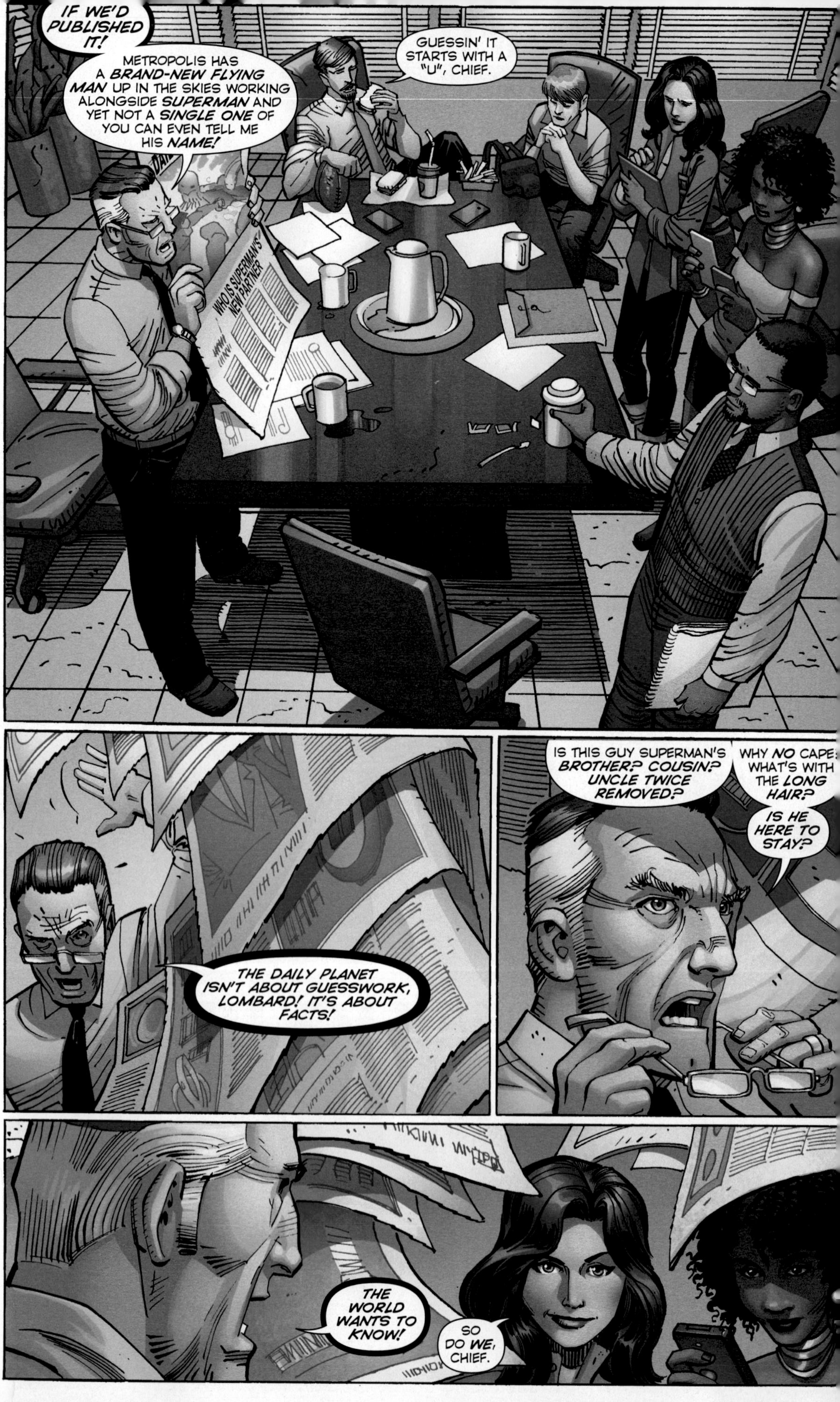
IF WE'D PUBLISHED IT!
METROPOLIS HAS A BRAND-NEW FLYING MAN UP IN THE SKIES WORKING ALONGSIDE SUPERMAN AND YET NOT A SINGLE ONE OF YOU CAN EVEN TELL ME HIS NAME!
WHO IS SUPERMAN'S NEW PARTNER
GUESSIN' IT STARTS WITH A "U", CHIEF.
THE DAILY PLANET ISN'T ABOUT GUESSWORK, LOMBARD! IT'S ABOUT FACTS!
IS THIS GUY SUPERMAN'S BROTHER? COUSIN? UNCLE TWICE REMOVED?
WHY NO CAPE? WHAT'S WITH THE LONG HAIR?
IS HE HERE TO STAY?
THE WORLD WANTS TO KNOW!
SO DO WE, CHIEF.

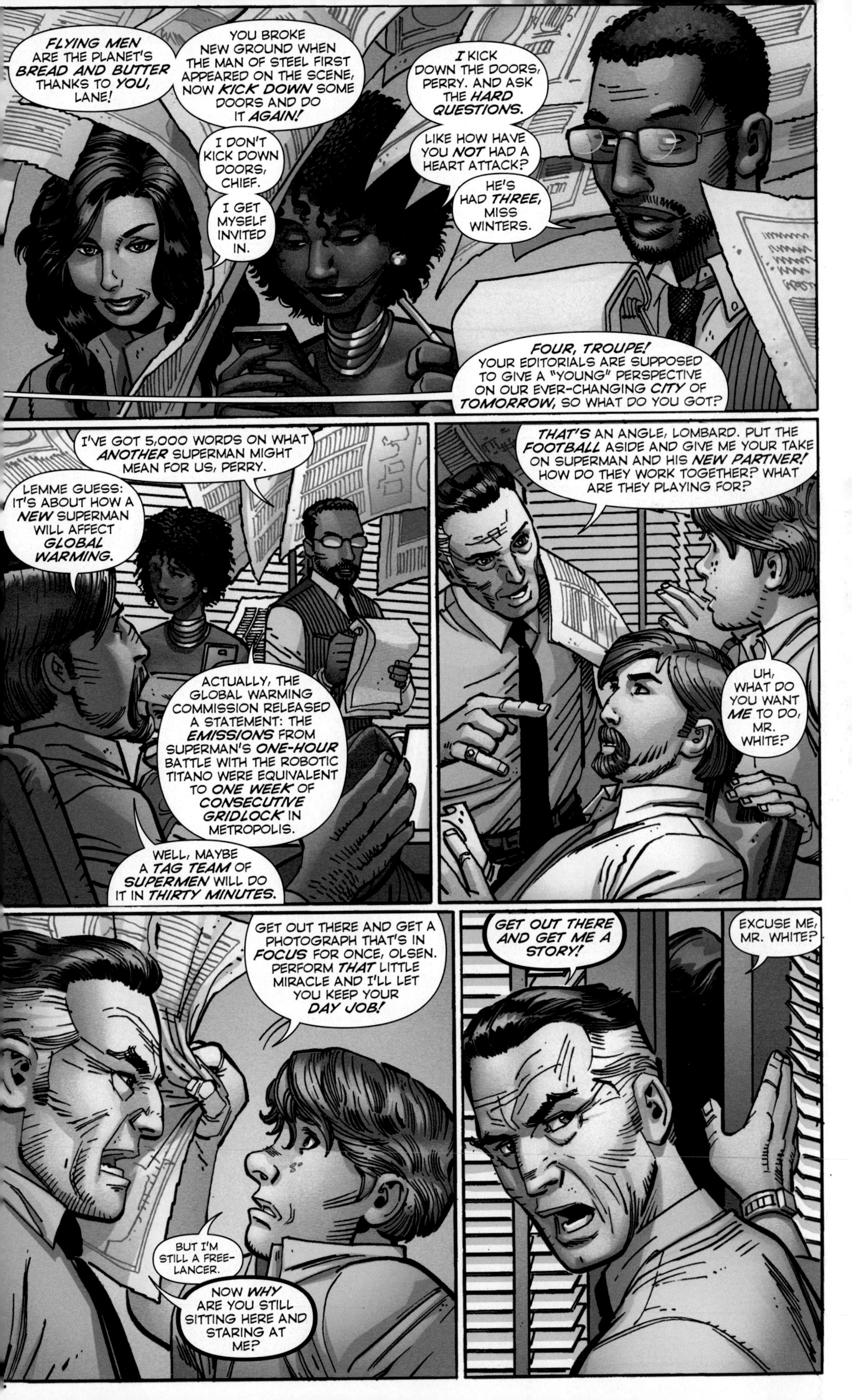

FLYING MEN ARE THE PLANET'S BREAD AND BUTTER THANKS TO YOU, LANE!
YOU BROKE NEW GROUND WHEN THE MAN OF STEEL FIRST APPEARED ON THE SCENE, NOW KICK DOWN SOME DOORS AND DO IT AGAIN!
I DON'T KICK DOWN DOORS, CHIEF.
I GET MYSELF INVITED IN.
I KICK DOWN THE DOORS, PERRY. AND ASK THE HARD QUESTIONS.
LIKE HOW HAVE YOU NOT HAD A HEART ATTACK?
HE'S HAD THREE, MISS WINTERS.
FOUR, TROUPE! YOUR EDITORIALS ARE SUPPOSED TO GIVE A "YOUNG" PERSPECTIVE ON OUR EVER-CHANGING CITY OF TOMORROW, SO WHAT DO YOU GOT?
I'VE GOT 5,000 WORDS ON WHAT ANOTHER SUPERMAN MIGHT MEAN FOR US, PERRY.
LEMME GUESS: IT'S ABOUT HOW A NEW SUPERMAN WILL AFFECT GLOBAL WARMING.
ACTUALLY, THE GLOBAL WARMING COMMISSION RELEASED A STATEMENT: THE EMISSIONS FROM SUPERMAN'S ONE-HOUR BATTLE WITH THE ROBOTIC TITANO WERE EQUIVALENT TO ONE WEEK OF CONSECUTIVE GRIDLOCK IN METROPOLIS.
WELL, MAYBE A TAG TEAM OF SUPERMEN WILL DO IT IN THIRTY MINUTES.
THAT'S AN ANGLE, LOMBARD. PUT THE FOOTBALL ASIDE AND GIVE ME YOUR TAKE ON SUPERMAN AND HIS NEW PARTNER! HOW DO THEY WORK TOGETHER? WHAT ARE THEY PLAYING FOR?
UH, WHAT DO YOU WANT ME TO DO, MR. WHITE?
GET OUT THERE AND GET A PHOTOGRAPH THAT'S IN FOCUS FOR ONCE, OLSEN. PERFORM THAT LITTLE MIRACLE AND I'LL LET YOU KEEP YOUR DAY JOB!
BUT I'M STILL A FREE-LANCER.
NOW WHY ARE YOU STILL SITTING HERE AND STARING AT ME?
GET OUT THERE AND GET ME A STORY!
EXCUSE ME, MR. WHITE?

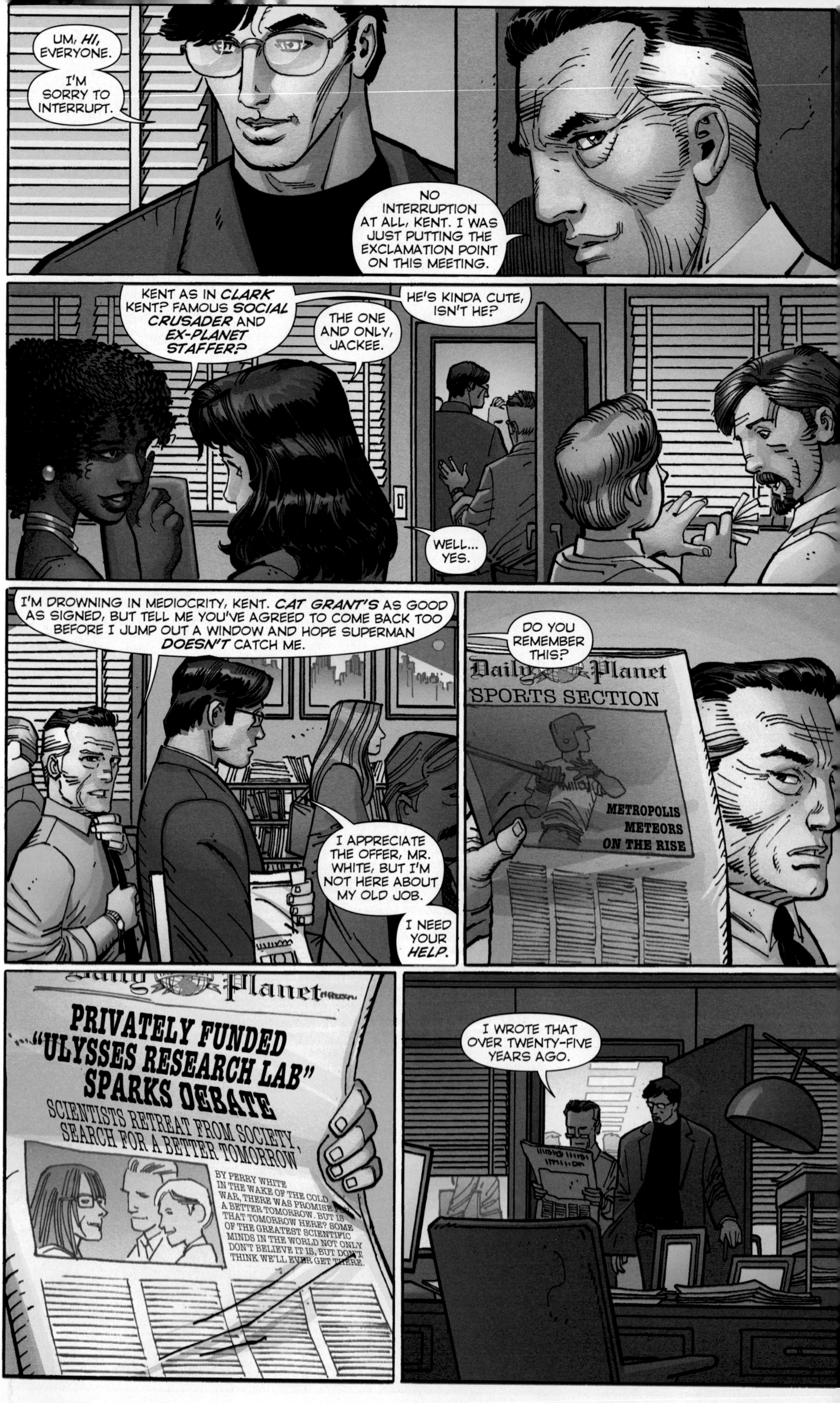
UM, HI, EVERYONE.
I'M SORRY TO INTERRUPT.
NO INTERRUPTION AT ALL, KENT. I WAS JUST PUTTING THE EXCLAMATION POINT ON THIS MEETING.
KENT AS IN CLARK KENT? FAMOUS SOCIAL CRUSADER AND EX-PLANET STAFFER?
THE ONE AND ONLY, JACKEE.
HE'S KINDA CUTE, ISN'T HE?
WELL... YES.
I'M DROWNING IN MEDIOCRITY, KENT. CAT GRANT'S AS GOOD AS SIGNED, BUT TELL ME YOU'VE AGREED TO COME BACK TOO BEFORE I JUMP OUT A WINDOW AND HOPE SUPERMAN DOESN'T CATCH ME.
I APPRECIATE THE OFFER, MR. WHITE, BUT I'M NOT HERE ABOUT MY OLD JOB.
I NEED YOUR HELP.
DO YOU REMEMBER THIS?
Daily Planet
SPORTS SECTION
METROPOLIS METEORS ON THE RISE
Planet
PRIVATELY FUNDED "ULYSSES RESEARCH LAB" SPARKS DEBATE
SCIENTISTS RETREAT FROM SOCIETY, SEARCH FOR A BETTER TOMORROW
BY PERRY WHITE
IN THE WAKE OF THE COLD WAR, THERE WAS PROMISE FOR A BETTER TOMORROW. BUT IS THAT TOMORROW HERE? SOME OF THE GREATEST SCIENTIFIC MINDS IN THE WORLD NOT ONLY DON'T BELIEVE IT IS, BUT DON'T THINK WE'LL EVER GET THERE.
I WROTE THAT OVER TWENTY-FIVE YEARS AGO.

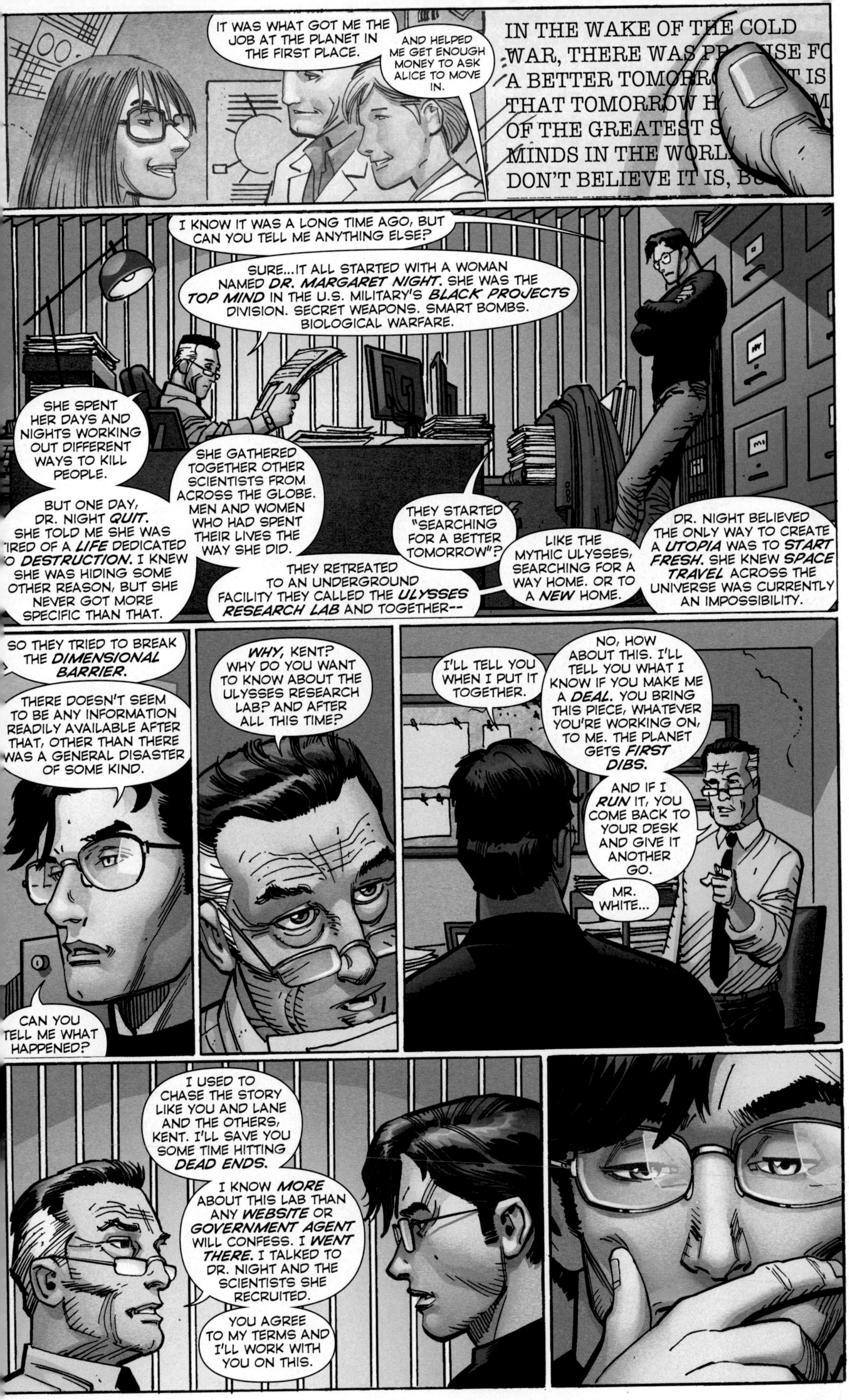

IT WAS WHAT GOT ME THE JOB AT THE PLANET IN THE FIRST PLACE.
AND HELPED ME GET ENOUGH MONEY TO ASK ALICE TO MOVE IN.
IN THE WAKE OF THE COLD WAR, THERE WAS PR
A BETTER TOMORRO
THAT TOMORROW H
OF THE GREATEST S
MINDS IN THE WORL
DON'T BELIEVE IT IS, BU
I KNOW IT WAS A LONG TIME AGO, BUT CAN YOU TELL ME ANYTHING ELSE?
SURE...IT ALL STARTED WITH A WOMAN NAMED DR. MARGARET NIGHT. SHE WAS THE TOP MIND IN THE U.S. MILITARY'S BLACK PROJECTS DIVISION. SECRET WEAPONS. SMART BOMBS. BIOLOGICAL WARFARE.
SHE SPENT HER DAYS AND NIGHTS WORKING OUT DIFFERENT WAYS TO KILL PEOPLE.
BUT ONE DAY, DR. NIGHT QUIT. SHE TOLD ME SHE WAS TIRED OF A LIFE DEDICATED TO DESTRUCTION. I KNEW SHE WAS HIDING SOME OTHER REASON, BUT SHE NEVER GOT MORE SPECIFIC THAN THAT.
SHE GATHERED TOGETHER OTHER SCIENTISTS FROM ACROSS THE GLOBE. MEN AND WOMEN WHO HAD SPENT THEIR LIVES THE WAY SHE DID.
THEY RETREATED TO AN UNDERGROUND FACILITY THEY CALLED THE ULYSSES RESEARCH LAB AND TOGETHER--
THEY STARTED "SEARCHING FOR A BETTER TOMORROW"?
LIKE THE MYTHIC ULYSSES, SEARCHING FOR A WAY HOME. OR TO A NEW HOME.
DR. NIGHT BELIEVED THE ONLY WAY TO CREATE A UTOPIA WAS TO START FRESH. SHE KNEW SPACE TRAVEL ACROSS THE UNIVERSE WAS CURRENTLY AN IMPOSSIBILITY.
SO THEY TRIED TO BREAK THE DIMENSIONAL BARRIER.
THERE DOESN'T SEEM TO BE ANY INFORMATION READILY AVAILABLE AFTER THAT, OTHER THAN THERE WAS A GENERAL DISASTER OF SOME KIND.
CAN YOU TELL ME WHAT HAPPENED?
WHY, KENT? WHY DO YOU WANT TO KNOW ABOUT THE ULYSSES RESEARCH LAB? AND AFTER ALL THIS TIME?
I'LL TELL YOU WHEN I PUT IT TOGETHER.
NO, HOW ABOUT THIS. I'LL TELL YOU WHAT I KNOW IF YOU MAKE ME A DEAL. YOU BRING THIS PIECE, WHATEVER YOU'RE WORKING ON, TO ME. THE PLANET GETS FIRST DIBS.
AND IF I RUN IT, YOU COME BACK TO YOUR DESK AND GIVE IT ANOTHER GO.
MR. WHITE...
I USED TO CHASE THE STORY LIKE YOU AND LANE AND THE OTHERS, KENT. I'LL SAVE YOU SOME TIME HITTING DEAD ENDS.
I KNOW MORE ABOUT THIS LAB THAN ANY WEBSITE OR GOVERNMENT AGENT WILL CONFESS. I WENT THERE. I TALKED TO DR. NIGHT AND THE SCIENTISTS SHE RECRUITED.
YOU AGREE TO MY TERMS AND I'LL WORK WITH YOU ON THIS.

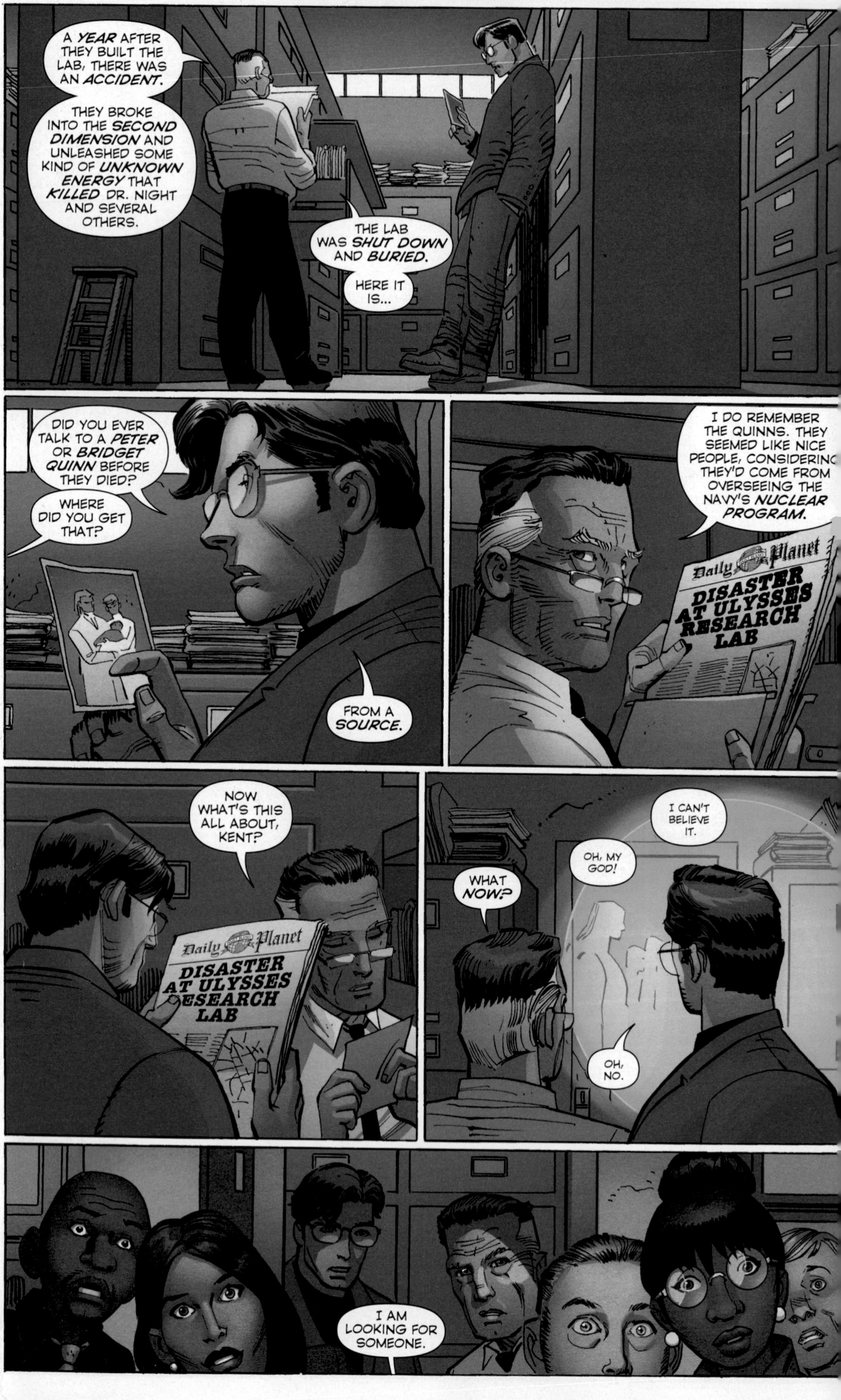
A YEAR AFTER THEY BUILT THE LAB, THERE WAS AN ACCIDENT.
THEY BROKE INTO THE SECOND DIMENSION AND UNLEASHED SOME KIND OF UNKNOWN ENERGY THAT KILLED DR. NIGHT AND SEVERAL OTHERS.
THE LAB WAS SHUT DOWN AND BURIED.
HERE IT IS...
DID YOU EVER TALK TO A PETER OR BRIDGET QUINN BEFORE THEY DIED?
WHERE DID YOU GET THAT?
FROM A SOURCE.
I DO REMEMBER THE QUINNS. THEY SEEMED LIKE NICE PEOPLE, CONSIDERING THEY'D COME FROM OVERSEEING THE NAVY'S NUCLEAR PROGRAM.
Daily Planet
DISASTER AT ULYSSES RESEARCH LAB
NOW WHAT'S THIS ALL ABOUT, KENT?
Daily Planet
DISASTER AT ULYSSES RESEARCH LAB
I CAN'T BELIEVE IT.
OH, MY GOD!
WHAT NOW?
OH, NO.
I AM LOOKING FOR SOMEONE.

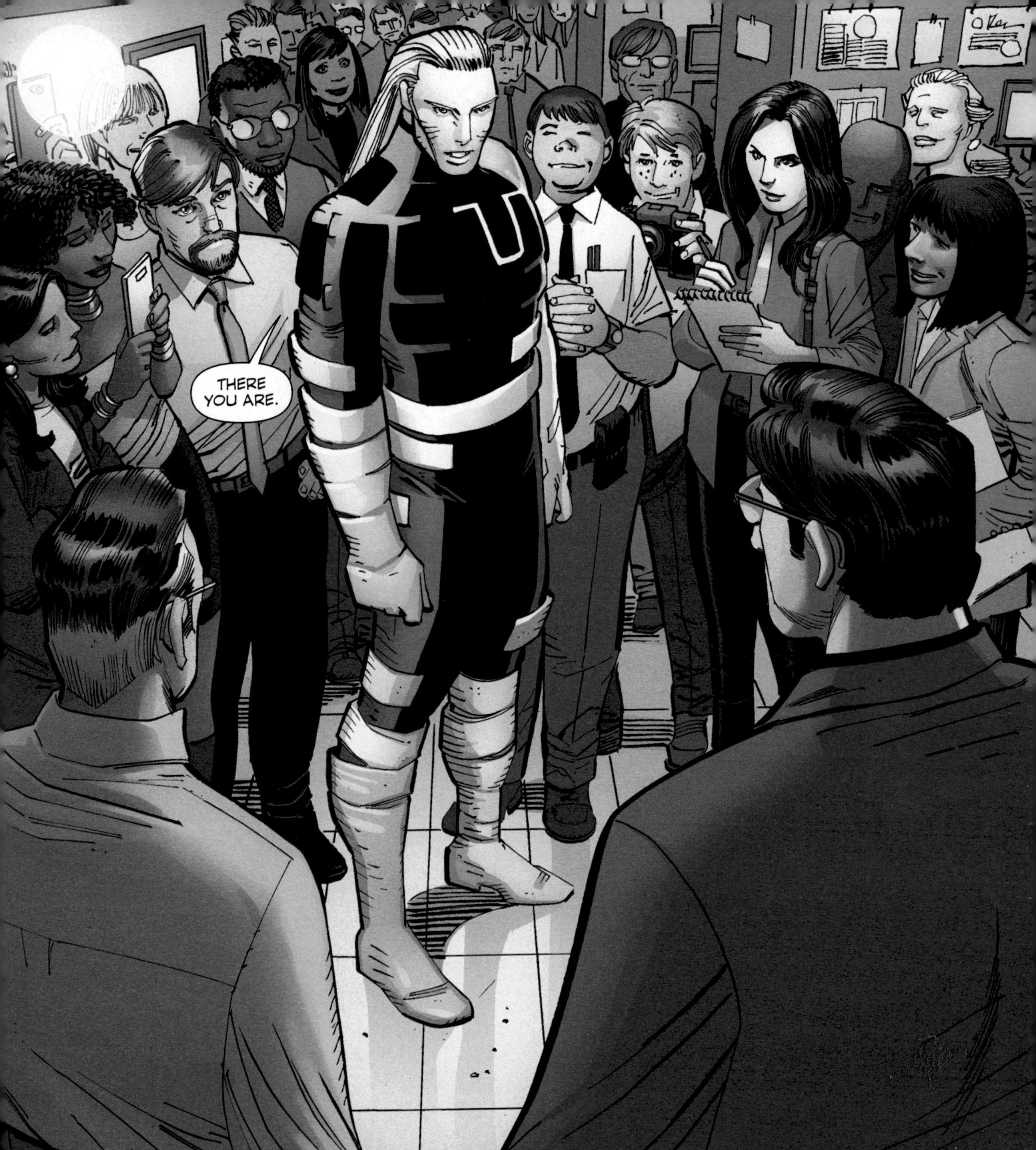
THERE YOU ARE.

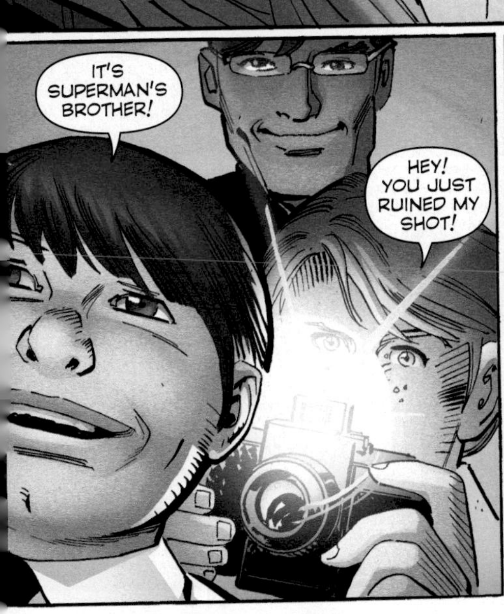
IT'S SUPERMAN'S BROTHER!
HEY! YOU JUST RUINED MY SHOT!

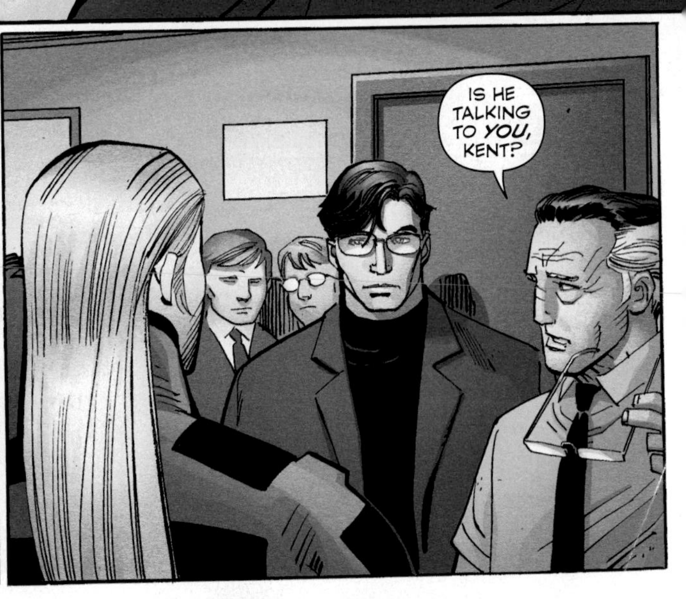
IS HE TALKING TO *YOU*, KENT?

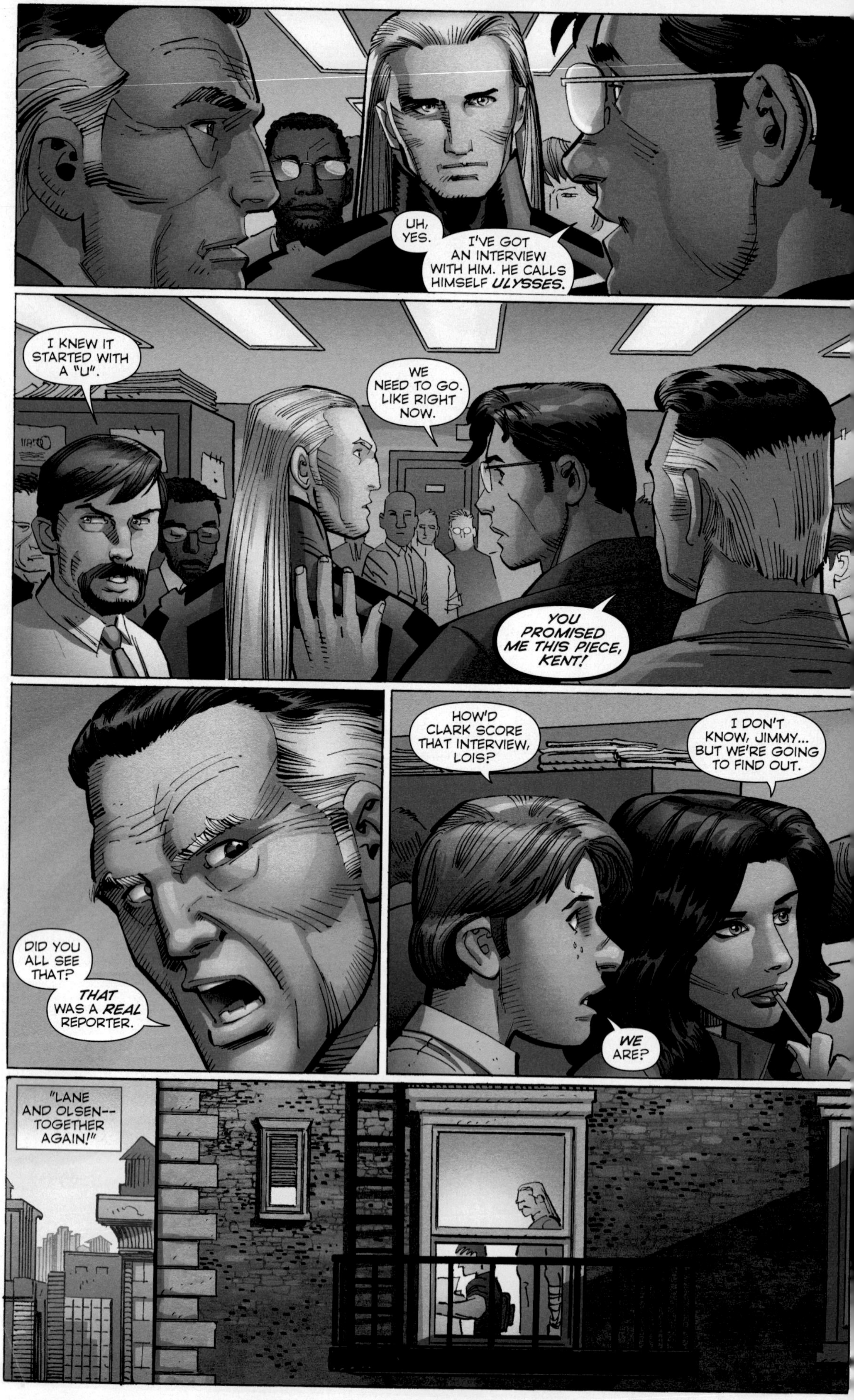
UH, YES.
I'VE GOT AN INTERVIEW WITH HIM. HE CALLS HIMSELF ULYSSES.
I KNEW IT STARTED WITH A "U".
WE NEED TO GO. LIKE RIGHT NOW.
YOU PROMISED ME THIS PIECE, KENT!
DID YOU ALL SEE THAT?
THAT WAS A REAL REPORTER.
HOW'D CLARK SCORE THAT INTERVIEW, LOIS?
I DON'T KNOW, JIMMY... BUT WE'RE GOING TO FIND OUT.
WE ARE?
"LANE AND OLSEN-- TOGETHER AGAIN!"

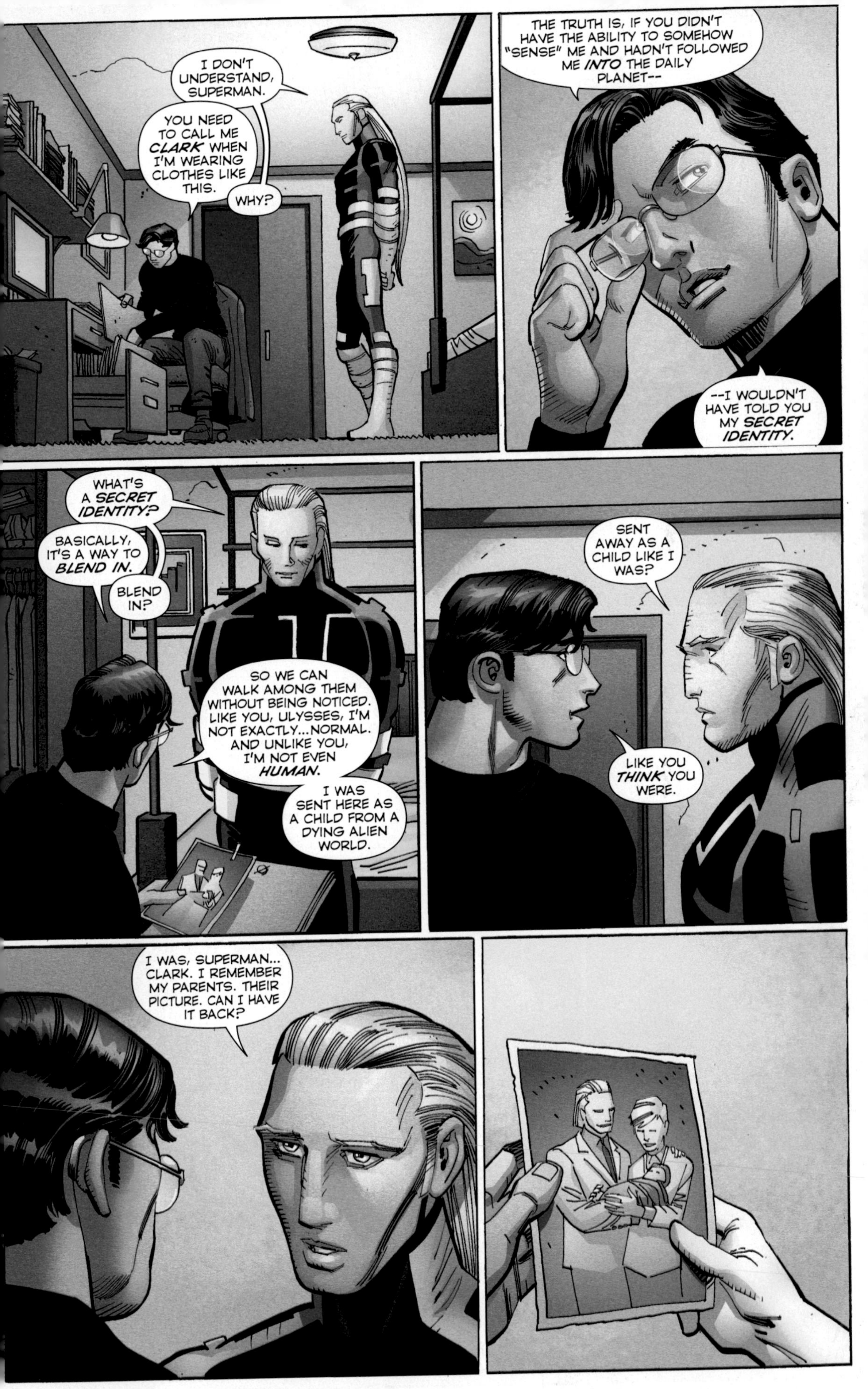
I DON'T UNDERSTAND, SUPERMAN.
YOU NEED TO CALL ME CLARK WHEN I'M WEARING CLOTHES LIKE THIS.
WHY?
THE TRUTH IS, IF YOU DIDN'T HAVE THE ABILITY TO SOMEHOW "SENSE" ME AND HADN'T FOLLOWED ME INTO THE DAILY PLANET--
--I WOULDN'T HAVE TOLD YOU MY SECRET IDENTITY.
WHAT'S A SECRET IDENTITY?
BASICALLY, IT'S A WAY TO BLEND IN.
BLEND IN?
SO WE CAN WALK AMONG THEM WITHOUT BEING NOTICED. LIKE YOU, ULYSSES, I'M NOT EXACTLY...NORMAL. AND UNLIKE YOU, I'M NOT EVEN HUMAN.
I WAS SENT HERE AS A CHILD FROM A DYING ALIEN WORLD.
SENT AWAY AS A CHILD LIKE I WAS?
LIKE YOU THINK YOU WERE.
I WAS, SUPERMAN... CLARK. I REMEMBER MY PARENTS. THEIR PICTURE. CAN I HAVE IT BACK?

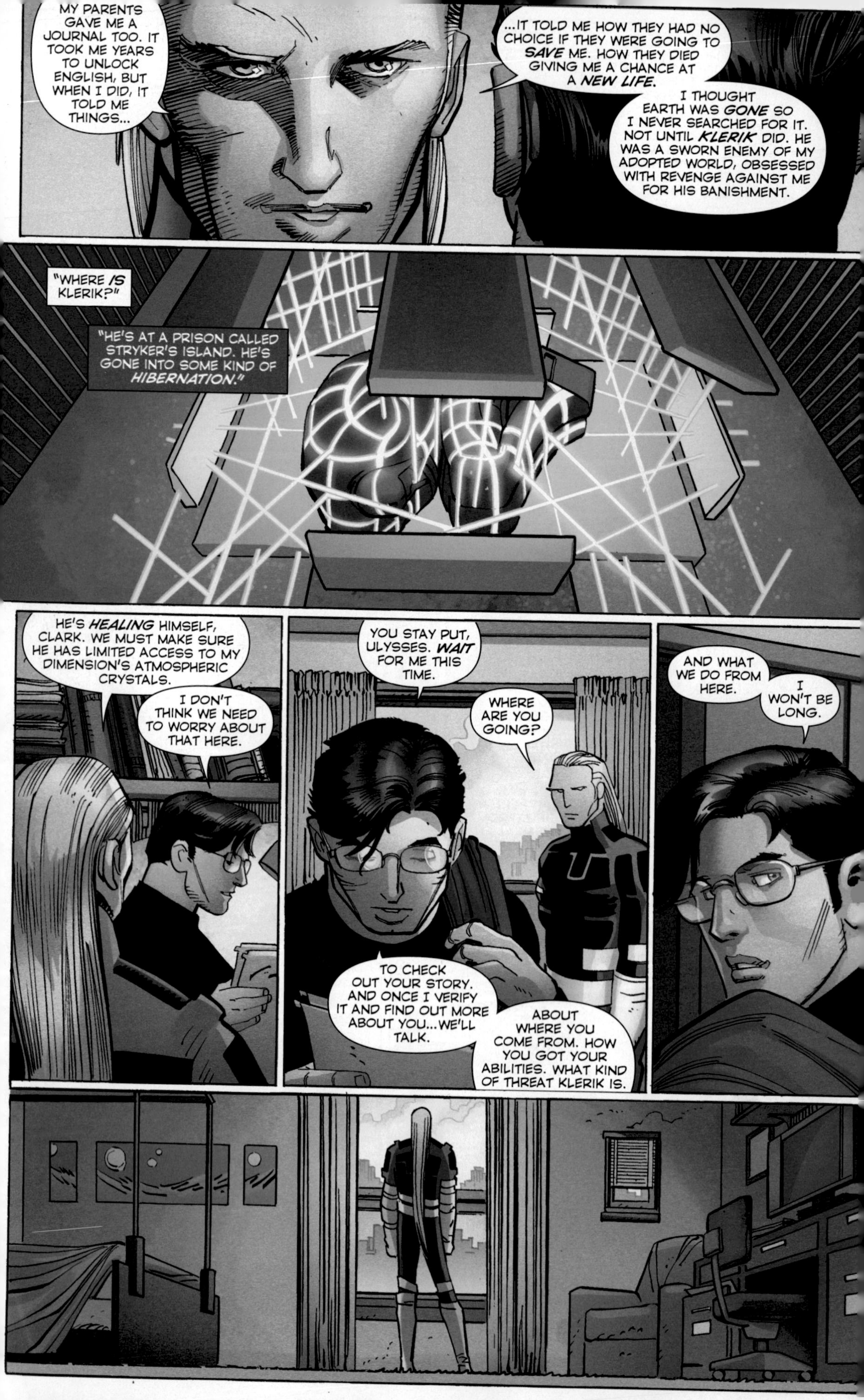
MY PARENTS GAVE ME A JOURNAL TOO. IT TOOK ME YEARS TO UNLOCK ENGLISH, BUT WHEN I DID, IT TOLD ME THINGS...
...IT TOLD ME HOW THEY HAD NO CHOICE IF THEY WERE GOING TO SAVE ME. HOW THEY DIED GIVING ME A CHANCE AT A NEW LIFE.
I THOUGHT EARTH WAS GONE SO I NEVER SEARCHED FOR IT. NOT UNTIL KLERIK DID. HE WAS A SWORN ENEMY OF MY ADOPTED WORLD, OBSESSED WITH REVENGE AGAINST ME FOR HIS BANISHMENT.
"WHERE IS KLERIK?"
"HE'S AT A PRISON CALLED STRYKER'S ISLAND. HE'S GONE INTO SOME KIND OF HIBERNATION."
HE'S HEALING HIMSELF, CLARK. WE MUST MAKE SURE HE HAS LIMITED ACCESS TO MY DIMENSION'S ATMOSPHERIC CRYSTALS.
I DON'T THINK WE NEED TO WORRY ABOUT THAT HERE.
YOU STAY PUT, ULYSSES. WAIT FOR ME THIS TIME.
WHERE ARE YOU GOING?
TO CHECK OUT YOUR STORY. AND ONCE I VERIFY IT AND FIND OUT MORE ABOUT YOU...WE'LL TALK.
ABOUT WHERE YOU COME FROM. HOW YOU GOT YOUR ABILITIES. WHAT KIND OF THREAT KLERIK IS.
AND WHAT WE DO FROM HERE.
I WON'T BE LONG.

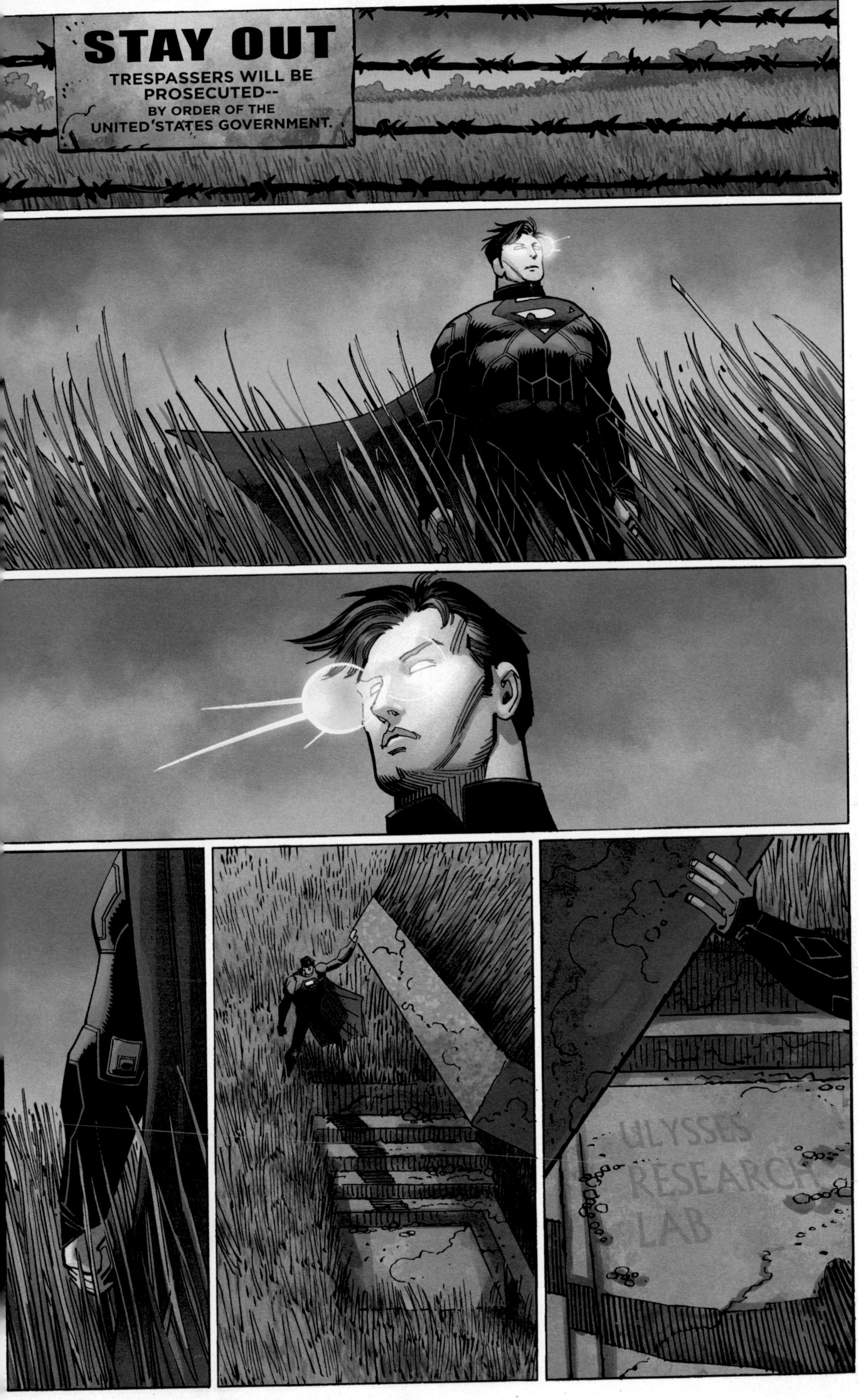
STAY OUT
TRESPASSERS WILL BE PROSECUTED--
BY ORDER OF THE UNITED STATES GOVERNMENT.
ULYSSES RESEARCH LAB

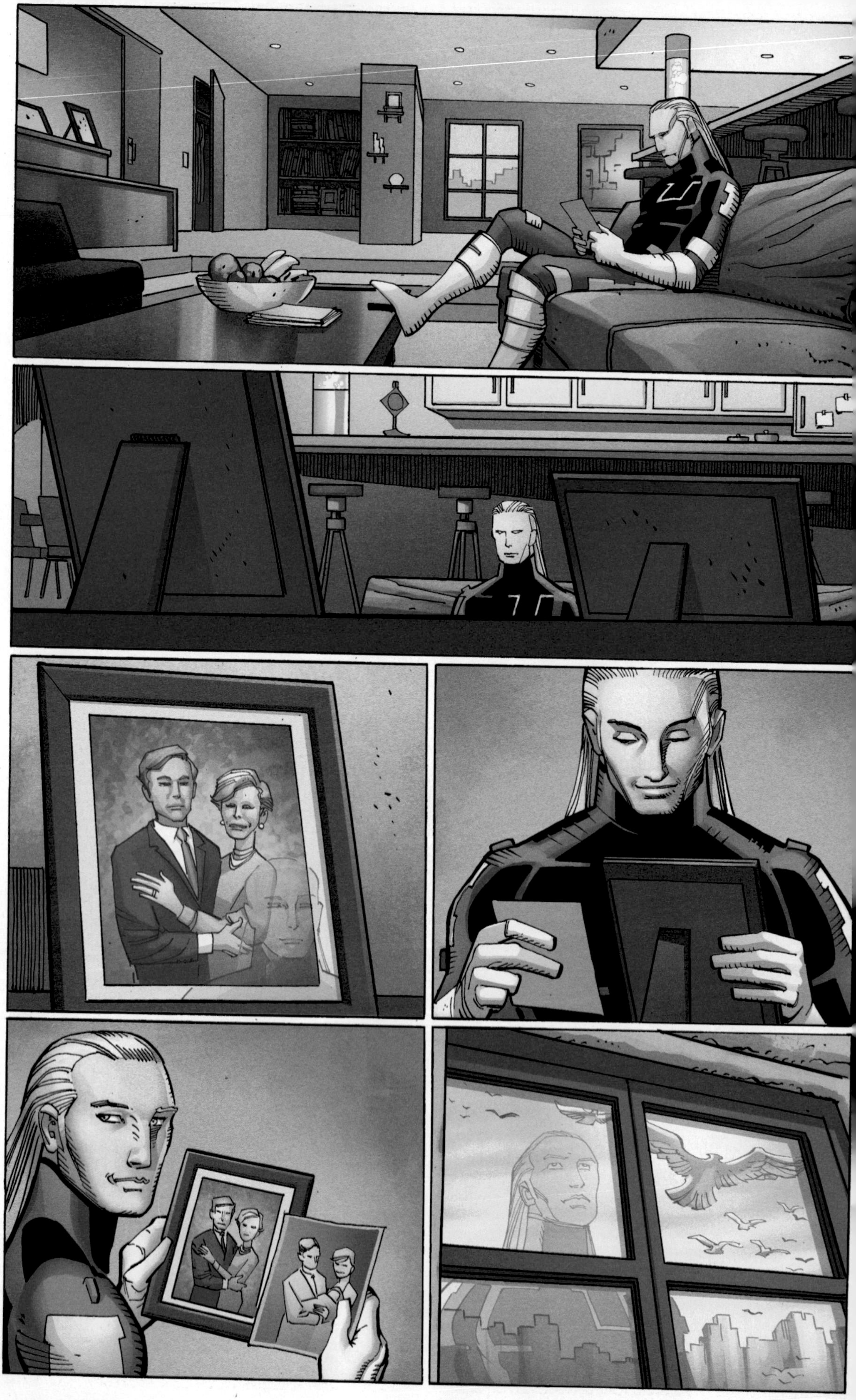

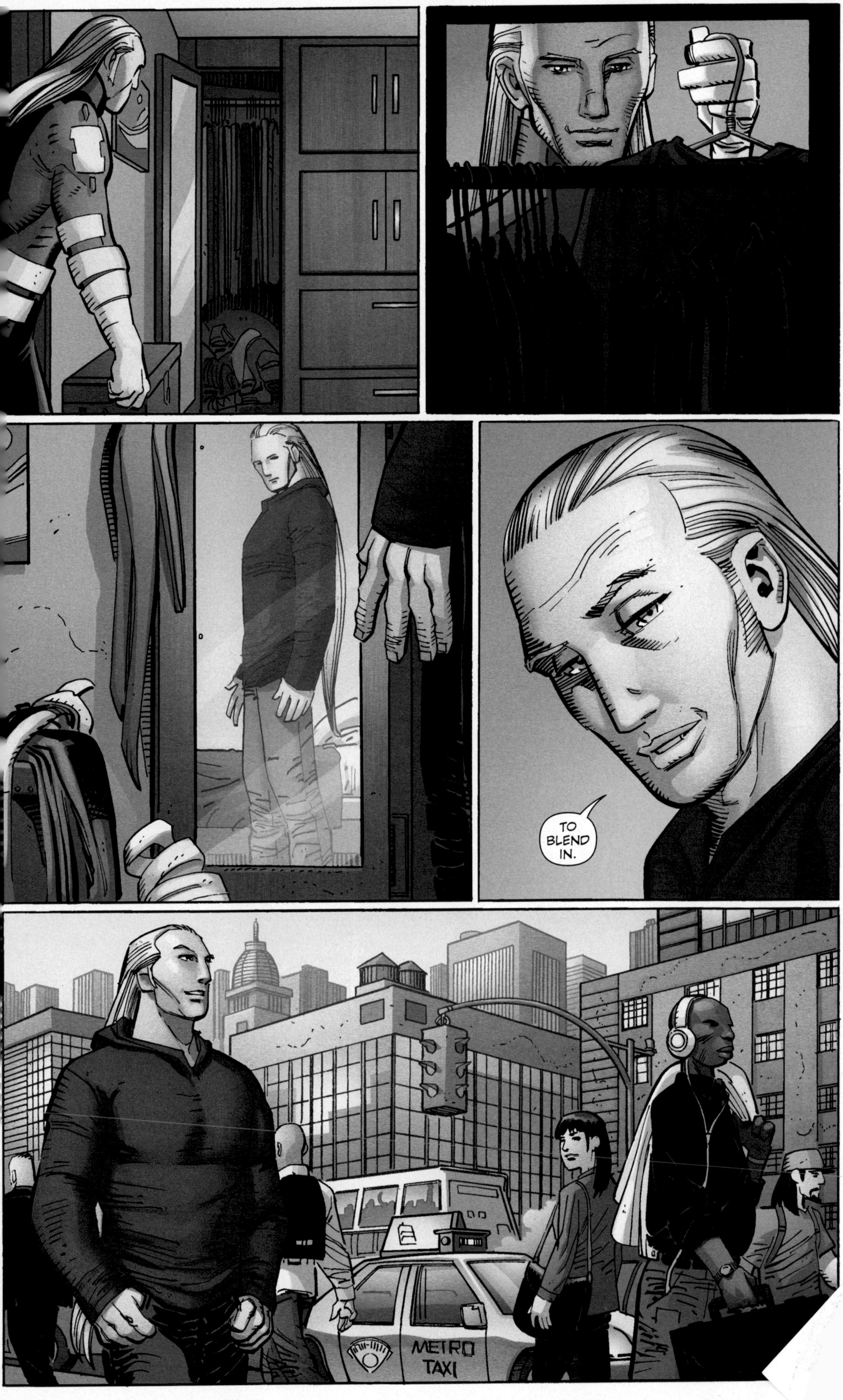
TO BLEND IN.
METRO TAXI

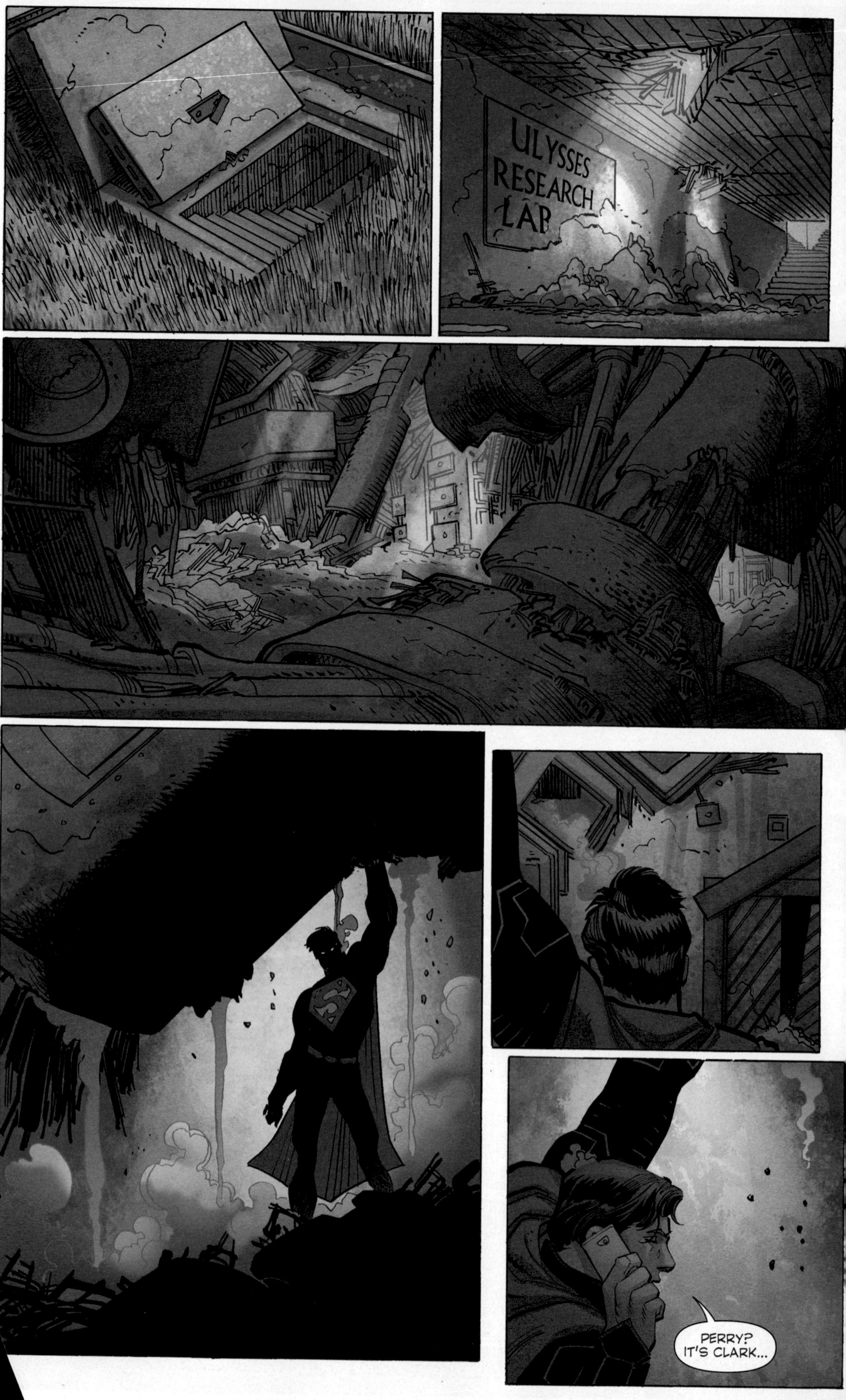
ULYSSES RESEARCH LAB
PERRY? IT'S CLARK...

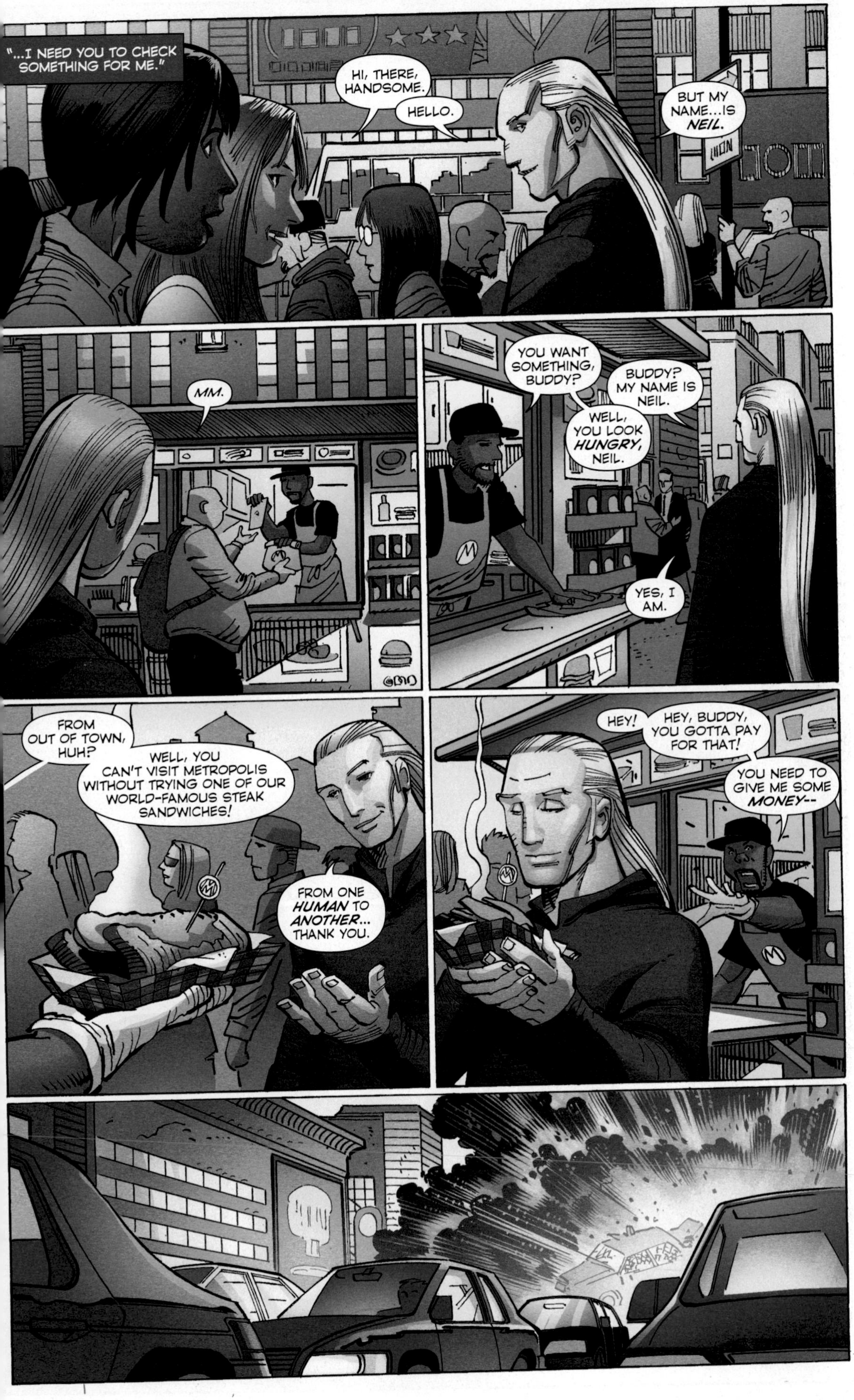
"...I NEED YOU TO CHECK SOMETHING FOR ME."
HI, THERE, HANDSOME.
HELLO.
BUT MY NAME...IS NEIL.
MM.
YOU WANT SOMETHING, BUDDY?
BUDDY? MY NAME IS NEIL.
WELL, YOU LOOK HUNGRY, NEIL.
YES, I AM.
FROM OUT OF TOWN, HUH?
WELL, YOU CAN'T VISIT METROPOLIS WITHOUT TRYING ONE OF OUR WORLD-FAMOUS STEAK SANDWICHES!
FROM ONE HUMAN TO ANOTHER... THANK YOU.
HEY!
HEY, BUDDY, YOU GOTTA PAY FOR THAT!
YOU NEED TO GIVE ME SOME MONEY--

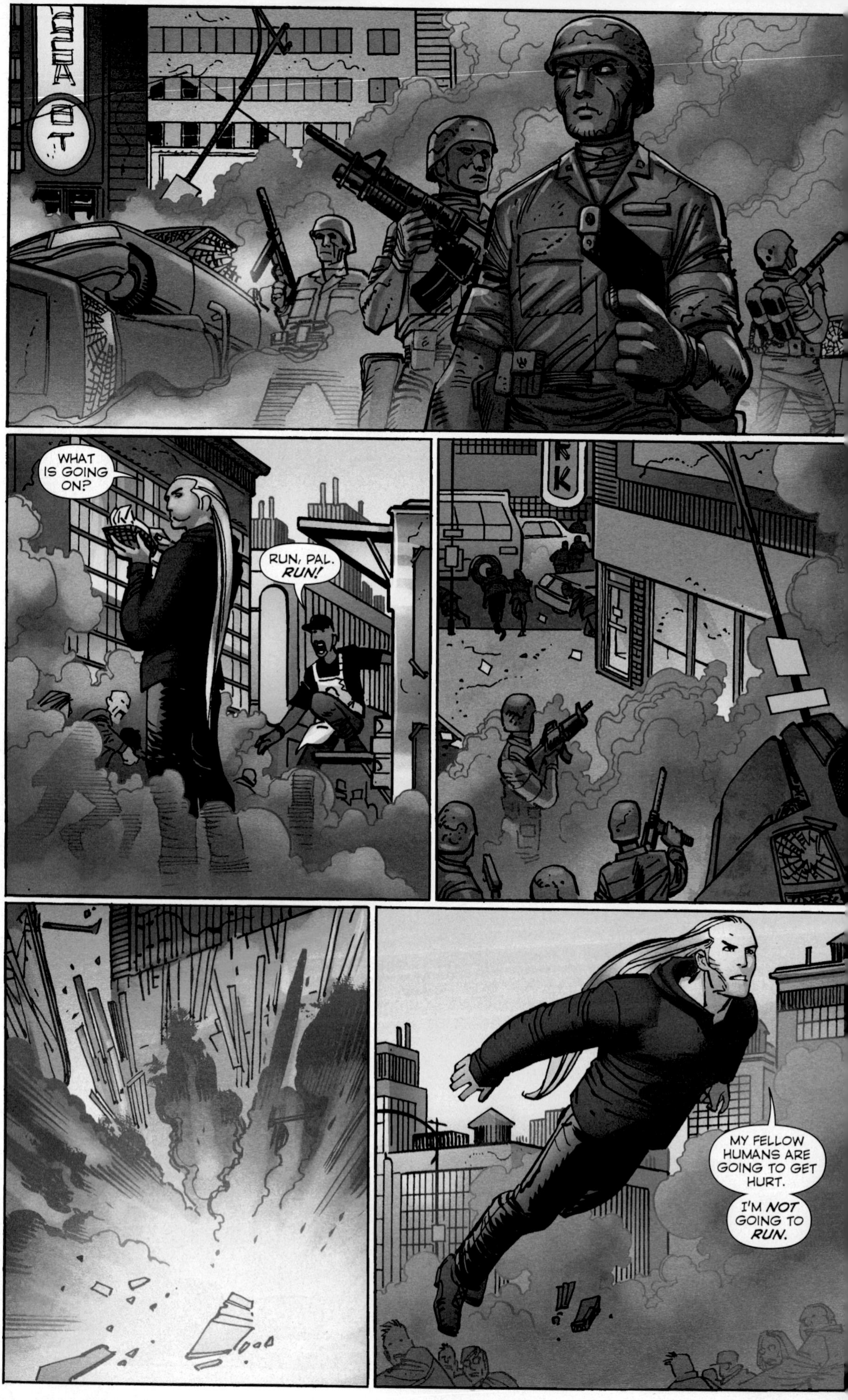
WHAT IS GOING ON?
RUN, PAL. *RUN!*
MY FELLOW HUMANS ARE GOING TO GET HURT.
I'M *NOT* GOING TO *RUN*.

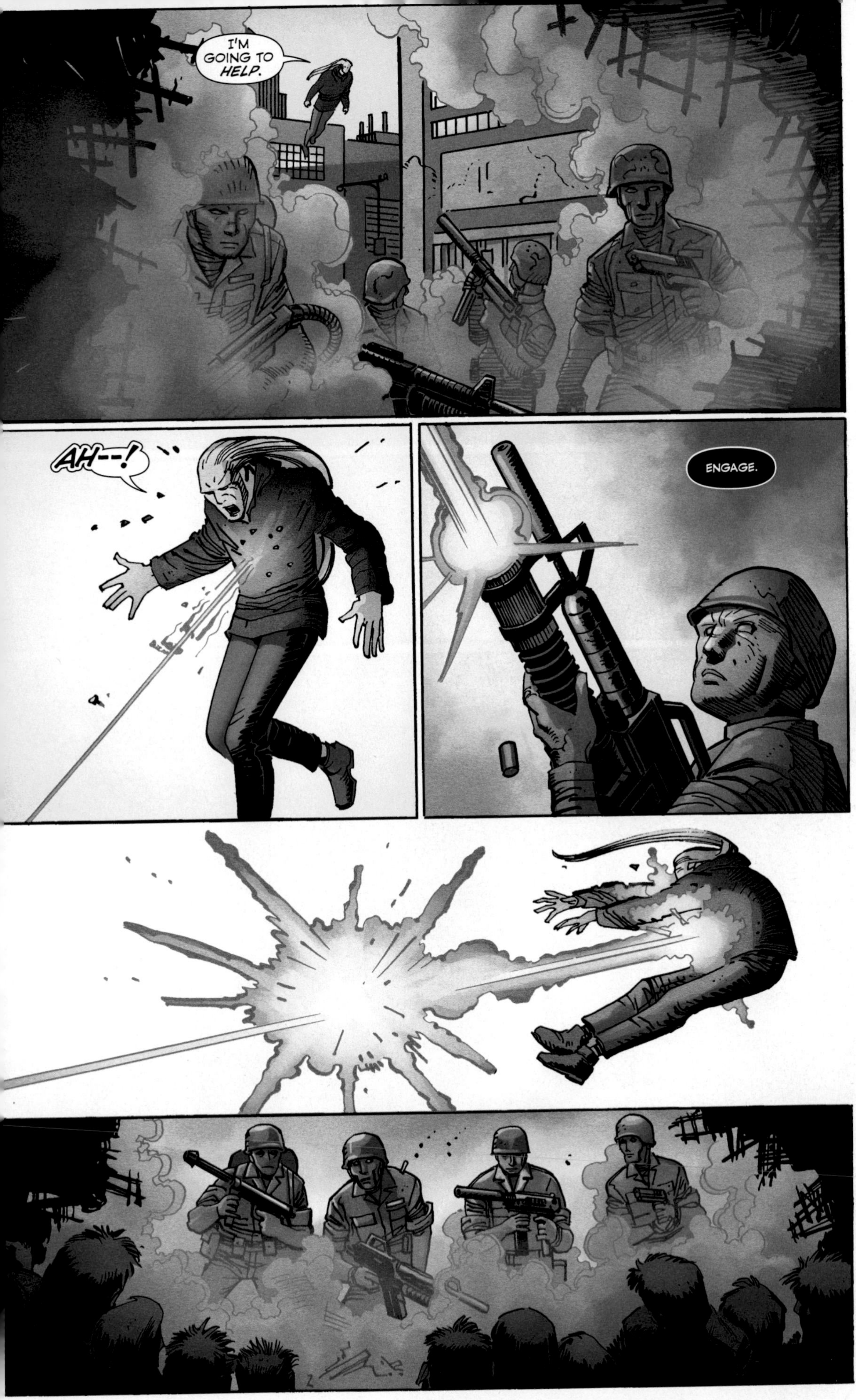

I'M GOING TO HELP.
AH--!
ENGAGE.

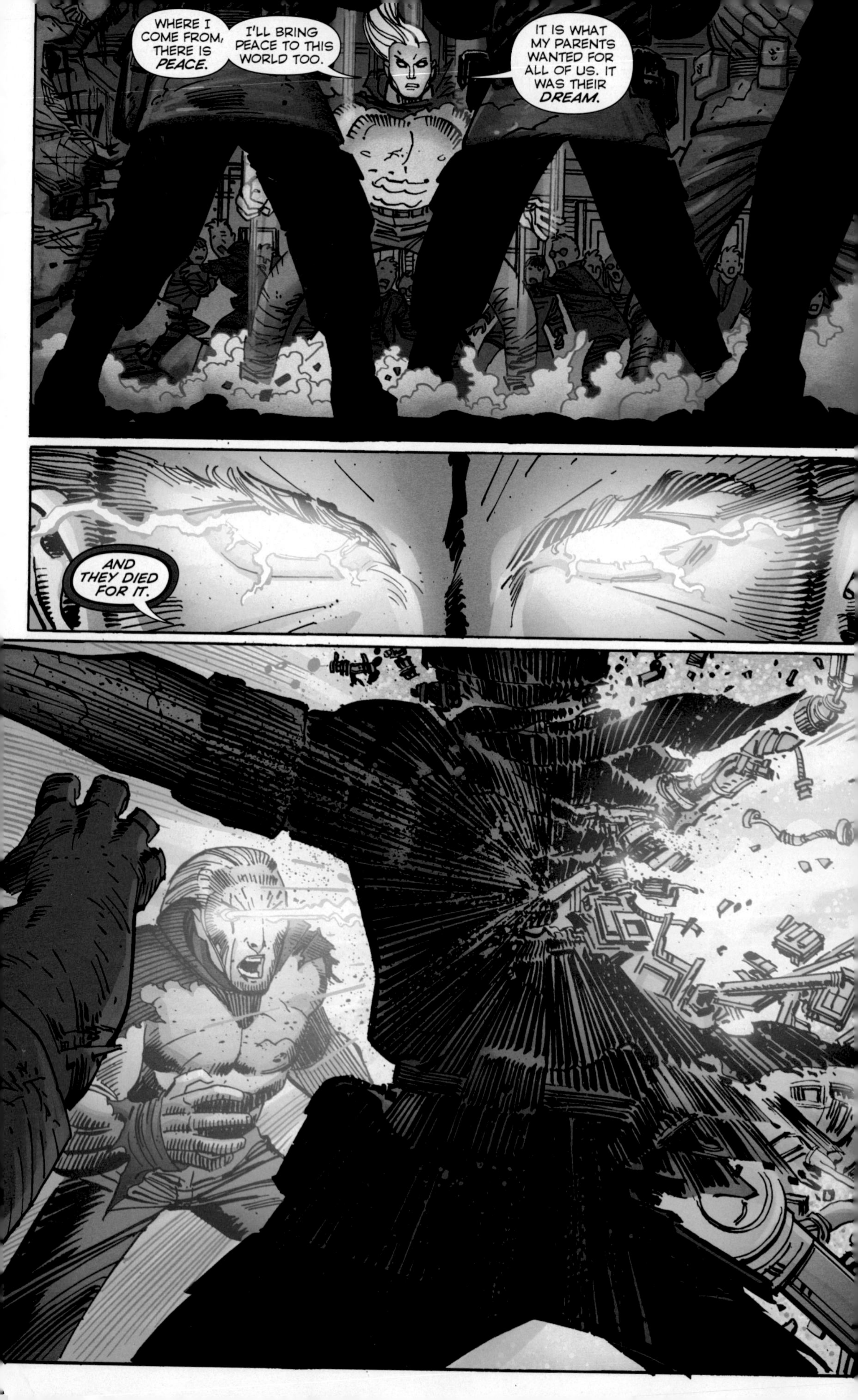
WHERE I COME FROM, THERE IS PEACE.
I'LL BRING PEACE TO THIS WORLD TOO.
IT IS WHAT MY PARENTS WANTED FOR ALL OF US. IT WAS THEIR DREAM.
AND THEY DIED FOR IT.

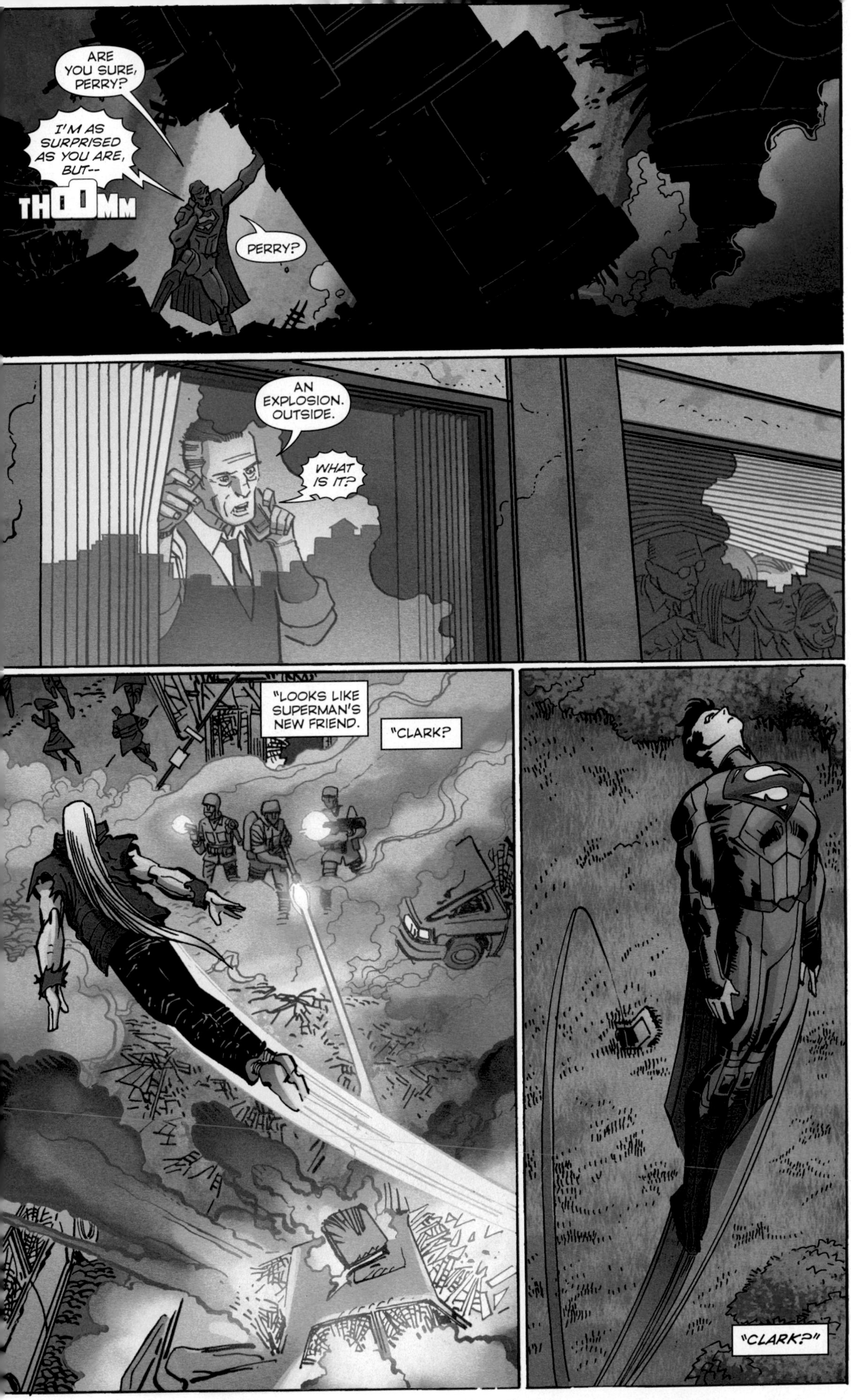
ARE YOU SURE, PERRY?
I'M AS SURPRISED AS YOU ARE, BUT--
THOOMM
PERRY?
AN EXPLOSION. OUTSIDE.
WHAT IS IT?
"LOOKS LIKE SUPERMAN'S NEW FRIEND.
"CLARK?
"CLARK?"

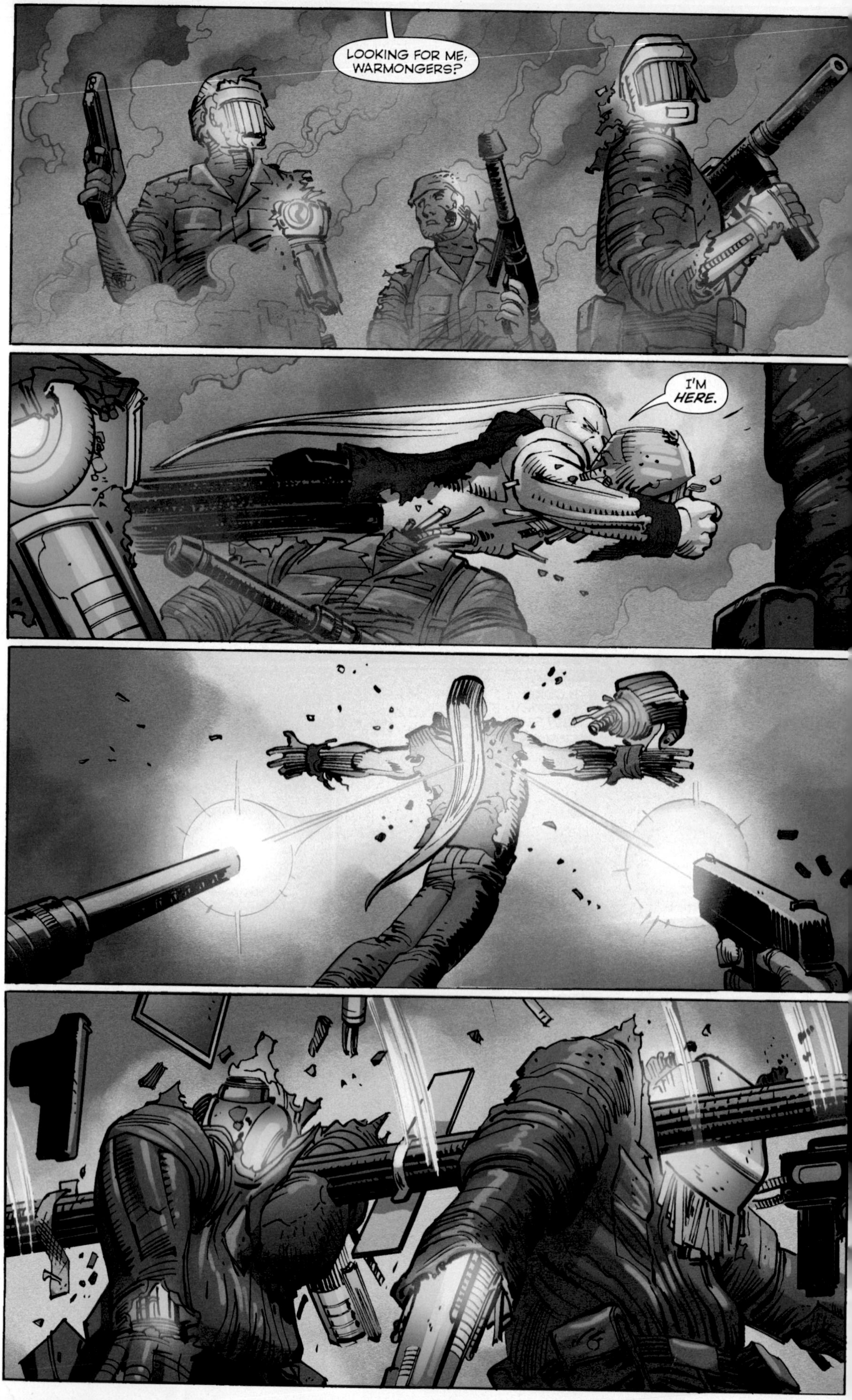
LOOKING FOR ME, WARMONGERS?
I'M *HERE.*

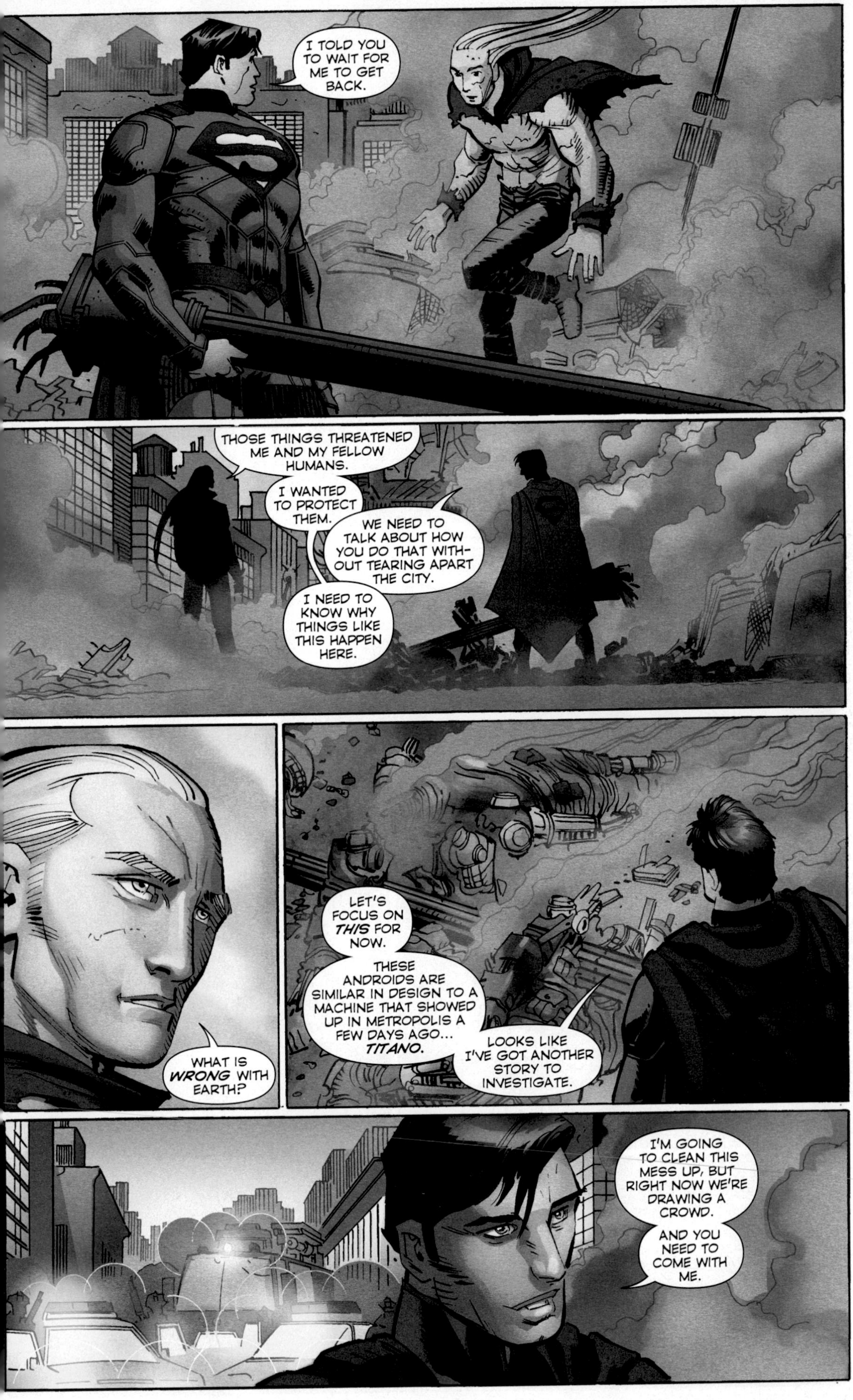
I TOLD YOU TO WAIT FOR ME TO GET BACK.
THOSE THINGS THREATENED ME AND MY FELLOW HUMANS.
I WANTED TO PROTECT THEM.
WE NEED TO TALK ABOUT HOW YOU DO THAT WITH-OUT TEARING APART THE CITY.
I NEED TO KNOW WHY THINGS LIKE THIS HAPPEN HERE.
WHAT IS *WRONG* WITH EARTH?
LET'S FOCUS ON *THIS* FOR NOW.
THESE ANDROIDS ARE SIMILAR IN DESIGN TO A MACHINE THAT SHOWED UP IN METROPOLIS A FEW DAYS AGO... *TITANO.*
LOOKS LIKE I'VE GOT ANOTHER STORY TO INVESTIGATE.
I'M GOING TO CLEAN THIS MESS UP, BUT RIGHT NOW WE'RE DRAWING A CROWD.
AND YOU NEED TO COME WITH ME.

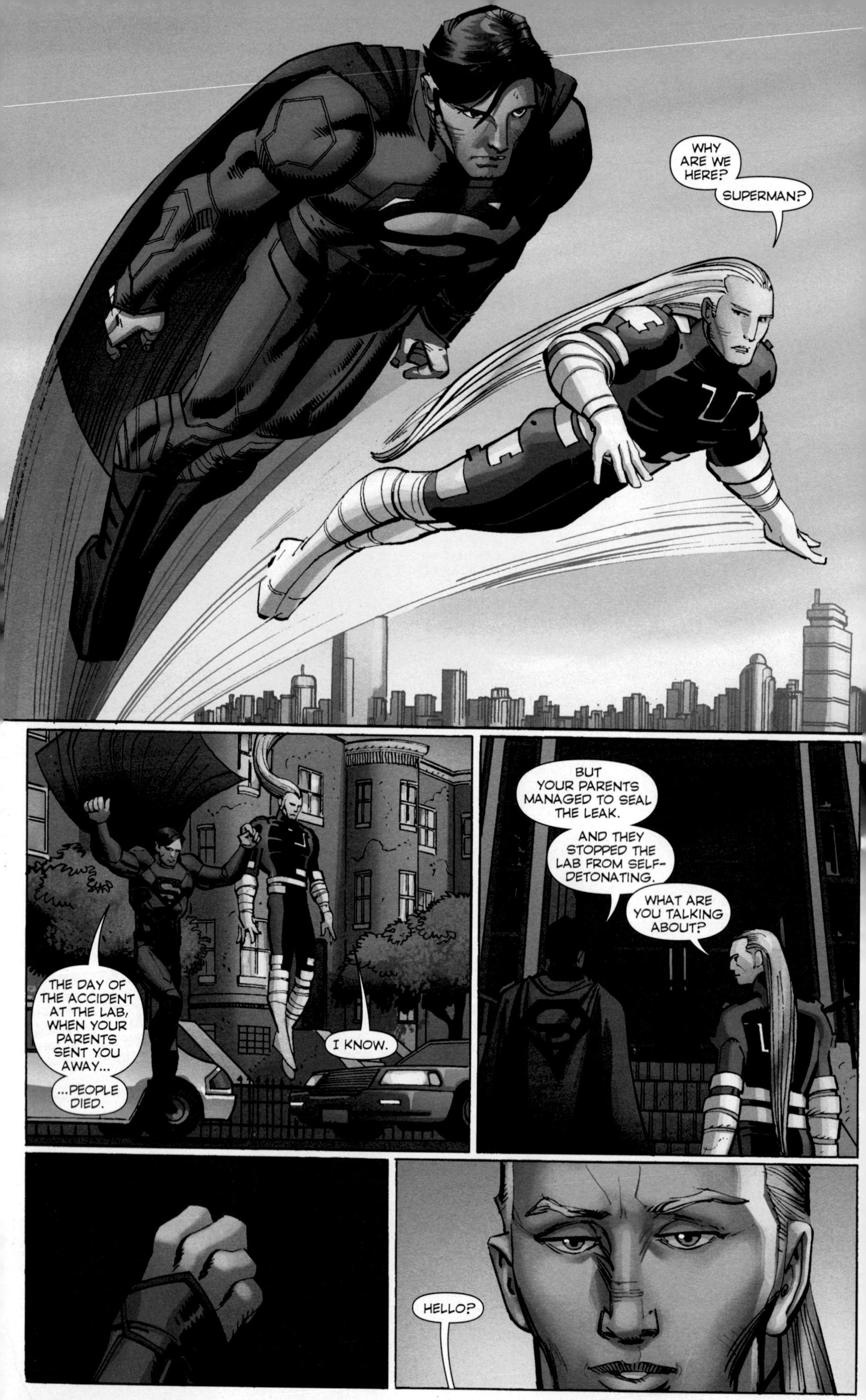
WHY ARE WE HERE?
SUPERMAN?
THE DAY OF THE ACCIDENT AT THE LAB, WHEN YOUR PARENTS SENT YOU AWAY...
...PEOPLE DIED.
I KNOW.
BUT YOUR PARENTS MANAGED TO SEAL THE LEAK.
AND THEY STOPPED THE LAB FROM SELF-DETONATING.
WHAT ARE YOU TALKING ABOUT?
HELLO?

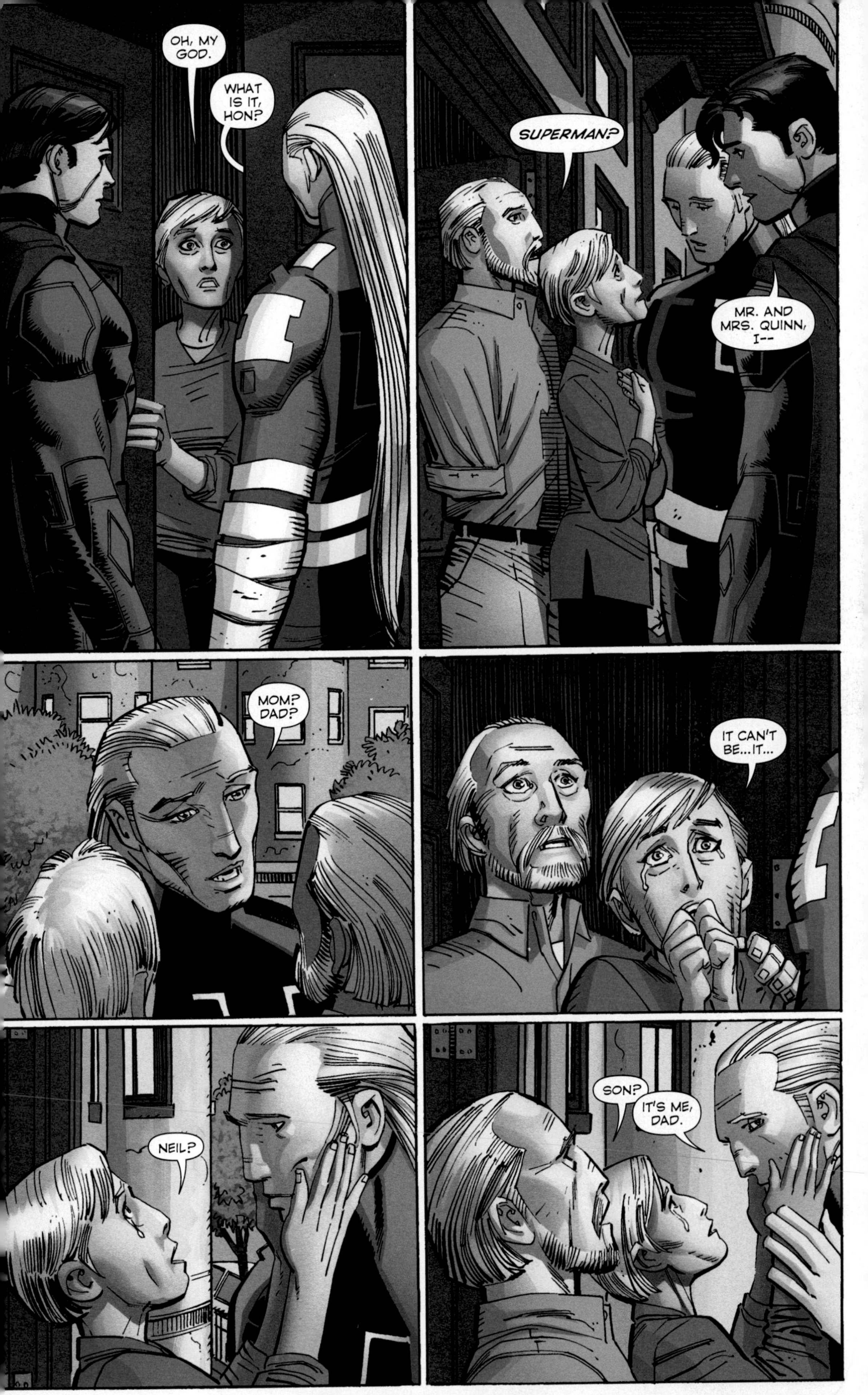
OH, MY GOD.
WHAT IS IT, HON?
SUPERMAN?
MR. AND MRS. QUINN, I--
MOM? DAD?
IT CAN'T BE...IT...
NEIL?
SON?
IT'S ME, DAD.

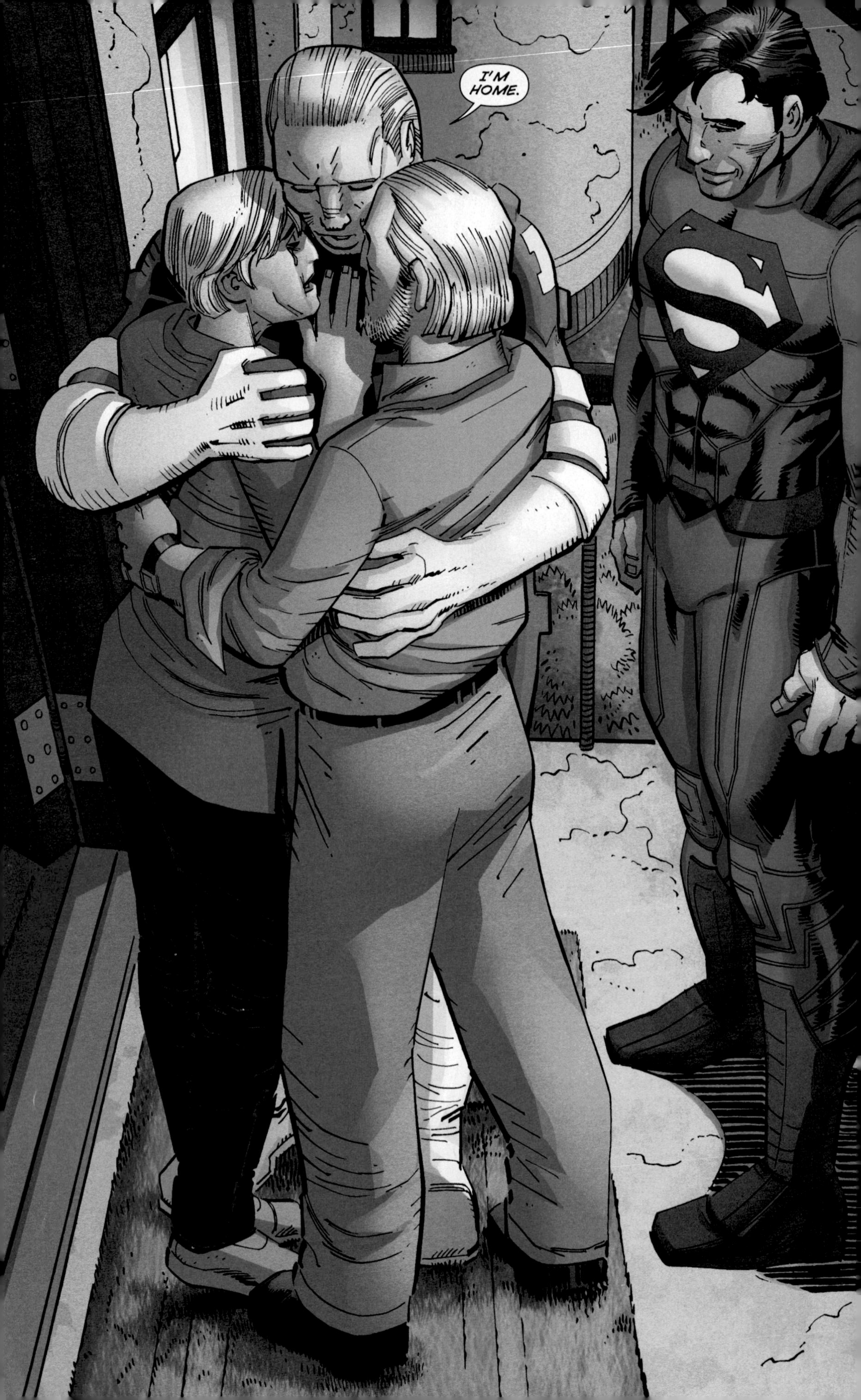
I'M HOME.

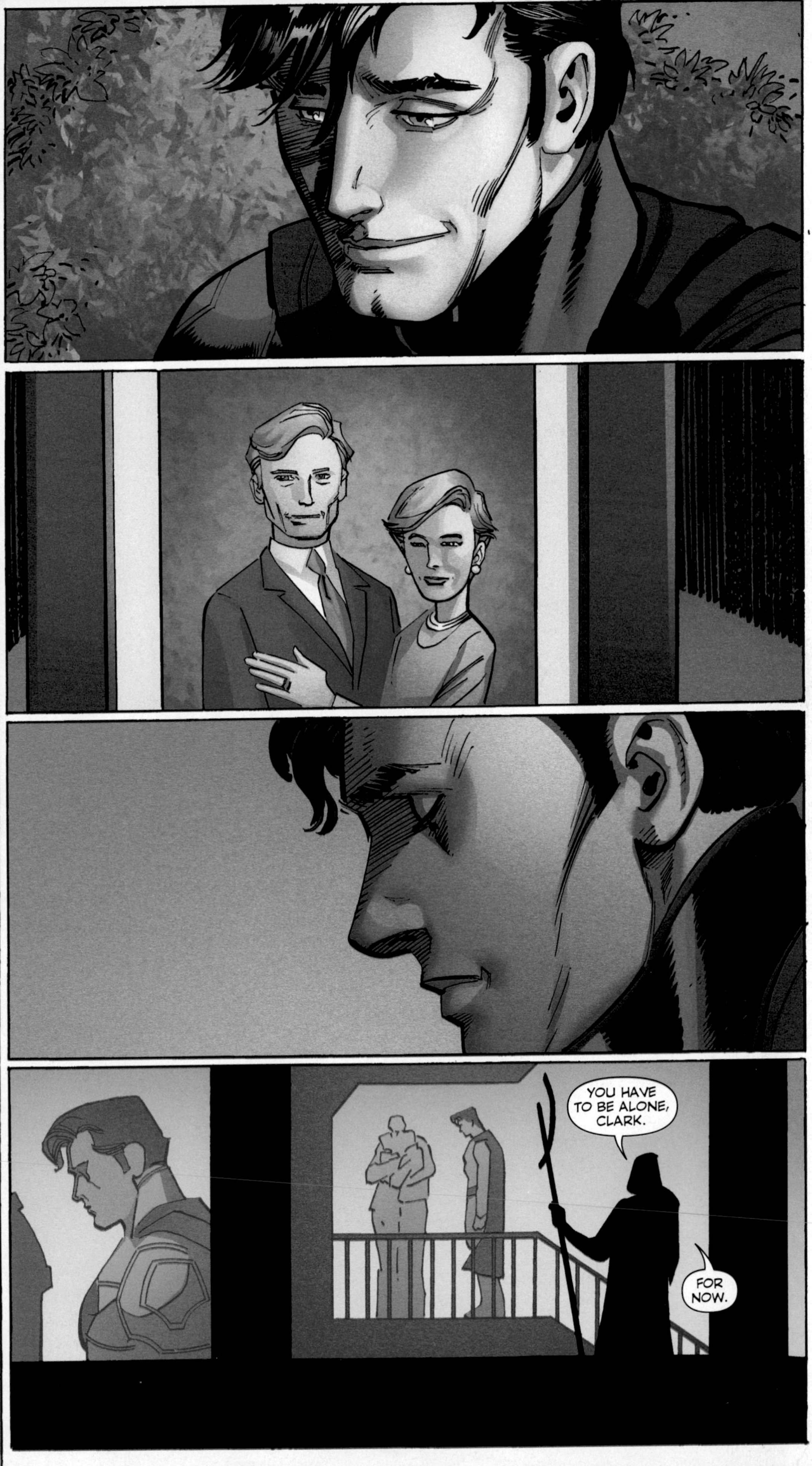
YOU HAVE TO BE ALONE, CLARK.
FOR NOW.

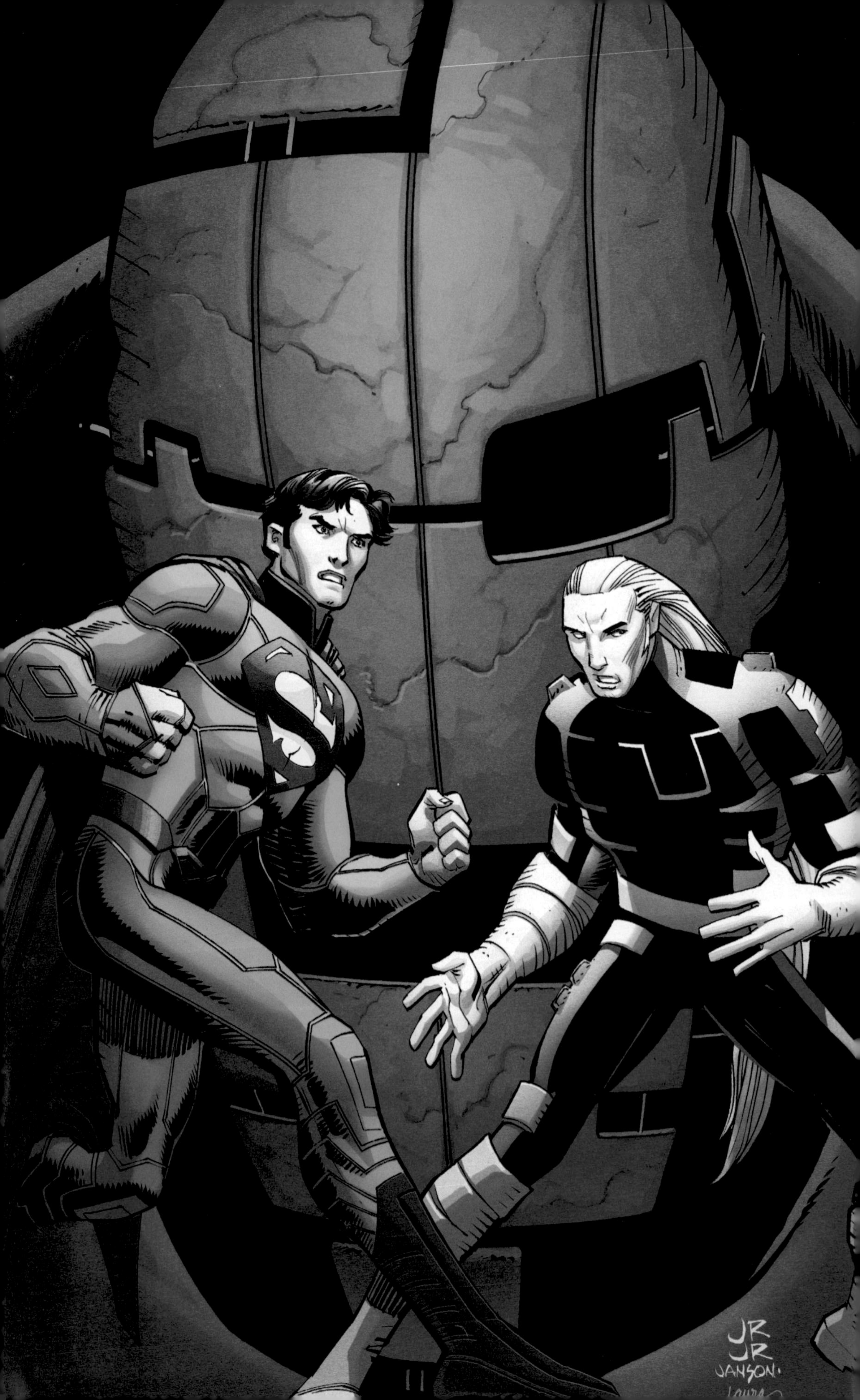
JR
JR
JANSON

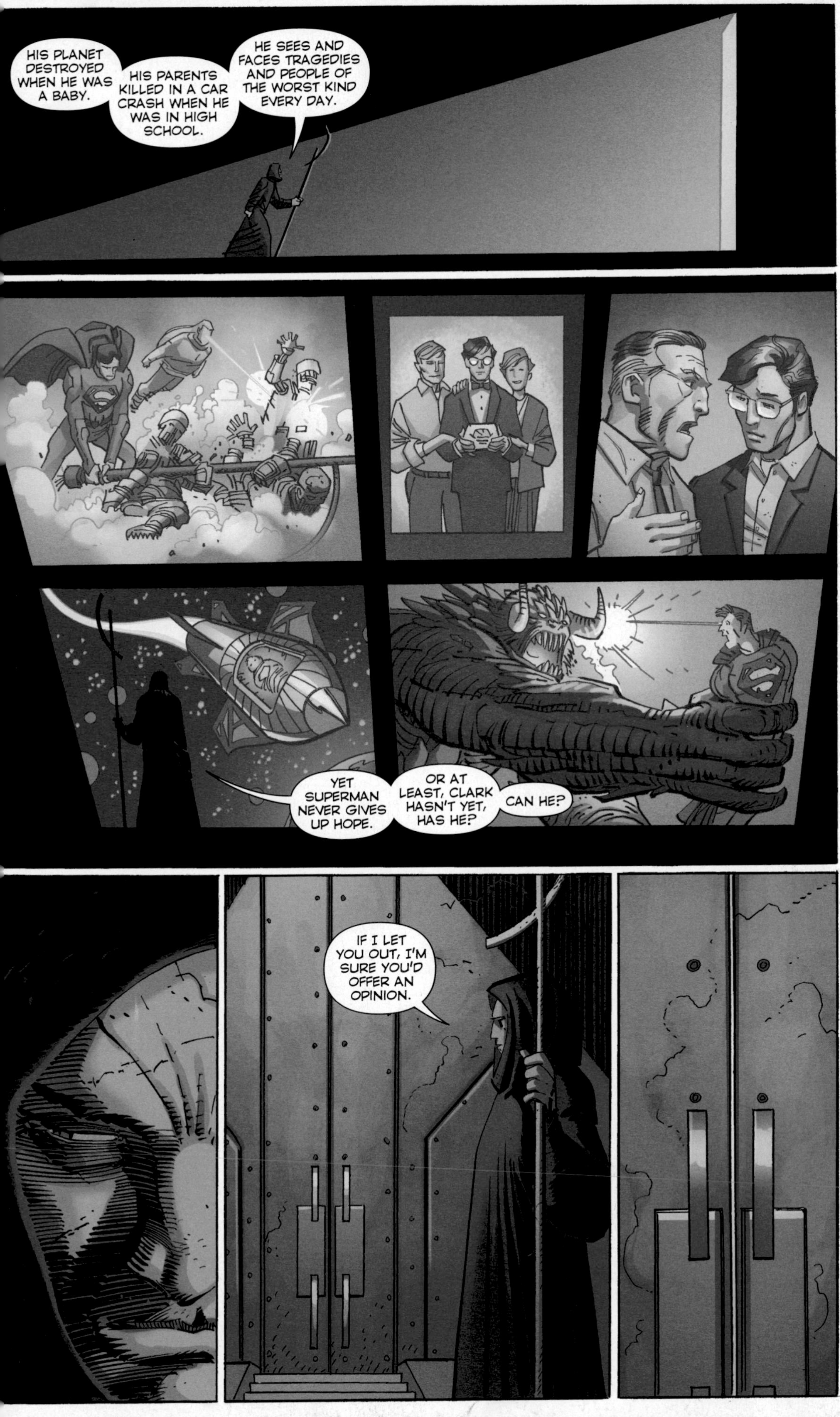
HIS PLANET DESTROYED WHEN HE WAS A BABY.
HIS PARENTS KILLED IN A CAR CRASH WHEN HE WAS IN HIGH SCHOOL.
HE SEES AND FACES TRAGEDIES AND PEOPLE OF THE WORST KIND EVERY DAY.
YET SUPERMAN NEVER GIVES UP HOPE.
OR AT LEAST, CLARK HASN'T YET, HAS HE?
CAN HE?
IF I LET YOU OUT, I'M SURE YOU'D OFFER AN OPINION.

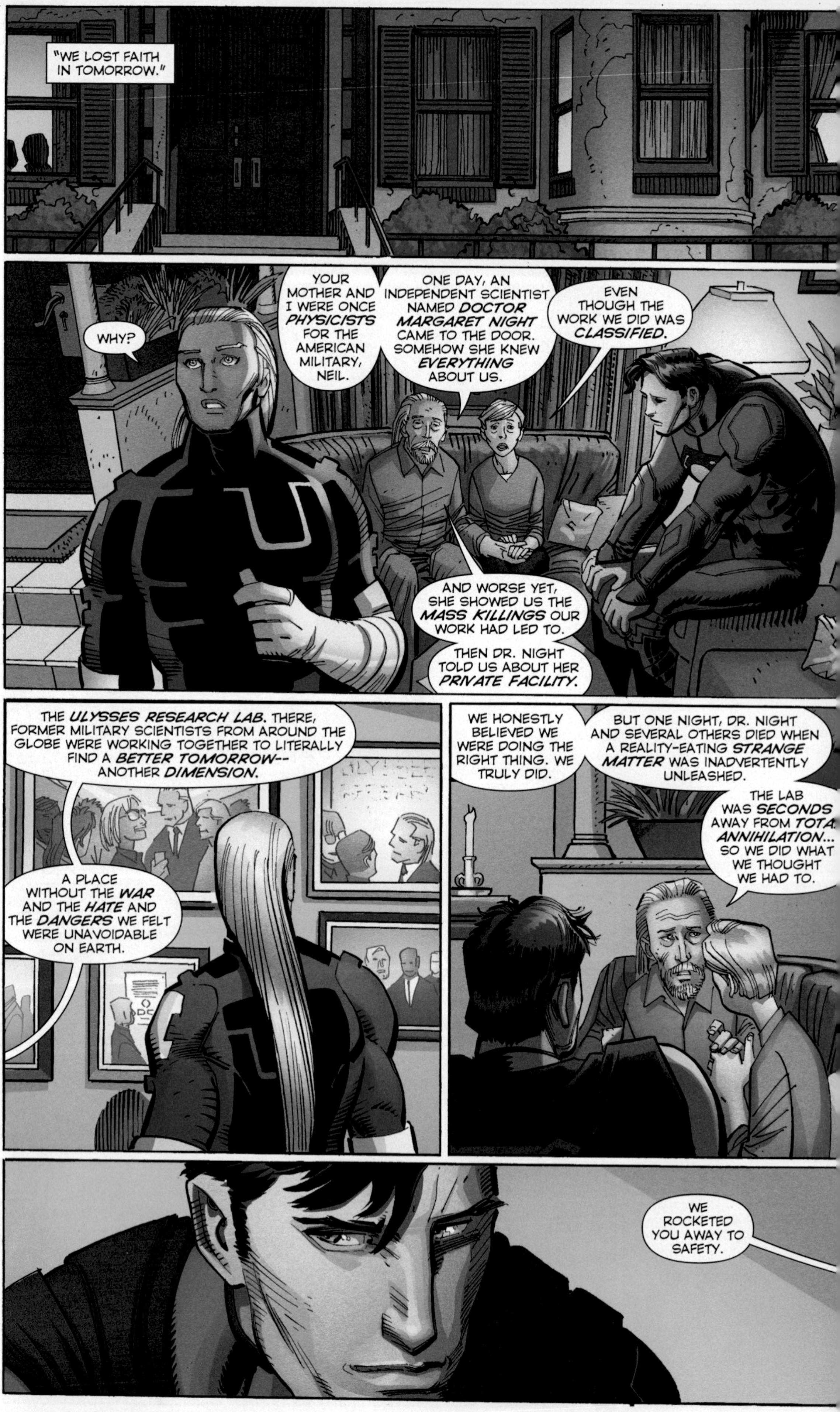
"WE LOST FAITH IN TOMORROW."
WHY?
YOUR MOTHER AND I WERE ONCE PHYSICISTS FOR THE AMERICAN MILITARY, NEIL.
ONE DAY, AN INDEPENDENT SCIENTIST NAMED DOCTOR MARGARET NIGHT CAME TO THE DOOR. SOMEHOW SHE KNEW EVERYTHING ABOUT US.
EVEN THOUGH THE WORK WE DID WAS CLASSIFIED.
AND WORSE YET, SHE SHOWED US THE MASS KILLINGS OUR WORK HAD LED TO.
THEN DR. NIGHT TOLD US ABOUT HER PRIVATE FACILITY.
THE ULYSSES RESEARCH LAB. THERE, FORMER MILITARY SCIENTISTS FROM AROUND THE GLOBE WERE WORKING TOGETHER TO LITERALLY FIND A BETTER TOMORROW-- ANOTHER DIMENSION.
A PLACE WITHOUT THE WAR AND THE HATE AND THE DANGERS WE FELT WERE UNAVOIDABLE ON EARTH.
WE HONESTLY BELIEVED WE WERE DOING THE RIGHT THING. WE TRULY DID.
BUT ONE NIGHT, DR. NIGHT AND SEVERAL OTHERS DIED WHEN A REALITY-EATING STRANGE MATTER WAS INADVERTENTLY UNLEASHED.
THE LAB WAS SECONDS AWAY FROM TOTAL ANNIHILATION... SO WE DID WHAT WE THOUGHT WE HAD TO.
WE ROCKETED YOU AWAY TO SAFETY.

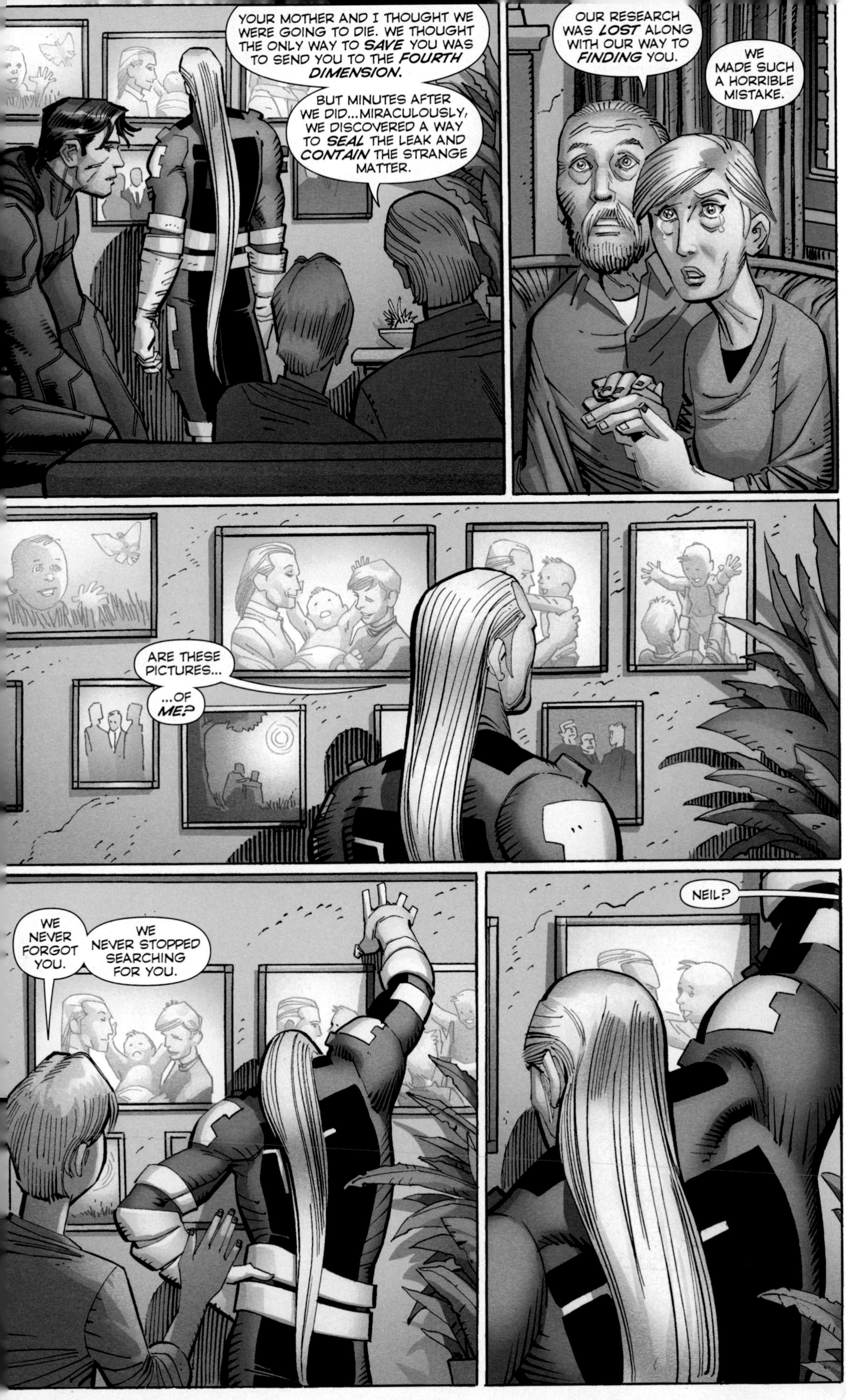
YOUR MOTHER AND I THOUGHT WE WERE GOING TO DIE. WE THOUGHT THE ONLY WAY TO SAVE YOU WAS TO SEND YOU TO THE FOURTH DIMENSION.
BUT MINUTES AFTER WE DID...MIRACULOUSLY, WE DISCOVERED A WAY TO SEAL THE LEAK AND CONTAIN THE STRANGE MATTER.
OUR RESEARCH WAS LOST ALONG WITH OUR WAY TO FINDING YOU.
WE MADE SUCH A HORRIBLE MISTAKE.
ARE THESE PICTURES...
...OF ME?
WE NEVER FORGOT YOU.
WE NEVER STOPPED SEARCHING FOR YOU.
NEIL?

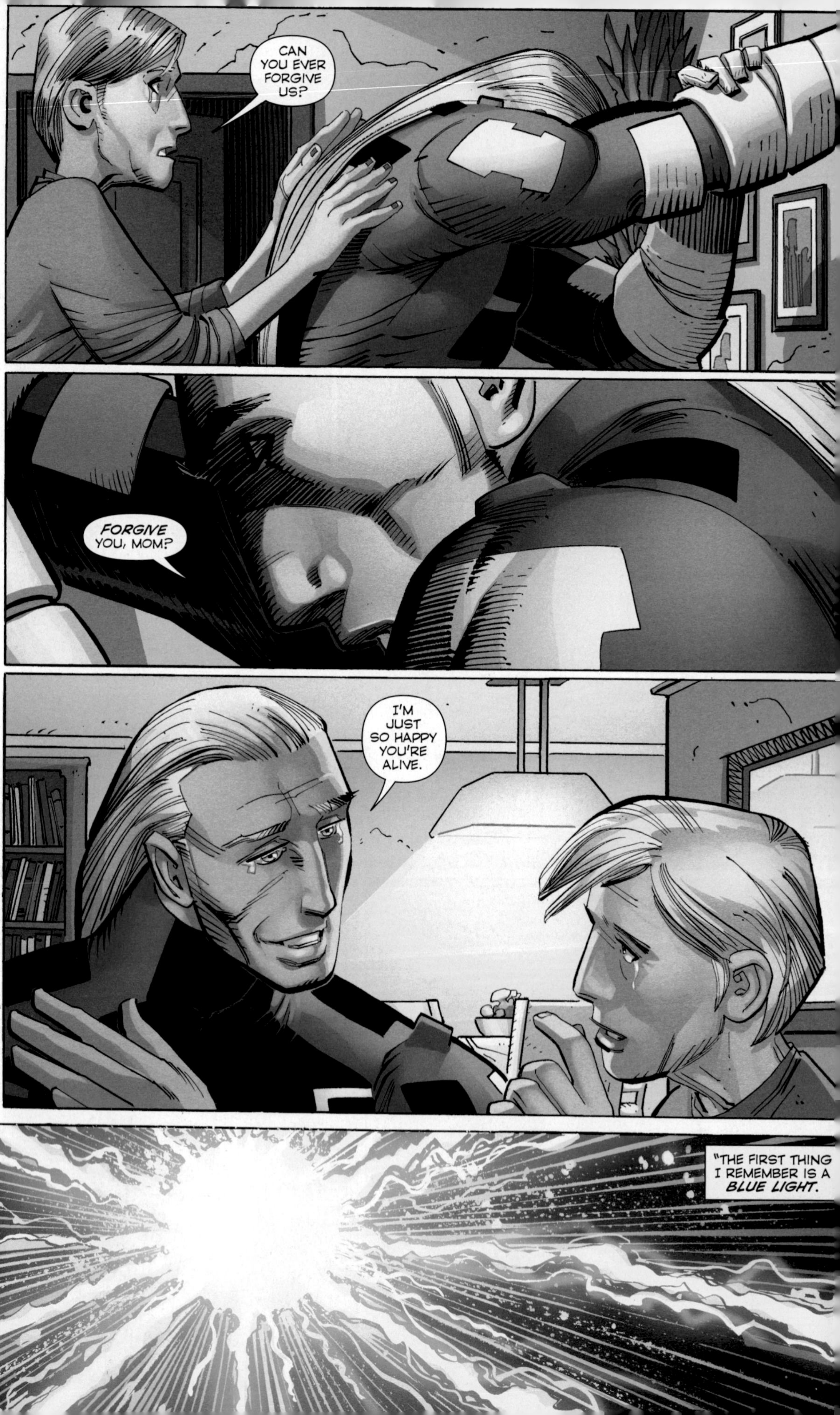
CAN YOU EVER FORGIVE US?
FORGIVE YOU, MOM?
I'M JUST SO HAPPY YOU'RE ALIVE.
"THE FIRST THING I REMEMBER IS A BLUE LIGHT.

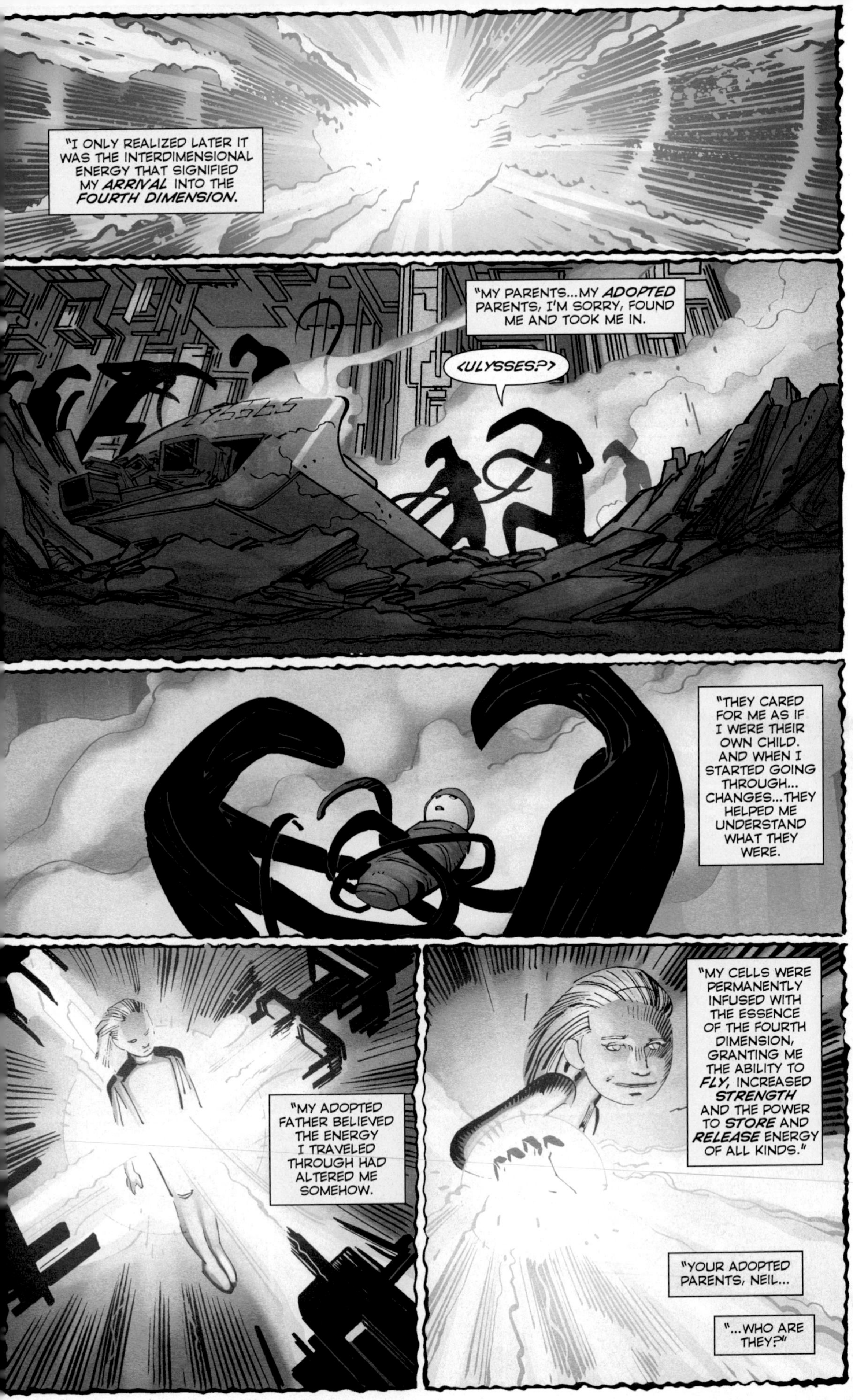
"I ONLY REALIZED LATER IT WAS THE INTERDIMENSIONAL ENERGY THAT SIGNIFIED MY ARRIVAL INTO THE FOURTH DIMENSION.
"MY PARENTS...MY ADOPTED PARENTS, I'M SORRY, FOUND ME AND TOOK ME IN.
<ULYSSES?>
ULYSSES
"THEY CARED FOR ME AS IF I WERE THEIR OWN CHILD. AND WHEN I STARTED GOING THROUGH... CHANGES...THEY HELPED ME UNDERSTAND WHAT THEY WERE.
"MY ADOPTED FATHER BELIEVED THE ENERGY I TRAVELED THROUGH HAD ALTERED ME SOMEHOW.
"MY CELLS WERE PERMANENTLY INFUSED WITH THE ESSENCE OF THE FOURTH DIMENSION, GRANTING ME THE ABILITY TO FLY, INCREASED STRENGTH AND THE POWER TO STORE AND RELEASE ENERGY OF ALL KINDS."
"YOUR ADOPTED PARENTS, NEIL...
"...WHO ARE THEY?"

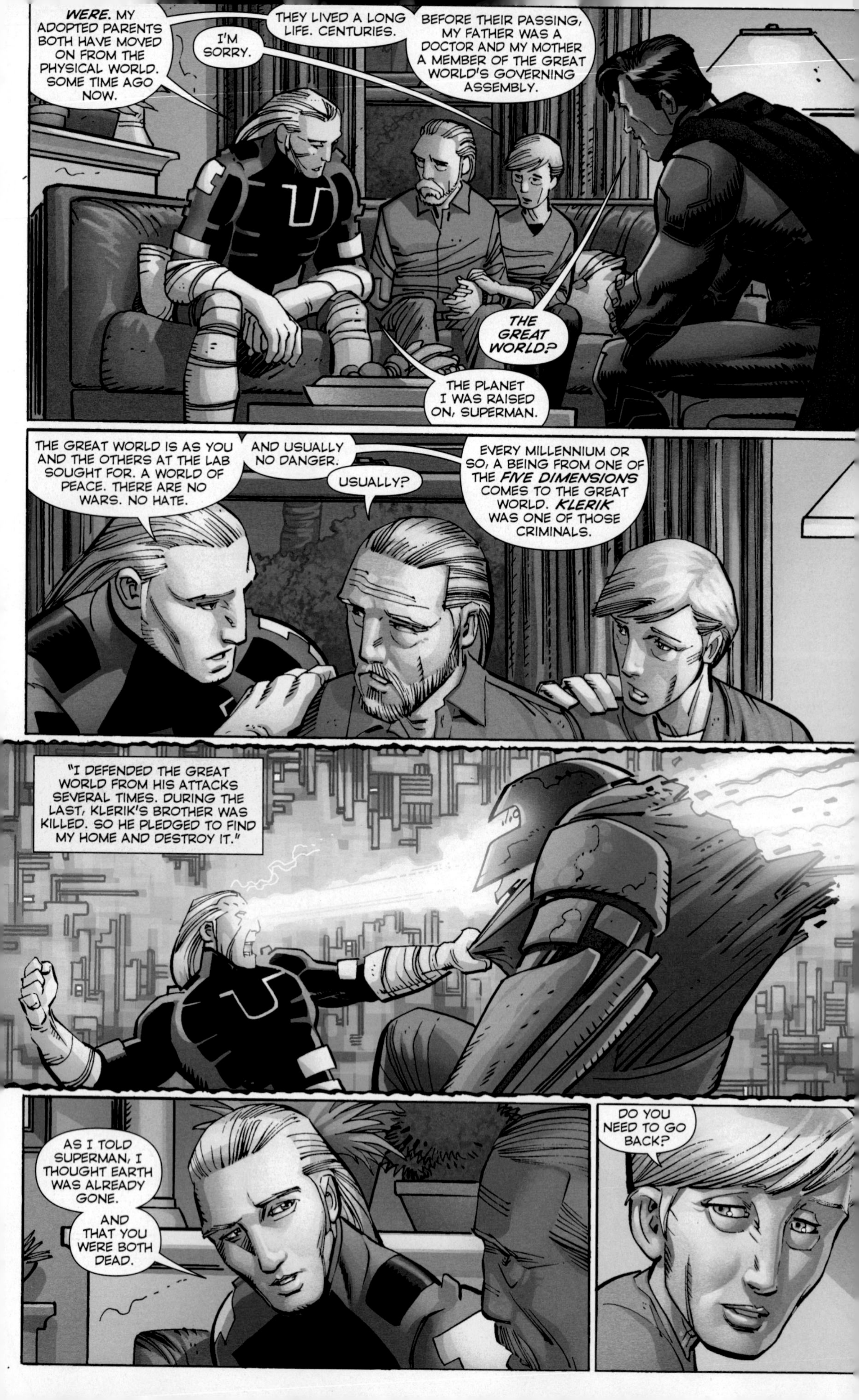
WERE. MY ADOPTED PARENTS BOTH HAVE MOVED ON FROM THE PHYSICAL WORLD. SOME TIME AGO NOW.
I'M SORRY.
THEY LIVED A LONG LIFE. CENTURIES.
BEFORE THEIR PASSING, MY FATHER WAS A DOCTOR AND MY MOTHER A MEMBER OF THE GREAT WORLD'S GOVERNING ASSEMBLY.
THE GREAT WORLD?
THE PLANET I WAS RAISED ON, SUPERMAN.
THE GREAT WORLD IS AS YOU AND THE OTHERS AT THE LAB SOUGHT FOR. A WORLD OF PEACE. THERE ARE NO WARS. NO HATE.
AND USUALLY NO DANGER.
USUALLY?
EVERY MILLENNIUM OR SO, A BEING FROM ONE OF THE *FIVE DIMENSIONS* COMES TO THE GREAT WORLD. *KLERIK* WAS ONE OF THOSE CRIMINALS.
"I DEFENDED THE GREAT WORLD FROM HIS ATTACKS SEVERAL TIMES. DURING THE LAST, KLERIK'S BROTHER WAS KILLED. SO HE PLEDGED TO FIND MY HOME AND DESTROY IT."
AS I TOLD SUPERMAN, I THOUGHT EARTH WAS ALREADY GONE.
AND THAT YOU WERE BOTH DEAD.
DO YOU NEED TO GO BACK?

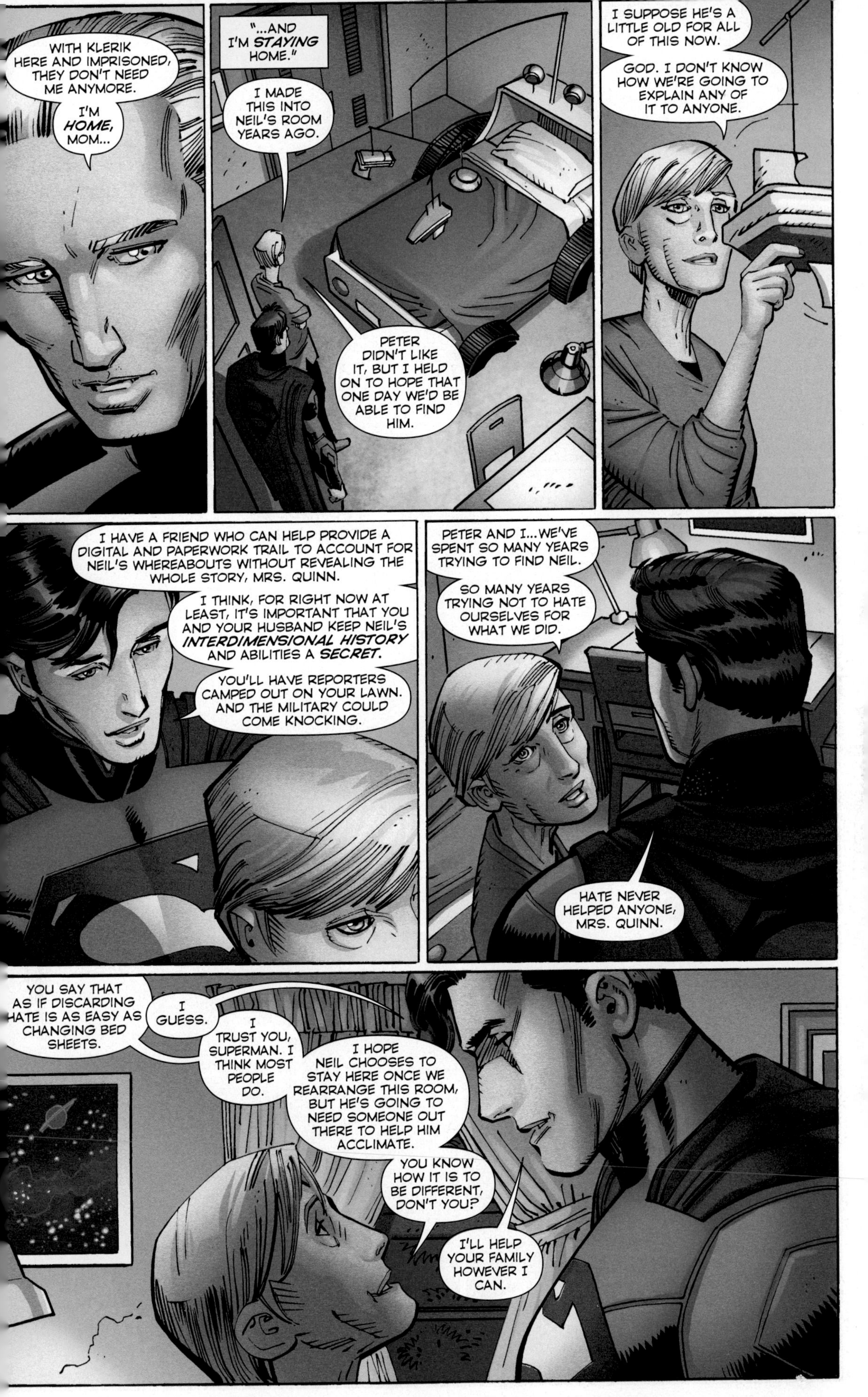
WITH KLERIK HERE AND IMPRISONED, THEY DON'T NEED ME ANYMORE.
I'M *HOME,* MOM...
"...AND I'M *STAYING* HOME."
I MADE THIS INTO NEIL'S ROOM YEARS AGO.
PETER DIDN'T LIKE IT, BUT I HELD ON TO HOPE THAT ONE DAY WE'D BE ABLE TO FIND HIM.
I SUPPOSE HE'S A LITTLE OLD FOR ALL OF THIS NOW.
GOD. I DON'T KNOW HOW WE'RE GOING TO EXPLAIN ANY OF IT TO ANYONE.
I HAVE A FRIEND WHO CAN HELP PROVIDE A DIGITAL AND PAPERWORK TRAIL TO ACCOUNT FOR NEIL'S WHEREABOUTS WITHOUT REVEALING THE WHOLE STORY, MRS. QUINN.
I THINK, FOR RIGHT NOW AT LEAST, IT'S IMPORTANT THAT YOU AND YOUR HUSBAND KEEP NEIL'S *INTERDIMENSIONAL HISTORY* AND ABILITIES A *SECRET.*
YOU'LL HAVE REPORTERS CAMPED OUT ON YOUR LAWN. AND THE MILITARY COULD COME KNOCKING.
PETER AND I...WE'VE SPENT SO MANY YEARS TRYING TO FIND NEIL.
SO MANY YEARS TRYING NOT TO HATE OURSELVES FOR WHAT WE DID.
HATE NEVER HELPED ANYONE, MRS. QUINN.
YOU SAY THAT AS IF DISCARDING HATE IS AS EASY AS CHANGING BED SHEETS.
I GUESS.
I TRUST YOU, SUPERMAN. I THINK MOST PEOPLE DO.
I HOPE NEIL CHOOSES TO STAY HERE ONCE WE REARRANGE THIS ROOM, BUT HE'S GOING TO NEED SOMEONE OUT THERE TO HELP HIM ACCLIMATE.
YOU KNOW HOW IT IS TO BE DIFFERENT, DON'T YOU?
I'LL HELP YOUR FAMILY HOWEVER I CAN.

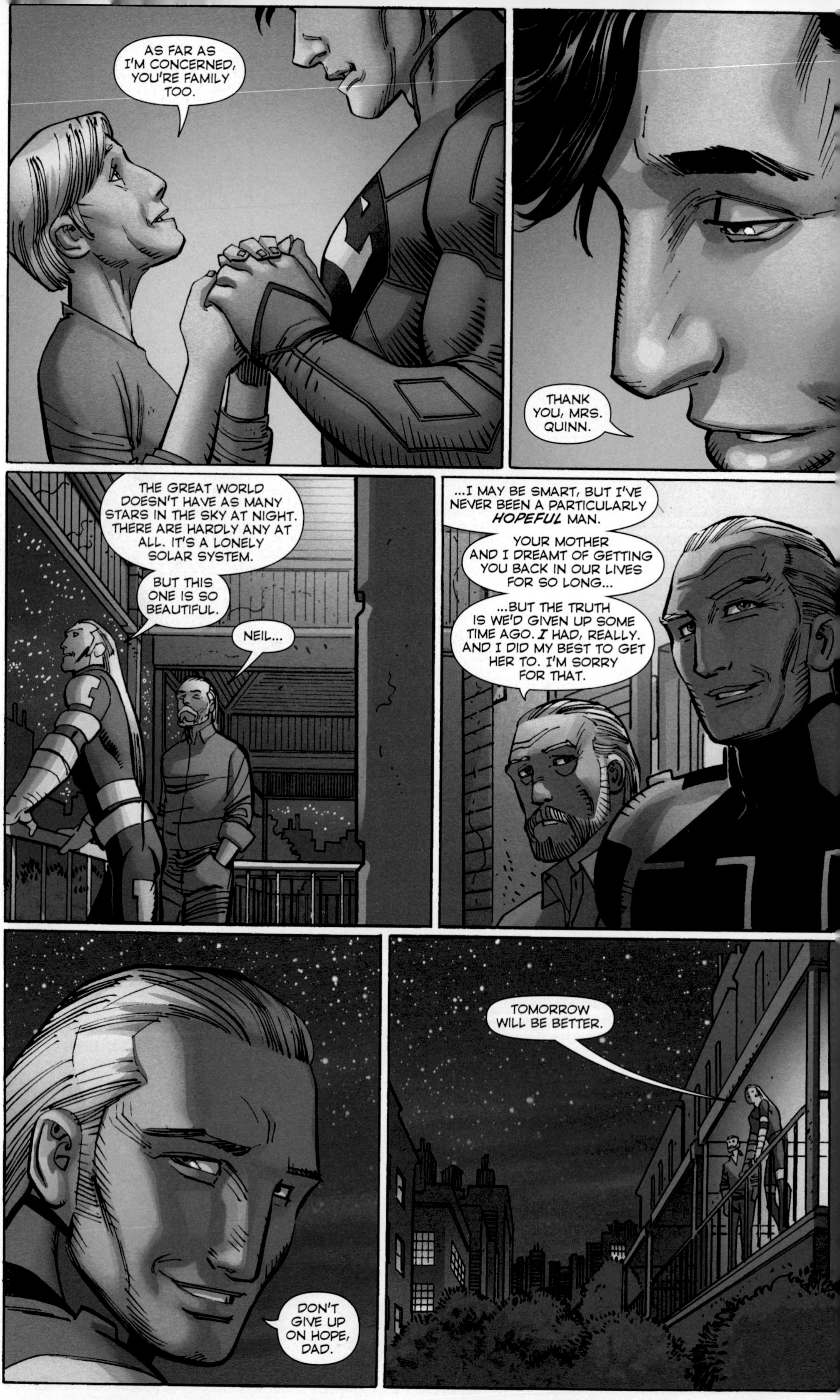
AS FAR AS I'M CONCERNED, YOU'RE FAMILY TOO.
THANK YOU, MRS. QUINN.
THE GREAT WORLD DOESN'T HAVE AS MANY STARS IN THE SKY AT NIGHT. THERE ARE HARDLY ANY AT ALL. IT'S A LONELY SOLAR SYSTEM.
BUT THIS ONE IS SO BEAUTIFUL.
NEIL...
...I MAY BE SMART, BUT I'VE NEVER BEEN A PARTICULARLY HOPEFUL MAN.
YOUR MOTHER AND I DREAMT OF GETTING YOU BACK IN OUR LIVES FOR SO LONG...
...BUT THE TRUTH IS WE'D GIVEN UP SOME TIME AGO. I HAD, REALLY. AND I DID MY BEST TO GET HER TO. I'M SORRY FOR THAT.
DON'T GIVE UP ON HOPE, DAD.
TOMORROW WILL BE BETTER.

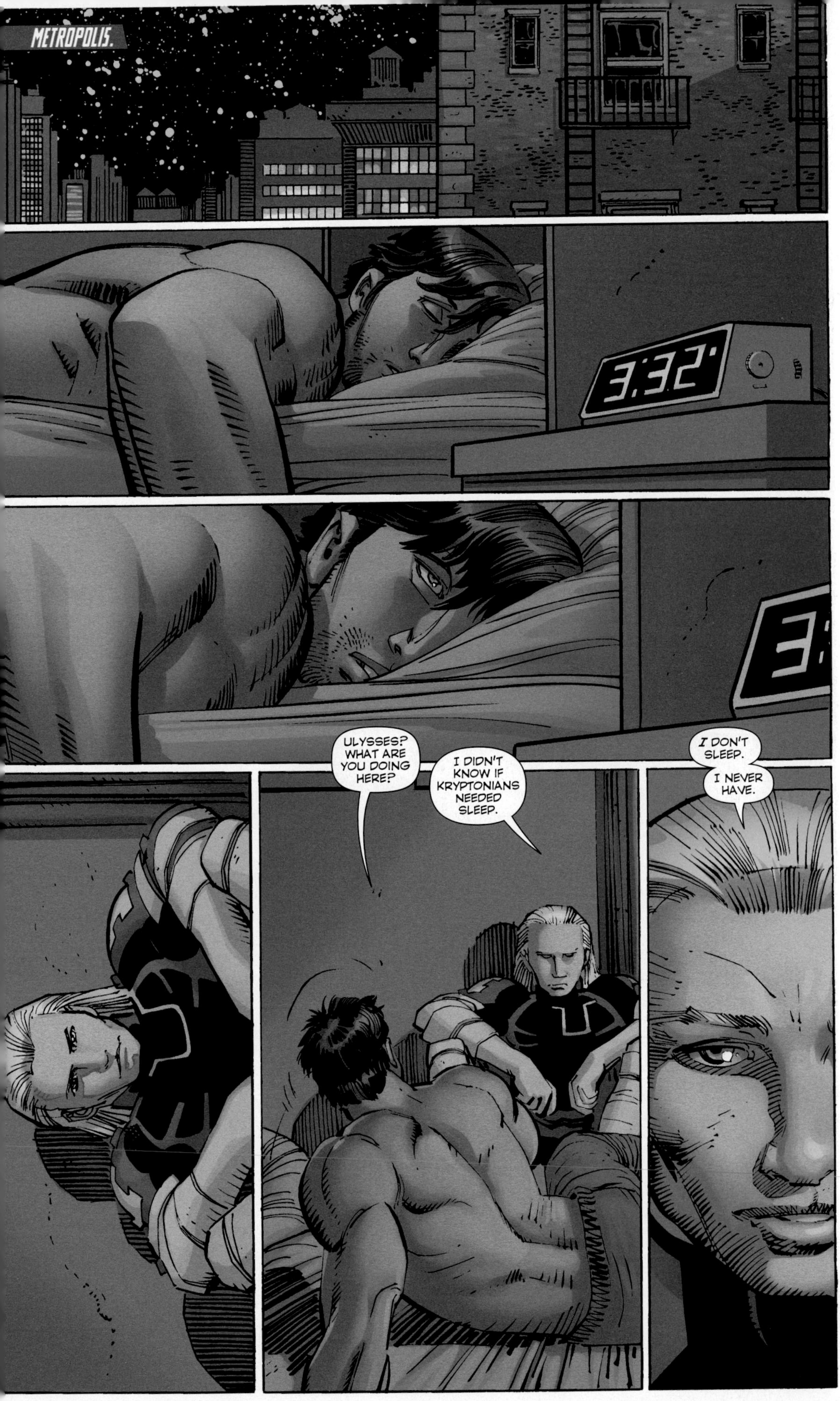
METROPOLIS.
3:32
ULYSSES? WHAT ARE YOU DOING HERE?
I DIDN'T KNOW IF KRYPTONIANS NEEDED SLEEP.
I DON'T SLEEP.
I NEVER HAVE.

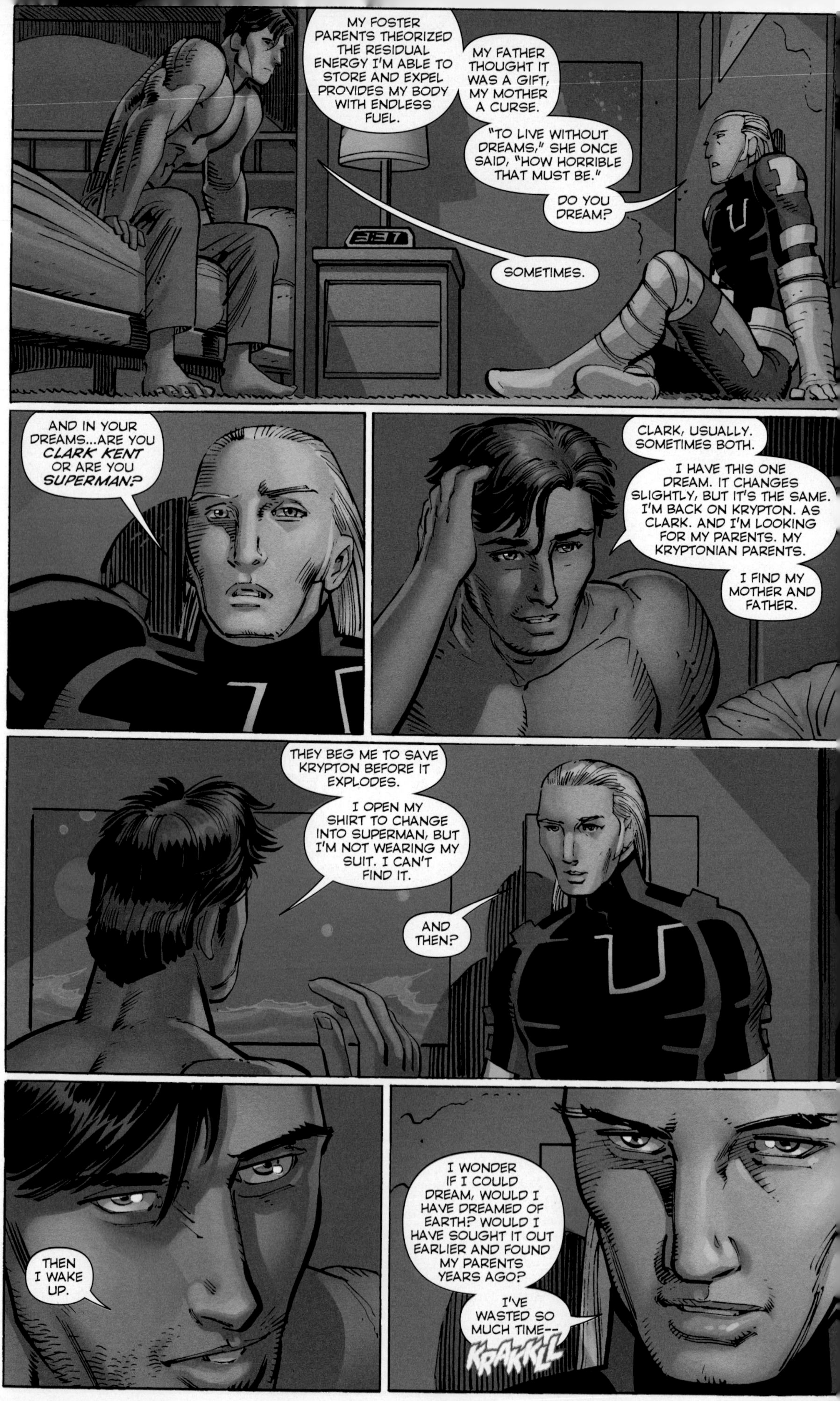
MY FOSTER PARENTS THEORIZED THE RESIDUAL ENERGY I'M ABLE TO STORE AND EXPEL PROVIDES MY BODY WITH ENDLESS FUEL.
MY FATHER THOUGHT IT WAS A GIFT, MY MOTHER A CURSE.
"TO LIVE WITHOUT DREAMS," SHE ONCE SAID, "HOW HORRIBLE THAT MUST BE."
DO YOU DREAM?
SOMETIMES.
AND IN YOUR DREAMS...ARE YOU *CLARK KENT* OR ARE YOU *SUPERMAN?*
CLARK, USUALLY. SOMETIMES BOTH.
I HAVE THIS ONE DREAM. IT CHANGES SLIGHTLY, BUT IT'S THE SAME. I'M BACK ON KRYPTON. AS CLARK. AND I'M LOOKING FOR MY PARENTS. MY KRYPTONIAN PARENTS.
I FIND MY MOTHER AND FATHER.
THEY BEG ME TO SAVE KRYPTON BEFORE IT EXPLODES.
I OPEN MY SHIRT TO CHANGE INTO SUPERMAN, BUT I'M NOT WEARING MY SUIT. I CAN'T FIND IT.
AND THEN?
THEN I WAKE UP.
I WONDER IF I COULD DREAM, WOULD I HAVE DREAMED OF EARTH? WOULD I HAVE SOUGHT IT OUT EARLIER AND FOUND MY PARENTS YEARS AGO?
I'VE WASTED SO MUCH TIME--
KRAKKLL

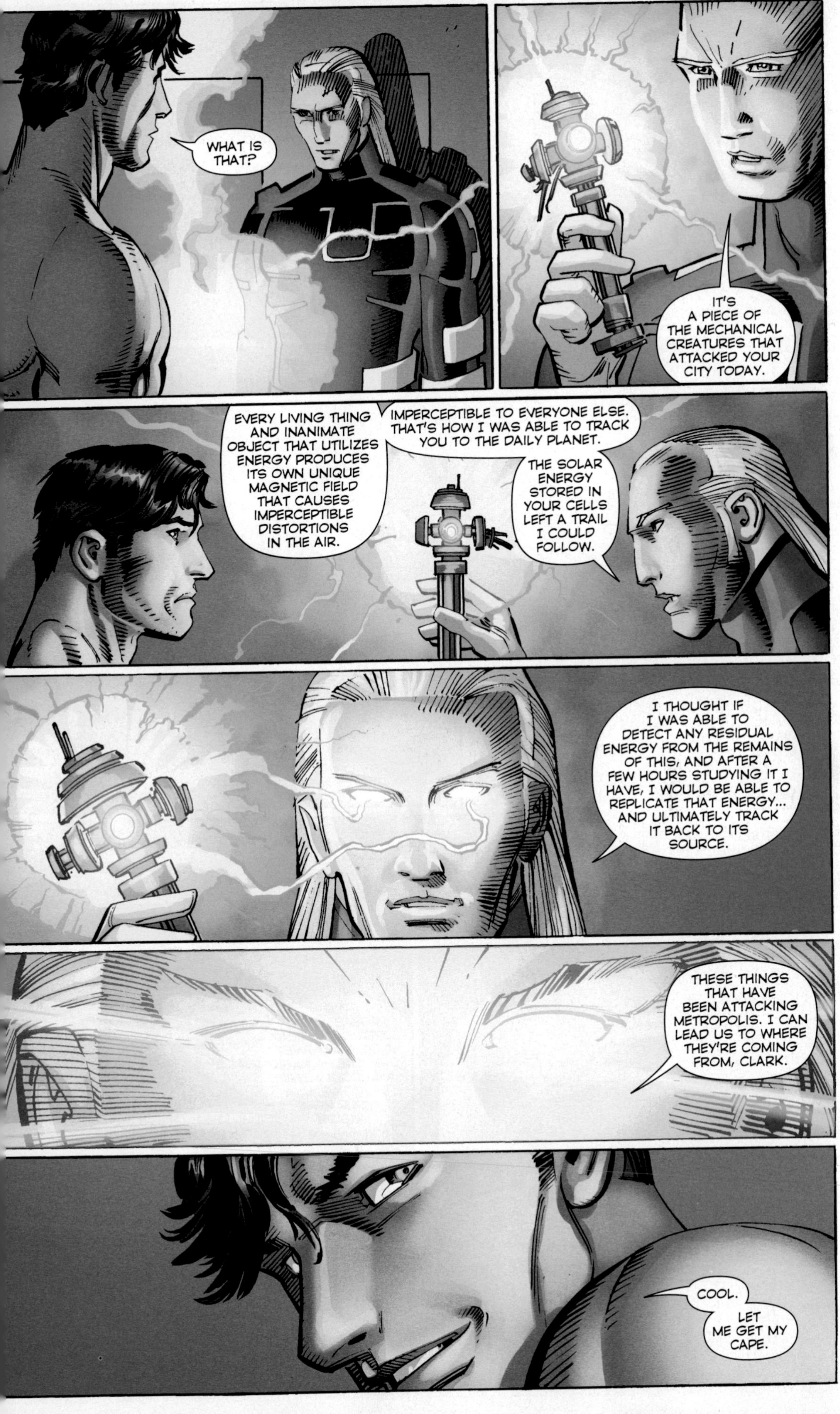
WHAT IS THAT?
IT'S A PIECE OF THE MECHANICAL CREATURES THAT ATTACKED YOUR CITY TODAY.
EVERY LIVING THING AND INANIMATE OBJECT THAT UTILIZES ENERGY PRODUCES ITS OWN UNIQUE MAGNETIC FIELD THAT CAUSES IMPERCEPTIBLE DISTORTIONS IN THE AIR.
IMPERCEPTIBLE TO EVERYONE ELSE. THAT'S HOW I WAS ABLE TO TRACK YOU TO THE DAILY PLANET.
THE SOLAR ENERGY STORED IN YOUR CELLS LEFT A TRAIL I COULD FOLLOW.
I THOUGHT IF I WAS ABLE TO DETECT ANY RESIDUAL ENERGY FROM THE REMAINS OF THIS, AND AFTER A FEW HOURS STUDYING IT I HAVE, I WOULD BE ABLE TO REPLICATE THAT ENERGY... AND ULTIMATELY TRACK IT BACK TO ITS SOURCE.
THESE THINGS THAT HAVE BEEN ATTACKING METROPOLIS. I CAN LEAD US TO WHERE THEY'RE COMING FROM, CLARK.
COOL.
LET ME GET MY CAPE.

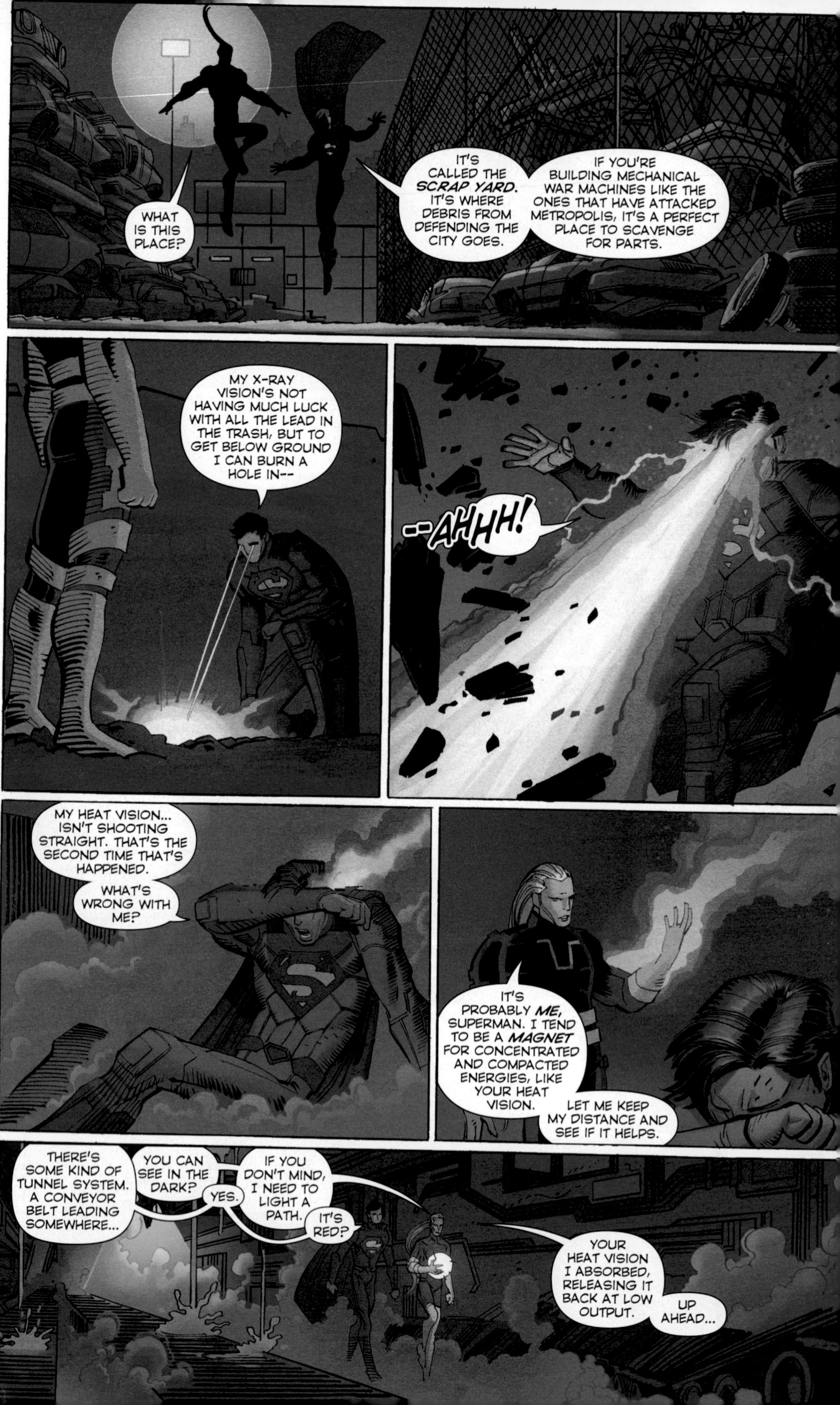
WHAT IS THIS PLACE?
IT'S CALLED THE SCRAP YARD. IT'S WHERE DEBRIS FROM DEFENDING THE CITY GOES.
IF YOU'RE BUILDING MECHANICAL WAR MACHINES LIKE THE ONES THAT HAVE ATTACKED METROPOLIS, IT'S A PERFECT PLACE TO SCAVENGE FOR PARTS.
MY X-RAY VISION'S NOT HAVING MUCH LUCK WITH ALL THE LEAD IN THE TRASH, BUT TO GET BELOW GROUND I CAN BURN A HOLE IN--
--AHHH!
MY HEAT VISION... ISN'T SHOOTING STRAIGHT. THAT'S THE SECOND TIME THAT'S HAPPENED.
WHAT'S WRONG WITH ME?
IT'S PROBABLY ME, SUPERMAN. I TEND TO BE A MAGNET FOR CONCENTRATED AND COMPACTED ENERGIES, LIKE YOUR HEAT VISION.
LET ME KEEP MY DISTANCE AND SEE IF IT HELPS.
THERE'S SOME KIND OF TUNNEL SYSTEM. A CONVEYOR BELT LEADING SOMEWHERE...
YOU CAN SEE IN THE DARK?
YES.
IF YOU DON'T MIND, I NEED TO LIGHT A PATH.
IT'S RED?
YOUR HEAT VISION I ABSORBED, RELEASING IT BACK AT LOW OUTPUT.
UP AHEAD...

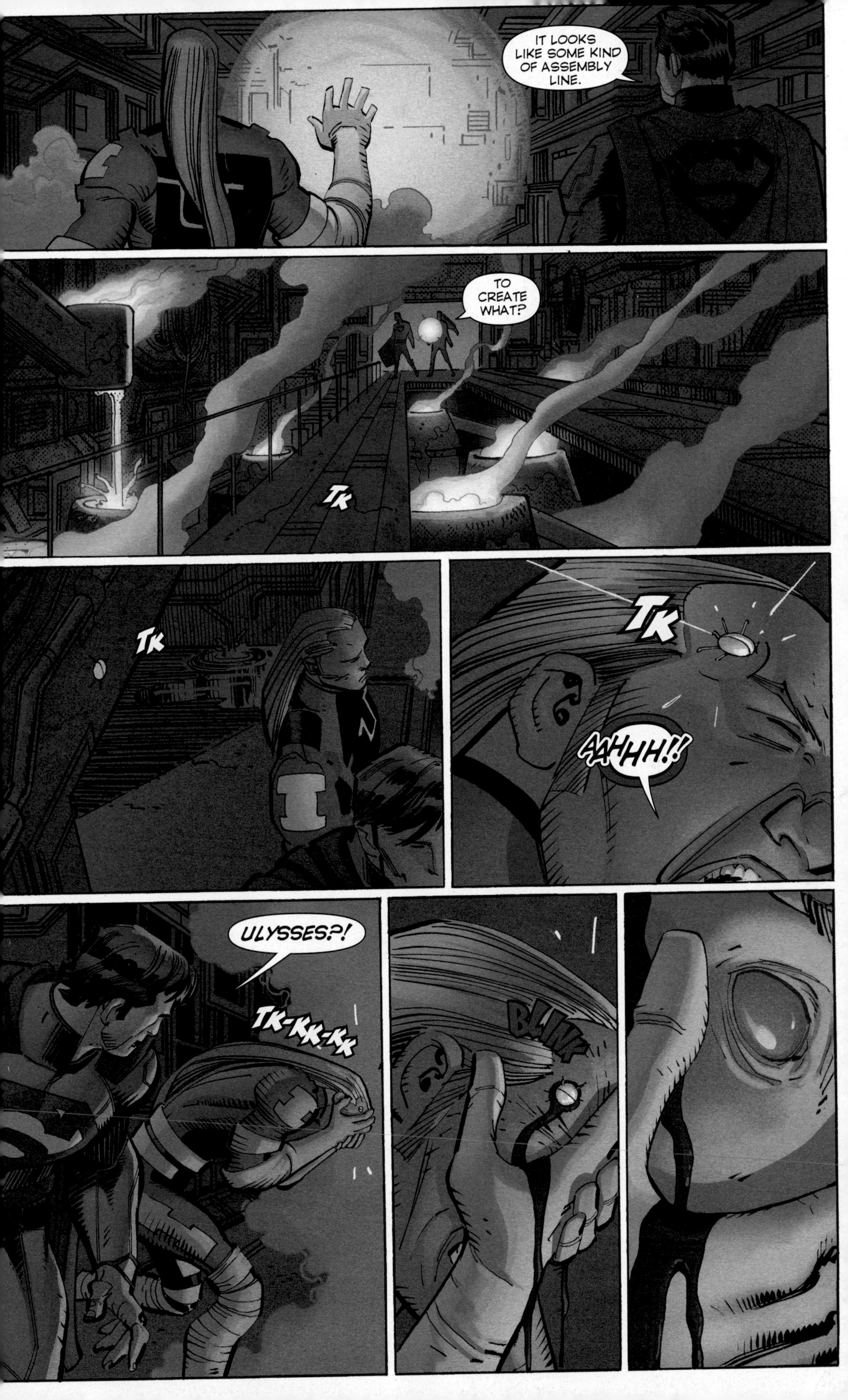
IT LOOKS LIKE SOME KIND OF ASSEMBLY LINE.
TO CREATE WHAT?
TK
TK
TK
AAHHH!!
ULYSSES?!
TK-KK-KK
BLINK

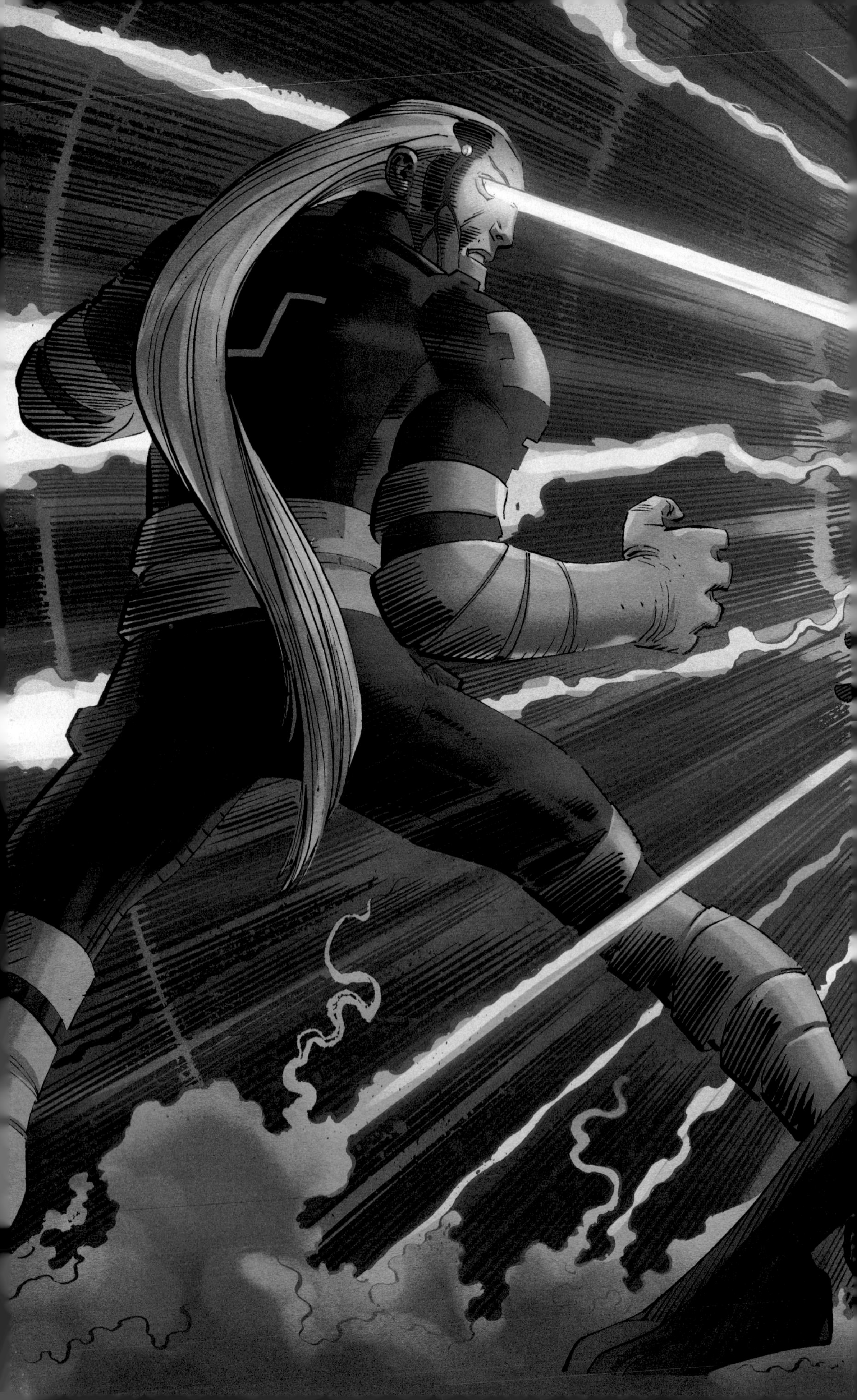

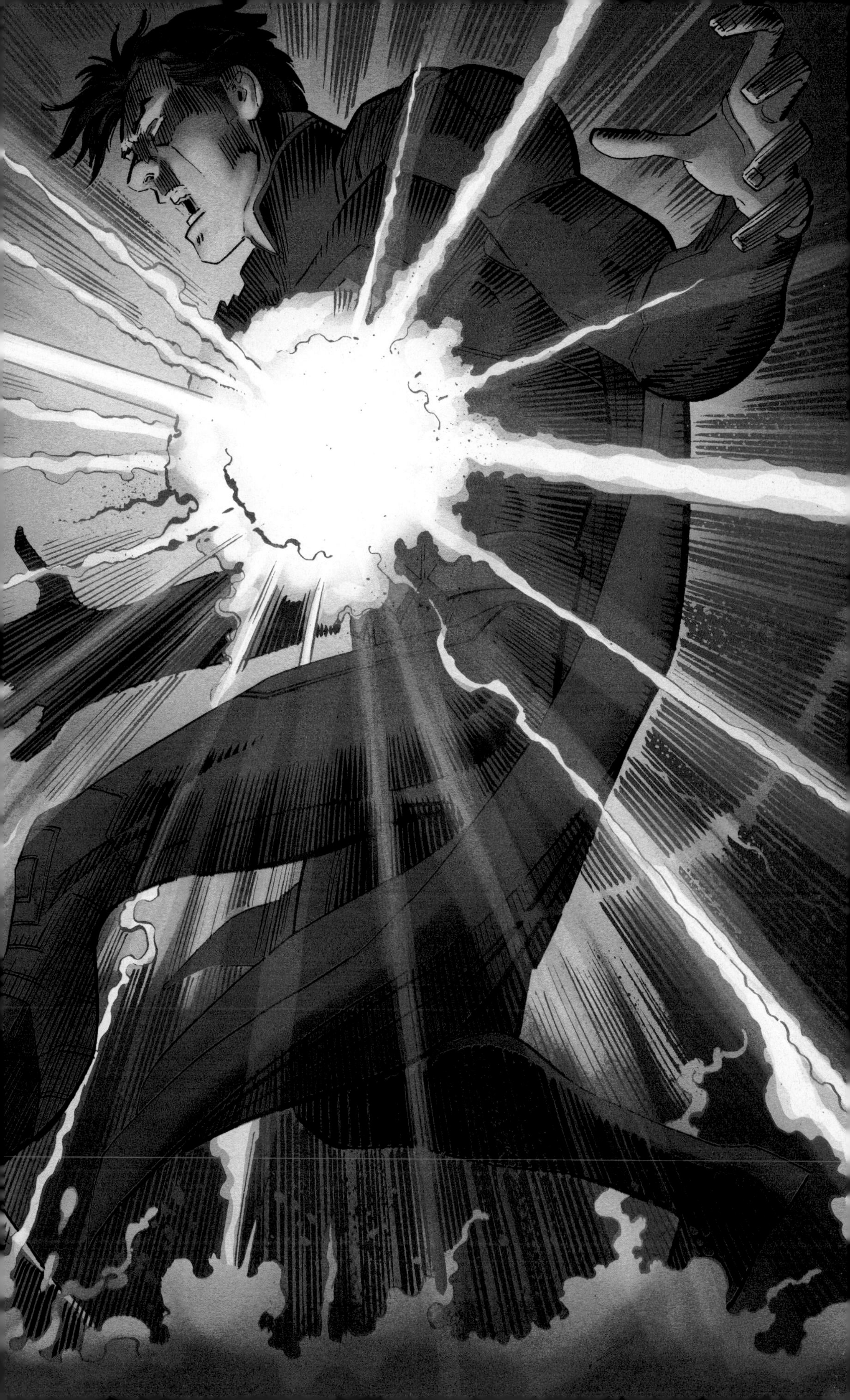

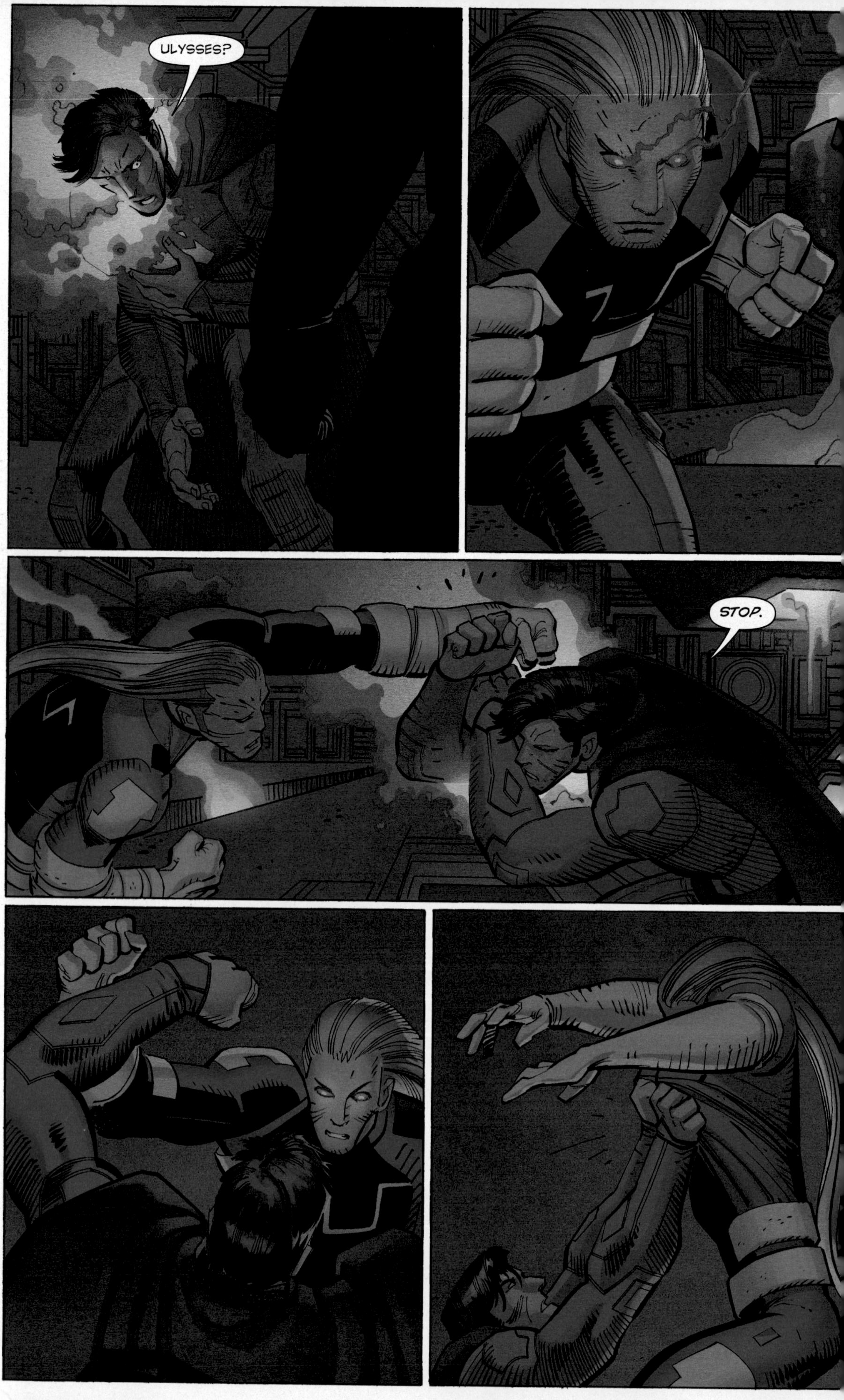
ULYSSES?
STOP.

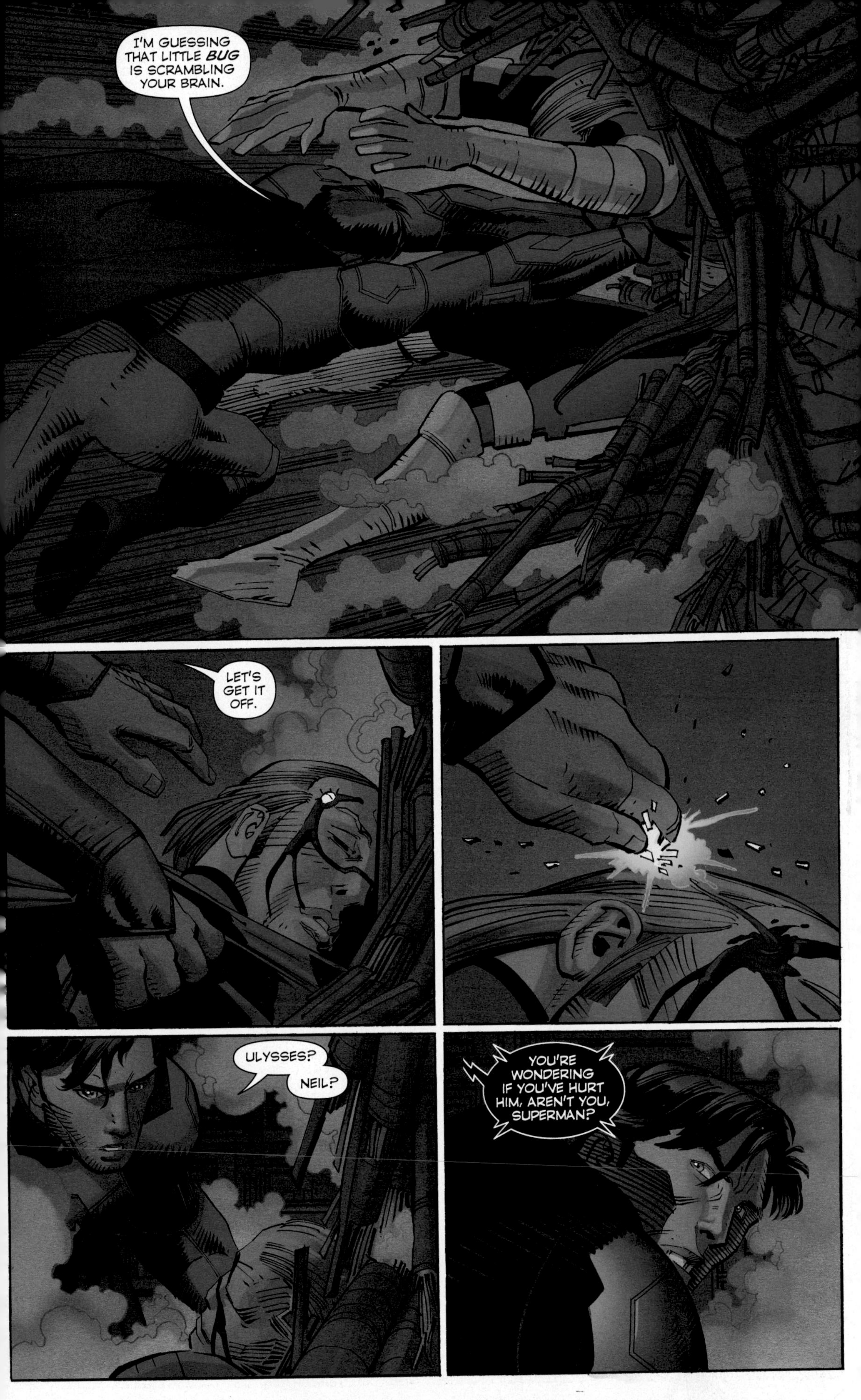
I'M GUESSING THAT LITTLE BUG IS SCRAMBLING YOUR BRAIN.
LET'S GET IT OFF.
ULYSSES?
NEIL?
YOU'RE WONDERING IF YOU'VE HURT HIM, AREN'T YOU, SUPERMAN?

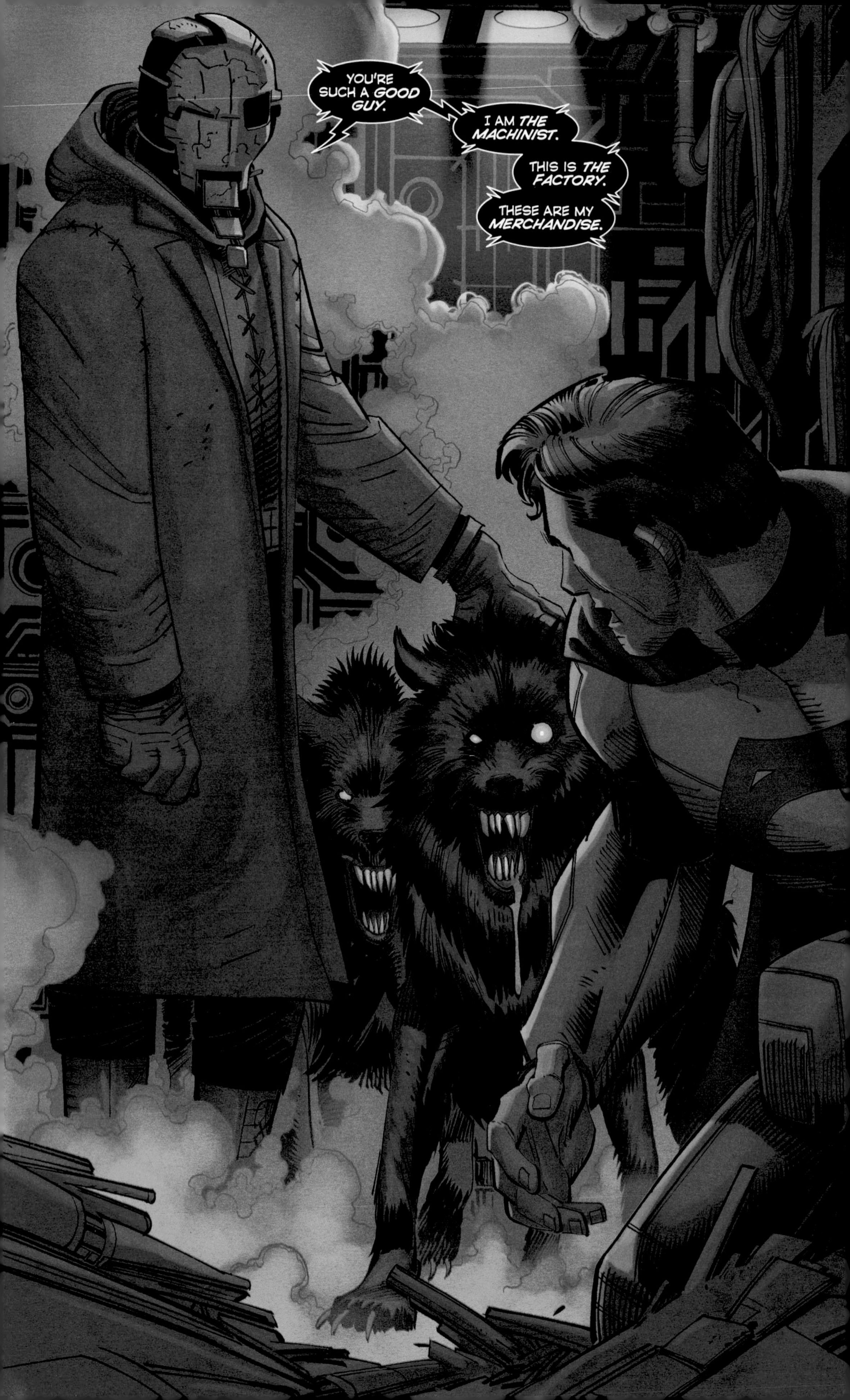
YOU'RE SUCH A GOOD GUY.
I AM THE MACHINIST.
THIS IS THE FACTORY.
THESE ARE MY MERCHANDISE.

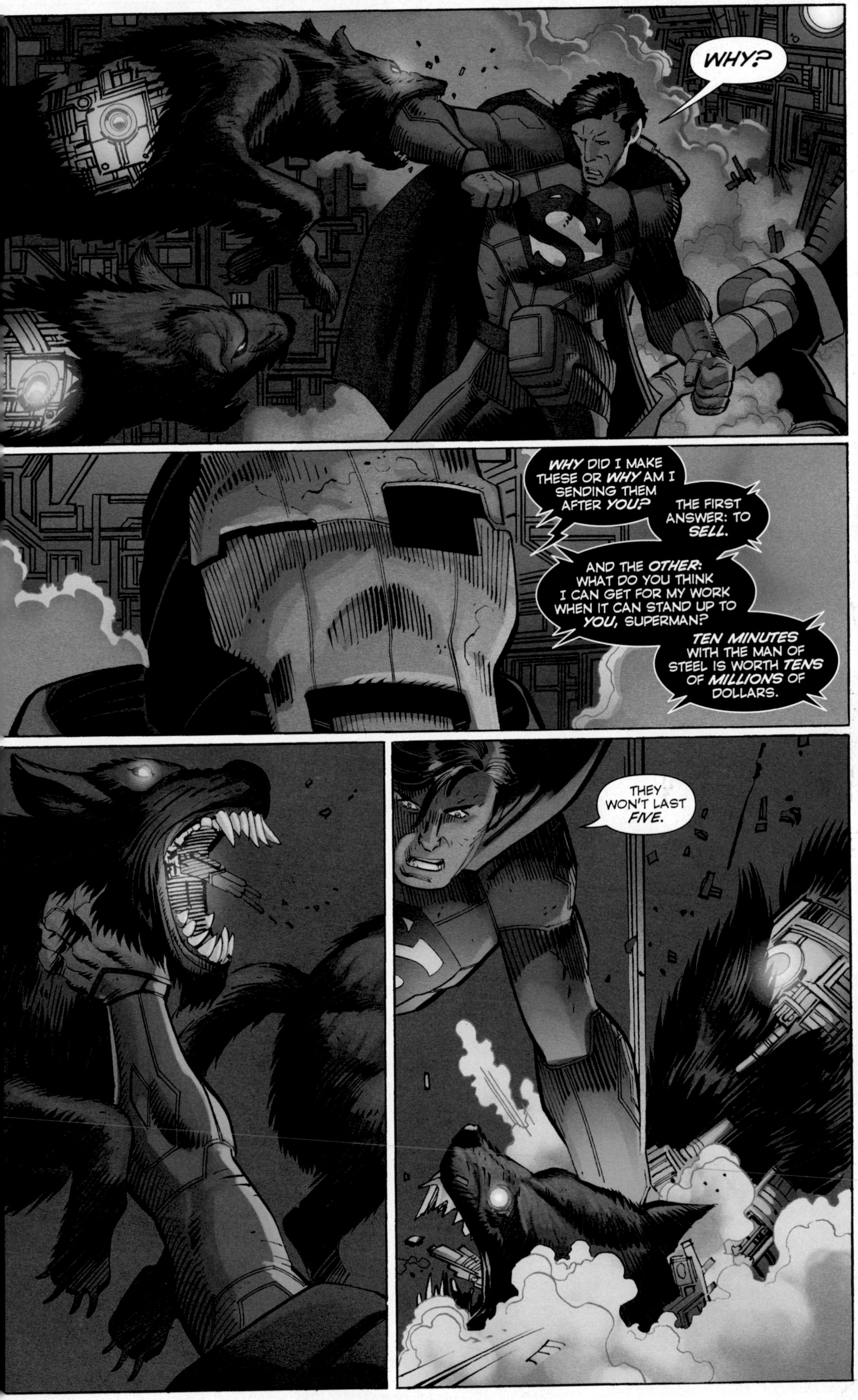
WHY?
WHY DID I MAKE THESE OR WHY AM I SENDING THEM AFTER YOU?
THE FIRST ANSWER: TO SELL.
AND THE OTHER: WHAT DO YOU THINK I CAN GET FOR MY WORK WHEN IT CAN STAND UP TO YOU, SUPERMAN?
TEN MINUTES WITH THE MAN OF STEEL IS WORTH TENS OF MILLIONS OF DOLLARS.
THEY WON'T LAST FIVE.

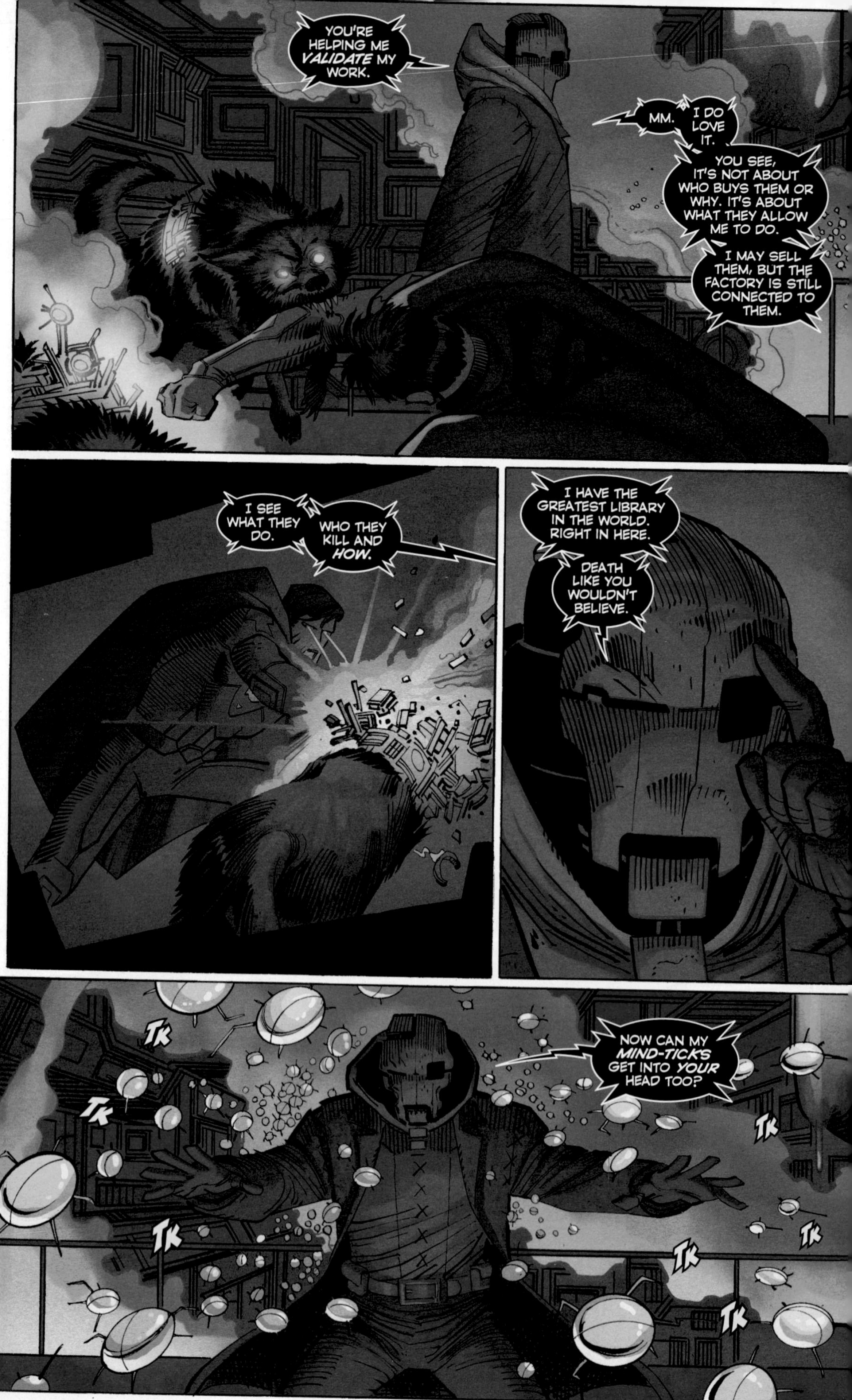
YOU'RE HELPING ME VALIDATE MY WORK.
MM.
I DO LOVE IT.
YOU SEE, IT'S NOT ABOUT WHO BUYS THEM OR WHY. IT'S ABOUT WHAT THEY ALLOW ME TO DO.
I MAY SELL THEM, BUT THE FACTORY IS STILL CONNECTED TO THEM.
I SEE WHAT THEY DO.
WHO THEY KILL AND HOW.
I HAVE THE GREATEST LIBRARY IN THE WORLD. RIGHT IN HERE.
DEATH LIKE YOU WOULDN'T BELIEVE.
TK
TK
NOW CAN MY MIND-TICKS GET INTO YOUR HEAD TOO?
TK
TK
TK
TK
TK

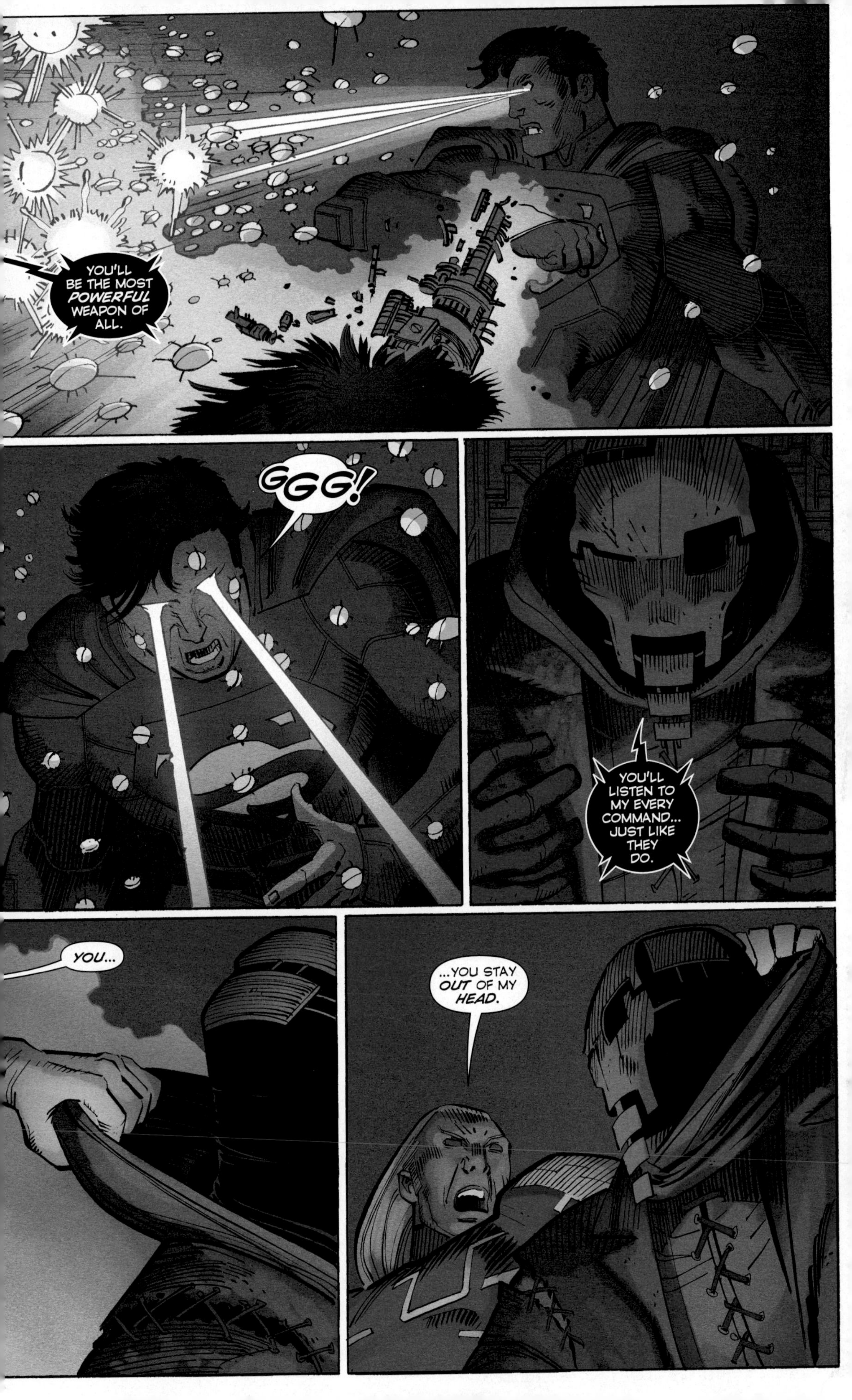
YOU'LL BE THE MOST *POWERFUL* WEAPON OF ALL.
GGG!
YOU'LL LISTEN TO MY EVERY COMMAND... JUST LIKE THEY DO.
YOU...
...YOU STAY *OUT* OF MY *HEAD.*

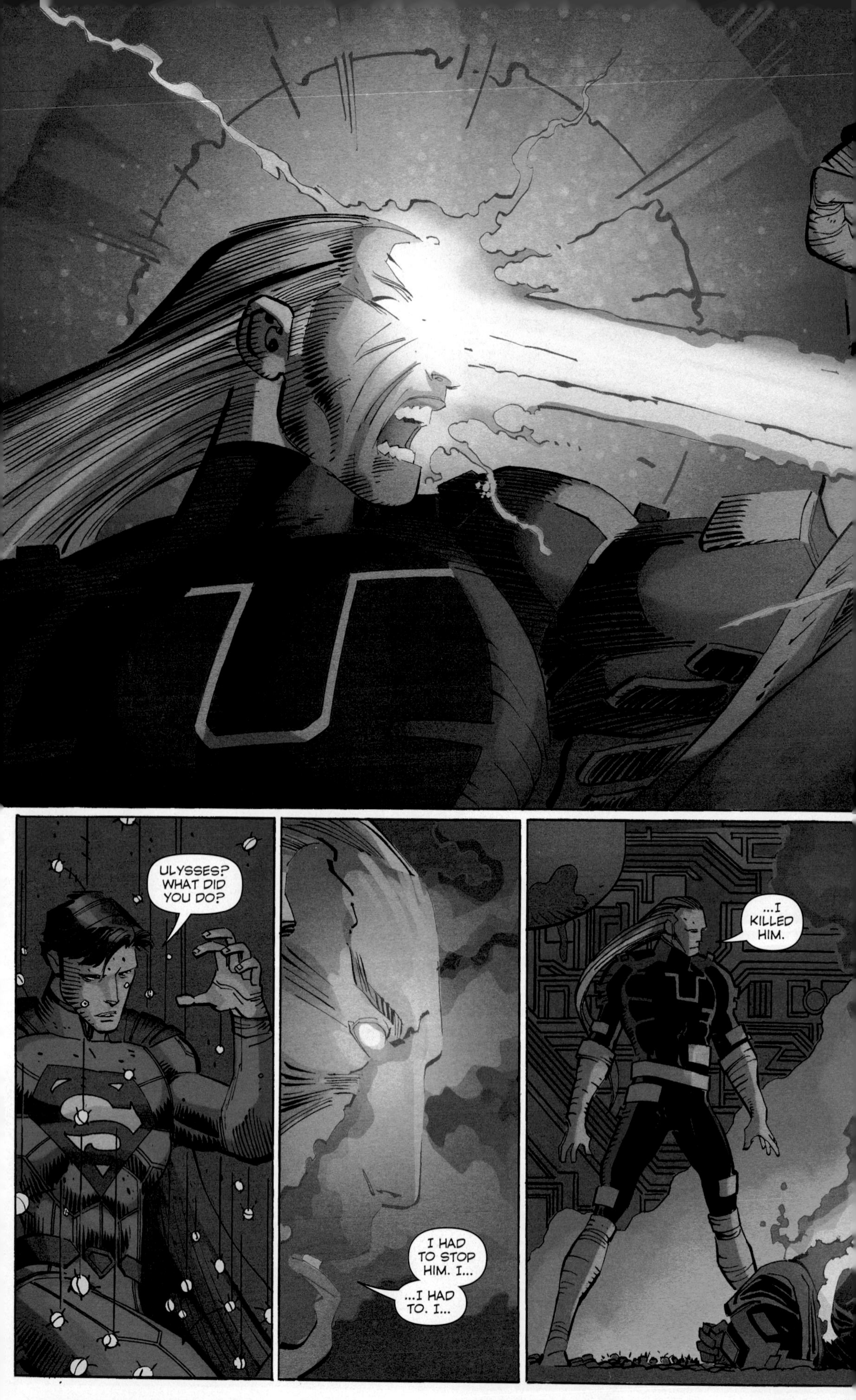
ULYSSES? WHAT DID YOU DO?
I HAD TO STOP HIM. I...
...I HAD TO. I...
...I KILLED HIM.

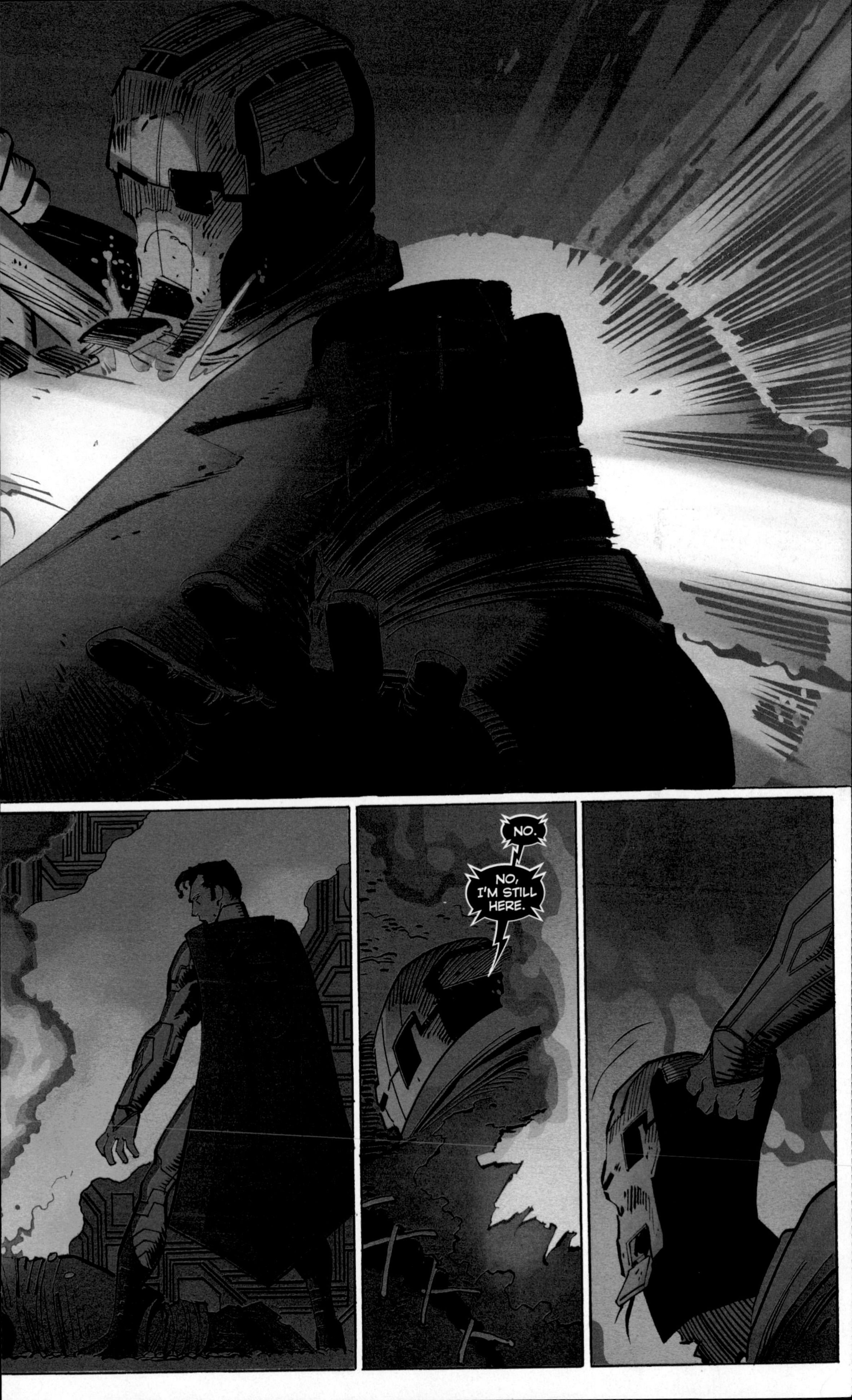
NO.
NO, I'M STILL HERE.

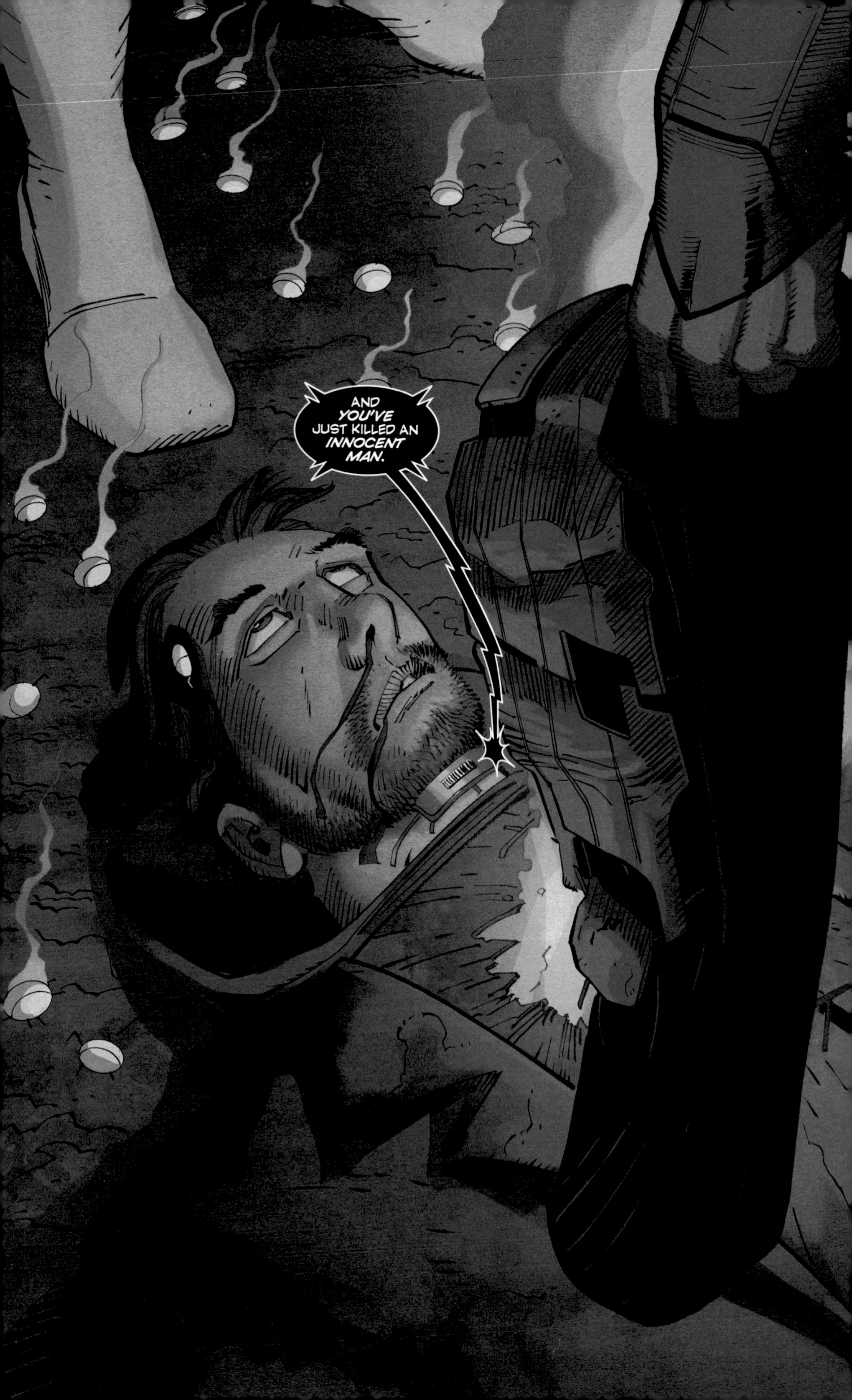
AND YOU'VE JUST KILLED AN INNOCENT MAN.

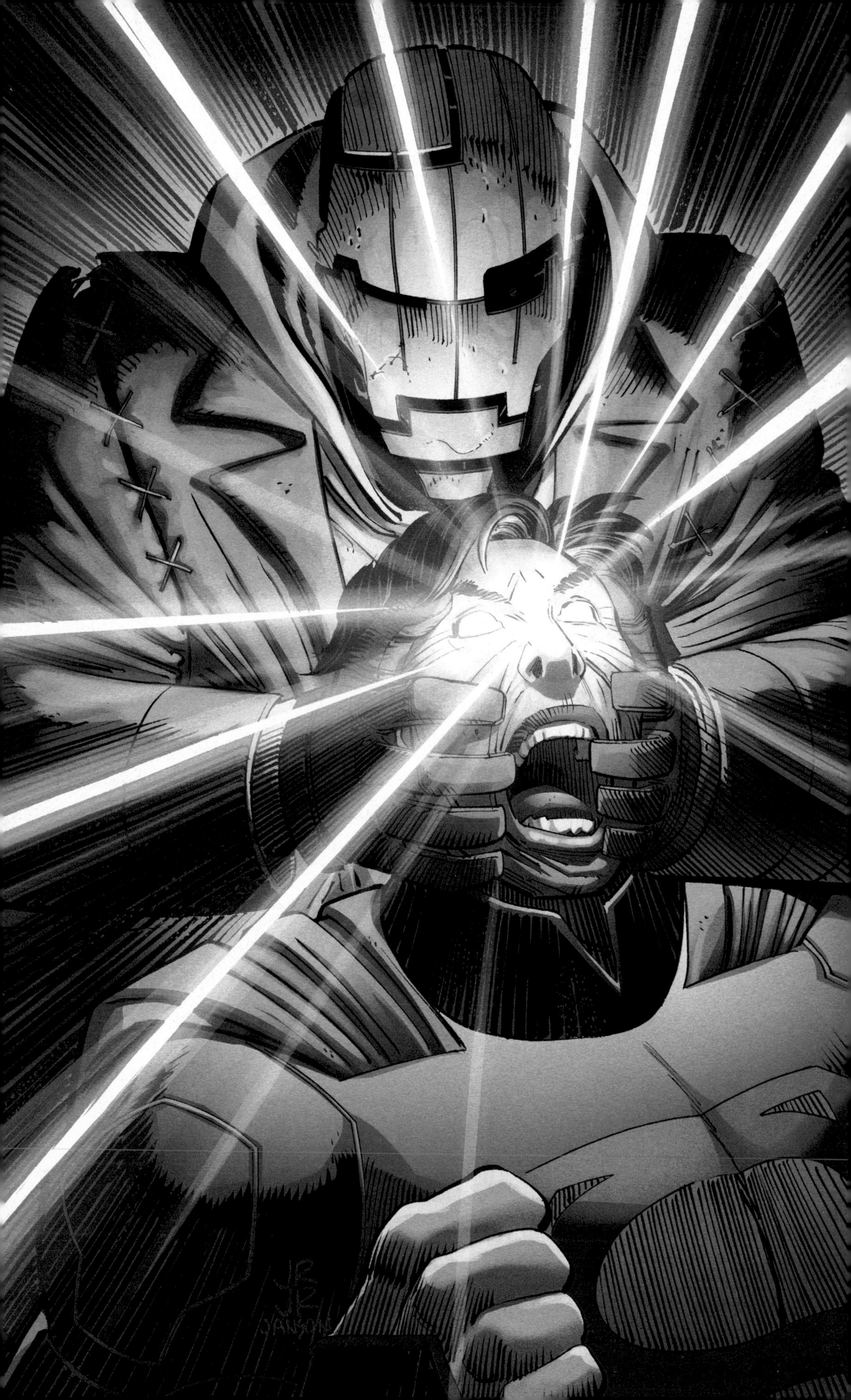
JR JR
JANSON

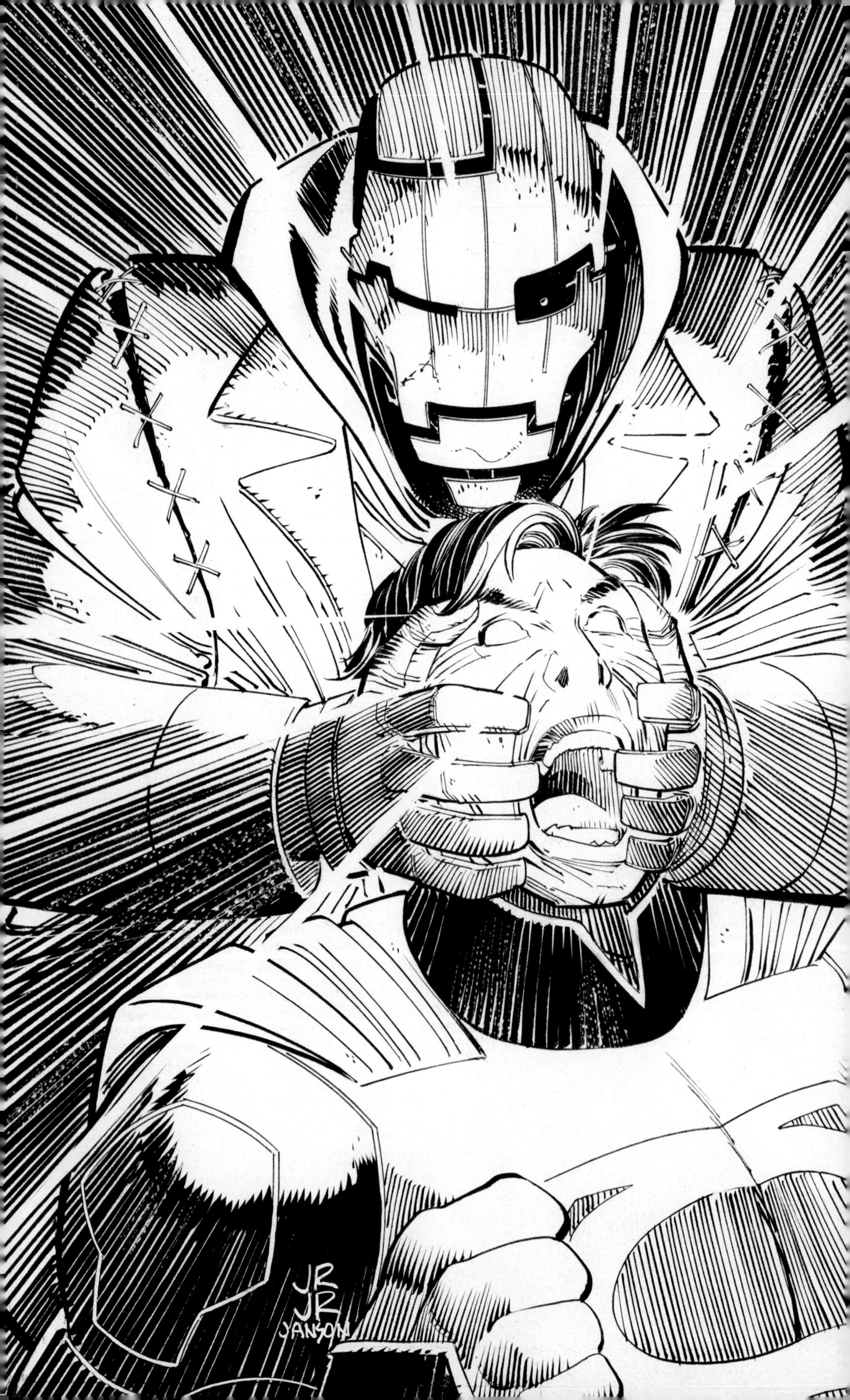
JR JR
JANSON

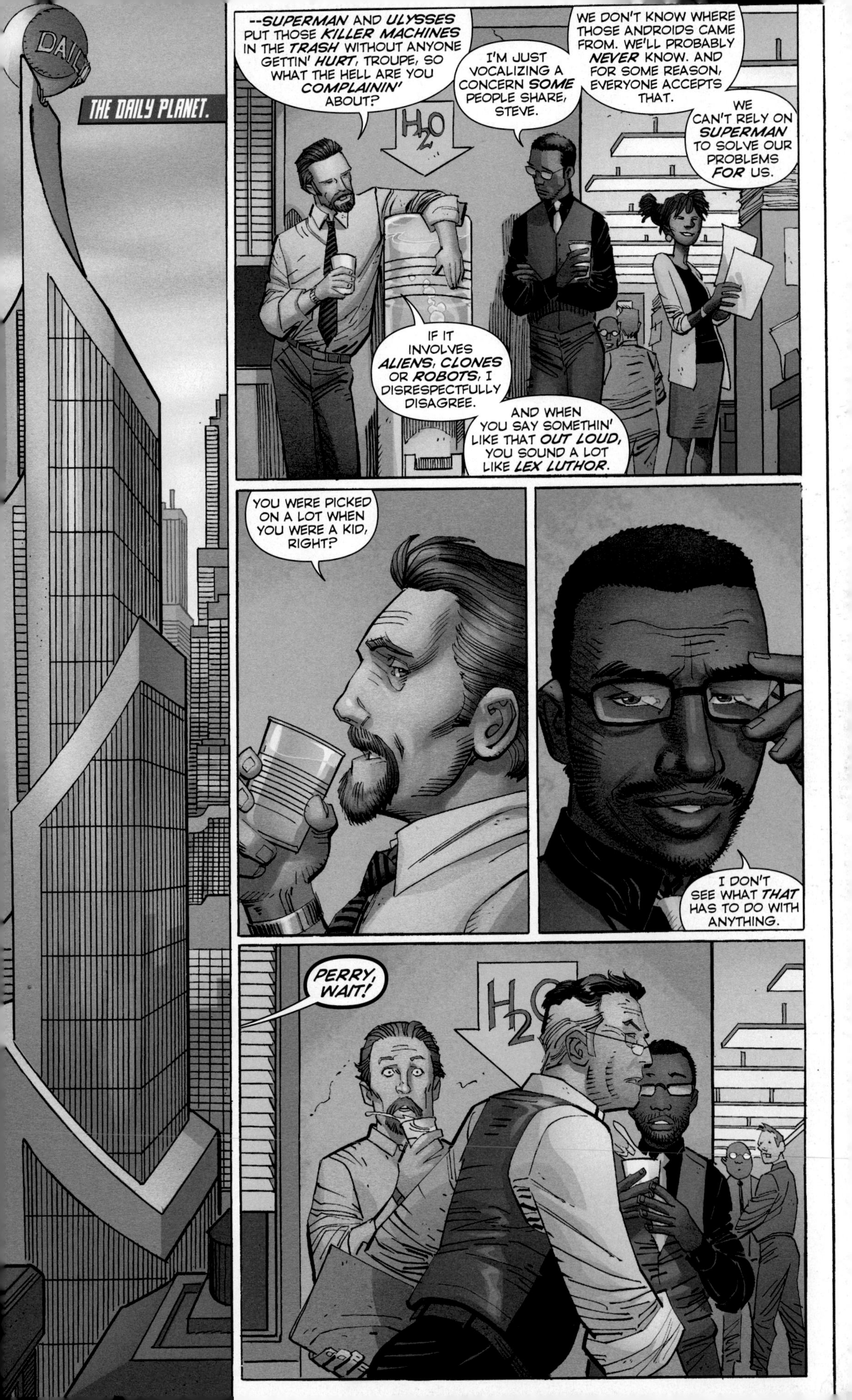

DAILY
THE DAILY PLANET.
--SUPERMAN AND ULYSSES PUT THOSE KILLER MACHINES IN THE TRASH WITHOUT ANYONE GETTIN' HURT, TROUPE, SO WHAT THE HELL ARE YOU COMPLAININ' ABOUT?
I'M JUST VOCALIZING A CONCERN SOME PEOPLE SHARE, STEVE.
WE DON'T KNOW WHERE THOSE ANDROIDS CAME FROM. WE'LL PROBABLY NEVER KNOW. AND FOR SOME REASON, EVERYONE ACCEPTS THAT.
WE CAN'T RELY ON SUPERMAN TO SOLVE OUR PROBLEMS FOR US.
H2O
IF IT INVOLVES ALIENS, CLONES OR ROBOTS, I DISRESPECTFULLY DISAGREE.
AND WHEN YOU SAY SOMETHIN' LIKE THAT OUT LOUD, YOU SOUND A LOT LIKE LEX LUTHOR.
YOU WERE PICKED ON A LOT WHEN YOU WERE A KID, RIGHT?
I DON'T SEE WHAT THAT HAS TO DO WITH ANYTHING.
PERRY, WAIT!

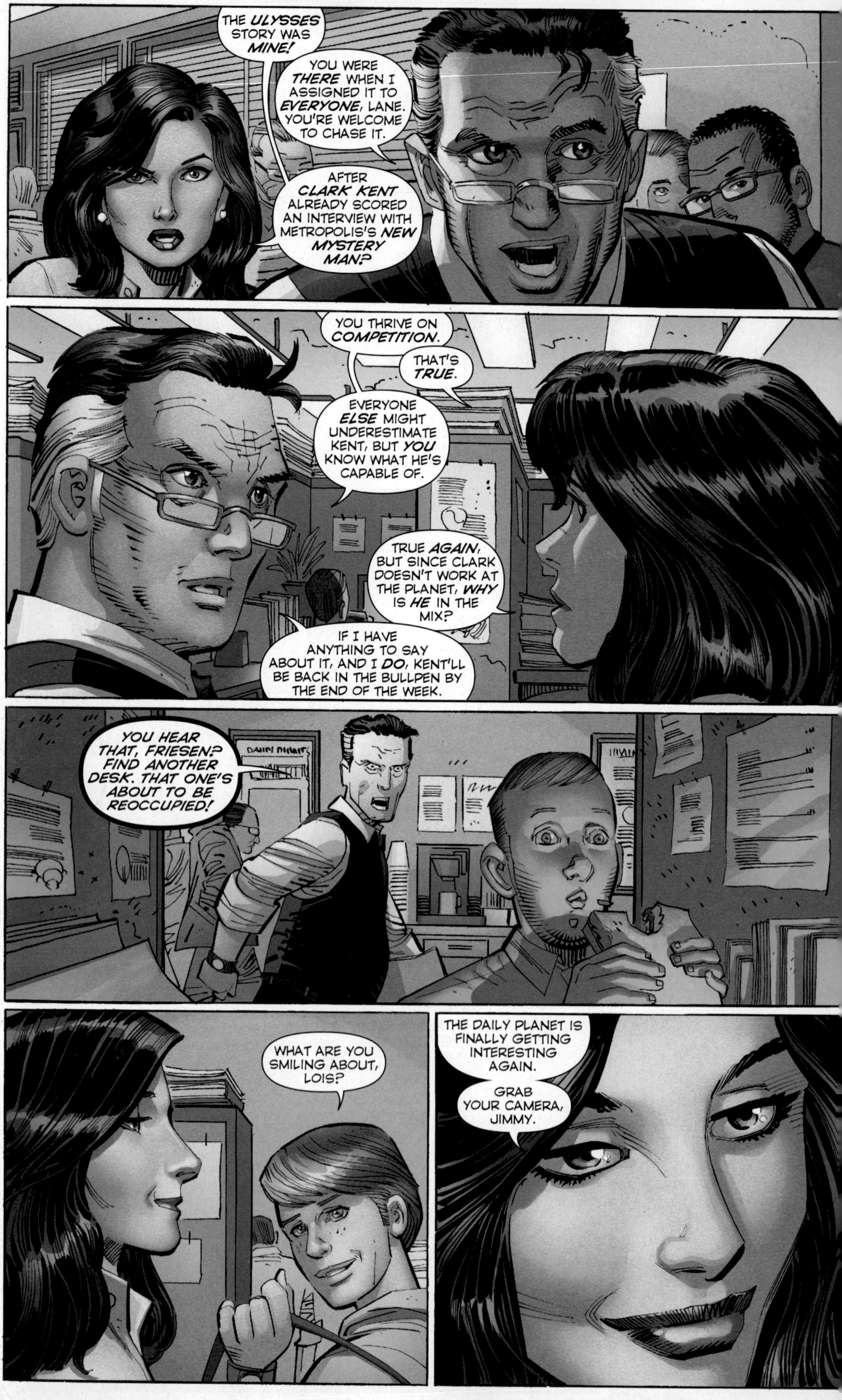
THE ULYSSES STORY WAS MINE!
YOU WERE THERE WHEN I ASSIGNED IT TO EVERYONE, LANE. YOU'RE WELCOME TO CHASE IT.
AFTER CLARK KENT ALREADY SCORED AN INTERVIEW WITH METROPOLIS'S NEW MYSTERY MAN?
YOU THRIVE ON COMPETITION.
THAT'S TRUE.
EVERYONE ELSE MIGHT UNDERESTIMATE KENT, BUT YOU KNOW WHAT HE'S CAPABLE OF.
TRUE AGAIN, BUT SINCE CLARK DOESN'T WORK AT THE PLANET, WHY IS HE IN THE MIX?
IF I HAVE ANYTHING TO SAY ABOUT IT, AND I DO, KENT'LL BE BACK IN THE BULLPEN BY THE END OF THE WEEK.
YOU HEAR THAT, FRIESEN? FIND ANOTHER DESK. THAT ONE'S ABOUT TO BE REOCCUPIED!
WHAT ARE YOU SMILING ABOUT, LOIS?
THE DAILY PLANET IS FINALLY GETTING INTERESTING AGAIN.
GRAB YOUR CAMERA, JIMMY.

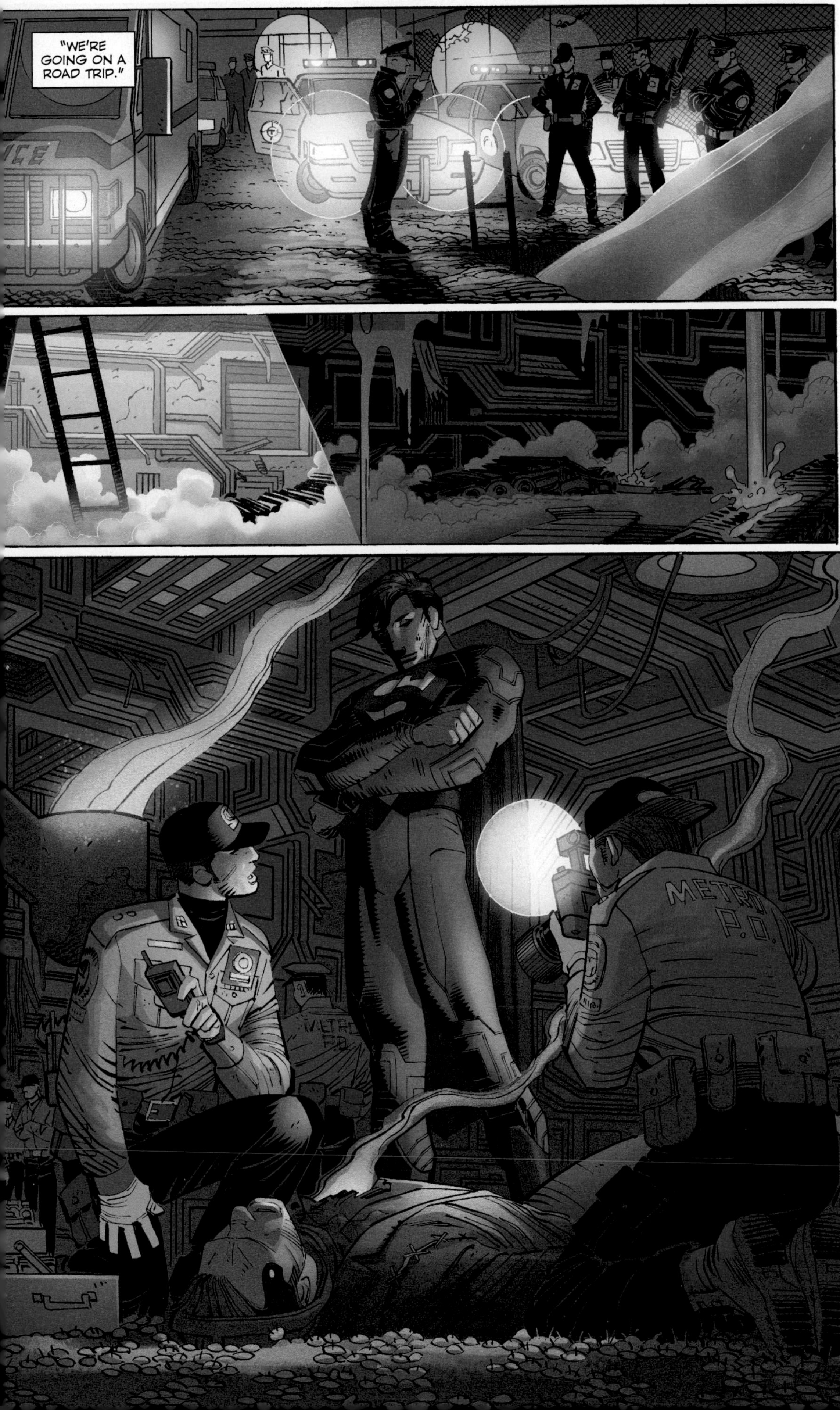
"WE'RE GOING ON A ROAD TRIP."
METRO P.D.

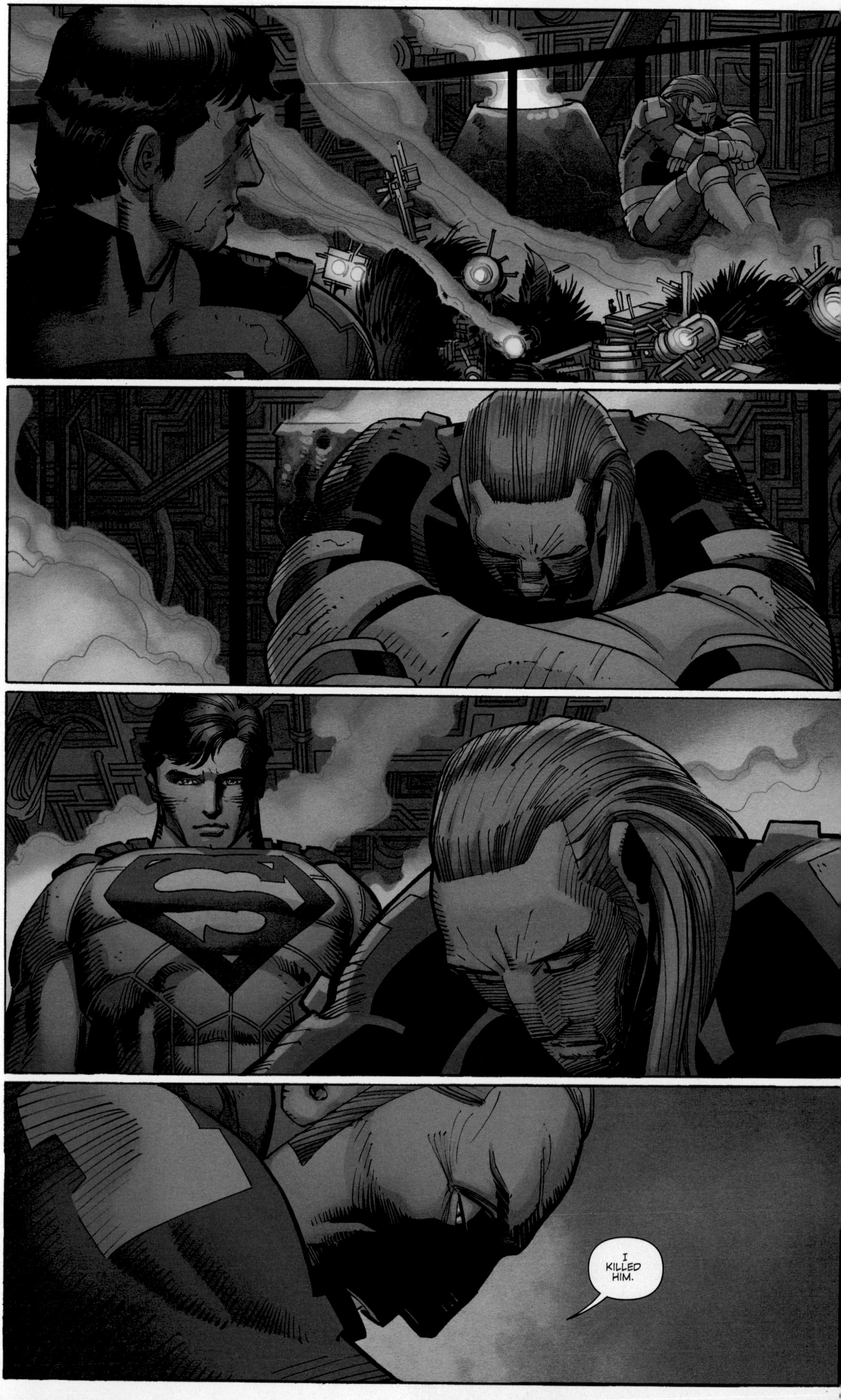
I KILLED HIM.

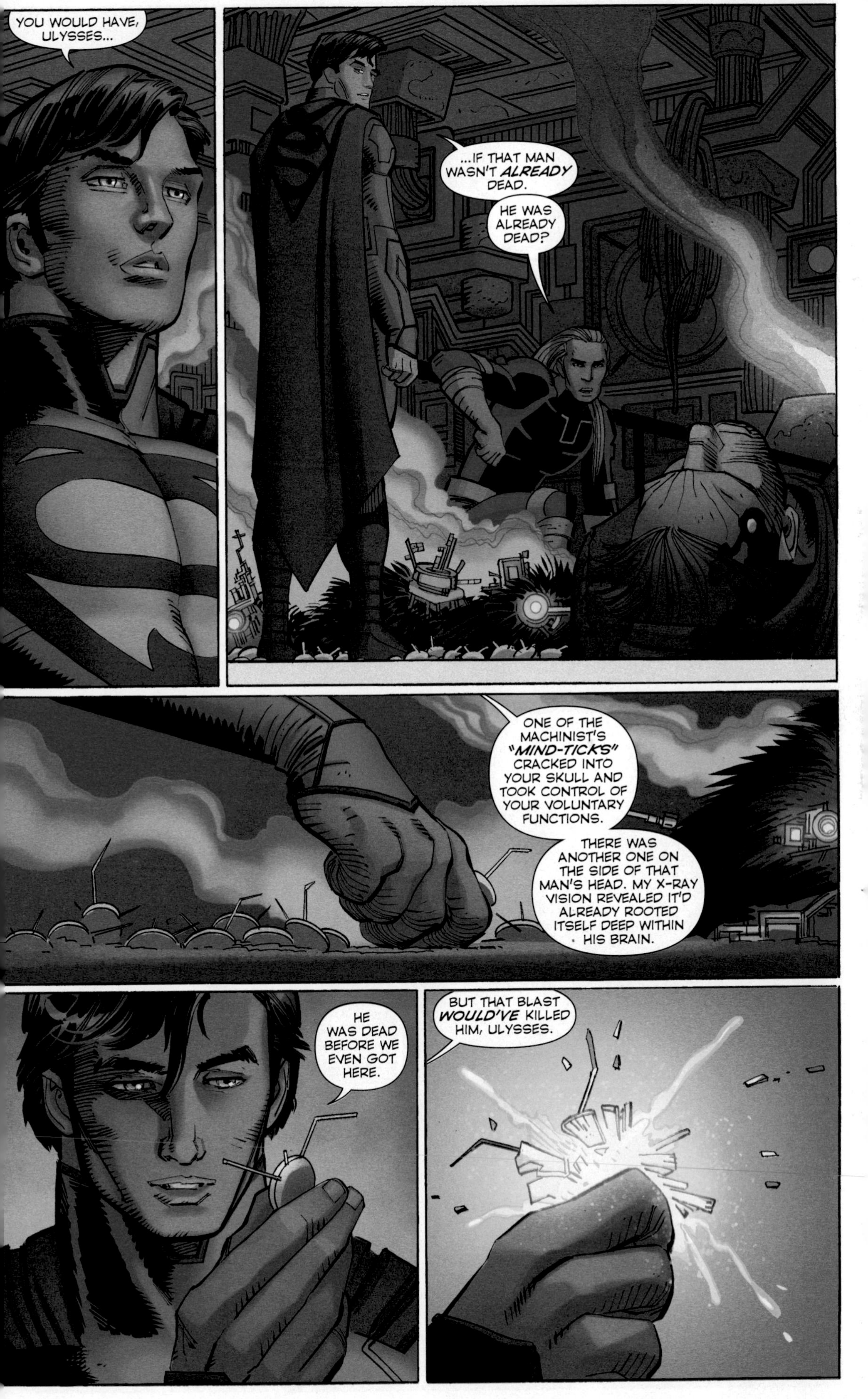
YOU WOULD HAVE, ULYSSES...
...IF THAT MAN WASN'T *ALREADY* DEAD.
HE WAS ALREADY DEAD?
ONE OF THE MACHINIST'S *"MIND-TICKS"* CRACKED INTO YOUR SKULL AND TOOK CONTROL OF YOUR VOLUNTARY FUNCTIONS.
THERE WAS ANOTHER ONE ON THE SIDE OF THAT MAN'S HEAD. MY X-RAY VISION REVEALED IT'D ALREADY ROOTED ITSELF DEEP WITHIN HIS BRAIN.
HE WAS DEAD BEFORE WE EVEN GOT HERE.
BUT THAT BLAST *WOULD'VE* KILLED HIM, ULYSSES.

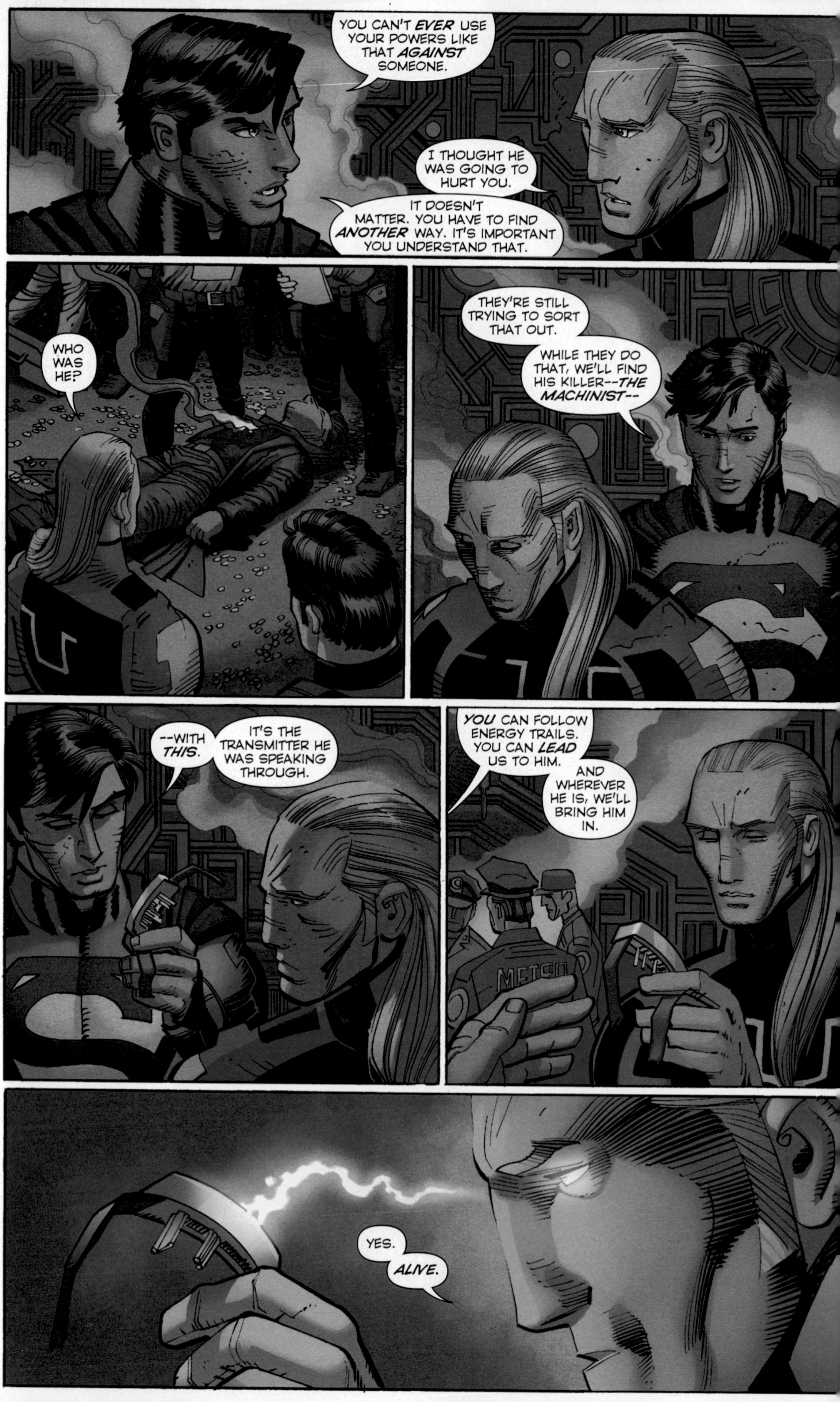

YOU CAN'T ***EVER*** USE YOUR POWERS LIKE THAT ***AGAINST*** SOMEONE.
I THOUGHT HE WAS GOING TO HURT YOU.
IT DOESN'T MATTER. YOU HAVE TO FIND ***ANOTHER*** WAY. IT'S IMPORTANT YOU UNDERSTAND THAT.
WHO WAS HE?
THEY'RE STILL TRYING TO SORT THAT OUT.
WHILE THEY DO THAT, WE'LL FIND HIS KILLER--***THE MACHINIST***--
--WITH ***THIS***.
IT'S THE TRANSMITTER HE WAS SPEAKING THROUGH.
YOU CAN FOLLOW ENERGY TRAILS. YOU CAN ***LEAD*** US TO HIM.
AND WHEREVER HE IS, WE'LL BRING HIM IN.
METRO
YES.
ALIVE.

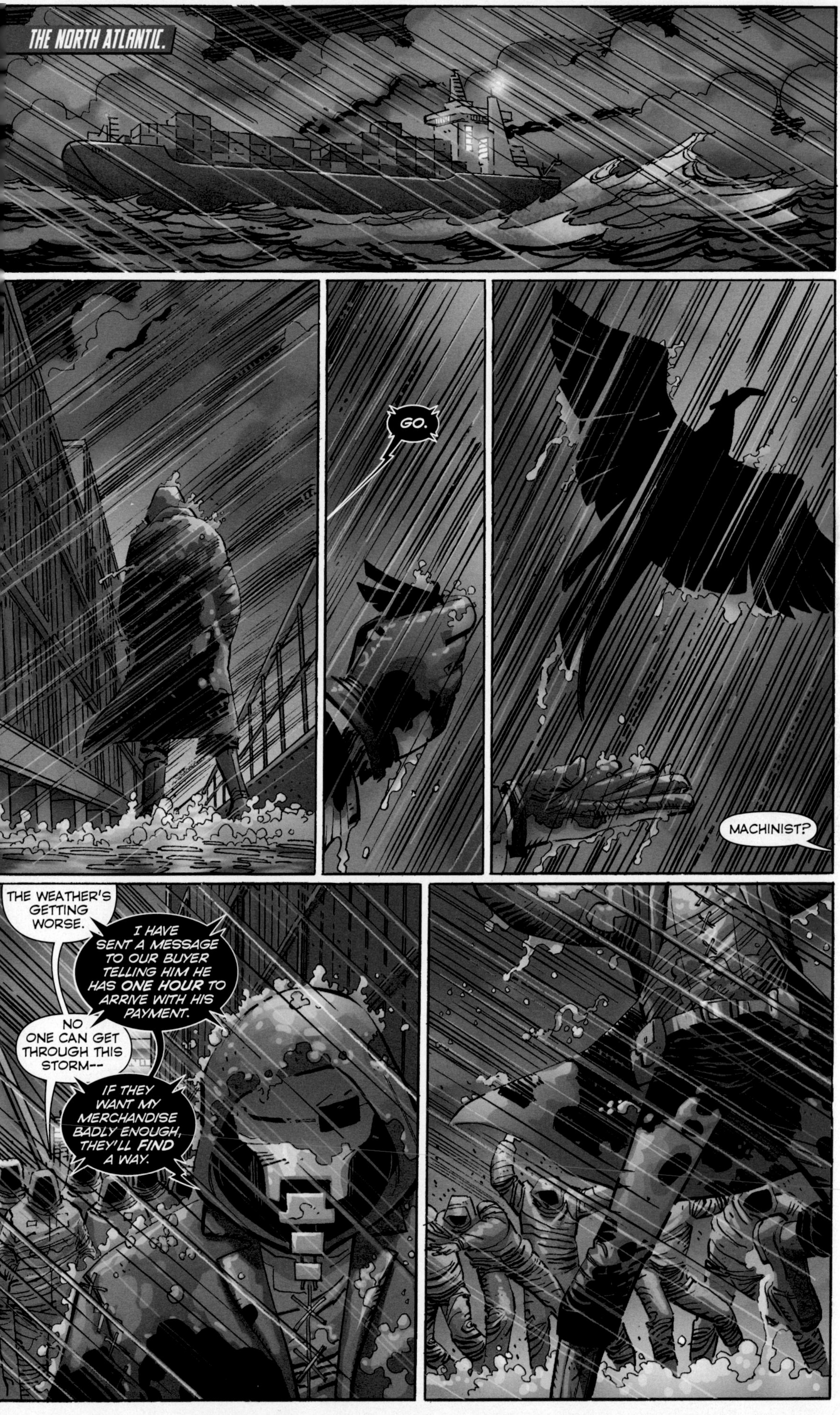
THE NORTH ATLANTIC.
GO.
MACHINIST?
THE WEATHER'S GETTING WORSE.
I HAVE SENT A MESSAGE TO OUR BUYER TELLING HIM HE HAS ONE HOUR TO ARRIVE WITH HIS PAYMENT.
NO ONE CAN GET THROUGH THIS STORM--
IF THEY WANT MY MERCHANDISE BADLY ENOUGH, THEY'LL FIND A WAY.

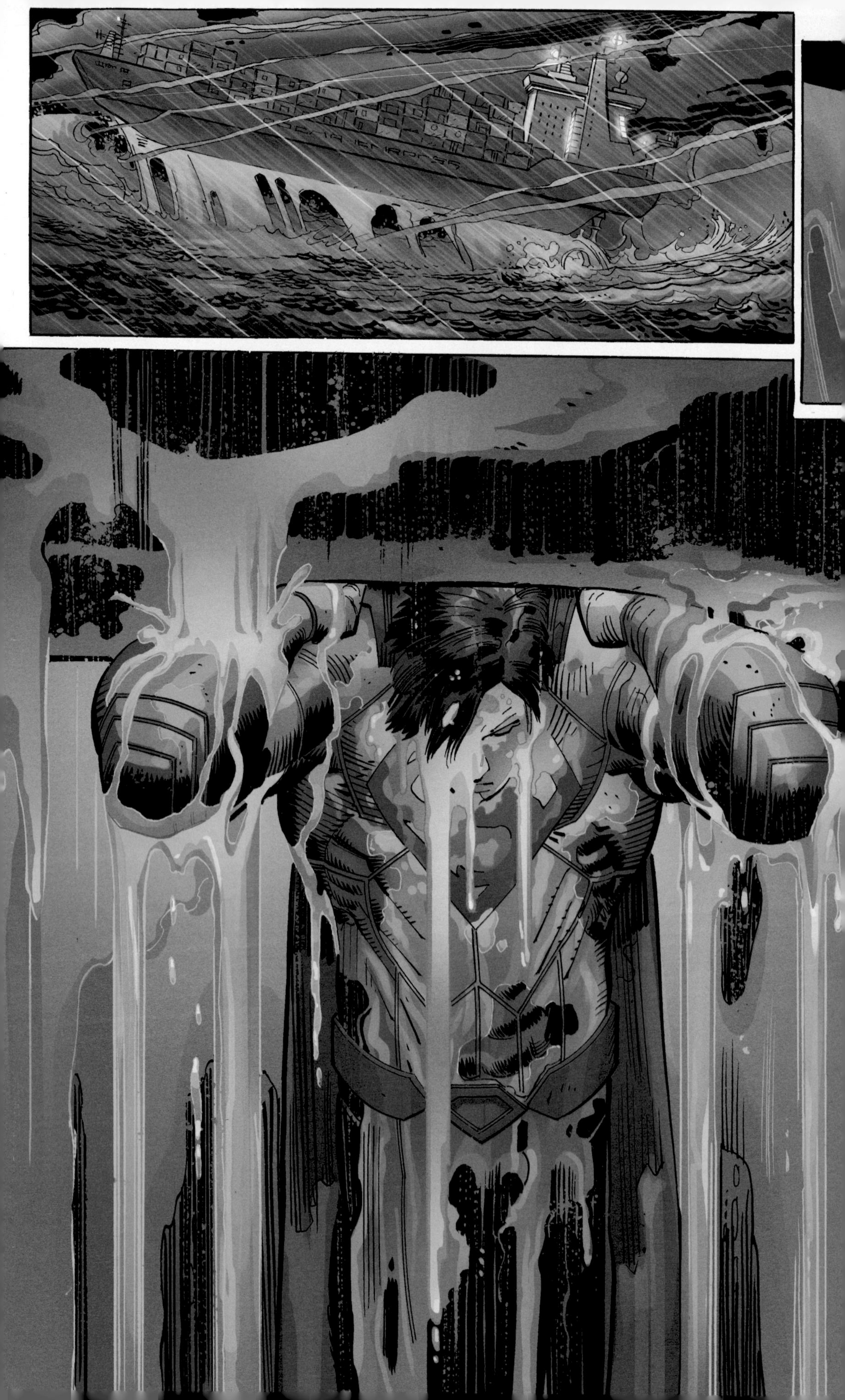

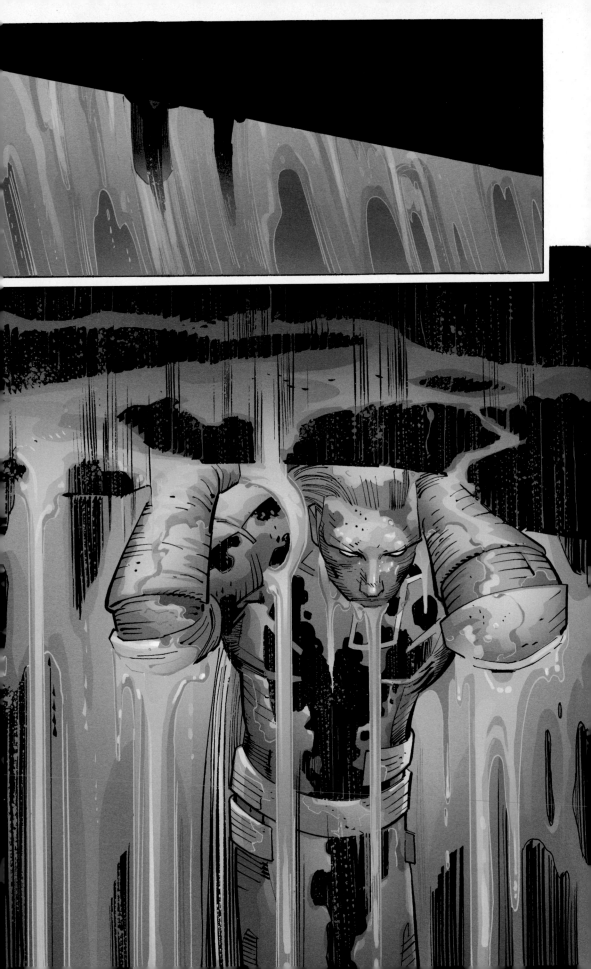

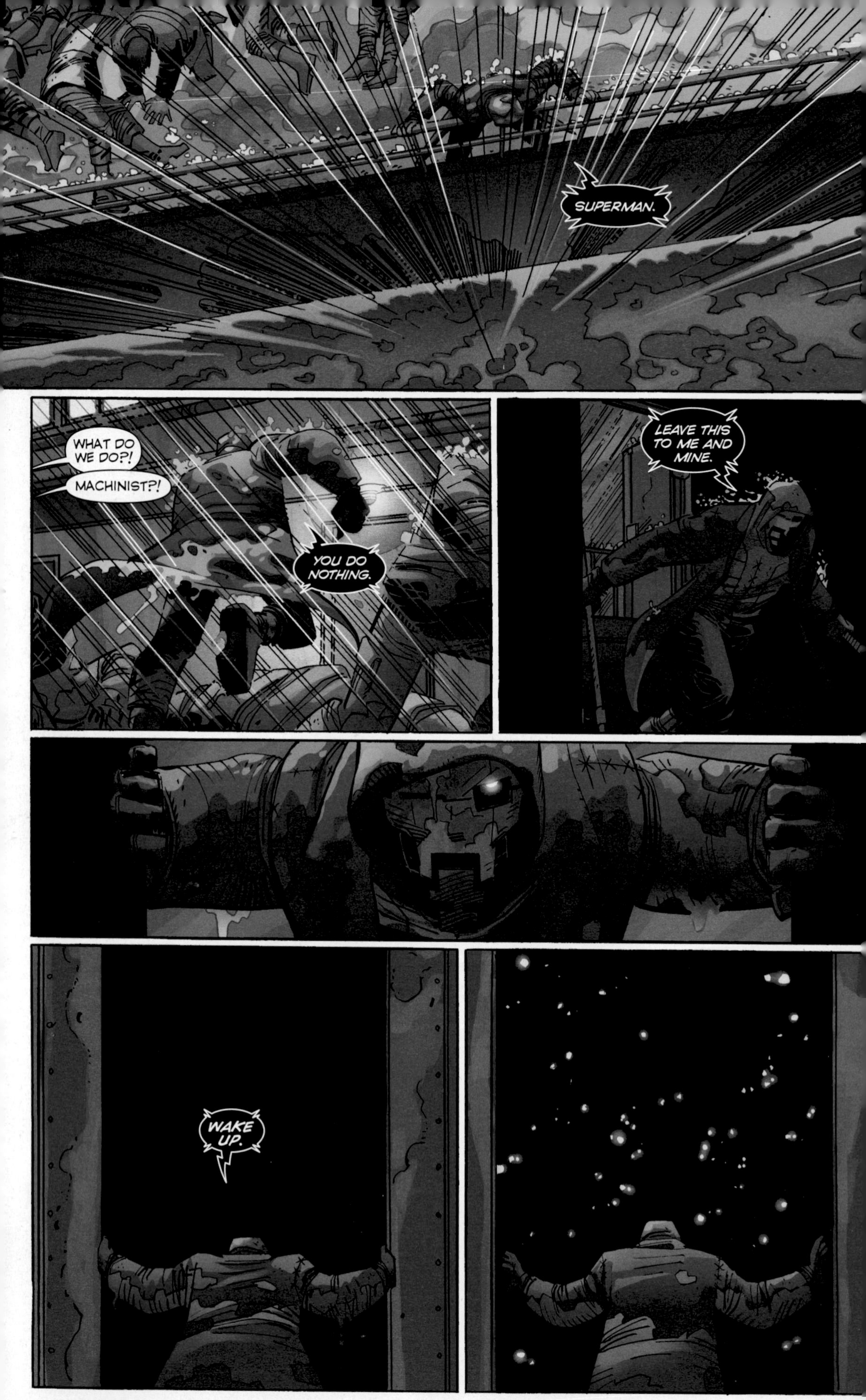
SUPERMAN.
WHAT DO WE DO?!
MACHINIST?!
YOU DO NOTHING.
LEAVE THIS TO ME AND MINE.
WAKE UP.

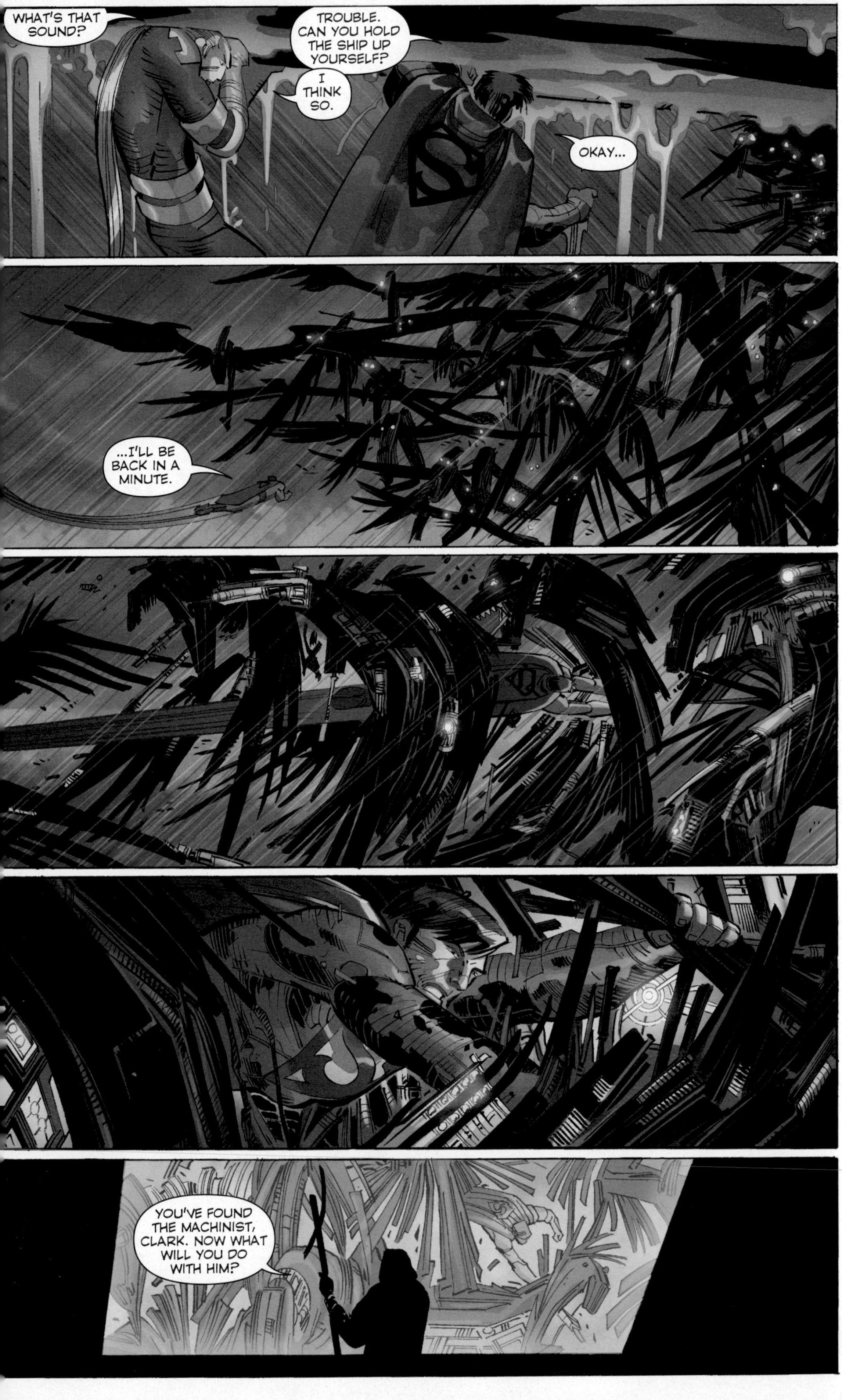
WHAT'S THAT SOUND?
TROUBLE. CAN YOU HOLD THE SHIP UP YOURSELF?
I THINK SO.
OKAY...
...I'LL BE BACK IN A MINUTE.
YOU'VE FOUND THE MACHINIST, CLARK. NOW WHAT WILL YOU DO WITH HIM?

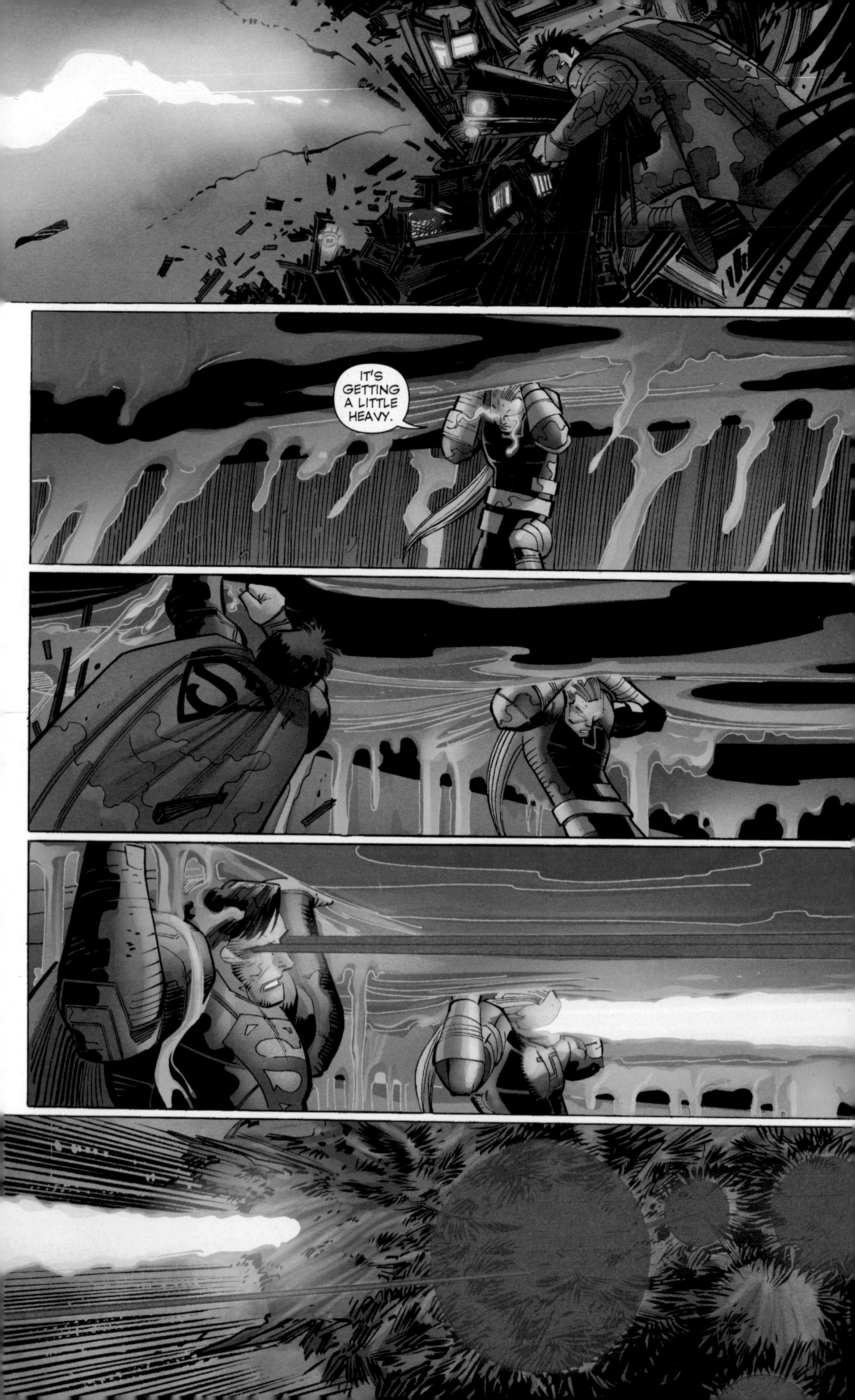
IT'S GETTING A LITTLE HEAVY.

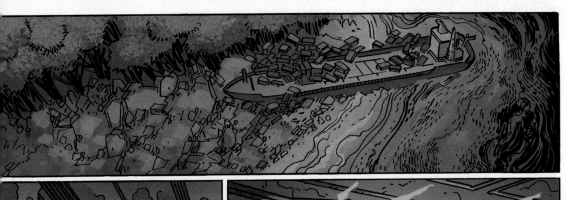

IS IT REALLY *HIM* THIS TIME?

I'M NOT SURE IT'S A *HIM.*

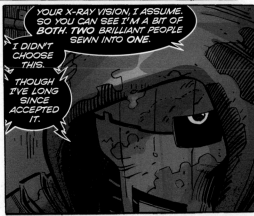

YOUR X-RAY VISION, I ASSUME. SO YOU CAN SEE I'M A BIT OF *BOTH.* TWO BRILLIANT PEOPLE SEWN INTO *ONE.*

I DIDN'T CHOOSE THIS.

THOUGH I'VE LONG SINCE ACCEPTED IT.

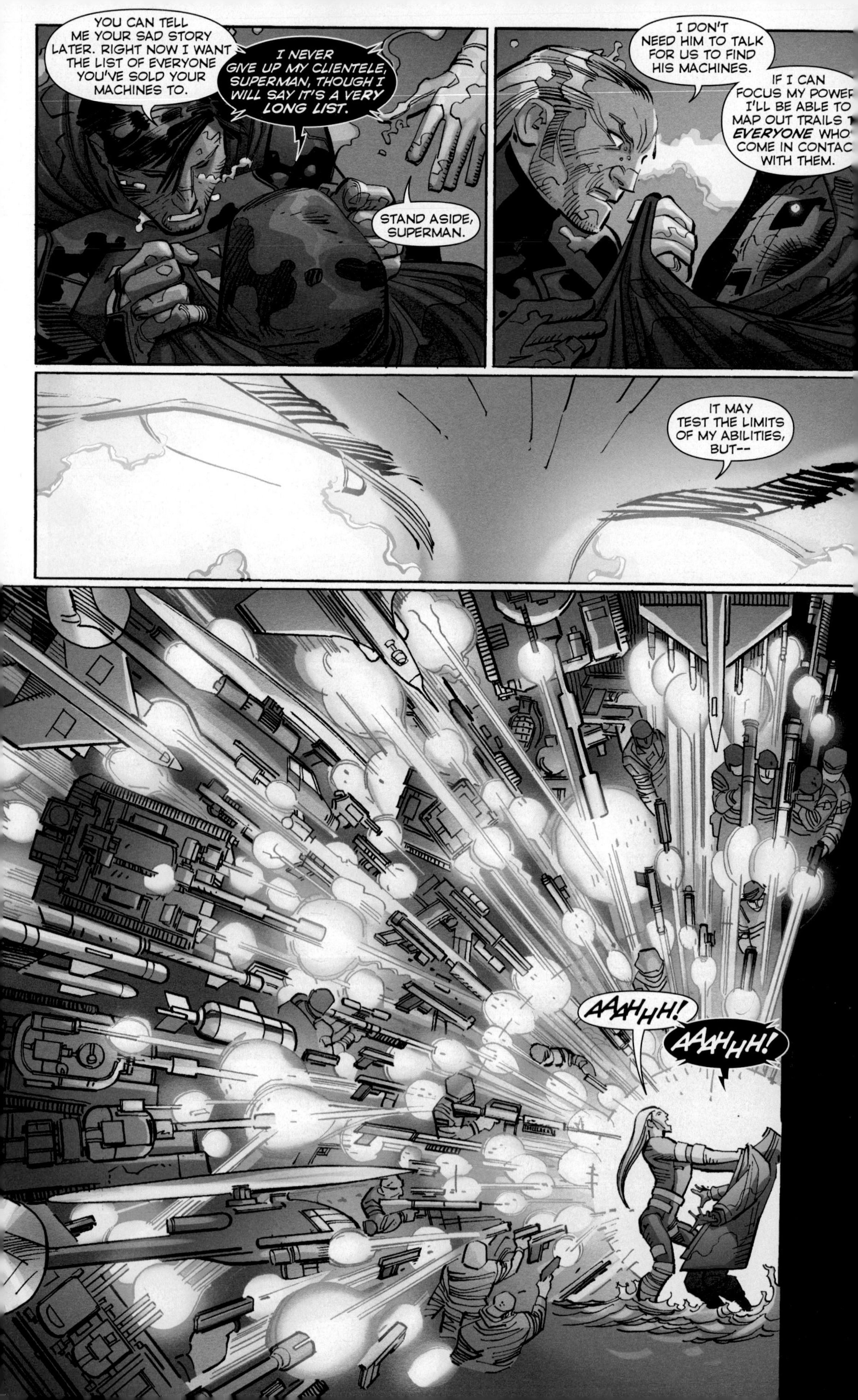
YOU CAN TELL ME YOUR SAD STORY LATER. RIGHT NOW I WANT THE LIST OF EVERYONE YOU'VE SOLD YOUR MACHINES TO.
I NEVER GIVE UP MY CLIENTELE, SUPERMAN, THOUGH I WILL SAY IT'S A VERY LONG LIST.
STAND ASIDE, SUPERMAN.
I DON'T NEED HIM TO TALK FOR US TO FIND HIS MACHINES.
IF I CAN FOCUS MY POWER I'LL BE ABLE TO MAP OUT TRAILS EVERYONE WHO COME IN CONTAC WITH THEM.
IT MAY TEST THE LIMITS OF MY ABILITIES, BUT--
AAAHHH!
AAAHHH!

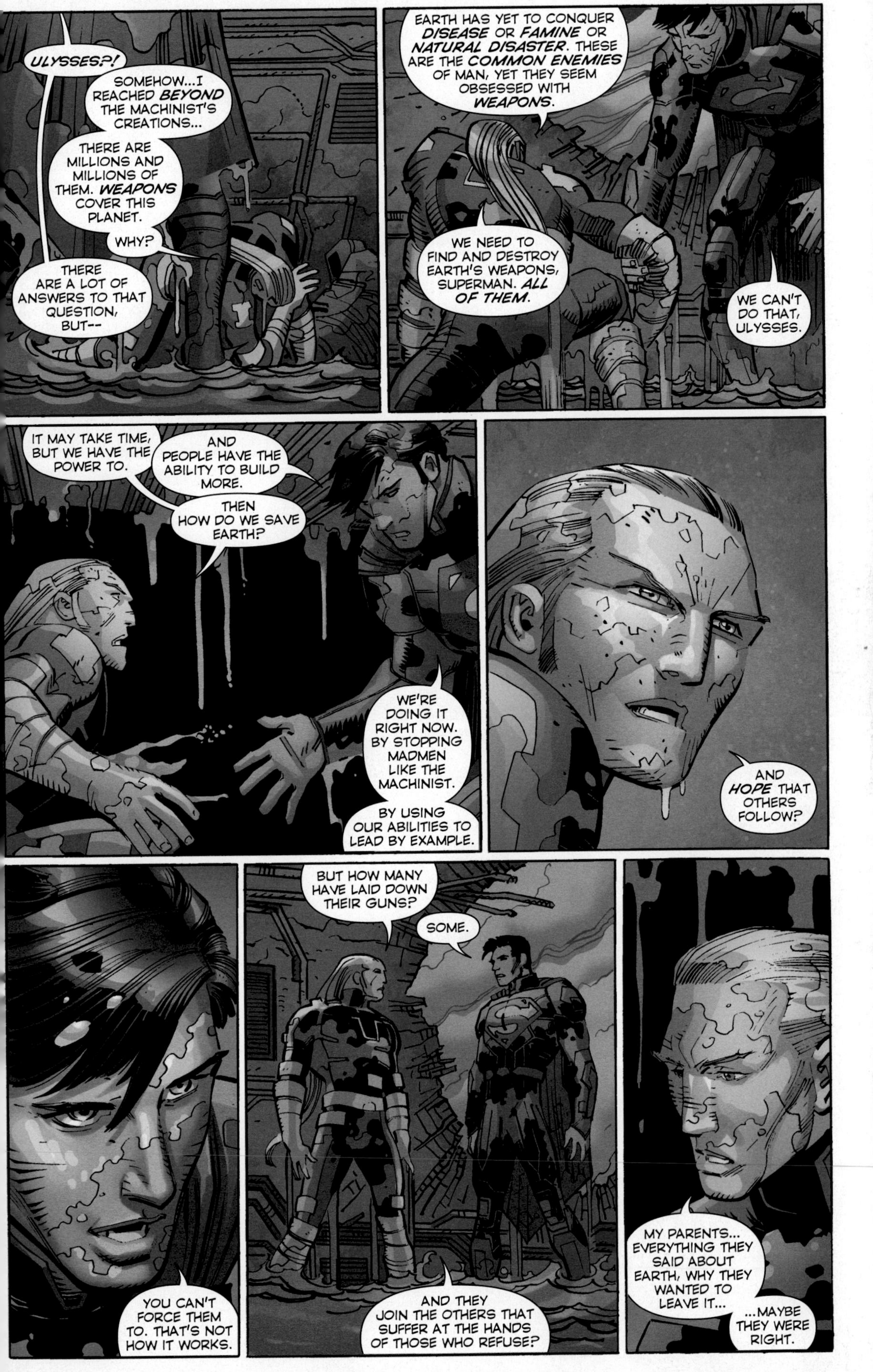
ULYSSES?!
SOMEHOW...I REACHED *BEYOND* THE MACHINIST'S CREATIONS...
THERE ARE MILLIONS AND MILLIONS OF THEM. *WEAPONS* COVER THIS PLANET.
WHY?
THERE ARE A LOT OF ANSWERS TO THAT QUESTION, BUT--
EARTH HAS YET TO CONQUER *DISEASE* OR *FAMINE* OR *NATURAL DISASTER*. THESE ARE THE *COMMON ENEMIES* OF MAN, YET THEY SEEM OBSESSED WITH *WEAPONS*.
WE NEED TO FIND AND DESTROY EARTH'S WEAPONS, SUPERMAN. *ALL OF THEM*.
WE CAN'T DO THAT, ULYSSES.
IT MAY TAKE TIME, BUT WE HAVE THE POWER TO.
AND PEOPLE HAVE THE ABILITY TO BUILD MORE.
THEN HOW DO WE SAVE EARTH?
WE'RE DOING IT RIGHT NOW. BY STOPPING MADMEN LIKE THE MACHINIST.
BY USING OUR ABILITIES TO LEAD BY EXAMPLE.
AND *HOPE* THAT OTHERS FOLLOW?
YOU CAN'T FORCE THEM TO. THAT'S NOT HOW IT WORKS.
BUT HOW MANY HAVE LAID DOWN THEIR GUNS?
SOME.
AND THEY JOIN THE OTHERS THAT SUFFER AT THE HANDS OF THOSE WHO REFUSE?
MY PARENTS... EVERYTHING THEY SAID ABOUT EARTH, WHY THEY WANTED TO LEAVE IT...
...MAYBE THEY WERE RIGHT.

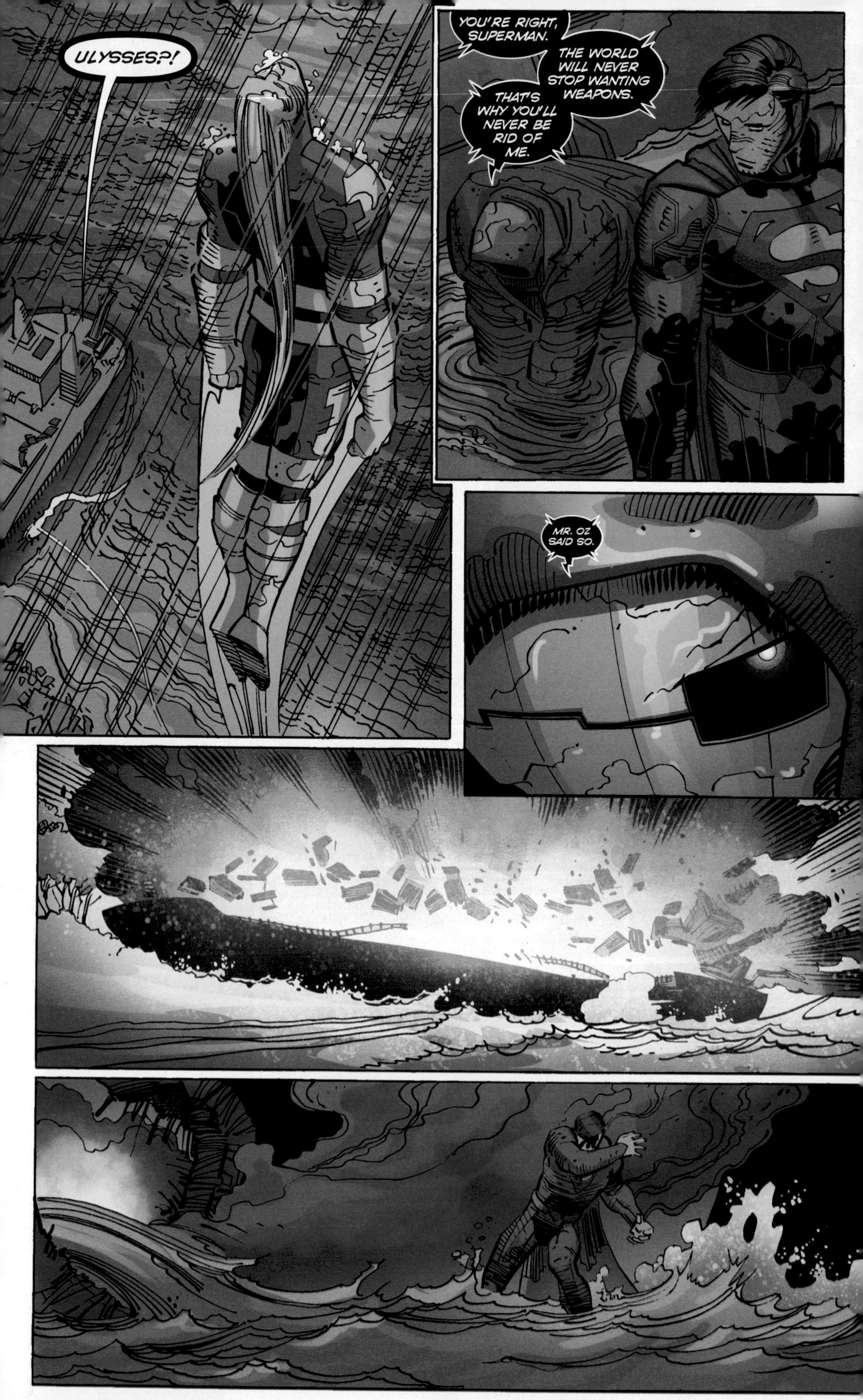
ULYSSES?!
YOU'RE RIGHT, SUPERMAN.
THE WORLD WILL NEVER STOP WANTING WEAPONS.
THAT'S WHY YOU'LL NEVER BE RID OF ME.
MR. OZ SAID SO.

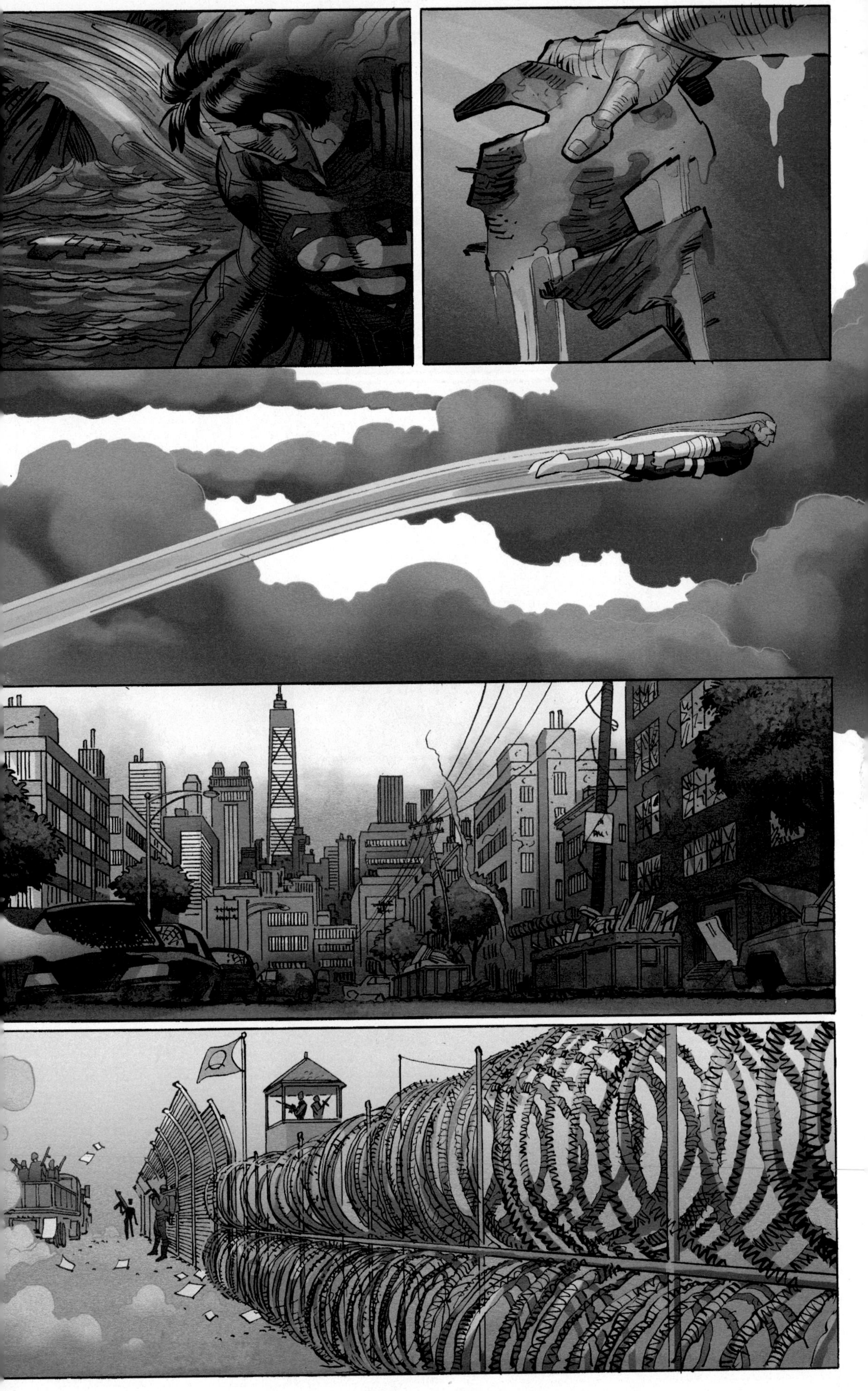

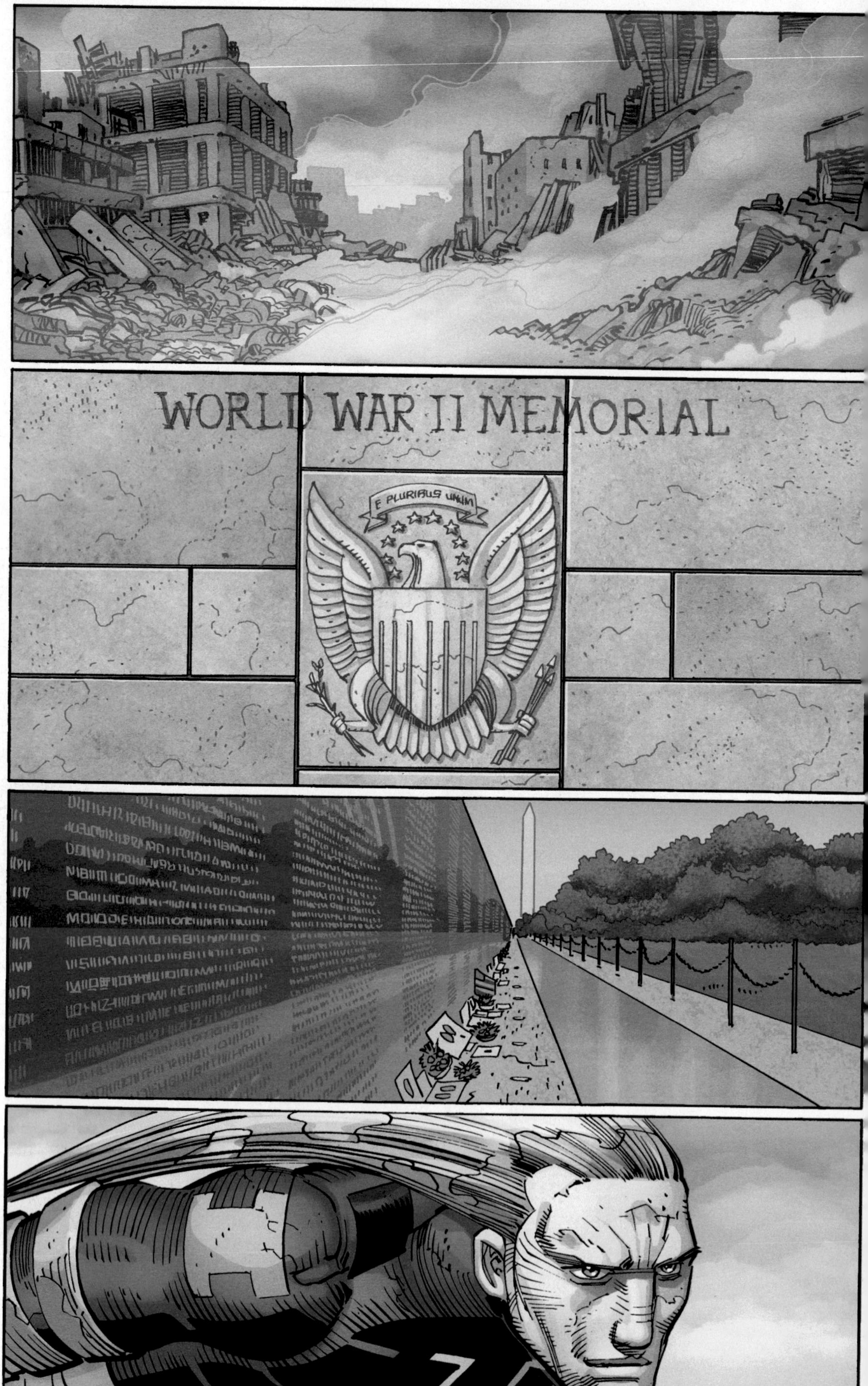
WORLD WAR II MEMORIAL
E PLURIBUS UNUM

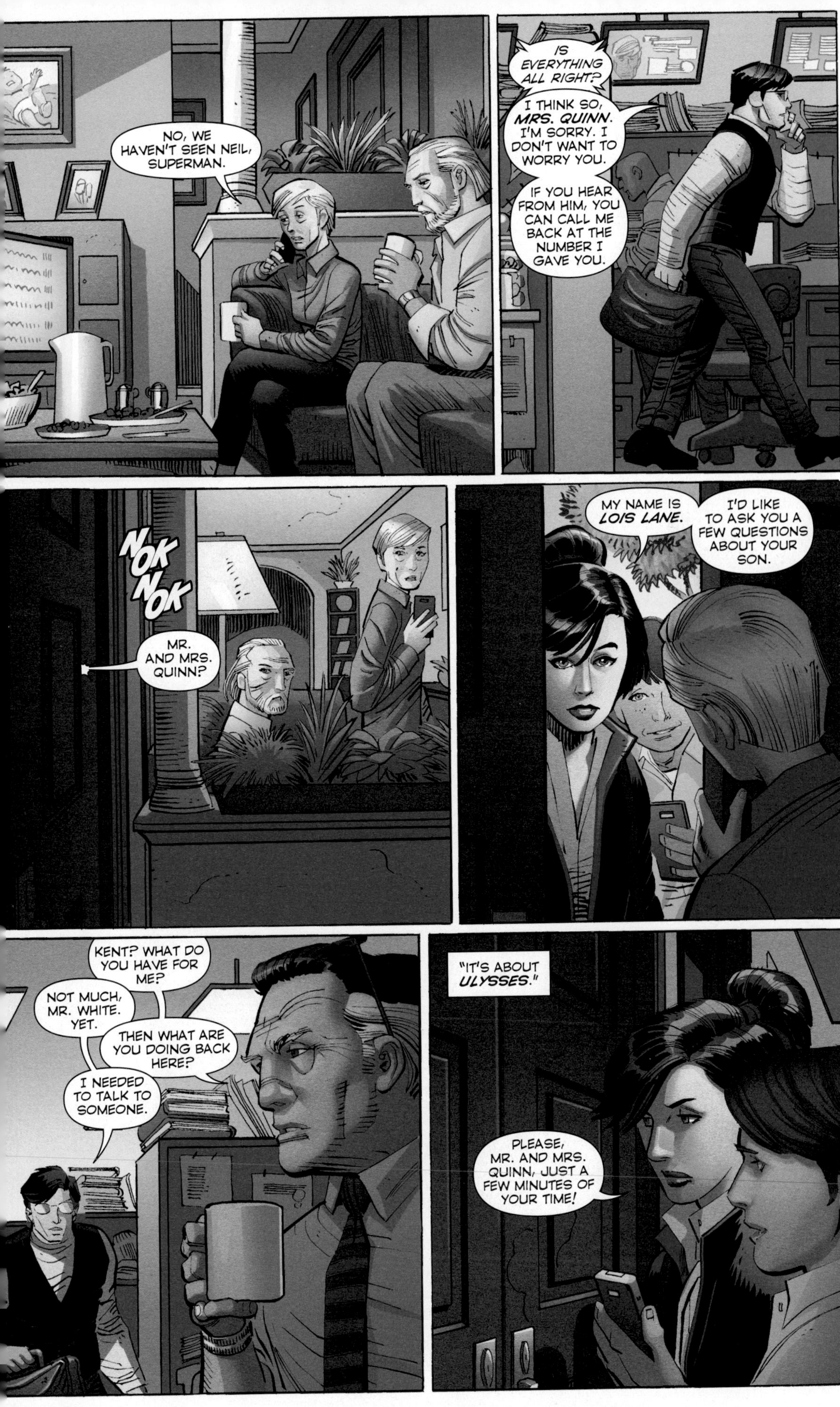
NO, WE HAVEN'T SEEN NEIL, SUPERMAN.
IS EVERYTHING ALL RIGHT?
I THINK SO, MRS. QUINN. I'M SORRY. I DON'T WANT TO WORRY YOU.
IF YOU HEAR FROM HIM, YOU CAN CALL ME BACK AT THE NUMBER I GAVE YOU.
NOK NOK NOK
MR. AND MRS. QUINN?
MY NAME IS LOIS LANE.
I'D LIKE TO ASK YOU A FEW QUESTIONS ABOUT YOUR SON.
KENT? WHAT DO YOU HAVE FOR ME?
NOT MUCH, MR. WHITE. YET.
THEN WHAT ARE YOU DOING BACK HERE?
I NEEDED TO TALK TO SOMEONE.
"IT'S ABOUT ULYSSES."
PLEASE, MR. AND MRS. QUINN, JUST A FEW MINUTES OF YOUR TIME!

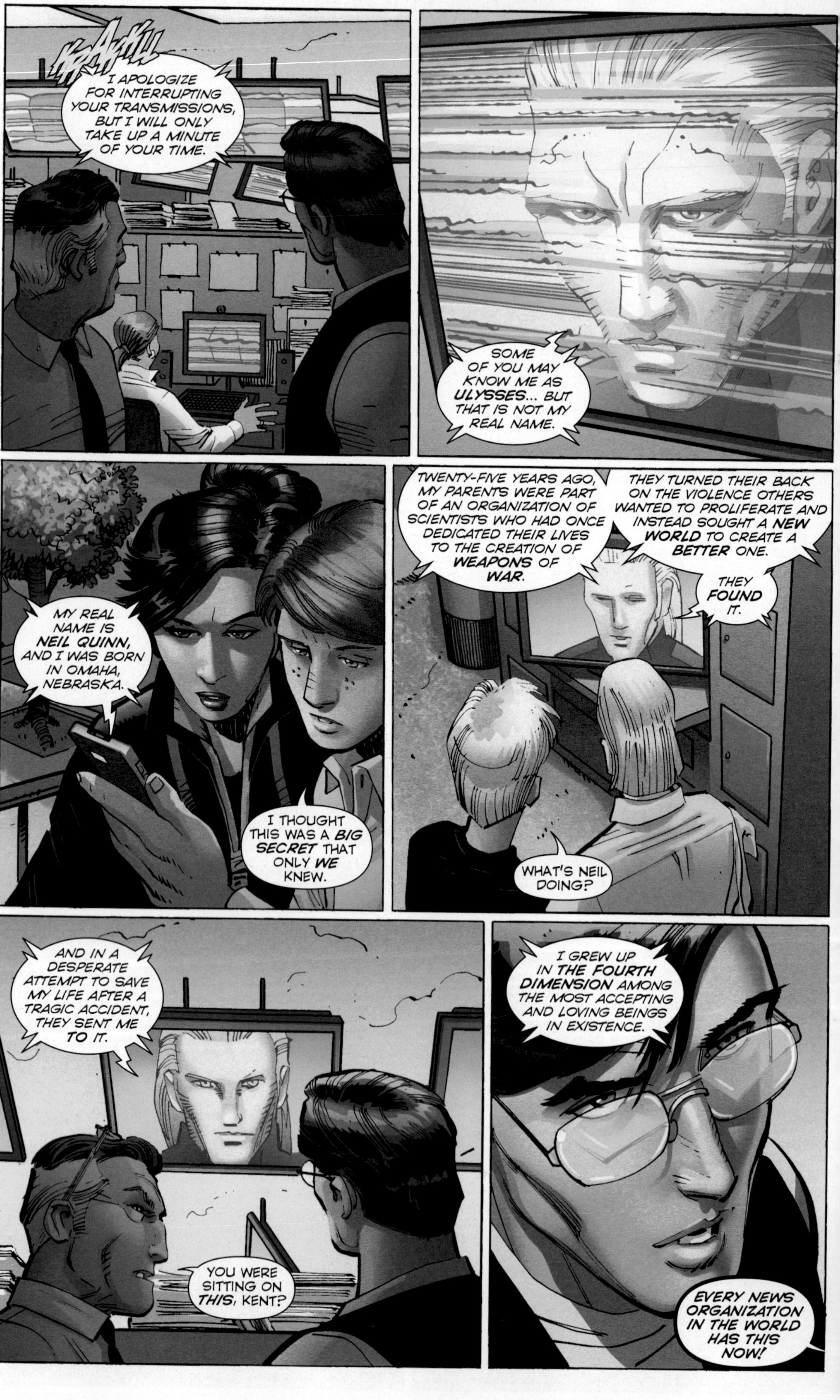
I APOLOGIZE FOR INTERRUPTING YOUR TRANSMISSIONS, BUT I WILL ONLY TAKE UP A MINUTE OF YOUR TIME.
SOME OF YOU MAY KNOW ME AS ***ULYSSES***... BUT THAT IS NOT MY REAL NAME.
MY REAL NAME IS ***NEIL QUINN,*** AND I WAS BORN IN OMAHA, NEBRASKA.
I THOUGHT THIS WAS A ***BIG SECRET*** THAT ONLY ***WE*** KNEW.
TWENTY-FIVE YEARS AGO, MY PARENTS WERE PART OF AN ORGANIZATION OF SCIENTISTS WHO HAD ONCE DEDICATED THEIR LIVES TO THE CREATION OF ***WEAPONS*** OF ***WAR***.
THEY TURNED THEIR BACK ON THE VIOLENCE OTHERS WANTED TO PROLIFERATE AND INSTEAD SOUGHT A ***NEW WORLD*** TO CREATE A ***BETTER*** ONE.
THEY ***FOUND*** IT.
WHAT'S NEIL DOING?
AND IN A DESPERATE ATTEMPT TO SAVE MY LIFE AFTER A TRAGIC ACCIDENT, THEY SENT ME ***TO IT***.
YOU WERE SITTING ON ***THIS***, KENT?
I GREW UP IN ***THE FOURTH DIMENSION*** AMONG THE MOST ACCEPTING AND LOVING BEINGS IN EXISTENCE.
EVERY NEWS ORGANIZATION IN THE WORLD HAS THIS NOW!

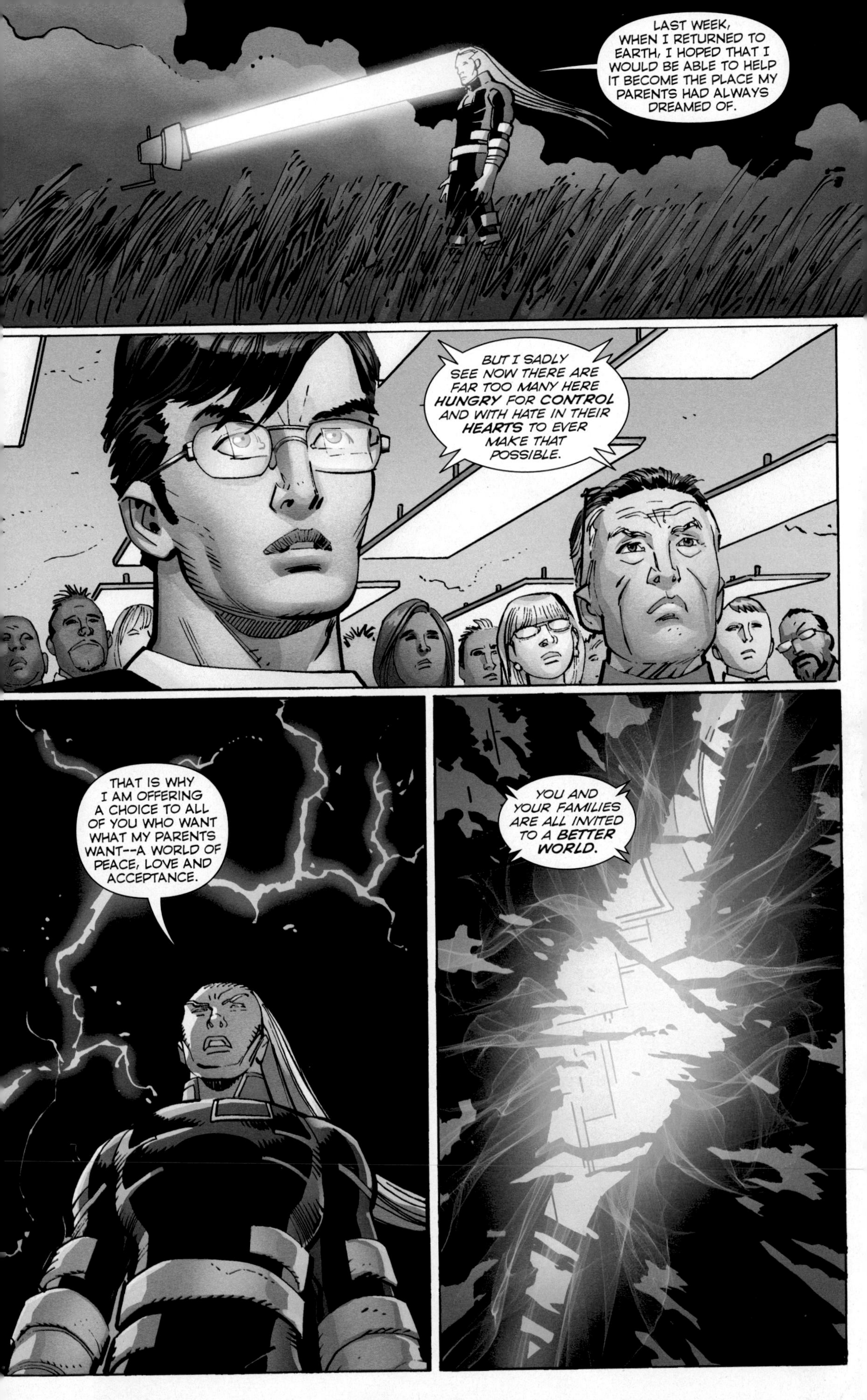
LAST WEEK, WHEN I RETURNED TO EARTH, I HOPED THAT I WOULD BE ABLE TO HELP IT BECOME THE PLACE MY PARENTS HAD ALWAYS DREAMED OF.
BUT I SADLY SEE NOW THERE ARE FAR TOO MANY HERE HUNGRY FOR CONTROL AND WITH HATE IN THEIR HEARTS TO EVER MAKE THAT POSSIBLE.
THAT IS WHY I AM OFFERING A CHOICE TO ALL OF YOU WHO WANT WHAT MY PARENTS WANT--A WORLD OF PEACE, LOVE AND ACCEPTANCE.
YOU AND YOUR FAMILIES ARE ALL INVITED TO A BETTER WORLD.

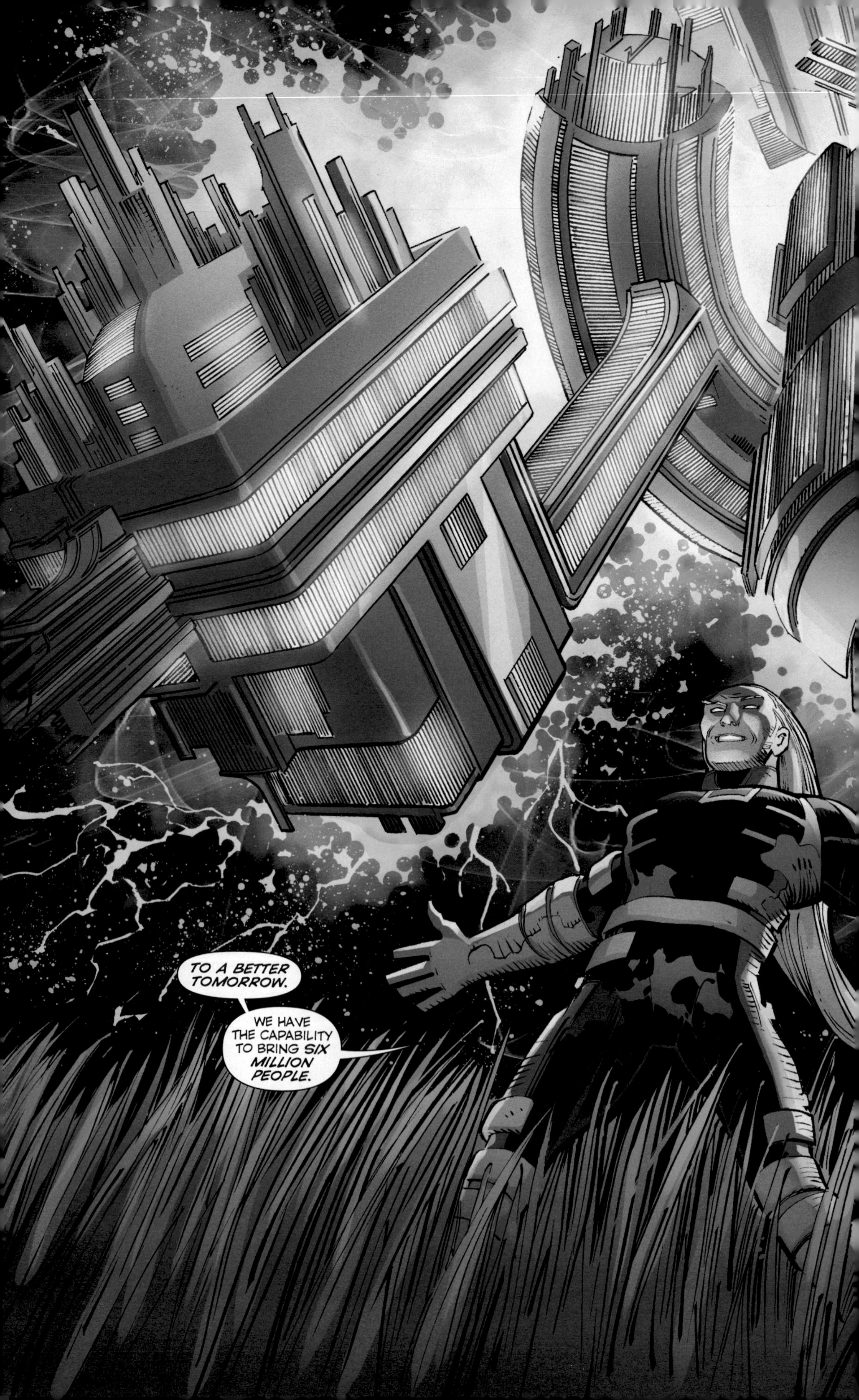
TO A BETTER TOMORROW.
WE HAVE THE CAPABILITY TO BRING SIX MILLION PEOPLE.

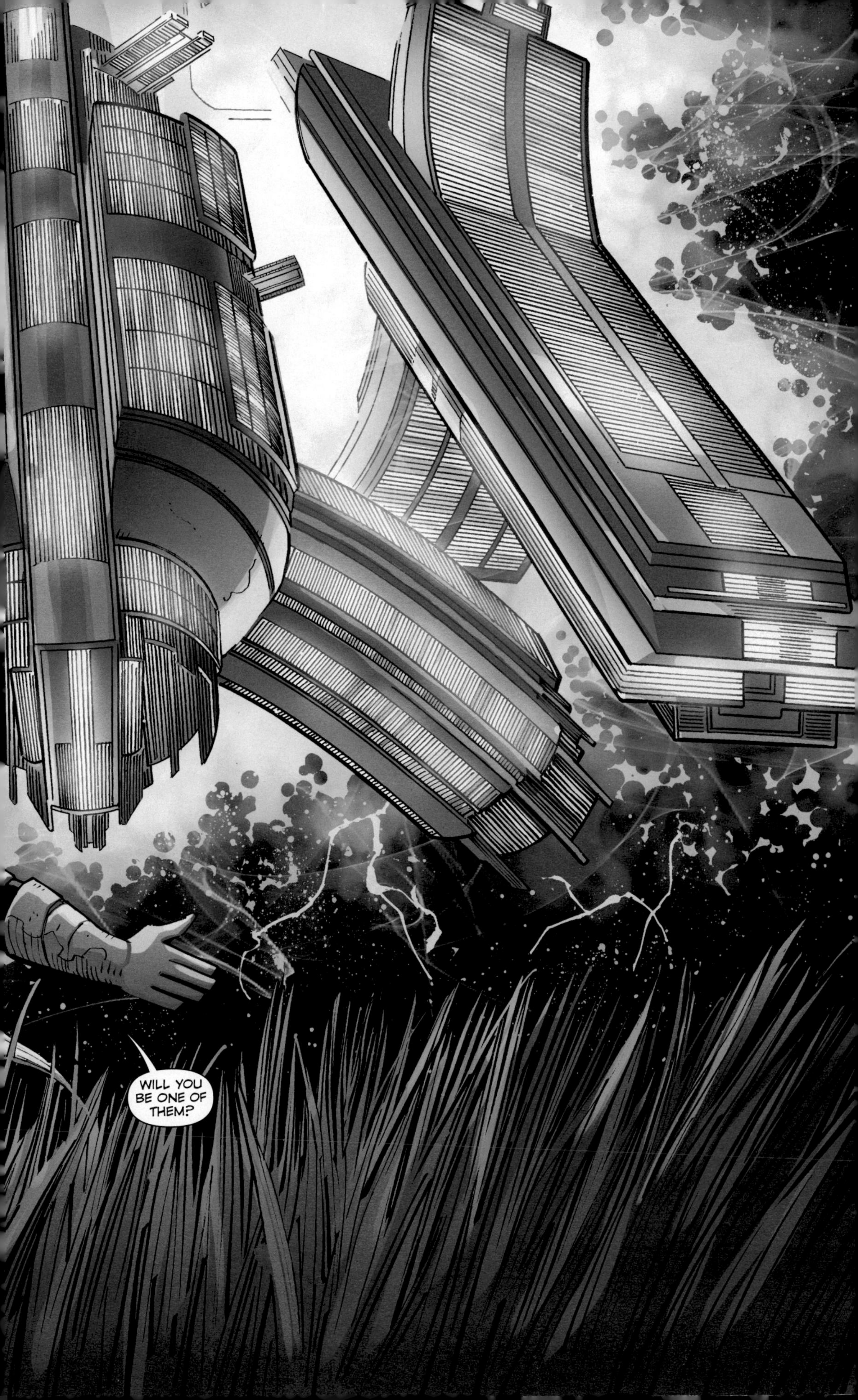
WILL YOU BE ONE OF THEM?

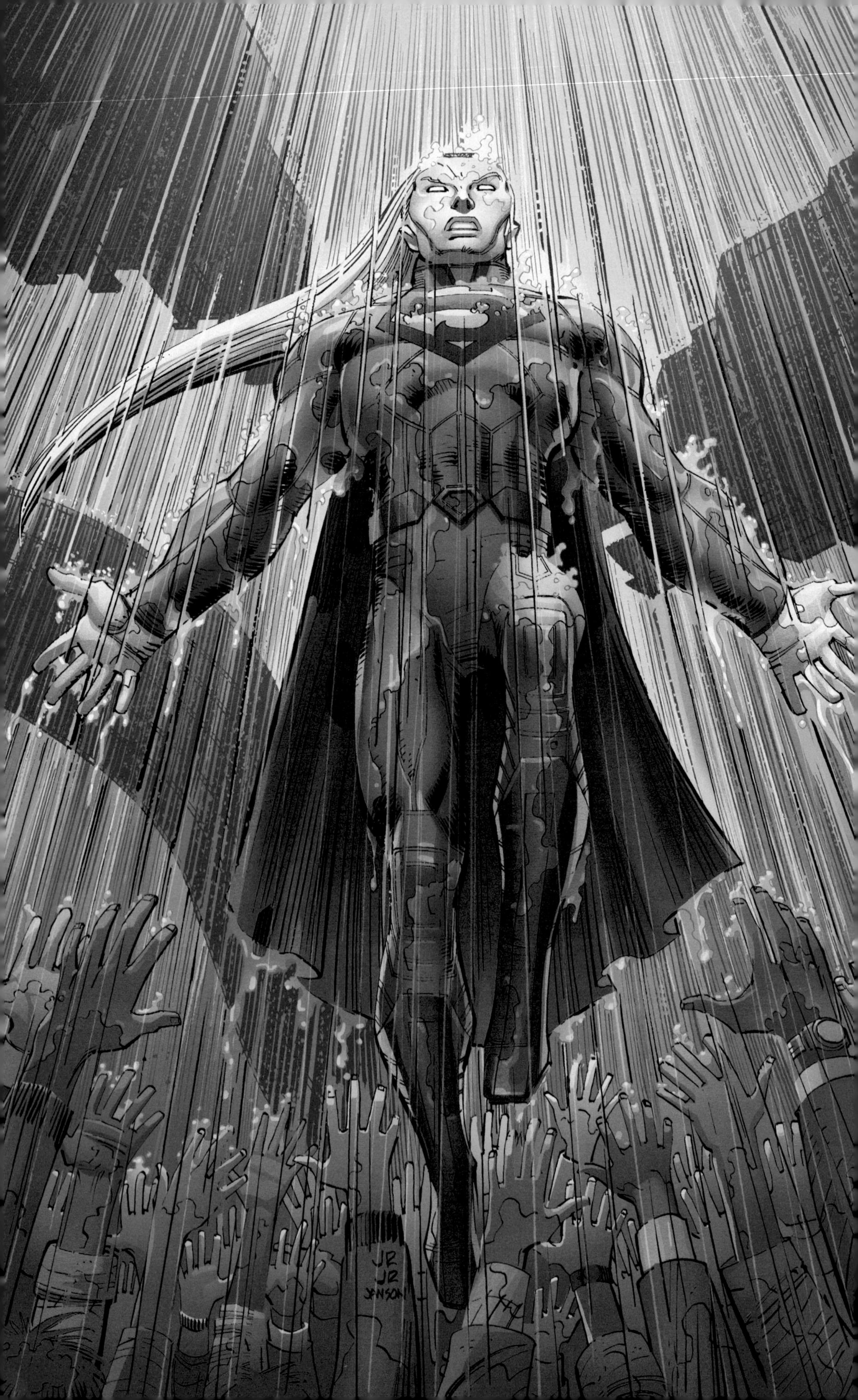
JR
JR
JANSON

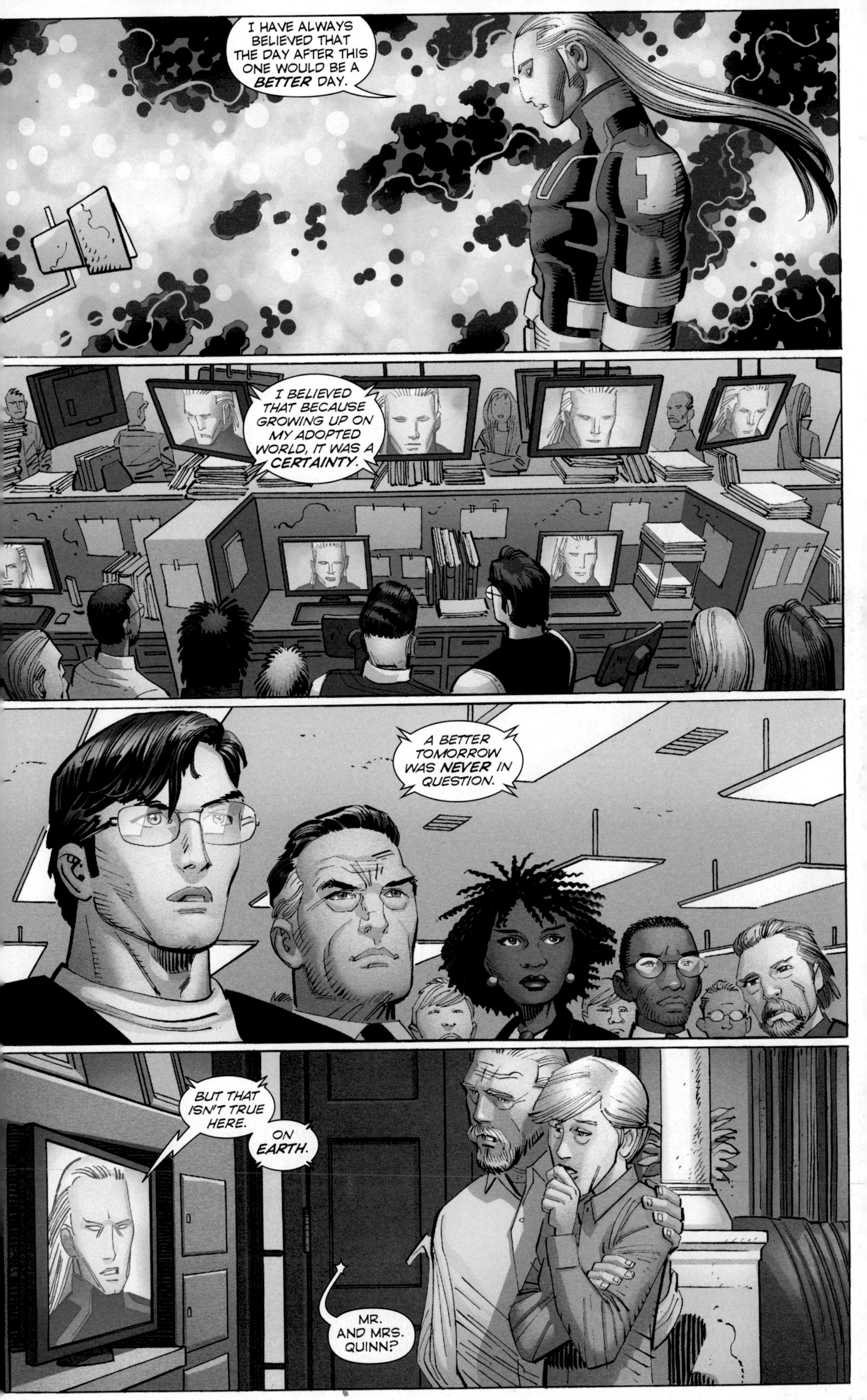
I HAVE ALWAYS BELIEVED THAT THE DAY AFTER THIS ONE WOULD BE A *BETTER* DAY.
I BELIEVED THAT BECAUSE GROWING UP ON MY ADOPTED WORLD, IT WAS A *CERTAINTY*.
A BETTER TOMORROW WAS *NEVER* IN QUESTION.
BUT THAT ISN'T TRUE HERE.
ON *EARTH*.
MR. AND MRS. QUINN?

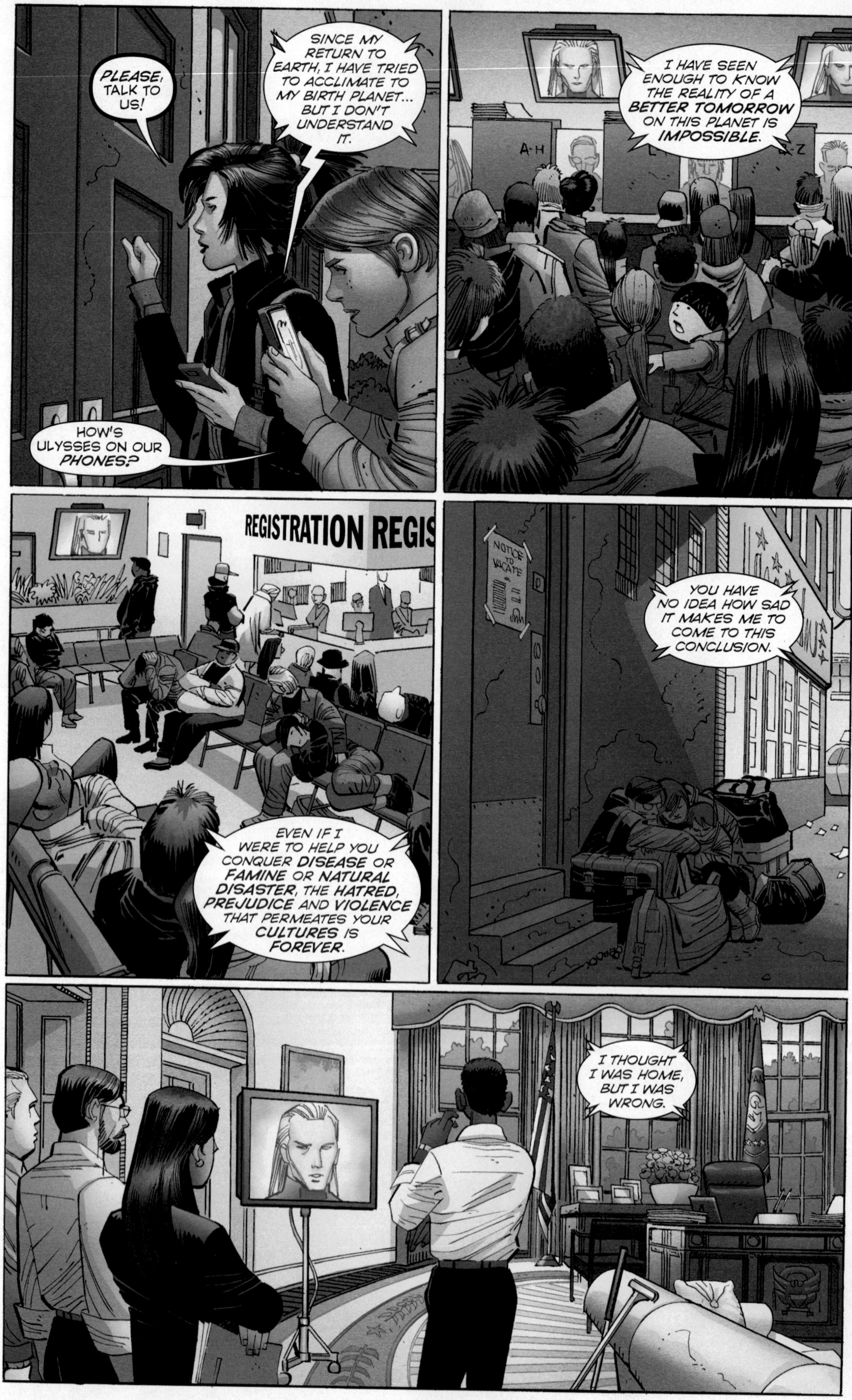
PLEASE, TALK TO US!
SINCE MY RETURN TO EARTH, I HAVE TRIED TO ACCLIMATE TO MY BIRTH PLANET... BUT I DON'T UNDERSTAND IT.
HOW'S ULYSSES ON OUR PHONES?
I HAVE SEEN ENOUGH TO KNOW THE REALITY OF A BETTER TOMORROW ON THIS PLANET IS IMPOSSIBLE.
A-H
REGISTRATION REGIS
EVEN IF I WERE TO HELP YOU CONQUER DISEASE OR FAMINE OR NATURAL DISASTER, THE HATRED, PREJUDICE AND VIOLENCE THAT PERMEATES YOUR CULTURES IS FOREVER.
NOTICE TO VACATE
YOU HAVE NO IDEA HOW SAD IT MAKES ME TO COME TO THIS CONCLUSION.
I THOUGHT I WAS HOME, BUT I WAS WRONG.

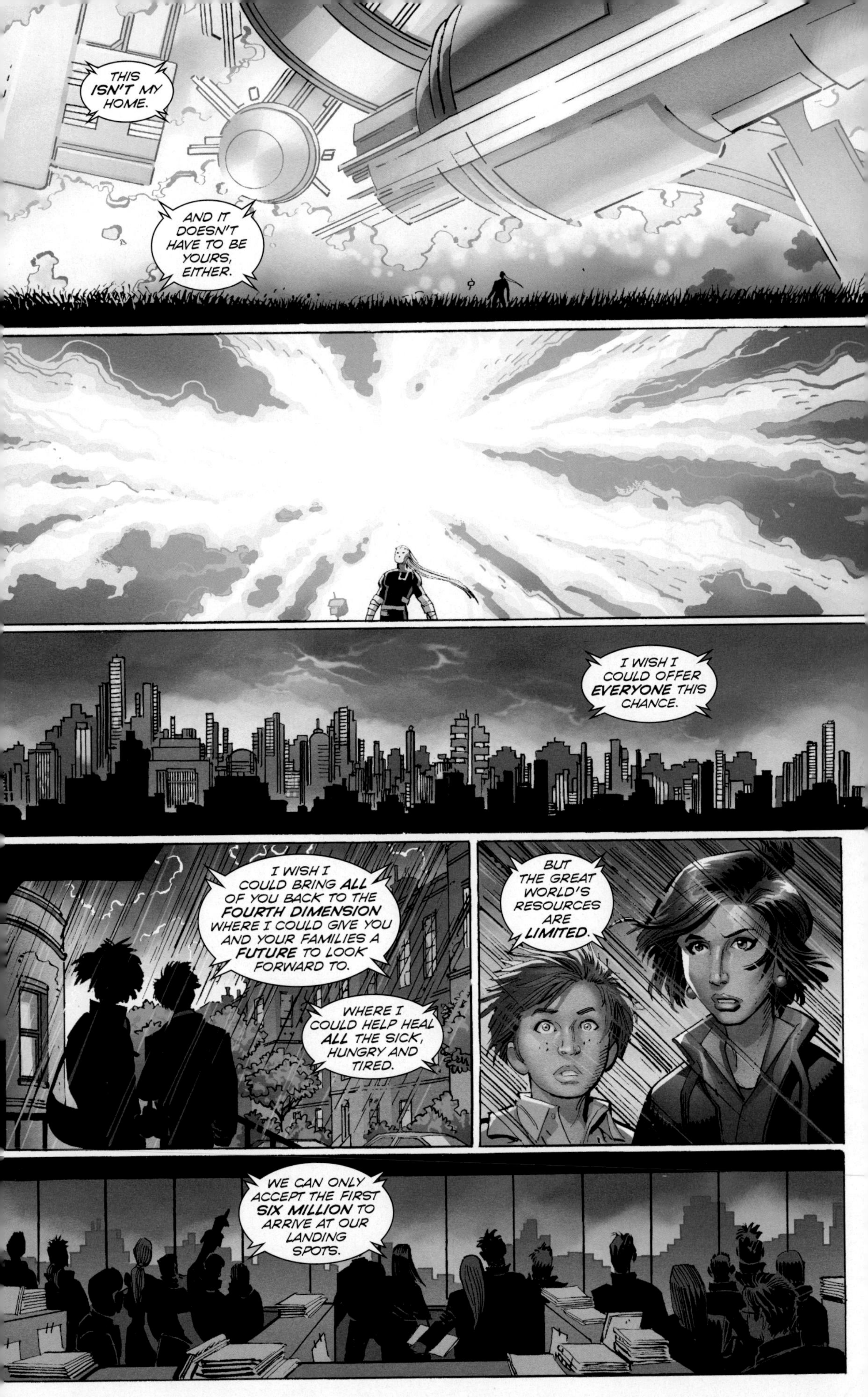
THIS ISN'T MY HOME.
AND IT DOESN'T HAVE TO BE YOURS, EITHER.
I WISH I COULD OFFER EVERYONE THIS CHANCE.
I WISH I COULD BRING ALL OF YOU BACK TO THE FOURTH DIMENSION WHERE I COULD GIVE YOU AND YOUR FAMILIES A FUTURE TO LOOK FORWARD TO.
WHERE I COULD HELP HEAL ALL THE SICK, HUNGRY AND TIRED.
BUT THE GREAT WORLD'S RESOURCES ARE LIMITED.
WE CAN ONLY ACCEPT THE FIRST SIX MILLION TO ARRIVE AT OUR LANDING SPOTS.

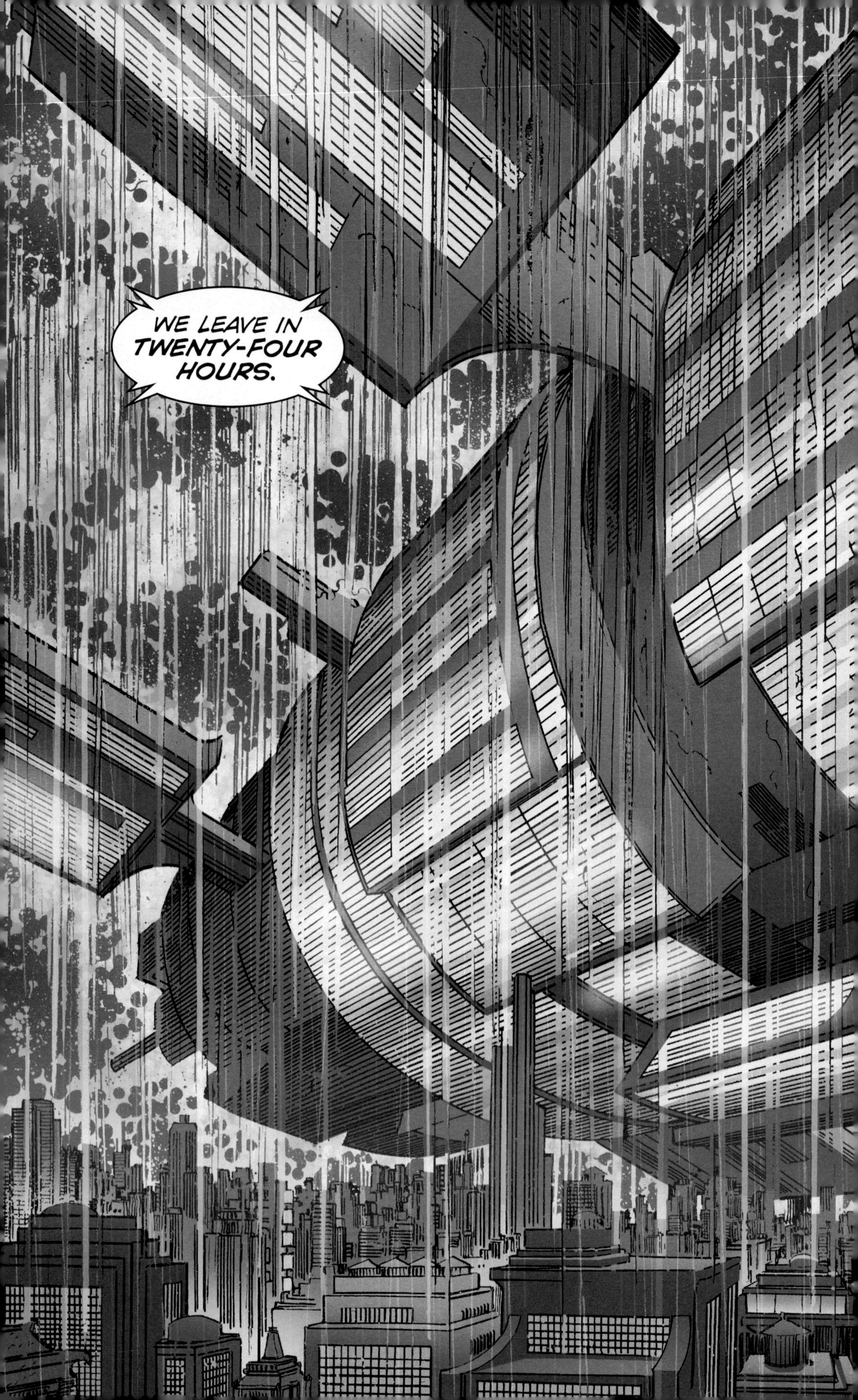
WE LEAVE IN TWENTY-FOUR HOURS.

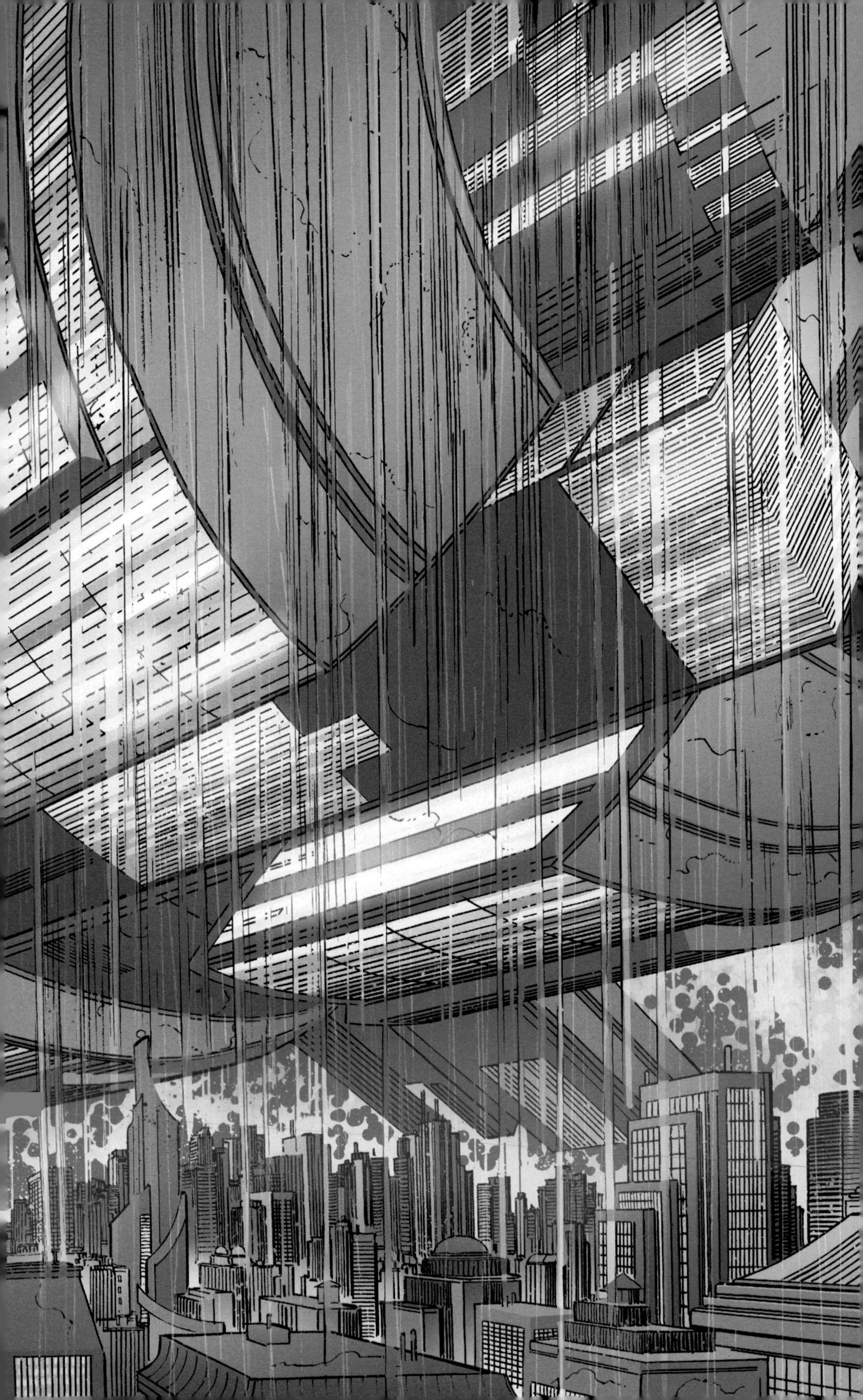

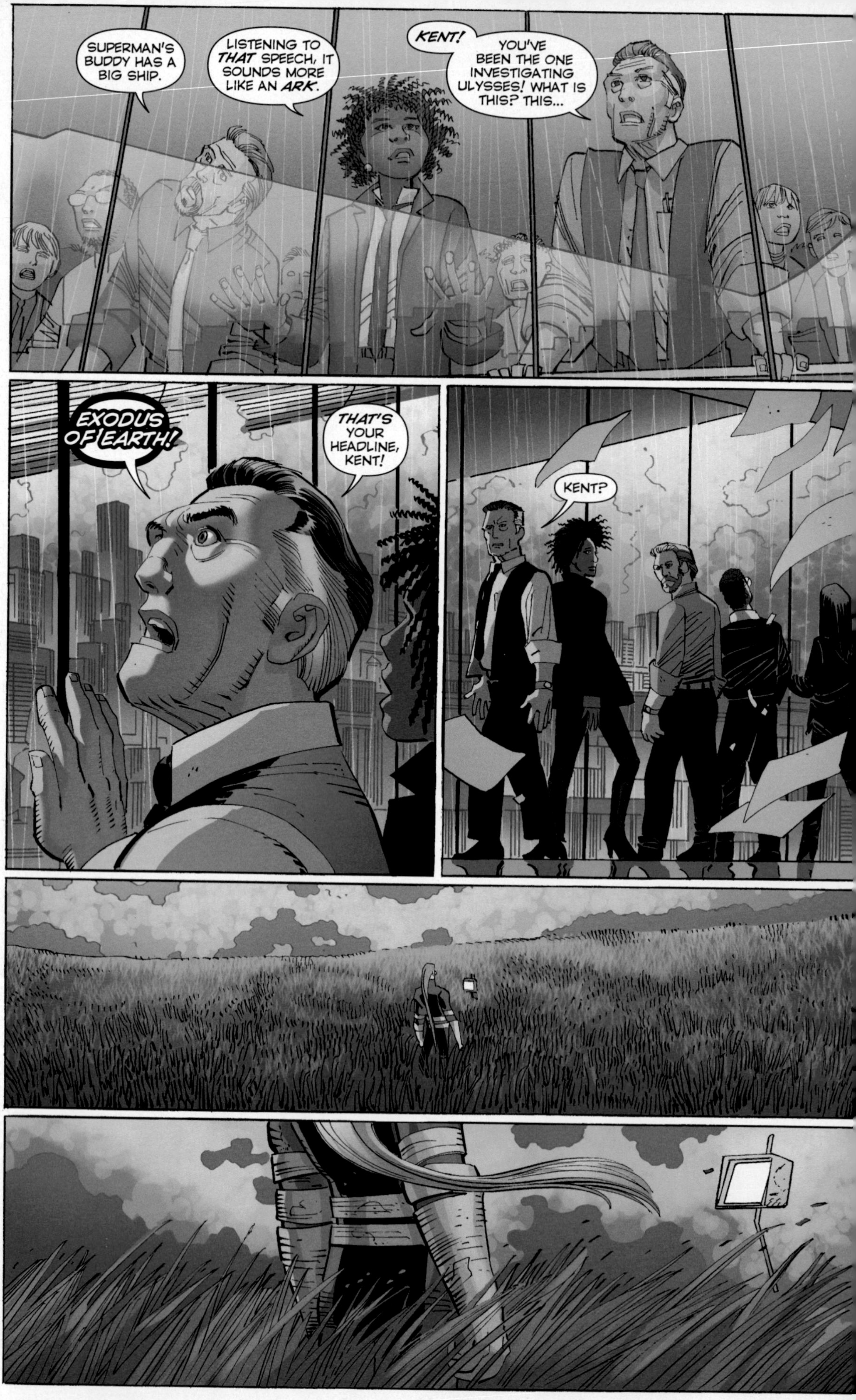
SUPERMAN'S BUDDY HAS A BIG SHIP.
LISTENING TO THAT SPEECH, IT SOUNDS MORE LIKE AN ARK.
KENT!
YOU'VE BEEN THE ONE INVESTIGATING ULYSSES! WHAT IS THIS? THIS...
EXODUS OF EARTH!
THAT'S YOUR HEADLINE, KENT!
KENT?

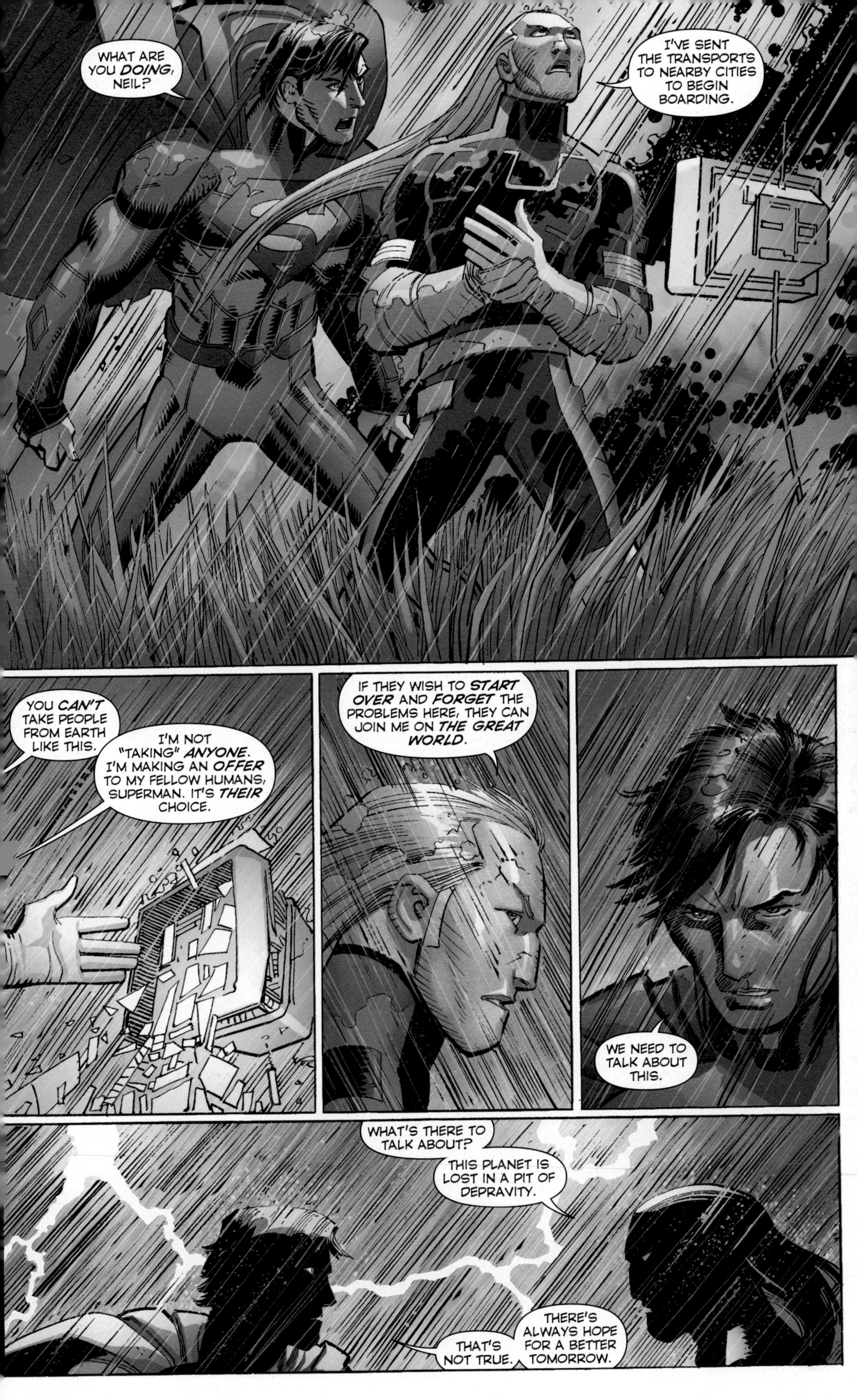
WHAT ARE YOU DOING, NEIL?
I'VE SENT THE TRANSPORTS TO NEARBY CITIES TO BEGIN BOARDING.
YOU CAN'T TAKE PEOPLE FROM EARTH LIKE THIS.
I'M NOT "TAKING" ANYONE. I'M MAKING AN OFFER TO MY FELLOW HUMANS, SUPERMAN. IT'S THEIR CHOICE.
IF THEY WISH TO START OVER AND FORGET THE PROBLEMS HERE, THEY CAN JOIN ME ON THE GREAT WORLD.
WE NEED TO TALK ABOUT THIS.
WHAT'S THERE TO TALK ABOUT?
THIS PLANET IS LOST IN A PIT OF DEPRAVITY.
THERE'S ALWAYS HOPE FOR A BETTER TOMORROW.
THAT'S NOT TRUE.

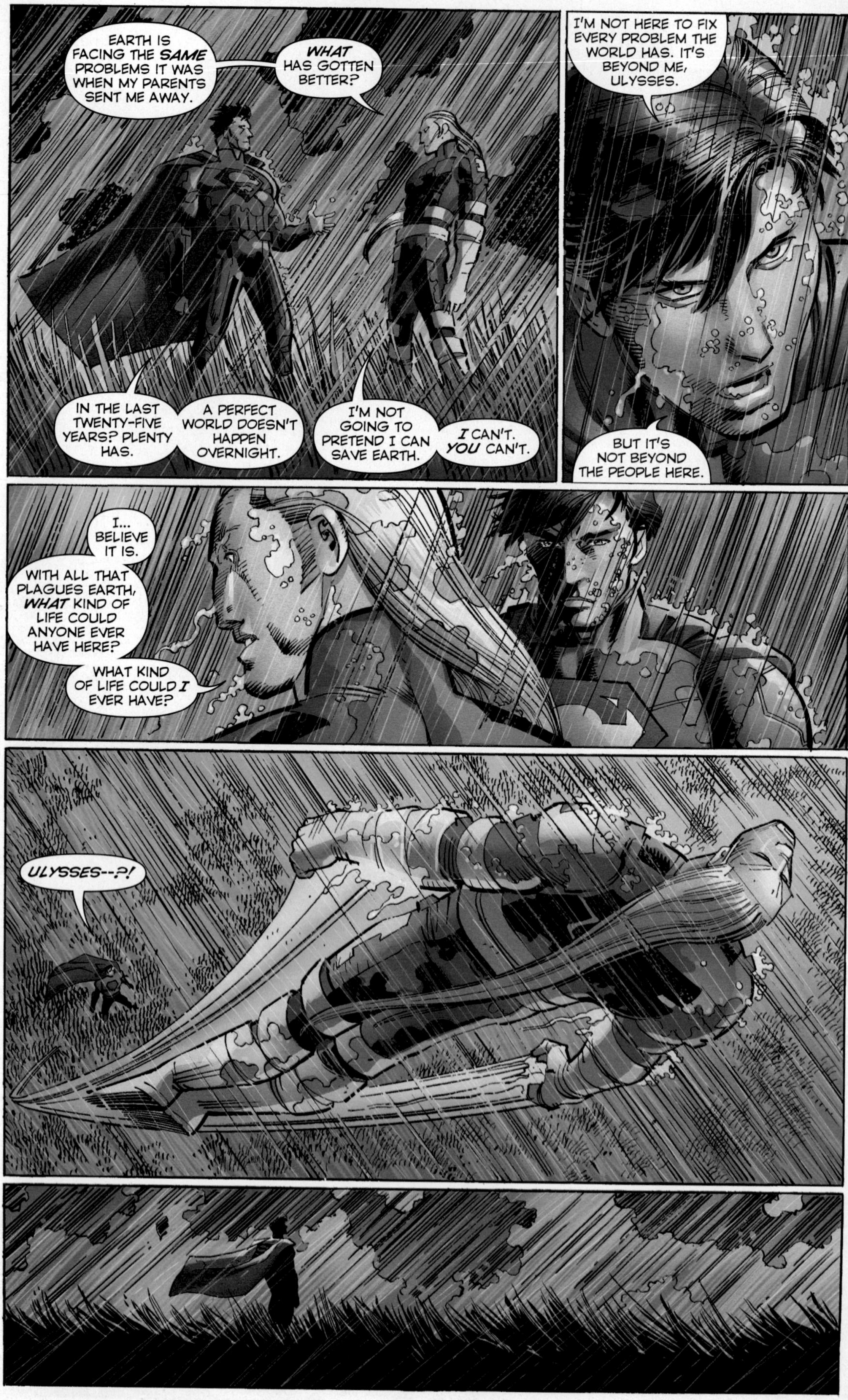
EARTH IS FACING THE SAME PROBLEMS IT WAS WHEN MY PARENTS SENT ME AWAY.
WHAT HAS GOTTEN BETTER?
IN THE LAST TWENTY-FIVE YEARS? PLENTY HAS.
A PERFECT WORLD DOESN'T HAPPEN OVERNIGHT.
I'M NOT GOING TO PRETEND I CAN SAVE EARTH.
I CAN'T. YOU CAN'T.
I'M NOT HERE TO FIX EVERY PROBLEM THE WORLD HAS. IT'S BEYOND ME, ULYSSES.
BUT IT'S NOT BEYOND THE PEOPLE HERE.
I... BELIEVE IT IS.
WITH ALL THAT PLAGUES EARTH, WHAT KIND OF LIFE COULD ANYONE EVER HAVE HERE?
WHAT KIND OF LIFE COULD I EVER HAVE?
ULYSSES--?!

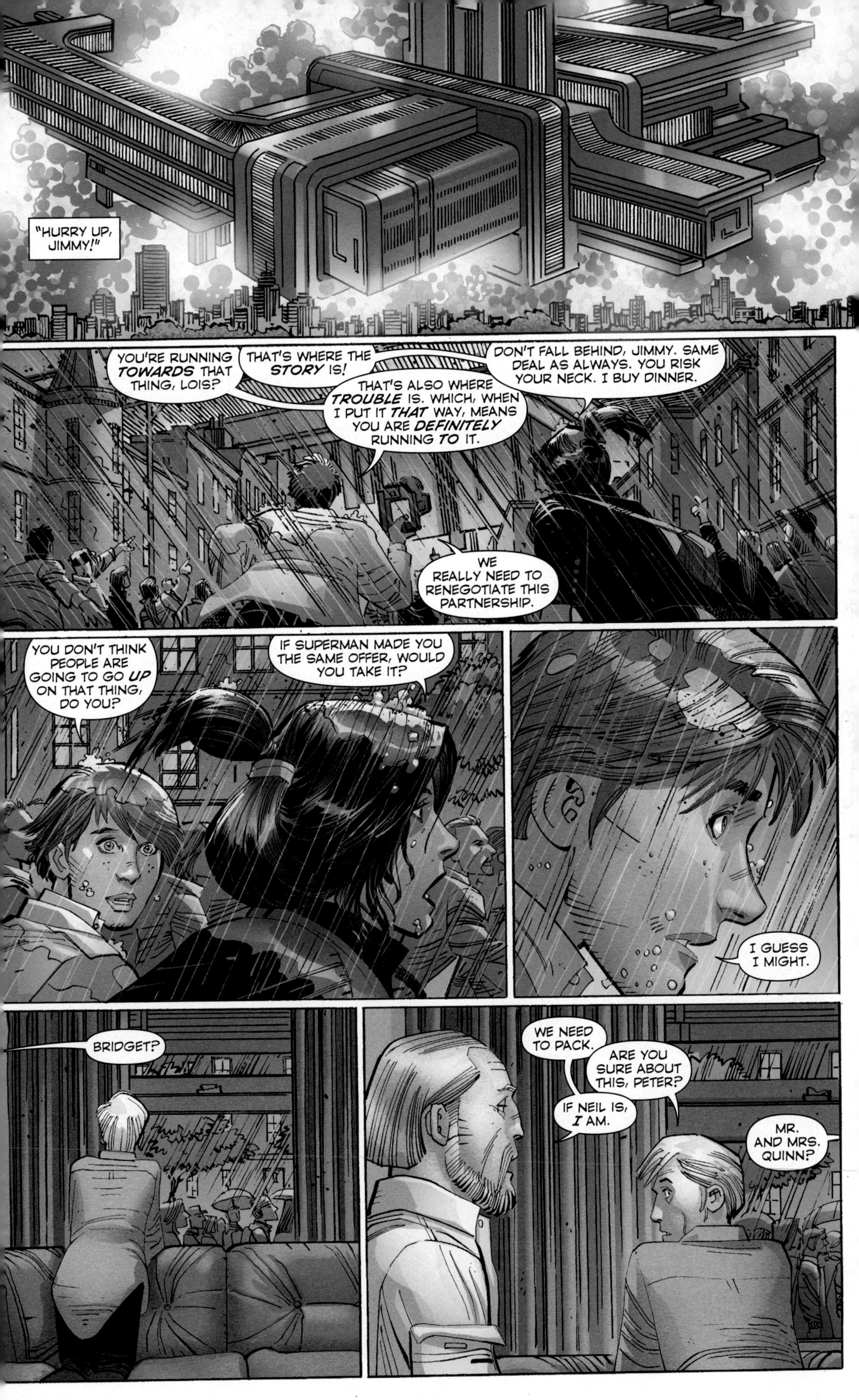
"HURRY UP, JIMMY!"
YOU'RE RUNNING TOWARDS THAT THING, LOIS?
THAT'S WHERE THE STORY IS!
THAT'S ALSO WHERE TROUBLE IS. WHICH, WHEN I PUT IT THAT WAY, MEANS YOU ARE DEFINITELY RUNNING TO IT.
DON'T FALL BEHIND, JIMMY. SAME DEAL AS ALWAYS. YOU RISK YOUR NECK. I BUY DINNER.
WE REALLY NEED TO RENEGOTIATE THIS PARTNERSHIP.
YOU DON'T THINK PEOPLE ARE GOING TO GO UP ON THAT THING, DO YOU?
IF SUPERMAN MADE YOU THE SAME OFFER, WOULD YOU TAKE IT?
I GUESS I MIGHT.
BRIDGET?
WE NEED TO PACK.
ARE YOU SURE ABOUT THIS, PETER?
IF NEIL IS, I AM.
MR. AND MRS. QUINN?

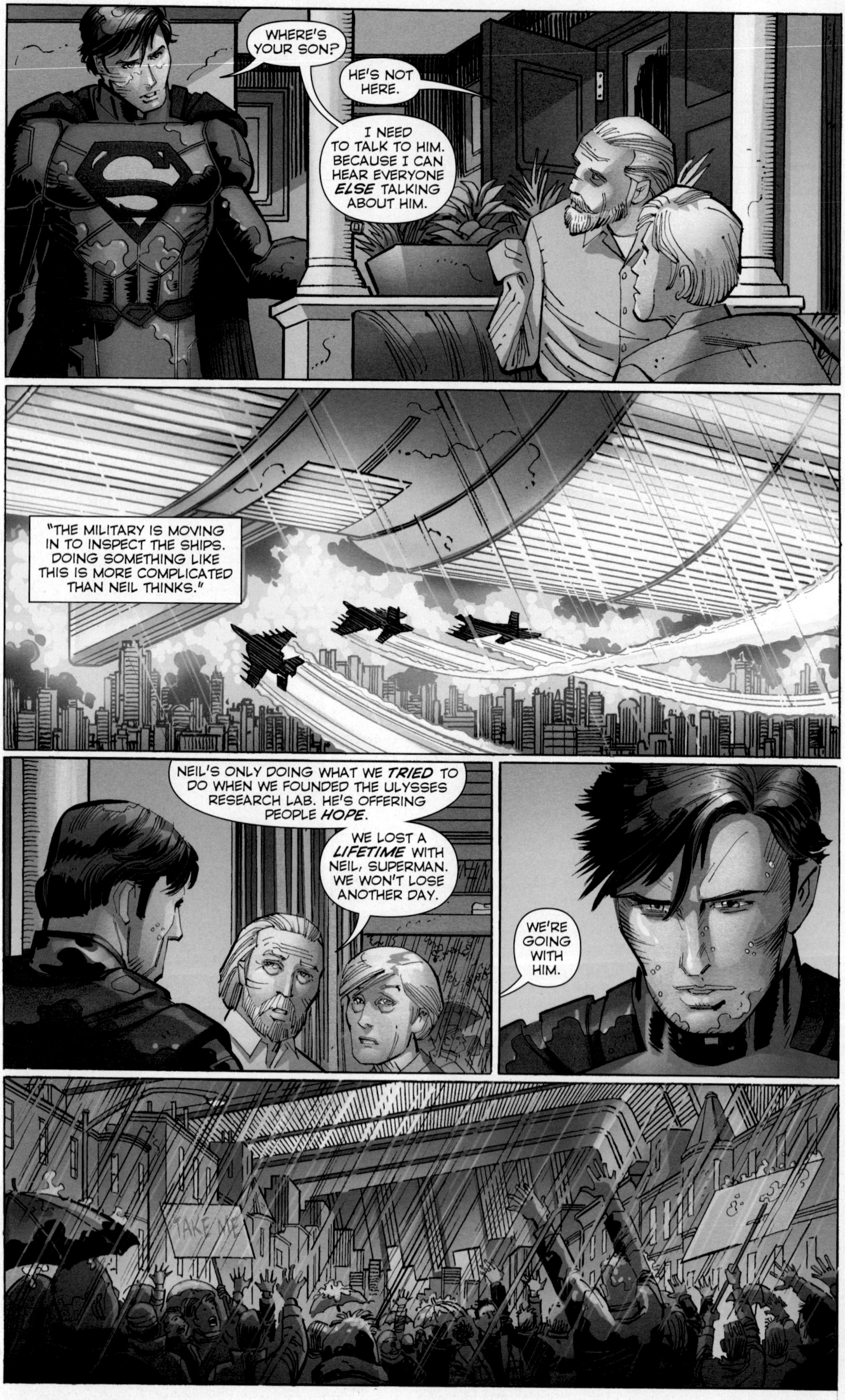
WHERE'S YOUR SON?
HE'S NOT HERE.
I NEED TO TALK TO HIM. BECAUSE I CAN HEAR EVERYONE *ELSE* TALKING ABOUT HIM.
"THE MILITARY IS MOVING IN TO INSPECT THE SHIPS. DOING SOMETHING LIKE THIS IS MORE COMPLICATED THAN NEIL THINKS."
NEIL'S ONLY DOING WHAT WE *TRIED* TO DO WHEN WE FOUNDED THE ULYSSES RESEARCH LAB. HE'S OFFERING PEOPLE *HOPE*.
WE LOST A *LIFETIME* WITH NEIL, SUPERMAN. WE WON'T LOSE ANOTHER DAY.
WE'RE GOING WITH HIM.
TAKE ME

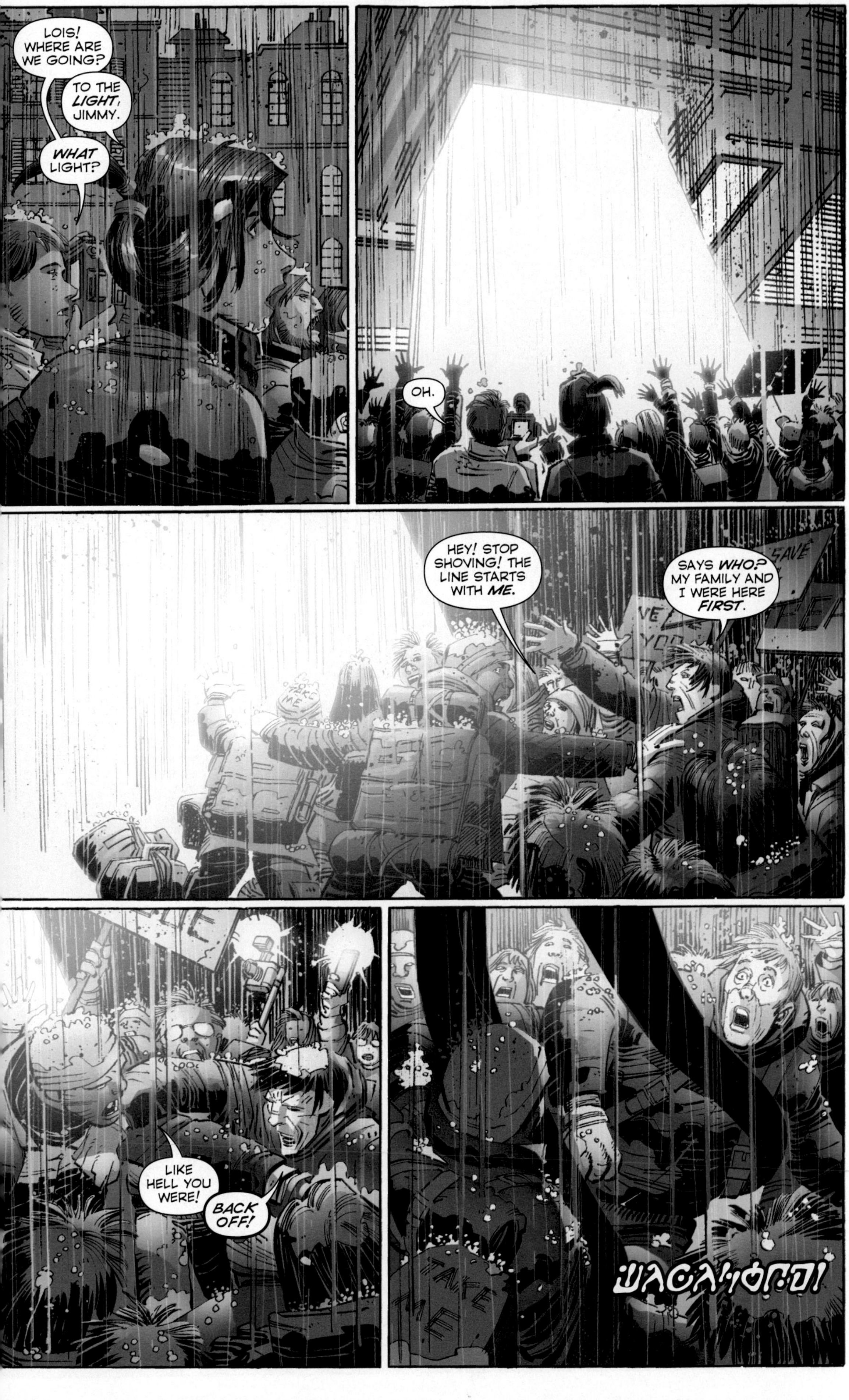
LOIS! WHERE ARE WE GOING?
TO THE *LIGHT*, JIMMY.
WHAT LIGHT?
OH.
HEY! STOP SHOVING! THE LINE STARTS WITH *ME*.
SAYS *WHO?* MY FAMILY AND I WERE HERE *FIRST*.
LIKE HELL YOU WERE!
BACK OFF!
TAKE ME

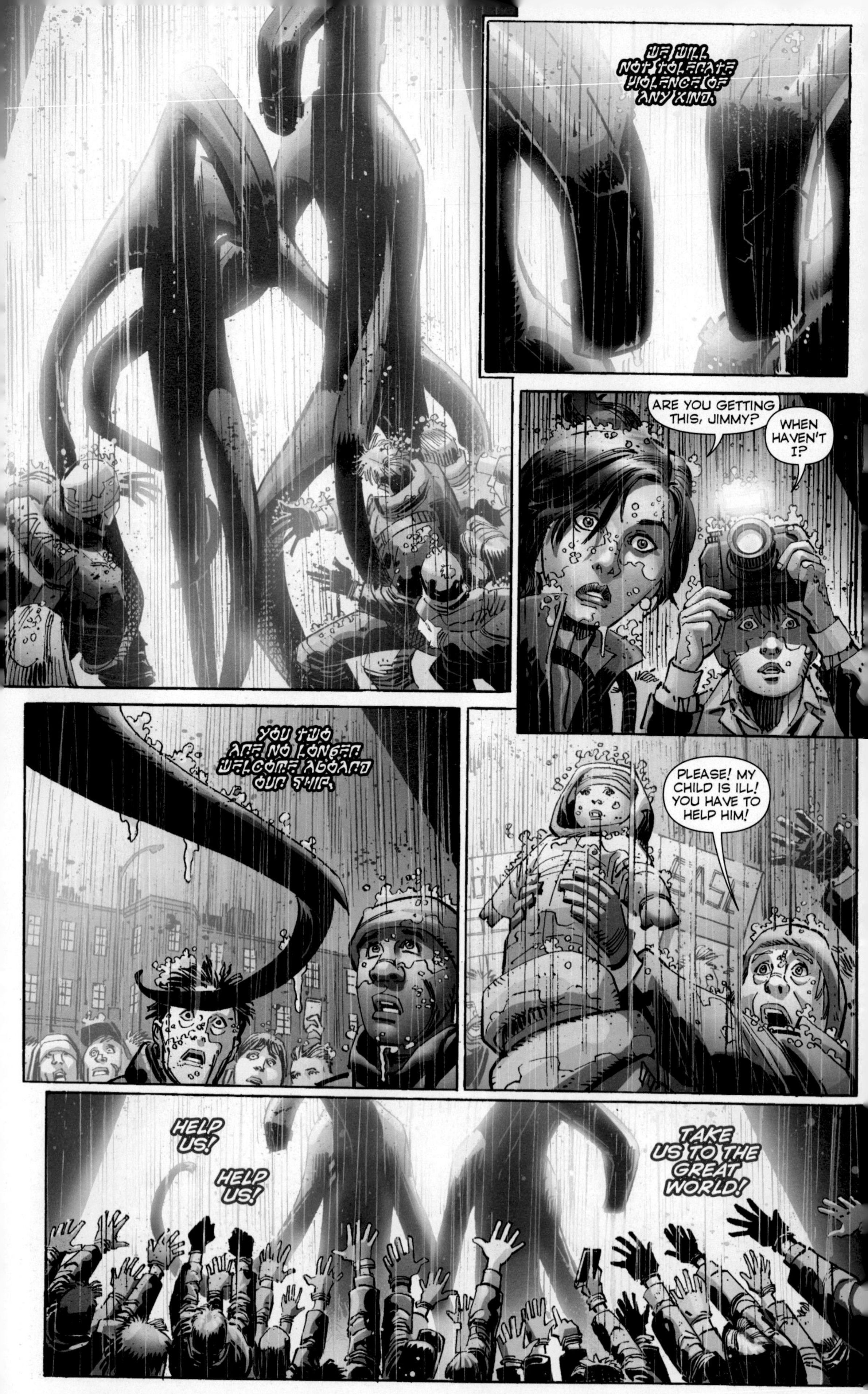
WE WILL NOT TOLERATE VIOLENCE OF ANY KIND.
ARE YOU GETTING THIS, JIMMY?
WHEN HAVEN'T I?
YOU TWO ARE NO LONGER WELCOME ABOARD OUR SHIP.
PLEASE! MY CHILD IS ILL! YOU HAVE TO HELP HIM!
HELP US!
HELP US!
TAKE US TO THE GREAT WORLD!

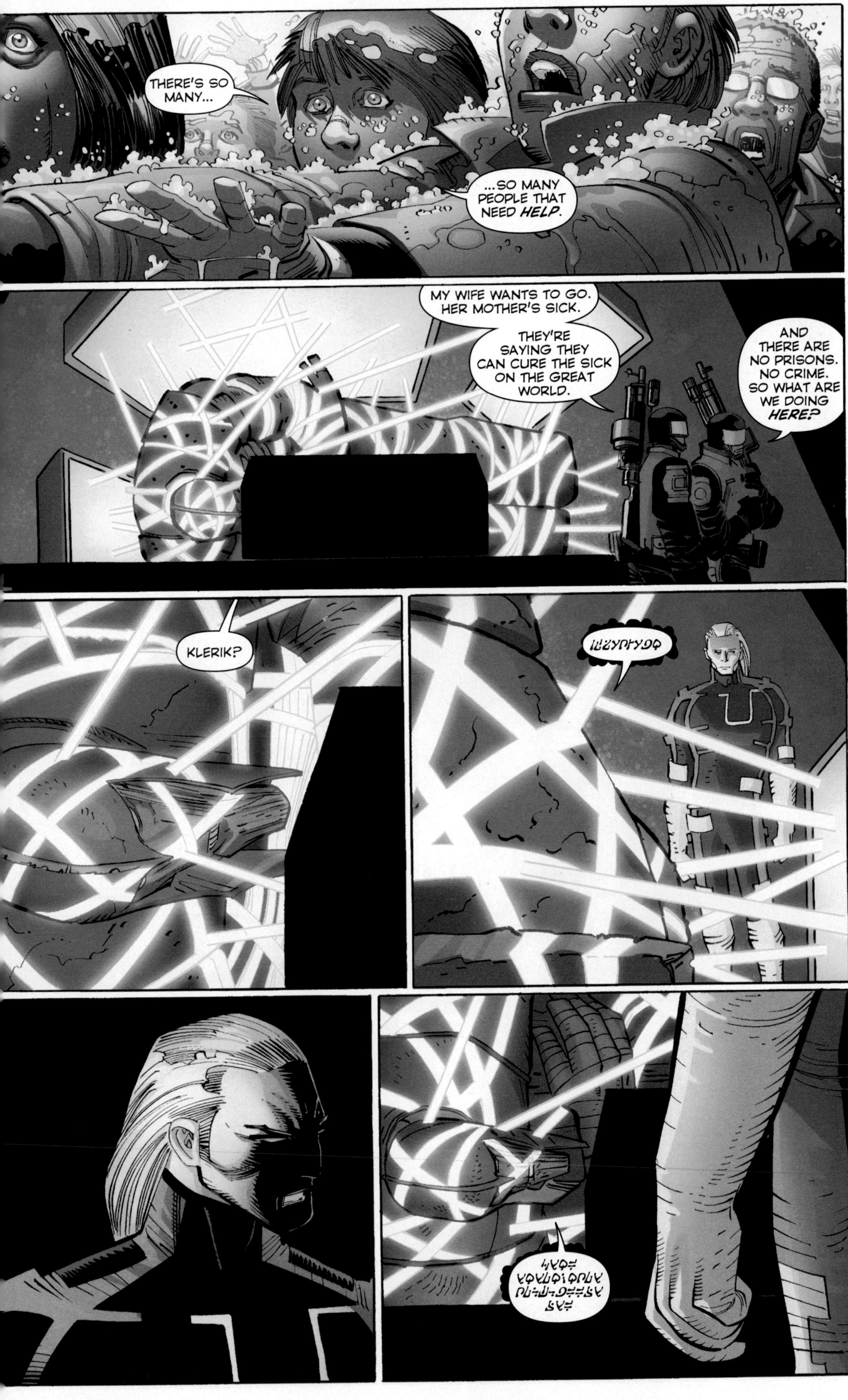
THERE'S SO MANY...
...SO MANY PEOPLE THAT NEED HELP.
MY WIFE WANTS TO GO. HER MOTHER'S SICK.
THEY'RE SAYING THEY CAN CURE THE SICK ON THE GREAT WORLD.
AND THERE ARE NO PRISONS. NO CRIME. SO WHAT ARE WE DOING HERE?
KLERIK?

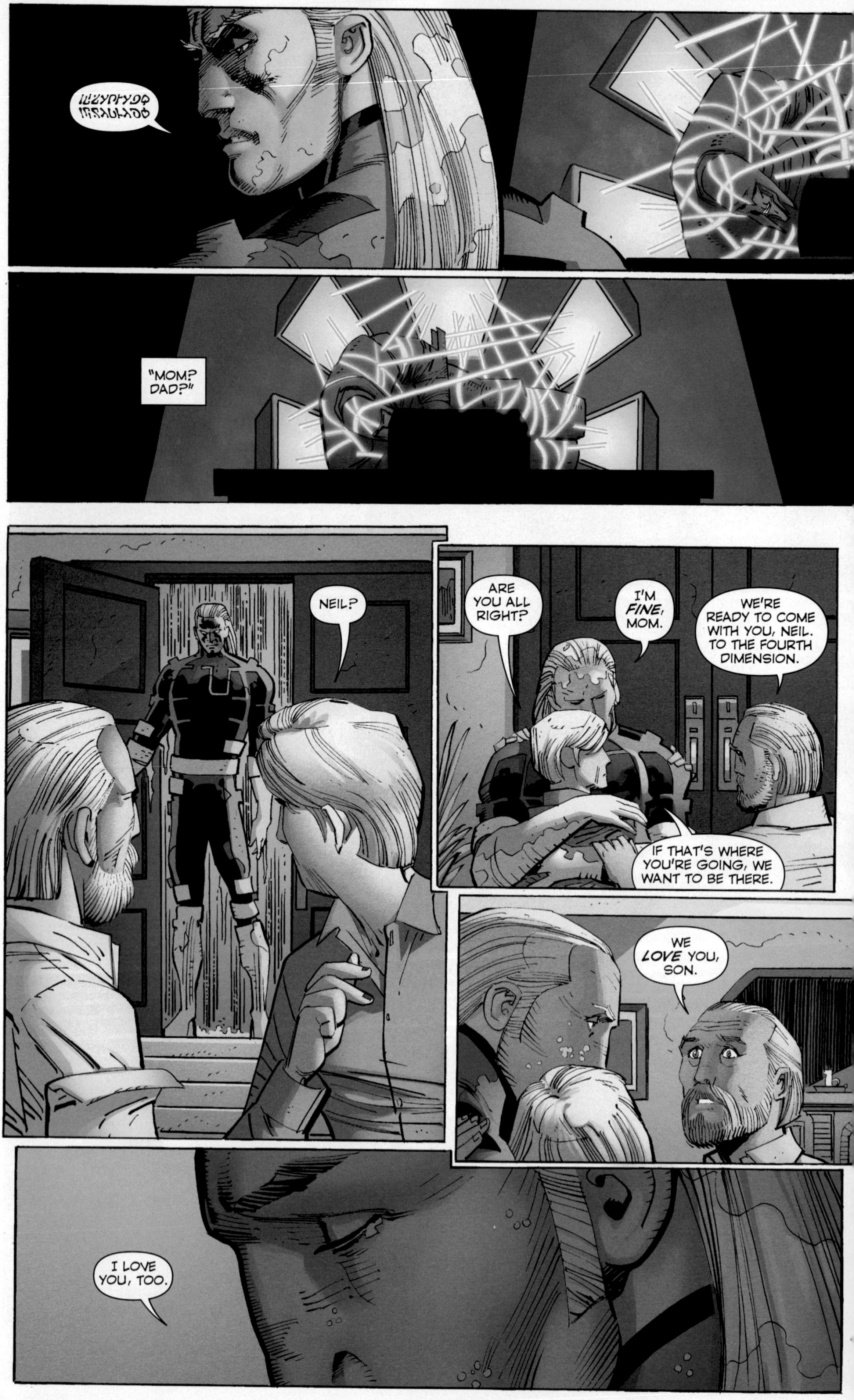
"MOM? DAD?"
NEIL?
ARE YOU ALL RIGHT?
I'M FINE, MOM.
WE'RE READY TO COME WITH YOU, NEIL. TO THE FOURTH DIMENSION.
IF THAT'S WHERE YOU'RE GOING, WE WANT TO BE THERE.
WE LOVE YOU, SON.
I LOVE YOU, TOO.

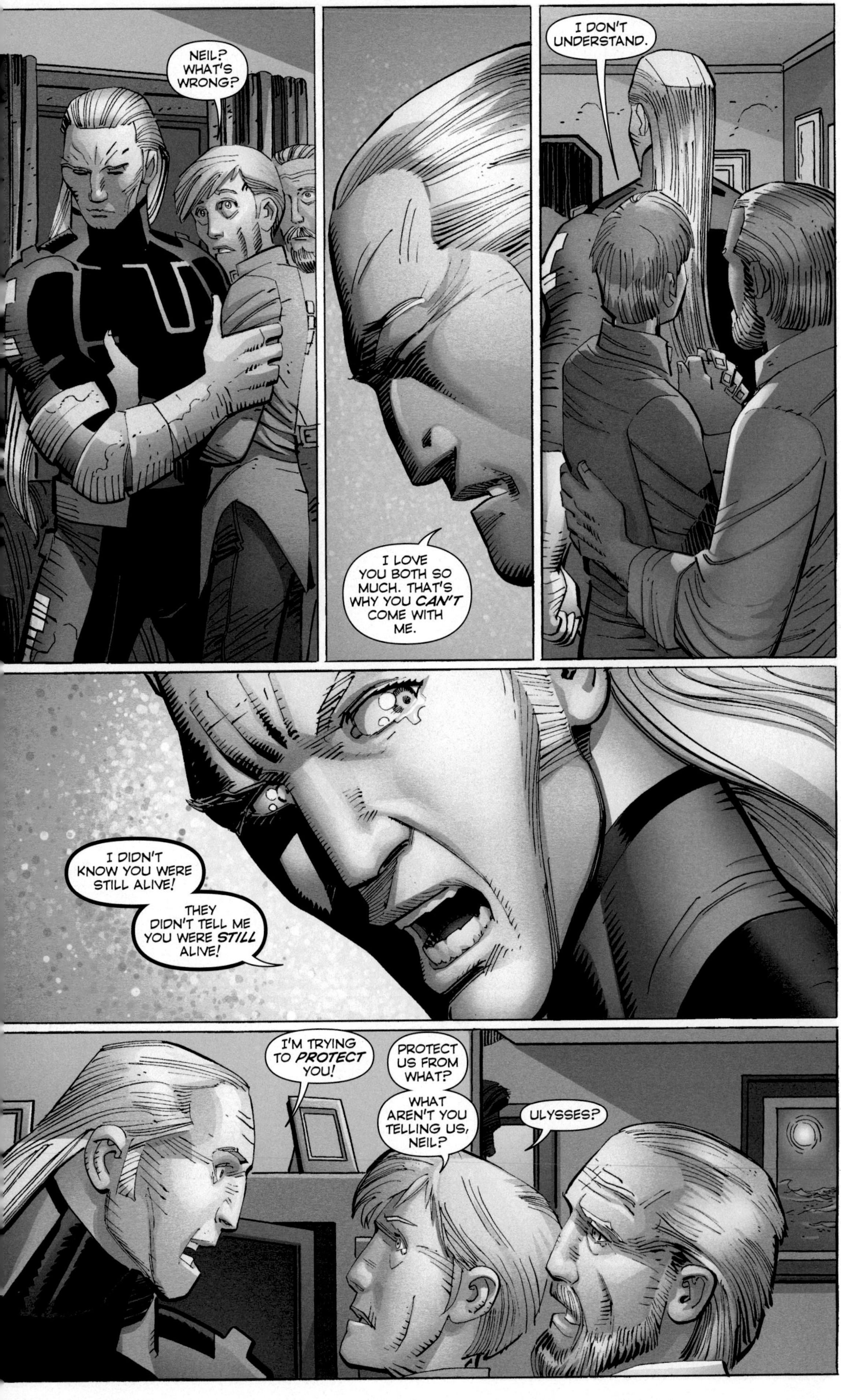
NEIL? WHAT'S WRONG?
I LOVE YOU BOTH SO MUCH. THAT'S WHY YOU *CAN'T* COME WITH ME.
I DON'T UNDERSTAND.
I DIDN'T KNOW YOU WERE STILL ALIVE!
THEY DIDN'T TELL ME YOU WERE *STILL* ALIVE!
I'M TRYING TO *PROTECT* YOU!
PROTECT US FROM WHAT?
WHAT AREN'T YOU TELLING US, NEIL?
ULYSSES?

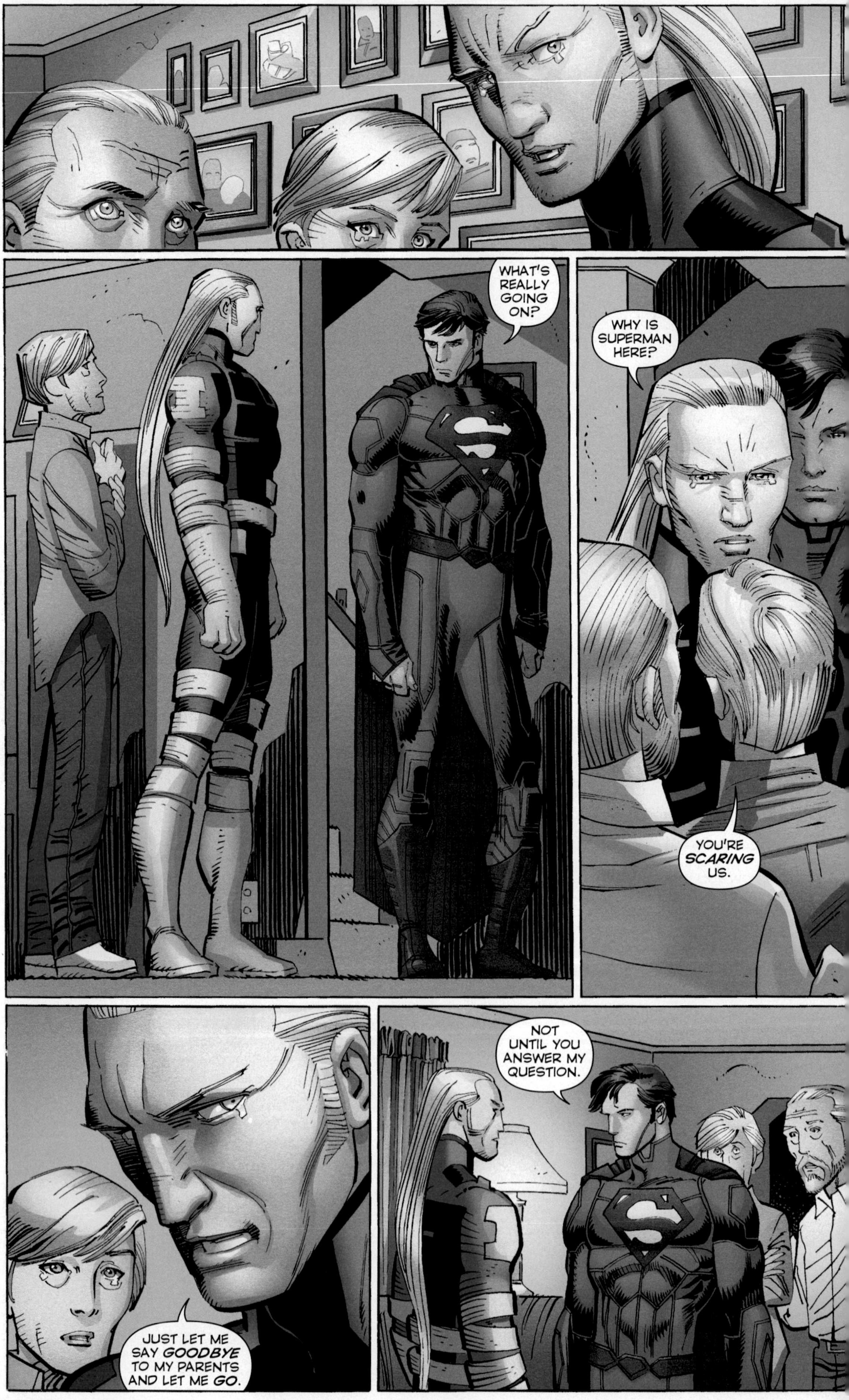
WHAT'S REALLY GOING ON?
WHY IS SUPERMAN HERE?
YOU'RE SCARING US.
JUST LET ME SAY GOODBYE TO MY PARENTS AND LET ME GO.
NOT UNTIL YOU ANSWER MY QUESTION.

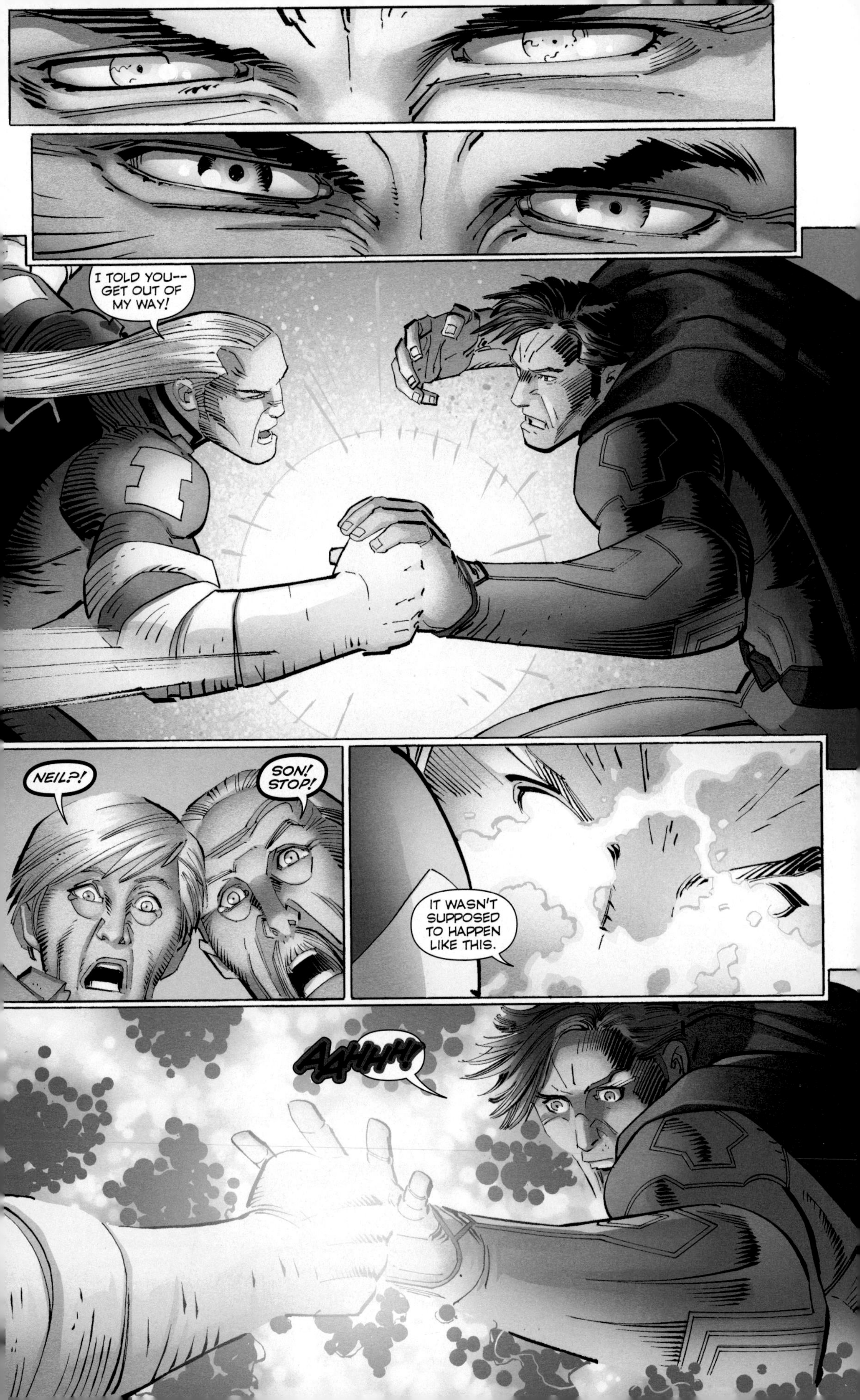
I TOLD YOU--
GET OUT OF
MY WAY!
NEIL?!
SON!
STOP!
IT WASN'T
SUPPOSED
TO HAPPEN
LIKE THIS.
AAHHH!

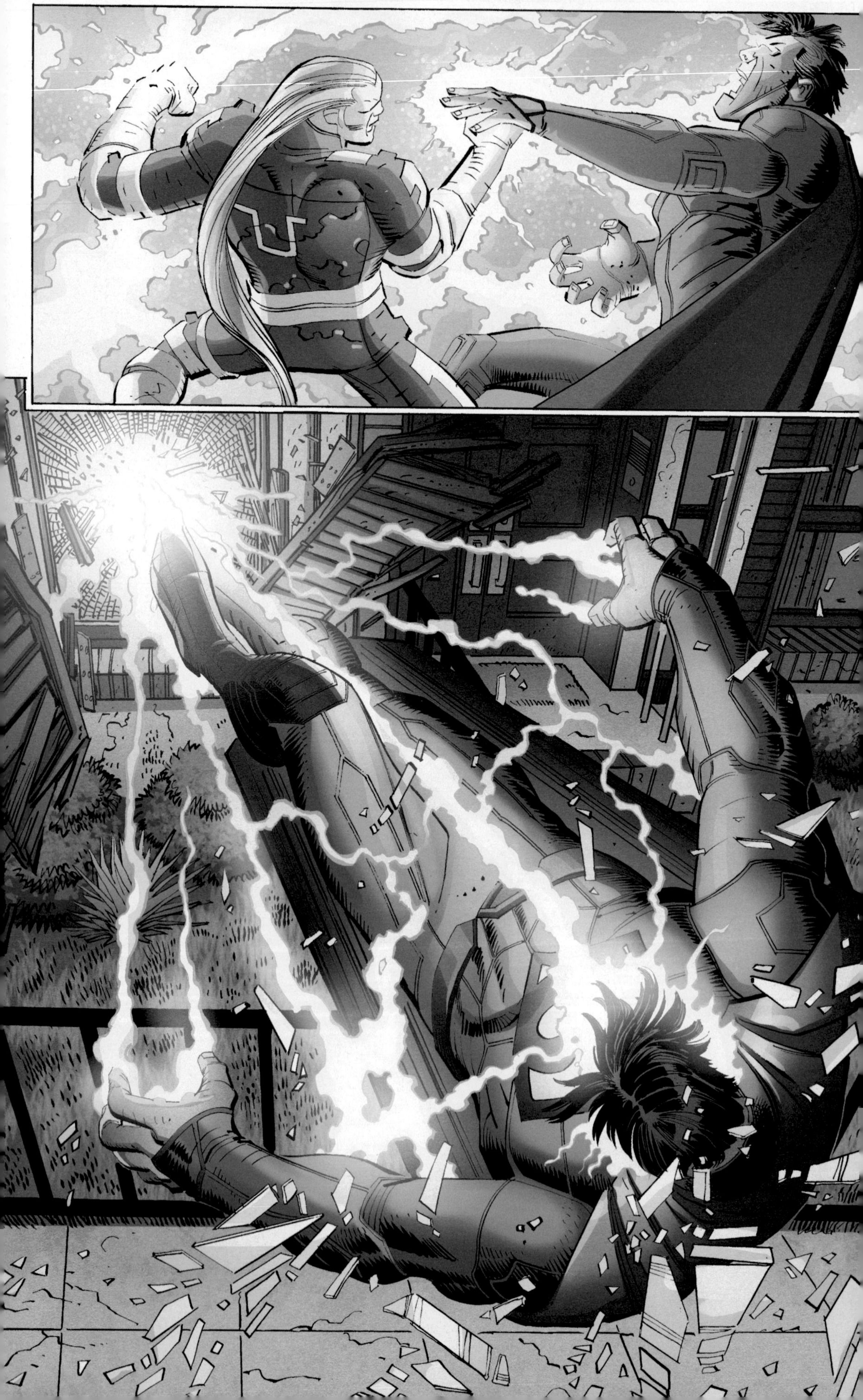

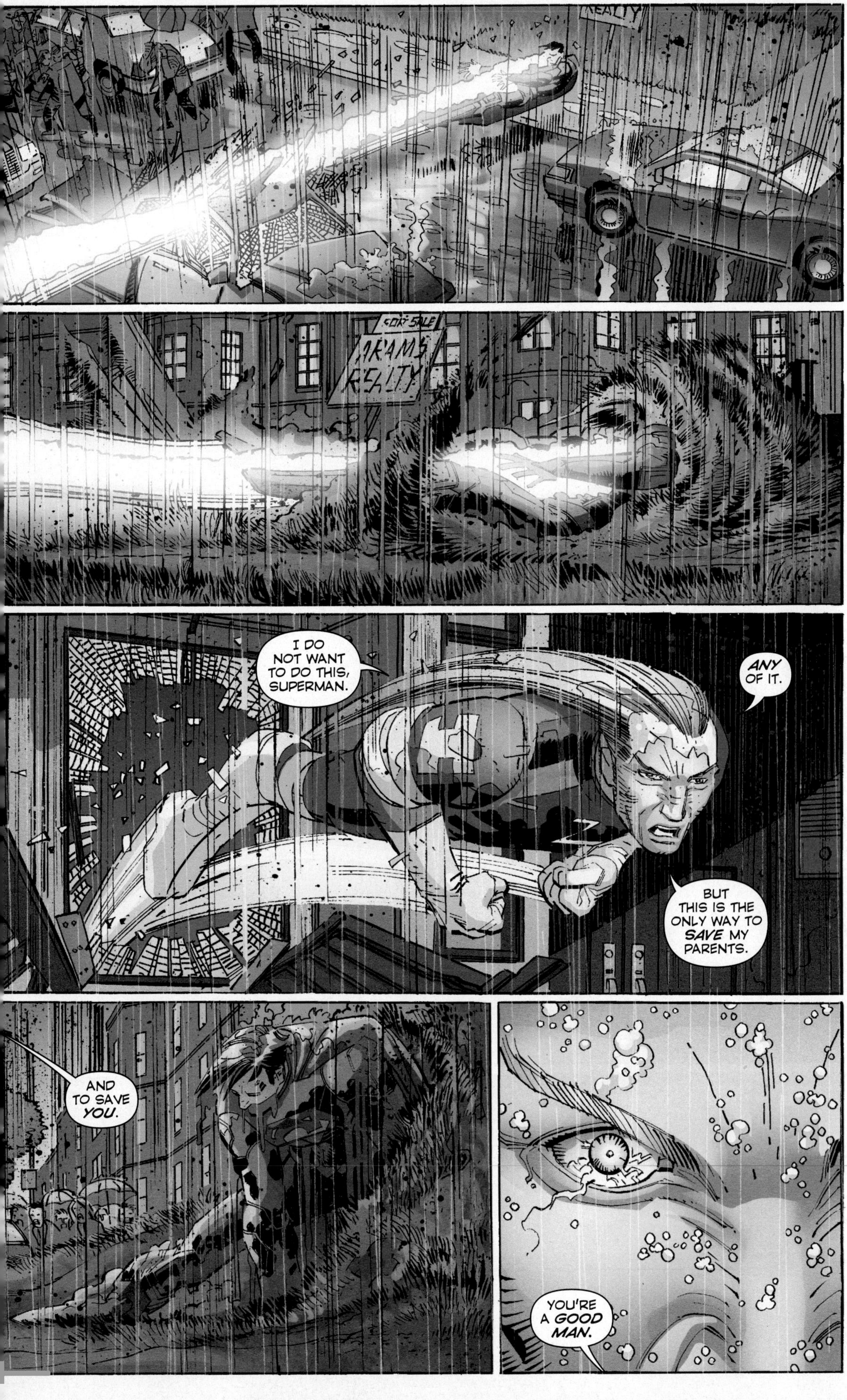
I DO NOT WANT TO DO THIS, SUPERMAN.
ANY OF IT.
BUT THIS IS THE ONLY WAY TO SAVE MY PARENTS.
AND TO SAVE YOU.
YOU'RE A GOOD MAN.

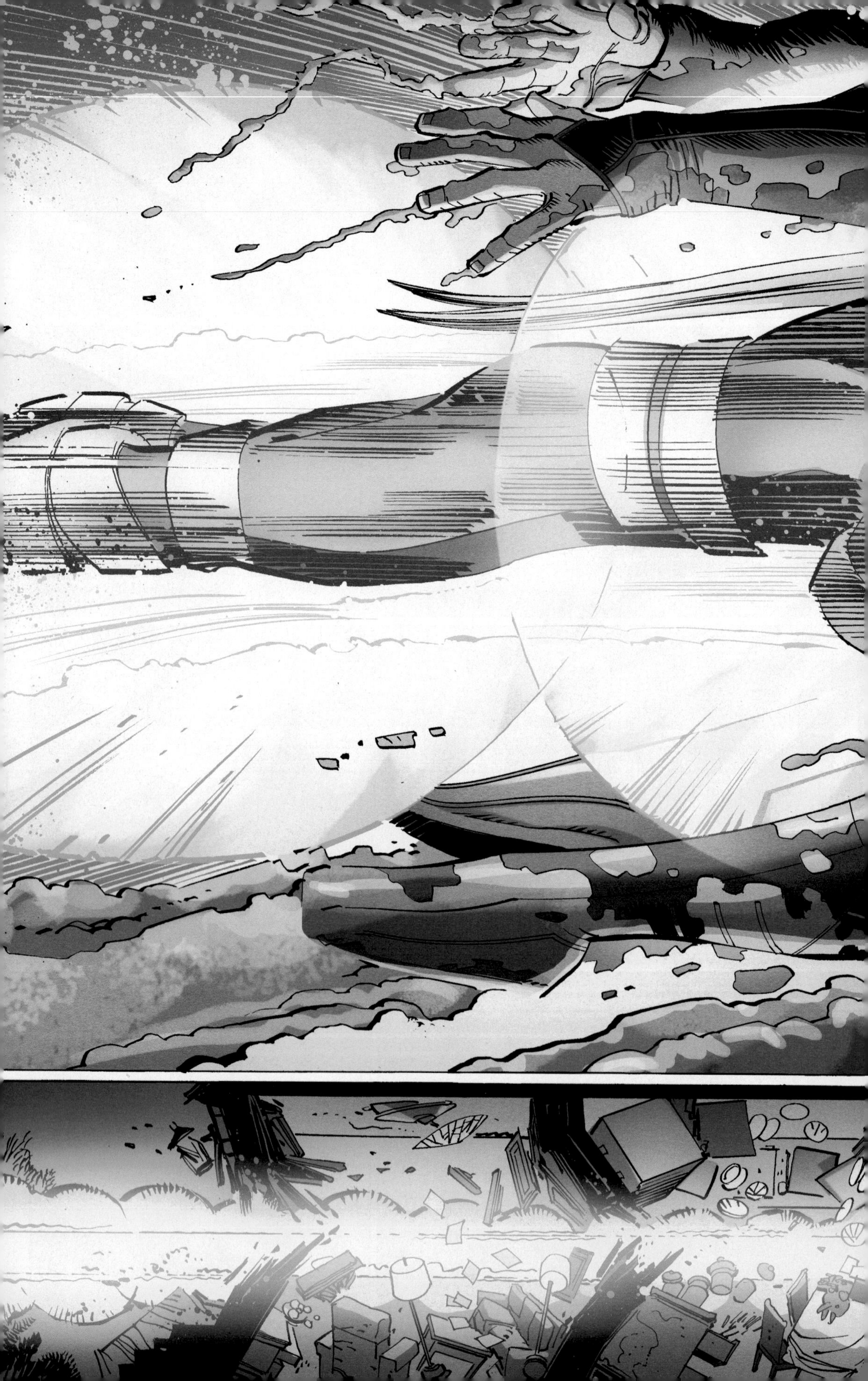

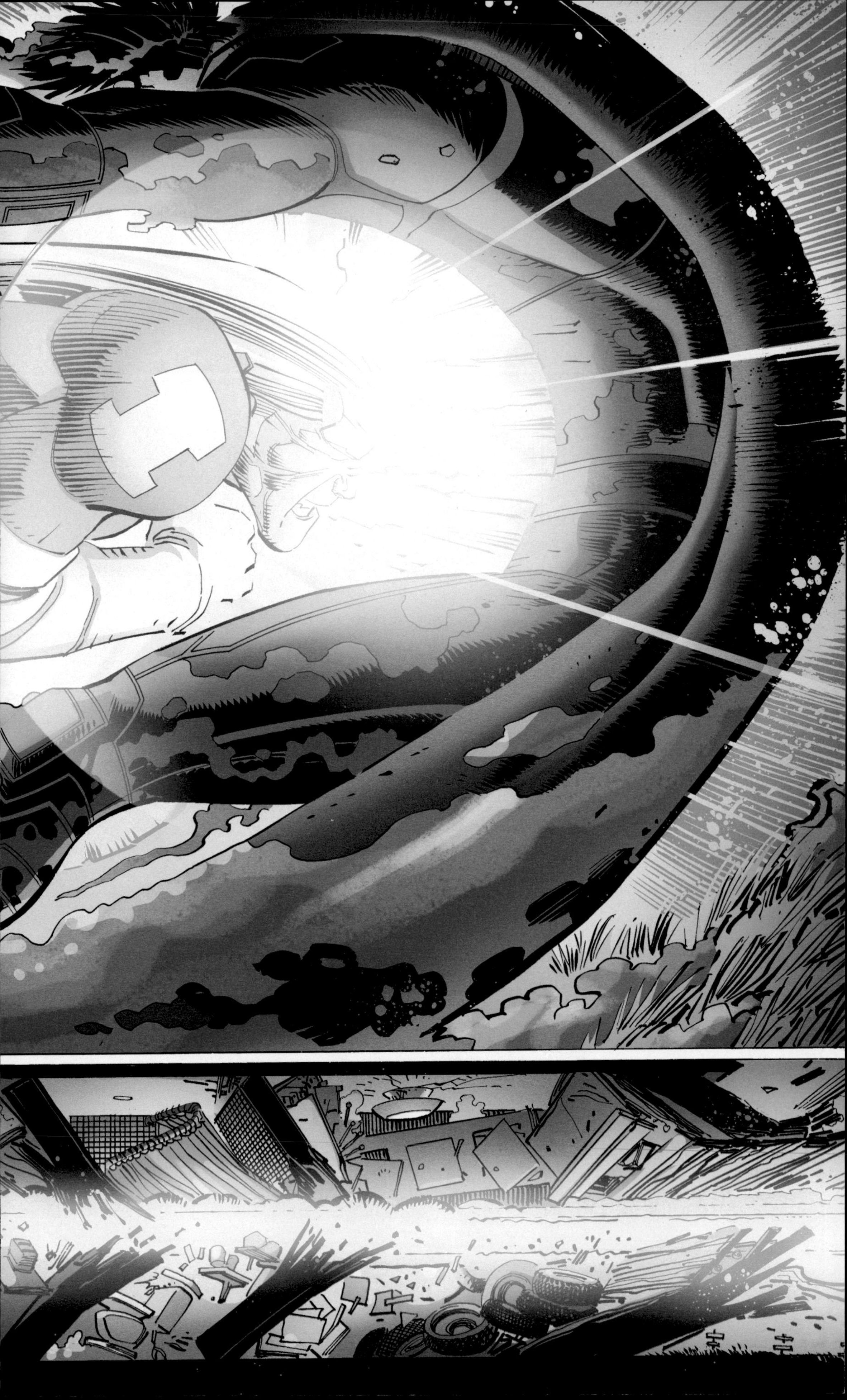

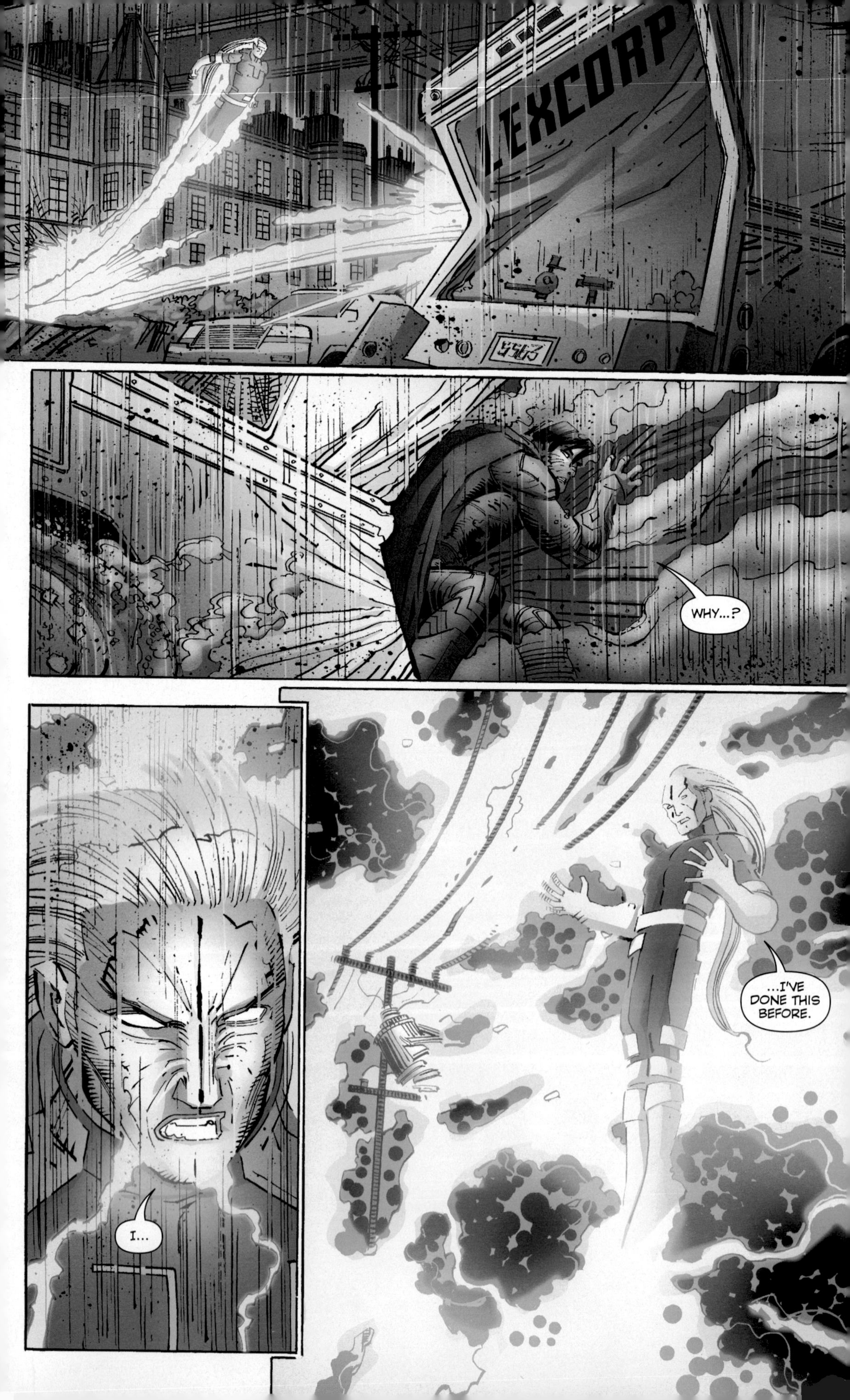
LEXCORP
5563
WHY...?
I...
...I'VE DONE THIS BEFORE.

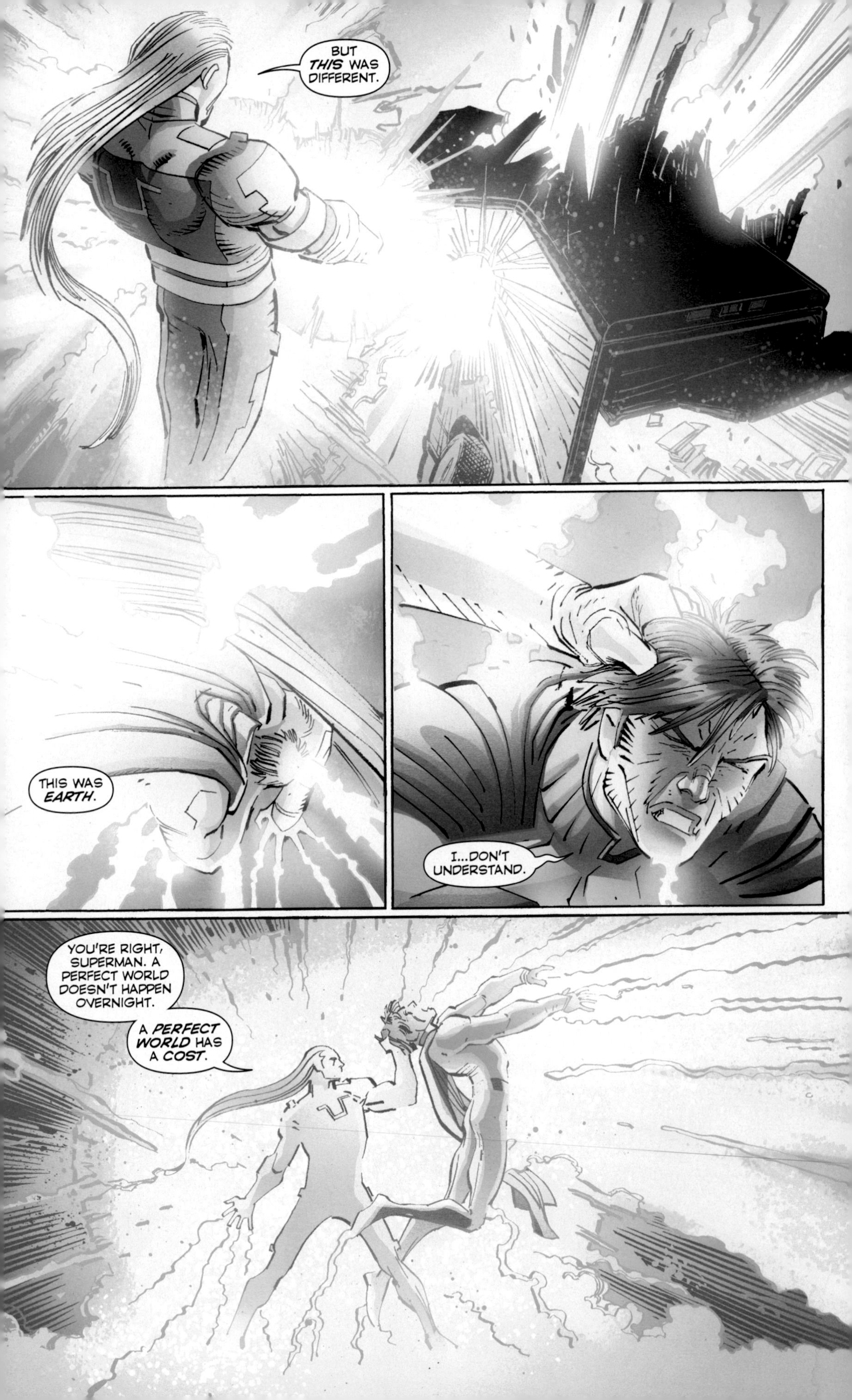
BUT *THIS* WAS DIFFERENT.
THIS WAS *EARTH*.
I...DON'T UNDERSTAND.
YOU'RE RIGHT, SUPERMAN. A PERFECT WORLD DOESN'T HAPPEN OVERNIGHT.
A *PERFECT WORLD* HAS A *COST*.

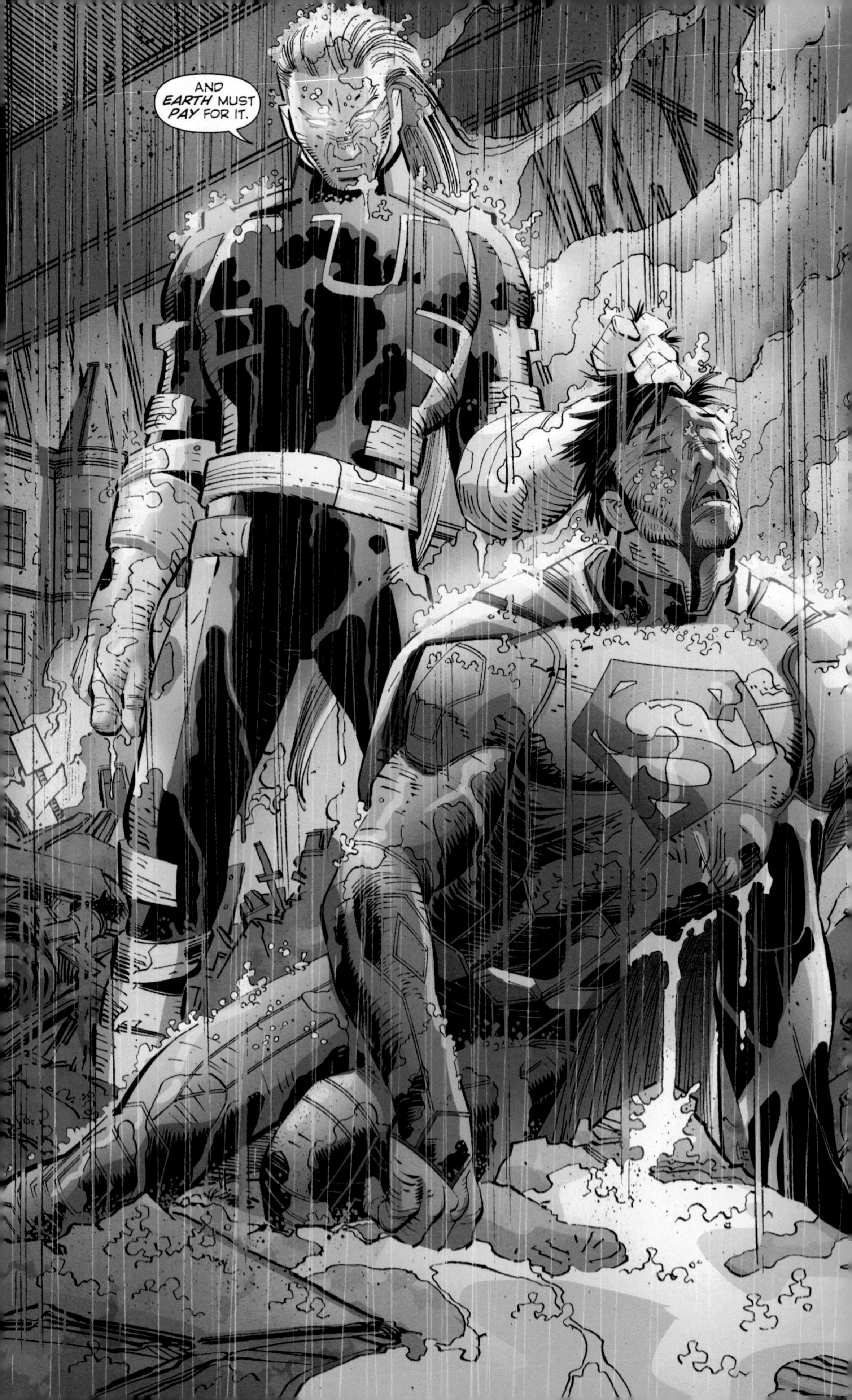
AND EARTH MUST PAY FOR IT.

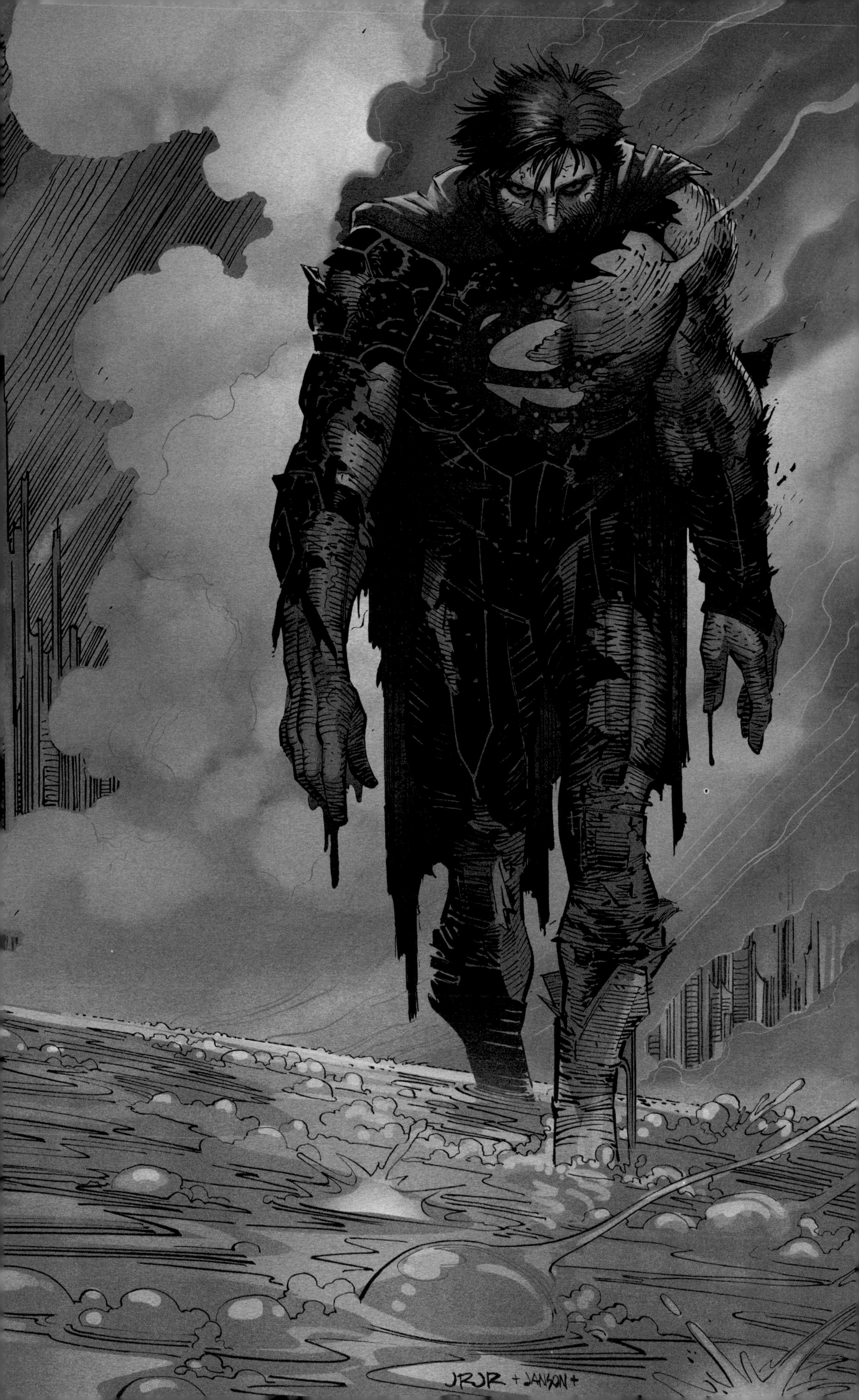
JRJR + JANSON +

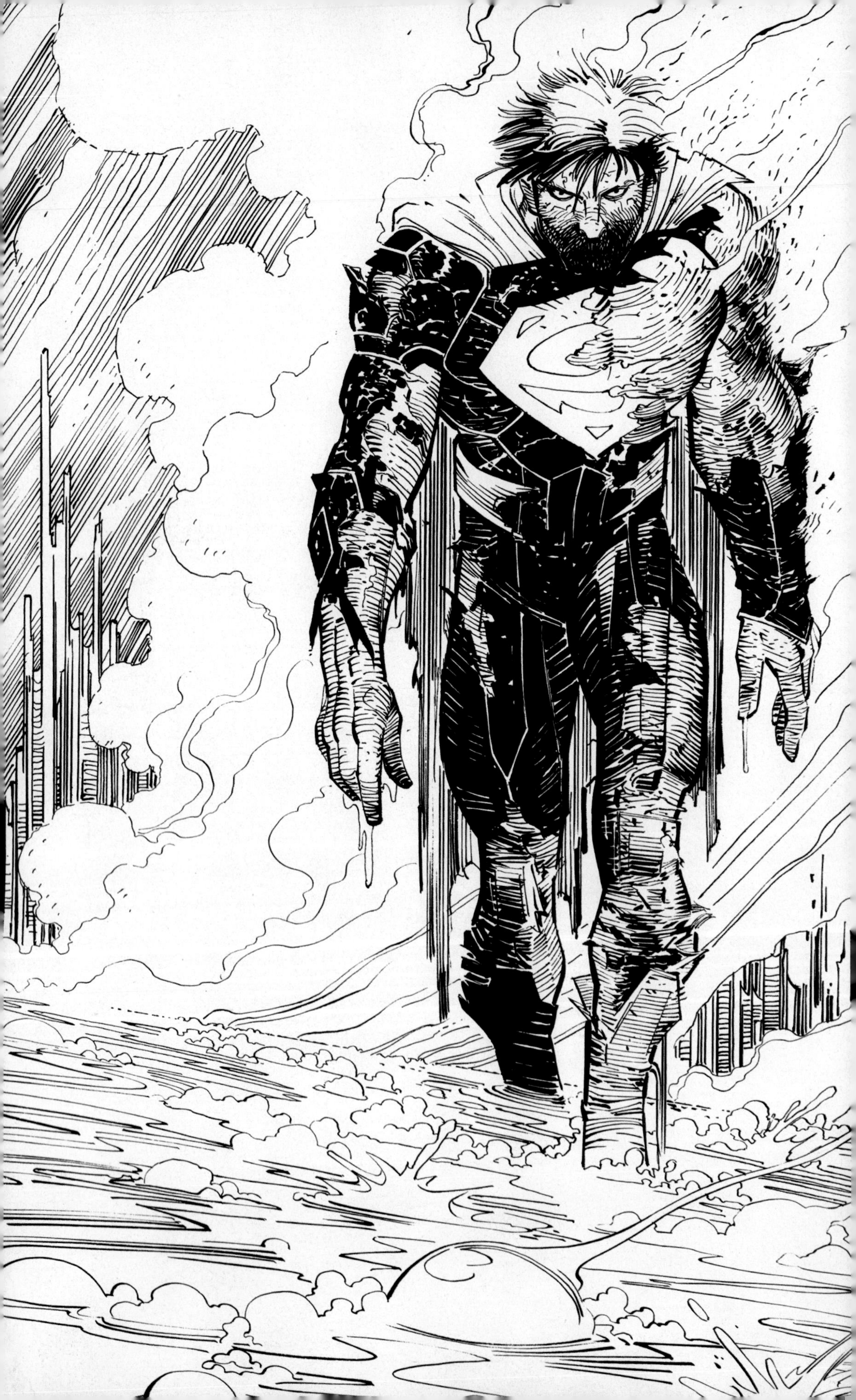

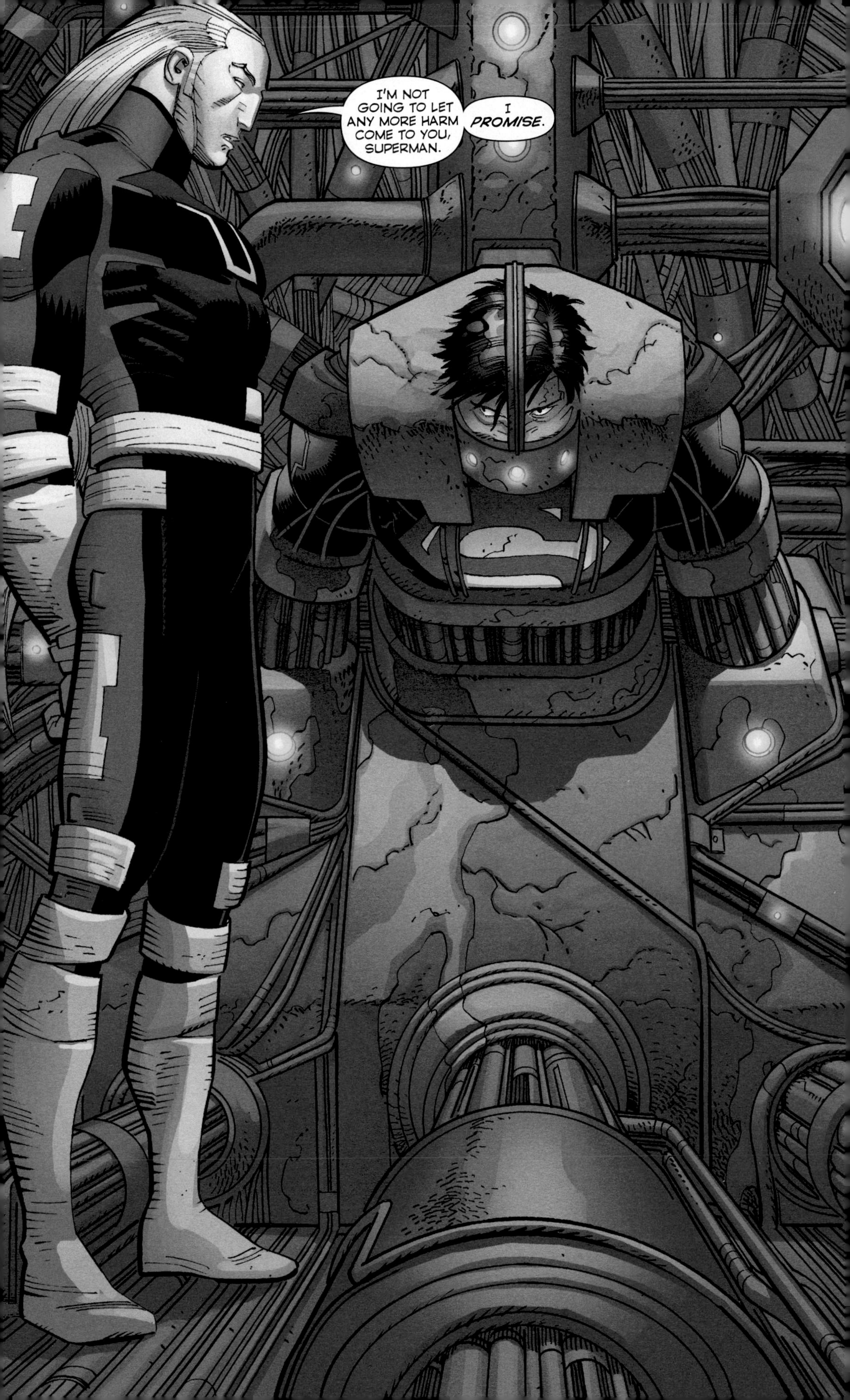
I'M NOT GOING TO LET ANY MORE HARM COME TO YOU, SUPERMAN.
I *PROMISE*.

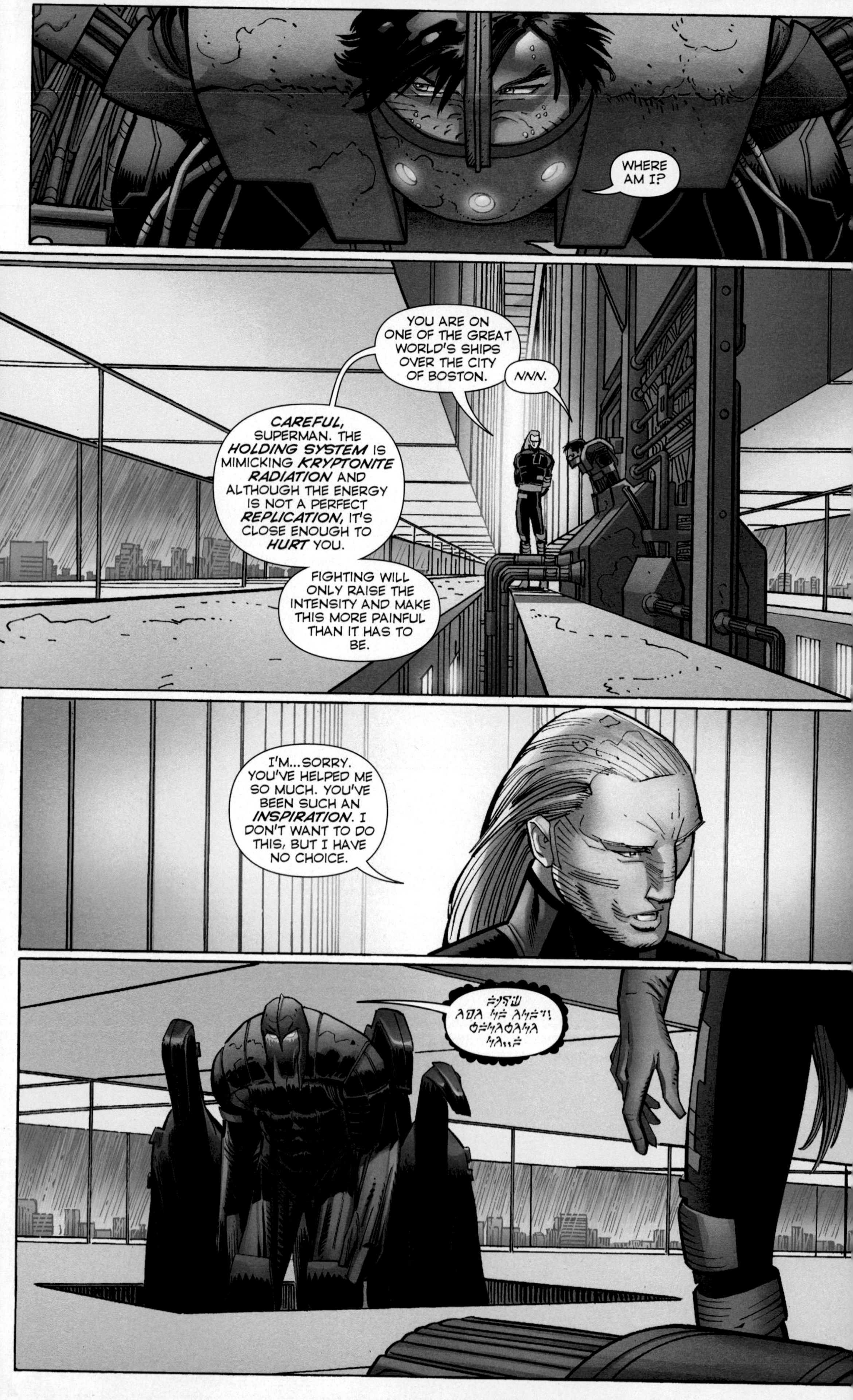
WHERE AM I?
YOU ARE ON ONE OF THE GREAT WORLD'S SHIPS OVER THE CITY OF BOSTON.
NNN.
CAREFUL, SUPERMAN. THE HOLDING SYSTEM IS MIMICKING KRYPTONITE RADIATION AND ALTHOUGH THE ENERGY IS NOT A PERFECT REPLICATION, IT'S CLOSE ENOUGH TO HURT YOU.
FIGHTING WILL ONLY RAISE THE INTENSITY AND MAKE THIS MORE PAINFUL THAN IT HAS TO BE.
I'M...SORRY. YOU'VE HELPED ME SO MUCH. YOU'VE BEEN SUCH AN INSPIRATION. I DON'T WANT TO DO THIS, BUT I HAVE NO CHOICE.

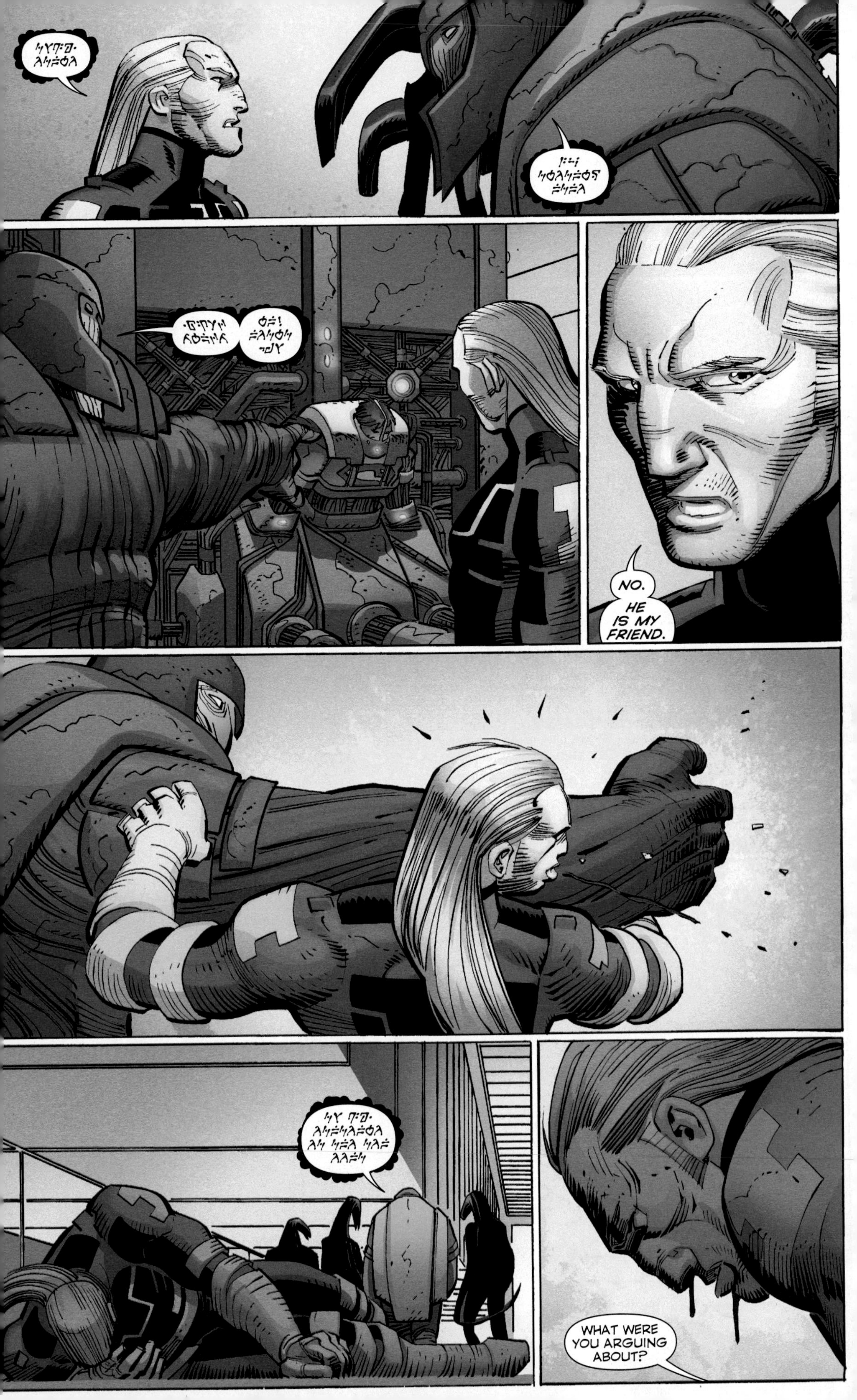
NO.
HE IS MY FRIEND.
WHAT WERE YOU ARGUING ABOUT?

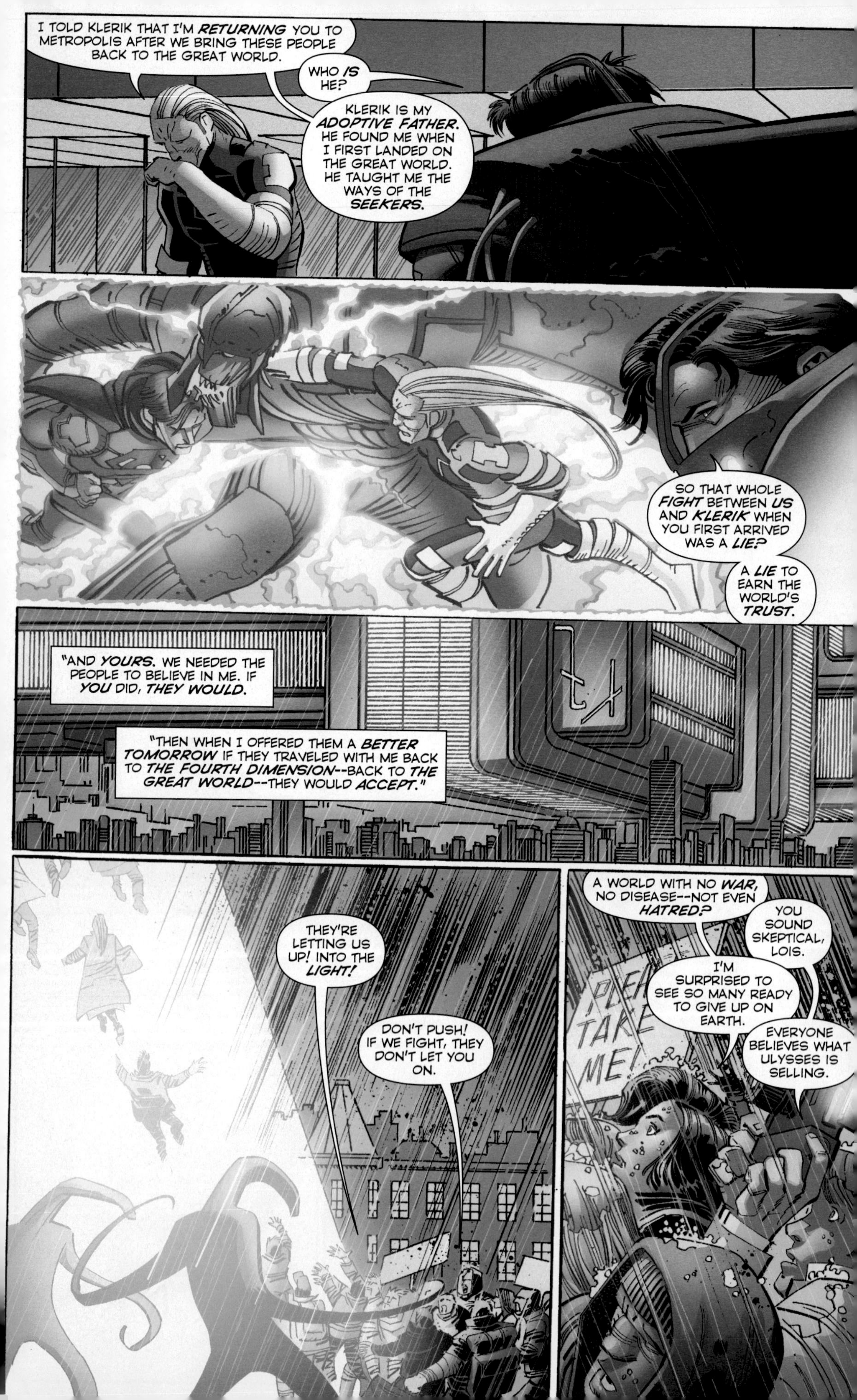

I TOLD KLERIK THAT I'M RETURNING YOU TO METROPOLIS AFTER WE BRING THESE PEOPLE BACK TO THE GREAT WORLD.
WHO IS HE?
KLERIK IS MY ADOPTIVE FATHER. HE FOUND ME WHEN I FIRST LANDED ON THE GREAT WORLD. HE TAUGHT ME THE WAYS OF THE SEEKERS.
SO THAT WHOLE FIGHT BETWEEN US AND KLERIK WHEN YOU FIRST ARRIVED WAS A LIE?
A LIE TO EARN THE WORLD'S TRUST.
"AND YOURS. WE NEEDED THE PEOPLE TO BELIEVE IN ME. IF YOU DID, THEY WOULD.
"THEN WHEN I OFFERED THEM A BETTER TOMORROW IF THEY TRAVELED WITH ME BACK TO THE FOURTH DIMENSION--BACK TO THE GREAT WORLD--THEY WOULD ACCEPT."
THEY'RE LETTING US UP! INTO THE LIGHT!
DON'T PUSH! IF WE FIGHT, THEY DON'T LET YOU ON.
A WORLD WITH NO WAR, NO DISEASE--NOT EVEN HATRED?
YOU SOUND SKEPTICAL, LOIS.
I'M SURPRISED TO SEE SO MANY READY TO GIVE UP ON EARTH.
EVERYONE BELIEVES WHAT ULYSSES IS SELLING.
TAKE ME!

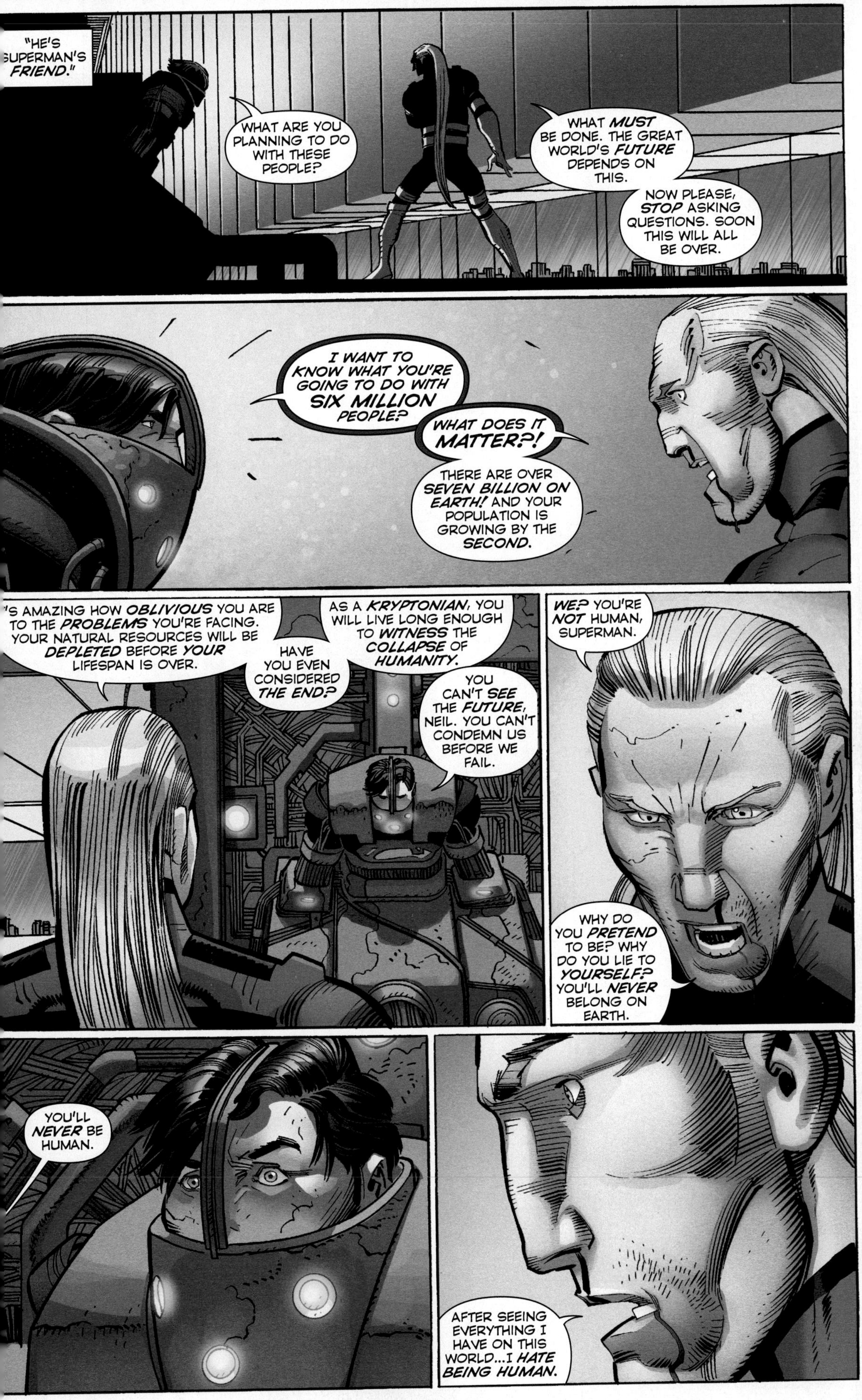

"HE'S SUPERMAN'S FRIEND."
WHAT ARE YOU PLANNING TO DO WITH THESE PEOPLE?
WHAT MUST BE DONE. THE GREAT WORLD'S FUTURE DEPENDS ON THIS.
NOW PLEASE, STOP ASKING QUESTIONS. SOON THIS WILL ALL BE OVER.
I WANT TO KNOW WHAT YOU'RE GOING TO DO WITH SIX MILLION PEOPLE?
WHAT DOES IT MATTER?!
THERE ARE OVER SEVEN BILLION ON EARTH! AND YOUR POPULATION IS GROWING BY THE SECOND.
'S AMAZING HOW OBLIVIOUS YOU ARE TO THE PROBLEMS YOU'RE FACING. YOUR NATURAL RESOURCES WILL BE DEPLETED BEFORE YOUR LIFESPAN IS OVER.
HAVE YOU EVEN CONSIDERED THE END?
AS A KRYPTONIAN, YOU WILL LIVE LONG ENOUGH TO WITNESS THE COLLAPSE OF HUMANITY.
YOU CAN'T SEE THE FUTURE, NEIL. YOU CAN'T CONDEMN US BEFORE WE FAIL.
WE? YOU'RE NOT HUMAN, SUPERMAN.
WHY DO YOU PRETEND TO BE? WHY DO YOU LIE TO YOURSELF? YOU'LL NEVER BELONG ON EARTH.
YOU'LL NEVER BE HUMAN.
AFTER SEEING EVERYTHING I HAVE ON THIS WORLD...I HATE BEING HUMAN.

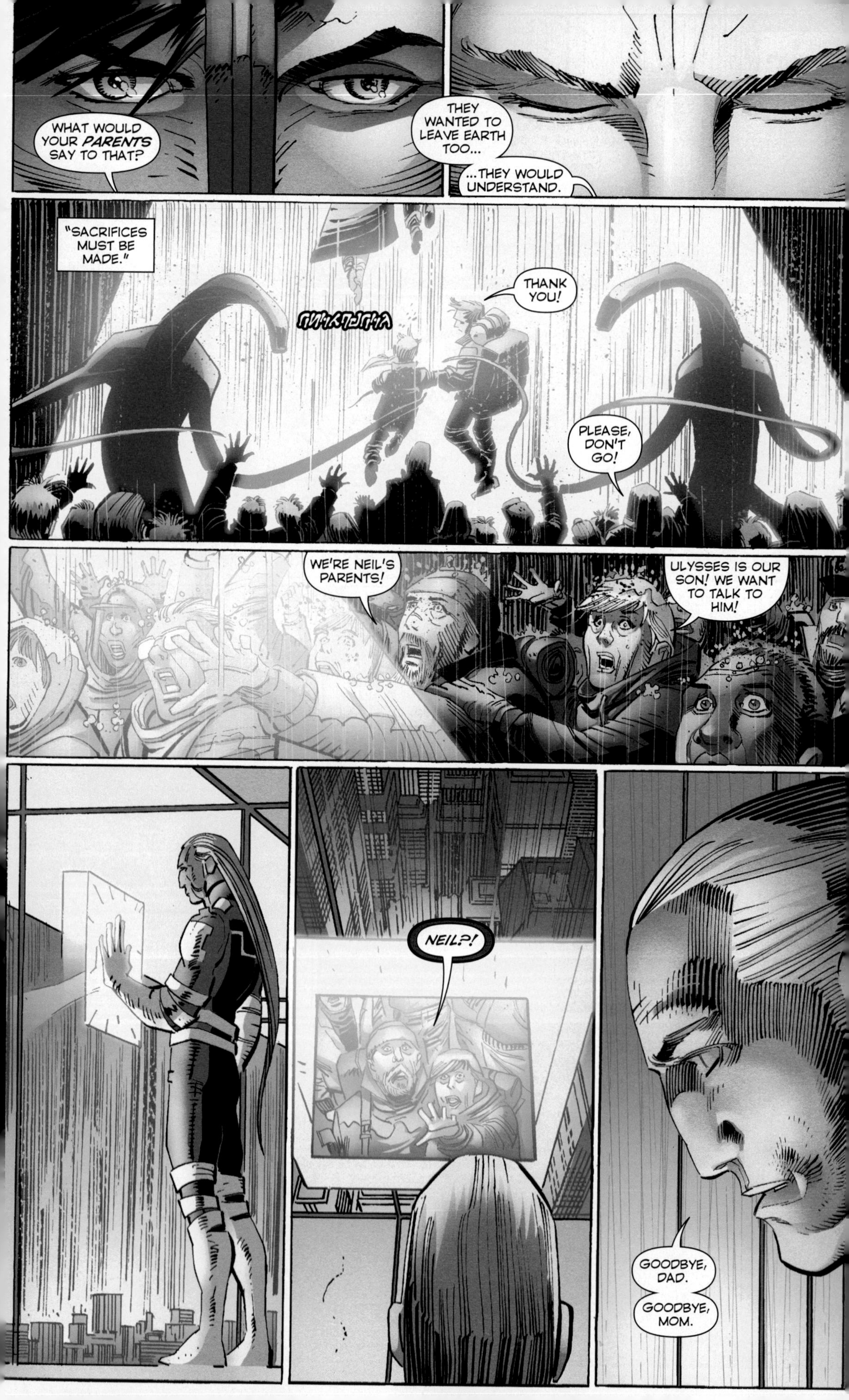
WHAT WOULD YOUR PARENTS SAY TO THAT?
THEY WANTED TO LEAVE EARTH TOO...
...THEY WOULD UNDERSTAND.
"SACRIFICES MUST BE MADE."
THANK YOU!
PLEASE, DON'T GO!
WE'RE NEIL'S PARENTS!
ULYSSES IS OUR SON! WE WANT TO TALK TO HIM!
NEIL?!
GOODBYE, DAD.
GOODBYE, MOM.

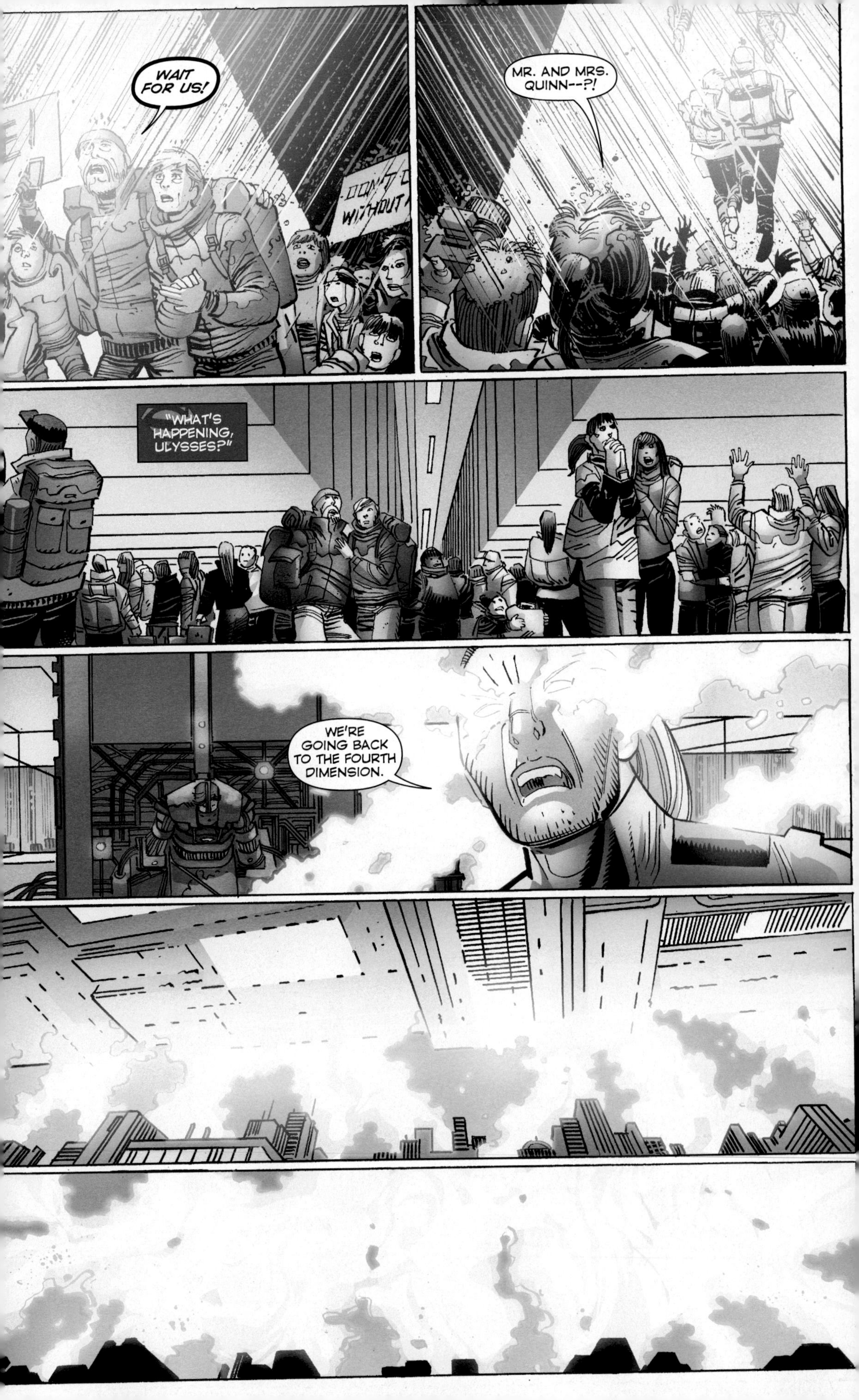

WAIT FOR US!
DON'T GO WITHOUT
MR. AND MRS. QUINN--?!
"WHAT'S HAPPENING, ULYSSES?"
WE'RE GOING BACK TO THE FOURTH DIMENSION.

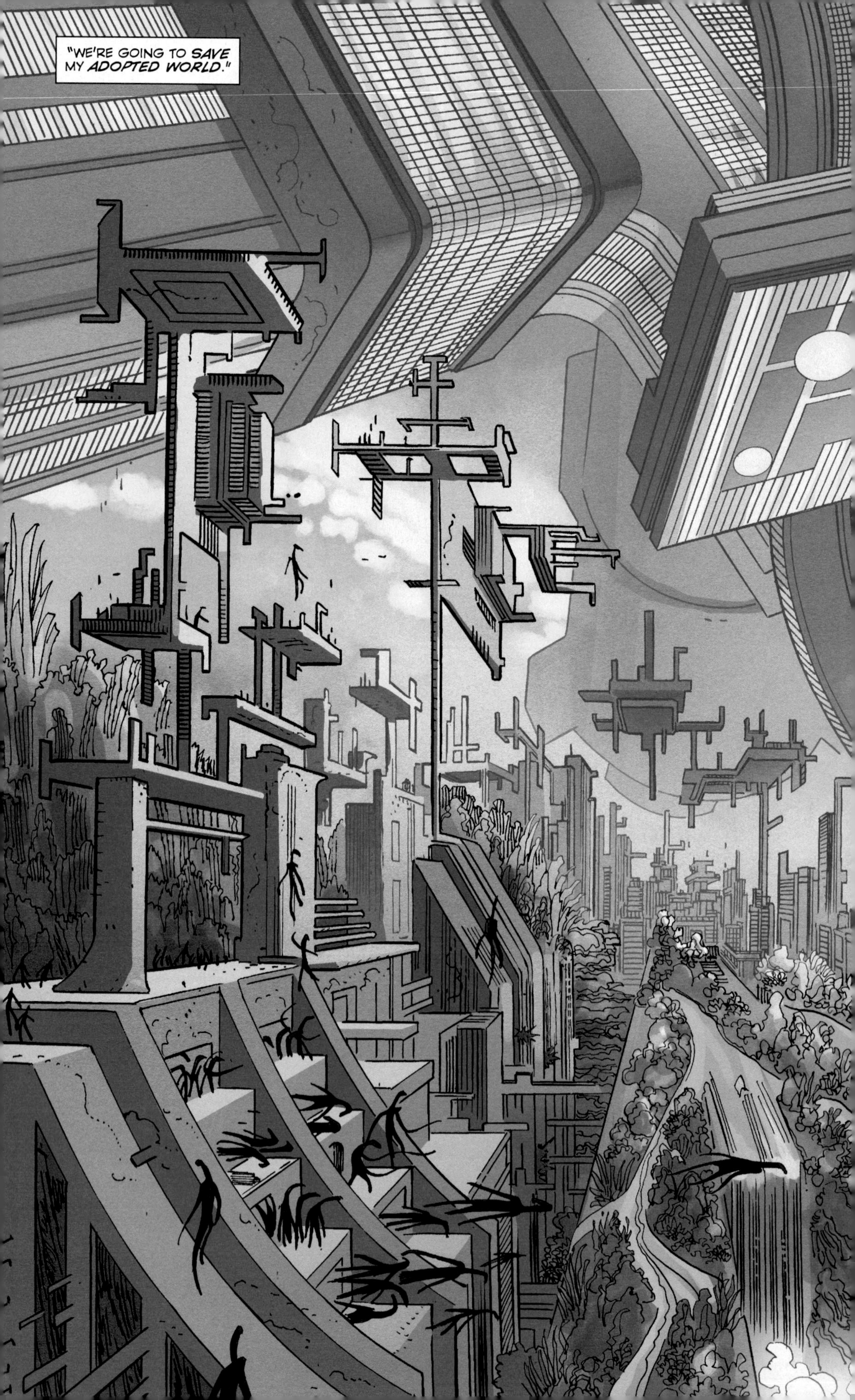
"WE'RE GOING TO SAVE MY ADOPTED WORLD."

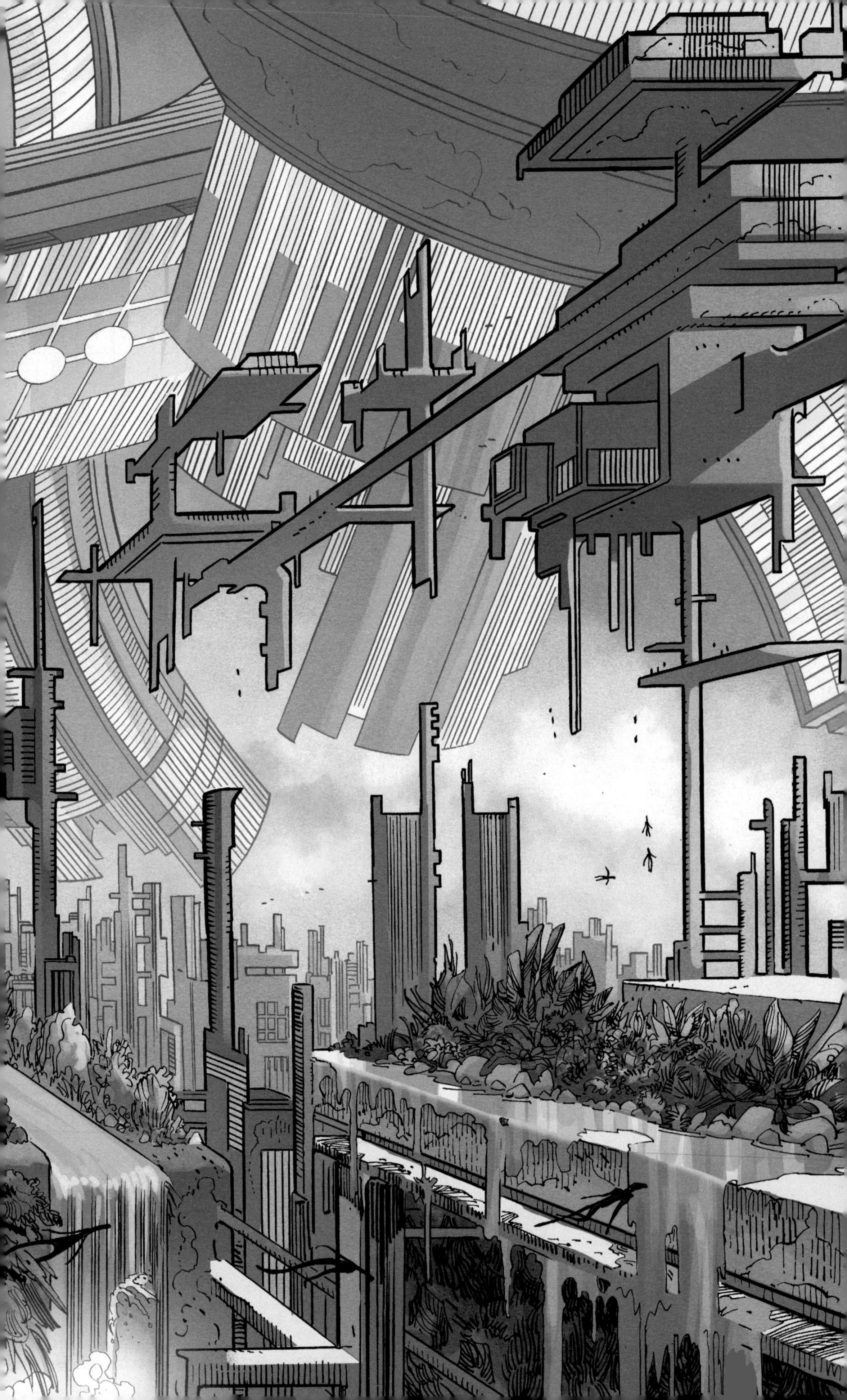

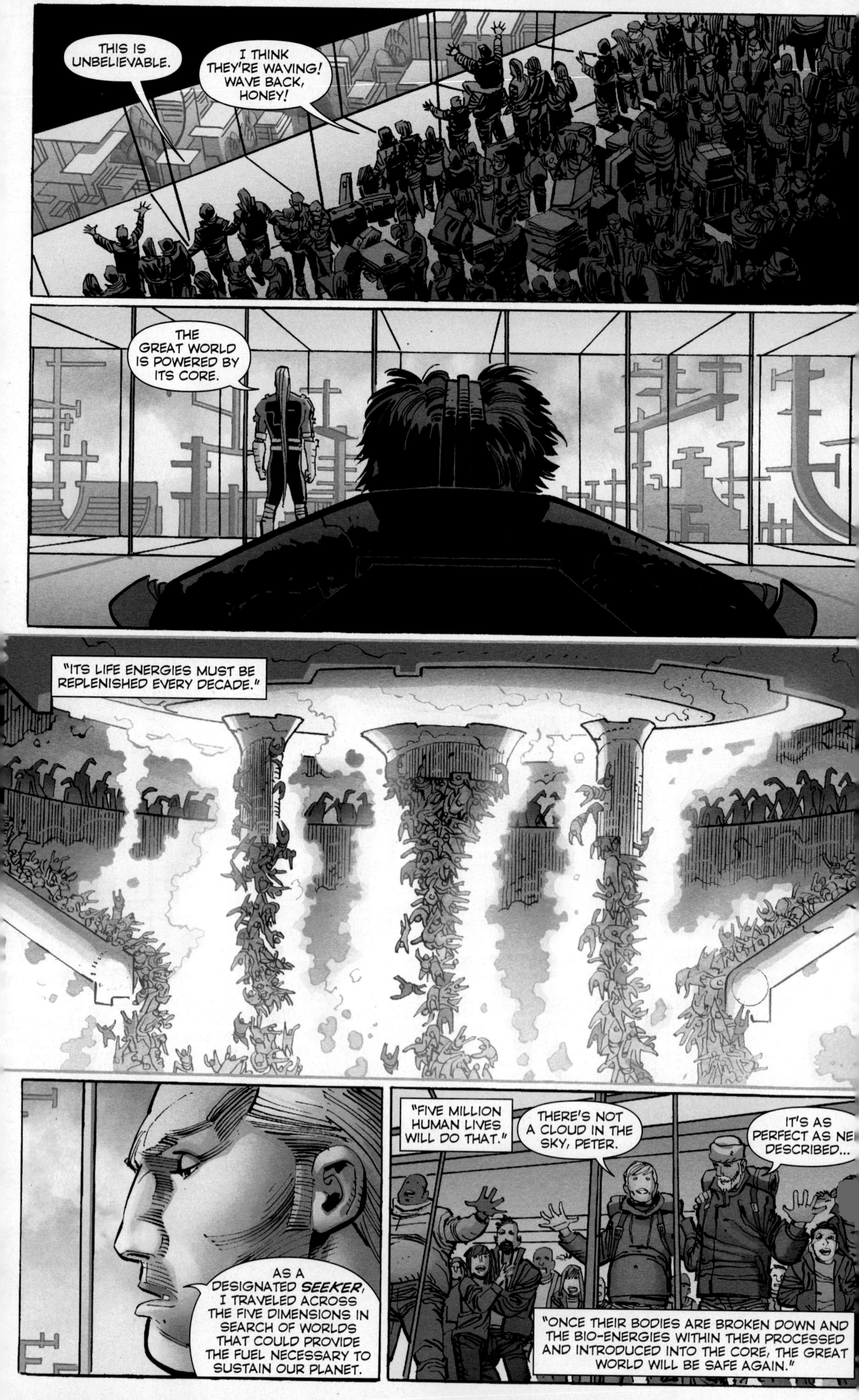
THIS IS UNBELIEVABLE.
I THINK THEY'RE WAVING! WAVE BACK, HONEY!
THE GREAT WORLD IS POWERED BY ITS CORE.
"ITS LIFE ENERGIES MUST BE REPLENISHED EVERY DECADE."
AS A DESIGNATED *SEEKER*, I TRAVELED ACROSS THE FIVE DIMENSIONS IN SEARCH OF WORLDS THAT COULD PROVIDE THE FUEL NECESSARY TO SUSTAIN OUR PLANET.
"FIVE MILLION HUMAN LIVES WILL DO THAT."
THERE'S NOT A CLOUD IN THE SKY, PETER.
IT'S AS PERFECT AS NE DESCRIBED...
"ONCE THEIR BODIES ARE BROKEN DOWN AND THE BIO-ENERGIES WITHIN THEM PROCESSED AND INTRODUCED INTO THE CORE, THE GREAT WORLD WILL BE SAFE AGAIN."

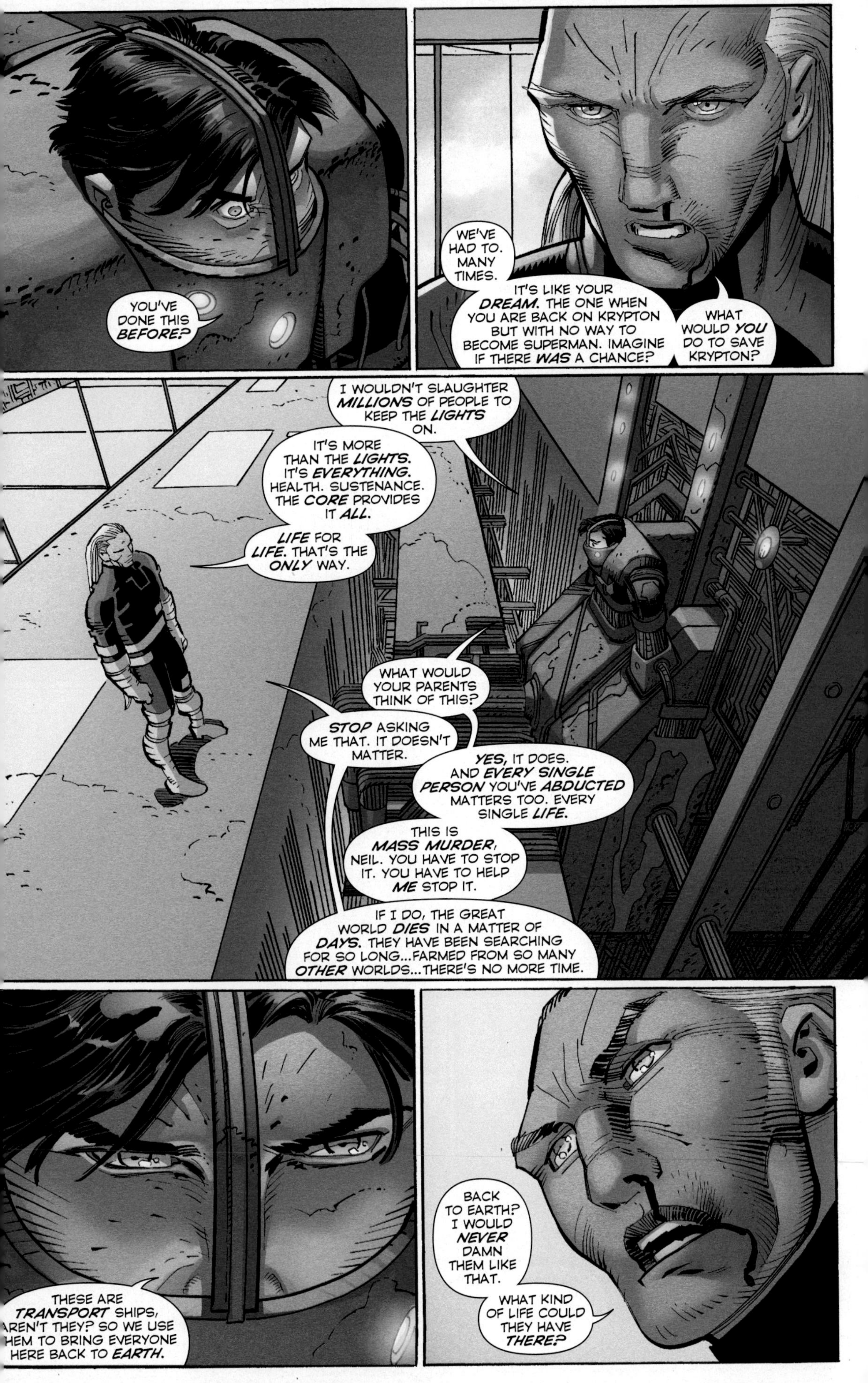
YOU'VE DONE THIS BEFORE?
WE'VE HAD TO. MANY TIMES.
IT'S LIKE YOUR DREAM. THE ONE WHEN YOU ARE BACK ON KRYPTON BUT WITH NO WAY TO BECOME SUPERMAN. IMAGINE IF THERE WAS A CHANCE?
WHAT WOULD YOU DO TO SAVE KRYPTON?
I WOULDN'T SLAUGHTER MILLIONS OF PEOPLE TO KEEP THE LIGHTS ON.
IT'S MORE THAN THE LIGHTS. IT'S EVERYTHING. HEALTH. SUSTENANCE. THE CORE PROVIDES IT ALL.
LIFE FOR LIFE. THAT'S THE ONLY WAY.
WHAT WOULD YOUR PARENTS THINK OF THIS?
STOP ASKING ME THAT. IT DOESN'T MATTER.
YES, IT DOES. AND EVERY SINGLE PERSON YOU'VE ABDUCTED MATTERS TOO. EVERY SINGLE LIFE.
THIS IS MASS MURDER, NEIL. YOU HAVE TO STOP IT. YOU HAVE TO HELP ME STOP IT.
IF I DO, THE GREAT WORLD DIES IN A MATTER OF DAYS. THEY HAVE BEEN SEARCHING FOR SO LONG...FARMED FROM SO MANY OTHER WORLDS...THERE'S NO MORE TIME.
THESE ARE TRANSPORT SHIPS, AREN'T THEY? SO WE USE THEM TO BRING EVERYONE HERE BACK TO EARTH.
BACK TO EARTH? I WOULD NEVER DAMN THEM LIKE THAT.
WHAT KIND OF LIFE COULD THEY HAVE THERE?

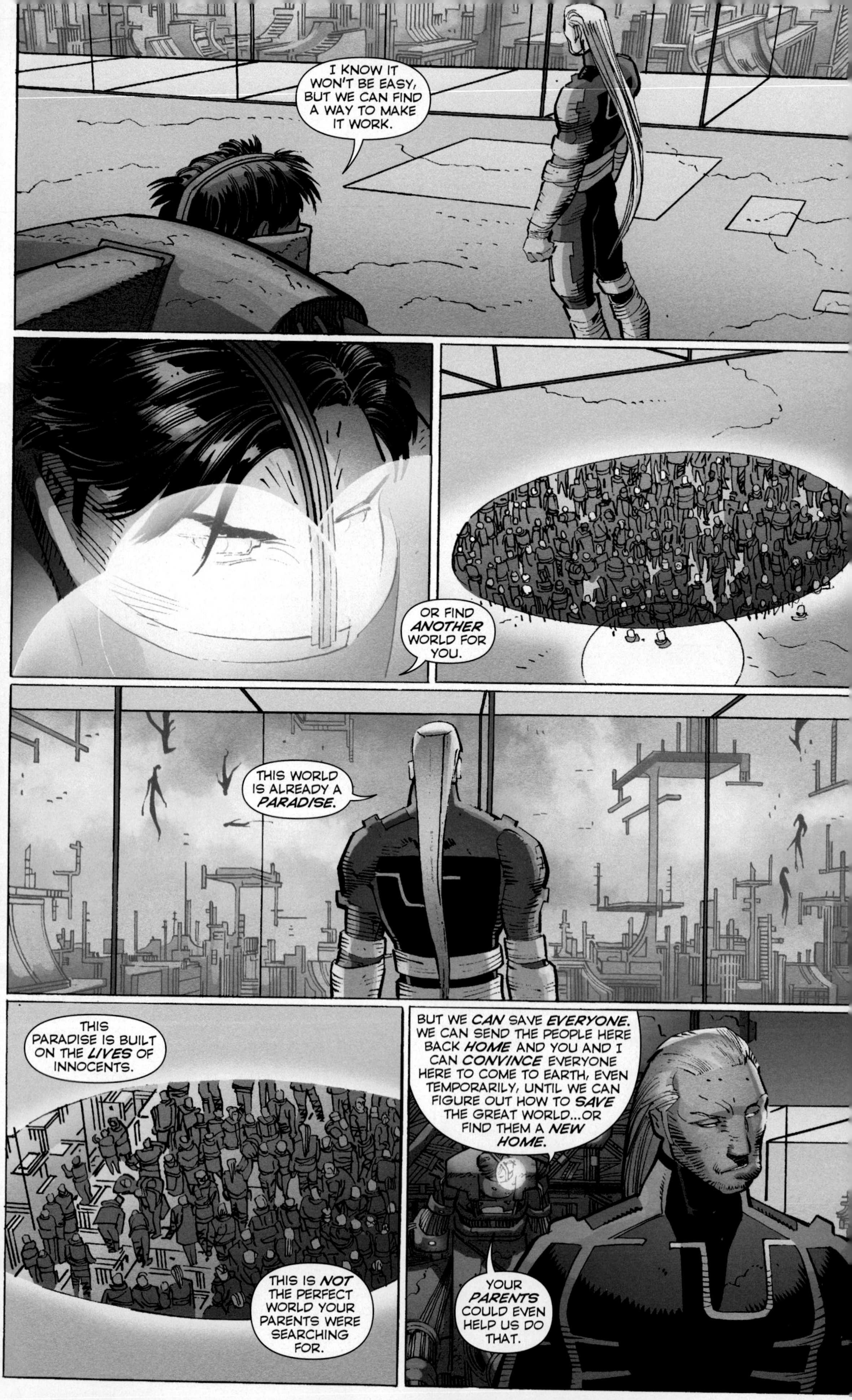
I KNOW IT WON'T BE EASY, BUT WE CAN FIND A WAY TO MAKE IT WORK.
OR FIND *ANOTHER* WORLD FOR YOU.
THIS WORLD IS ALREADY A *PARADISE.*
THIS PARADISE IS BUILT ON THE *LIVES* OF INNOCENTS.
THIS IS *NOT* THE PERFECT WORLD YOUR PARENTS WERE SEARCHING FOR.
BUT WE *CAN* SAVE *EVERYONE.* WE CAN SEND THE PEOPLE HERE BACK *HOME* AND YOU AND I CAN *CONVINCE* EVERYONE HERE TO COME TO EARTH, EVEN TEMPORARILY, UNTIL WE CAN FIGURE OUT HOW TO *SAVE* THE GREAT WORLD...OR FIND THEM A *NEW HOME.*
YOUR *PARENTS* COULD EVEN HELP US DO THAT.

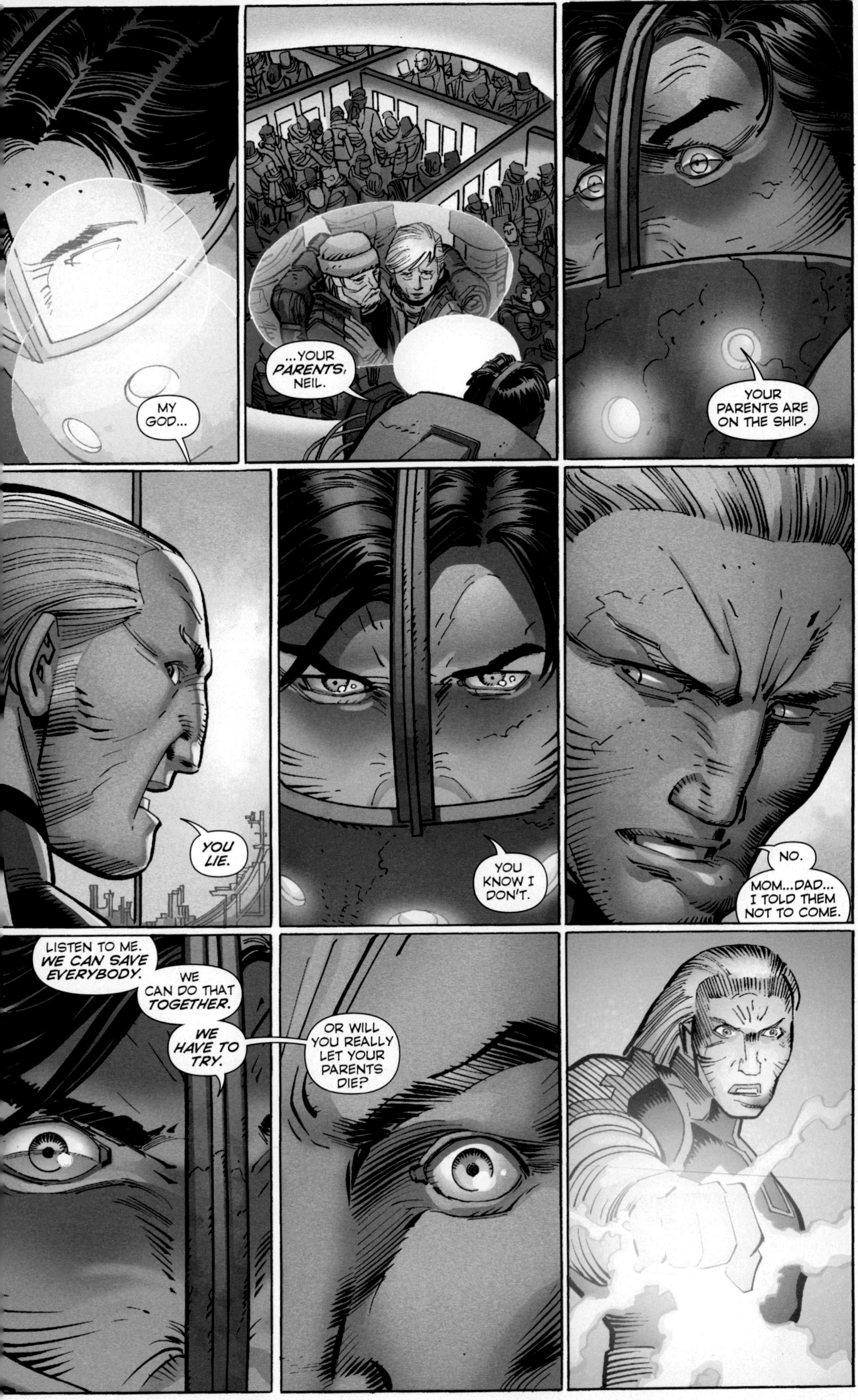
MY GOD...
...YOUR PARENTS, NEIL.
YOUR PARENTS ARE ON THE SHIP.
YOU LIE.
YOU KNOW I DON'T.
NO.
MOM...DAD... I TOLD THEM NOT TO COME.
LISTEN TO ME. WE CAN SAVE EVERYBODY.
WE CAN DO THAT TOGETHER.
WE HAVE TO TRY.
OR WILL YOU REALLY LET YOUR PARENTS DIE?

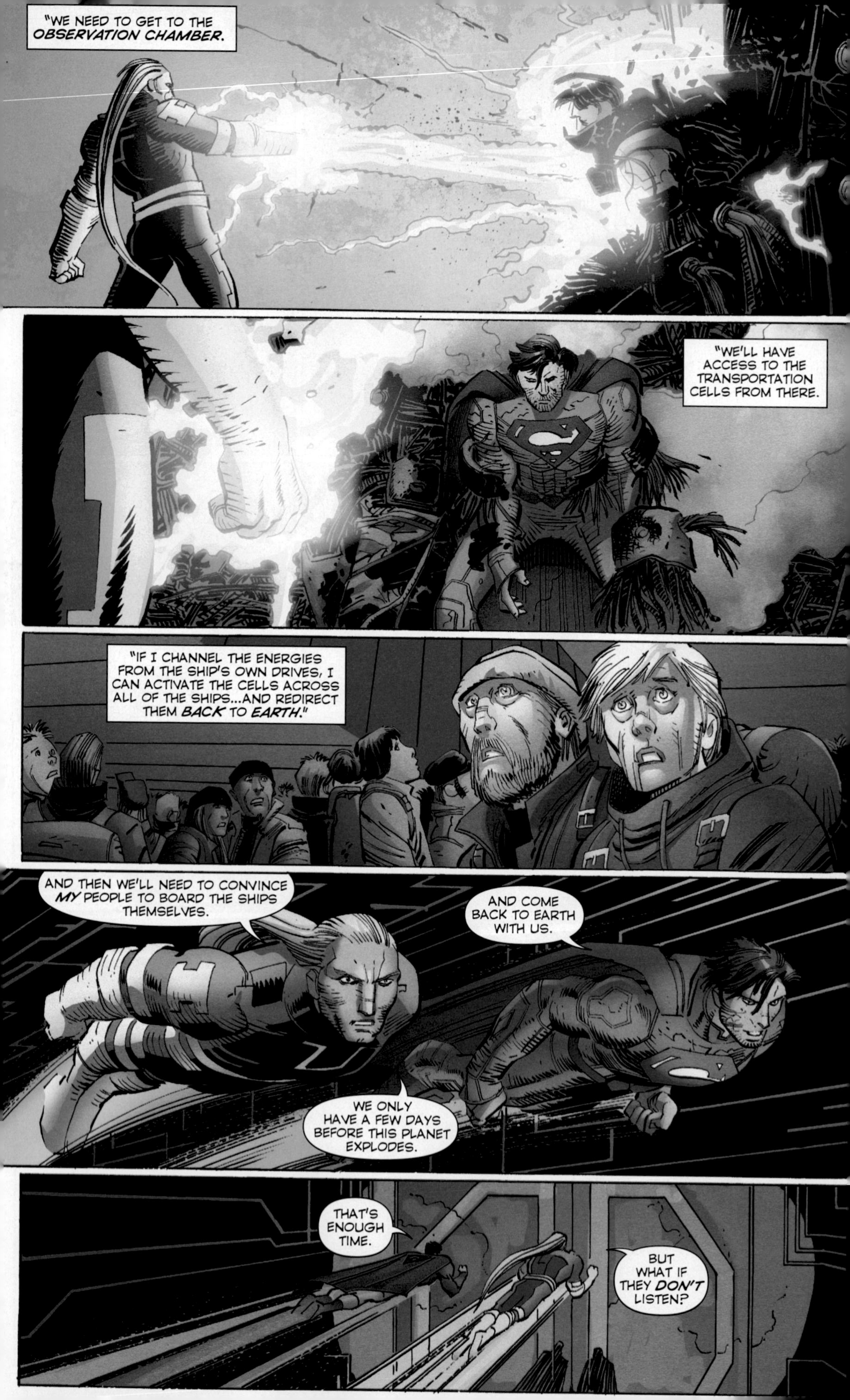
"WE NEED TO GET TO THE OBSERVATION CHAMBER.
"WE'LL HAVE ACCESS TO THE TRANSPORTATION CELLS FROM THERE.
"IF I CHANNEL THE ENERGIES FROM THE SHIP'S OWN DRIVES, I CAN ACTIVATE THE CELLS ACROSS ALL OF THE SHIPS...AND REDIRECT THEM BACK TO EARTH."
AND THEN WE'LL NEED TO CONVINCE MY PEOPLE TO BOARD THE SHIPS THEMSELVES.
AND COME BACK TO EARTH WITH US.
WE ONLY HAVE A FEW DAYS BEFORE THIS PLANET EXPLODES.
THAT'S ENOUGH TIME.
BUT WHAT IF THEY DON'T LISTEN?

MAKE THEM LISTEN.

...ᗺᑀ!

...ᗅᑀ...

I NEED ACCESS TO THE *FUEL* IN THE *DRIVES* SO I CAN *ABSORB* IT. THAT *CIRCULAR DOOR* ON THE FLOOR--

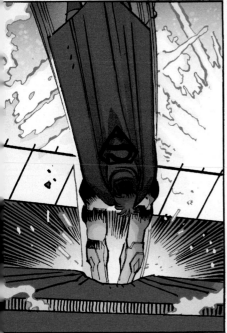

GOT IT.

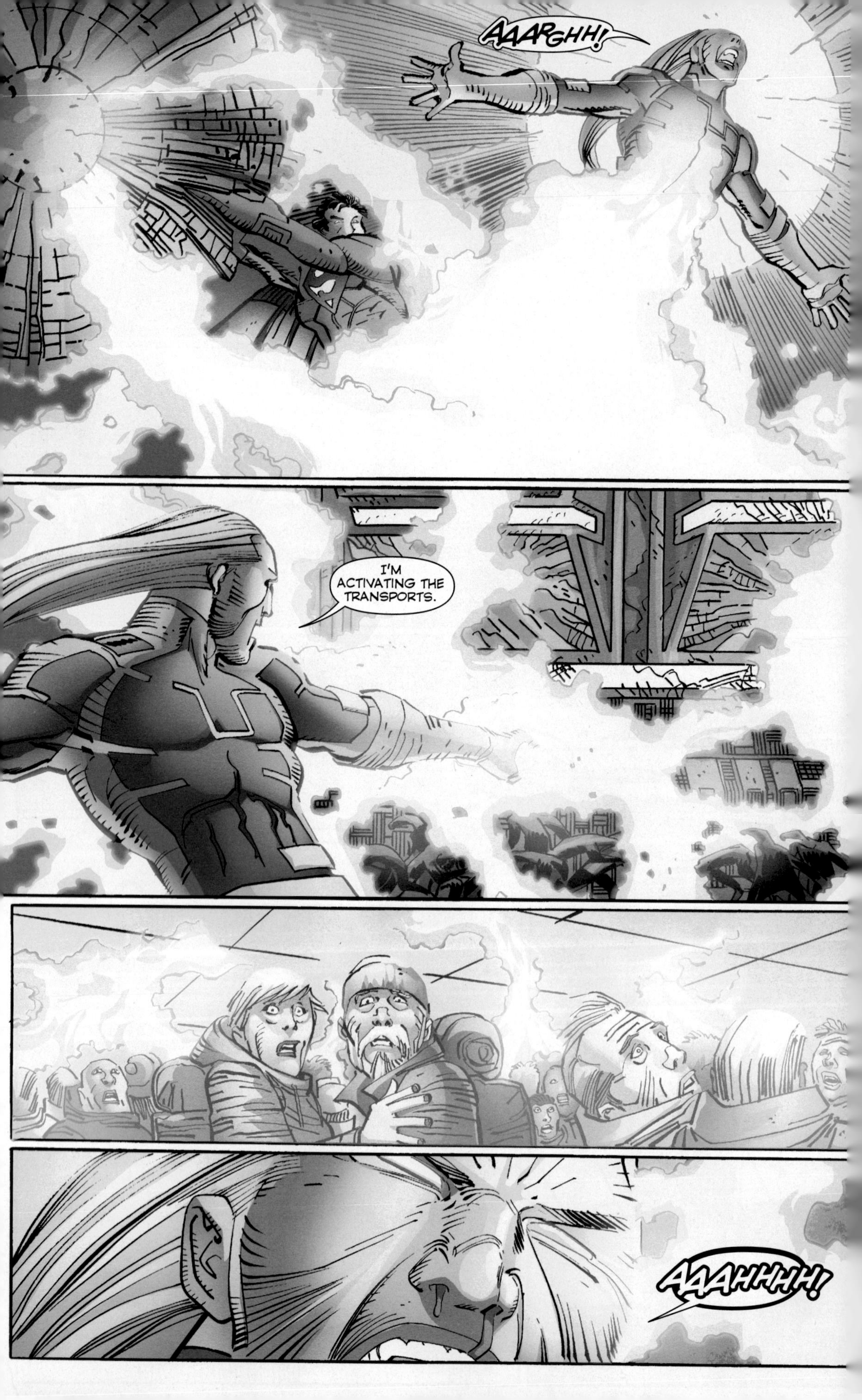
AAARGHH!
I'M ACTIVATING THE TRANSPORTS.
AAAHHHH!

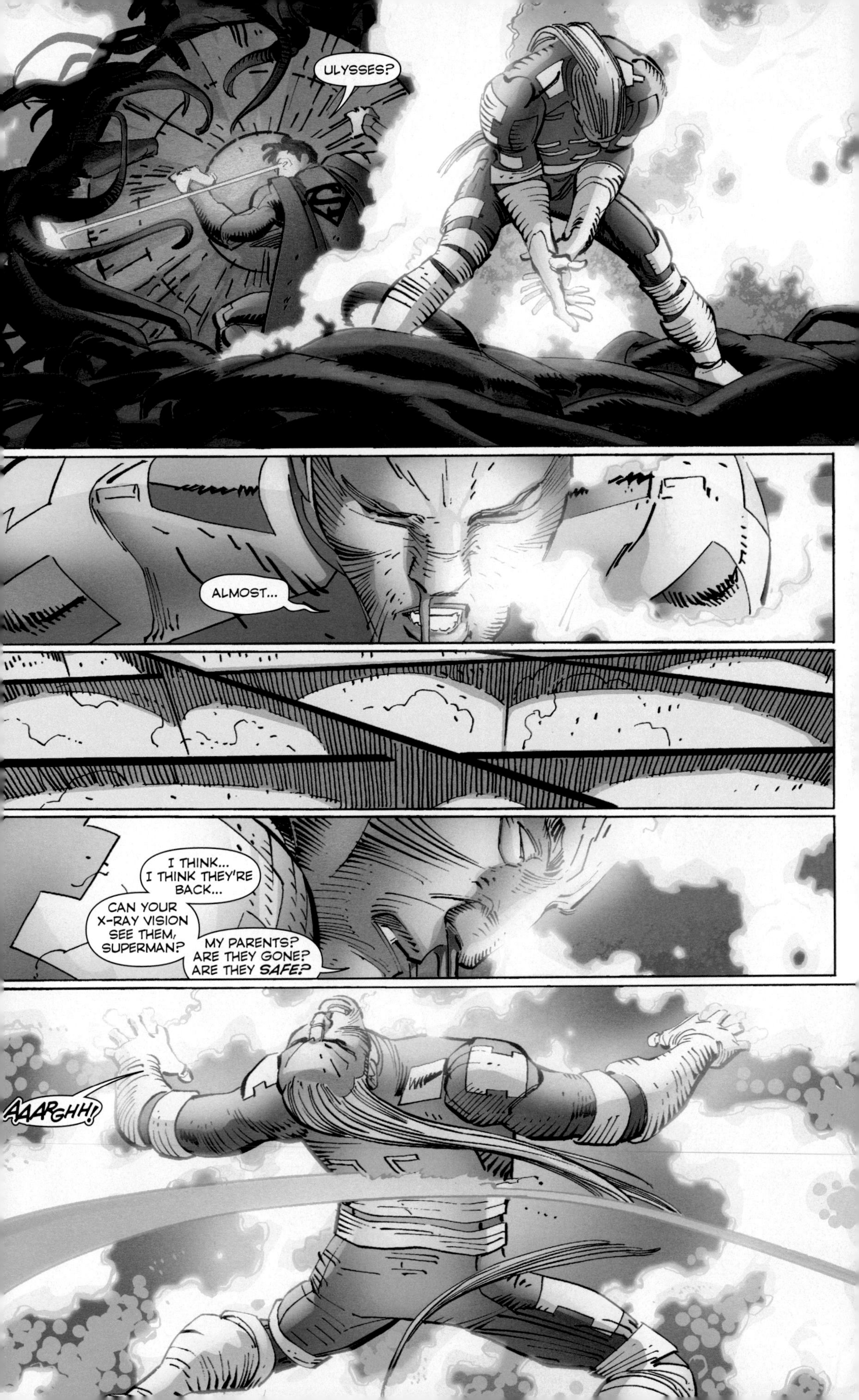
ULYSSES?
ALMOST...
I THINK... I THINK THEY'RE BACK...
CAN YOUR X-RAY VISION SEE THEM, SUPERMAN?
MY PARENTS? ARE THEY GONE? ARE THEY *SAFE?*
AAARGHH!

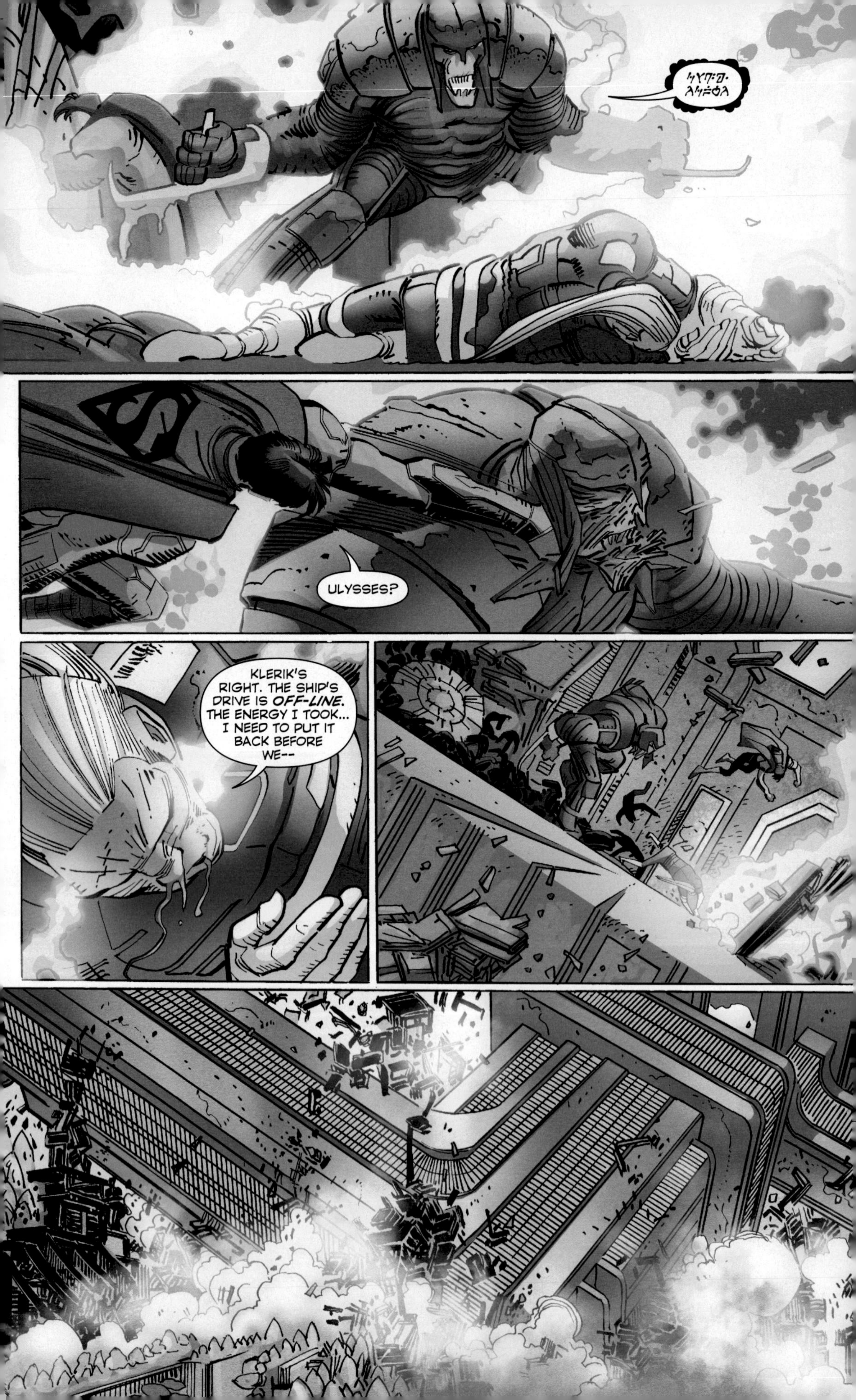
ULYSSES?
KLERIK'S RIGHT. THE SHIP'S DRIVE IS *OFF-LINE.* THE ENERGY I TOOK... I NEED TO PUT IT BACK BEFORE WE--

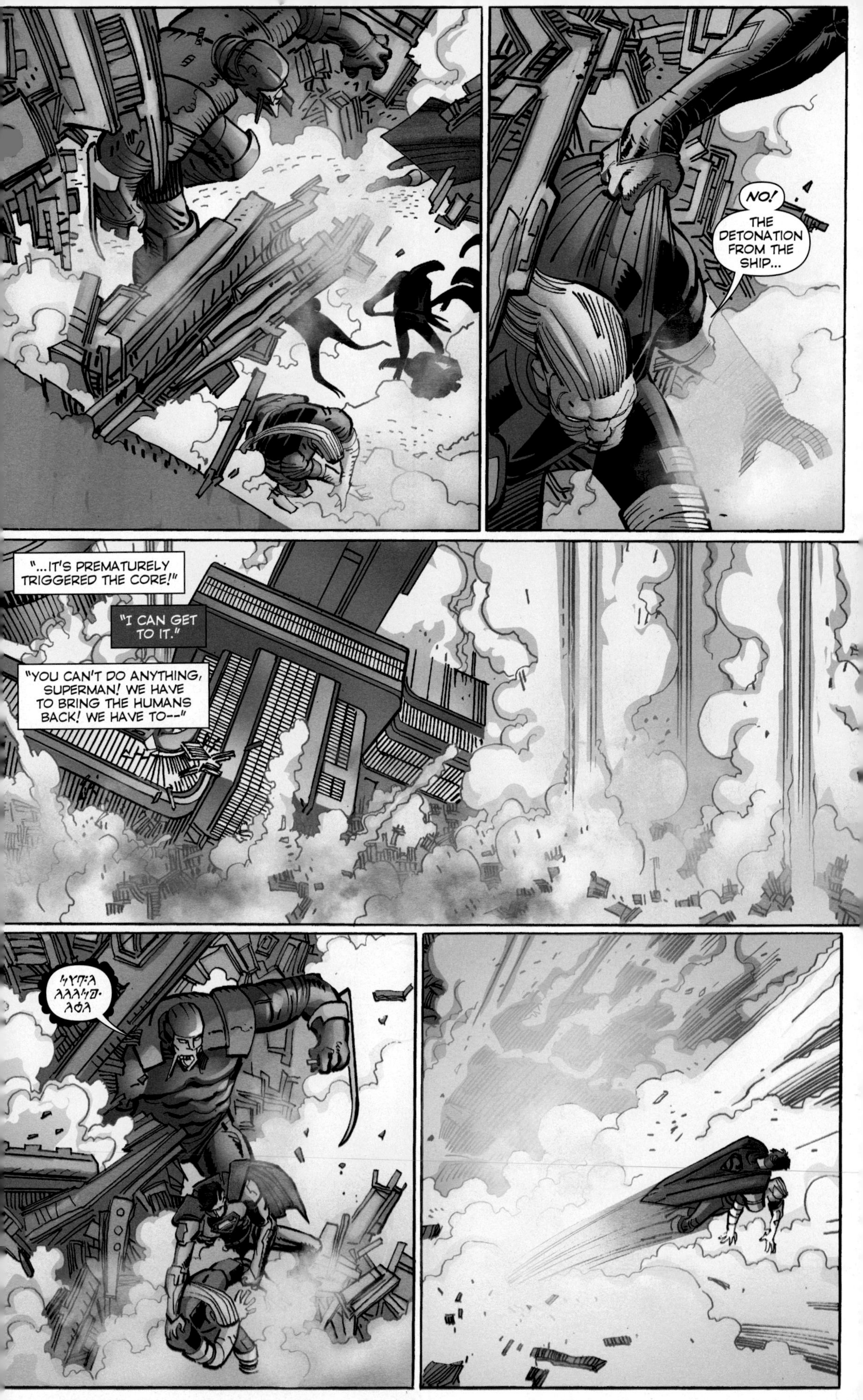
NO!
THE DETONATION FROM THE SHIP...
"...IT'S PREMATURELY TRIGGERED THE CORE!"
"I CAN GET TO IT."
"YOU CAN'T DO ANYTHING, SUPERMAN! WE HAVE TO BRING THE HUMANS BACK! WE HAVE TO--"

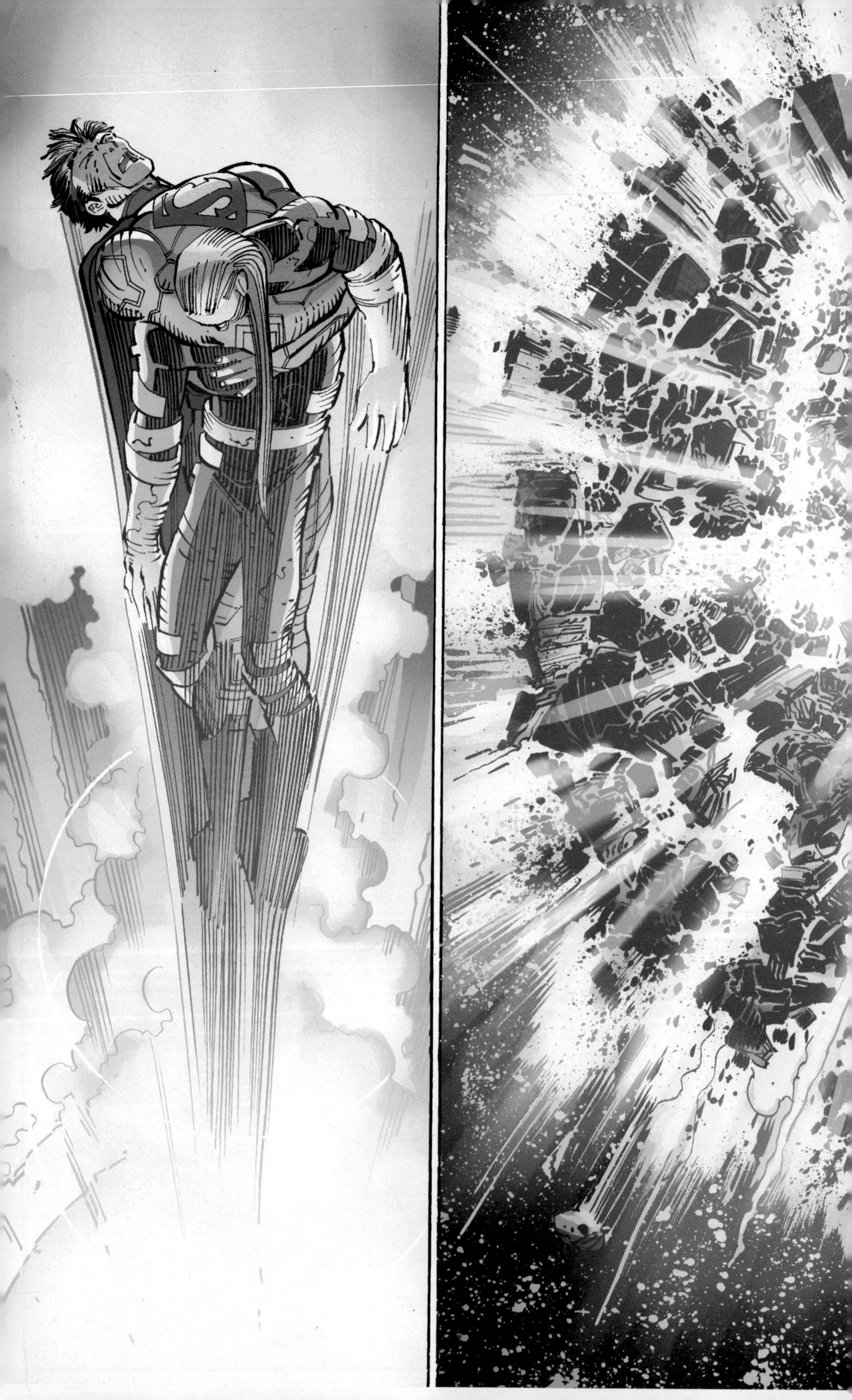

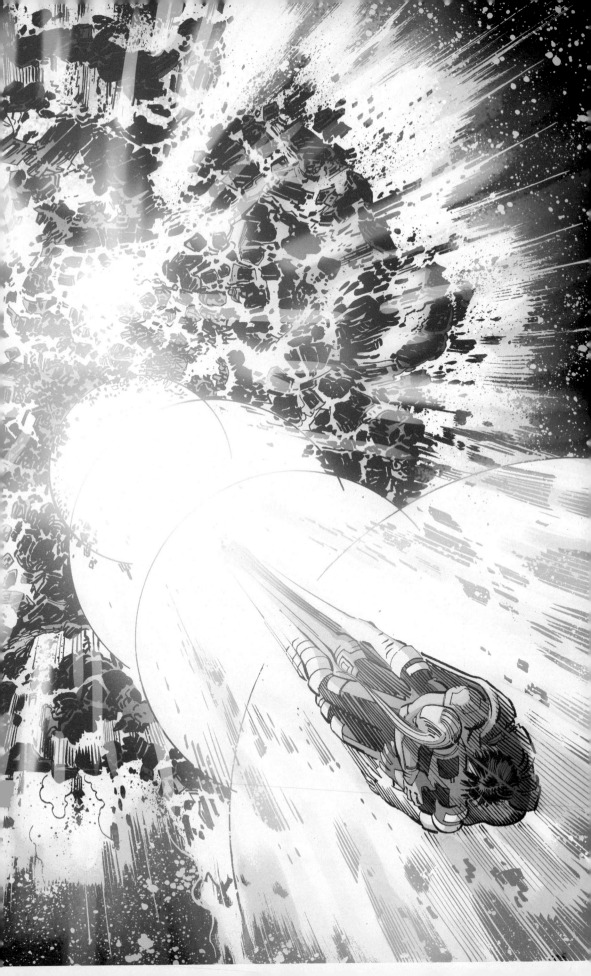

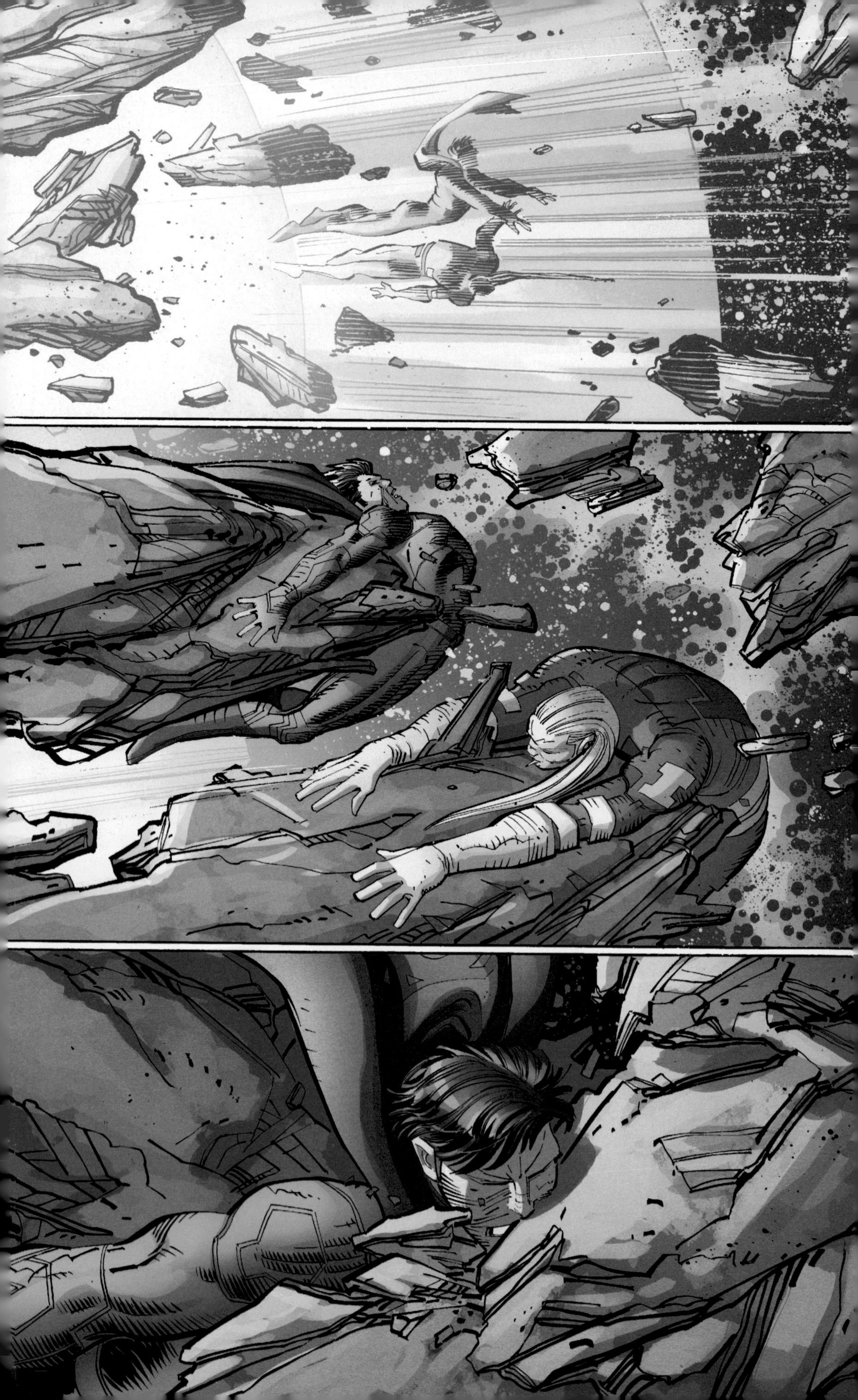

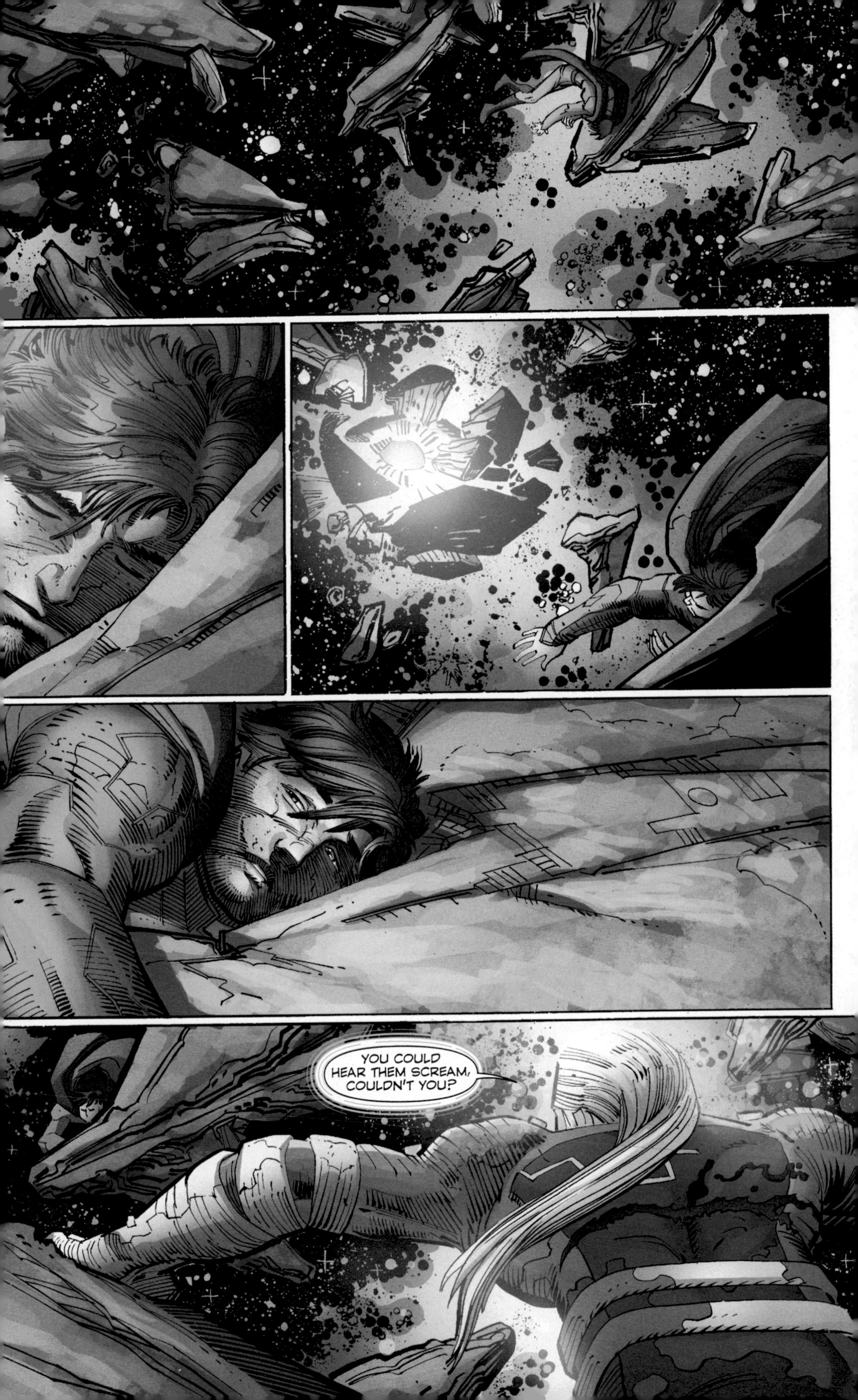
YOU COULD HEAR THEM SCREAM, COULDN'T YOU?

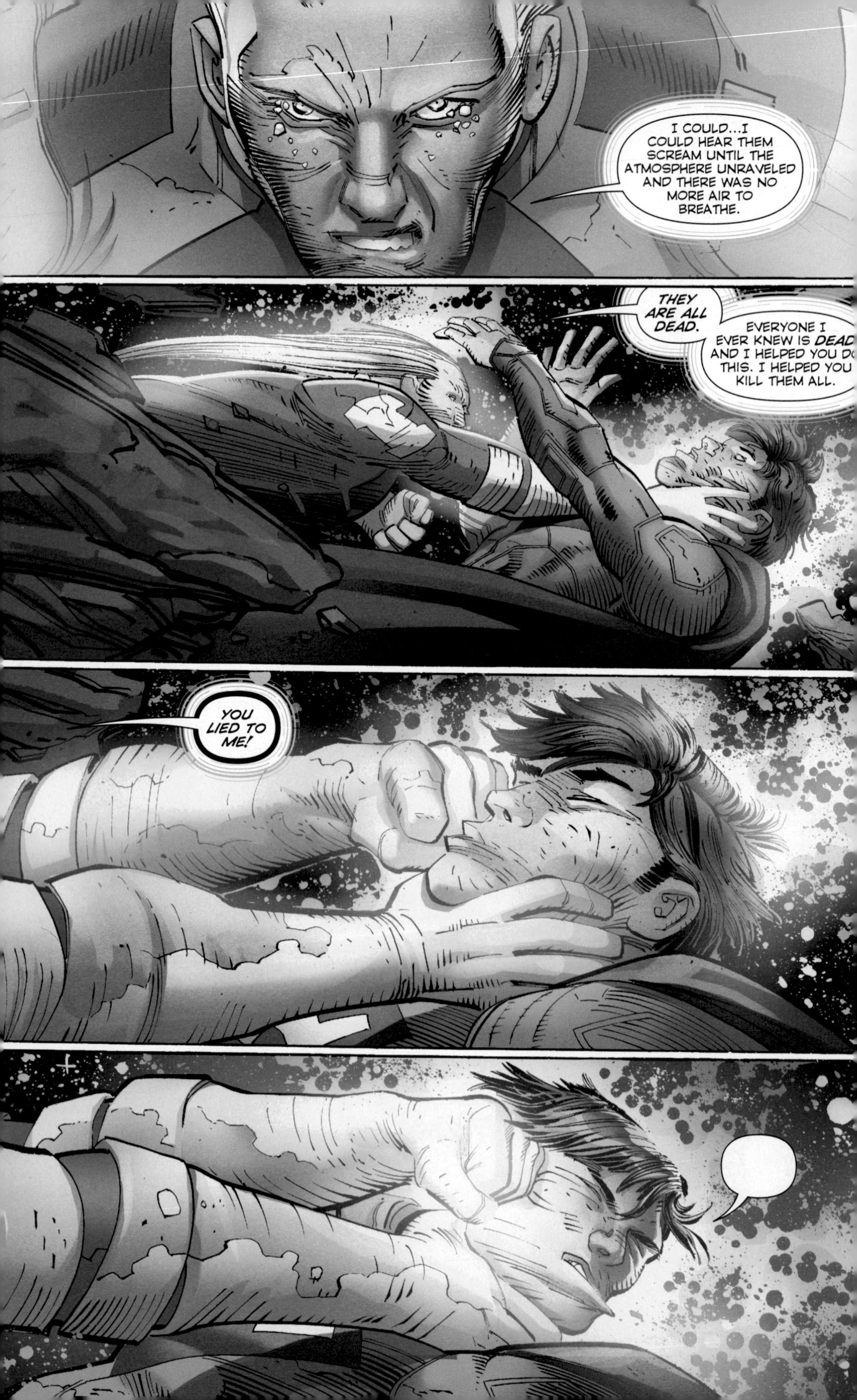
I COULD...I COULD HEAR THEM SCREAM UNTIL THE ATMOSPHERE UNRAVELED AND THERE WAS NO MORE AIR TO BREATHE.
THEY ARE ALL DEAD.
EVERYONE I EVER KNEW IS DEAD AND I HELPED YOU DO THIS. I HELPED YOU KILL THEM ALL.
YOU LIED TO ME!

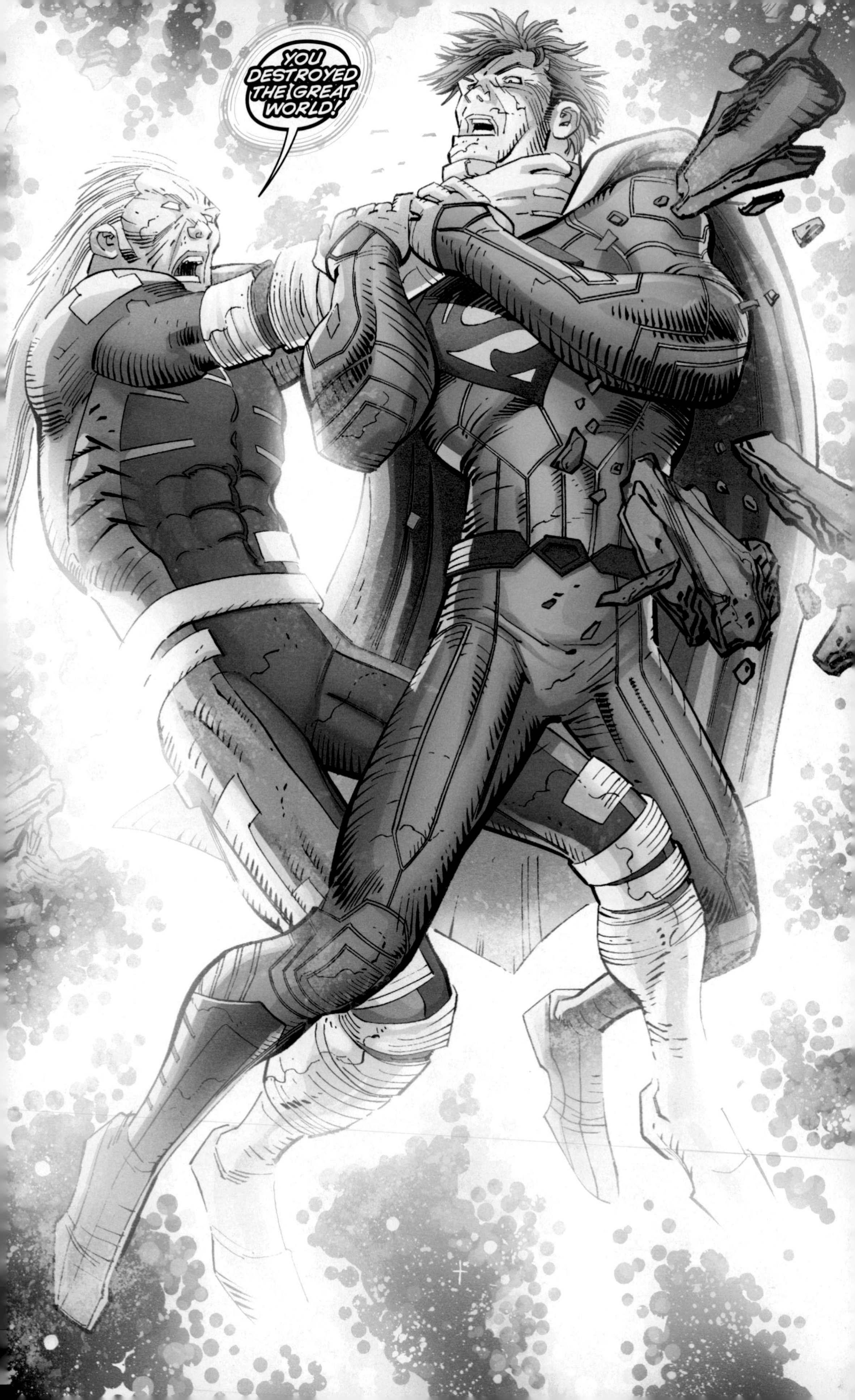
YOU DESTROYED THE GREAT WORLD!

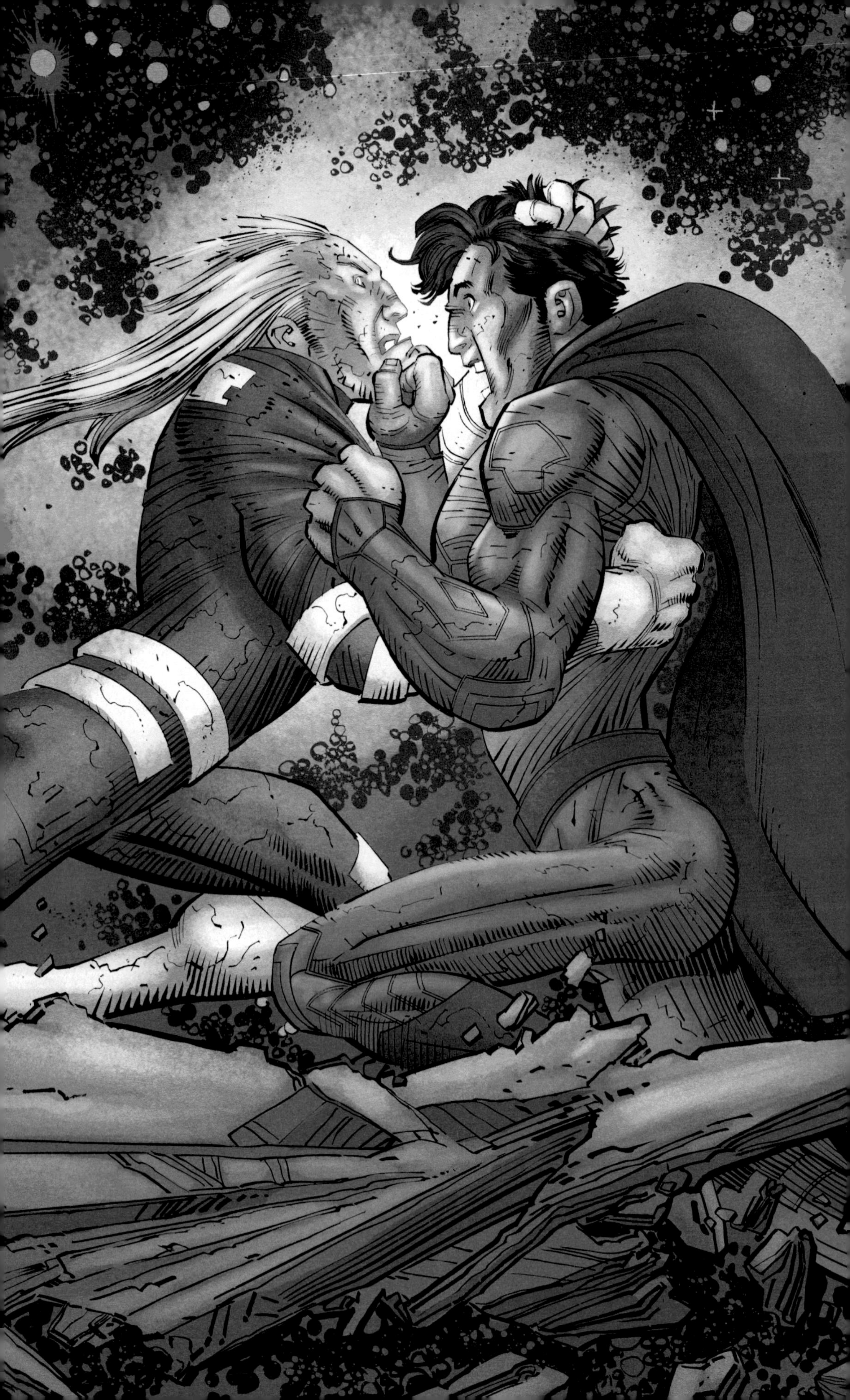

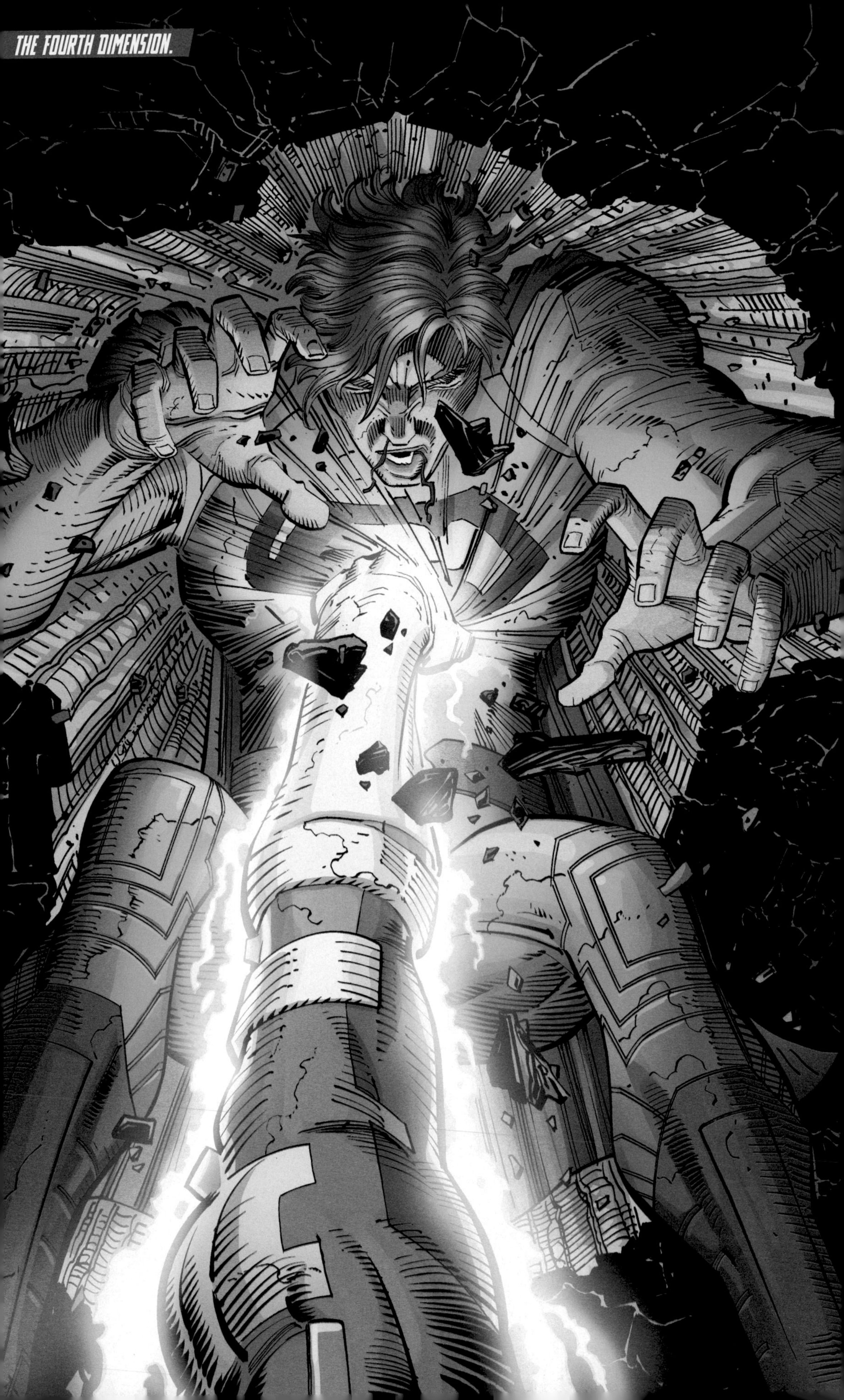
THE FOURTH DIMENSION.

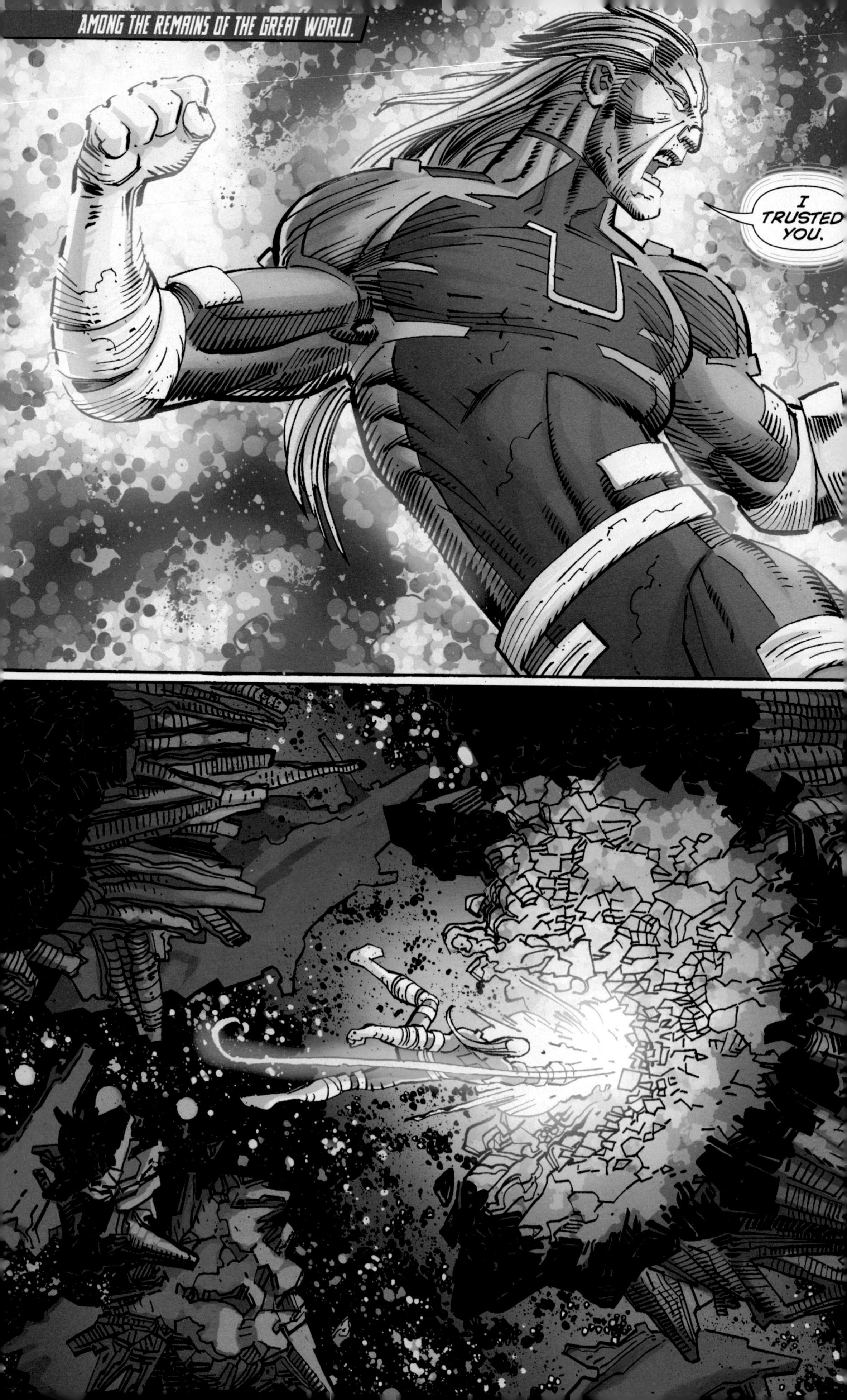
AMONG THE REMAINS OF THE GREAT WORLD.
I TRUSTED YOU.

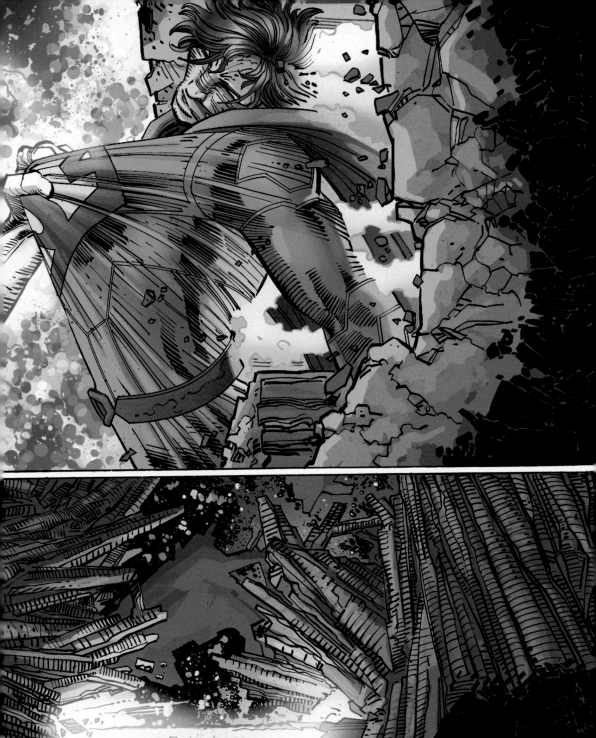
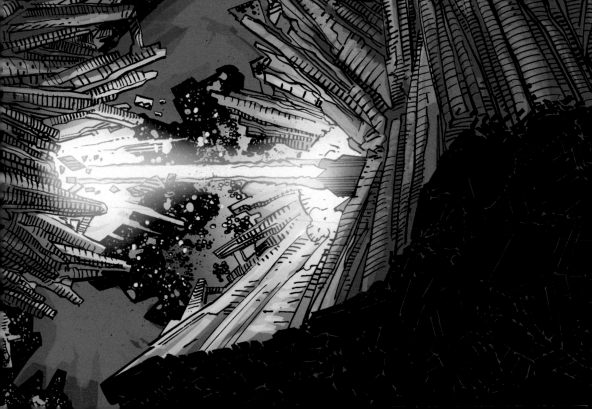

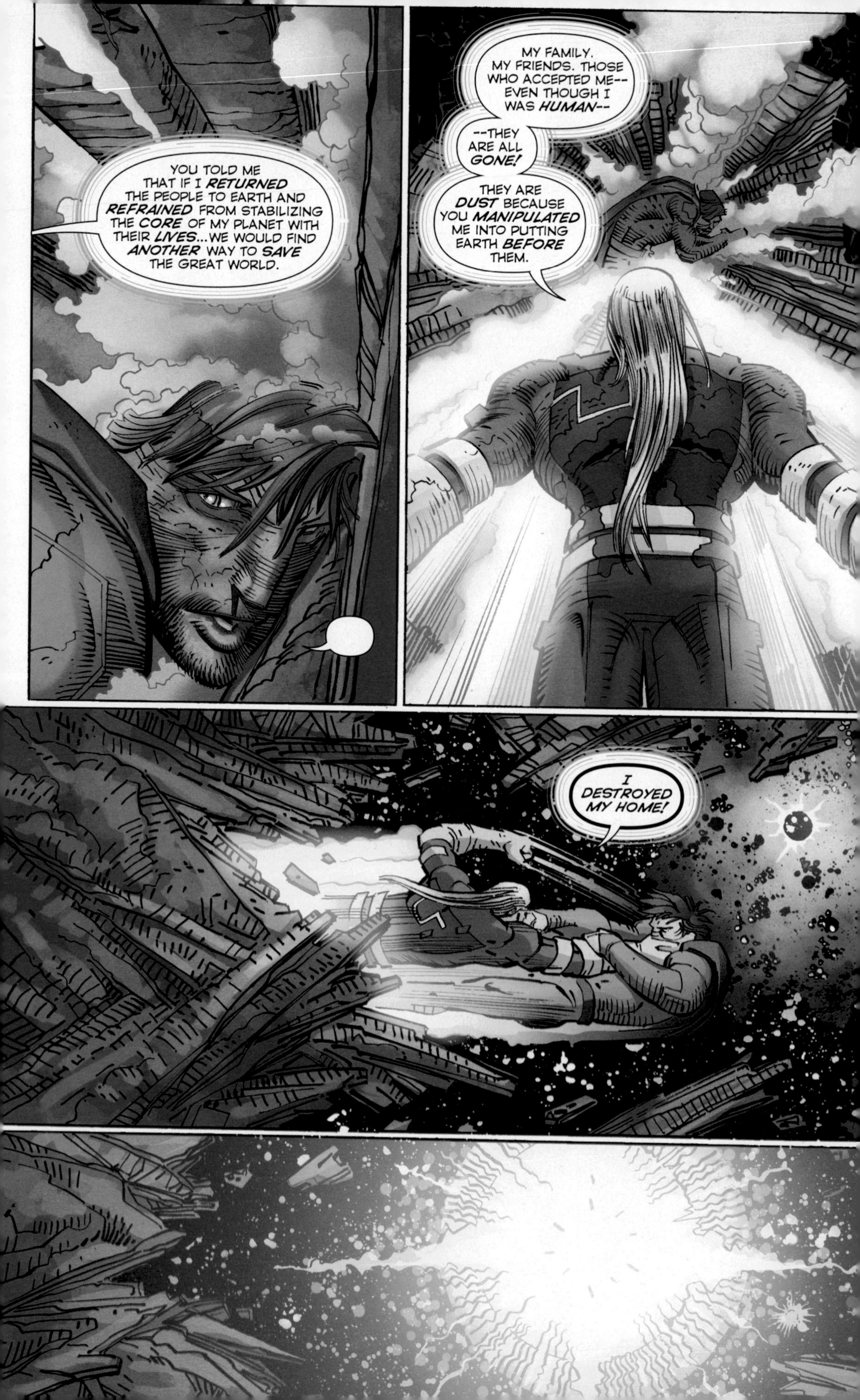

YOU TOLD ME THAT IF I RETURNED THE PEOPLE TO EARTH AND REFRAINED FROM STABILIZING THE CORE OF MY PLANET WITH THEIR LIVES...WE WOULD FIND ANOTHER WAY TO SAVE THE GREAT WORLD.
MY FAMILY. MY FRIENDS. THOSE WHO ACCEPTED ME--EVEN THOUGH I WAS HUMAN--
--THEY ARE ALL GONE!
THEY ARE DUST BECAUSE YOU MANIPULATED ME INTO PUTTING EARTH BEFORE THEM.
I DESTROYED MY HOME!

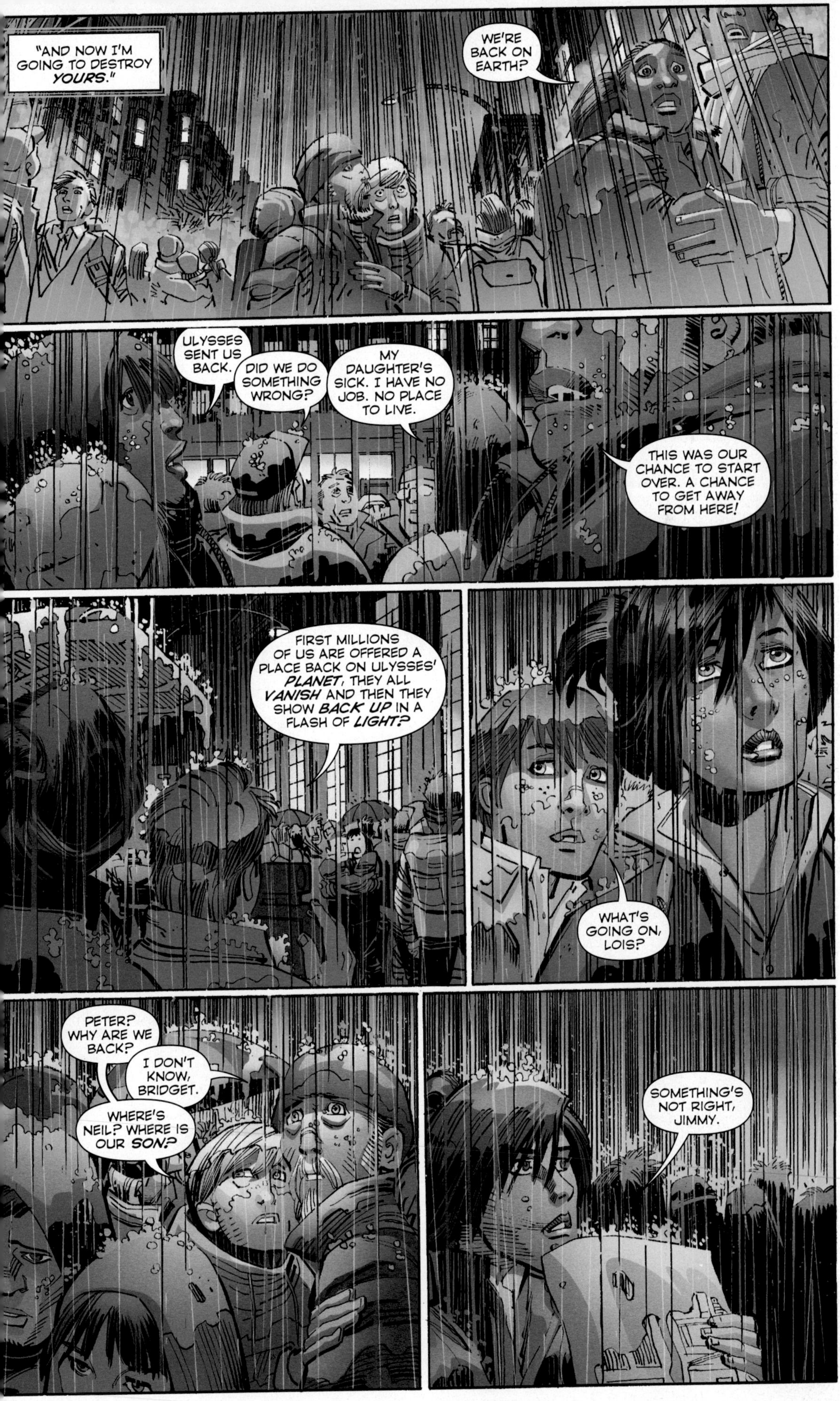
"AND NOW I'M GOING TO DESTROY YOURS."
WE'RE BACK ON EARTH?
ULYSSES SENT US BACK.
DID WE DO SOMETHING WRONG?
MY DAUGHTER'S SICK. I HAVE NO JOB. NO PLACE TO LIVE.
THIS WAS OUR CHANCE TO START OVER. A CHANCE TO GET AWAY FROM HERE!
FIRST MILLIONS OF US ARE OFFERED A PLACE BACK ON ULYSSES' PLANET, THEY ALL VANISH AND THEN THEY SHOW BACK UP IN A FLASH OF LIGHT?
WHAT'S GOING ON, LOIS?
PETER? WHY ARE WE BACK?
I DON'T KNOW, BRIDGET.
WHERE'S NEIL? WHERE IS OUR SON?
SOMETHING'S NOT RIGHT, JIMMY.

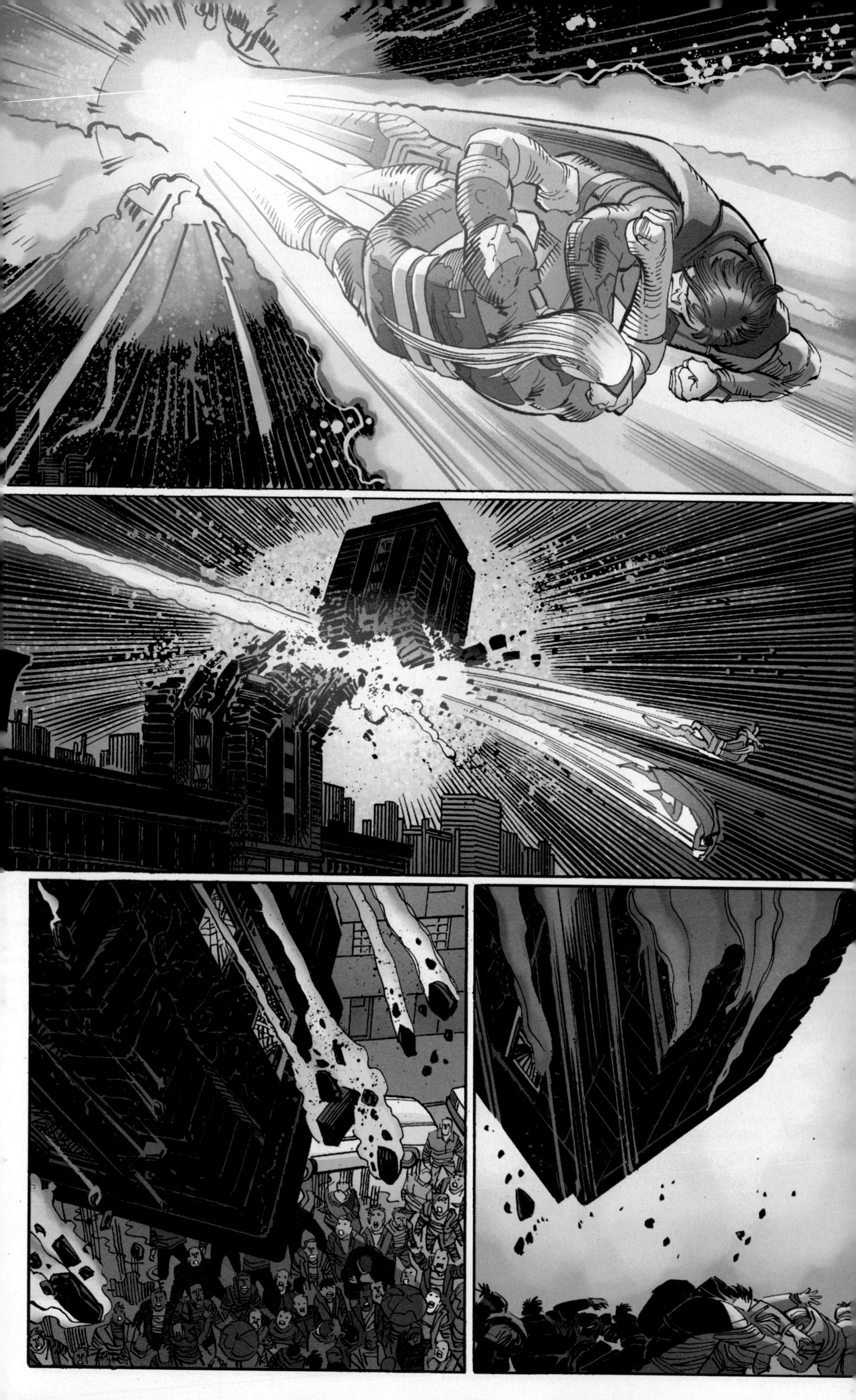

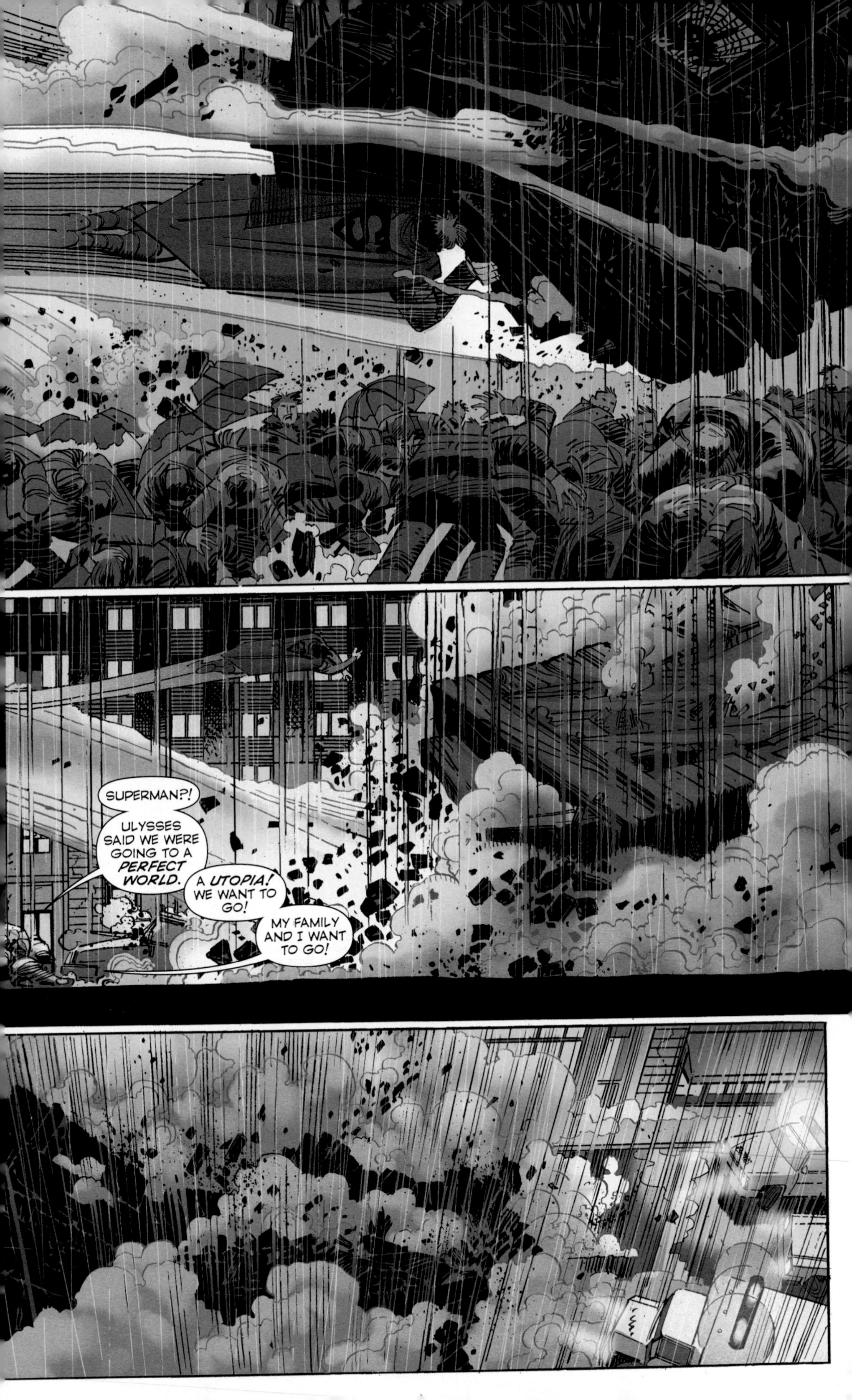
SUPERMAN?!
ULYSSES SAID WE WERE GOING TO A PERFECT WORLD.
A UTOPIA! WE WANT TO GO!
MY FAMILY AND I WANT TO GO!

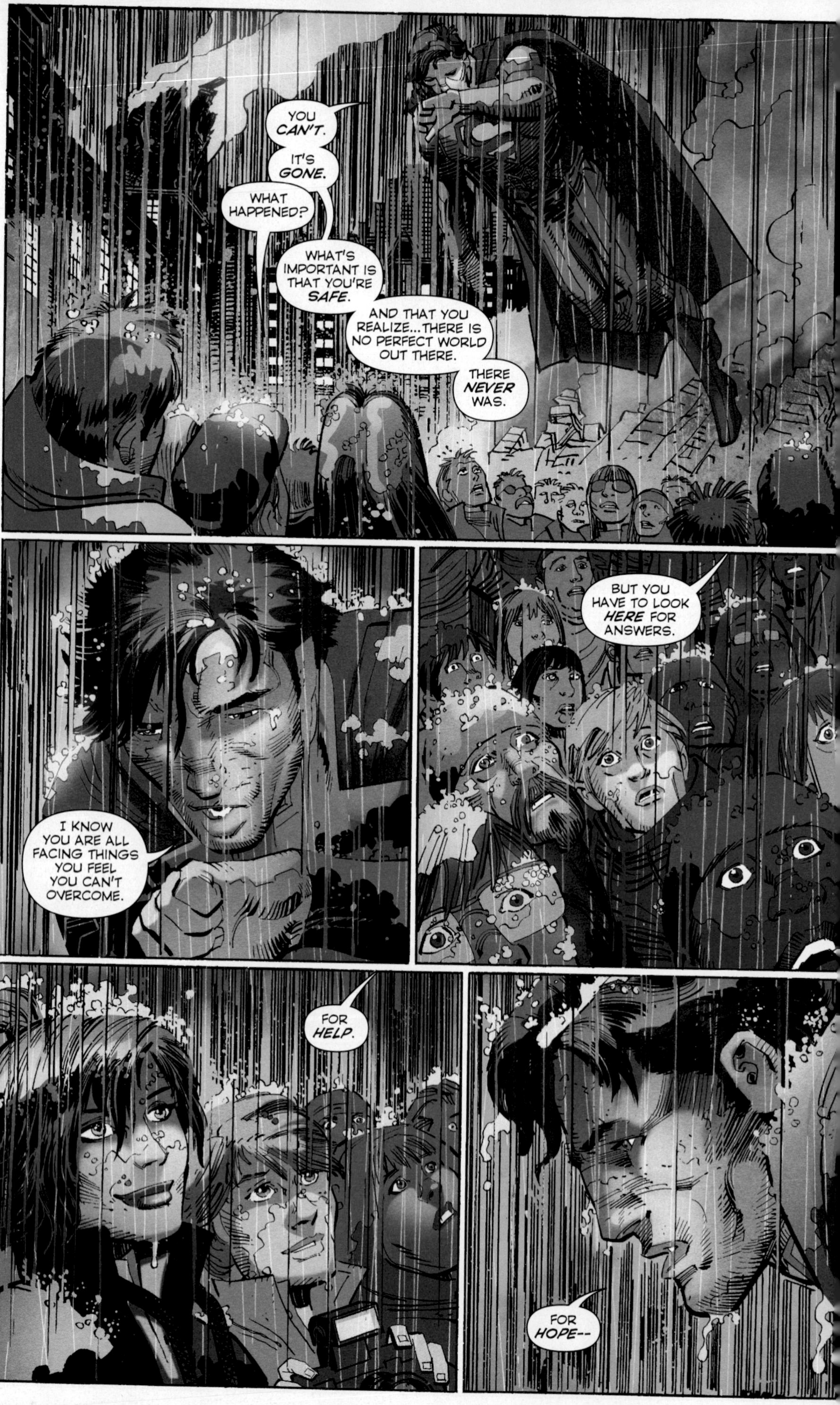
YOU CAN'T.
IT'S GONE.
WHAT HAPPENED?
WHAT'S IMPORTANT IS THAT YOU'RE SAFE.
AND THAT YOU REALIZE...THERE IS NO PERFECT WORLD OUT THERE.
THERE NEVER WAS.
I KNOW YOU ARE ALL FACING THINGS YOU FEEL YOU CAN'T OVERCOME.
BUT YOU HAVE TO LOOK HERE FOR ANSWERS.
FOR HELP.
FOR HOPE--

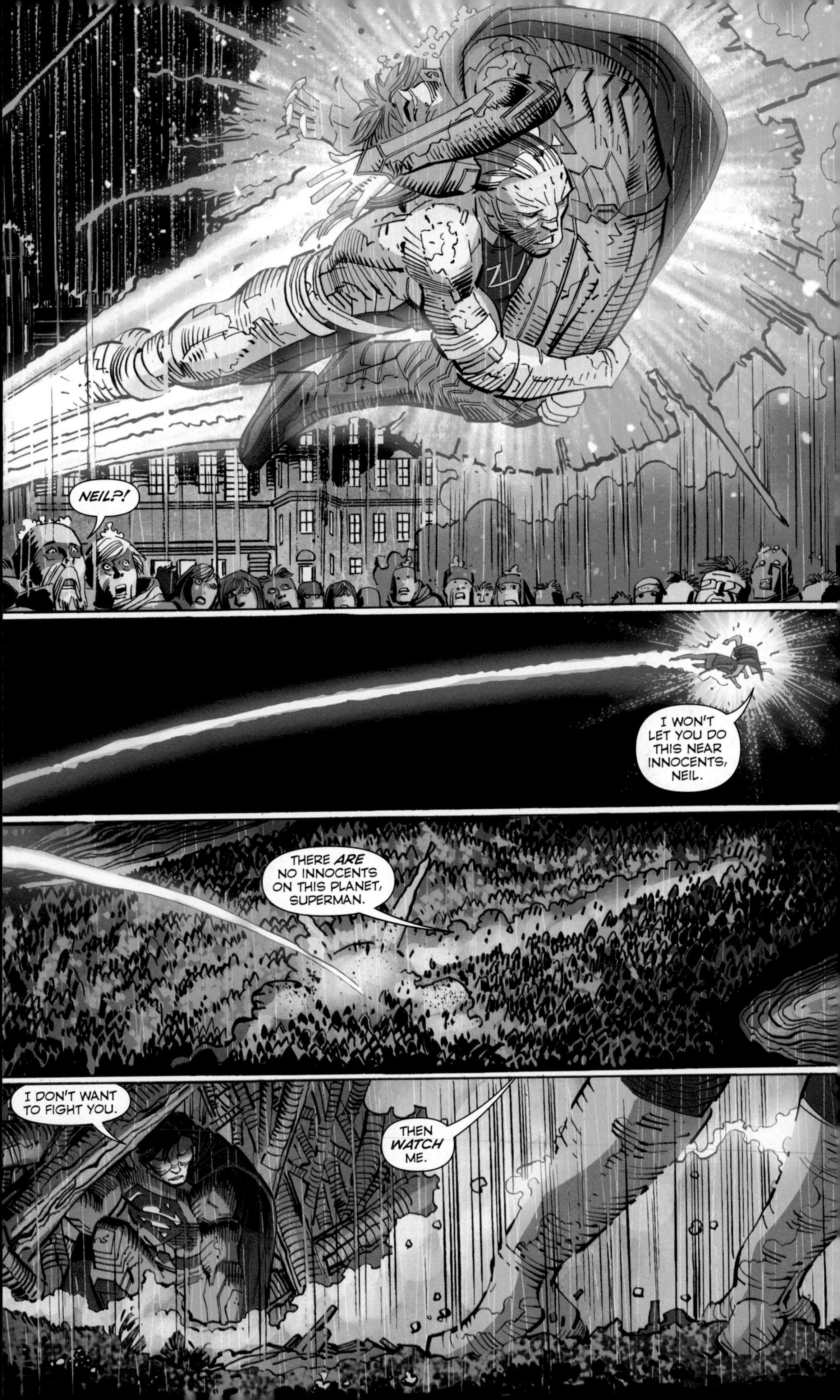
NEIL?!
I WON'T LET YOU DO THIS NEAR INNOCENTS, NEIL.
THERE ARE NO INNOCENTS ON THIS PLANET, SUPERMAN.
I DON'T WANT TO FIGHT YOU.
THEN WATCH ME.

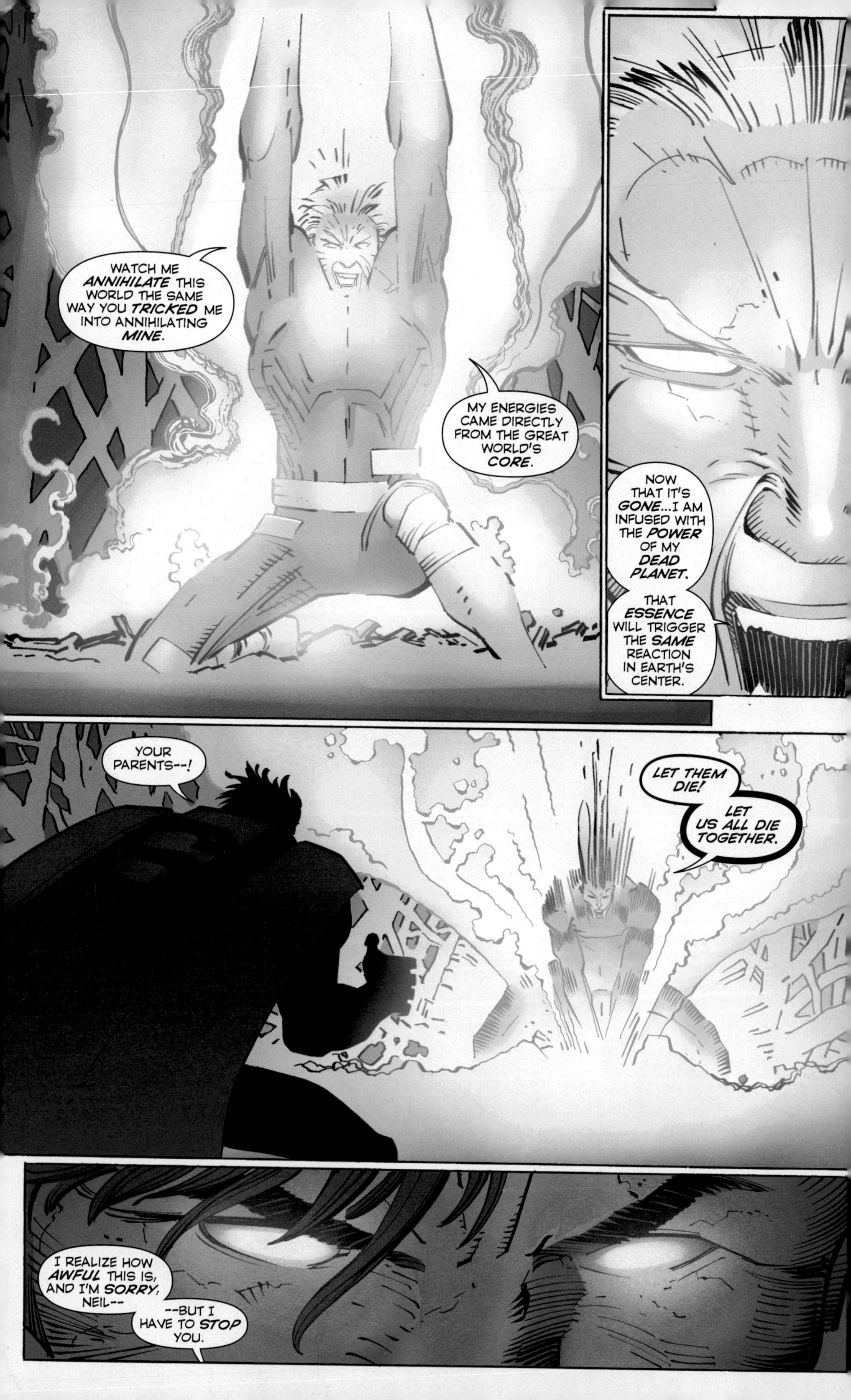

WATCH ME ANNIHILATE THIS WORLD THE SAME WAY YOU TRICKED ME INTO ANNIHILATING MINE.
MY ENERGIES CAME DIRECTLY FROM THE GREAT WORLD'S CORE.
NOW THAT IT'S GONE...I AM INFUSED WITH THE POWER OF MY DEAD PLANET.
THAT ESSENCE WILL TRIGGER THE SAME REACTION IN EARTH'S CENTER.
YOUR PARENTS--!
LET THEM DIE!
LET US ALL DIE TOGETHER.
I REALIZE HOW AWFUL THIS IS, AND I'M SORRY, NEIL--
--BUT I HAVE TO STOP YOU.

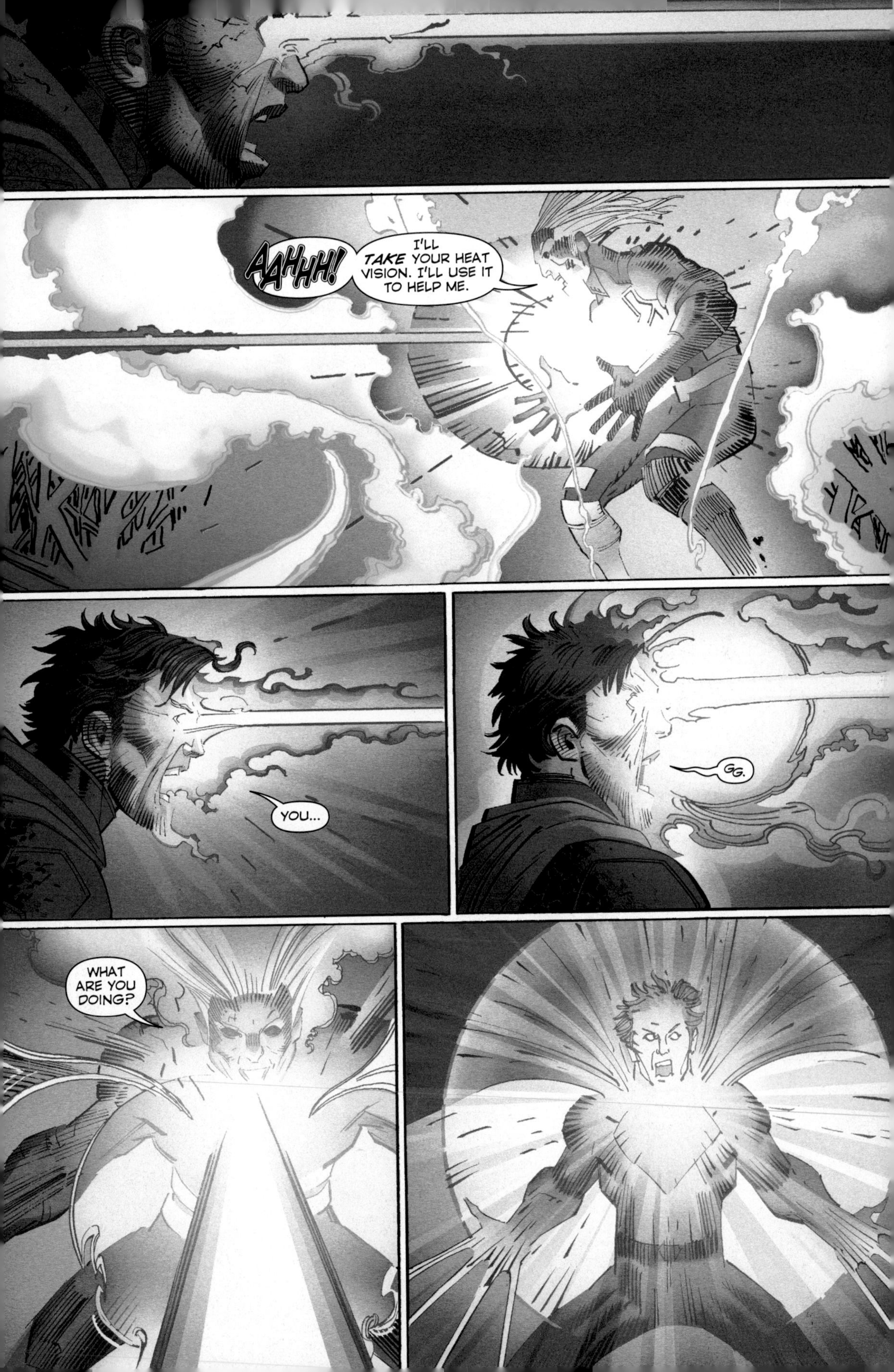
AAHHH!
I'LL TAKE YOUR HEAT VISION. I'LL USE IT TO HELP ME.
YOU...
GG.
WHAT ARE YOU DOING?

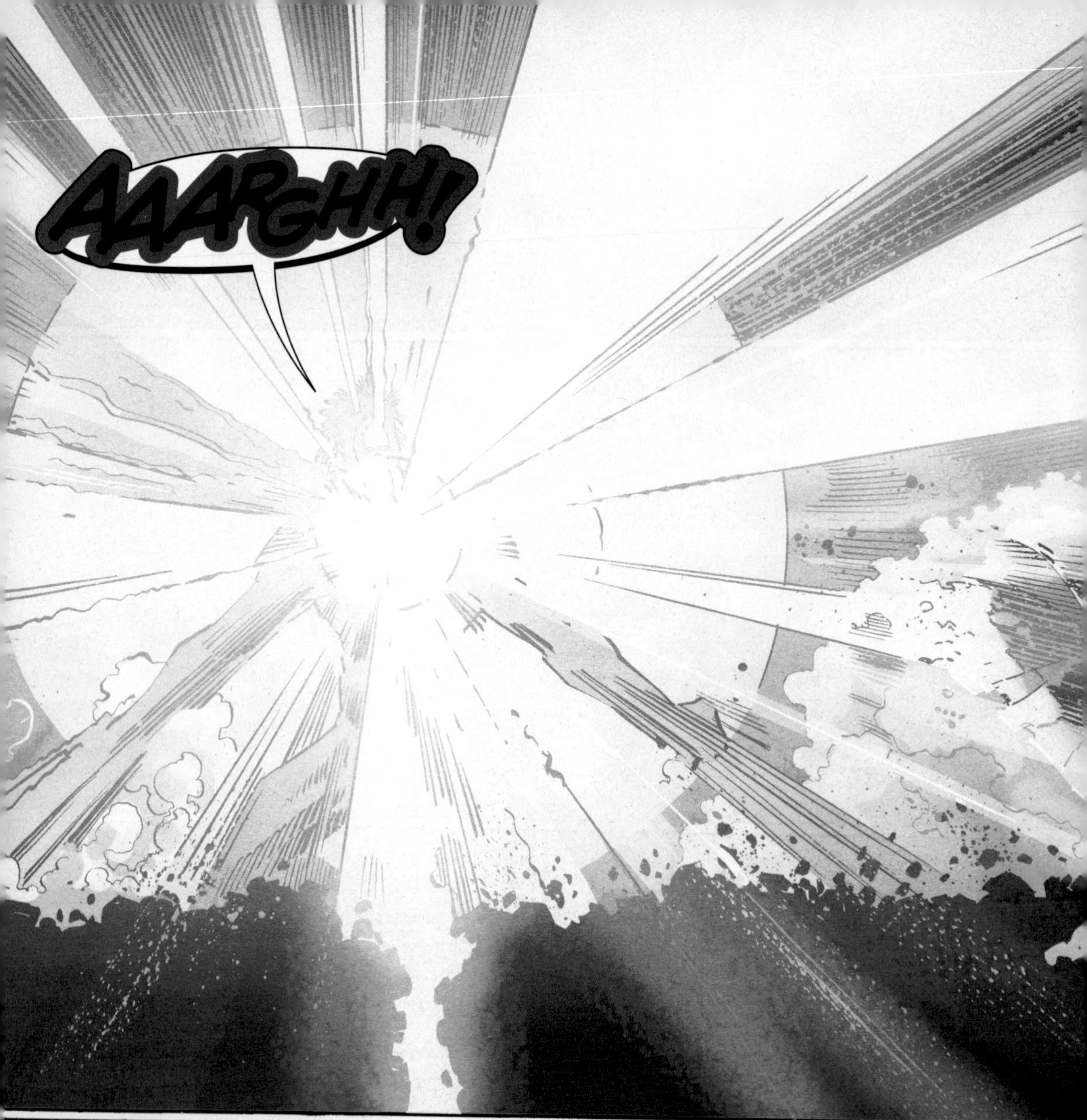
AAARGHH!
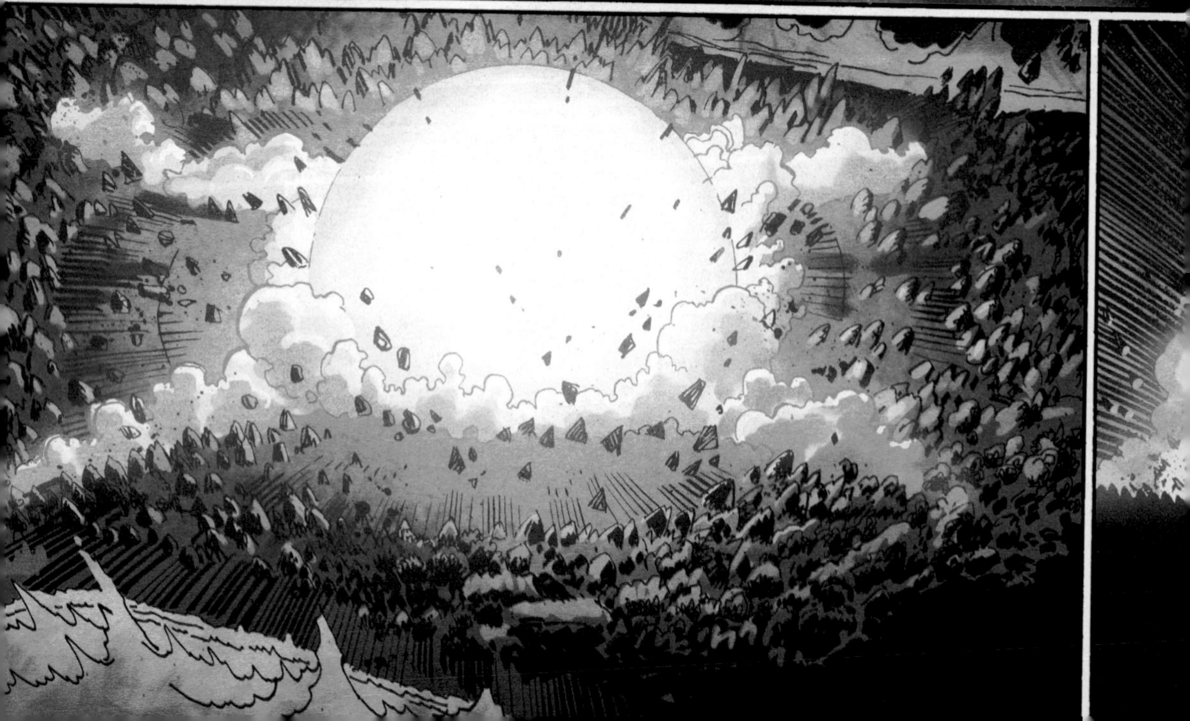

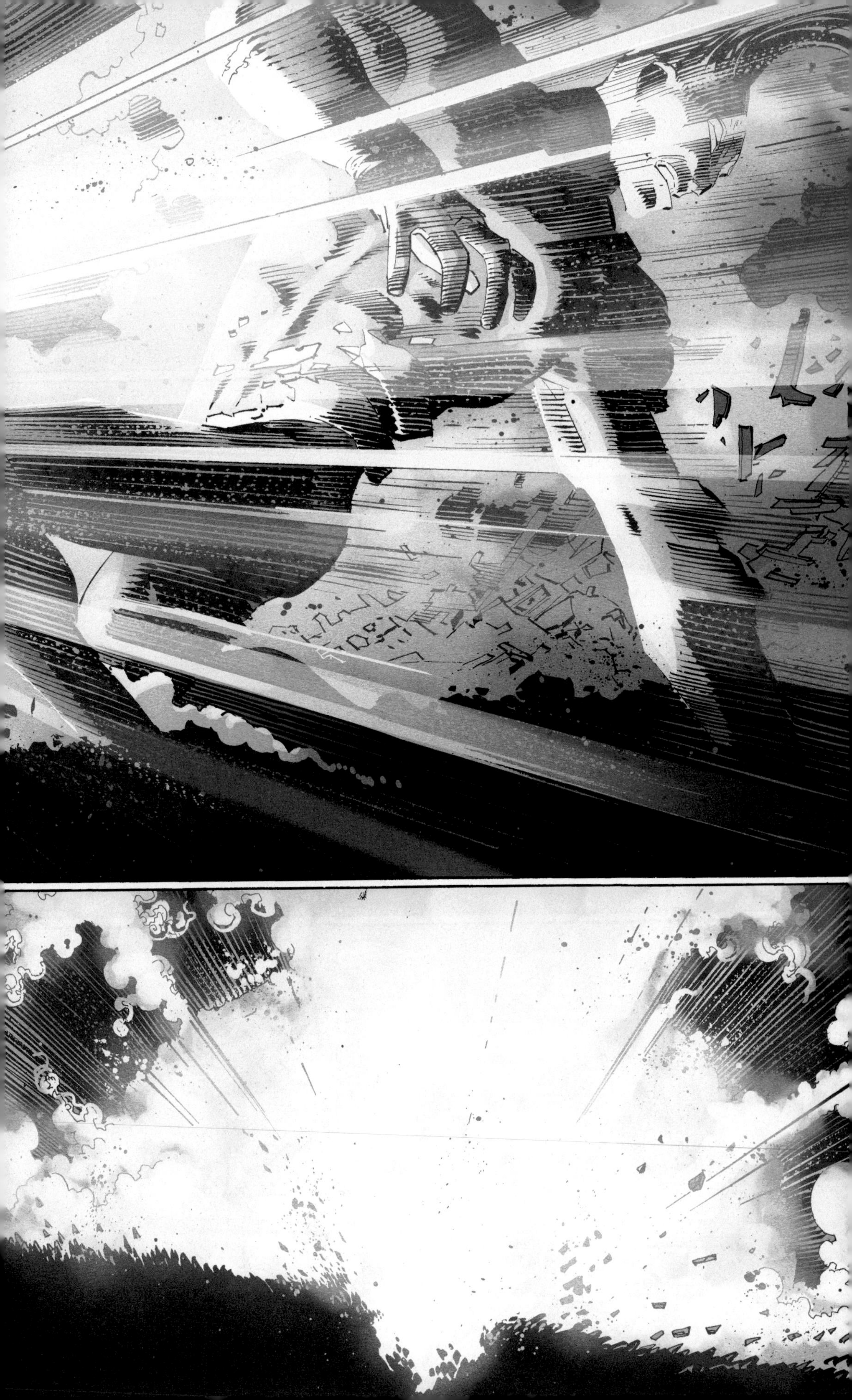

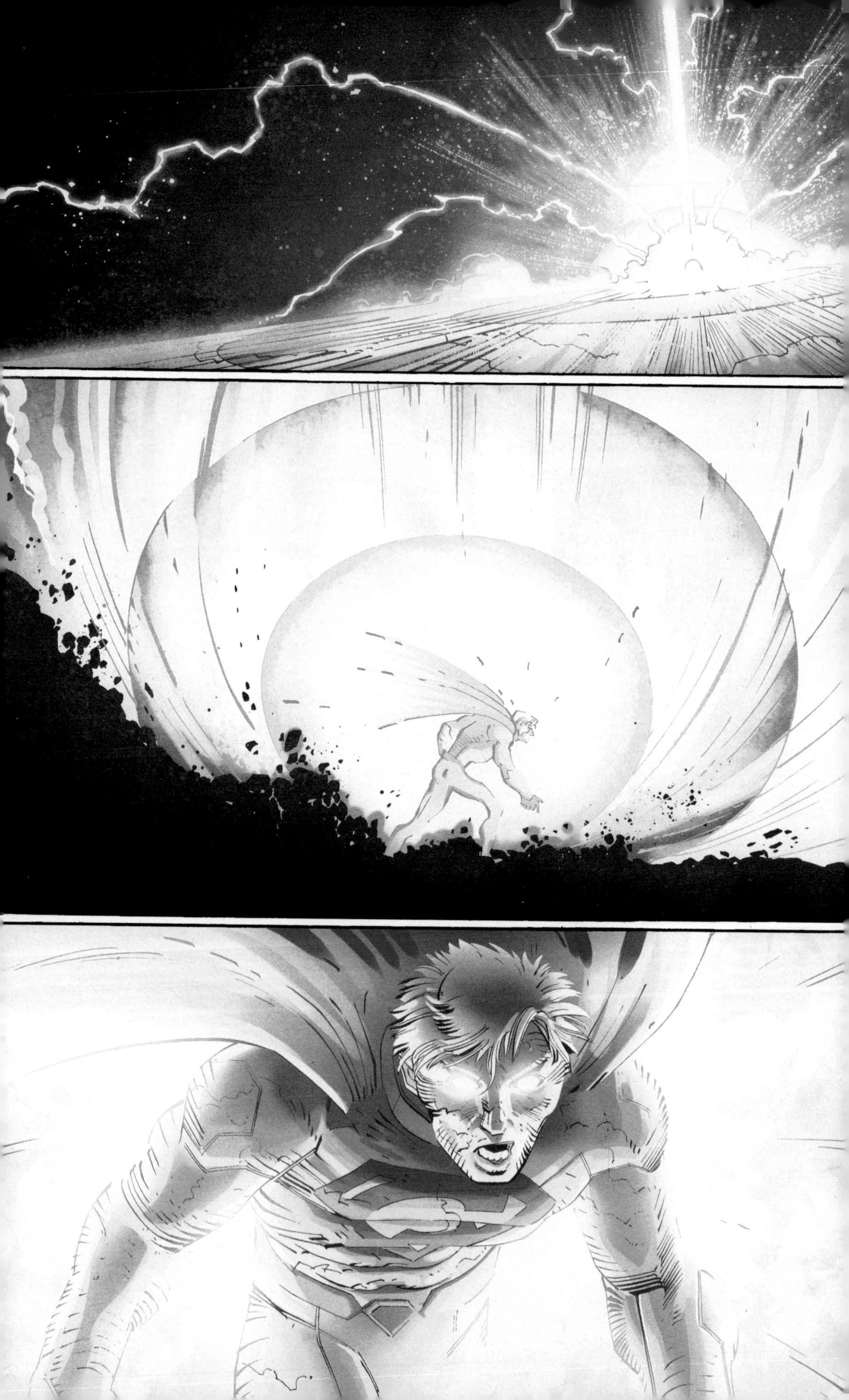

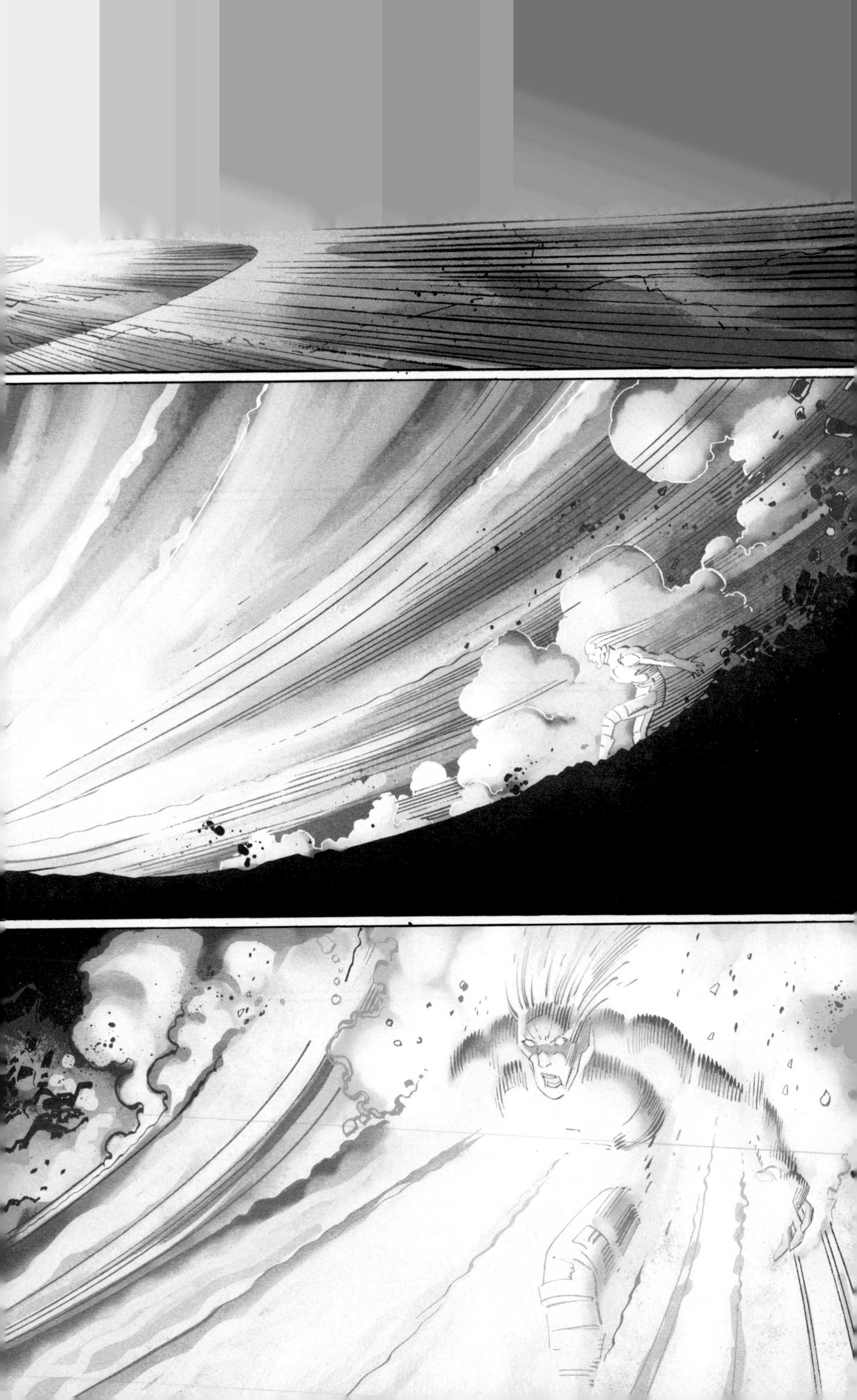

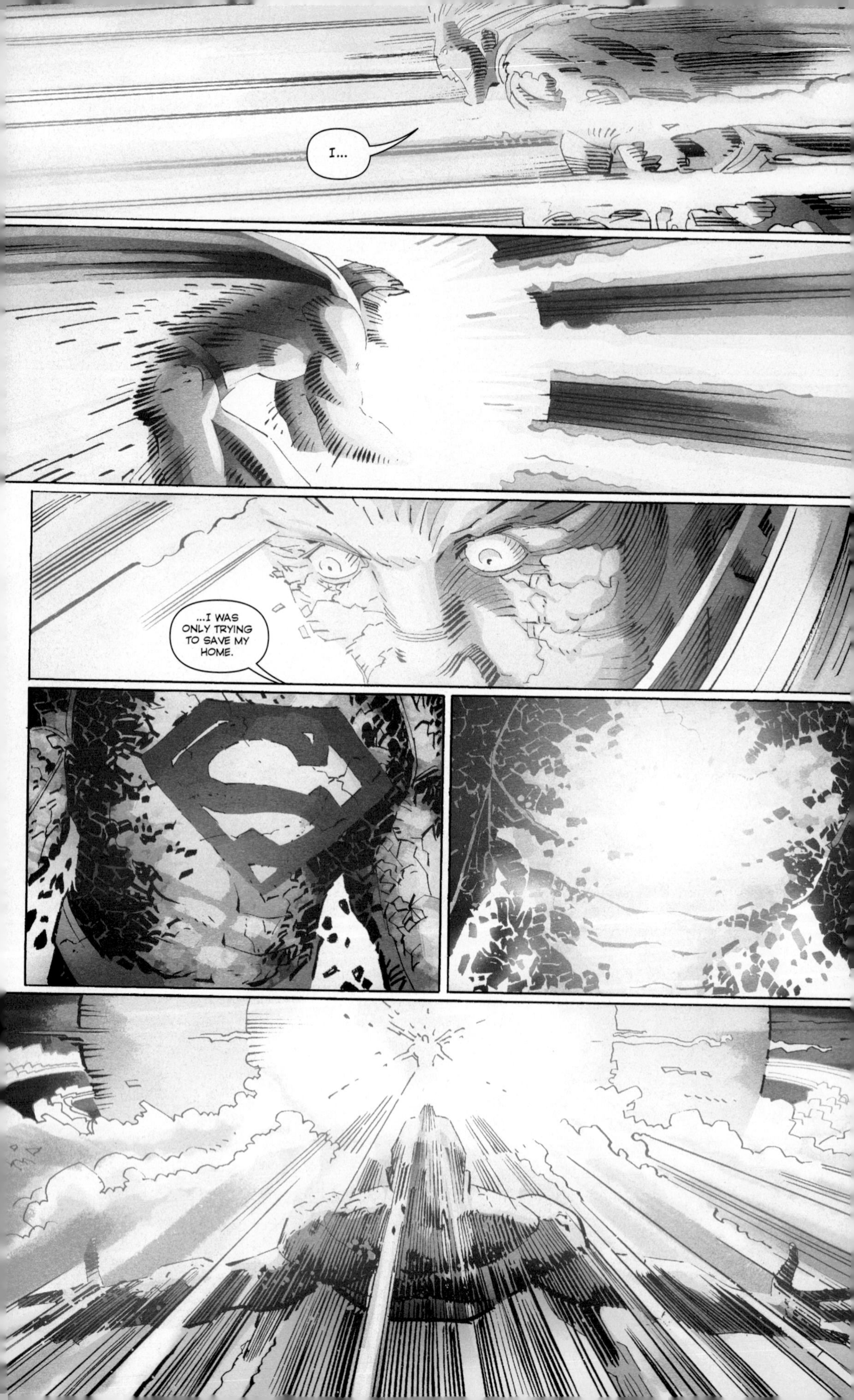
I...
...I WAS ONLY TRYING TO SAVE MY HOME.

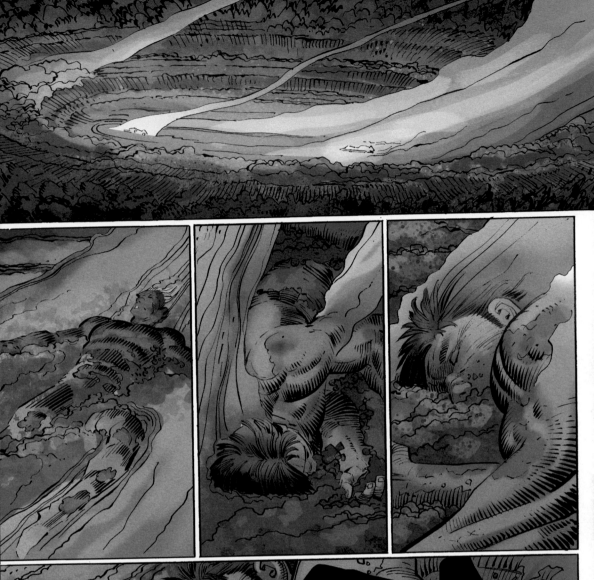

SUPERMAN.

EVERYTHING'S GOING TO BE ALL RIGHT.

HNNN?

WHO...?

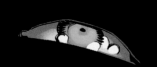

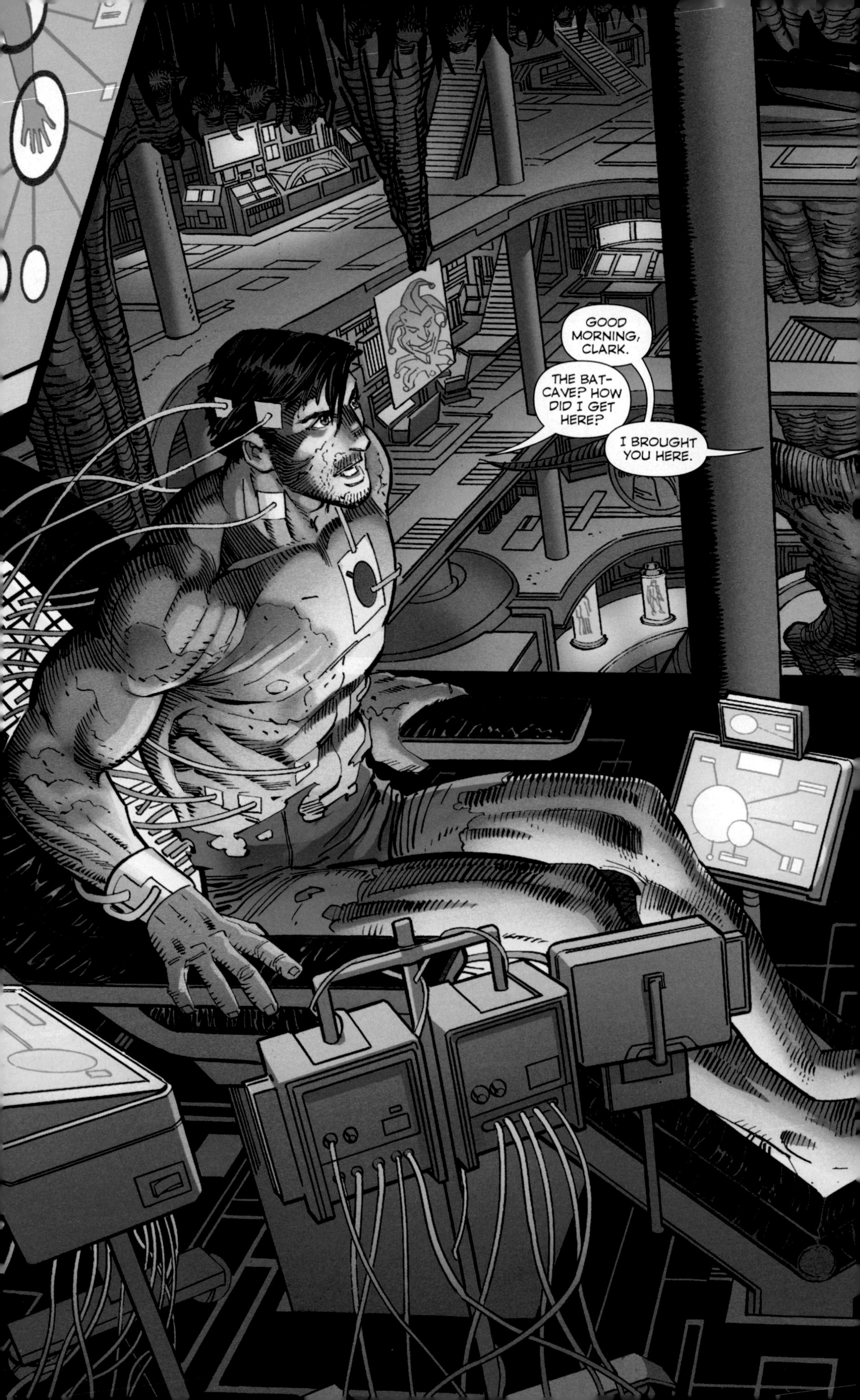
GOOD MORNING, CLARK.
THE BAT-CAVE? HOW DID I GET HERE?
I BROUGHT YOU HERE.

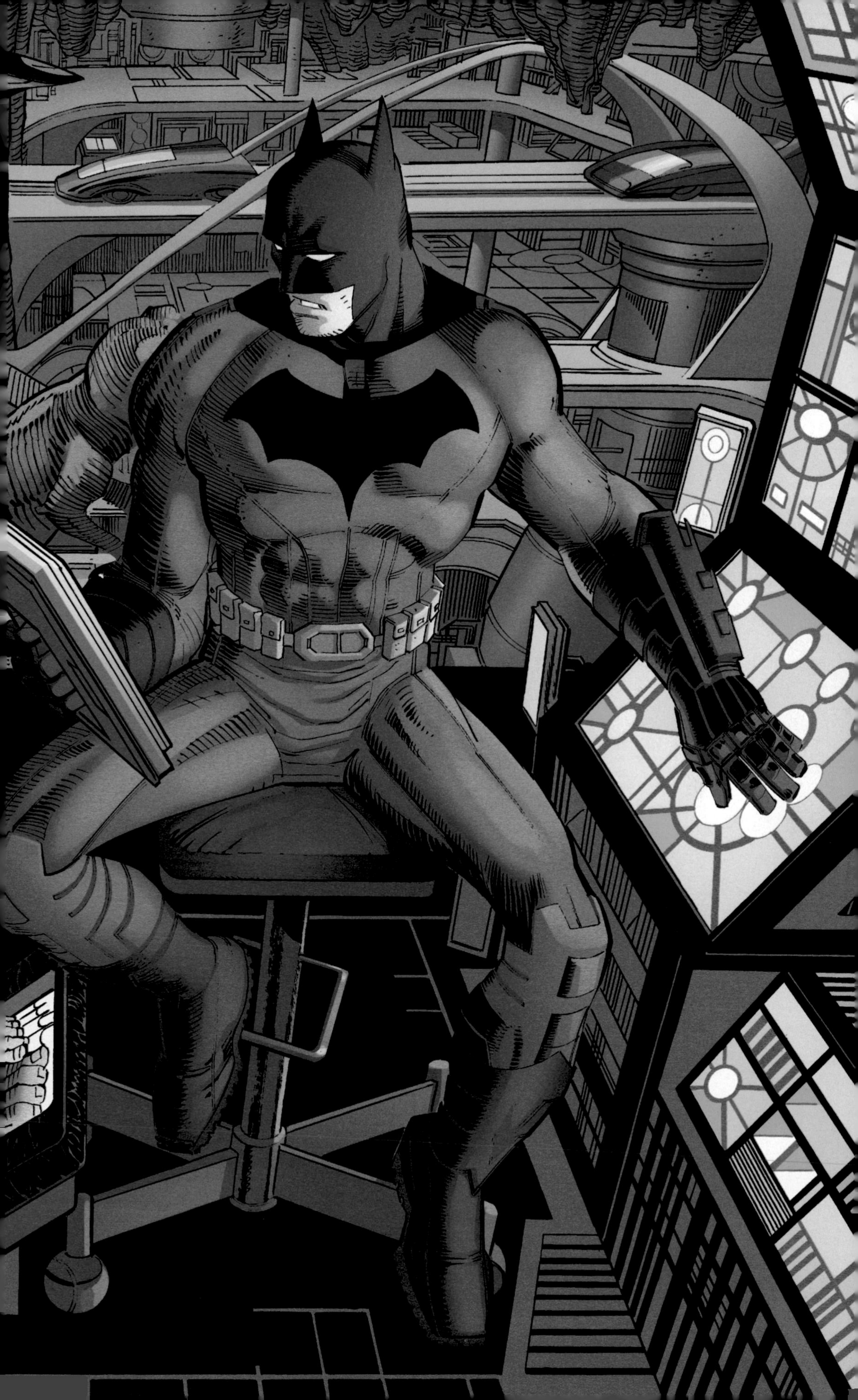

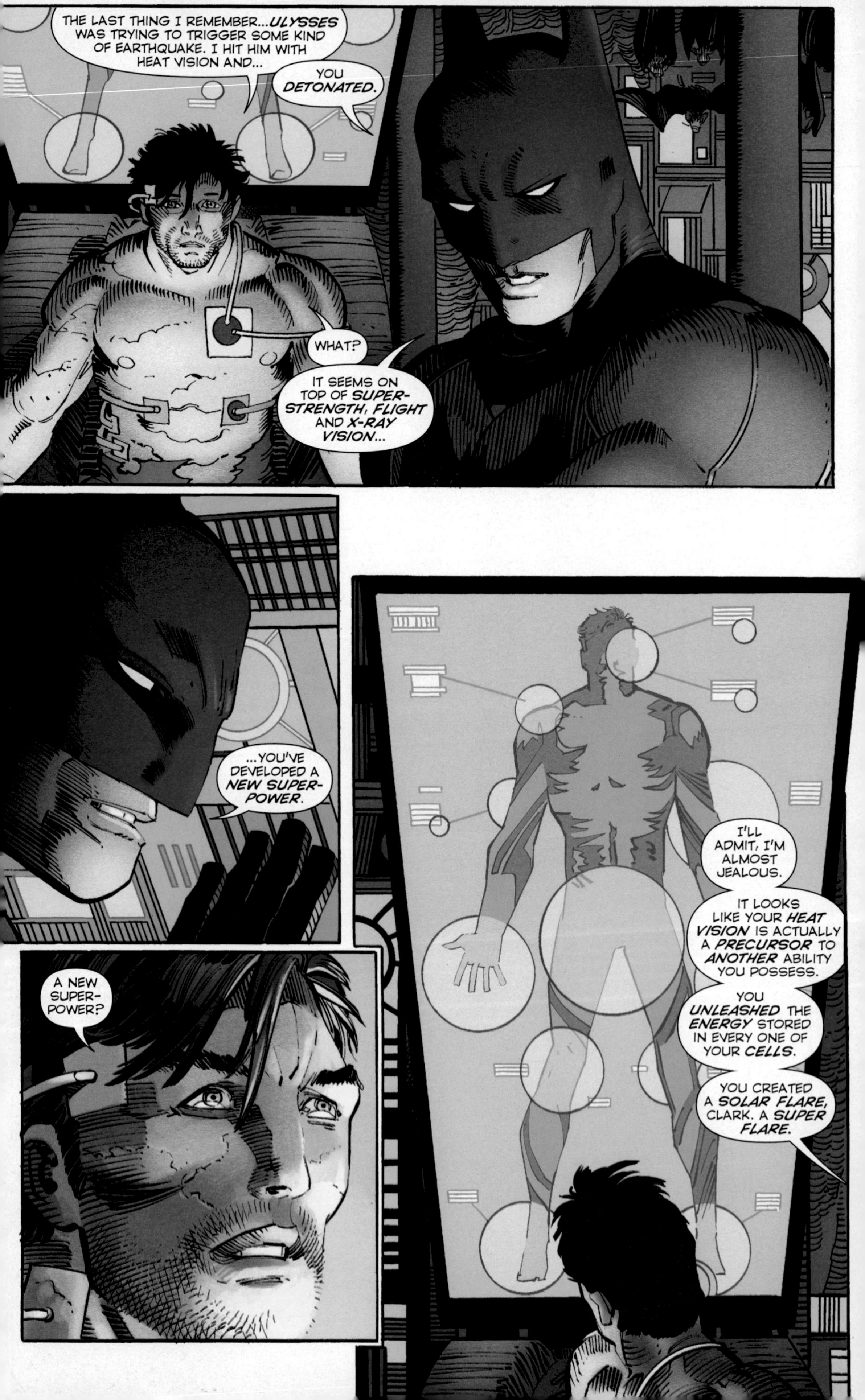
THE LAST THING I REMEMBER...ULYSSES WAS TRYING TO TRIGGER SOME KIND OF EARTHQUAKE. I HIT HIM WITH HEAT VISION AND...
YOU DETONATED.
WHAT?
IT SEEMS ON TOP OF SUPER-STRENGTH, FLIGHT AND X-RAY VISION...
...YOU'VE DEVELOPED A NEW SUPER-POWER.
A NEW SUPER-POWER?
I'LL ADMIT, I'M ALMOST JEALOUS.
IT LOOKS LIKE YOUR HEAT VISION IS ACTUALLY A PRECURSOR TO ANOTHER ABILITY YOU POSSESS.
YOU UNLEASHED THE ENERGY STORED IN EVERY ONE OF YOUR CELLS.
YOU CREATED A SOLAR FLARE, CLARK. A SUPER FLARE.

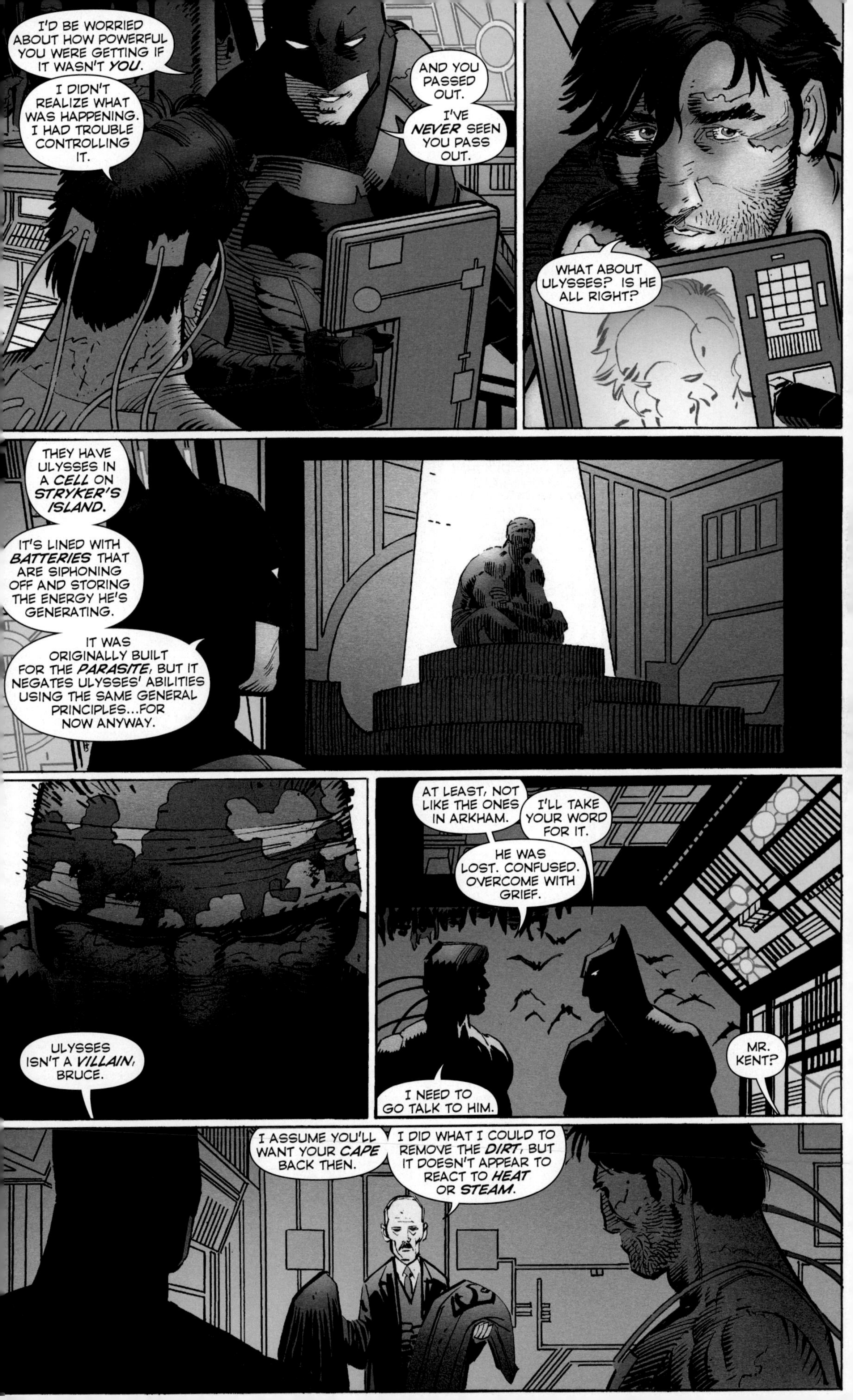
I'D BE WORRIED ABOUT HOW POWERFUL YOU WERE GETTING IF IT WASN'T YOU.
I DIDN'T REALIZE WHAT WAS HAPPENING. I HAD TROUBLE CONTROLLING IT.
AND YOU PASSED OUT.
I'VE NEVER SEEN YOU PASS OUT.
WHAT ABOUT ULYSSES? IS HE ALL RIGHT?
THEY HAVE ULYSSES IN A CELL ON STRYKER'S ISLAND.
IT'S LINED WITH BATTERIES THAT ARE SIPHONING OFF AND STORING THE ENERGY HE'S GENERATING.
IT WAS ORIGINALLY BUILT FOR THE PARASITE, BUT IT NEGATES ULYSSES' ABILITIES USING THE SAME GENERAL PRINCIPLES...FOR NOW ANYWAY.
ULYSSES ISN'T A VILLAIN, BRUCE.
AT LEAST, NOT LIKE THE ONES IN ARKHAM.
I'LL TAKE YOUR WORD FOR IT.
HE WAS LOST. CONFUSED. OVERCOME WITH GRIEF.
I NEED TO GO TALK TO HIM.
MR. KENT?
I ASSUME YOU'LL WANT YOUR CAPE BACK THEN.
I DID WHAT I COULD TO REMOVE THE DIRT, BUT IT DOESN'T APPEAR TO REACT TO HEAT OR STEAM.

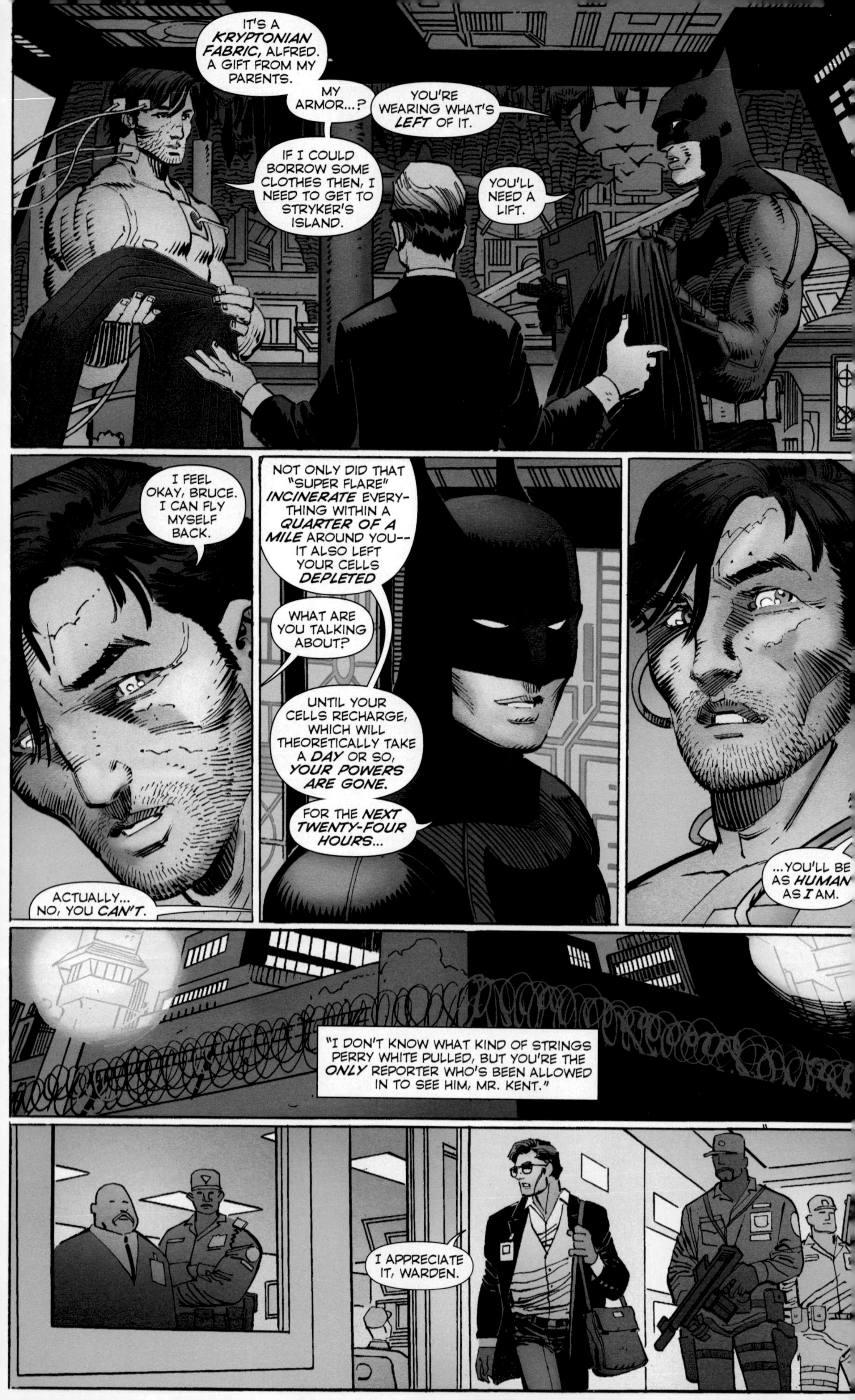
IT'S A KRYPTONIAN FABRIC, ALFRED. A GIFT FROM MY PARENTS.
MY ARMOR...?
YOU'RE WEARING WHAT'S LEFT OF IT.
IF I COULD BORROW SOME CLOTHES THEN, I NEED TO GET TO STRYKER'S ISLAND.
YOU'LL NEED A LIFT.
I FEEL OKAY, BRUCE. I CAN FLY MYSELF BACK.
ACTUALLY... NO, YOU CAN'T.
NOT ONLY DID THAT "SUPER FLARE" INCINERATE EVERY-THING WITHIN A QUARTER OF A MILE AROUND YOU-- IT ALSO LEFT YOUR CELLS DEPLETED
WHAT ARE YOU TALKING ABOUT?
UNTIL YOUR CELLS RECHARGE, WHICH WILL THEORETICALLY TAKE A DAY OR SO, YOUR POWERS ARE GONE.
FOR THE NEXT TWENTY-FOUR HOURS...
...YOU'LL BE AS HUMAN AS I AM.
"I DON'T KNOW WHAT KIND OF STRINGS PERRY WHITE PULLED, BUT YOU'RE THE ONLY REPORTER WHO'S BEEN ALLOWED IN TO SEE HIM, MR. KENT."
I APPRECIATE IT, WARDEN.

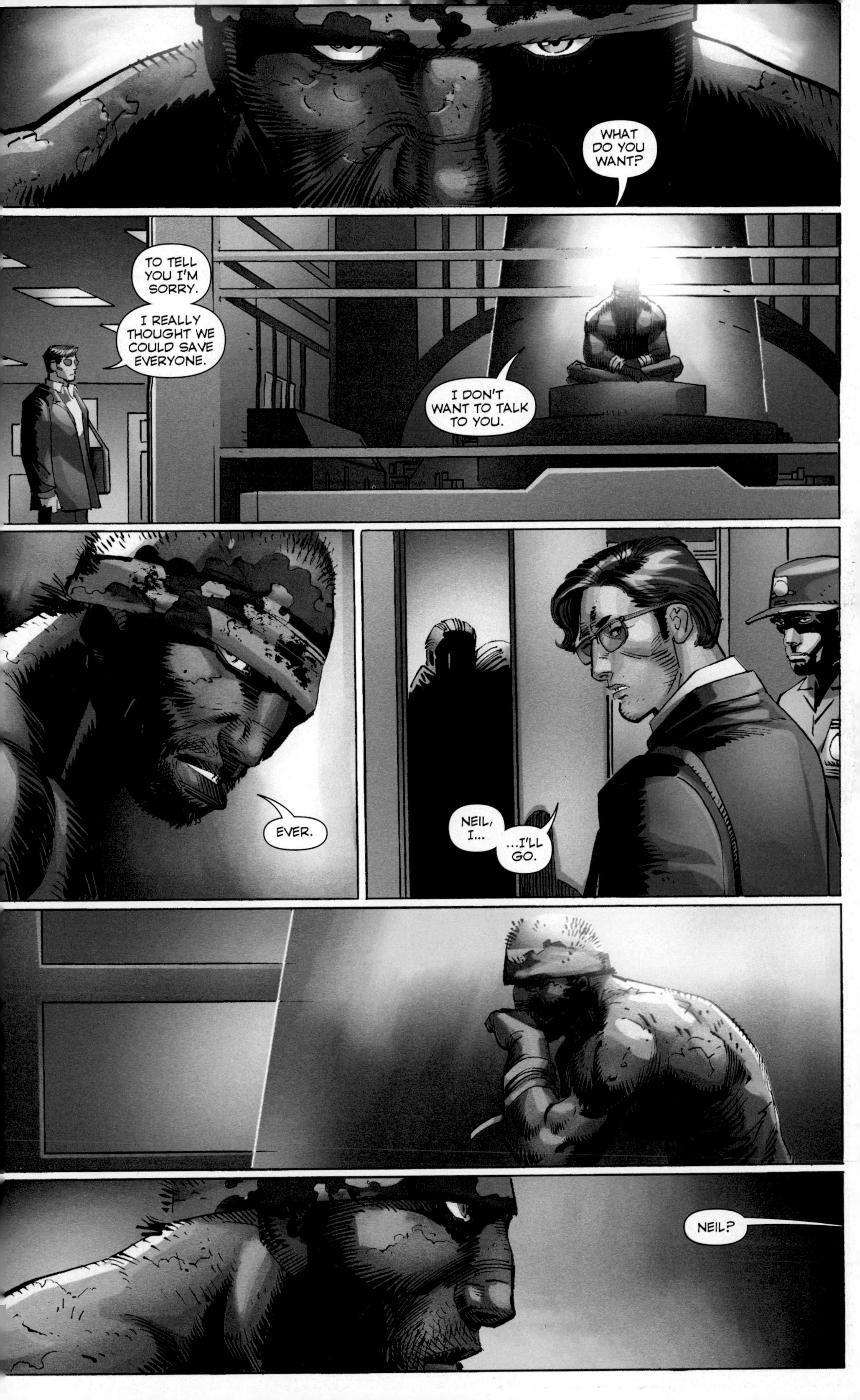
WHAT DO YOU WANT?
TO TELL YOU I'M SORRY.
I REALLY THOUGHT WE COULD SAVE EVERYONE.
I DON'T WANT TO TALK TO YOU.
EVER.
NEIL, I...
...I'LL GO.
NEIL?

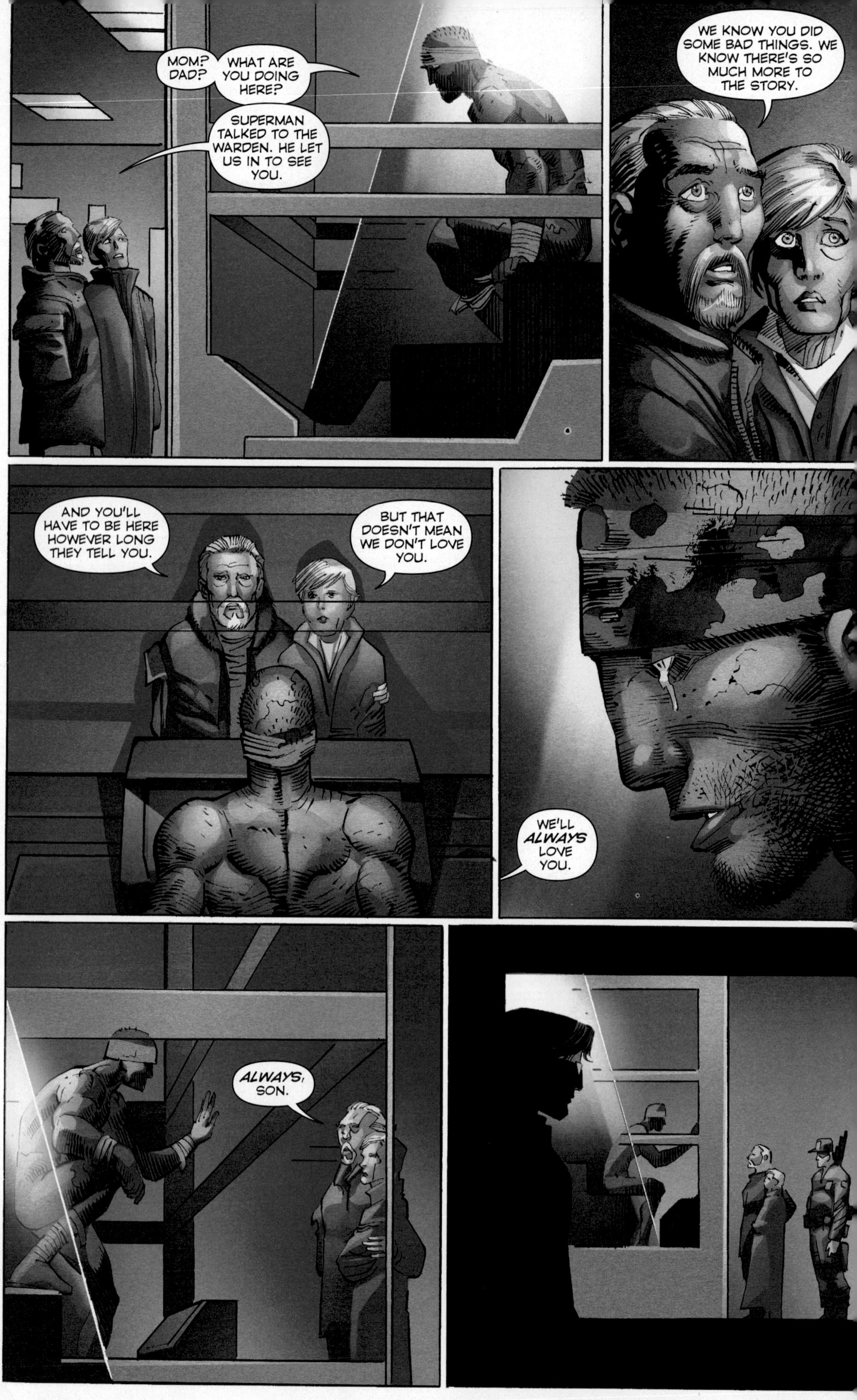
MOM? DAD?
WHAT ARE YOU DOING HERE?
SUPERMAN TALKED TO THE WARDEN. HE LET US IN TO SEE YOU.
WE KNOW YOU DID SOME BAD THINGS. WE KNOW THERE'S SO MUCH MORE TO THE STORY.
AND YOU'LL HAVE TO BE HERE HOWEVER LONG THEY TELL YOU.
BUT THAT DOESN'T MEAN WE DON'T LOVE YOU.
WE'LL *ALWAYS* LOVE YOU.
ALWAYS, SON.

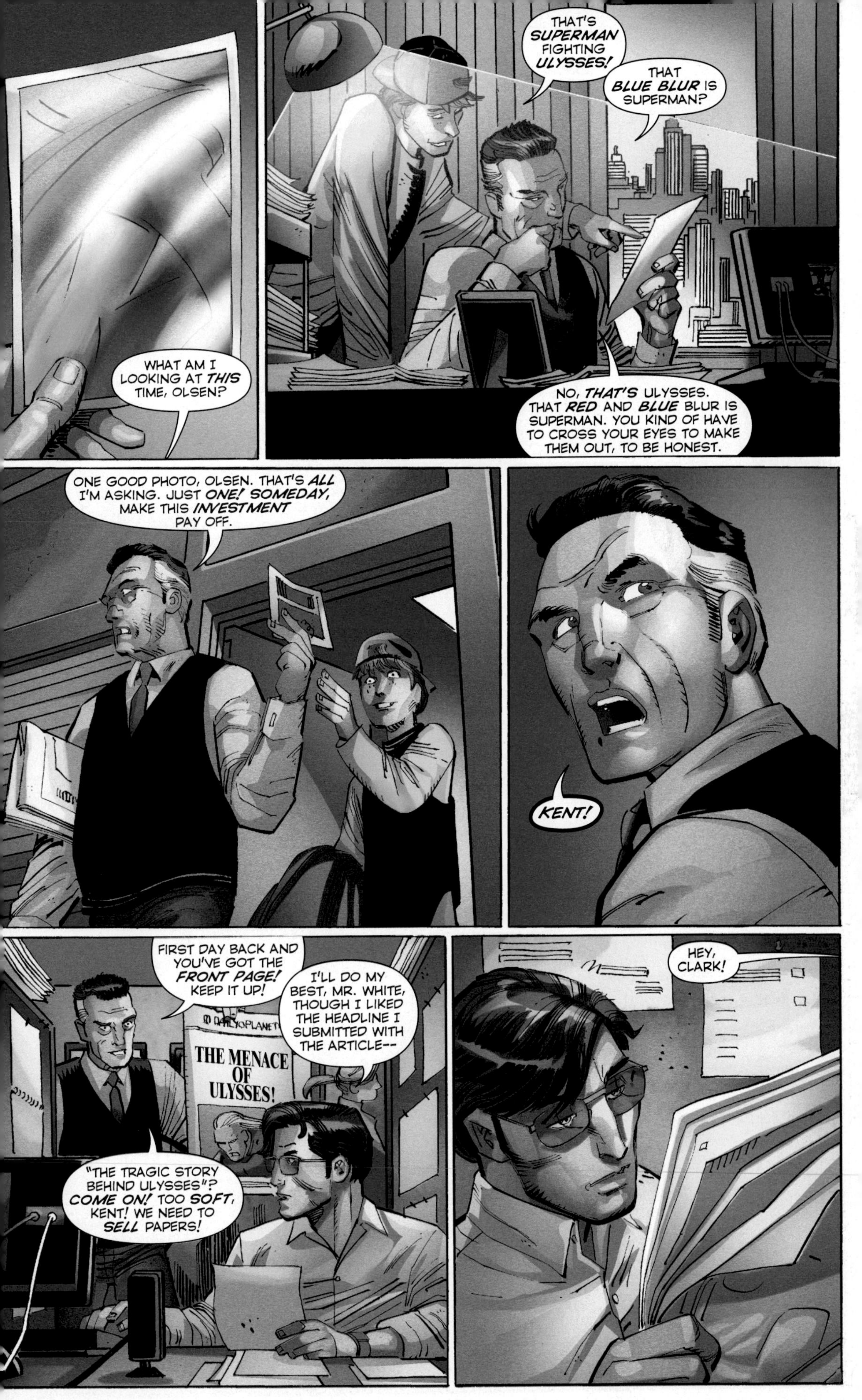
WHAT AM I LOOKING AT THIS TIME, OLSEN?
THAT'S SUPERMAN FIGHTING ULYSSES!
THAT BLUE BLUR IS SUPERMAN?
NO, THAT'S ULYSSES. THAT RED AND BLUE BLUR IS SUPERMAN. YOU KIND OF HAVE TO CROSS YOUR EYES TO MAKE THEM OUT, TO BE HONEST.
ONE GOOD PHOTO, OLSEN. THAT'S ALL I'M ASKING. JUST ONE! SOMEDAY, MAKE THIS INVESTMENT PAY OFF.
KENT!
FIRST DAY BACK AND YOU'VE GOT THE FRONT PAGE! KEEP IT UP!
I'LL DO MY BEST, MR. WHITE, THOUGH I LIKED THE HEADLINE I SUBMITTED WITH THE ARTICLE--
DAILY PLANET
THE MENACE OF ULYSSES!
"THE TRAGIC STORY BEHIND ULYSSES"? COME ON! TOO SOFT, KENT! WE NEED TO SELL PAPERS!
HEY, CLARK!

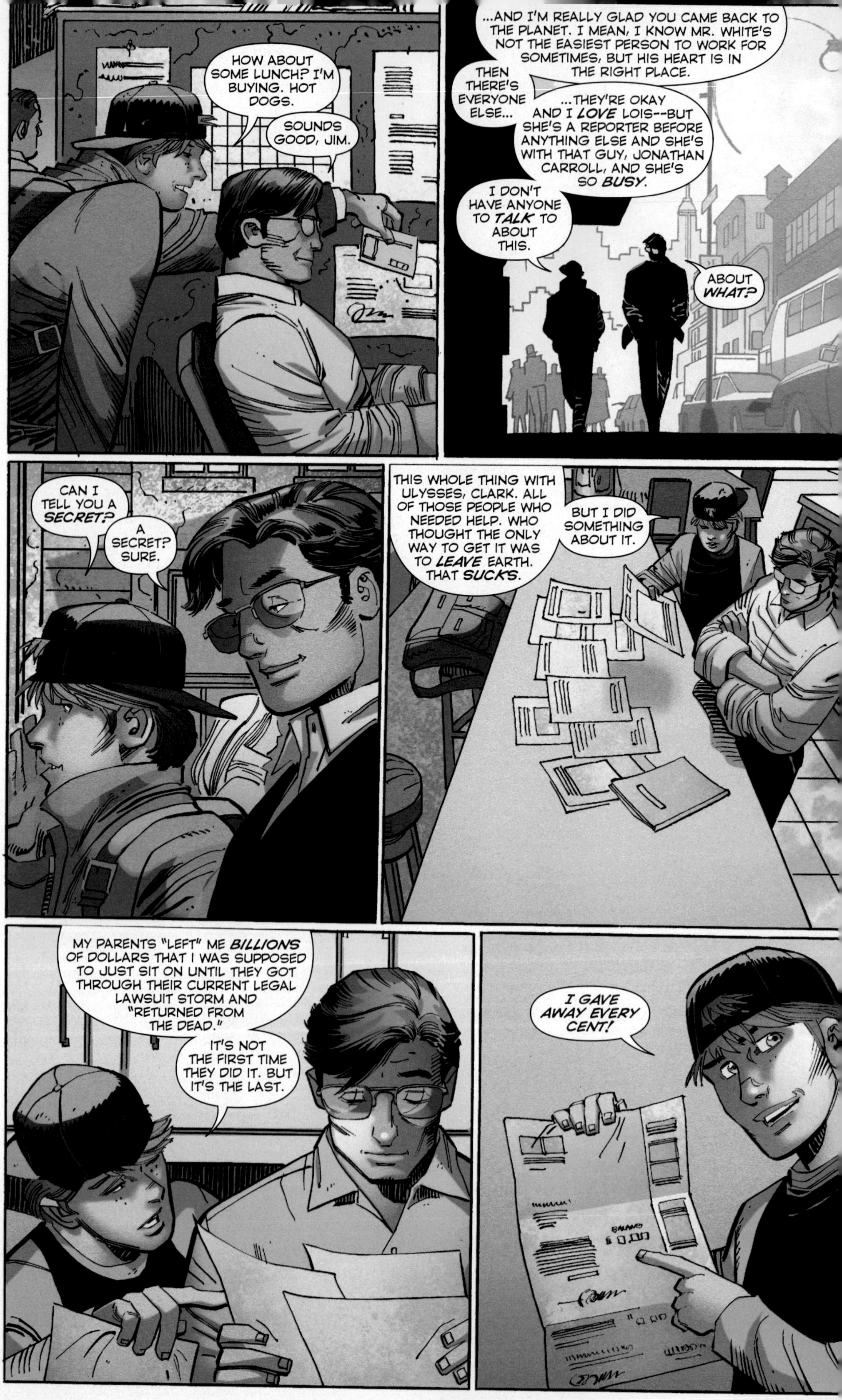
HOW ABOUT SOME LUNCH? I'M BUYING. HOT DOGS.
SOUNDS GOOD, JIM.
...AND I'M REALLY GLAD YOU CAME BACK TO THE PLANET. I MEAN, I KNOW MR. WHITE'S NOT THE EASIEST PERSON TO WORK FOR SOMETIMES, BUT HIS HEART IS IN THE RIGHT PLACE.
THEN THERE'S EVERYONE ELSE...
...THEY'RE OKAY AND I LOVE LOIS--BUT SHE'S A REPORTER BEFORE ANYTHING ELSE AND SHE'S WITH THAT GUY, JONATHAN CARROLL, AND SHE'S SO BUSY.
I DON'T HAVE ANYONE TO TALK TO ABOUT THIS.
ABOUT WHAT?
CAN I TELL YOU A SECRET?
A SECRET? SURE.
THIS WHOLE THING WITH ULYSSES, CLARK. ALL OF THOSE PEOPLE WHO NEEDED HELP. WHO THOUGHT THE ONLY WAY TO GET IT WAS TO LEAVE EARTH. THAT SUCKS.
BUT I DID SOMETHING ABOUT IT.
MY PARENTS "LEFT" ME BILLIONS OF DOLLARS THAT I WAS SUPPOSED TO JUST SIT ON UNTIL THEY GOT THROUGH THEIR CURRENT LEGAL LAWSUIT STORM AND "RETURNED FROM THE DEAD."
IT'S NOT THE FIRST TIME THEY DID IT. BUT IT'S THE LAST.
I GAVE AWAY EVERY CENT!

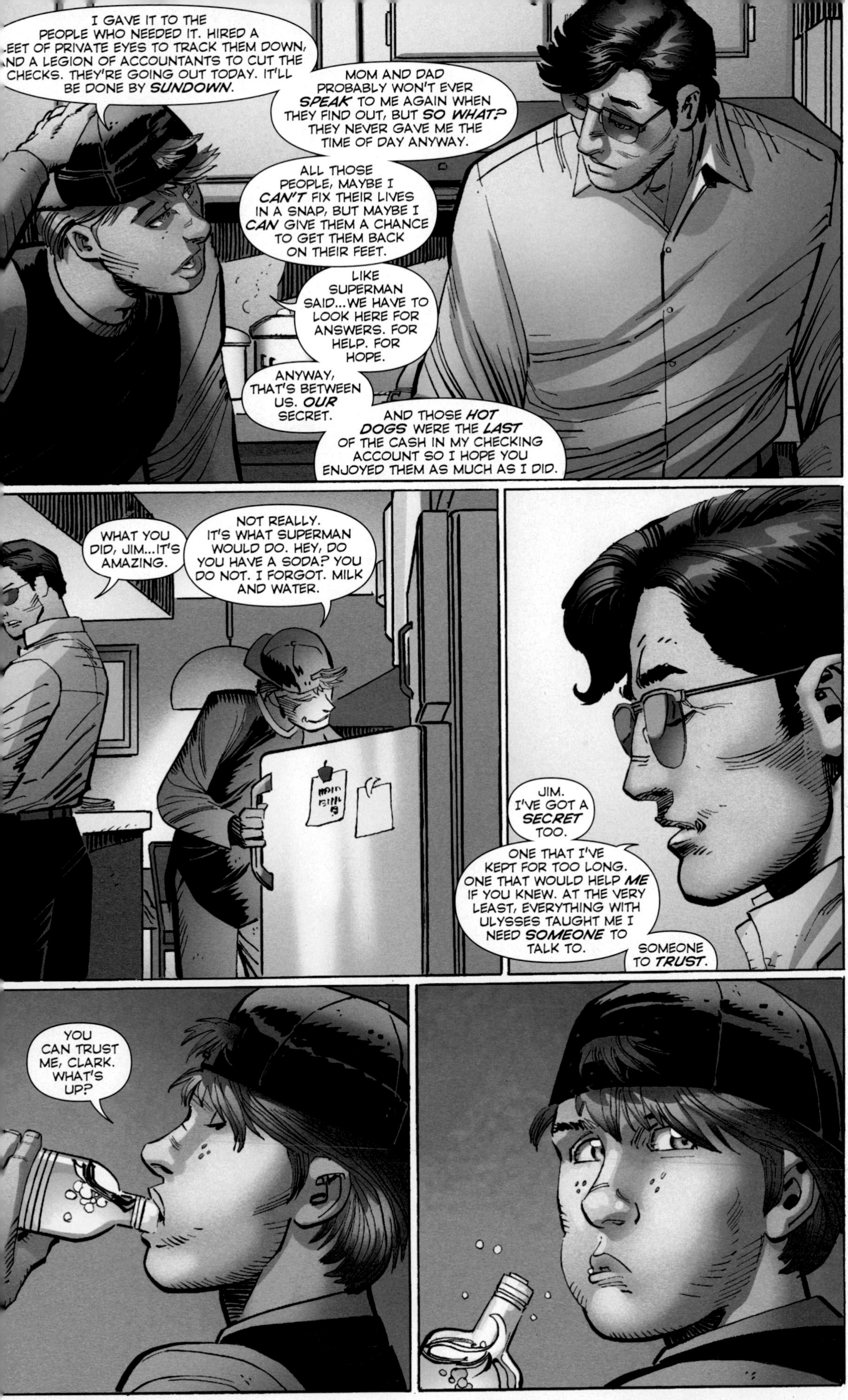
I GAVE IT TO THE PEOPLE WHO NEEDED IT. HIRED A EET OF PRIVATE EYES TO TRACK THEM DOWN, ND A LEGION OF ACCOUNTANTS TO CUT THE CHECKS. THEY'RE GOING OUT TODAY. IT'LL BE DONE BY SUNDOWN.
MOM AND DAD PROBABLY WON'T EVER SPEAK TO ME AGAIN WHEN THEY FIND OUT, BUT SO WHAT? THEY NEVER GAVE ME THE TIME OF DAY ANYWAY.
ALL THOSE PEOPLE, MAYBE I CAN'T FIX THEIR LIVES IN A SNAP, BUT MAYBE I CAN GIVE THEM A CHANCE TO GET THEM BACK ON THEIR FEET.
LIKE SUPERMAN SAID...WE HAVE TO LOOK HERE FOR ANSWERS. FOR HELP. FOR HOPE.
ANYWAY, THAT'S BETWEEN US. OUR SECRET.
AND THOSE HOT DOGS WERE THE LAST OF THE CASH IN MY CHECKING ACCOUNT SO I HOPE YOU ENJOYED THEM AS MUCH AS I DID.
WHAT YOU DID, JIM...IT'S AMAZING.
NOT REALLY. IT'S WHAT SUPERMAN WOULD DO. HEY, DO YOU HAVE A SODA? YOU DO NOT. I FORGOT. MILK AND WATER.
JIM. I'VE GOT A SECRET TOO.
ONE THAT I'VE KEPT FOR TOO LONG. ONE THAT WOULD HELP ME IF YOU KNEW. AT THE VERY LEAST, EVERYTHING WITH ULYSSES TAUGHT ME I NEED SOMEONE TO TALK TO.
SOMEONE TO TRUST.
YOU CAN TRUST ME, CLARK. WHAT'S UP?

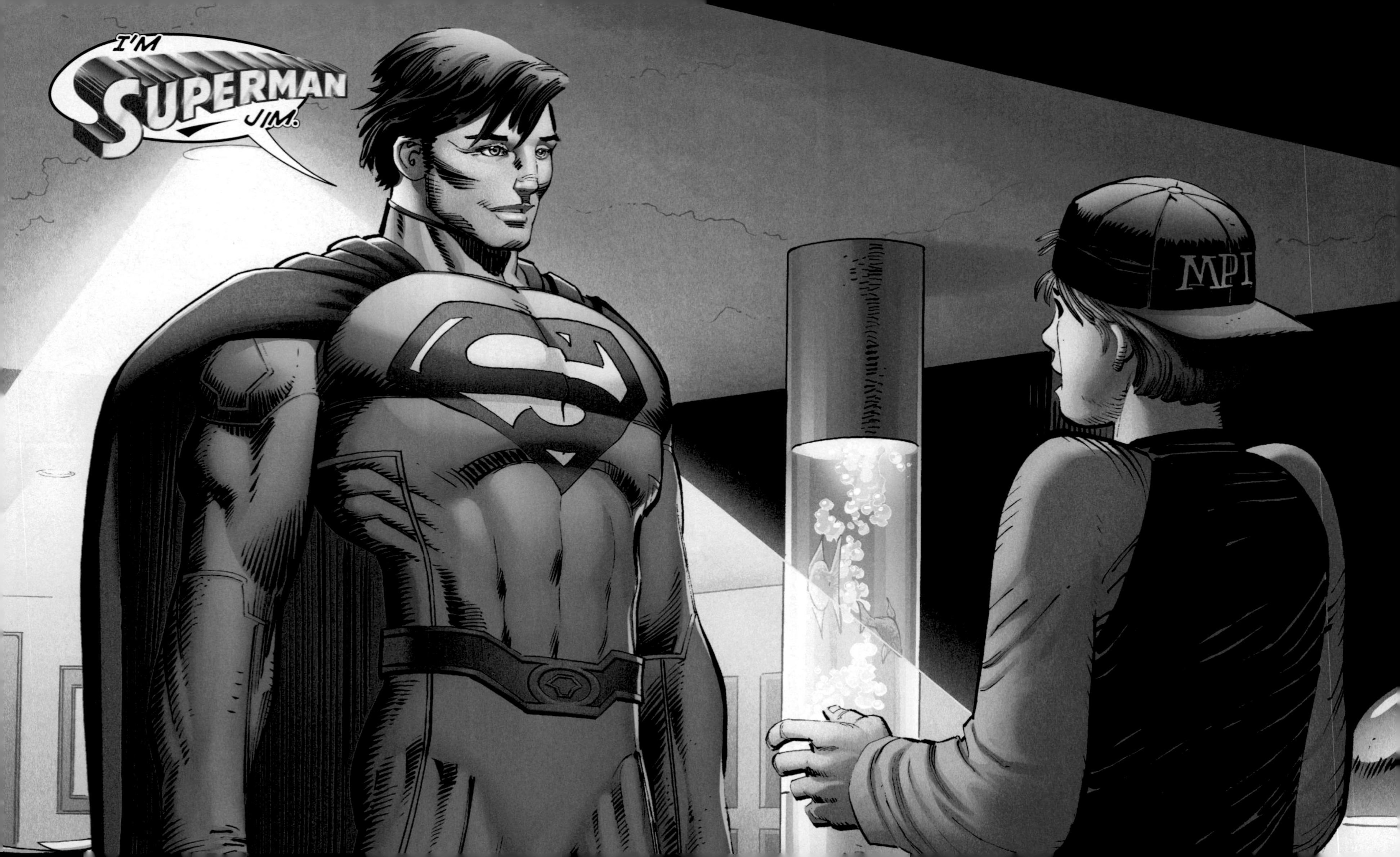
I'M SUPERMAN, JIM.
MPI

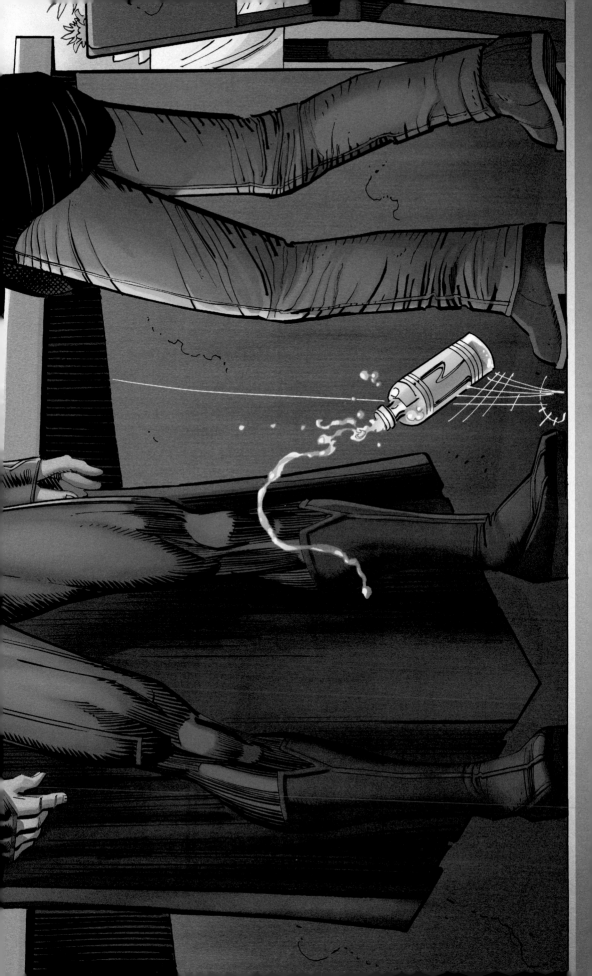

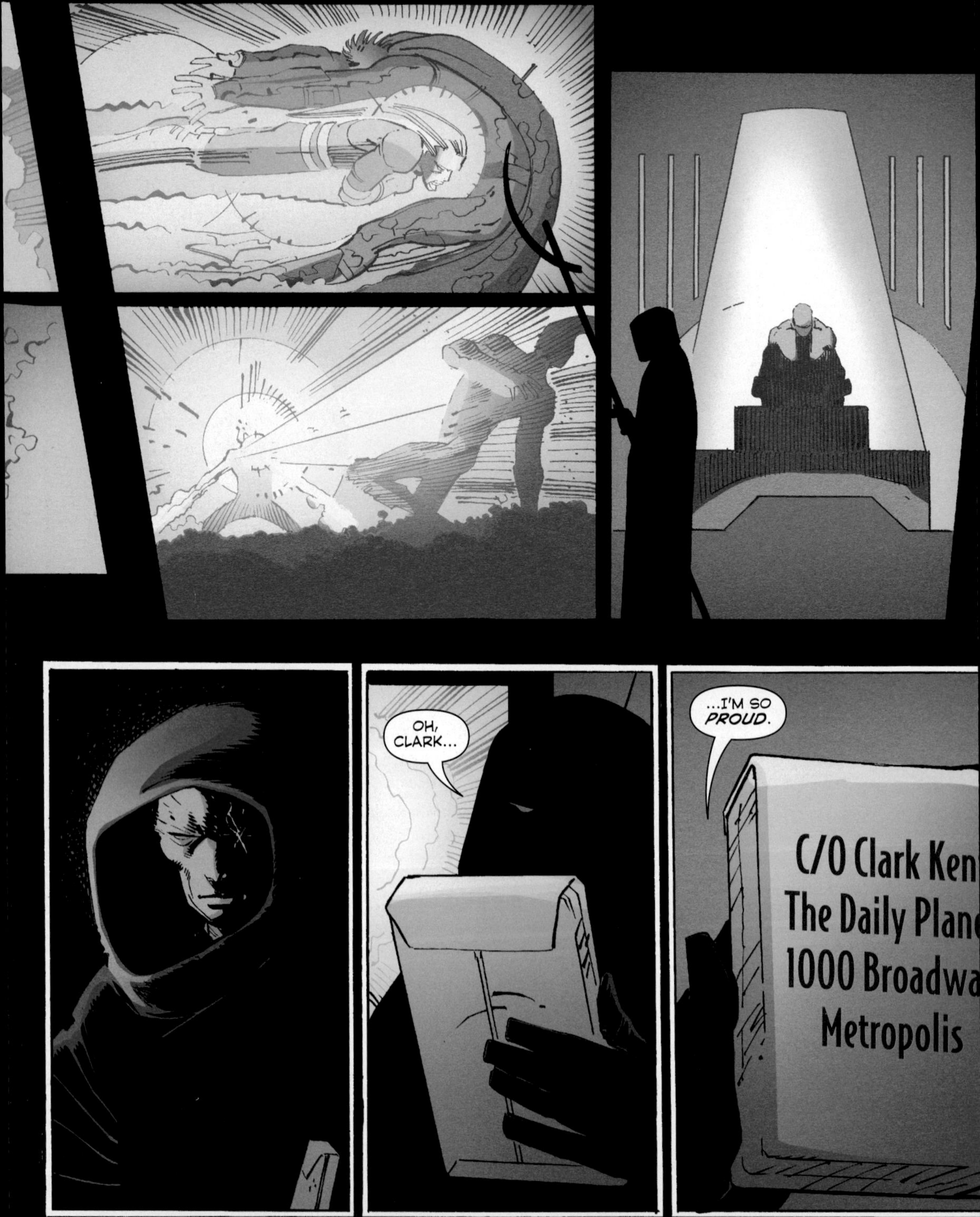
OH, CLARK...
...I'M SO PROUD.
C/O Clark Ken
The Daily Plane
1000 Broadwa
Metropolis

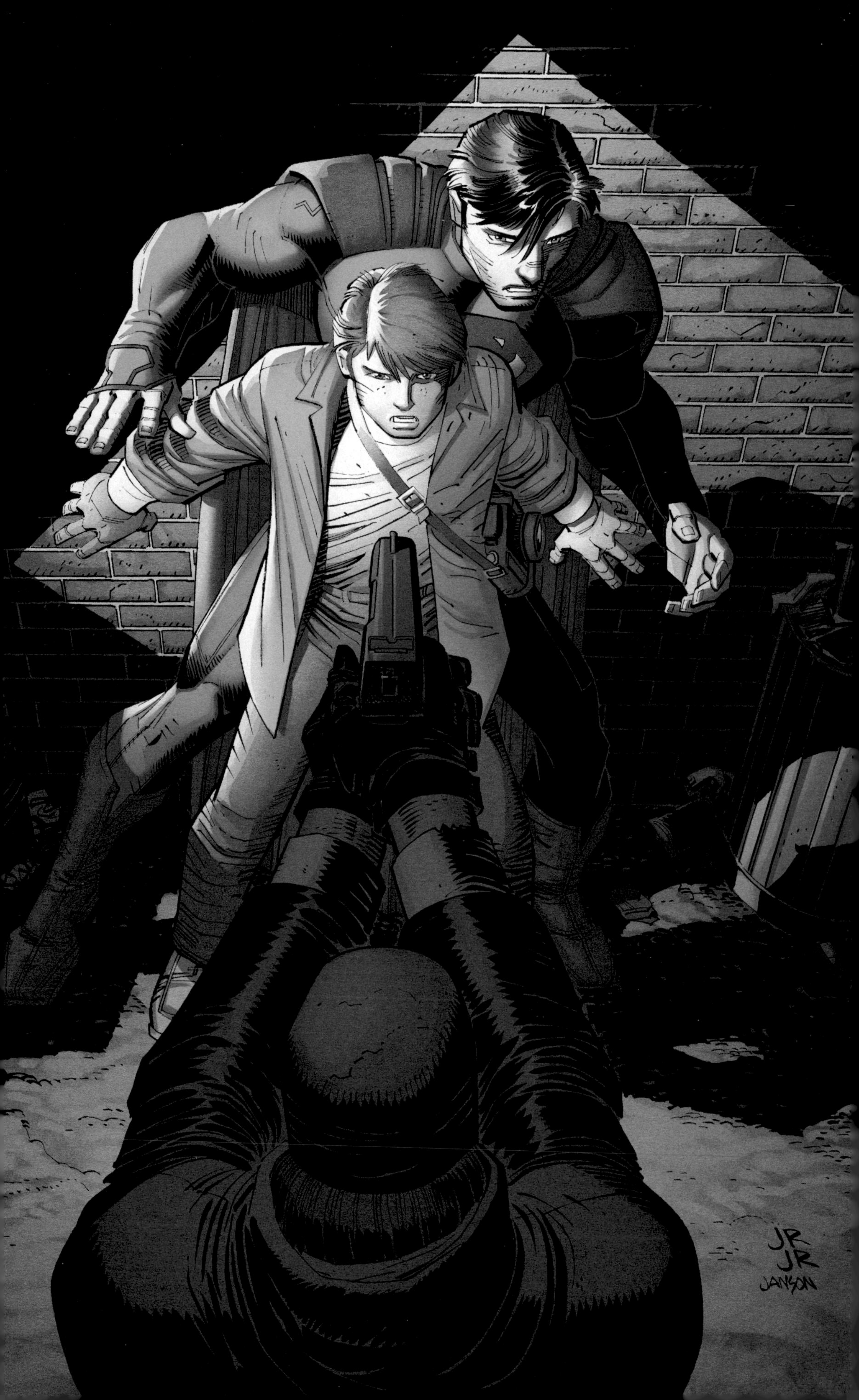
JR
JR
JANSON

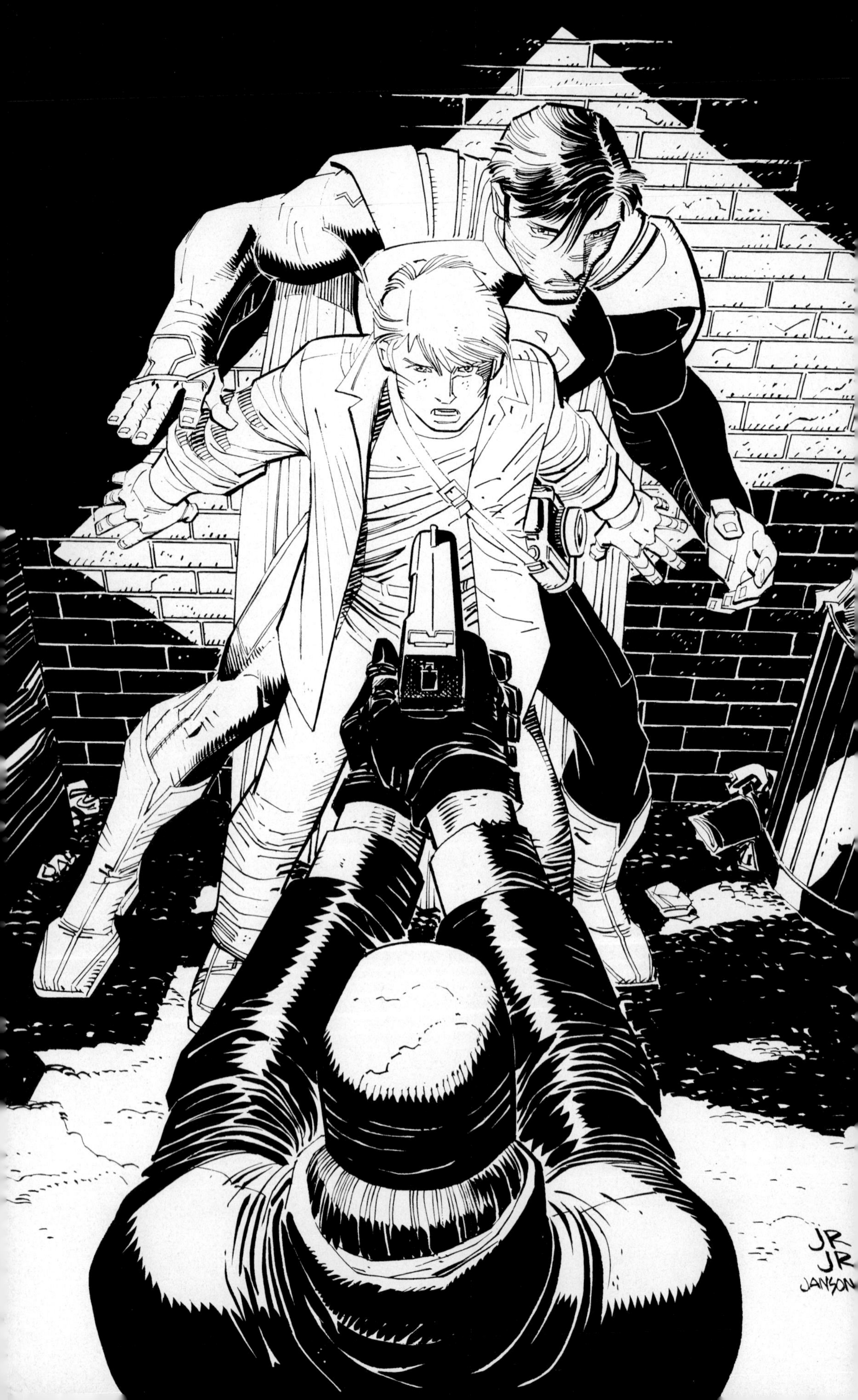
JR
JR
JANSON

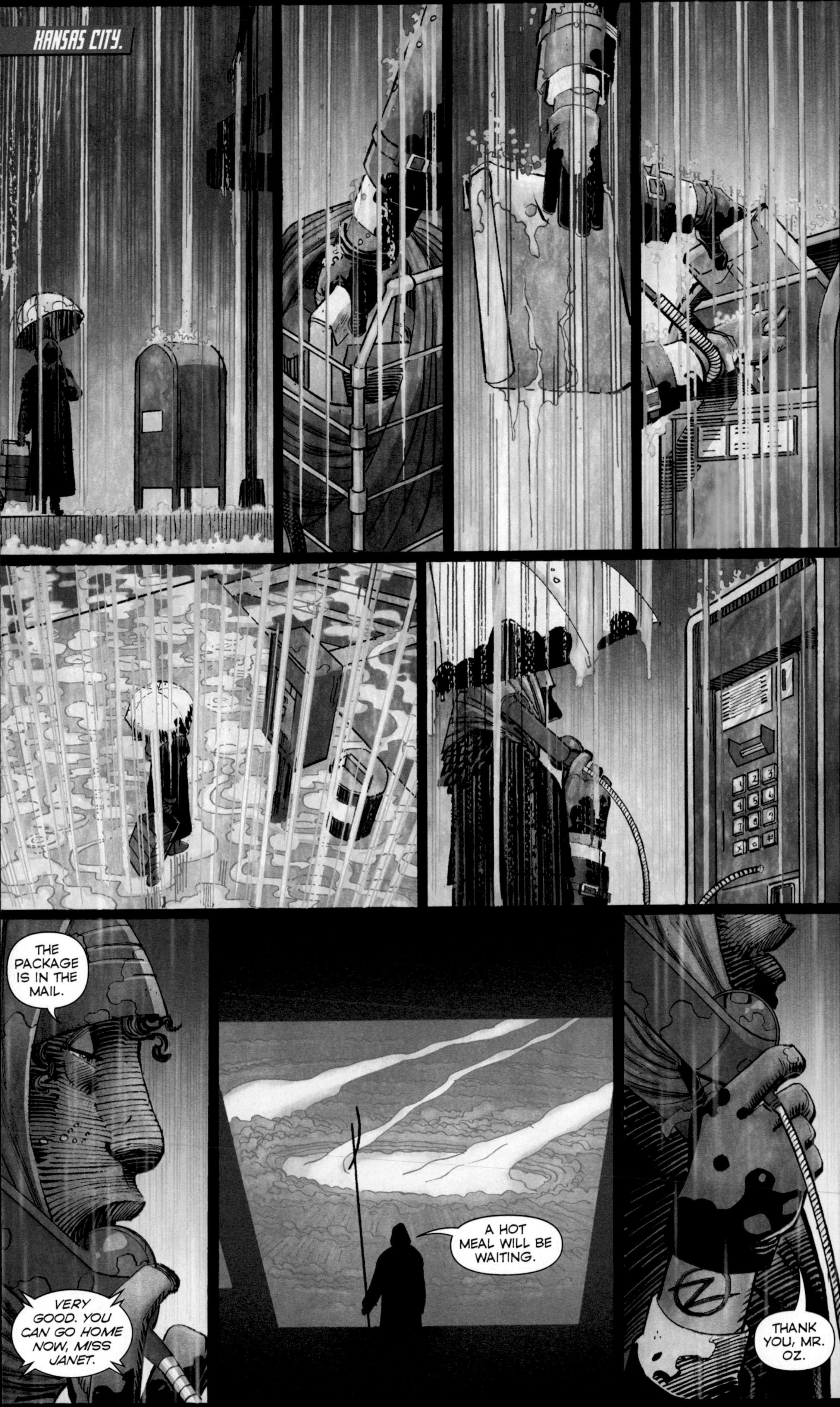
KANSAS CITY.
THE PACKAGE IS IN THE MAIL.
VERY GOOD. YOU CAN GO HOME NOW, MISS JANET.
A HOT MEAL WILL BE WAITING.
THANK YOU, MR. OZ.

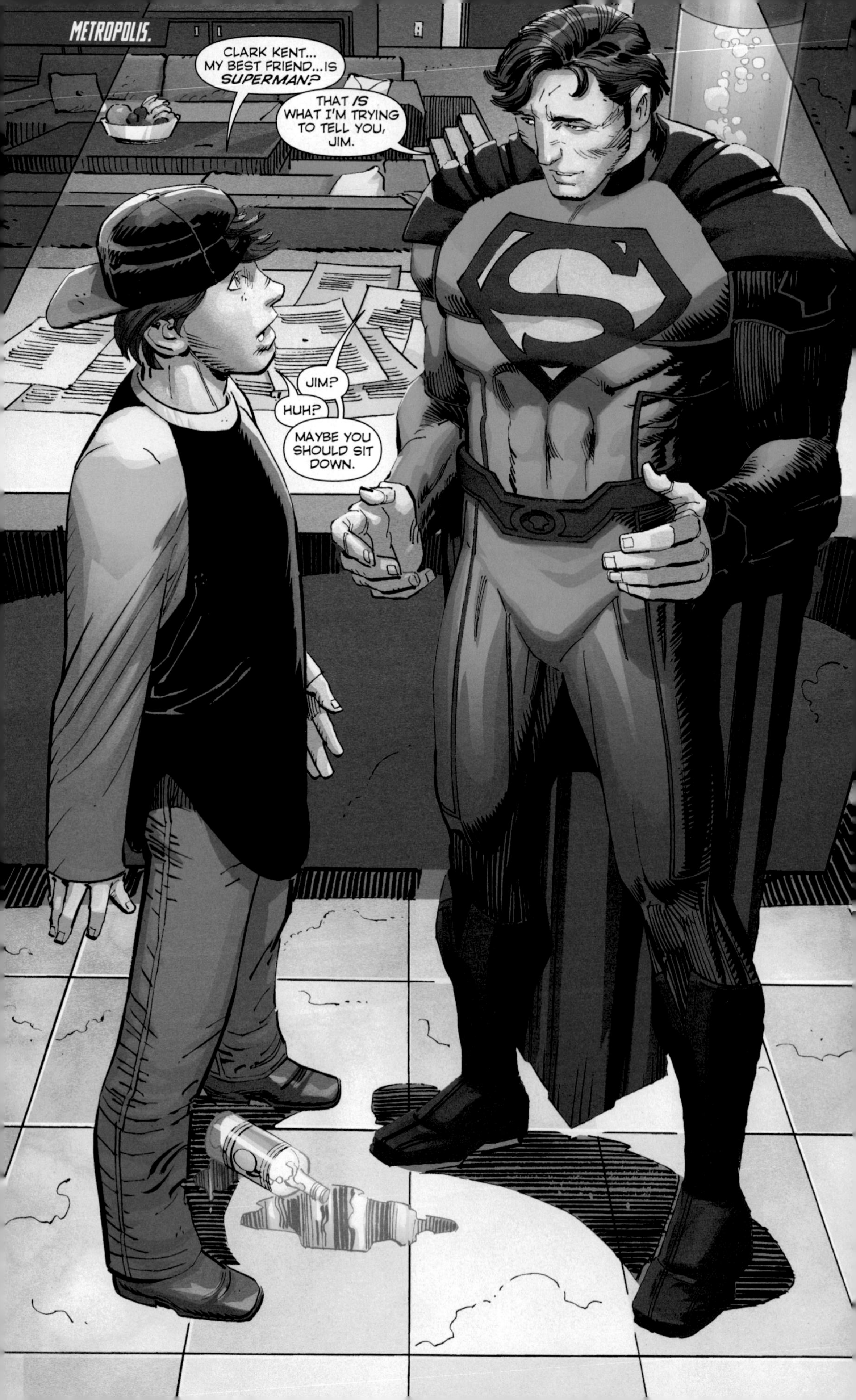
METROPOLIS.
CLARK KENT... MY BEST FRIEND...IS SUPERMAN?
THAT IS WHAT I'M TRYING TO TELL YOU, JIM.
JIM?
HUH?
MAYBE YOU SHOULD SIT DOWN.

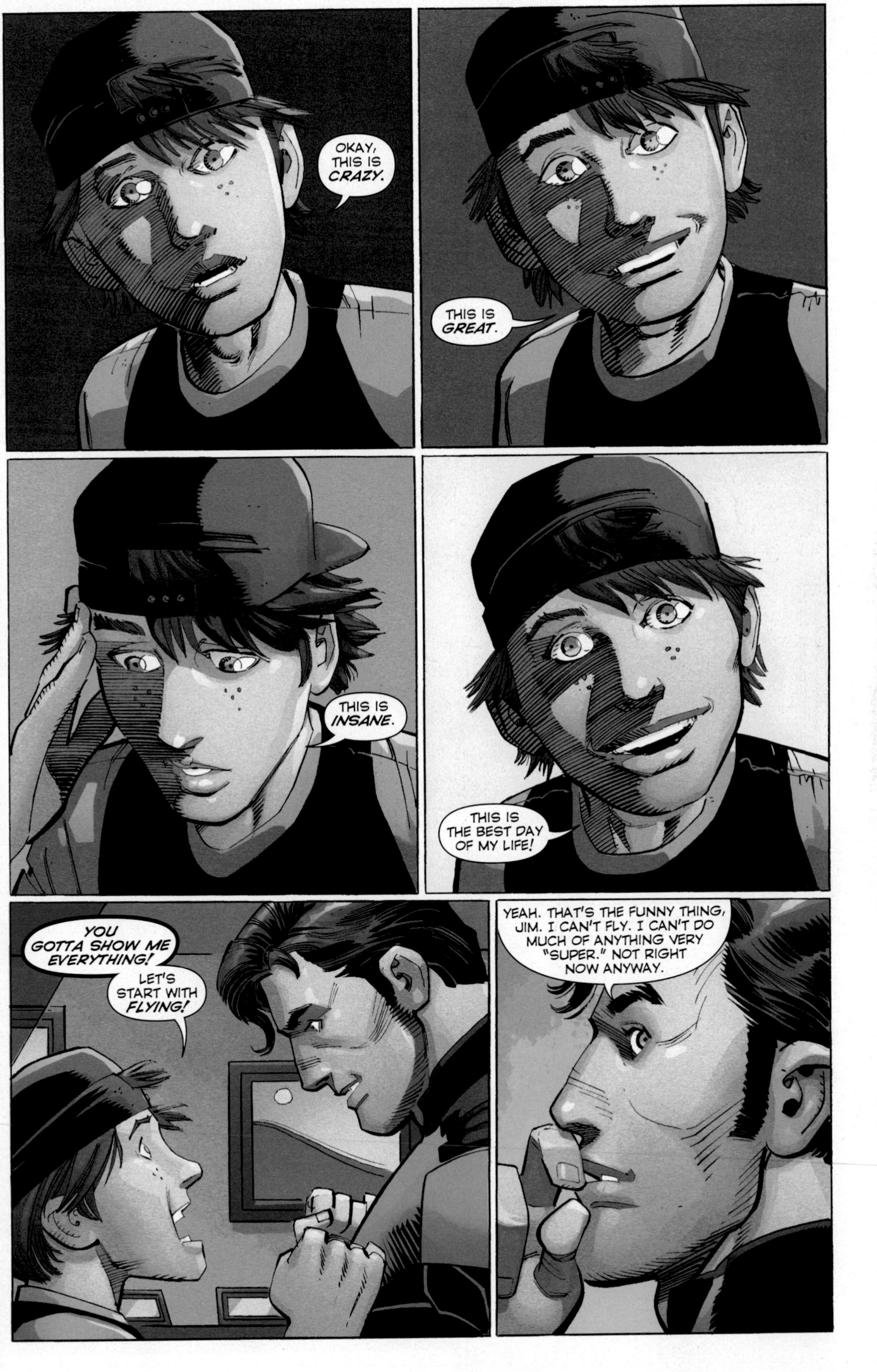
OKAY, THIS IS CRAZY.
THIS IS GREAT.
THIS IS INSANE.
THIS IS THE BEST DAY OF MY LIFE!
YOU GOTTA SHOW ME EVERYTHING!
LET'S START WITH FLYING!
YEAH. THAT'S THE FUNNY THING, JIM. I CAN'T FLY. I CAN'T DO MUCH OF ANYTHING VERY "SUPER." NOT RIGHT NOW ANYWAY.

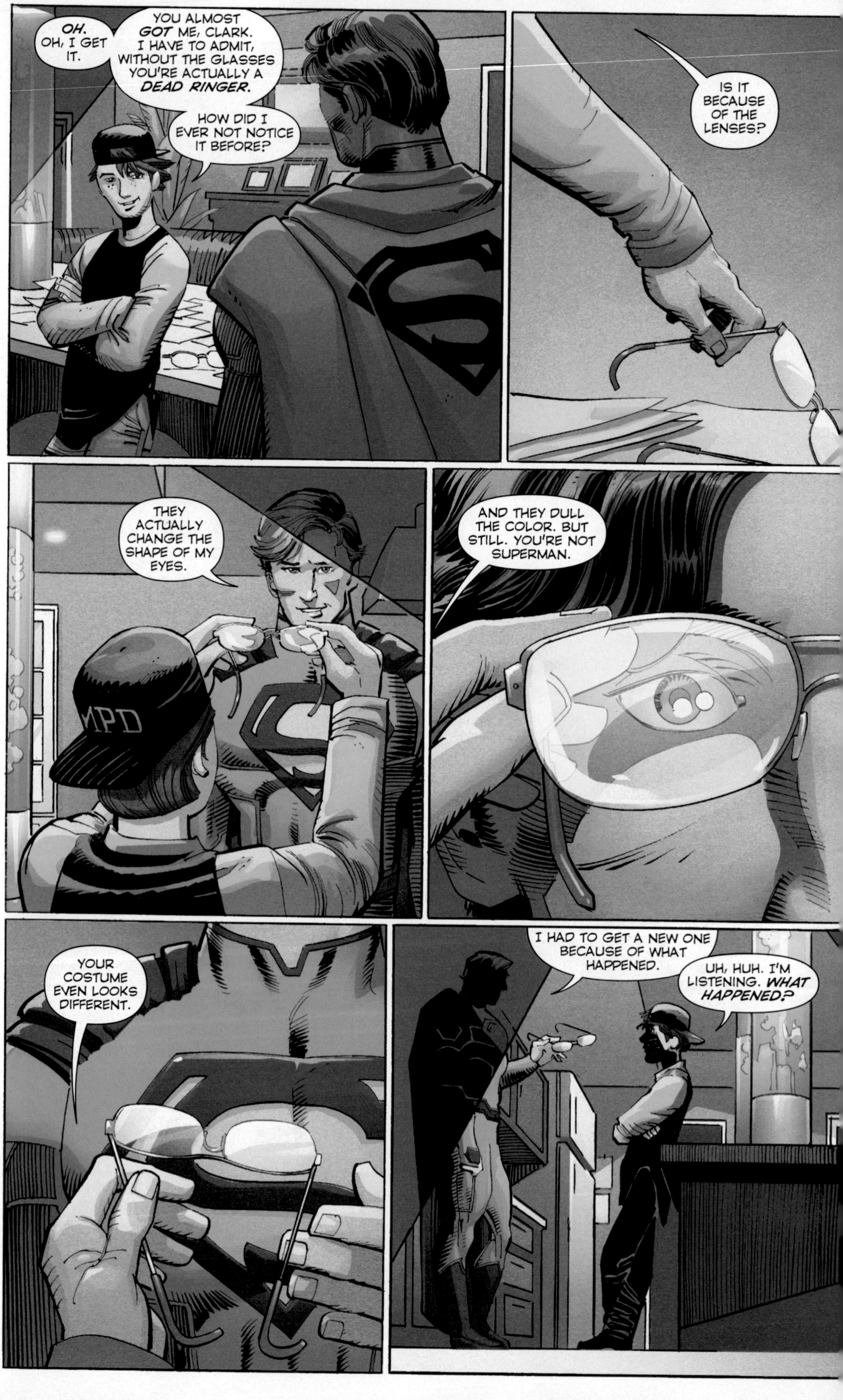

OH. OH, I GET IT.
YOU ALMOST *GOT* ME, CLARK. I HAVE TO ADMIT, WITHOUT THE GLASSES YOU'RE ACTUALLY A *DEAD RINGER.*
HOW DID I EVER NOT NOTICE IT BEFORE?
IS IT BECAUSE OF THE LENSES?
THEY ACTUALLY CHANGE THE SHAPE OF MY EYES.
AND THEY DULL THE COLOR. BUT STILL. YOU'RE NOT SUPERMAN.
MPD
YOUR COSTUME EVEN LOOKS DIFFERENT.
I HAD TO GET A NEW ONE BECAUSE OF WHAT HAPPENED.
UH, HUH. I'M LISTENING. *WHAT HAPPENED?*

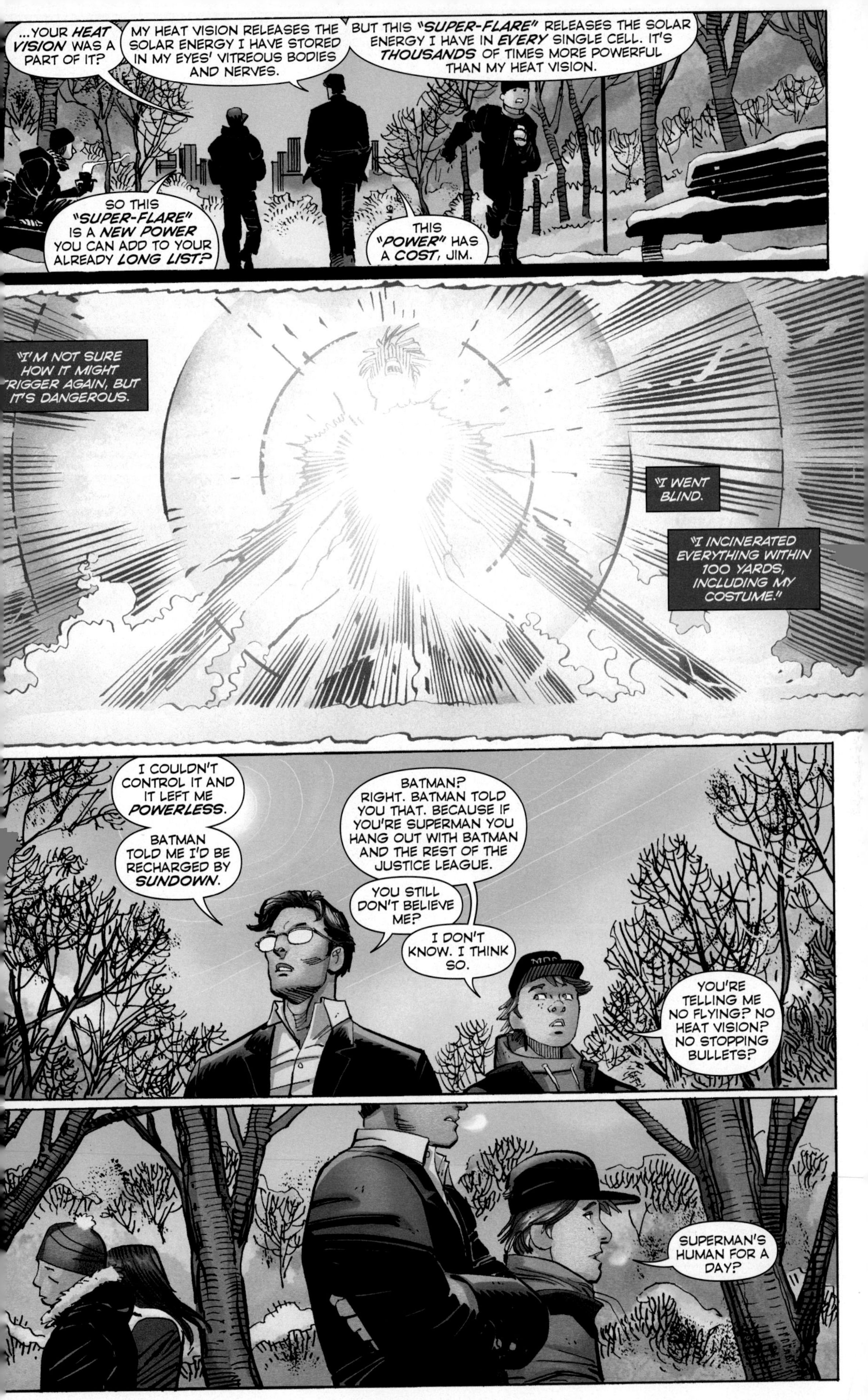
...YOUR HEAT VISION WAS A PART OF IT?
MY HEAT VISION RELEASES THE SOLAR ENERGY I HAVE STORED IN MY EYES' VITREOUS BODIES AND NERVES.
BUT THIS "SUPER-FLARE" RELEASES THE SOLAR ENERGY I HAVE IN EVERY SINGLE CELL. IT'S THOUSANDS OF TIMES MORE POWERFUL THAN MY HEAT VISION.
SO THIS "SUPER-FLARE" IS A NEW POWER YOU CAN ADD TO YOUR ALREADY LONG LIST?
THIS "POWER" HAS A COST, JIM.
"I'M NOT SURE HOW IT MIGHT TRIGGER AGAIN, BUT IT'S DANGEROUS.
"I WENT BLIND.
"I INCINERATED EVERYTHING WITHIN 100 YARDS, INCLUDING MY COSTUME."
I COULDN'T CONTROL IT AND IT LEFT ME POWERLESS.
BATMAN TOLD ME I'D BE RECHARGED BY SUNDOWN.
BATMAN? RIGHT. BATMAN TOLD YOU THAT. BECAUSE IF YOU'RE SUPERMAN YOU HANG OUT WITH BATMAN AND THE REST OF THE JUSTICE LEAGUE.
YOU STILL DON'T BELIEVE ME?
I DON'T KNOW. I THINK SO.
YOU'RE TELLING ME NO FLYING? NO HEAT VISION? NO STOPPING BULLETS?
SUPERMAN'S HUMAN FOR A DAY?

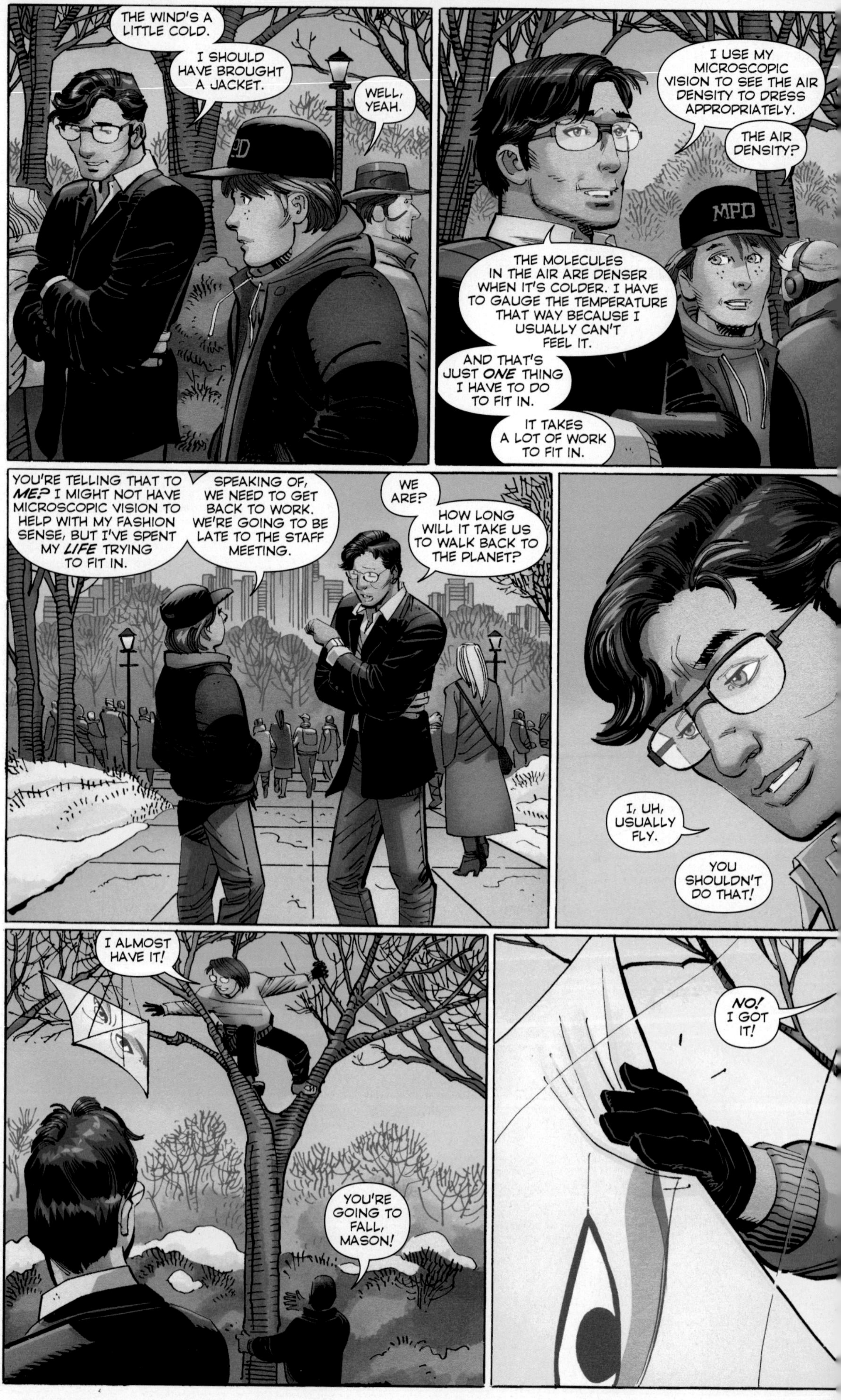
THE WIND'S A LITTLE COLD.
I SHOULD HAVE BROUGHT A JACKET.
WELL, YEAH.
I USE MY MICROSCOPIC VISION TO SEE THE AIR DENSITY TO DRESS APPROPRIATELY.
THE AIR DENSITY?
THE MOLECULES IN THE AIR ARE DENSER WHEN IT'S COLDER. I HAVE TO GAUGE THE TEMPERATURE THAT WAY BECAUSE I USUALLY CAN'T FEEL IT.
AND THAT'S JUST ONE THING I HAVE TO DO TO FIT IN.
IT TAKES A LOT OF WORK TO FIT IN.
YOU'RE TELLING THAT TO ME? I MIGHT NOT HAVE MICROSCOPIC VISION TO HELP WITH MY FASHION SENSE, BUT I'VE SPENT MY LIFE TRYING TO FIT IN.
SPEAKING OF, WE NEED TO GET BACK TO WORK. WE'RE GOING TO BE LATE TO THE STAFF MEETING.
WE ARE?
HOW LONG WILL IT TAKE US TO WALK BACK TO THE PLANET?
I, UH, USUALLY FLY.
YOU SHOULDN'T DO THAT!
I ALMOST HAVE IT!
YOU'RE GOING TO FALL, MASON!
NO! I GOT IT!

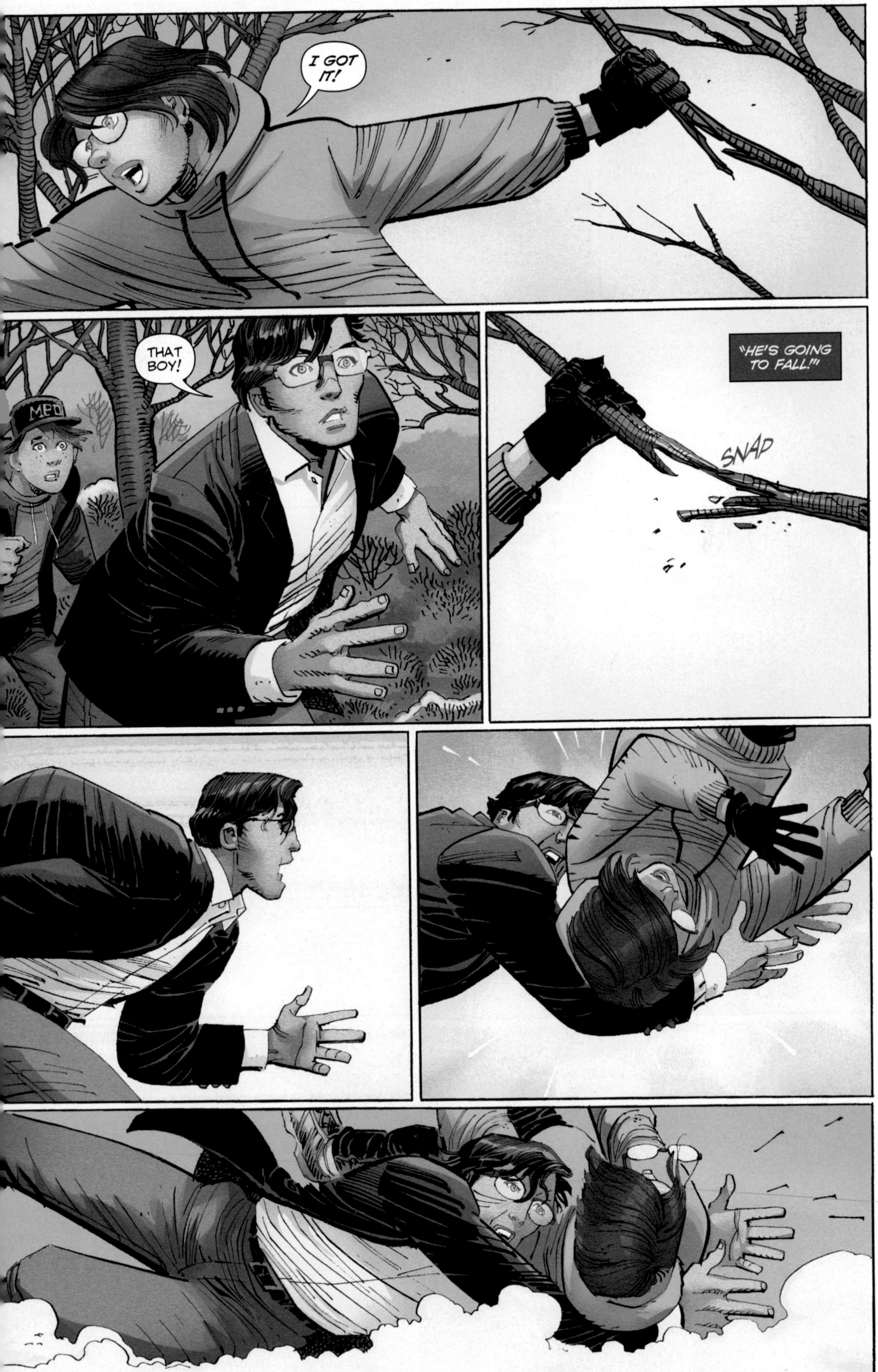
I GOT IT!
THAT BOY!
MPD
"HE'S GOING TO FALL!"
SNAP

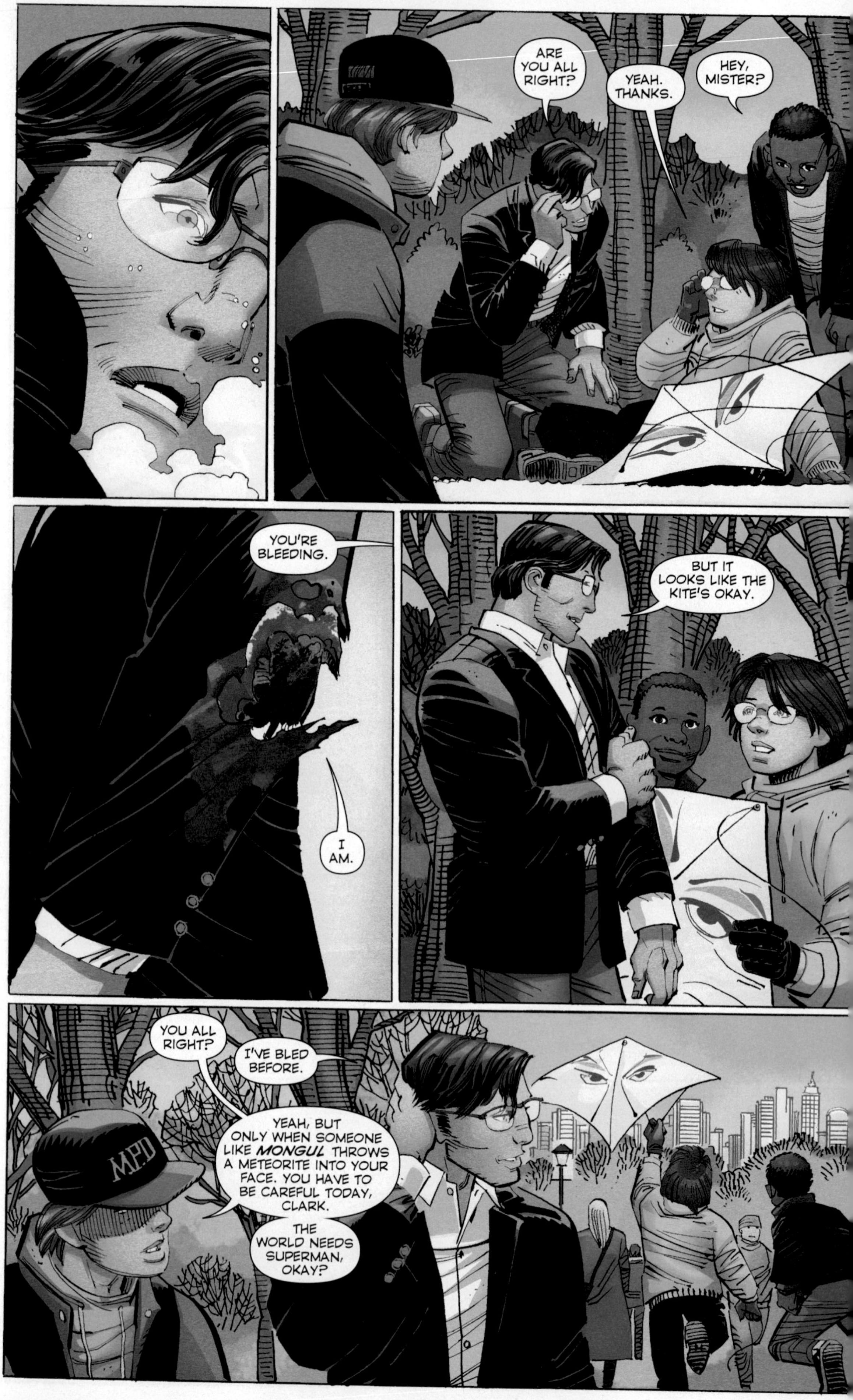

ARE YOU ALL RIGHT?
YEAH. THANKS.
HEY, MISTER?
YOU'RE BLEEDING.
I AM.
BUT IT LOOKS LIKE THE KITE'S OKAY.
YOU ALL RIGHT?
I'VE BLED BEFORE.
YEAH, BUT ONLY WHEN SOMEONE LIKE *MONGUL* THROWS A METEORITE INTO YOUR FACE. YOU HAVE TO BE CAREFUL TODAY, CLARK.
THE WORLD NEEDS SUPERMAN, OKAY?
M.P.D.

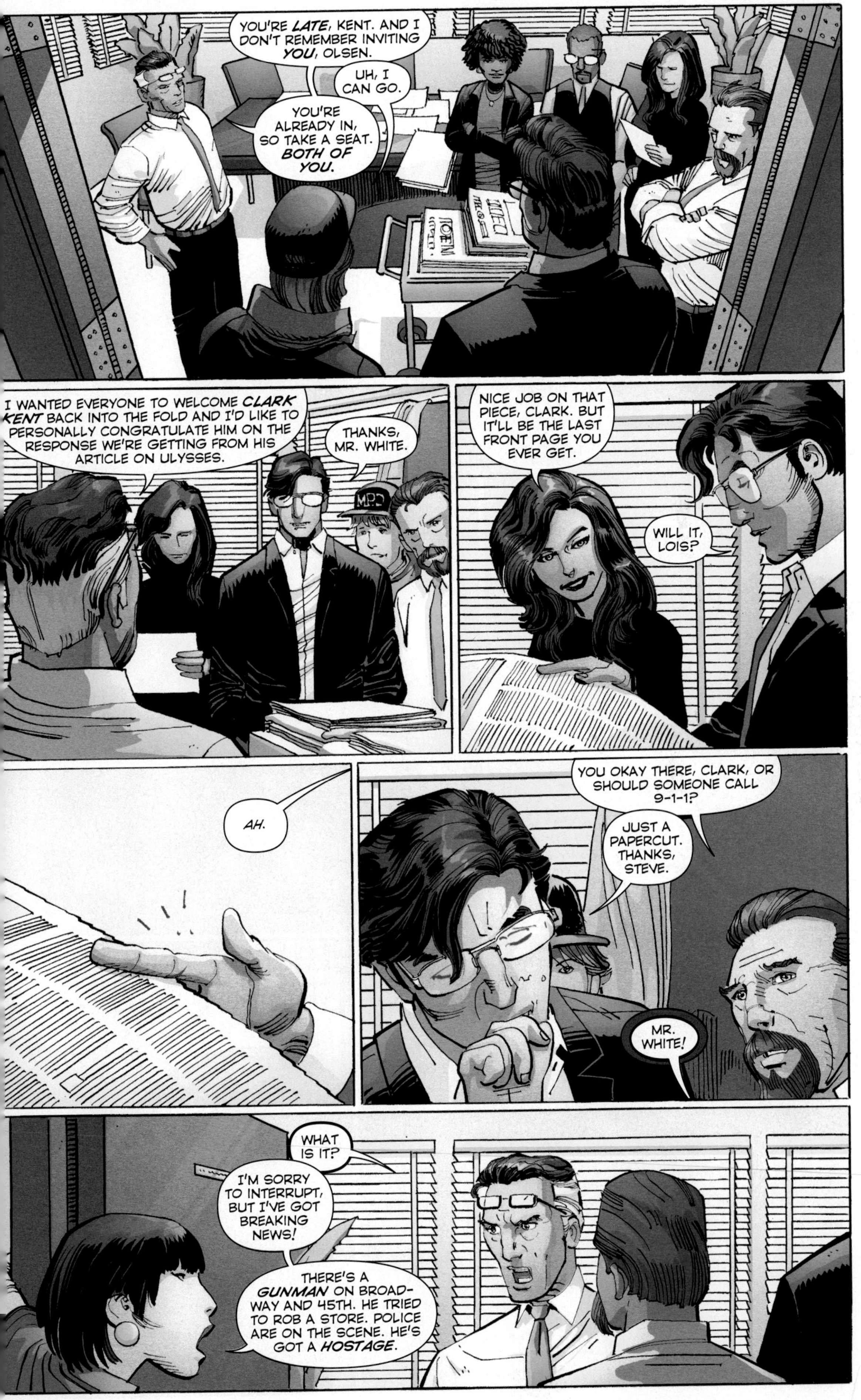
YOU'RE LATE, KENT. AND I DON'T REMEMBER INVITING YOU, OLSEN.
UH, I CAN GO.
YOU'RE ALREADY IN, SO TAKE A SEAT. BOTH OF YOU.
I WANTED EVERYONE TO WELCOME CLARK KENT BACK INTO THE FOLD AND I'D LIKE TO PERSONALLY CONGRATULATE HIM ON THE RESPONSE WE'RE GETTING FROM HIS ARTICLE ON ULYSSES.
THANKS, MR. WHITE.
MPD
NICE JOB ON THAT PIECE, CLARK. BUT IT'LL BE THE LAST FRONT PAGE YOU EVER GET.
WILL IT, LOIS?
AH.
YOU OKAY THERE, CLARK, OR SHOULD SOMEONE CALL 9-1-1?
JUST A PAPERCUT. THANKS, STEVE.
MR. WHITE!
WHAT IS IT?
I'M SORRY TO INTERRUPT, BUT I'VE GOT BREAKING NEWS!
THERE'S A GUNMAN ON BROADWAY AND 45TH. HE TRIED TO ROB A STORE. POLICE ARE ON THE SCENE. HE'S GOT A HOSTAGE.

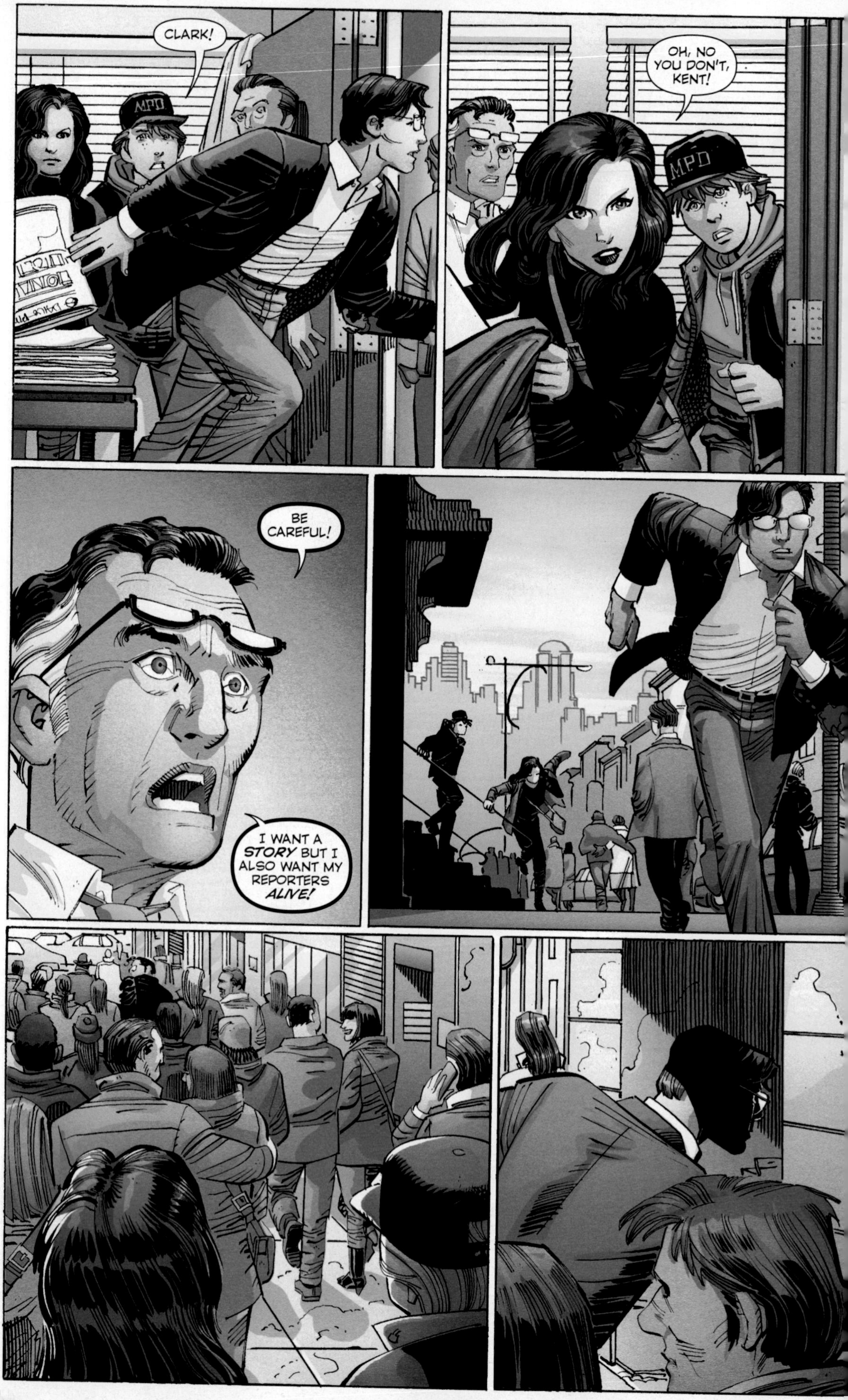
CLARK!
OH, NO YOU DON'T, KENT!
BE CAREFUL!
I WANT A STORY BUT I ALSO WANT MY REPORTERS ALIVE!

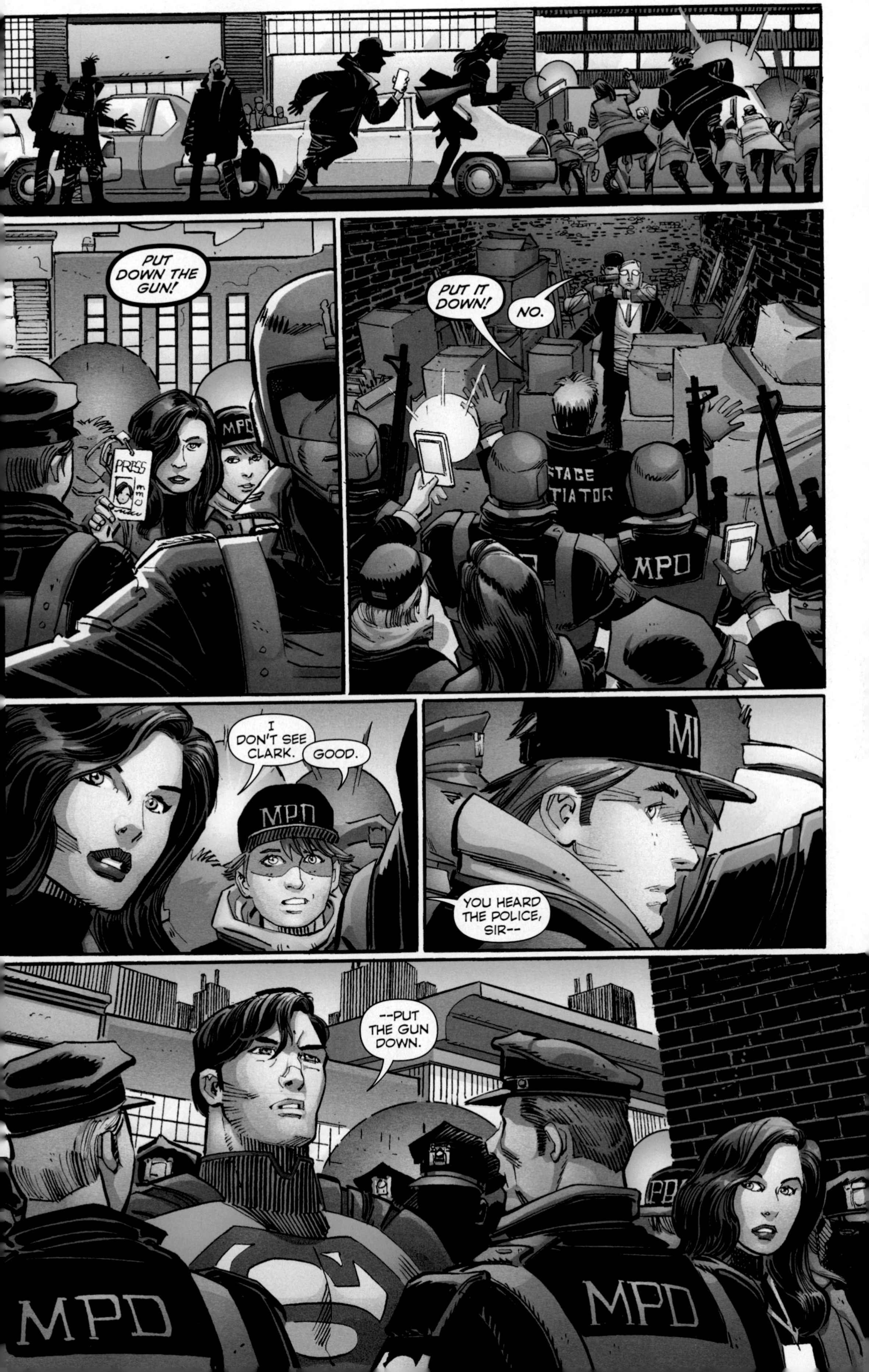
PUT DOWN THE GUN!
PUT IT DOWN!
NO.
STAGE
TIATOR
MPD
PRESS
MPD
I DON'T SEE CLARK.
GOOD.
MPD
YOU HEARD THE POLICE, SIR--
--PUT THE GUN DOWN.
MPD
MPD

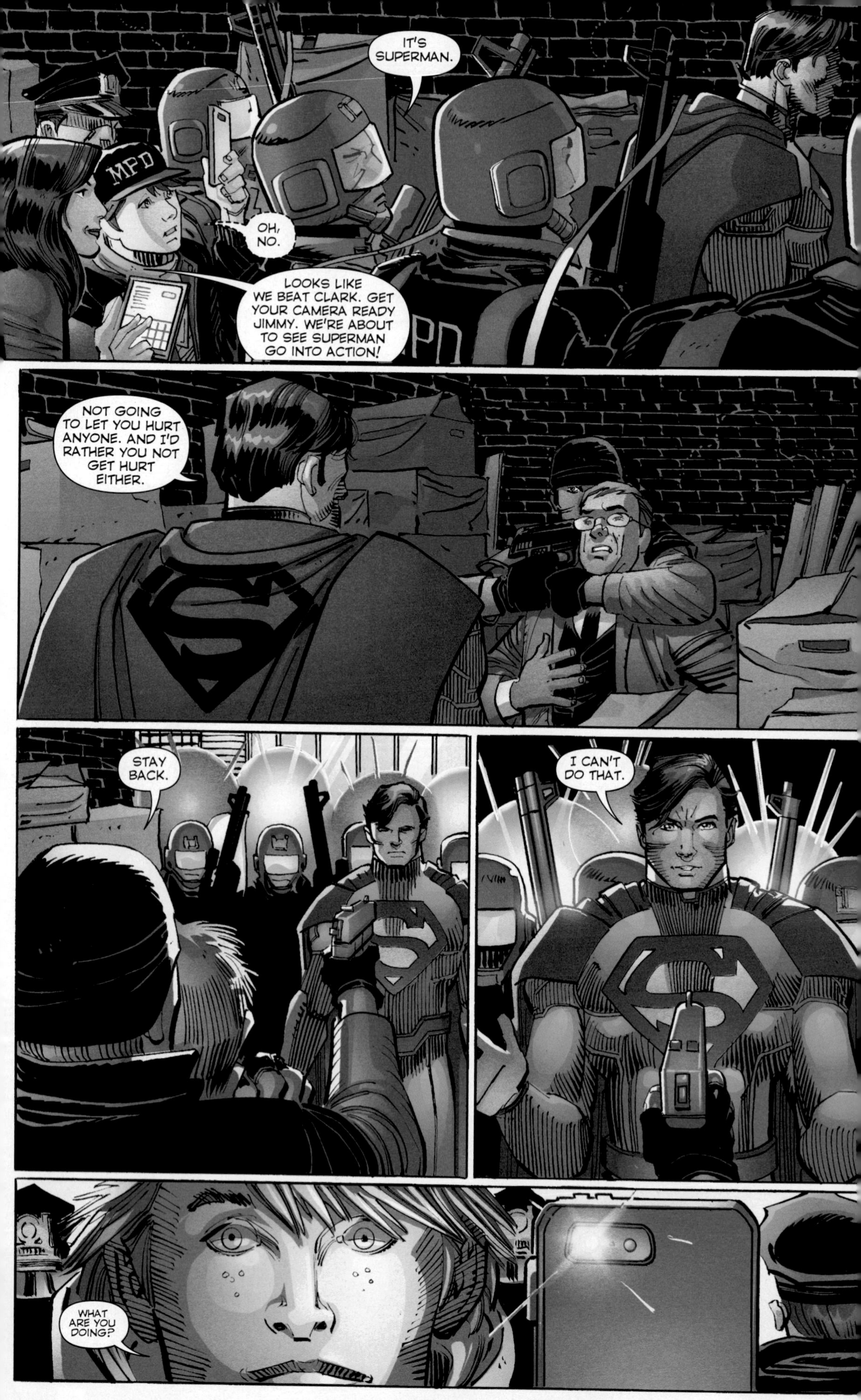
IT'S SUPERMAN.
OH, NO.
LOOKS LIKE WE BEAT CLARK. GET YOUR CAMERA READY JIMMY. WE'RE ABOUT TO SEE SUPERMAN GO INTO ACTION!
NOT GOING TO LET YOU HURT ANYONE. AND I'D RATHER YOU NOT GET HURT EITHER.
STAY BACK.
I CAN'T DO THAT.
WHAT ARE YOU DOING?

YOU KNOW WHAT HAPPENS WHEN PEOPLE SHOOT ME, DON'T YOU?

STAY BACK!

THEY WASTE BULLETS.

I SAID STAY BACK! I WILL SHOOT.

YOU DON'T WANT TO DO THAT.

YOU HAVEN'T HURT ANYONE YET. YOU CAN STILL SURRENDER. YOU CAN SERVE YOUR TIME, BECAUSE YOU'RE GOING TO HAVE TO DO TIME, BUT YOU CAN DO IT WITH INTEGRITY.

THEY'D PUT ME AWAY FOR YEARS.

FOR WHAT YOU'VE DONE, A FEW. BUT LESS IF YOU GIVE UP NOW WITHOUT PULLING THAT TRIGGER. YOU'LL STILL HAVE YOUR LIFE AHEAD OF YOU.

MAKE THE RIGHT CHOICE.

PLEASE.

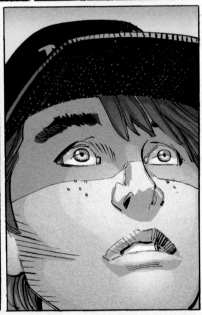

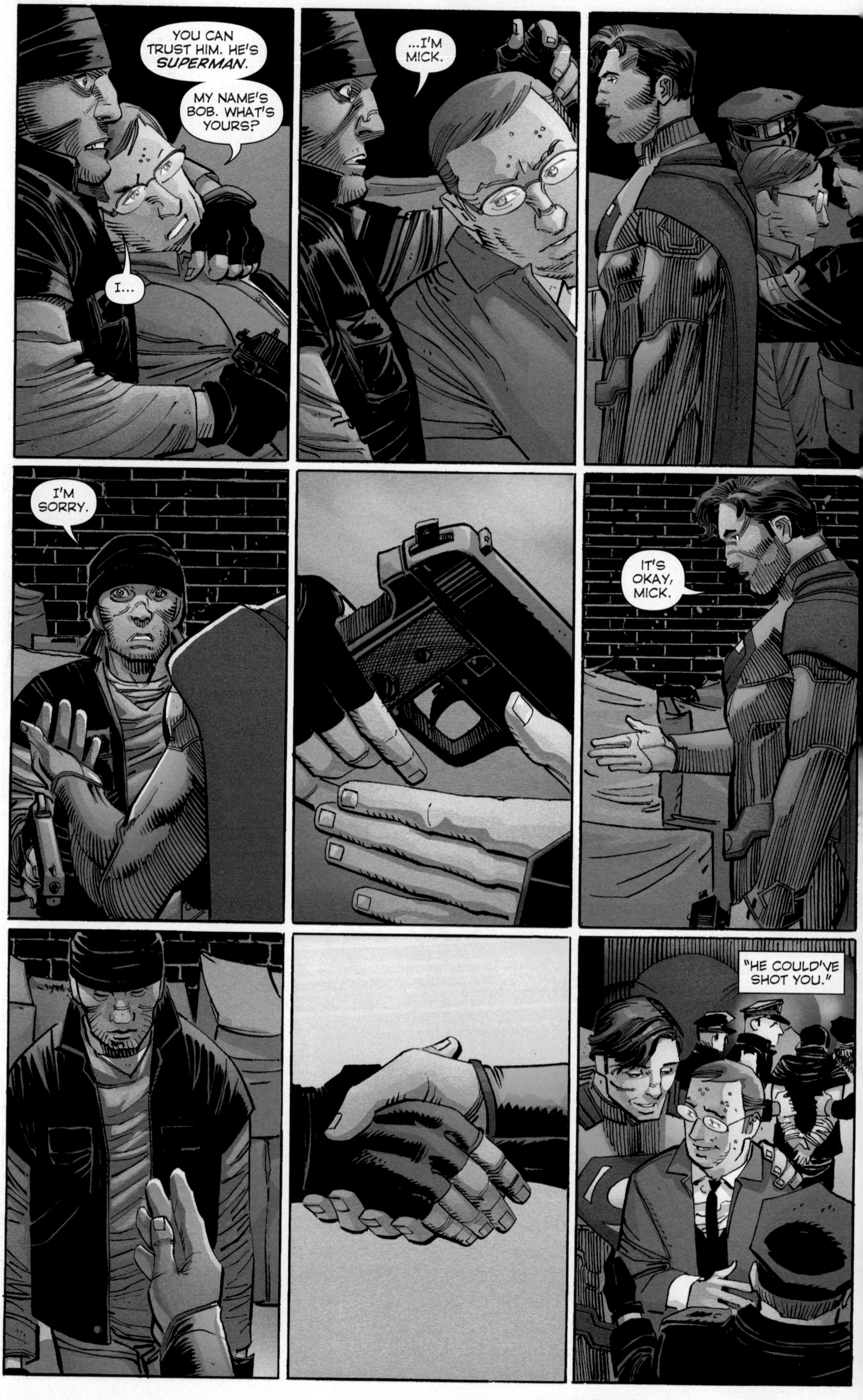
YOU CAN TRUST HIM. HE'S *SUPERMAN*.
MY NAME'S BOB. WHAT'S YOURS?
I...
...I'M MICK.
I'M SORRY.
IT'S OKAY, MICK.
"HE COULD'VE SHOT YOU."

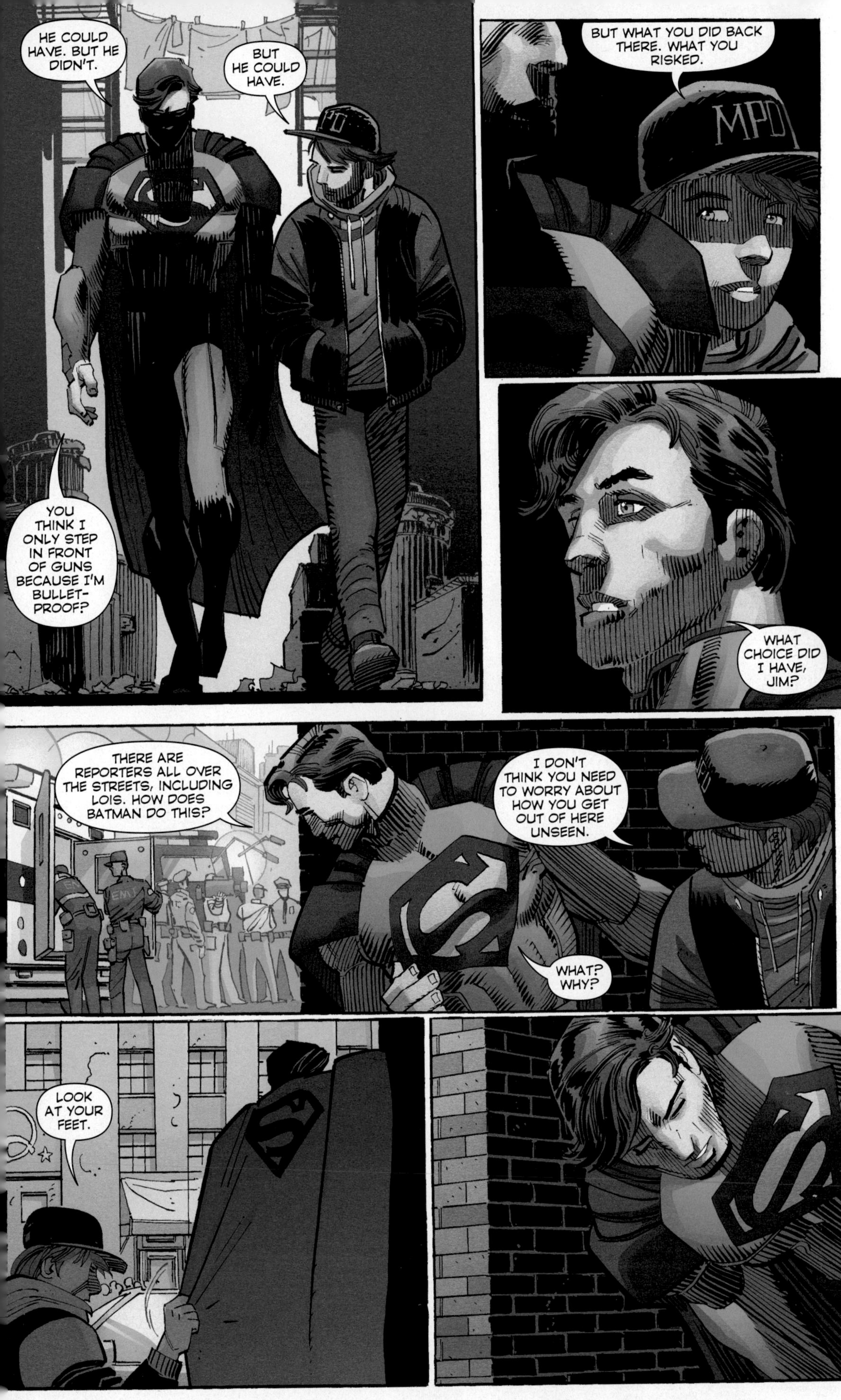
HE COULD HAVE. BUT HE DIDN'T.
BUT HE COULD HAVE.
YOU THINK I ONLY STEP IN FRONT OF GUNS BECAUSE I'M BULLET-PROOF?
BUT WHAT YOU DID BACK THERE. WHAT YOU RISKED.
MPD
WHAT CHOICE DID I HAVE, JIM?
THERE ARE REPORTERS ALL OVER THE STREETS, INCLUDING LOIS. HOW DOES BATMAN DO THIS?
I DON'T THINK YOU NEED TO WORRY ABOUT HOW YOU GET OUT OF HERE UNSEEN.
WHAT? WHY?
LOOK AT YOUR FEET.

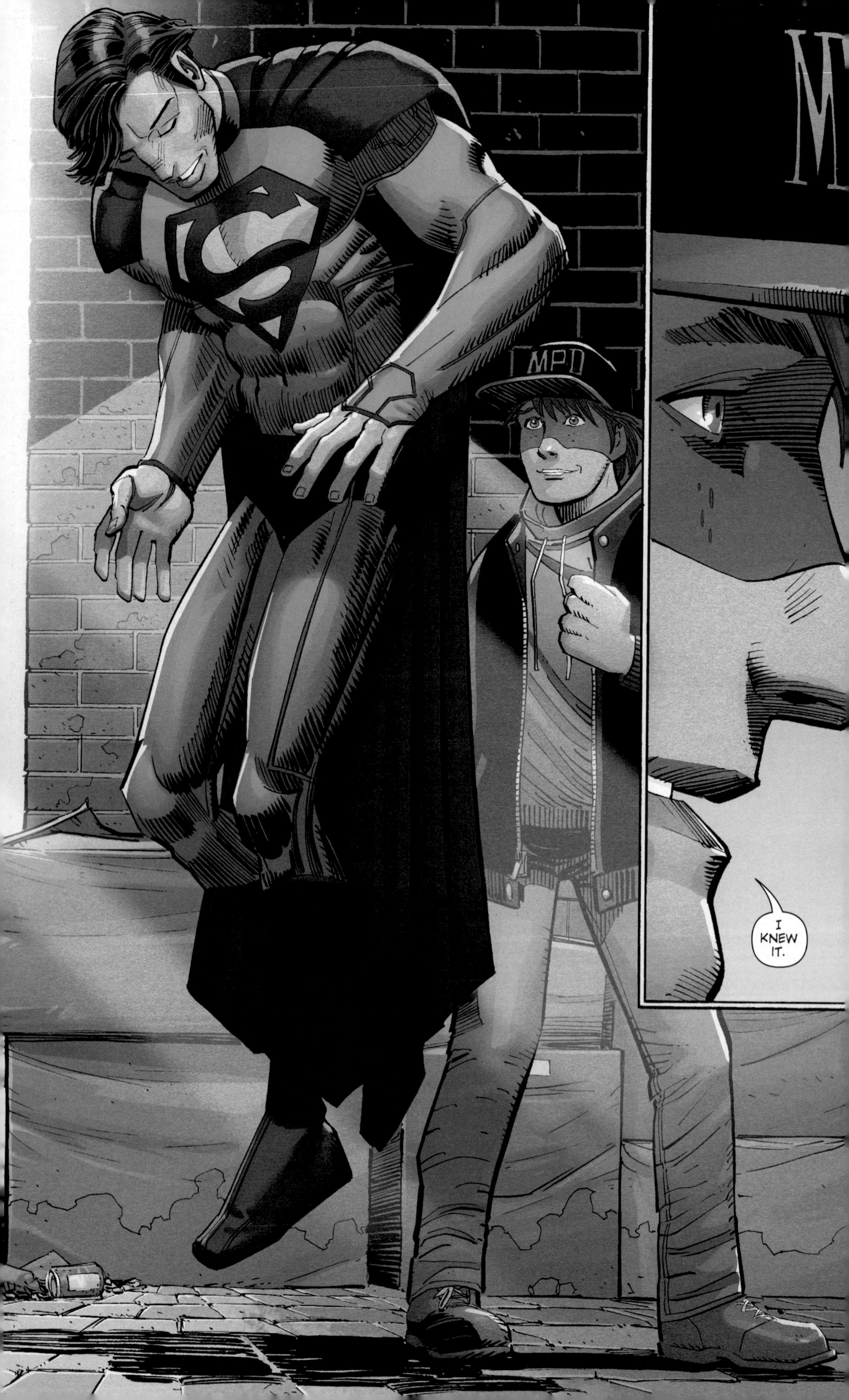
MPD
I KNEW IT.

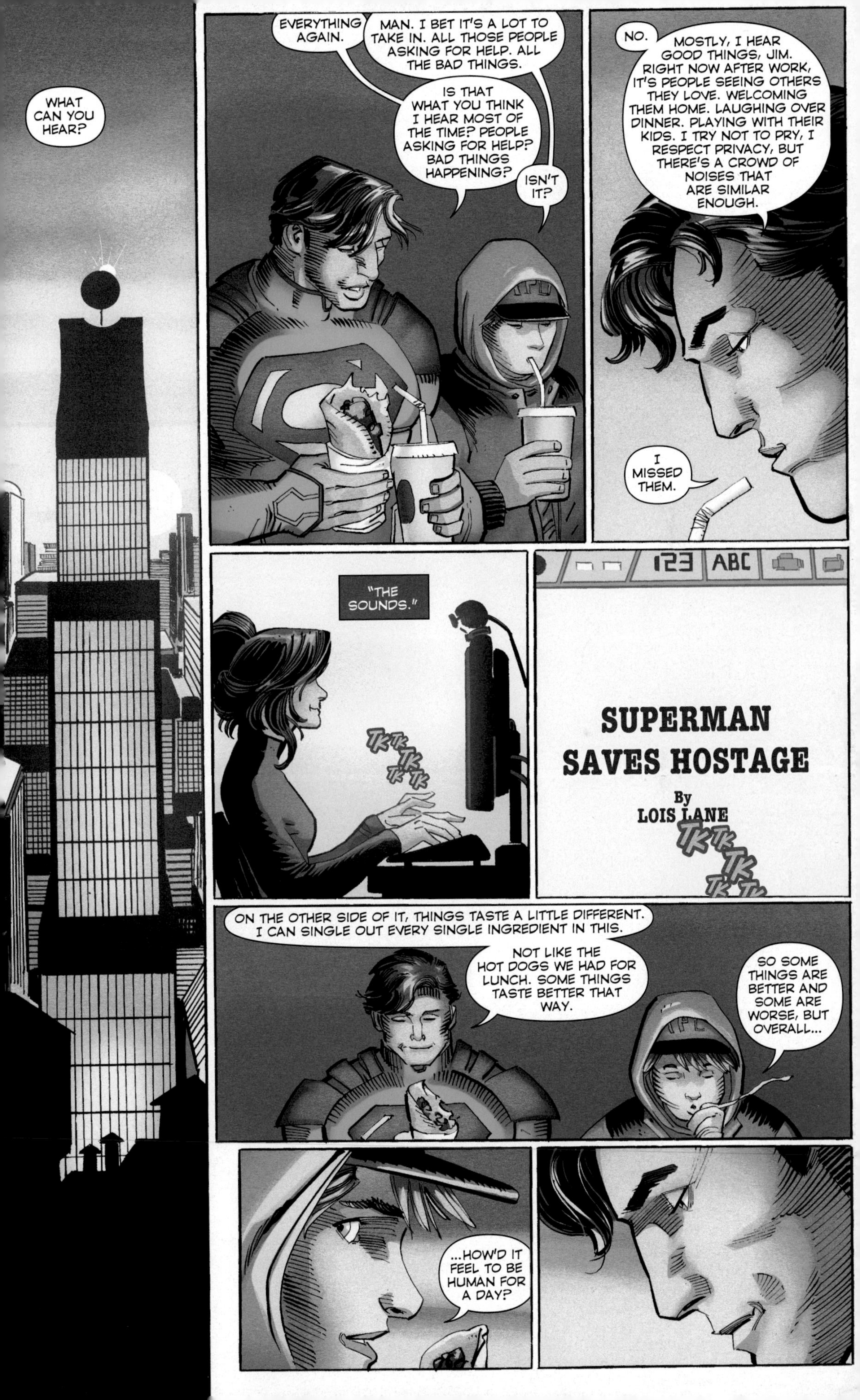
WHAT CAN YOU HEAR?
EVERYTHING AGAIN.
MAN. I BET IT'S A LOT TO TAKE IN. ALL THOSE PEOPLE ASKING FOR HELP. ALL THE BAD THINGS.
IS THAT WHAT YOU THINK I HEAR MOST OF THE TIME? PEOPLE ASKING FOR HELP? BAD THINGS HAPPENING?
ISN'T IT?
NO.
MOSTLY, I HEAR GOOD THINGS, JIM. RIGHT NOW AFTER WORK, IT'S PEOPLE SEEING OTHERS THEY LOVE. WELCOMING THEM HOME. LAUGHING OVER DINNER. PLAYING WITH THEIR KIDS. I TRY NOT TO PRY, I RESPECT PRIVACY, BUT THERE'S A CROWD OF NOISES THAT ARE SIMILAR ENOUGH.
I MISSED THEM.
"THE SOUNDS."
TK TK TK TK TK
123 ABC
SUPERMAN SAVES HOSTAGE
By LOIS LANE
TK TK TK TK
ON THE OTHER SIDE OF IT, THINGS TASTE A LITTLE DIFFERENT. I CAN SINGLE OUT EVERY SINGLE INGREDIENT IN THIS.
NOT LIKE THE HOT DOGS WE HAD FOR LUNCH. SOME THINGS TASTE BETTER THAT WAY.
SO SOME THINGS ARE BETTER AND SOME ARE WORSE, BUT OVERALL...
...HOW'D IT FEEL TO BE HUMAN FOR A DAY?

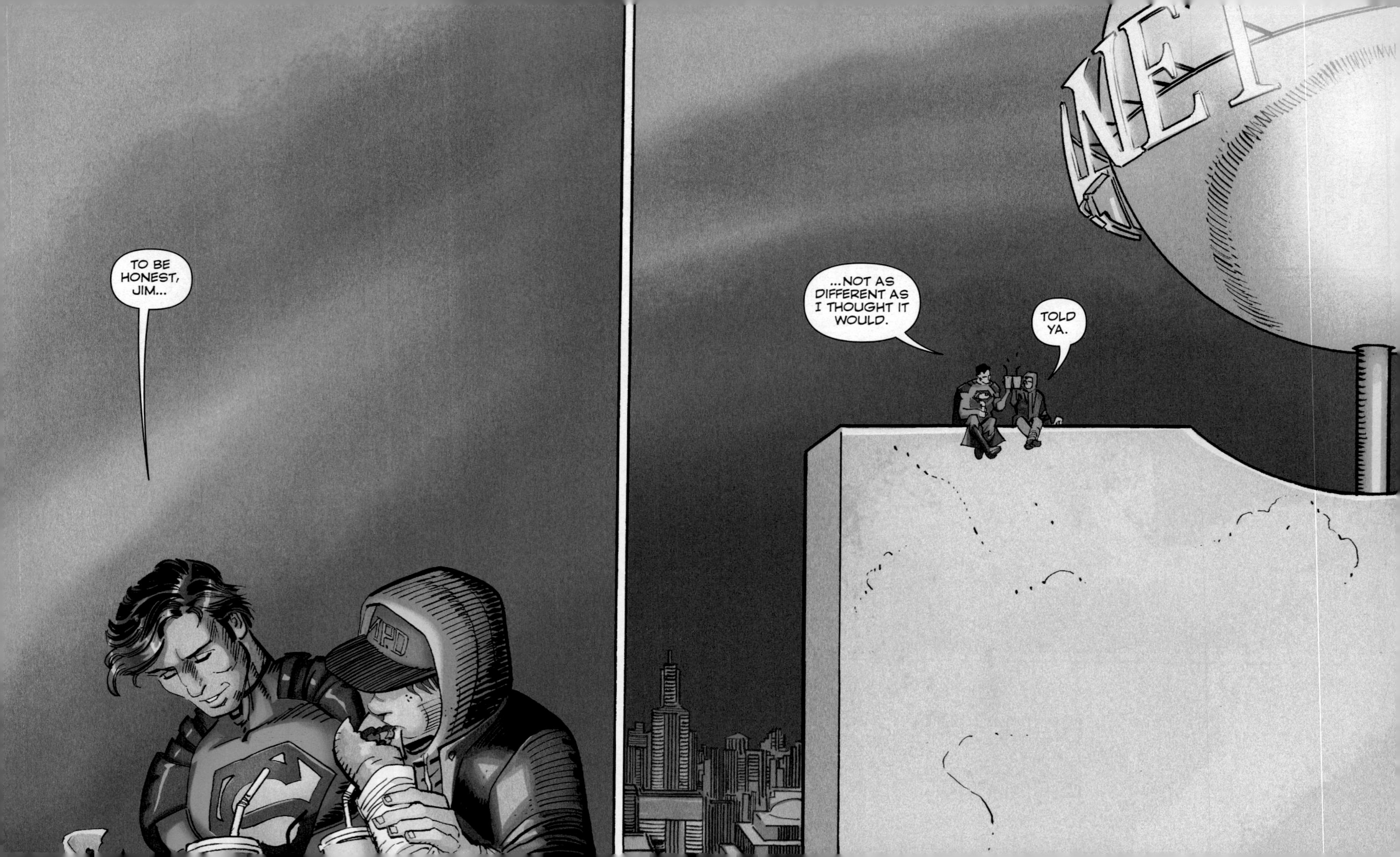
TO BE HONEST, JIM...
...NOT AS DIFFERENT AS I THOUGHT IT WOULD.
TOLD YA.

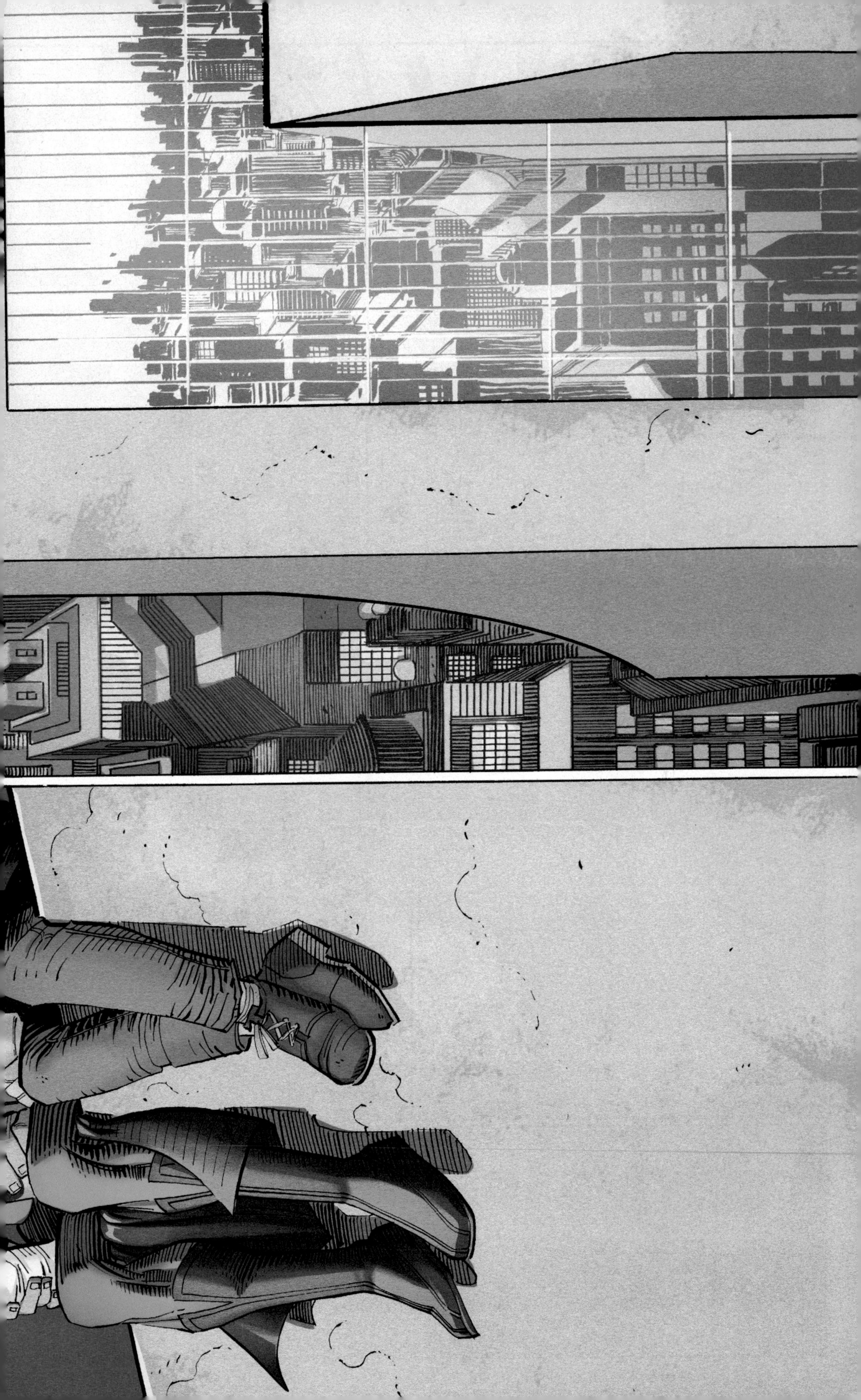

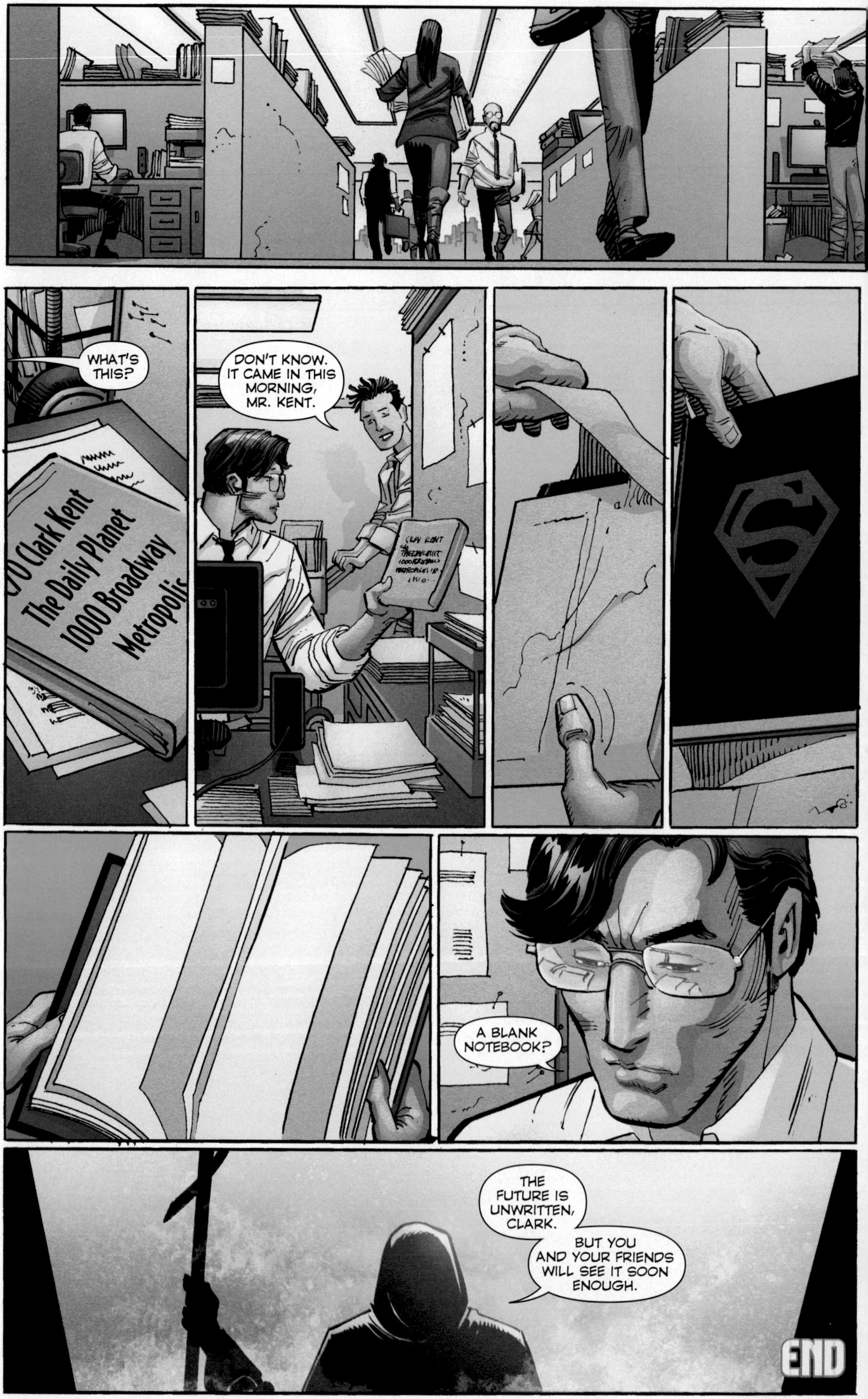

WHAT'S THIS?
DON'T KNOW. IT CAME IN THIS MORNING, MR. KENT.
C/O Clark Kent
The Daily Planet
1000 Broadway
Metropolis
A BLANK NOTEBOOK?
THE FUTURE IS UNWRITTEN, CLARK.
BUT YOU AND YOUR FRIENDS WILL SEE IT SOON ENOUGH.
END

SUPERMAN

Promotional image by JOHN ROMITA JR., KLAUS JANSON & LAURA MARTIN

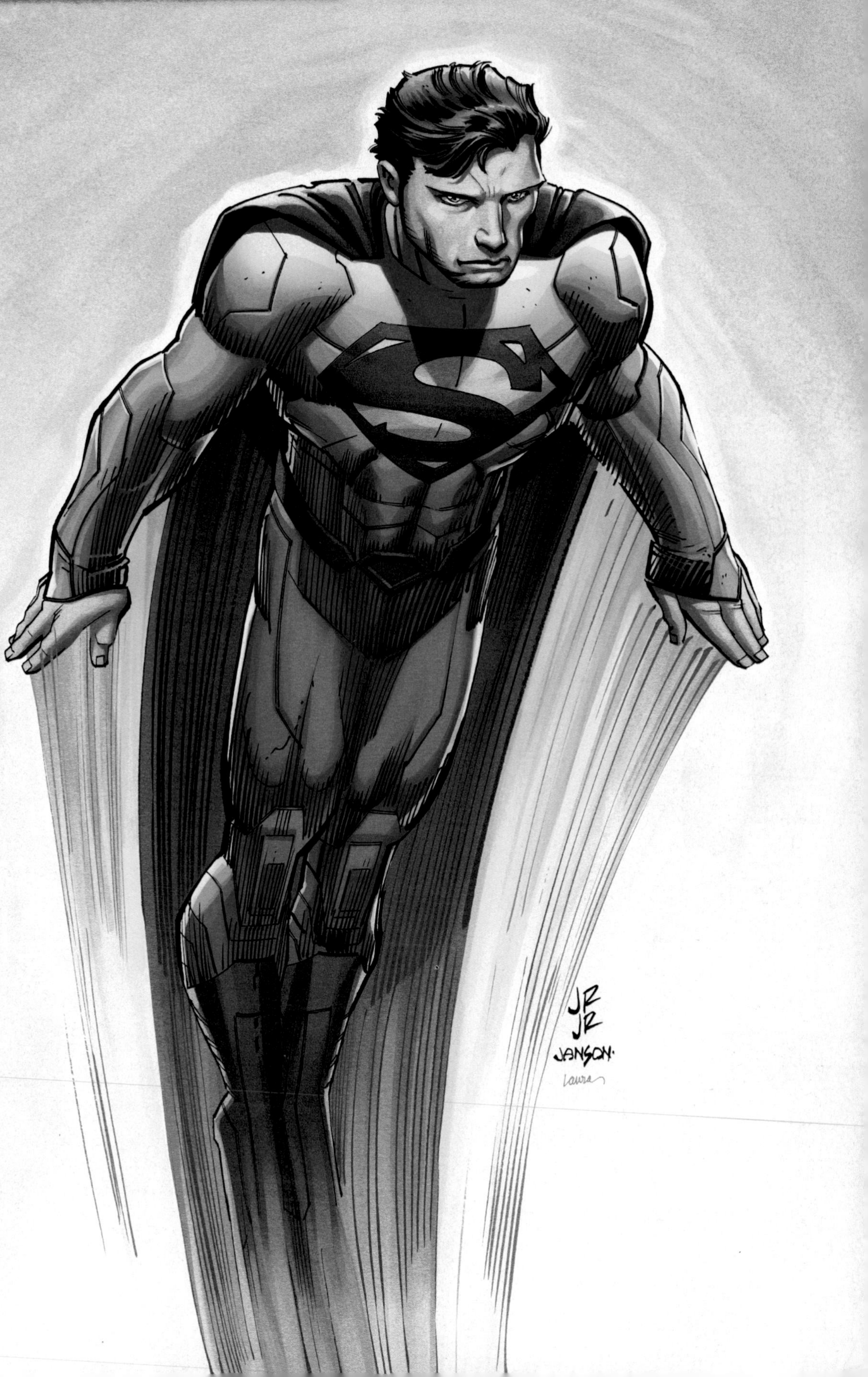

SUPERMAN #32

Full wrap-around cover by JOHN ROMITA JR., KLAUS JANSON & LAURA MARTIN

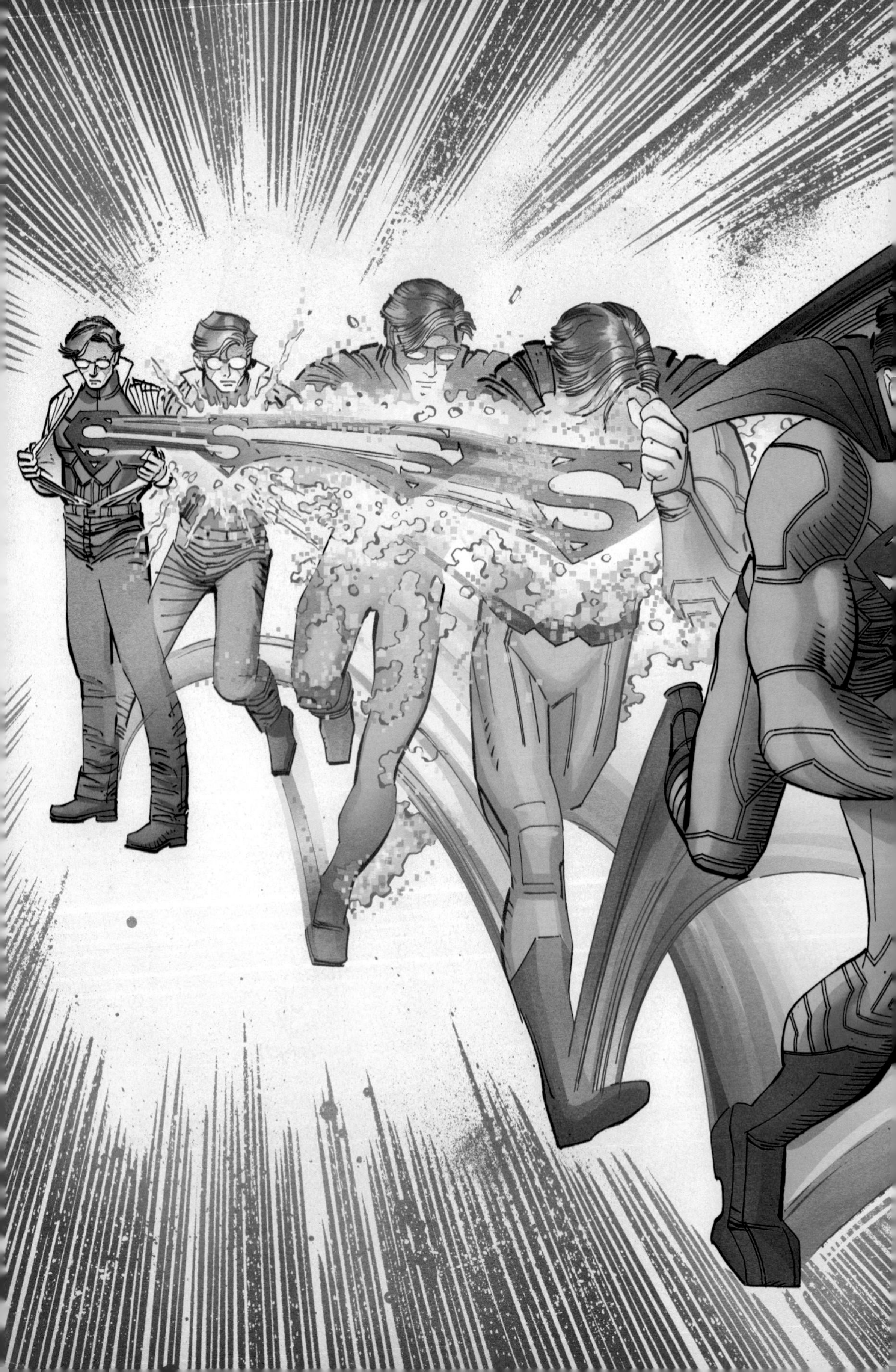

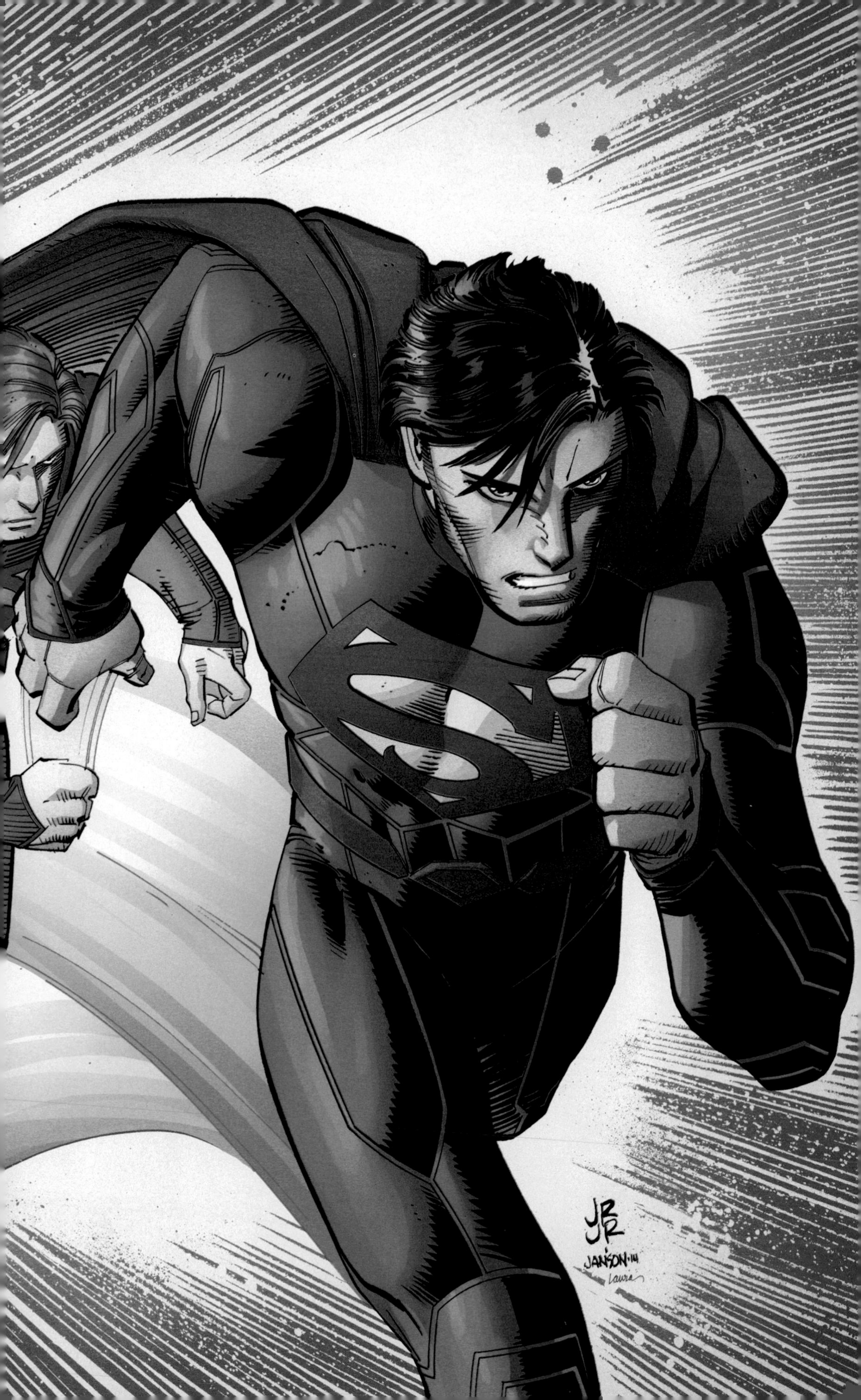
JANSON·14

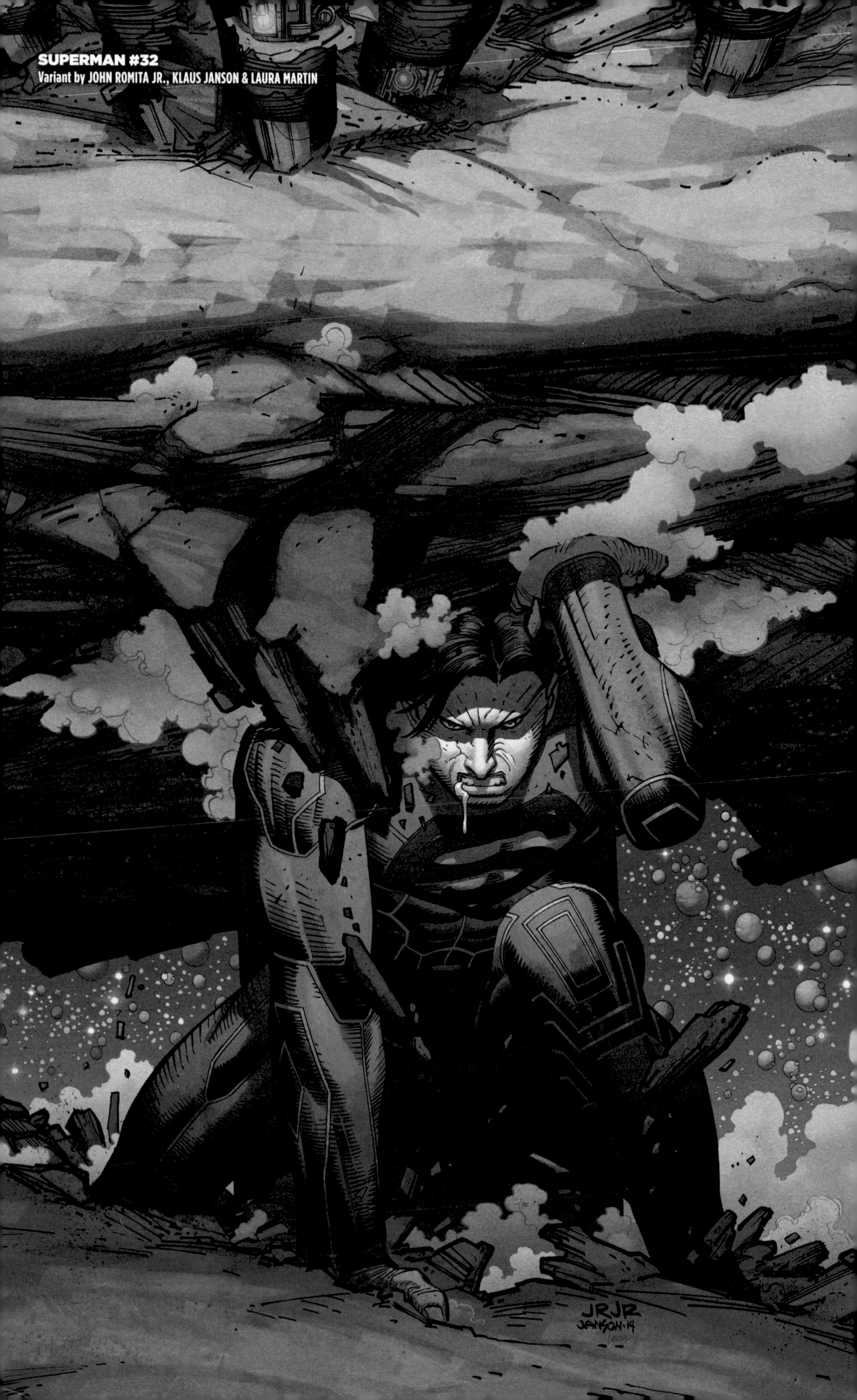
JRJR
JANSON·14

SUPERMAN #32
Variant by JOHN ROMITA JR., KLAUS JANSON & LAURA MARTIN

SUPERMAN #32
Bombshell variant by ANT LUCIA

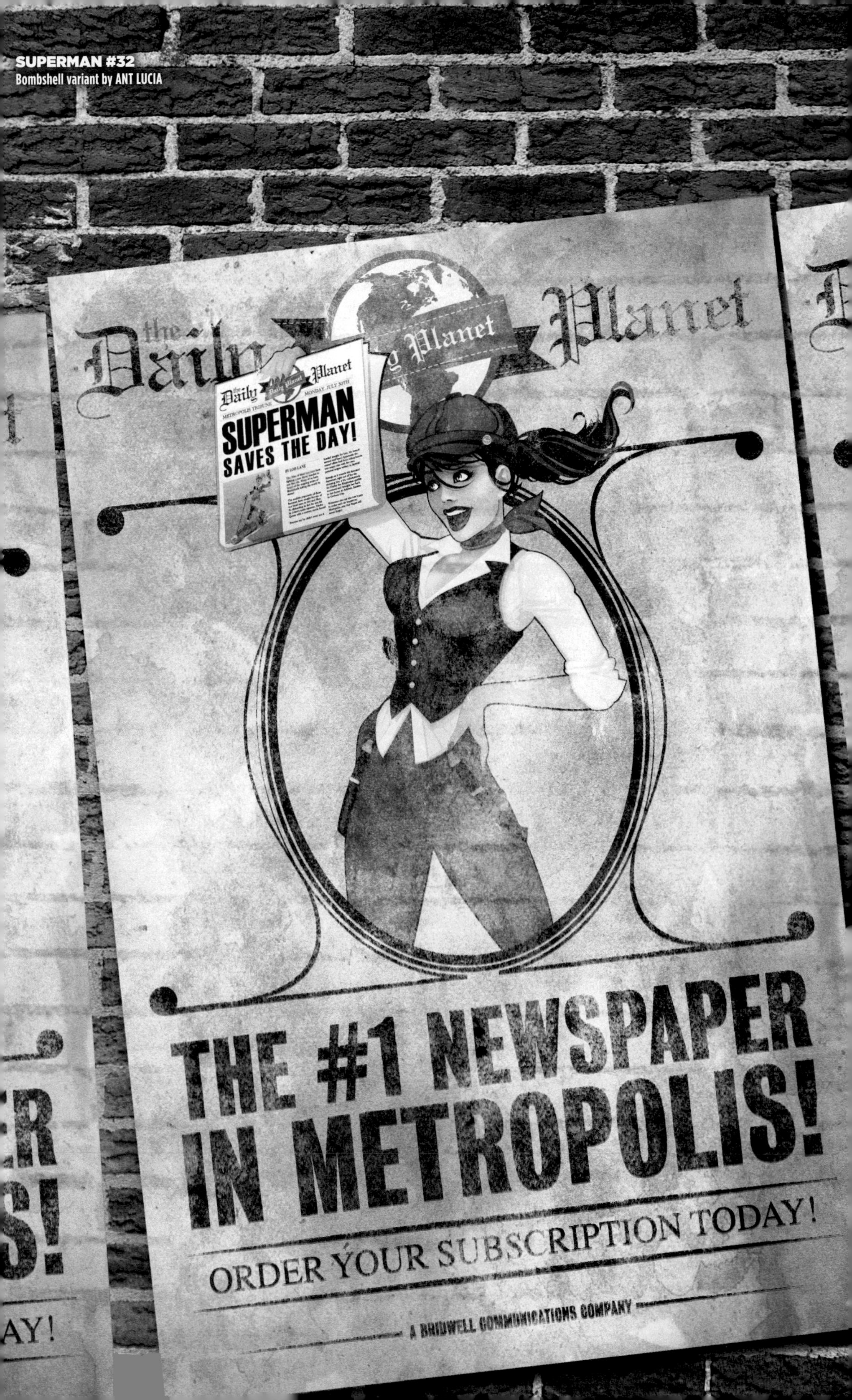
the Daily Planet
Daily Planet
SUPERMAN
SAVES THE DAY!
THE #1 NEWSPAPER
IN METROPOLIS!
ORDER YOUR SUBSCRIPTION TODAY!
A BRIDWELL COMMUNICATIONS COMPANY

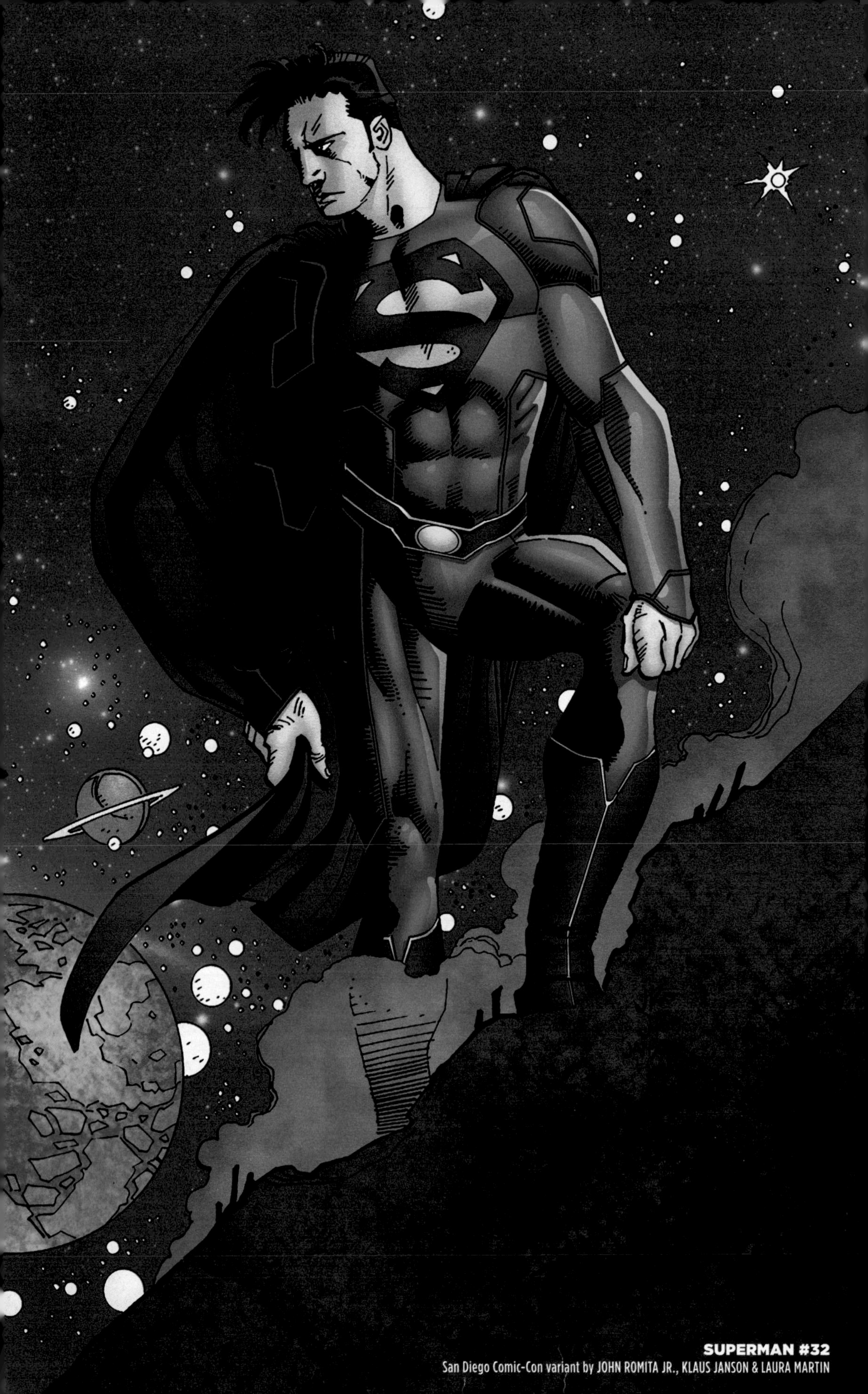

SUPERMAN #32
San Diego Comic-Con variant by JOHN ROMITA JR., KLAUS JANSON & LAURA MARTIN

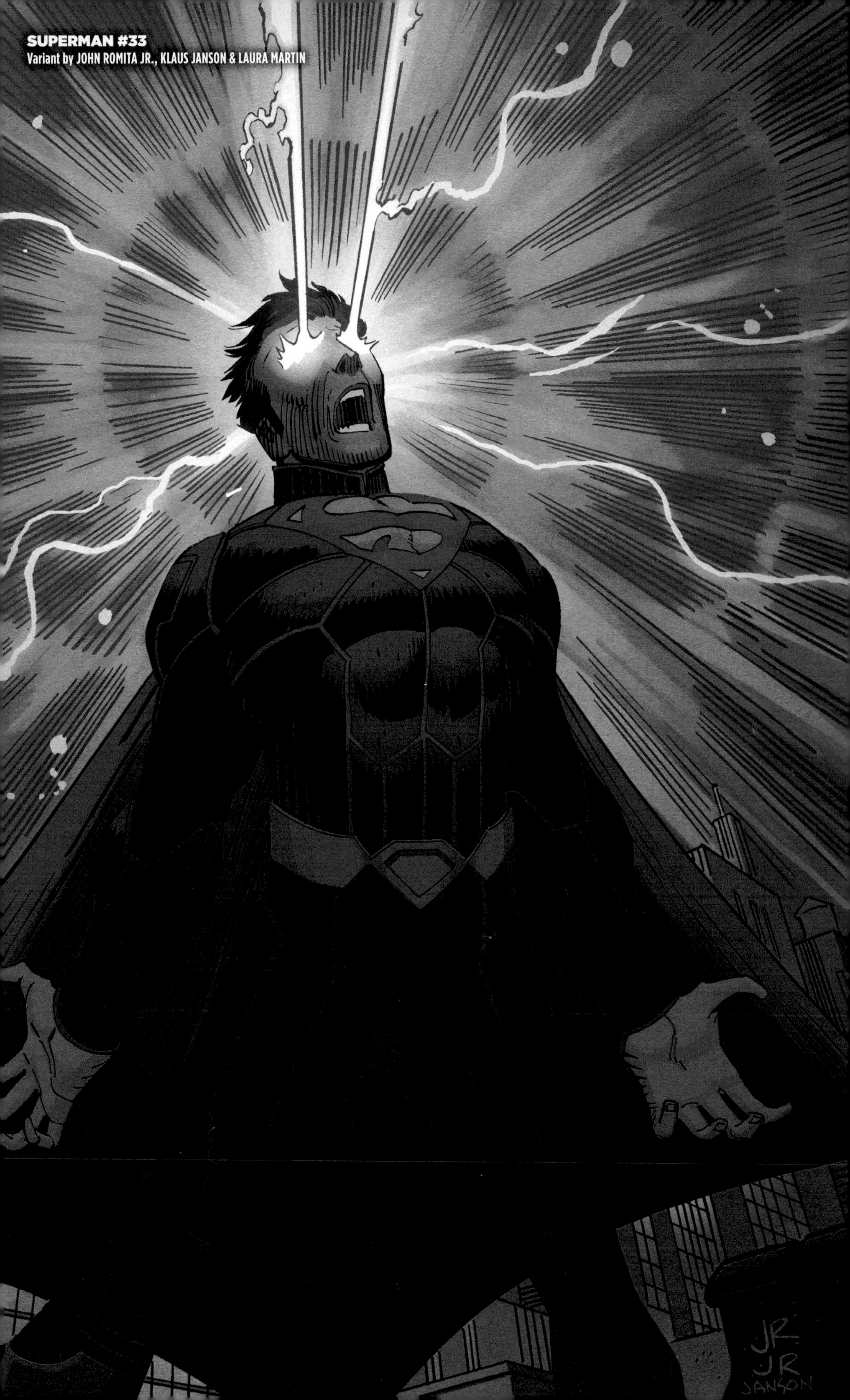
JR.
JR
JANSON

SUPERMAN #33
Variant by JOHN ROMITA JR., KLAUS JANSON & LAURA MARTIN

SUPERMAN #33

Batman 75th anniversary variant by ERIK LARSEN

SUPERMAN #34
Variant by JOHN ROMITA JR., KLAUS JANSON & LAURA MARTIN

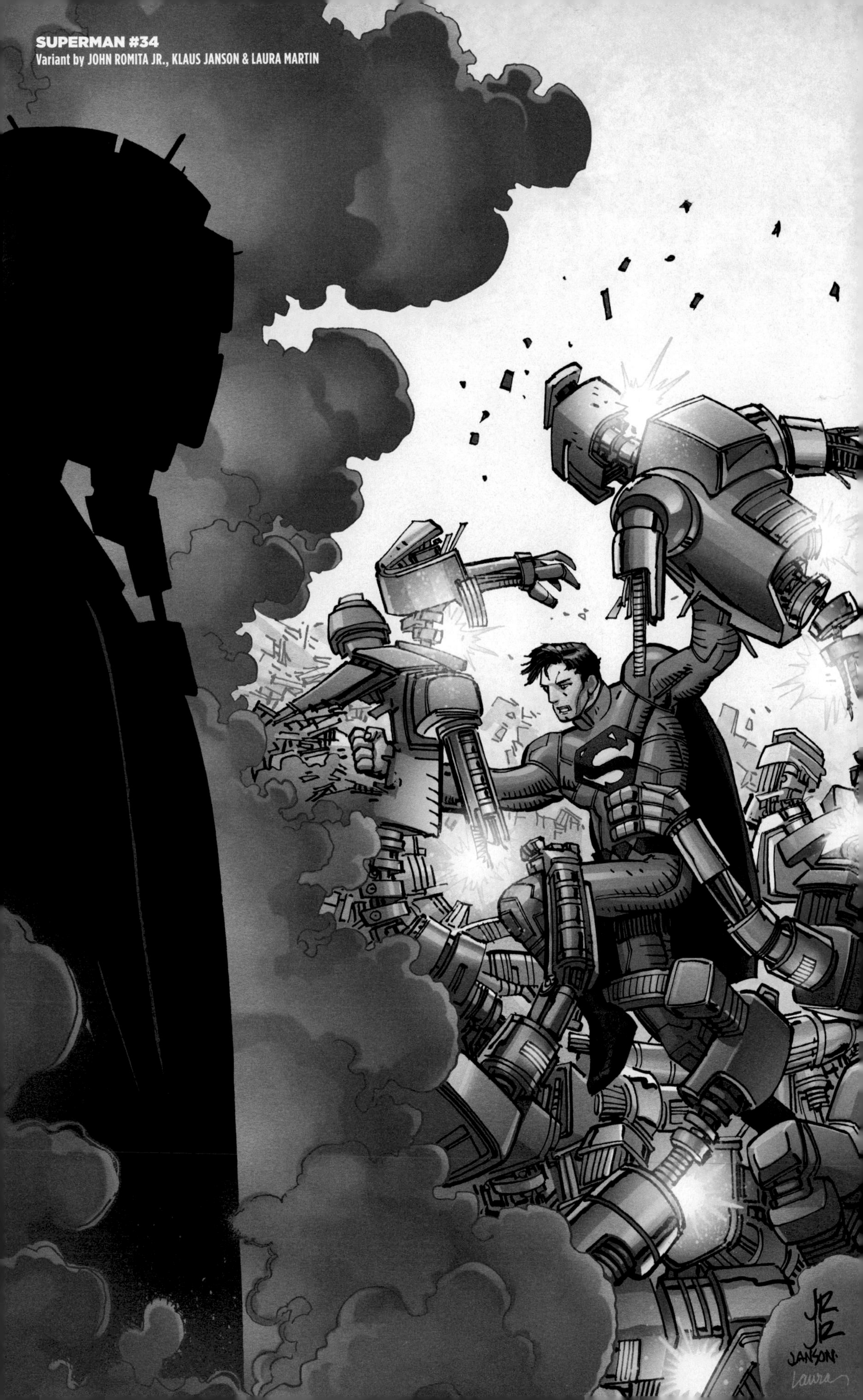
JR JR
JANSON
Laura

SUPERMAN #34
Variant by JOHN ROMITA, KLAUS JANSON & LAURA MARTIN

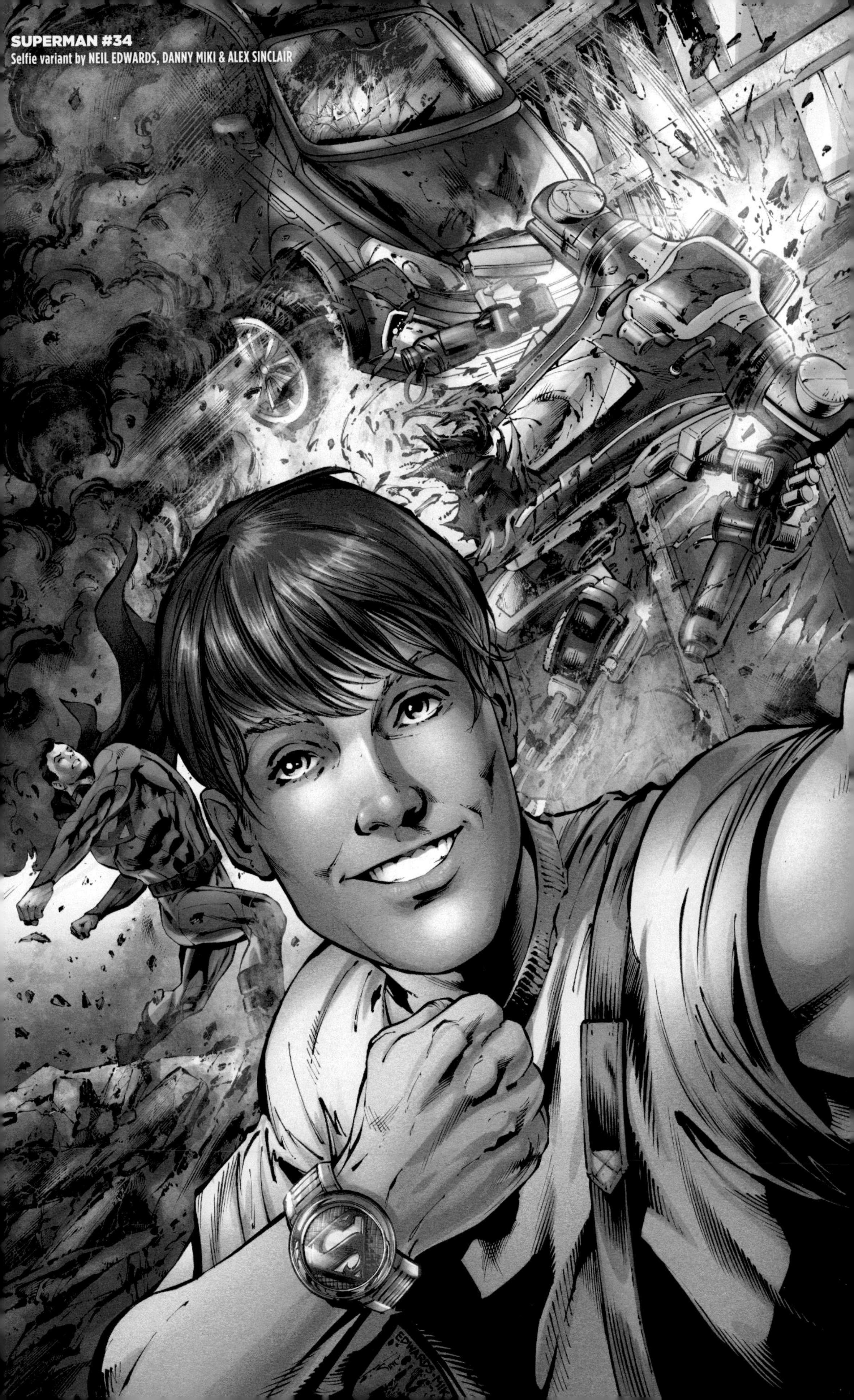

SUPERMAN #34
Selfie variant by NEIL EDWARDS, DANNY MIKI & ALEX SINCLAIR

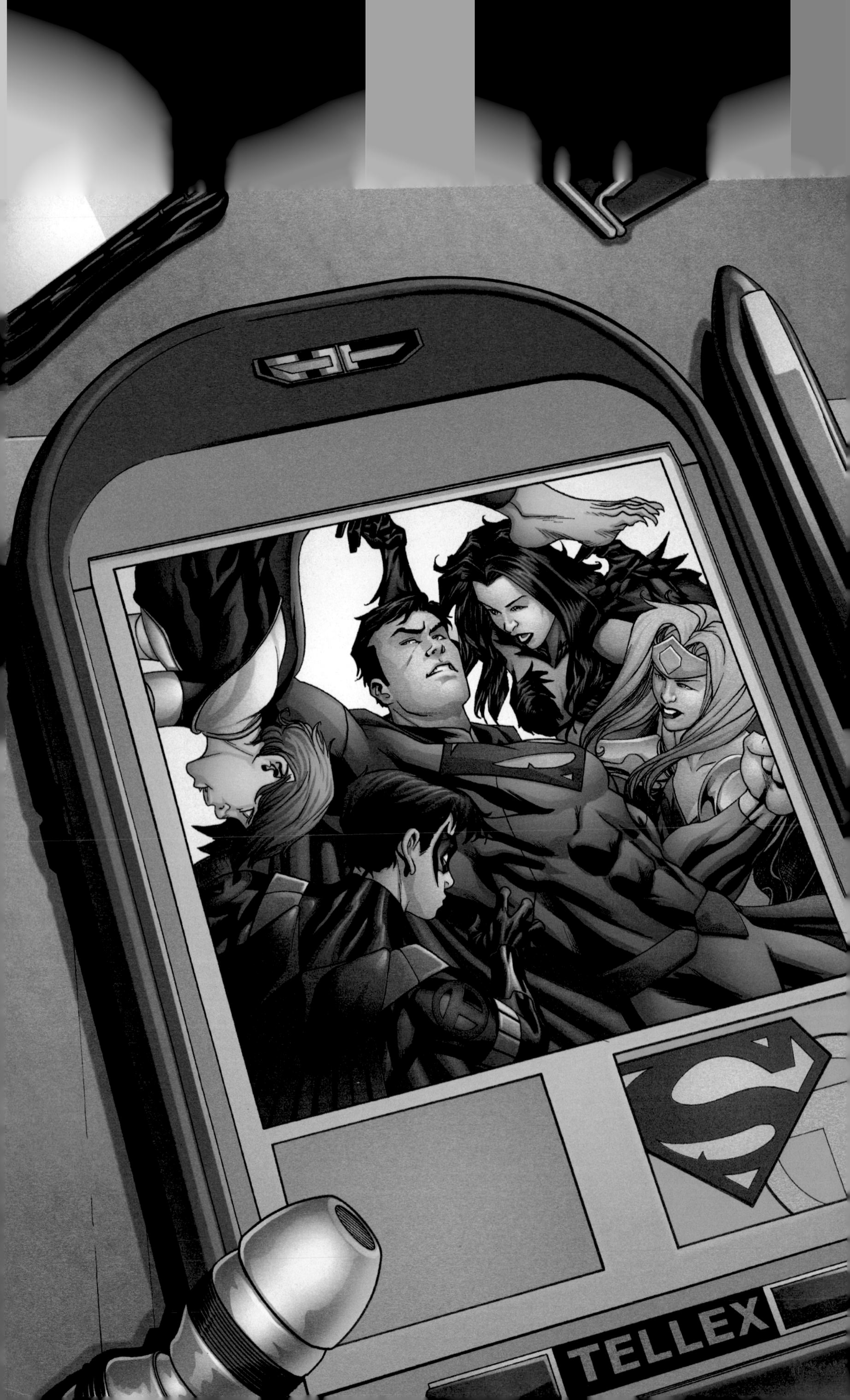
TELLEX

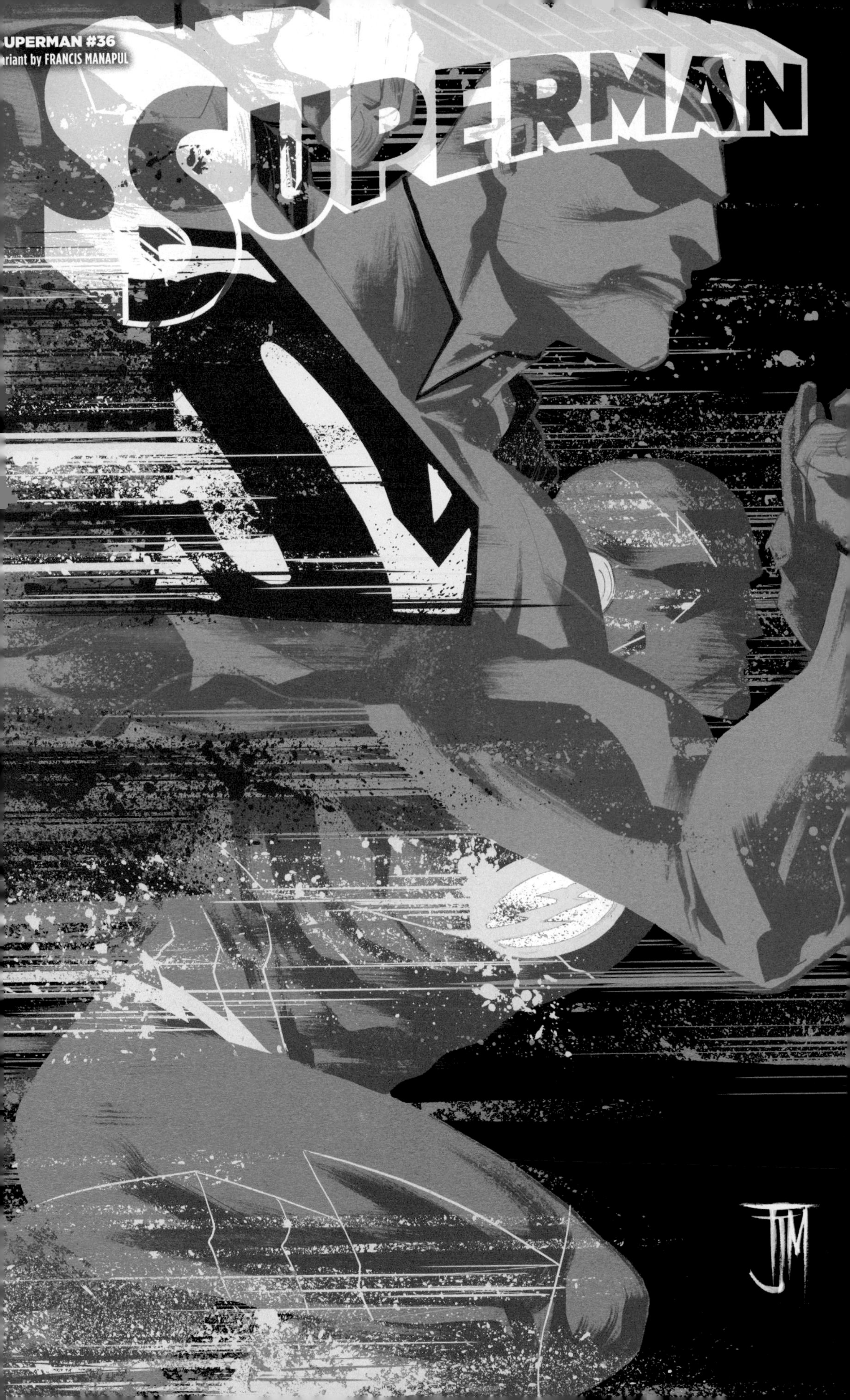
SUPERMAN

UPERMAN #36
ariant by FRANCIS MANAPUL

SUPERMAN #36

Variant by JOHN ROMITA JR., KLAUS JANSON & LAURA MARTIN

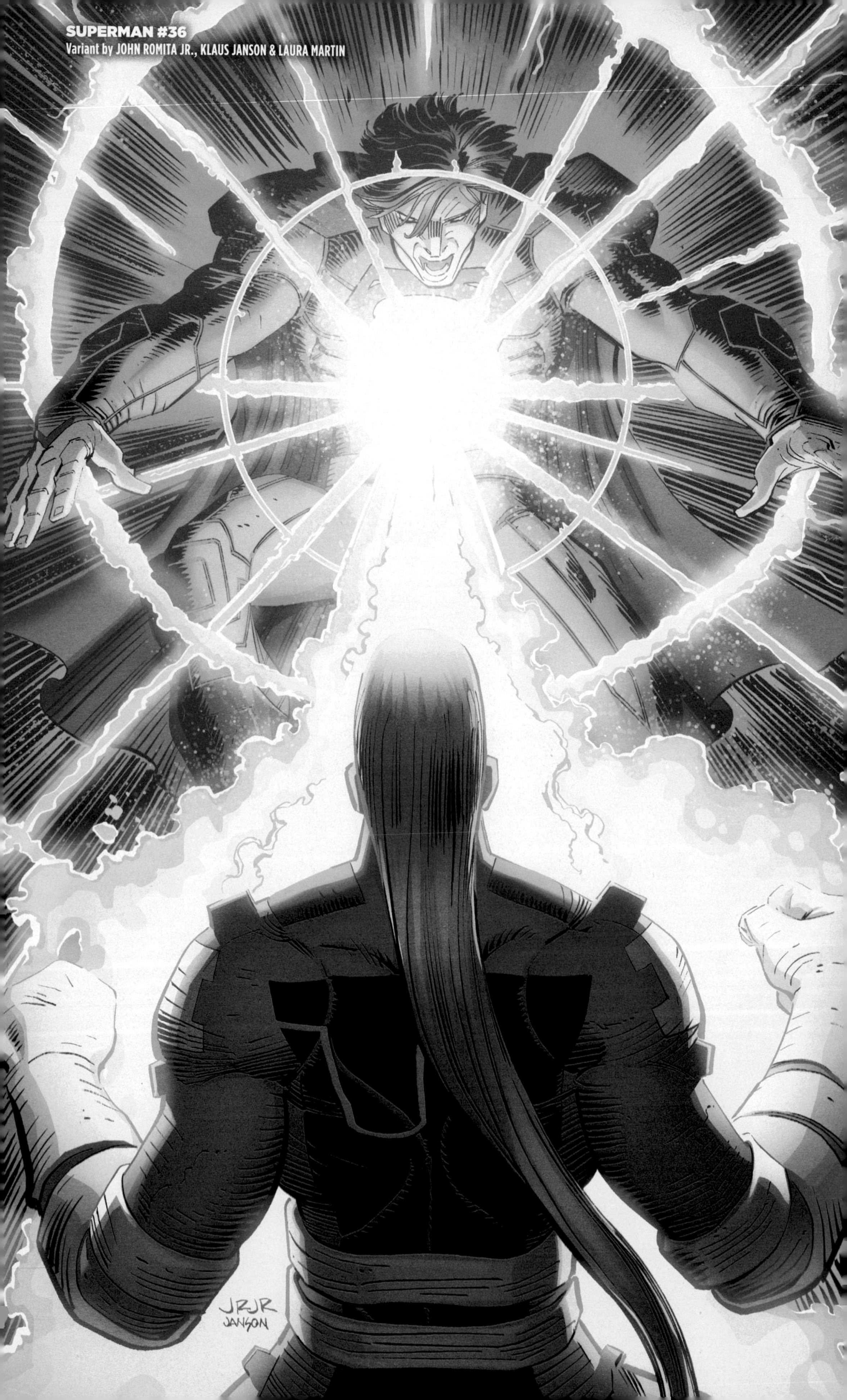
JRJR
JANSON

SUPERMAN #36
LEGO variant

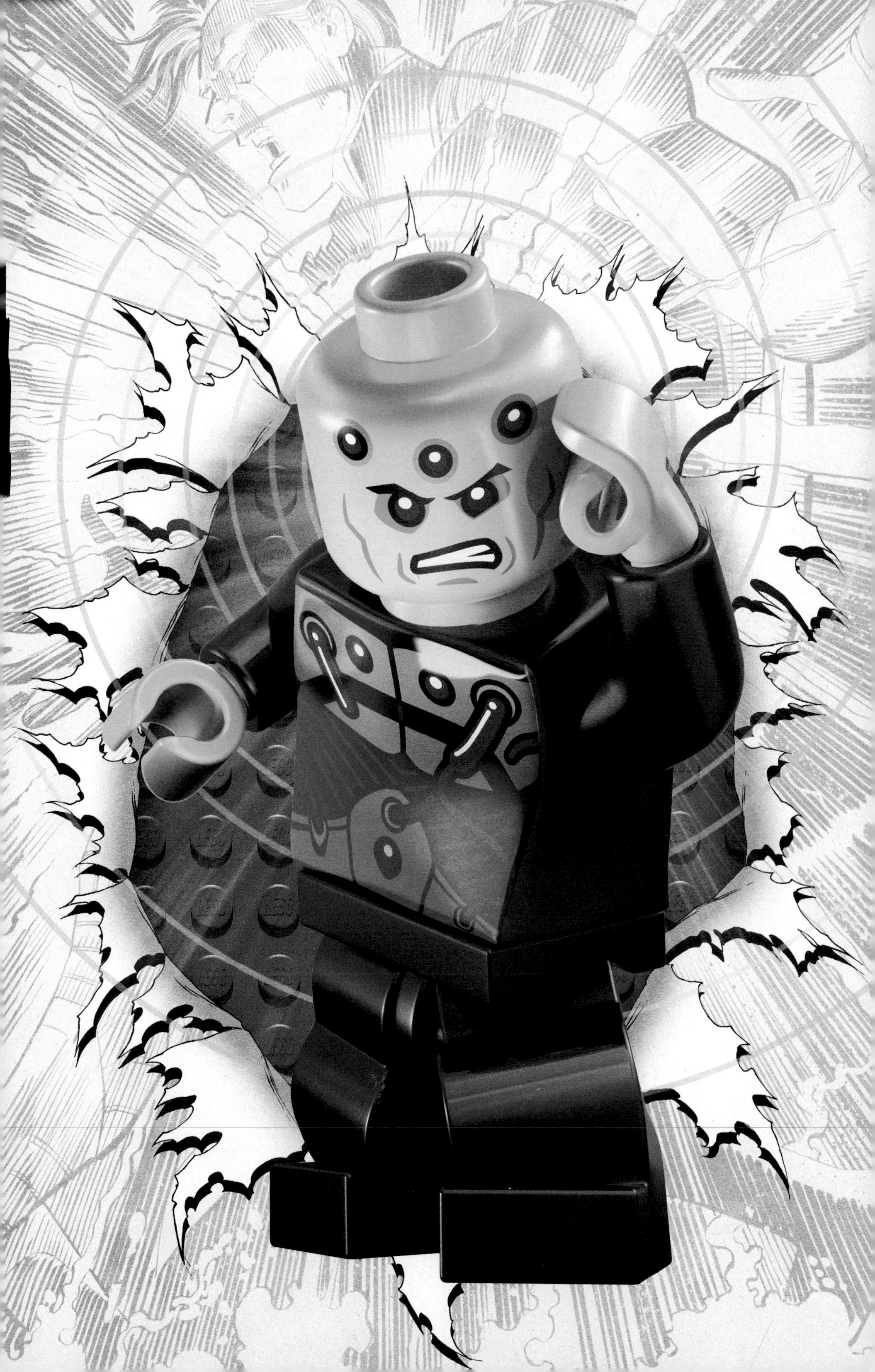

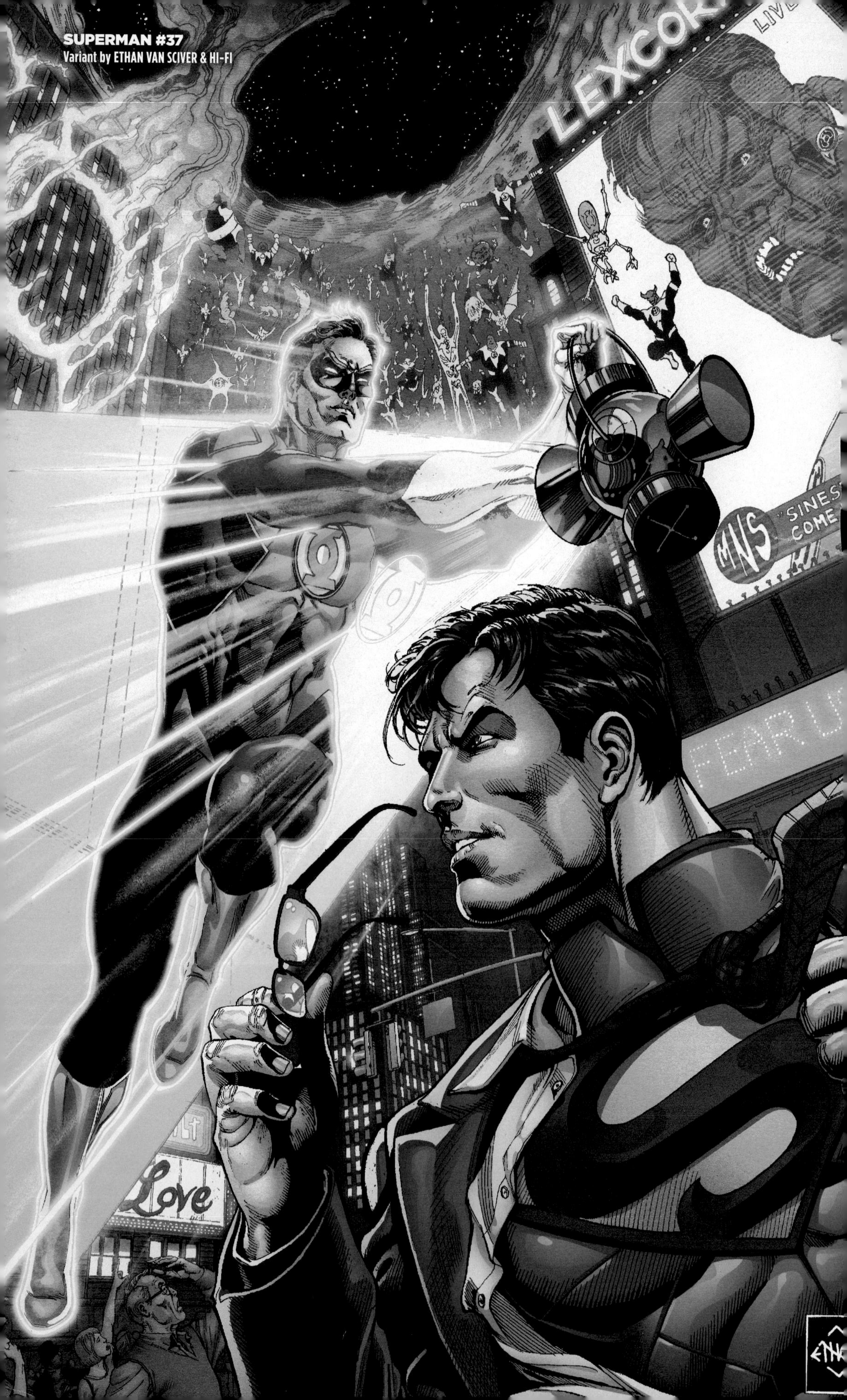
LEXCOR
Love

SUPERMAN #37
Variant by ETHAN VAN SCIVER & HI-FI

SUPERMAN #35
Monster variant by JASON PEARSON

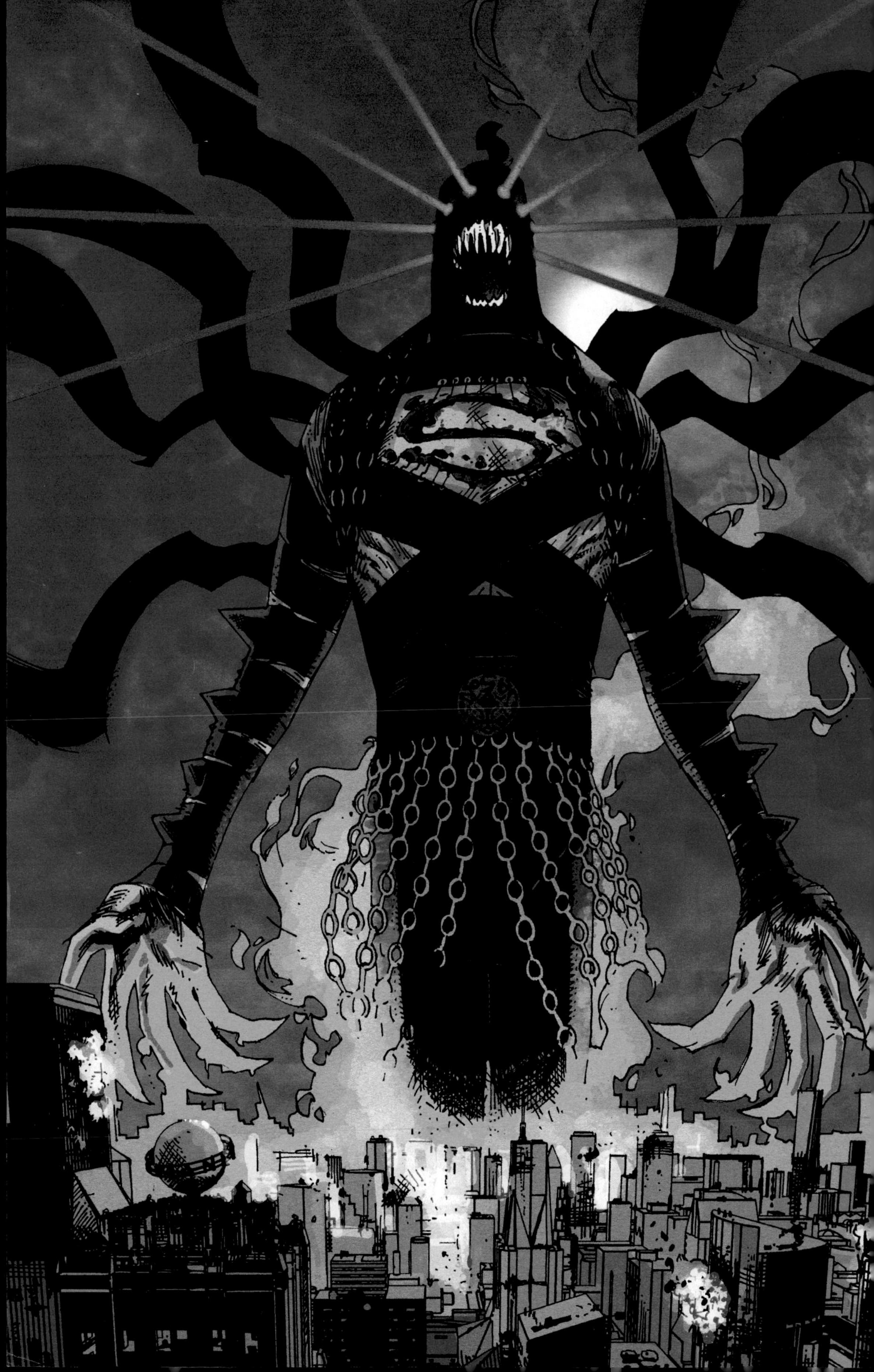

SUPERMAN #35
Variant by JOHN ROMITA JR., KLAUS JANSON & LAURA MARTIN

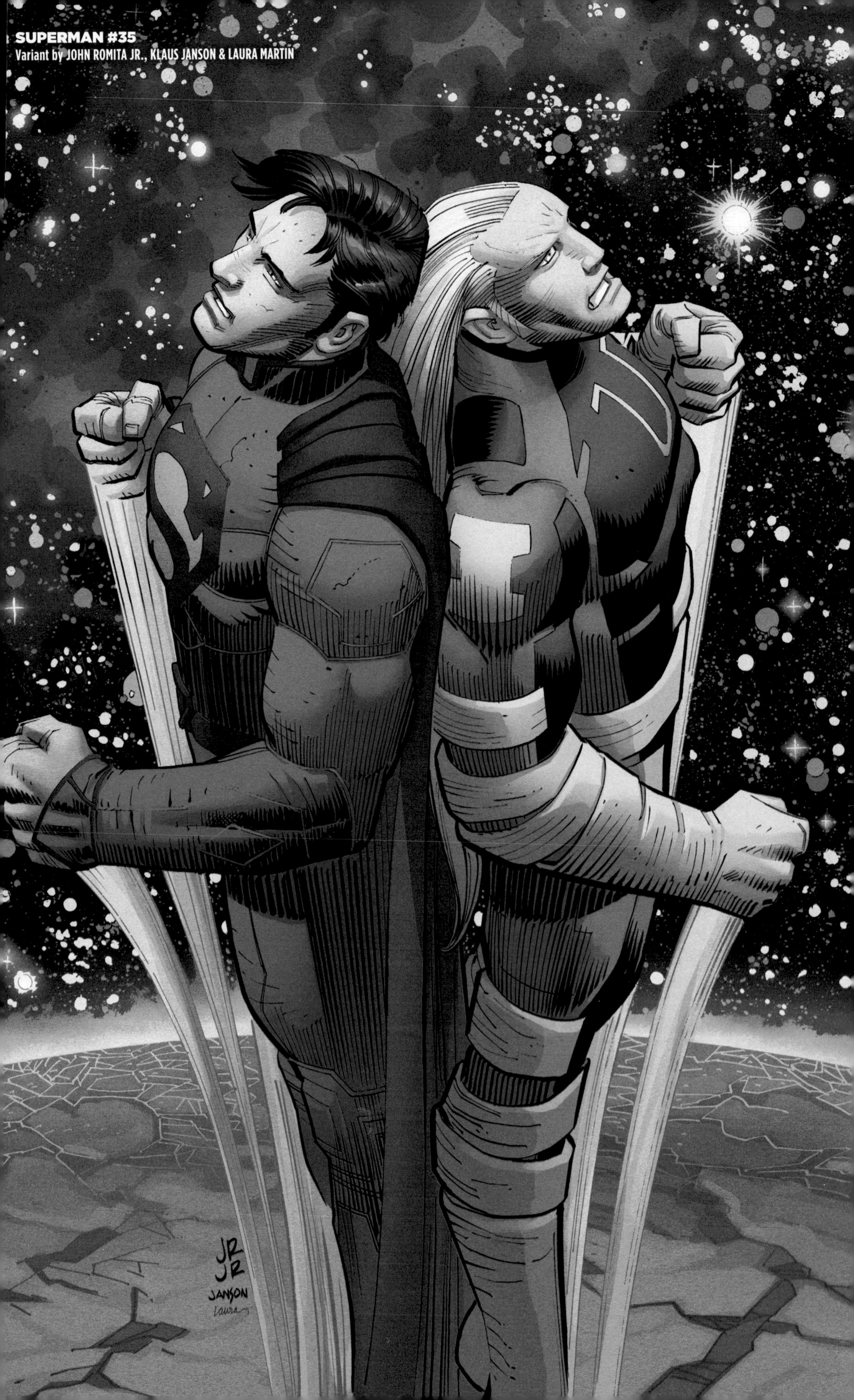
JR
JR
JANSON
Laura

SUPERMAN #37
Variant by JOHN ROMITA JR., KLAUS JANSON & LAURA MARTIN

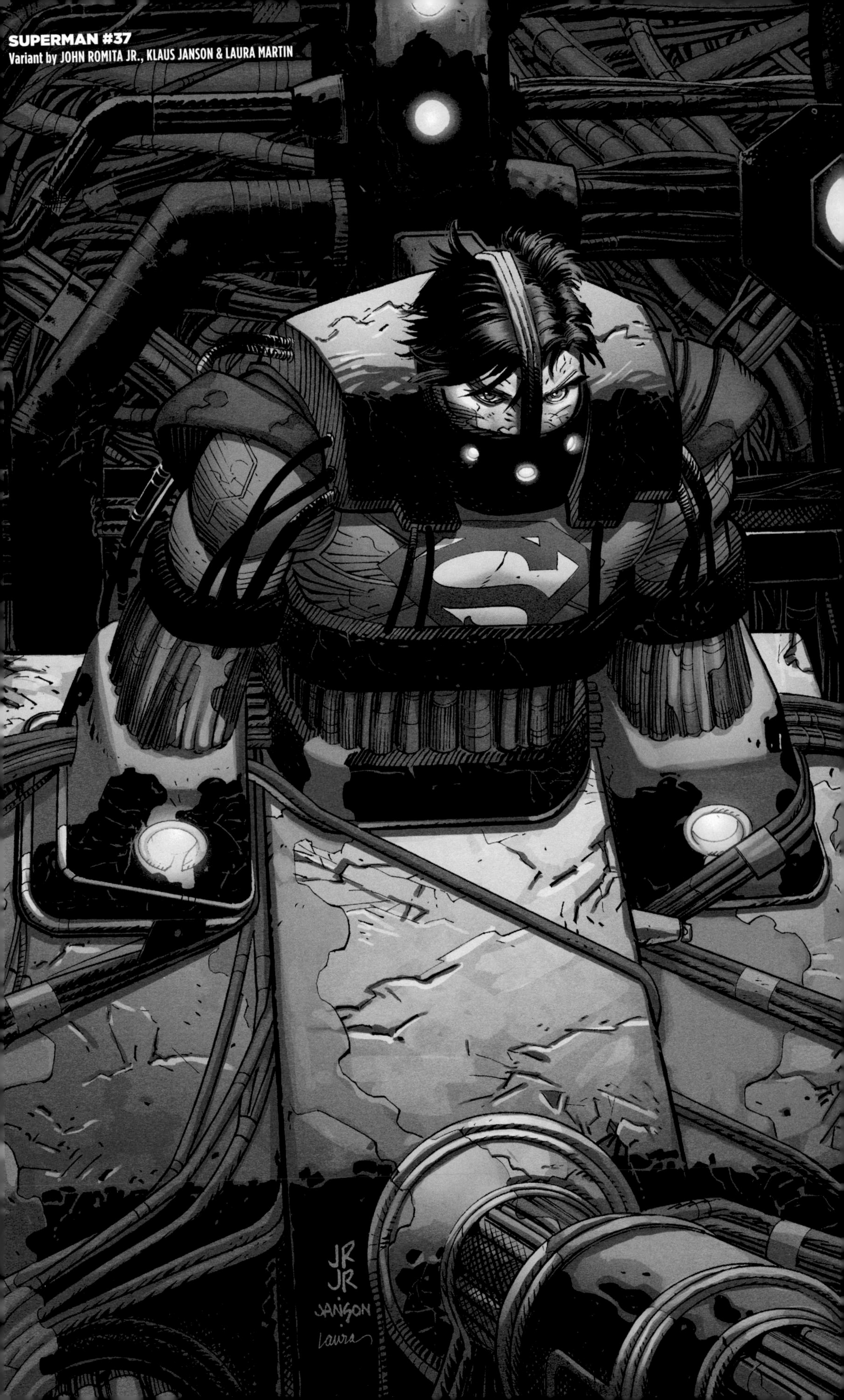
JR
JR
JANSON
Laura

SUPERMAN #37
Variant by DARWYN COOKE

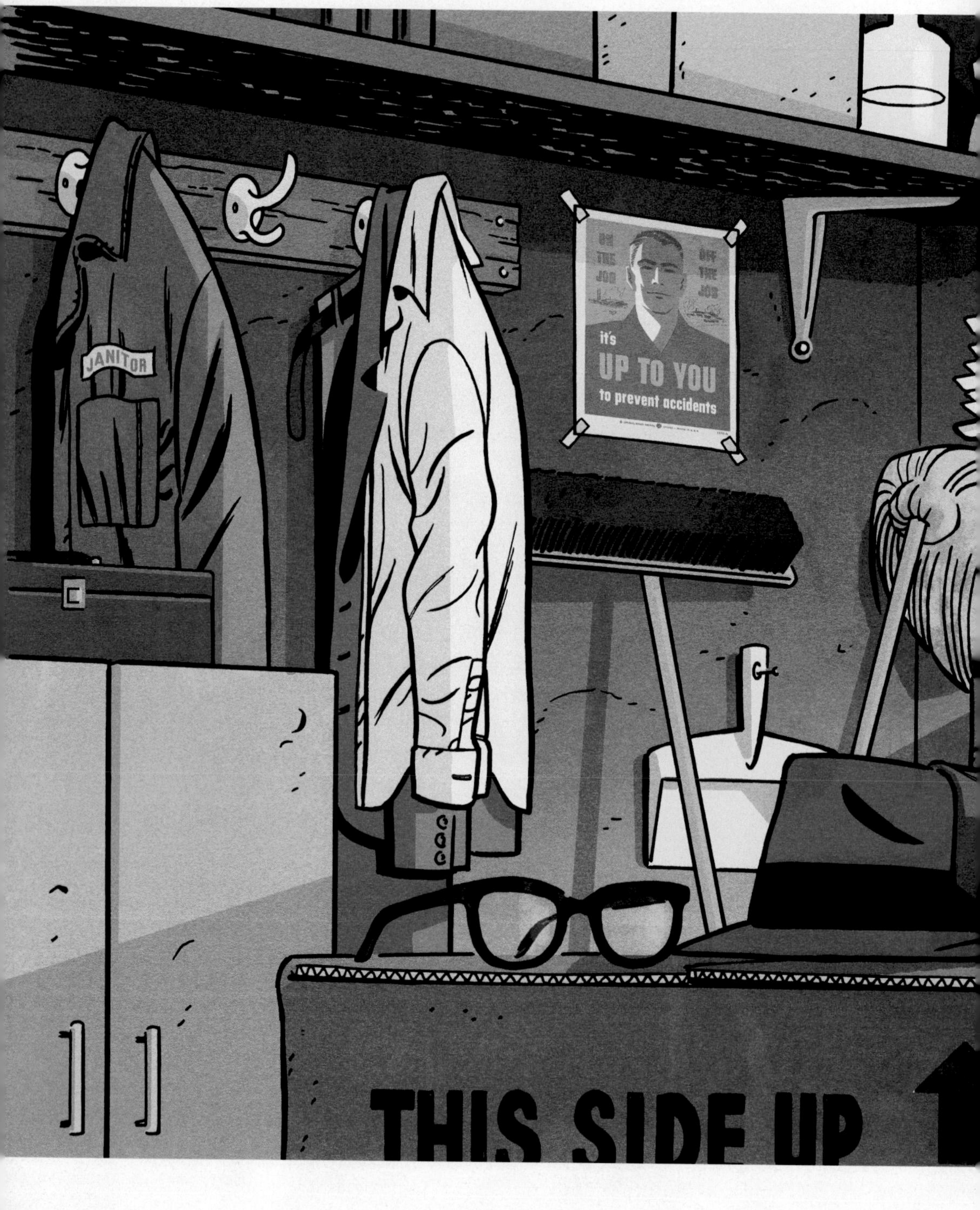
JANITOR
ON THE JOB
OFF THE JOB
it's
UP TO YOU
to prevent accidents
THIS SIDE UP

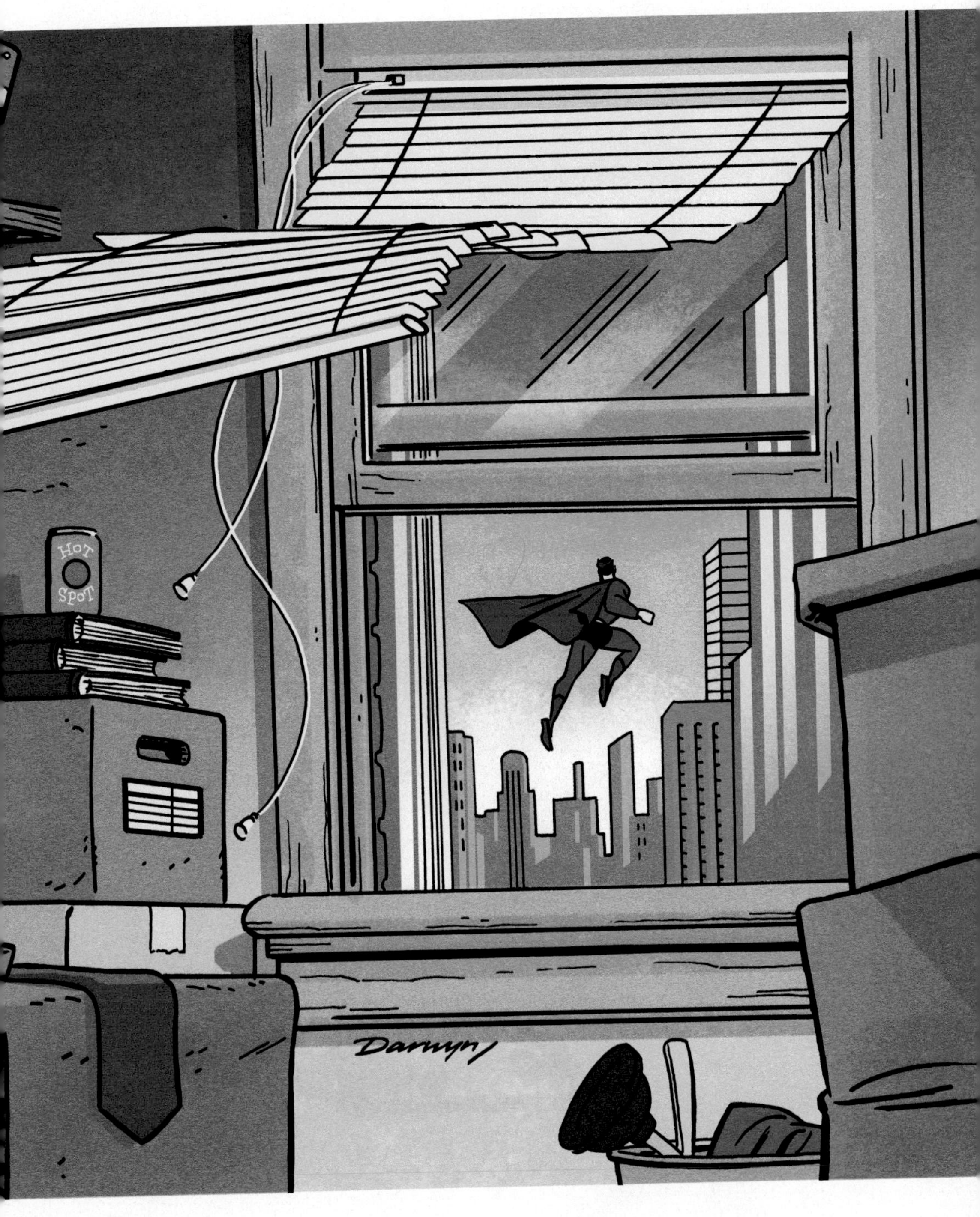
HOT SPOT
Darwyn

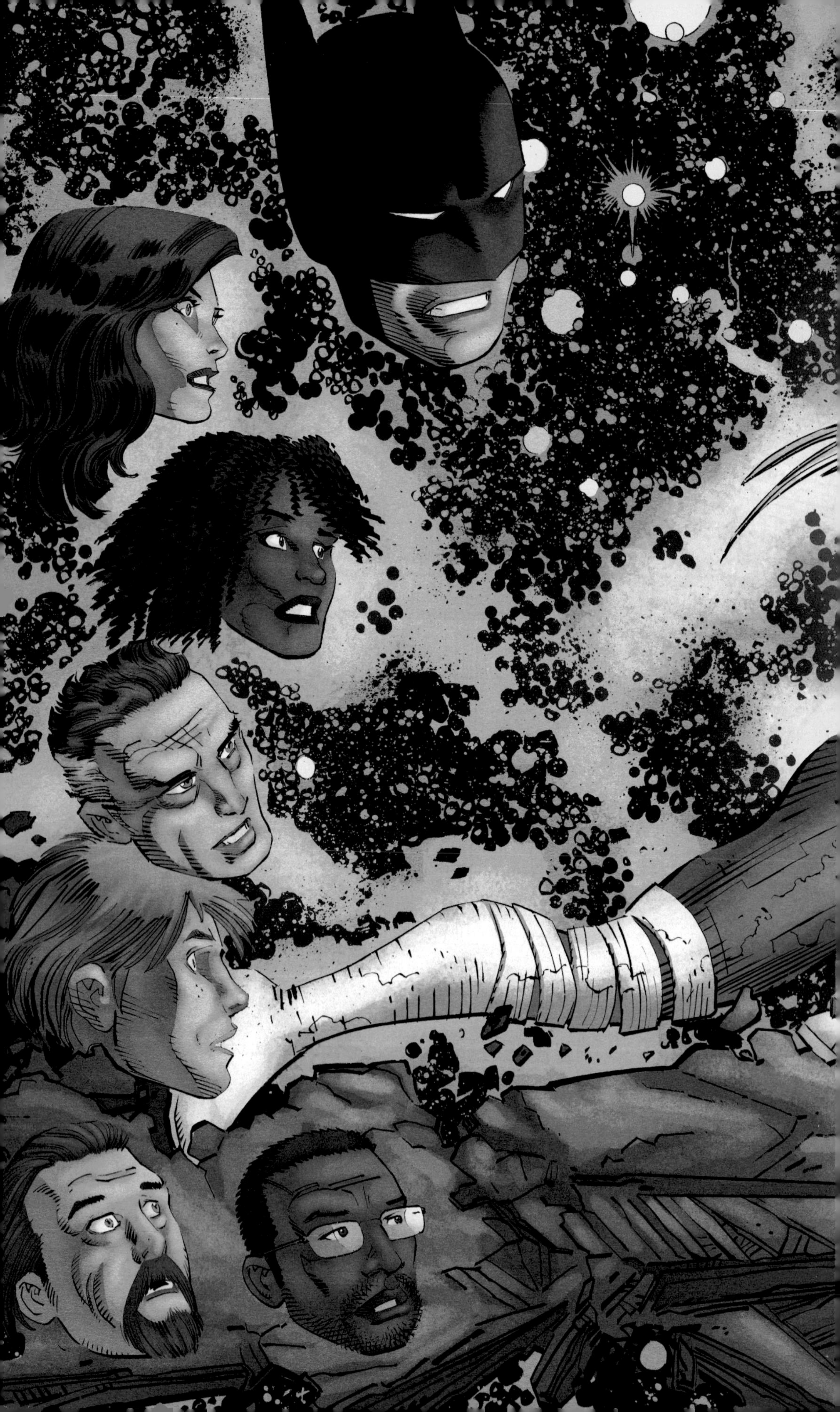

SUPERMAN #38

Full wrap-around cover by JOHN ROMITA JR., KLAUS JANSON & LAURA MARTIN

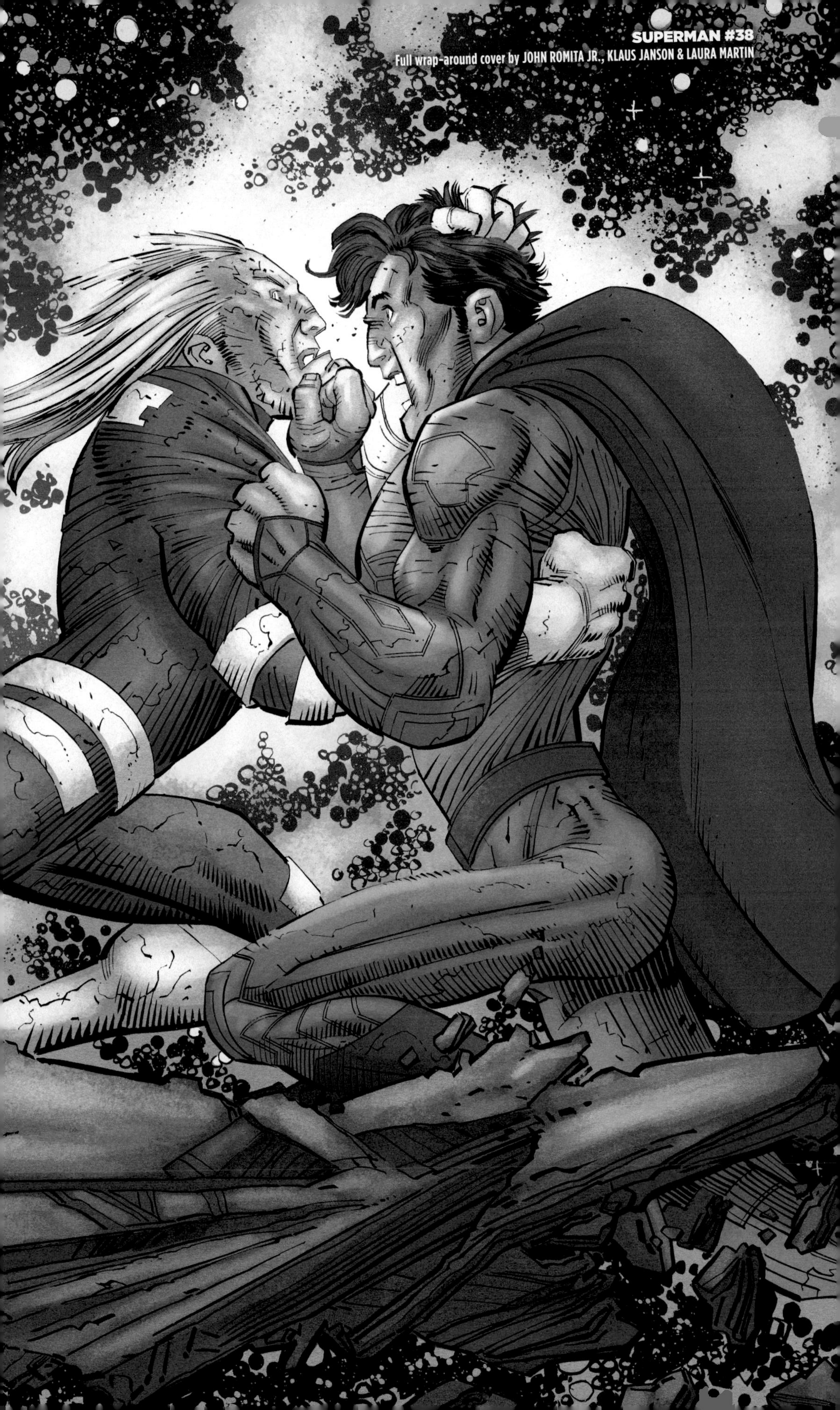

SUPERMAN #38
Variant cover by LEE MODER & MIKE ATIYEH

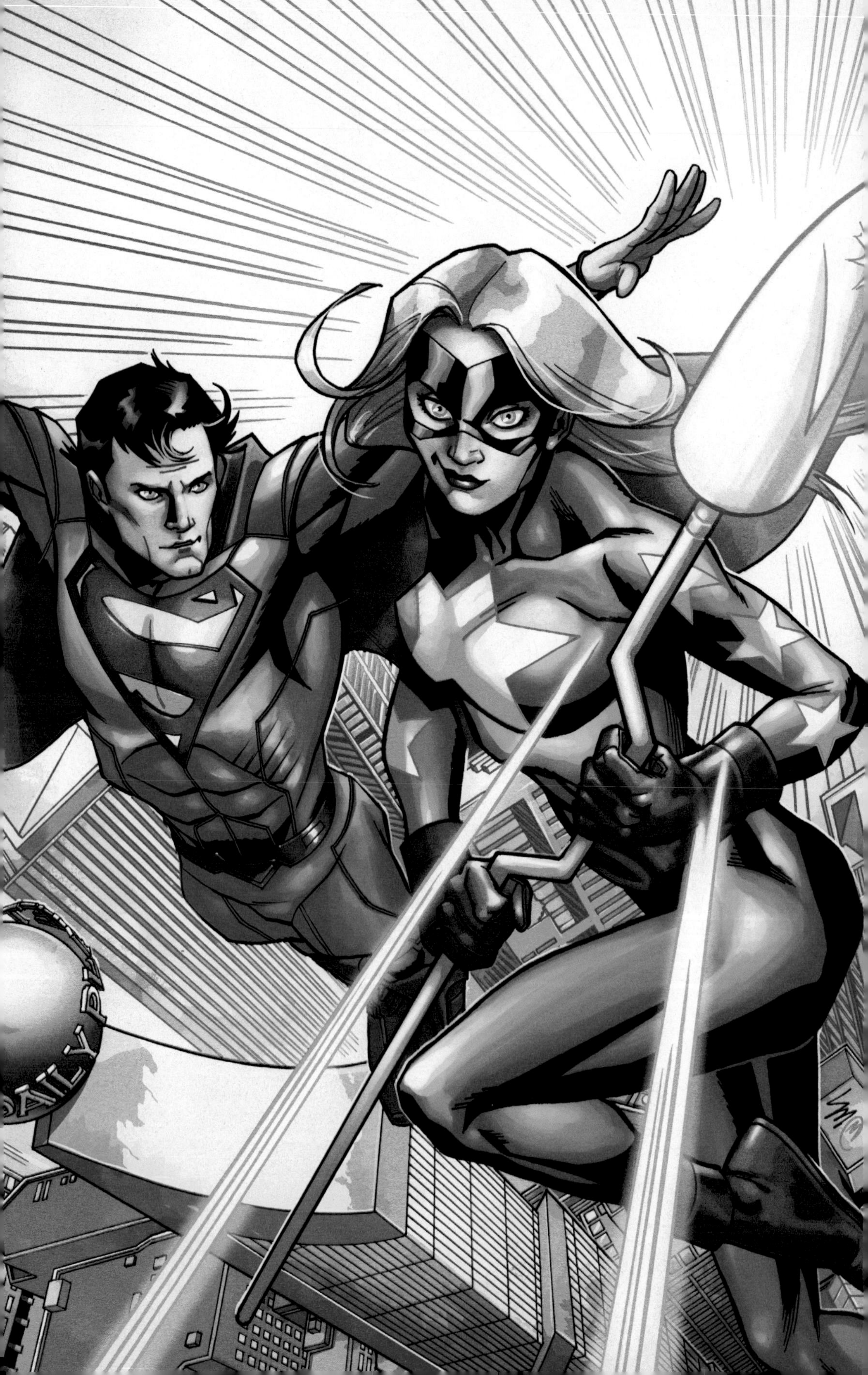

UPERMAN #38
riant by JOHN ROMITA JR., KLAUS JANSON & LAURA MARTIN

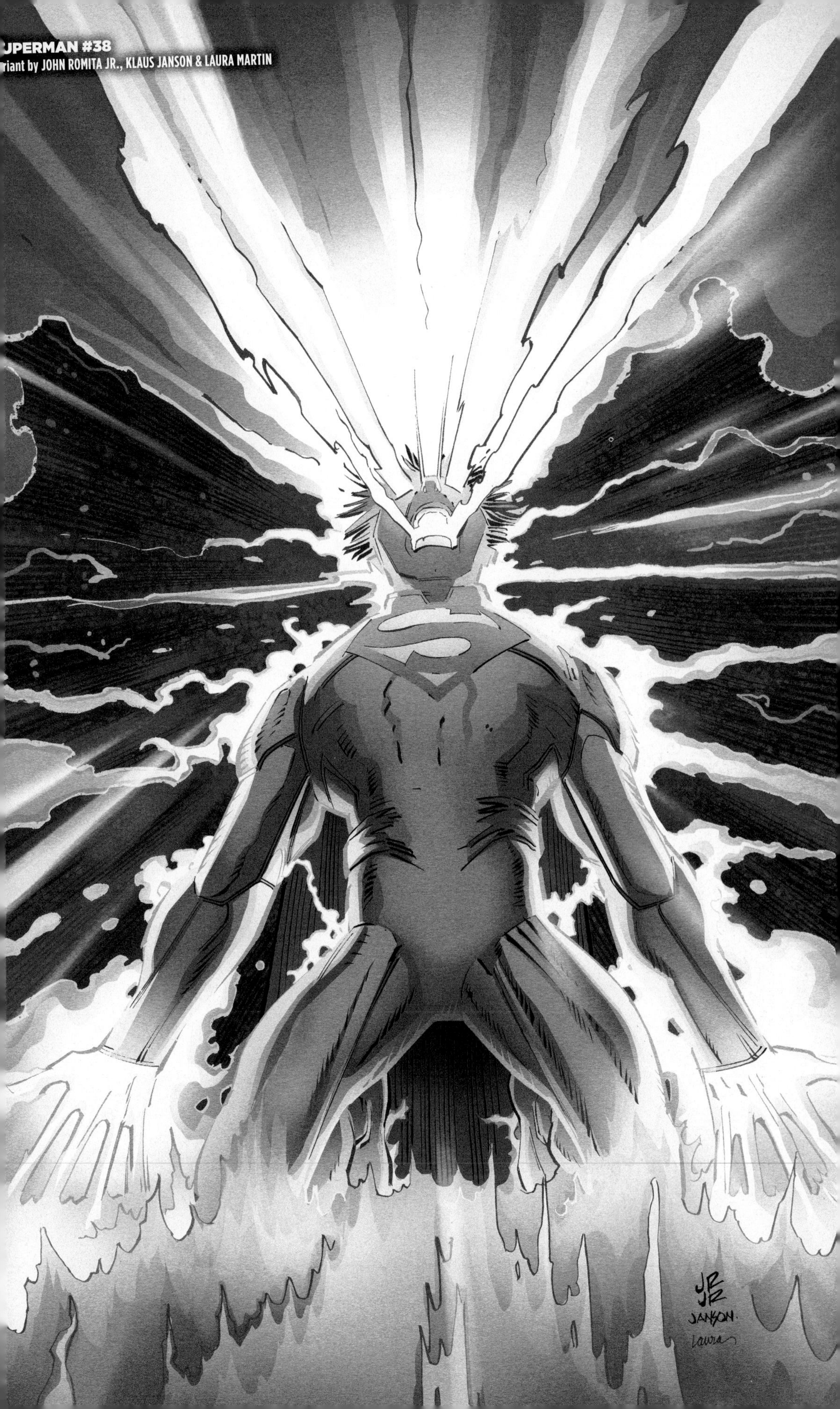
JR JR
JANSON.
Laura

SUPERMAN #38
Flash 75th Anniversary variant by KEVIN NOWLAN, AFTER CURT SWAN & SHELDON MOLDOFF

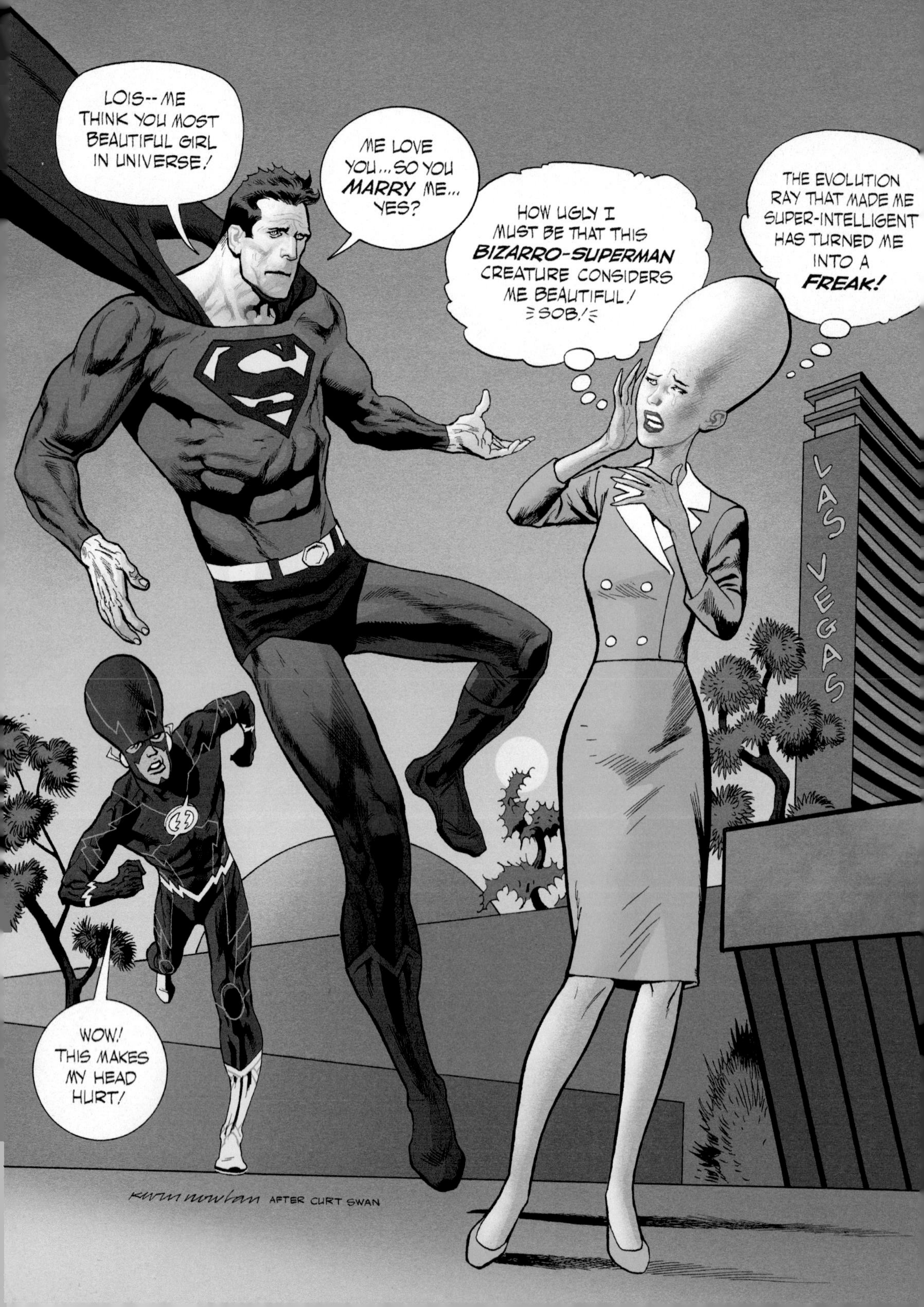
LOIS-- ME THINK YOU MOST BEAUTIFUL GIRL IN UNIVERSE!
ME LOVE YOU... SO YOU MARRY ME... YES?
HOW UGLY I MUST BE THAT THIS BIZARRO-SUPERMAN CREATURE CONSIDERS ME BEAUTIFUL! ≡SOB!≡
THE EVOLUTION RAY THAT MADE ME SUPER-INTELLIGENT HAS TURNED ME INTO A FREAK!
LAS VEGAS
WOW! THIS MAKES MY HEAD HURT!
KEVIN NOWLAN AFTER CURT SWAN

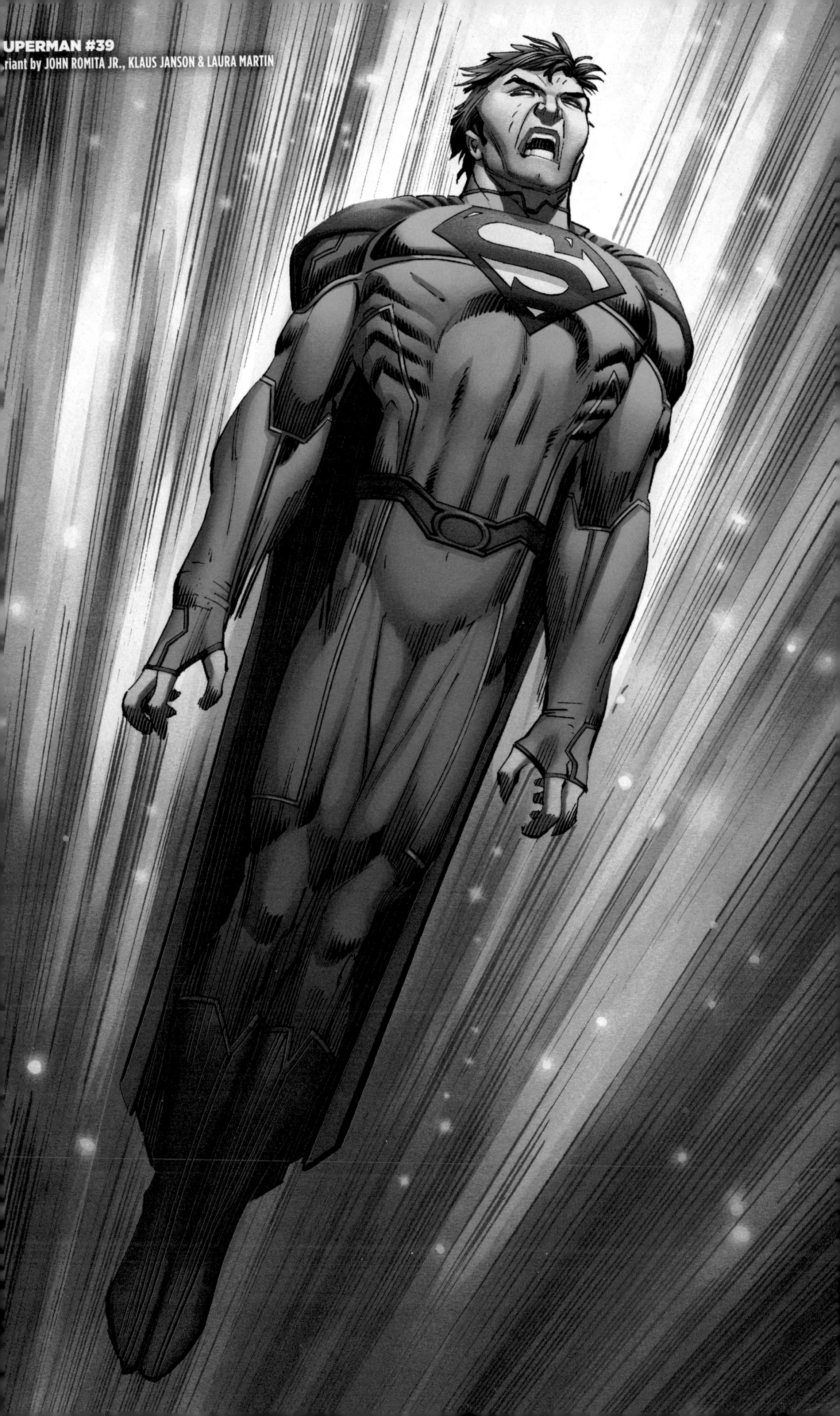

UPERMAN #39
riant by JOHN ROMITA JR., KLAUS JANSON & LAURA MARTIN

SUPERMAN #39
Variant by SHANE DAVIS, MICHELLE DELECKI & BARBARA CIARDO

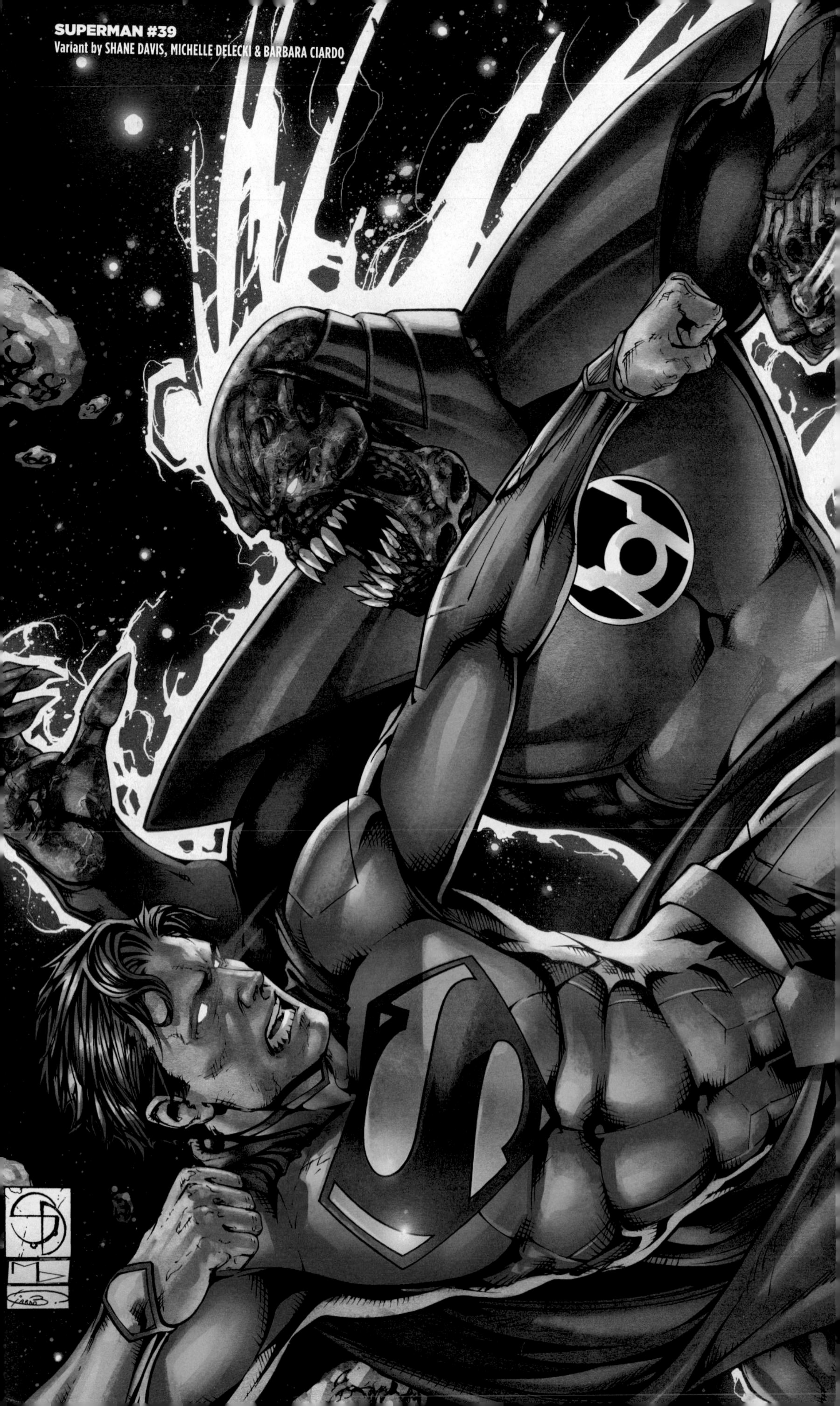

SUPERMAN #39
Harley Quinn variant by AMANDA CONNER & PAUL MOUNTS

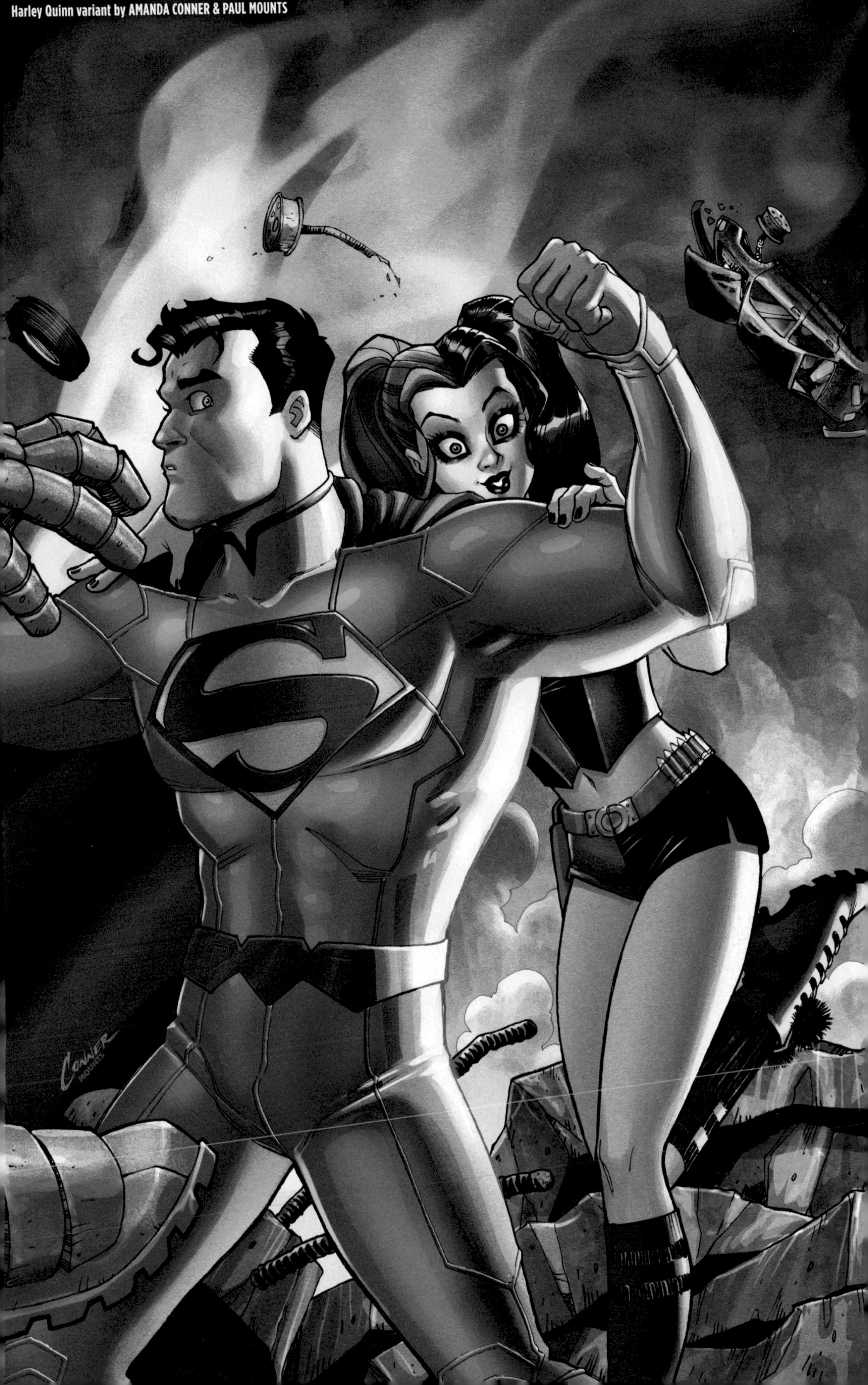

SUPERMAN SKETCH BOOK
DESIGNS, SKETCHES AND MORE FROM LEGENDARY ARTIST JOHN ROMITA JR.

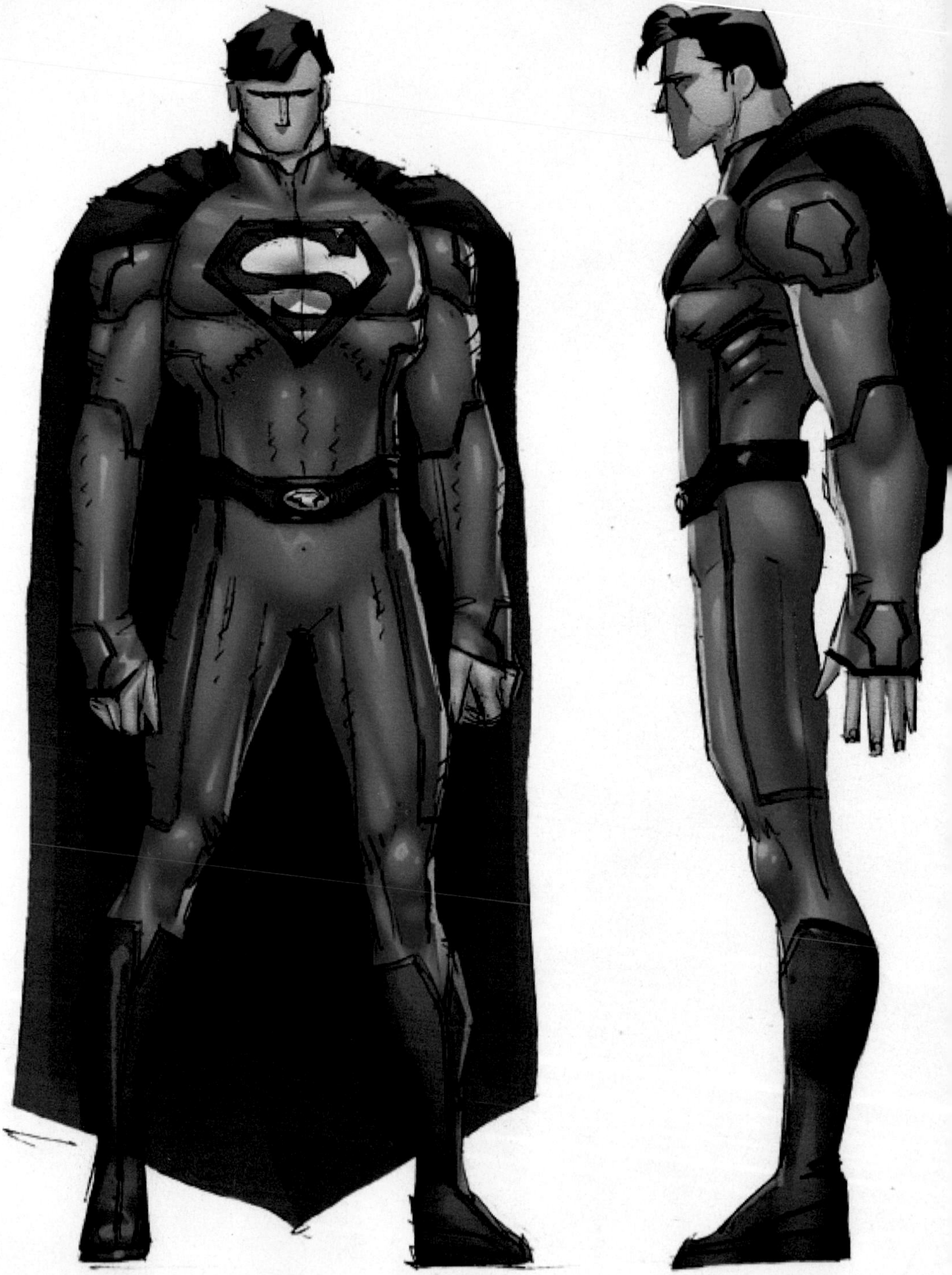

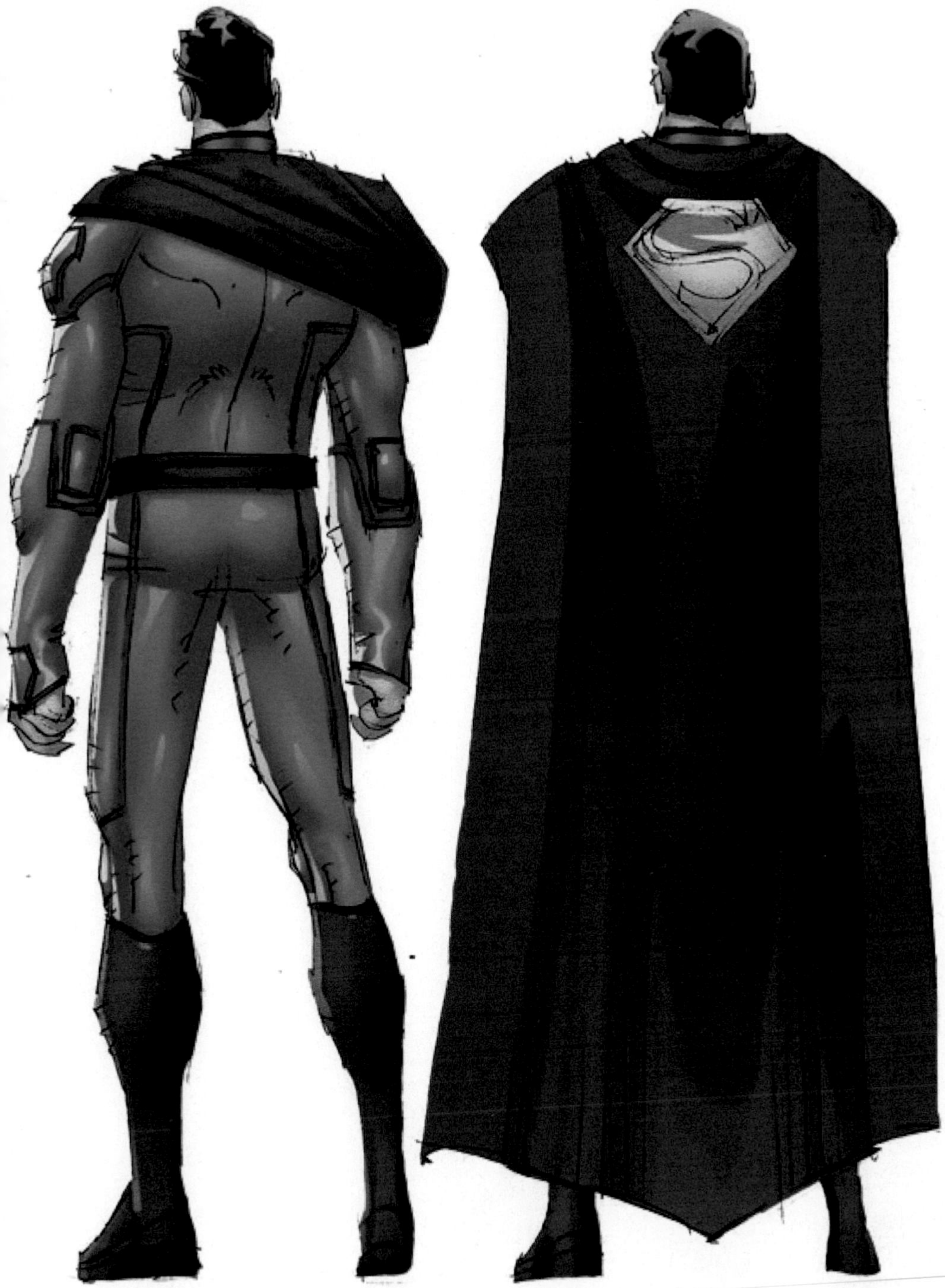

Taking on his first DC Comics job, John Romita Jr. got to reimagine the Superman cast as well as new characters, both friend and foe. He also got a chance to redo the New 52 version of Superman's costume!

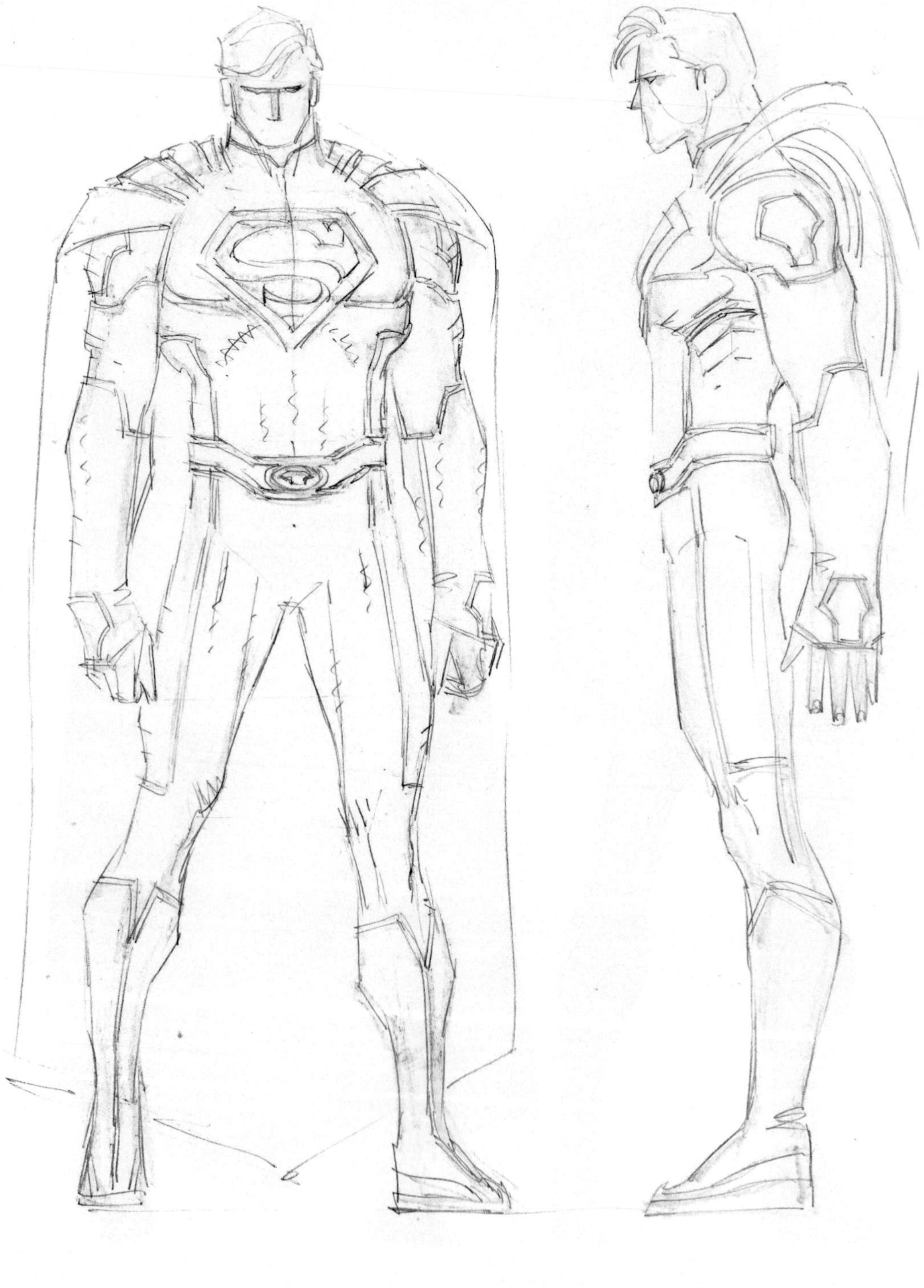

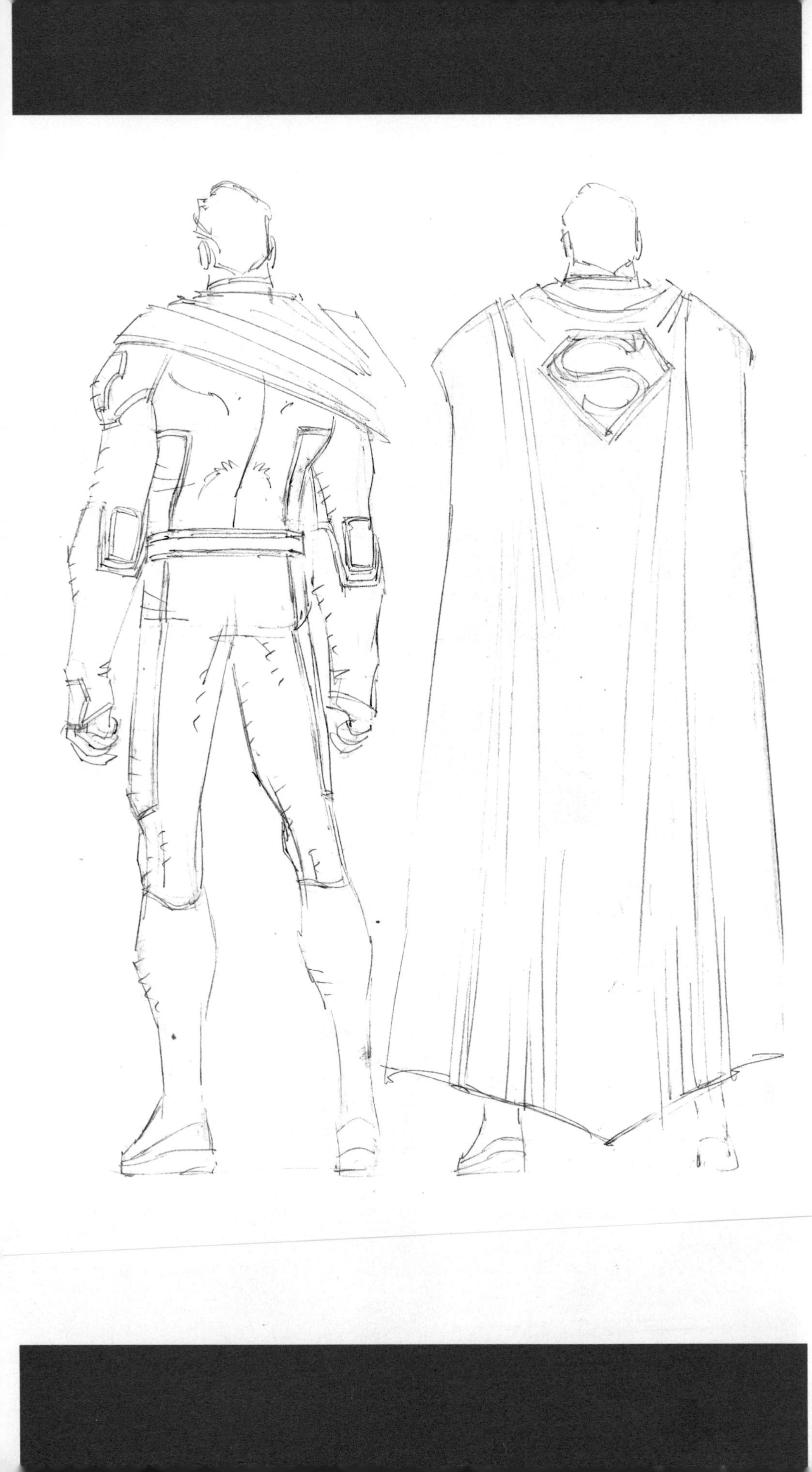

ULYSSES
WHAT DOES HE LOOK LIKE?

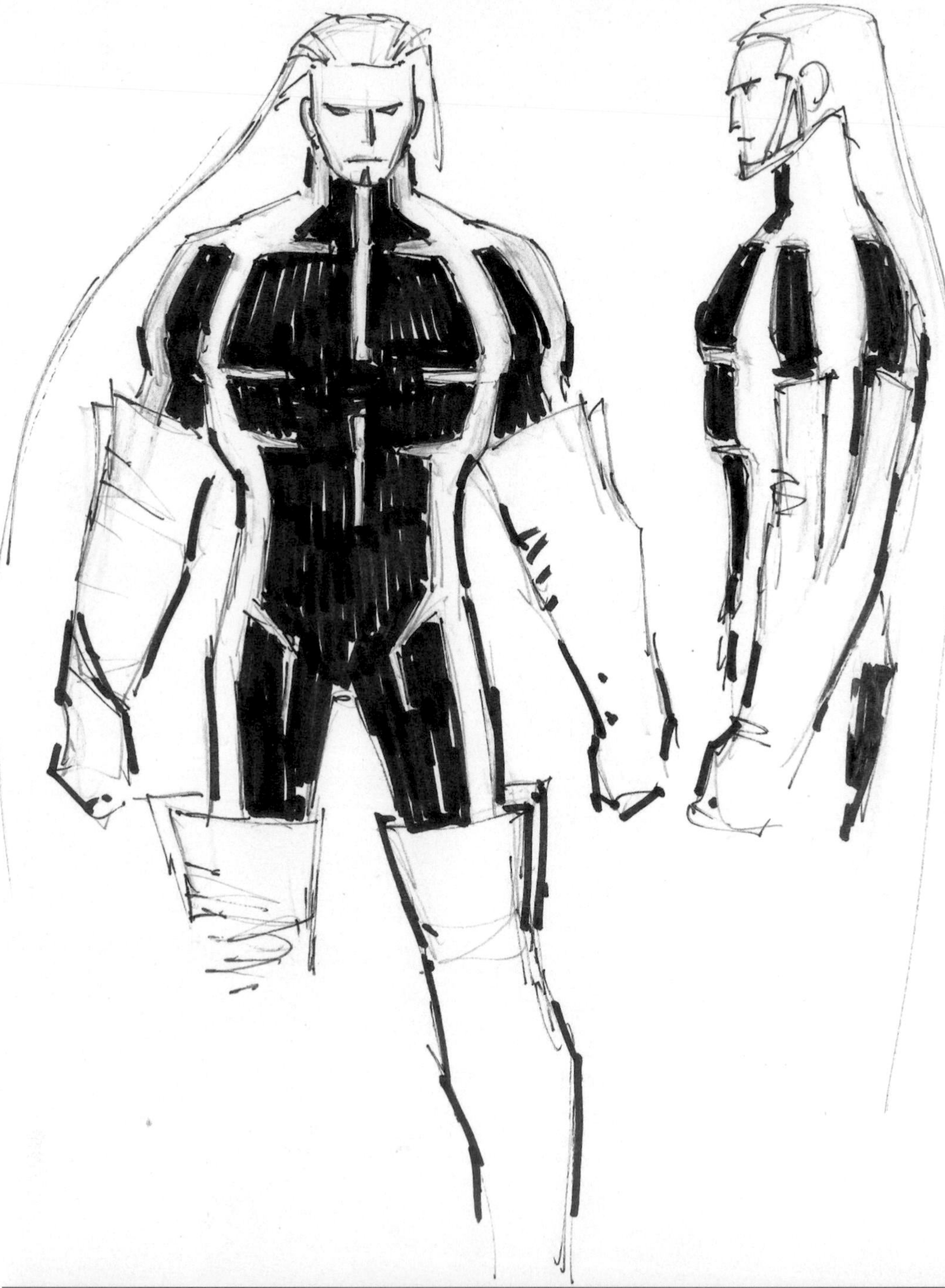

Geoff's note to John—
"I'm envisioning someone that reflects Superman in some way, it shouldn't simply mirror him. I'm not sure if he needs a cape—maybe when he first shows up he doesn't have one and then gets one after being influenced by Superman.

Does he have a beard? He should have a great hero's smile. For the first few issues we will think and portray him as a hero. He only gets dark later.

Physically, I'm thinking he's much like Superman at least in terms of size. He should have a different hair color obviously. I'm envisioning blonde, but am open."

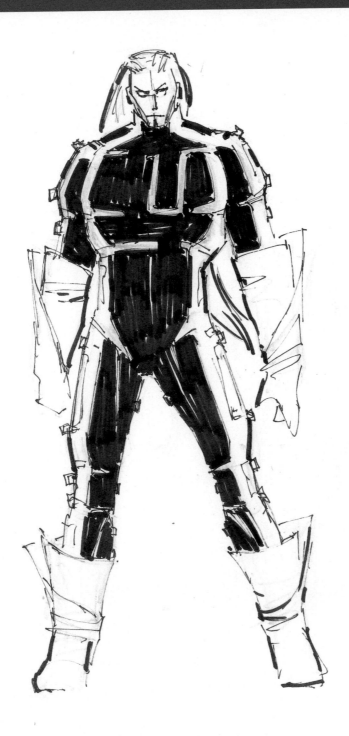

ULYSSES
THE HERO (25 years old)

HERO
ULYSSES ?
FLOOR LENGTH
PLATINUM
BLONDE

25 year after the accident at the Ulysses Research Center, Neil Quinn will return to Earth, as surprised by its existence as Superman would be to discovering Krypton hadn't exploded.

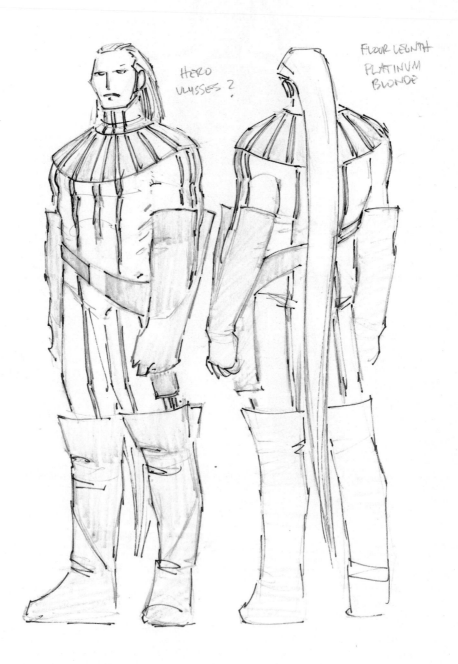

VILLAIN
COSTUME

HERO
FACE

Despite Superman's protests, Ulysses announces to the world that he understands why his parents sent
him away from Earth—that the future is bleak—and that the only way to a better tomorrow is quite
literally to come back with him to his world.

VILLAIN
ULYSSES

-- DIFFERENT FROM HERO VERSION ?

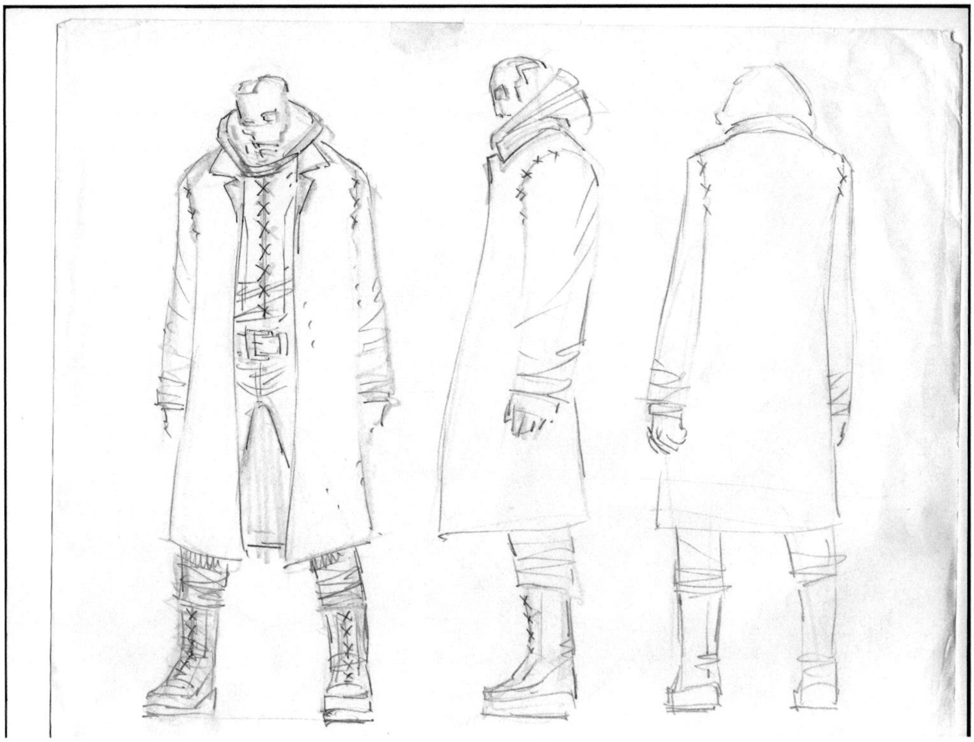

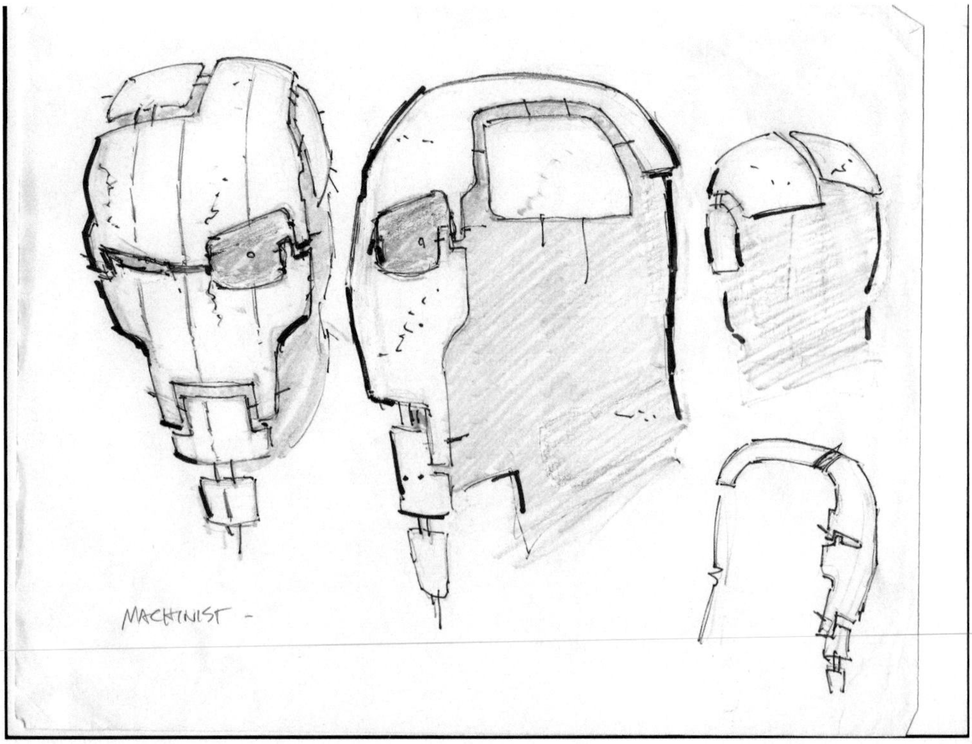
MACHINIST -

THE MACHINIST standing in all his unnatural and twisted dark glory. Oddly, he began as another old foe of Superman's.

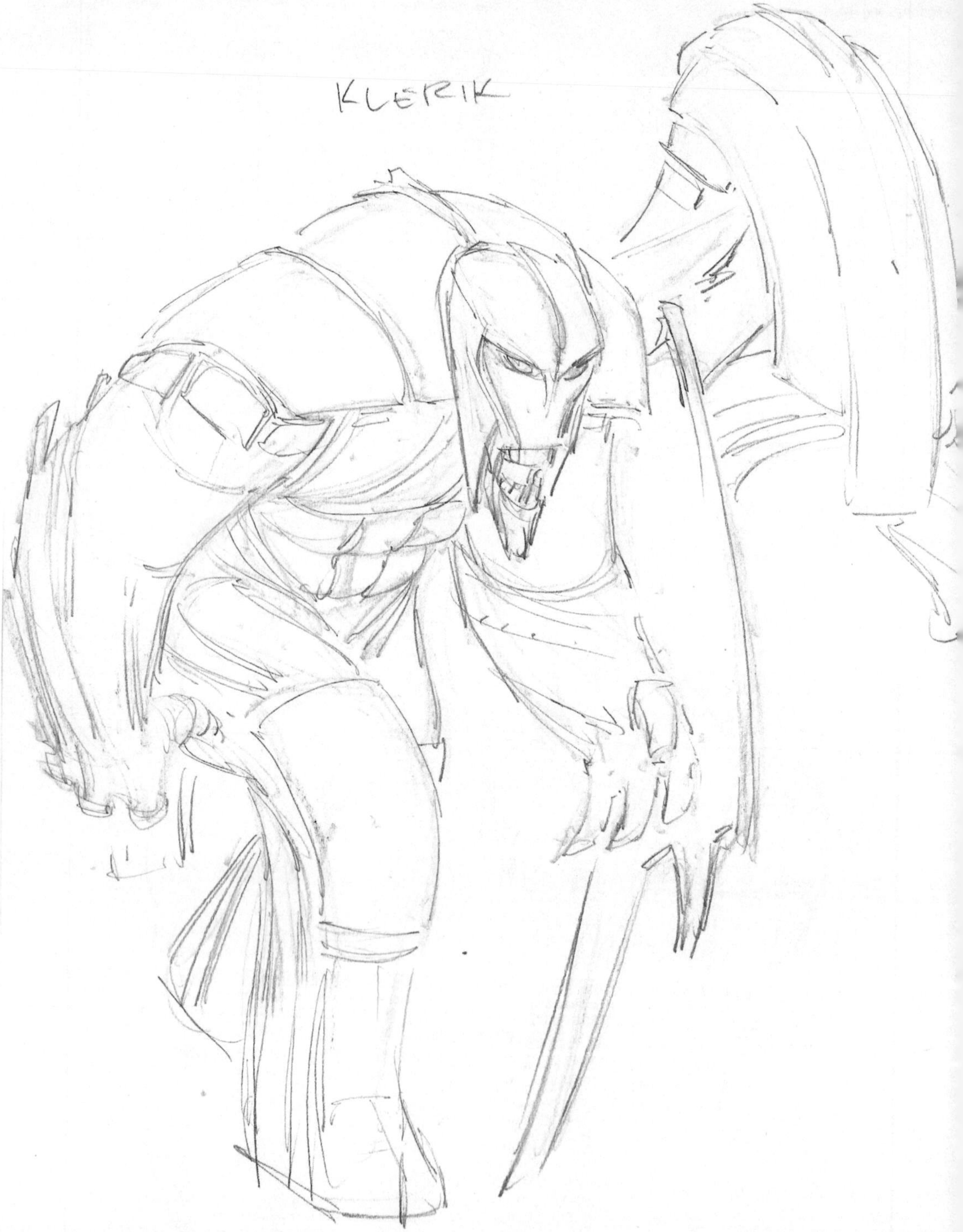
KLERIK

JACKEE WINTERS
POLITICAL CORRESPONDENT

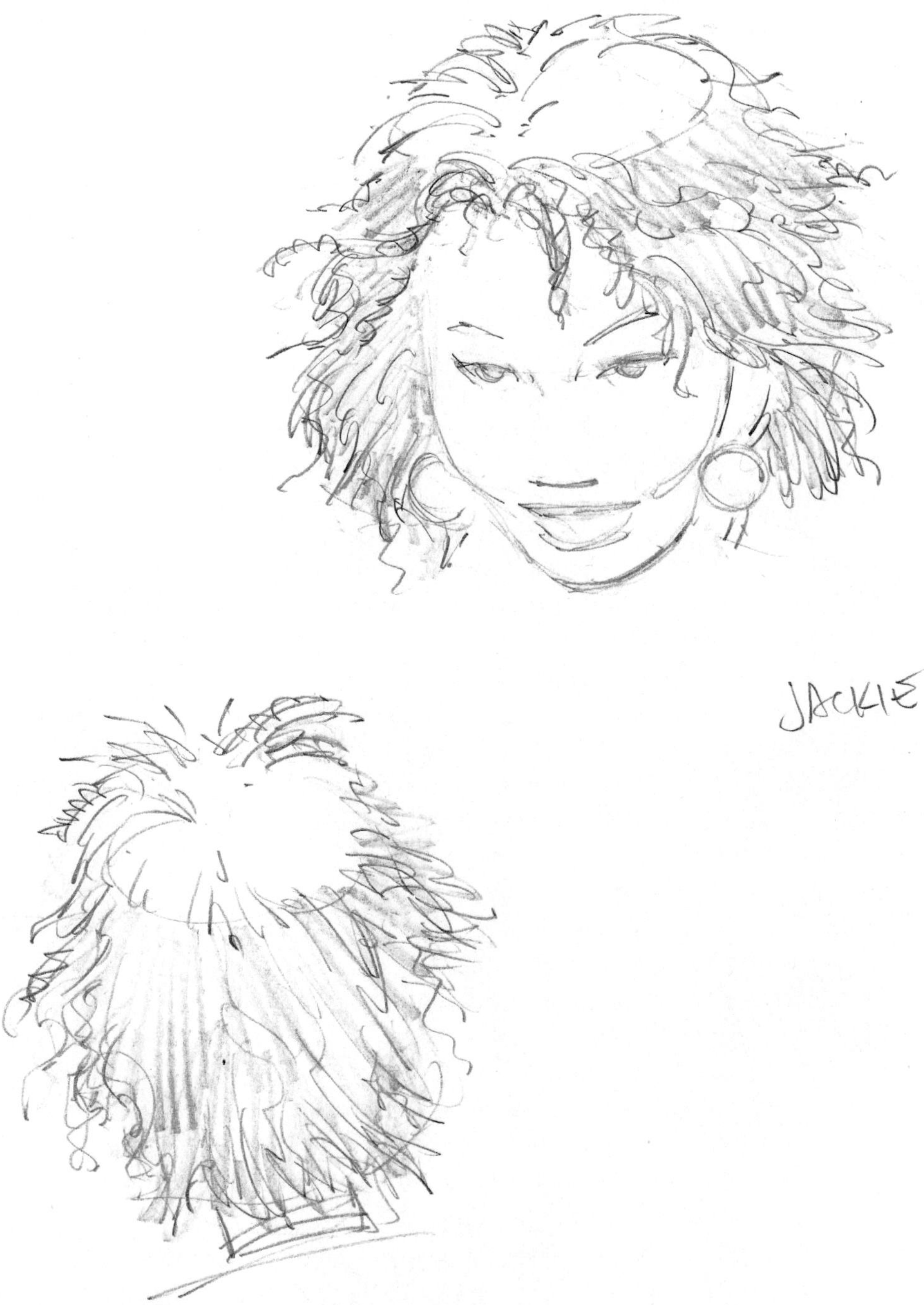
JACKIE

Brand-new character introduced at The Side Car bar with Lois. Jackee smiles more often times than not, never loses her cool, unassuming but incredibly shrewd. She asks the hard questions and tears into the answers.

But there are rumors that Jackee was once involved with groups like Wikileaks. That she has made enemies in high places. She has a past that could catch up with her. And she knows it.

Friend to Lois. Tech-savvy with multiple smartphones, including one that's totally off the grid. Coffee drinker.

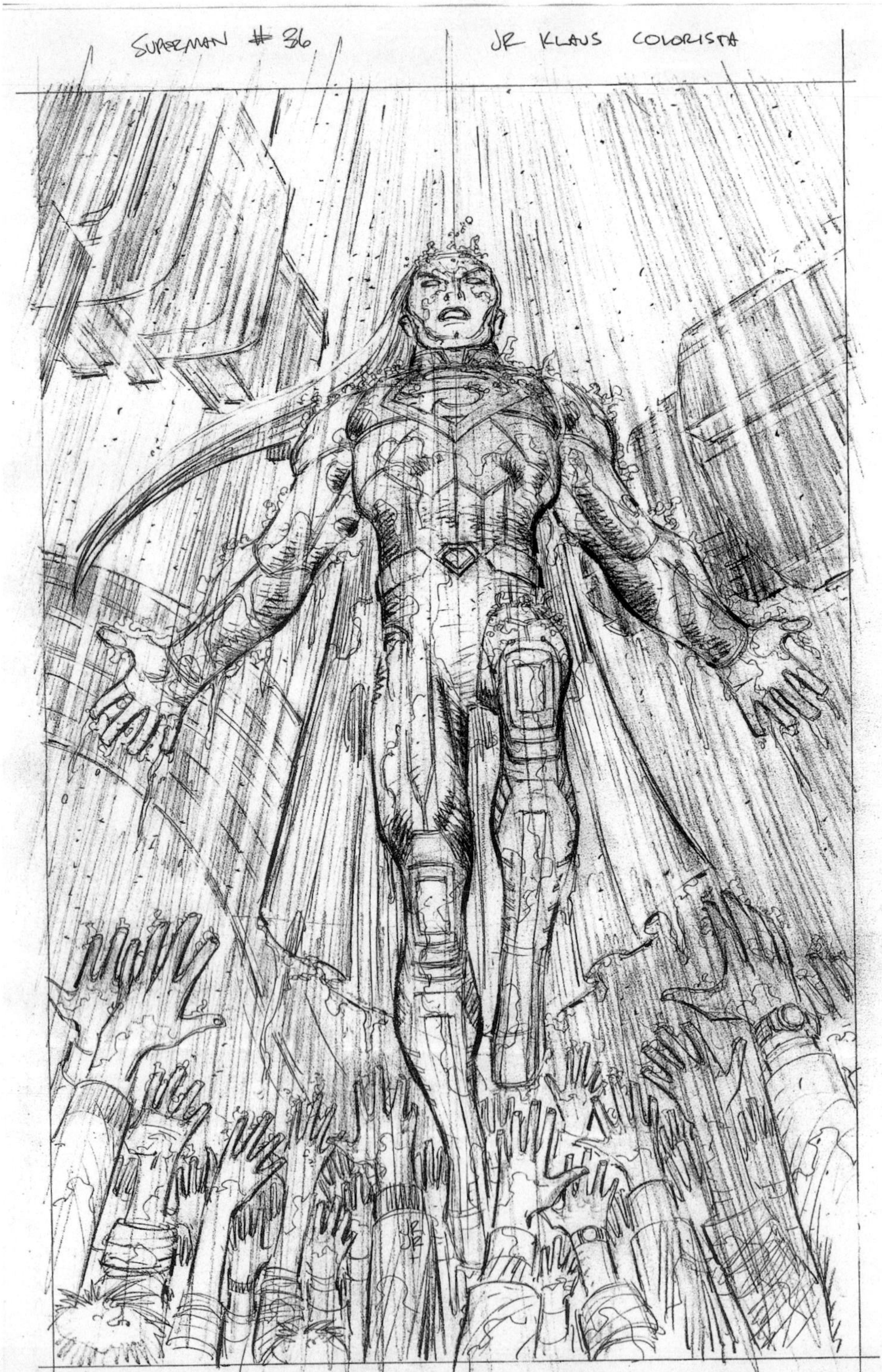
SUPERMAN #36
JR KLAUS COLORISTA